QUEEN OF NAVARRE
Jeanne d'Albret
1528–1572

JEANNE D'ALBRET, QUEEN OF NAVARRE

QUEEN OF NAVARRE

Jeanne d'Albret

1528–1572

By

Nancy Lyman Roelker

THE BELKNAP PRESS OF

HARVARD UNIVERSITY PRESS

CAMBRIDGE, MASSACHUSETTS

1968

Designed by Burton J Jones

Library of Congress Catalog Card Number 68–54024

Printed in the United States of America

FOR

MY MOTHER

AND OTHERS WHO HAVE SHARED THE ADVENTURE

Nancy L. Roelker

ACKNOWLEDGMENTS

The sources on Jeanne d'Albret are widely scattered in France and there is also considerable documentation in London and Geneva. Several summers of research were therefore required to assemble the materials for a full-scale biography. A grant from the American Philosophical Society in 1960 enabled me to make the preliminary forays and to plan the amount of time necessary in each place. The research was completed and the first draft written in 1965–66, thanks to a Fellowship from the John Simon Guggenheim Memorial Foundation.

At each stage I benefited from the assistance of many persons and institutions. Space forbids mention of each debt owed to the staffs of the Houghton Library at Harvard, the Bibliothèque Nationale and Archives Nationales in Paris, the Archives Départementales des Basses-Pyrénées in Pau, and de l'Orme in Alençon, the Bibliothèque de la Faculté des Lettres at the University of Bordeaux, the British Museum and the Public Records Office in London, the Bibliothèque Municipale in La Rochelle and the Bibliothèque Publique et Universitaire and the Musée Historique de la Réformation in Geneva, all of whom assisted me to locate and decipher the sources. Mademoiselle Olga de Sainte-Affrique in La Rochelle and Monsieur Alain Dufour in Geneva have been particularly helpful in innumerable ways. Nor is it possible to thank personally the many specialists in local history I met in the departmental and communal archives, without whose knowledge of the regional sources and generous interest in my project this book would have been much less complete. To M. le pasteur Henri Bosc, Librarian, and the other officers of the Société de l'Histoire du Protestantisme français, in Paris, I shall be eternally grateful for the fact that they gave me working-space for months at a time. By far the greatest proportion of the work was done in the Bibliothèque, and M. Bosc also put me in touch with other scholars working on sixteenth-century Huguenot subjects.

Among the fellow-historians who generously gave of their learning, advice, and time, I am especially indebted to four who also read the manuscript with great care and made substantial contributions to the final product: William F. Church of Brown University, Myron P.

ACKNOWLEDGMENTS

Gilmore of Harvard University, Natalie Z. Davis of the University of Toronto, and Robert M. Kingdon of the University of Wisconsin. Since the 1860's specialists in the French Wars of Religion have repeatedly asserted that one of the chief gaps in the field was a full study of Jeanne d'Albret. Several undertook the task but died before they could complete it, as mentioned in the Bibliographical Comment. Professor Kingdon's encouragement was the chief factor in my decision to resume the task, and his constant supply of information and suggestions has been the greatest single help in enabling me to complete it. Several of my students have brought me precious nuggets of information and have helped with problems of research, especially Laura Maslow Armand and Charmarie Jenkins Webb. The indispensable contributions of these colleagues does not mean that they should be blamed for weaknesses in the book, however, since the responsibility for the research and interpretation is exclusively my own.

As I wished to address the book to the general reader as well as to historians, and to produce a personal biography as well as a study of Jeanne's career and times, I also drew on the expertise of friends who are not historians. Erik Erikson of Harvard and members of his Seminar on Life History and History provided me with fresh insights into the material in 1963–64, while Dr. Gregory N. Rochlin of the Harvard Medical School read the manuscript and helped me to phrase my conclusions accurately in layman's language. If the book has any literary merit, the fine editorial hand, tact, and patience of Hermine Isaacs Popper are largely responsible. Finally, I wish to thank Pauline W. Shannon for the skill, speed, and enthusiasm with which she typed the manuscript and Ann Louise Coffin McLaughlin of the Harvard University Press for final corrections, improvements, and pleasant hours in the publication process.

NANCY LYMAN ROELKER

Cambridge, Massachusetts
April 1968

CONTENTS

CONTENTS

CONTENTS

ILLUSTRATIONS

MAPS

(drawn by Samuel H. Bryant)

QUEEN OF NAVARRE
Jeanne d'Albret
1528–1572

SIMPLIFIED GENEALOGICAL CHART

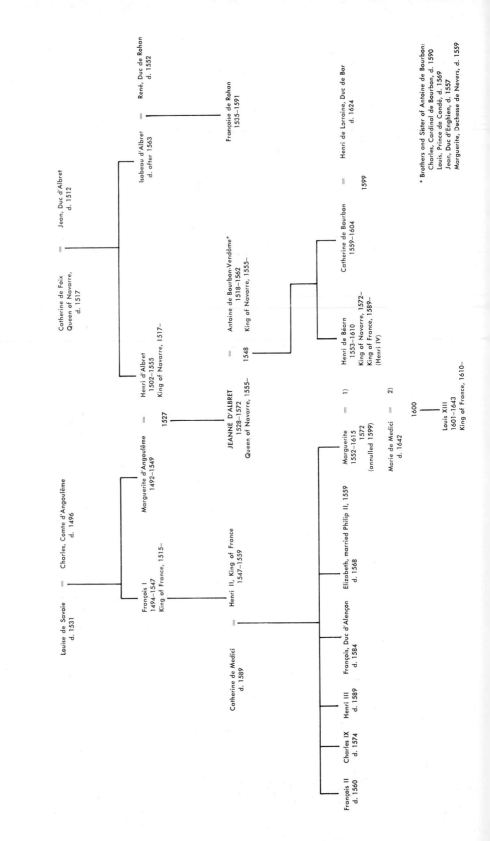

PROLOGUE

O! for a Muse of Fire, that would ascend
The brightest heaven of invention;
A kingdom for a stage, princes to act
And monarchs to behold the swelling scene . . .
And let us, ciphers to this great accompt,
On your imaginary forces work . . .
Piece out our imperfections with your thoughts:
Into a thousand parts divide one man . . .
For 'tis your thoughts that now must deck our kings,
Carry them here and there, jumping o'er times,
Turning the accomplishment of many years
Into an hour-glass; for the which supply
Admit me Chorus to this history . . .

Shakespeare, *Henry V*, Prologue

Western Europe in the year of Jeanne's birth, 1528, was dominated by three young monarchs: Charles V, Holy Roman Emperor since 1519, whose inherited lands included Spain, southern Italy, and the Low Countries as well as the Hapsburg lands in Central Europe; his rival, François I, Jeanne's uncle, King of France; and Henry VIII of England, who sometimes played the two continental powers off against each other to the advantage of his own kingdom. The continuing rivalry between the Hapsburg and the Valois, especially in northern Italy, produced a series of wars which had begun in the 1490's and were to outlast both François I and Henry VIII (both died in 1547) and to affect the development of modern Europe in many ways.

François' reign had begun with a spectacular success, when he gained possession of Milan by winning the Battle of Marignano (September 1515); but ten years later, at the Battle of Pavia, he was defeated, captured, and obliged to spend a year in Spain as Charles' prisoner and to sign the ignominious Treaty of Madrid, by which François had to cede Burgundy, renounce his Italian claims, and agree to deliver his two sons to Charles as hostages. During his enforced absence, France was governed by his mother, Louise de Savoie, as Regent. (His father, Charles, Comte d'Angoulême,* had died in 1496, leaving Louise a widow at the age of nineteen, with two children under five.) A woman of intense ambition and considerable political ability, resembled in these respects by her granddaughter Jeanne, Louise had seen her highest hopes fulfilled when François, hitherto only Comte d'Angoulême and Duc de Valois, became King of France. This was in accord with what she regarded as the "destiny" of her "Caesar."

Louise, who frequently referred to herself and her children as "the Trinity," had brought up her daughter to idolize her younger brother. Marguerite was François' constant companion and served him in many ways, notably as official hostess and supervisor of his household, but often also as his deputy.[1] From the beginning of his reign, François had showered honors on his sister. He had designated her husband, Charles, Duc d'Alençon, as his heir, and given the enormous wealth of the house of Armagnac to Marguerite and her descendants. Marguerite was usually at her brother's side; foreign ambassadors and those who curried royal favor sought her help. "With her mother, she was a sort of viceroy."[2] Marguerite's most important public service was her trip to Spain in the autumn of 1525 to negotiate with the Emperor for her brother's release. All Europe followed the King's sister in her strenuous four-month journey, fraught with danger. She arrived in Madrid, after three weeks on the road, to find François so critically ill that he did not recognize her. She would not leave his side and spent several days in ardent prayer. His fever suddenly dropped and he recovered his senses. Later he was often to say that she had saved his life. Nursing him back to health was her real accomplishment, since she was unable to soften the terms of the treaty. When the Emperor learned of a plot for François' escape it was feared that he would not extend Marguerite's safe-conduct to permit her return. Rumors in the chanceries of Europe and entries in private diaries reflected the widespread concern. When she arrived in France, just in time for Christmas, "Marguerite reached the height of her glory. To the court, bedazzled by the code of chivalry, she was a heroine."[3]

Marguerite was then thirty-three years old and a widow. The Duc

---

* French names, titles, and offices for which there is no English equivalent are left in French; other foreign titles have been Anglicized.

d'Alençon, wholly undistinguished even on the battlefield, had escaped capture at Pavia but fell ill and died soon afterward. Although Marguerite tended him devotedly to the end, the marriage does not seem to have been a happy one and she had turned increasingly to religion. Since the early 1520's she had been closely associated with Briçonnet, Bishop of Meaux, around whom was gathered a group of humanists representing the early stages of the Reformation in France. By the time of the voyage to Spain, Marguerite was well-launched on her own personal career as a woman of letters and patroness of the developing French Renaissance.

François' interest in the arts was focused largely on the construction and ornamentation of royal residences like Fontainebleau and Chambord, which provided suitable settings for the court and the hunt—the passion of the *Roi Chevalier*. He encouraged the new scholarship in its less controversial aspects by founding royal lectureships in Greek, Hebrew, Oriental languages, and mathematics, and by collecting manuscripts and precious books (the nucleus of the Bibliothèque Nationale), but he was not a scholar himself. His attitude toward the "new thinking" hardened in a conservative direction as soon as it became evident that a potential challenge to royal authority was involved. Marguerite, on the contrary, was deeply committed to the "reform from within" which characterized the initial phase of the Reformation.

In 1528 it was not at all evident that this movement was doomed to fail and western Christendom to be torn between warring sects. Especially since Martin Luther had nailed his ninety-five theses on the door of the church at Wittenburg (1517), it had become respectable, even fashionable, to advocate abolition of the abuses that encrusted Roman Catholicism. As late as 1541 some members of the College of Cardinals still hoped to work out a compromise with the Lutherans. In France, the King's sister added her voice to those of the humanist-reformers and on several occasions in the 1520's obtained for them her brother's protection from the ecclesiastical authorities. Marguerite thus occupied an influential position in the intellectual movements of the day as well as a unique place at the court of France.

The court, a complex phenomenon already, although less institutionalized and more nomadic than it was to become in the seventeenth century, revolved around the King, with the fortunes of individuals and families rising and falling with royal favor.[4] Far more than either of his wives, the King's mother and sister held important positions in this constellation, which Marguerite, at least, earned with hard work and at the cost of considerable sacrifice. Family ties aside, it served François well to have at hand an able woman on whose devotion he could count absolutely. Other prominent ladies, notably the Duchesse d'Etampes (Anne de Pisselieu) who became François' official mistress in the year of Jeanne's birth, exploited royal favor for their own ends. It was an era of new men in the royal entourage. Many of François' early intimates had died at Pavia. When he returned from Spain the vacuum was filled by certain great nobles—but not by royal cousins. The last independent branch of the ruling family (the House of Bourbon) had fallen into disgrace when Charles de Bourbon, head of the family and Constable of France, had turned traitor and led the Hapsburg troops against the French in Italy.

For the greater part of François' reign the most important nobleman at the court (and in the kingdom) was Anne de Montmorency, "first gentleman," Grand Master, and, finally, Constable of France. The Montmorencys possessed extensive lands and dominated more vassals than any other "private" family in the kingdom. For generations they had held important royal offices and their prestige was great, but they had not become courtiers. The Constable, eclipsed toward the end of François' reign, rose to an even more important position in the reign of François' son, Henri II (1547–1559), to whom he was both intimate friend and chief adviser, and he played a vital role in the civil wars until his death in 1567. Montmorency was a staunch Catholic, of the old-fashioned conservative stamp, very devoted to the crown. When his three nephews, the Châtillon brothers, became leaders of the Calvinist movement in the 1550's, it was a complicating factor, but family ties and royalist sentiment were strong and the Constable was able to exert a moderating and unifying influence as long as he lived.

As Montmorency's star waned in the 1540's, that of the first Duc de Guise was rising. In the generation of Henri II, his sons Charles, Cardinal de Lorraine, and François, Duc de Guise, would amass so many titles and such vast wealth, thanks to royal favor and personal ability, that they (with their vassals) would form a rival party to the Montmorencys. The crystallization of these factions, which formed the basic politico-religious configuration of the second half-century, lay in the future in 1528, but the elements were all present.

The time had not yet come when the highest ranking French nobles regularly spent much time at court. They were not yet wholly dependent on the crown; regional autonomy, and even rebellion, flourished. In the first half of the sixteenth century the great nobles could follow an independent policy and carry with them a large number of their vassals and retainers, as the career of the Constable de Bourbon proves.[5] As far as possible from the Ile-de-France, between the Basque country and the central Pyrenees, lay the domains of one such family, the Comtes de Foix, Sovereign Lords of Béarn, who called themselves "kings" of Navarre, although only the rump of that kingdom north of the Pyrenees remained in their hands since Ferdinand of Aragon had conquered the larger portion to the south in 1512. Ever since that year "the Navarre question" had been a minor cause of friction between the crowns of France and Spain; very minor indeed to the Valois, who had too many real quarrels with the Hapsburgs to risk anything in behalf of a "king" of Navarre who would thus become a more difficult vassal to control. For the Hapsburgs, there was considerable nuisance-value in the possession of Pampeluna, the ancient capital, and in repeated opportunities either to proceed to the conquest of the rest of Navarre or to make a deal with its king as part of the Hapsburg struggle with France. Charles V, after he succeeded his grandfather Ferdinand as King of Spain, exploited this situation to the utmost. He could do so because the Navarre question was the all-absorbing concern of Henri d'Albret (1502–1555), King of Navarre and Jeanne's father.

Henri had been born and spent the first nine years of his life on the Spanish side of the Pyrenees. When the King of Spain took over Haute Navarre in 1512, Henri fled with his mother, Catherine de Foix, from whom he inherited Béarn and what was left of Navarre. Charles Dartigue, a scholar who has studied Henri as an administrator of Béarn, says, "from this school of continuous anguish Henri had learned one lesson: how to maneuver between those more powerful than himself and how to seize opportunities in order to turn them to his own immediate advantage."[6] The experience left Henri with the single desire of recovering Spanish Navarre by whatever means and marked him for life with the attitude of a ruler-in-exile. After his mother's death in 1517, when he assumed the title of King, Henri spent some time at the French court, where he was conspicuous for his Gascon temperament, casual love affairs, and luxurious style of life. At the age of fourteen, at Blois, where he was an intimate companion of François I, Henri d'Albret maintained a household of eighty-two persons at a cost of 3000 livres tournois a month. Easily angered or roused to enthusiasm, he was just as quickly discouraged and never could be depended upon to fulfill an obligation. The principal male influence on the adolescent Henri was his grandfather Alain d'Albret, a famous Gascon adventurer who taught him to surmount obstacles by dissimulation. Although as a young man Henri was torn between a golden captivity at the Valois court and the liberty of Béarn, he managed to make the most of both in his lifetime of fifty-two years. He proved to be an outstanding administrator in Béarn. As Dartigue says, "where he was really master, he knew how to unite great courtesy with a very firm grip."

In contrast to Marguerite's first husband, Henri d'Albret distinguished himself at Pavia, was taken prisoner at his King's side, then made a dramatic escape (down a rope ladder) in typical Gascon fashion, which was the admiration of the French court.[7] Thus, the disaster of Pavia had been mitigated in chivalrous terms by two feats of exceptional "prowess": that of the King of Navarre and that of Marguerite. It was not unnatural in the circumstances that the Gascon should become a suitor for the hand of the King's widowed sister. Ten years her junior, handsome, a hero in her eyes because of his service to François, Henri d'Albret seemed to offer Marguerite all the qualities that Alençon had lacked. To the "King of Navarre," the marriage appeared as a providential opportunity. He expected that the Navarre question would acquire top priority when he became the King's brother-in-law.

They were married in great splendor at St. Germain-en-Laye in January 1527. Henri d'Albret became one of the *grands seigneurs* of France, and Marguerite "had come a long way from the day she married Charles d'Alençon, virtually without a dowry."[8] Congratulations poured in from the powers of Europe and Marguerite's influence continued to grow. Erasmus sought her opinion on philosophical and religious issues; Cardinal Wolsey paid special court to her during his visit to France. In the months following her second marriage, the Queen of Navarre even plunged deeply into the municipal politics of Florence, declaring not only that she loved the City of the Lilies but that she considered herself an adopted Florentine.[9]

When she became pregnant, in the spring of 1528, Marguerite was gayer than ever before in her life and nothing seemed to tire her, not even the elaborate festivities of the marriage of her cousin Renée de

France (daughter of Louis XII) and Hercule d'Este. The court poets outdid each other in extravagant praise of "the pearl of princesses," the "Marguerite of marguerites."[10] By October she daily expected the birth of her daughter—she had felt from the start that it would be a daughter —and feared only that it would happen in her brother's absence. As she said, "my daughter would not dare to come into the world without the King's permission." She swore that if such a misfortune occurred she would have her brother's latest letter read aloud during the delivery instead of the traditional *Oraison de Sainte Marguerite*.[11]

Labor began on the night of November 15, and for several hours it seemed that she would not survive. François, fortunately on hand, and their mother were at her side. They commanded the court and the city to offer special prayers and Marguerite herself vowed to undertake a pilgrimage to Notre Dame de Lorette if she lived. The prayers were answered at five o'clock in the afternoon of November 16, when the Queen of Navarre gave birth normally to her first child—and the only one that ever lived—Jeanne d'Albret, Princess of the Blood on her mother's side, heiress of much of southwestern France on her father's.[12]

I

THE TWIG IS BENT

1 5 2 8 – 1 5 3 7

FRANCE learned officially of Jeanne's existence on January 7, 1529, when François I permitted the addition of one new "master" in every city where there were incorporated guilds, "in honor of the birth of Jeanne de Navarre, the King's niece."[1] This was a tribute to the devoted sister who had always put him and his affairs above everything else. Nor did motherhood curtail Marguerite's activities.[2] Immediately after Jeanne's birth she undertook to reconcile with the Sorbonne one of her protégés in Alençon, Pierre Caroli, who was accused of heretical preaching. Her efforts were moderately successful, but she failed in the more important case of Louis Berquin, a gentleman-scholar in Paris who was condemned for the second time on April 16, 1529, and executed the following day despite her pleas. A truce in the war with Charles V in that year involved her again in international affairs. The Peace of Cambrai (August 1529) was the work of two women, Margaret of Austria, representing her nephew the Emperor, and Louise de Savoie, representing her son, François I. Marguerite de Navarre took part in at least the cere- monial aspects of the peace conference and Clément Marot,* in his *Traité de la Paix,* compared the three royal ladies to three goddesses. Historians assume that Marguerite was not included in the serious negotiations because it seems obvious that François I had made up his mind to sacrifice Navarre. Henri d'Albret, who had been pressing his claims,

---

* Clément Marot, 1495–1544, lyric poet and translator of the Psalms into French. A retainer of Marguerite's, he often wrote poems for family occasions.

was deeply humiliated and angry—not for the last time. The royal policy would provide him with increasing incentive to turn away from the French crown and create a painful situation for Marguerite.

For several months afterward Marguerite served her brother in a familiar capacity, supervisor of his children. When François went to meet his new wife (the Emperor's sister, Eleanor) Marguerite was not allowed to accompany him, partly because she was pregnant again and travel was considered risky for her health. She was restless and complained bitterly of her "exile," as she did whenever she was separated from her brother. Louise de Savoie, seeking ways to distract her, invited Madame de Montmorency, who was also expecting a child, to come to court and keep her company. The most important diversion, however, was a "visit" from her husband and infant daughter, at Blois in March 1530.[3] With the exception of her uncle's act creating the new guild-masters, this is the first mention of Jeanne in contemporary sources since her birth a year and four months earlier. The poets, who before Jeanne's birth had hailed Marguerite as "sister, wife, and mother of kings," neglect even to mention Jeanne's christening or the names of her god-parents.[4]

It is not surprising that the infant Princess provided no news for chroniclers of court gossip as yet. Female offspring, even in the royal family, were of little interest, except when they married or bore children, and Jeanne may already have been far removed from the public eye, in the care of her mother's friend Aymée de Lafayette, Baillive of Caen, who lived at Lonray on the outskirts of Alençon. Aymée is not listed as *gouvernante* until 1532, but it is possible that her position as foster-mother was merely regularized in financial terms at that time.[5] No correspondence between Marguerite and Aymée has survived, although the Queen of Navarre was a prolific writer of letters. The hundreds calendared by Jourda include letters of condolence and congratulation and letters conferring protection or favors on her vassals, retainers, and friends.[6] But whatever correspondence there was between Marguerite and Aymée has unfortunately disappeared in the course of the centuries.

Jeanne is not even mentioned in Marguerite's letters before 1532. This is not surprising in letters concerned with public affairs—Marguerite's correspondents of the period include the Pope, Margaret of Austria, and various German princes—or in exchanges with poets and scholars. Her letters to François I and Montmorency, however, usually include personal matters. She speaks frequently of the health of Madame de Montmorency and Louise de Savoie, and reports news of the King's children. There are several references to her own second pregnancy, and in July 1530 (her son Jean was born on the 14th), she wrote to the King, "you say that your children are also mine, and I do not disclaim the honor, because I love them more than those [sic] I have borne." She adds that if the child she is awaiting, whom the King calls his own, "could have come into the world through my mouth, he would have done so today because when the good news [the deliverance of the two Princes from their captivity in Spain] was announced he leapt up in my womb in order to hear better."[7] To Montmorency she expresses irritation that the birth is delayed because she cannot join the court.[8] She claims that the return of the Princes is the greatest joy of her life, thanking God for having made Montmorency the instrument of their deliverance.[9]

No details of the brief family reunion at Blois have survived. Henri d'Albret left to join the escort of the Princes in April 1530, and Marguerite herself followed as soon as she recovered from childbirth, presumably sending Jeanne back to Alençon with Aymée. Later in the year, Marguerite and Henri d'Albret spent some weeks there. This must have been the last really happy period of Marguerite's life. Her newborn son died on Christmas Day of the same year; relations with her husband became increasingly strained; and she and Jeanne were never at ease with each other. Marguerite developed a profound melancholy, which is reflected in her writing and in her intensified search for comfort in religion.

Many scholars have written about Marguerite's personal beliefs, a controversial subject outside the range of this study.[10] Two facts important to a biographer of her daughter are undisputed. Marguerite never left the Roman church; nevertheless, she spent so much time and energy protecting reformers and even persons condemned for heresy, that for four hundred years Catholic historians have blamed her for weakening the church, while Protestant historians have credited her with spreading the reform.

Some of Jeanne's earliest memories may have been of Marguerite as the sponsor of the reform in Alençon—although not during the 1530 visit, when she was not yet two years old. The following year Marguerite was preoccupied by the death of Louise de Savoie, the publication of *Le Miroir de l'âme pécheresse,* the coronation of her new sister-in-law, and

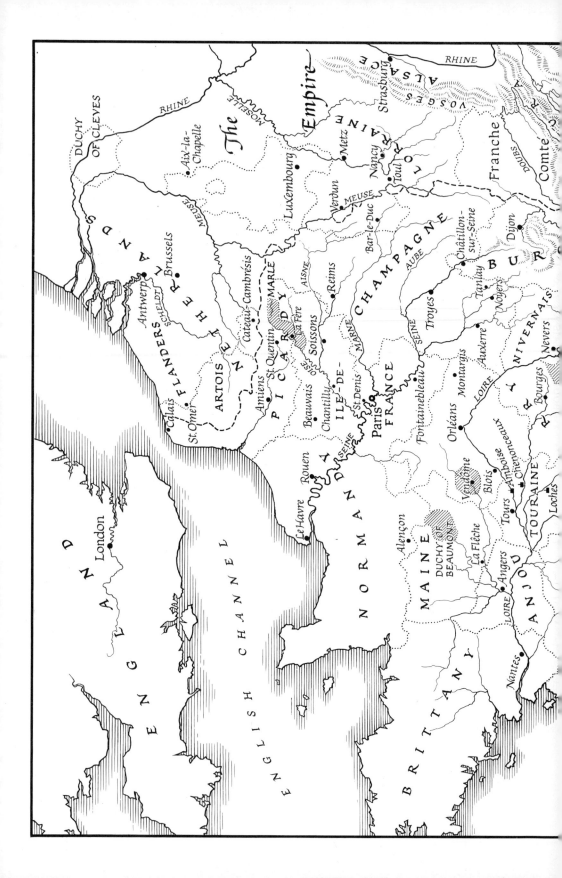

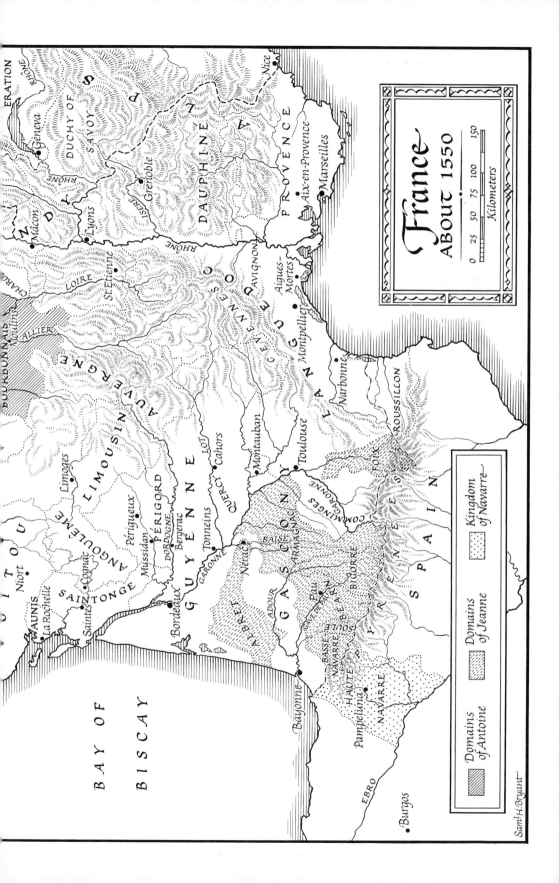

France
ABOUT 1550

0 25 50 75 100 150
Kilometers

Domains
of Antoine

Domains
of Jeanne

Kingdom
of Navarre

BAY OF BISCAY

RHONE
ERATION
DUCHY OF SAVOY
Geneva
Lyons
St. Etienne
Grenoble
Isère
DAUPHINE
PROVENCE
Nice
Aix-en-Provence
Marseilles
Macon
Moulins
ALLIER
BOURBONNAIS
LOIRE
AUVERGNE
CÉVENNES
LANGUEDOC
Avignon
Aigues-Mortes
Montpellier
Narbonne
ROUSSILLON
LIMOUSIN
Limoges
Périgueux
PÉRIGORD
Mussidan
DORDOGNE
Bergerac
Cahors
QUERCY
LOT
Montauban
Toulouse
FOIX
COMMINGES
GARONNE
SPAIN
ANGOULEME
Cognac
Saintes
SAINTONGE
Tonneins
GARONNE
GUYENNE
Bordeaux
ALBRET
Nérac
BAISE
ADOUR
ARMAGNAC
GASCONY
PYRENEES
Niort
POITOU
La Rochelle
AUNIS
CHAR...
RHONE
CHARENTE
Bayonne
BASSE-NAVARRE
HAUTE-NAVARRE
Pampeluna
NAVARRE
Pau
GAVE DE PAU
BEARN
SOULE
BIGORRE
Burgos
EBRO

Sam'l. H. Bryant

political activities accompanying the rise of Montmorency. Affairs in Alençon had to wait. In 1532, although every important person who came to the French court paid his respects to the King's sister and she was busy with public affairs, Marguerite did make two trips to Alençon. An awkward situation there erupted in a crisis the following year, when two of her subjects mutilated statues in the chapel of St. Blaise, and the Parlement of Paris (the highest court in France), which investigated the incident on orders from the King, accused three local priests of inciting the perpetrators of the crime. The King thereupon named commissioners to investigate the state of religion in Alençon, declaring the local justices incompetent. This embarrassed Marguerite, who, while encouraging reform, prided herself on the absence of "sedition" in her domains. In the Alençon crisis, she ordered her officers to submit fully to the royal authorities;[11] to her brother she wrote disassociating herself from the episode.[12]

Marguerite's religious views created even greater difficulties at court, where Gérard Roussel,* her chaplain and a critic of the Church, was causing a sensation with his Lenten sermons, preaching the Gospel "with great liberty" and, according to Erasmus, condemning the cult of saints. Noel Béda, self-appointed defender of the faith and spokesman for the Sorbonne, drew up a list of heretical propositions advocated by Roussel. The liberals struck back when Marot published verses satirizing the Faculty of Theology. Paris was in a state of agitation and mutual recrimination. The D'Albrets urged François I to prevent an uprising, and on May 18, 1533, the King exiled Béda on the grounds that he was disturbing the peace—postponing the question of Roussel's alleged heresy. François wrote Marguerite that his high opinion of her was in no way diminished, a welcome assurance.

The Queen of Navarre did not attempt to avoid the consequences of the attack on Roussel. She supported him strongly and took him under her protection pending his trial. She showed that she considered her own position at stake when she wrote Montmorency, "Would I have retained in my service for five years one guilty of emitting poison?"[13] That Marguerite was justified in taking the attack personally was proved later in the year, when students at the Collège de Navarre insulted her

---

* Gérard Roussel (died 1555) became Bishop of Oloron (one of the two sees in Béarn) thanks to the sponsorship of Marguerite. The spread of the reform there is attributed to his influence.

in a satirical performance and the Sorbonne placed *Le Miroir* (published two years earlier) on a list of prohibited books. François I again took up his sister's defense and the Faculty of Theology fell back on the lame excuse that the book had been published without its authorization. The real explanation of the attack may lie in the fact that the new edition contained a translation of the Sixth Psalm by Marot. The King's sister was guilty of sanctioning the "new thinking." Thanks to the King's support, Marguerite was vindicated and the Sorbonne yielded, but the incident remained a source of irritation and hurt pride to the Queen of Navarre. (This quarrel with the Faculty of Theology did not prevent her from being on good terms with Pope Clement VII, who commended her piety and granted her exemption from fasting.)[14]

While it is unlikely that Jeanne was informed of these events, there was undoubtedly gossip and speculation in the servants' quarters at Lonray, and Jeanne must have overheard references to them, even if she appeared not to. Significantly, the only episode of her childhood (prior to the Cleves marriage) about which we know from Jeanne herself concerns Marguerite's religious opinions and the anger they provoked in Henri d'Albret. In a letter to the Vicomte de Gourdon,* written in August 1555, when she was twenty-seven years old, Jeanne said, "I well remember the great annoyance shown years ago by most honored father and lord . . . when [Marguerite] was praying in her room with the ministers, Roussel and Farel . . . how he slapped her on the cheek and forbade her to meddle in doctrinal matters . . . he shook a stick at me, which has cost me bitter tears and kept me fearful and compliant until they had both died."[15]

Known facts about Roussel place this episode before 1536, and it is unlikely to have occurred before 1534, since Henri d'Albret was himself still sponsoring Roussel in 1533. It should probably be placed in the latter months of 1534 or in 1535. This is plausible; at that time not only Roussel but Marot and Calvin himself took refuge at Marguerite's court

---

* Nicolas de Flotard, Vicomte de Gourdon. (See Haag, V, 119.) For the context of this important letter see Chapter V. There is some question about the authenticity of the nine letters (copies) from Jeanne to Gourdon in the Bibliothèque Nationale. The style of some of them, including this one, leads me to accept those, as did Jourda (*Marguerite d'Angoulême*), I, 181, note). Jeanne erred, however, in naming Farel (1489–1565), who was not in France during these years, but in Switzerland, where he played an important role in the introduction of the reform in Geneva. She might easily have mistaken the names of some of the persons in Marguerite's entourage at court, whom she saw infrequently, as a young child.

in Nérac, after tension over the new religious ideas erupted in *l'affaire des placards.* The appearance throughout Paris of handbills attacking the church (October 1534) marks the turn of the French Reformation from the initial, intellectual stage to the aggressive stage, later institutionalized by Calvin. The effects were dramatic, and from then on both François I and Henri d'Albret opposed the reformers. The letter to Gourdon indicates that Jeanne was aware at the age of six or seven that her mother's religious views were "dangerous" and that the relationship between her parents was affected by them. Clearly it was an unforgettable experience, and the context of Jeanne's letter—her decision to embrace Calvinism—shows that she had been cautioned by it to proceed carefully in matters of religion.

Other events of these early years may have affected Jeanne at the time as well as later. In the 1530's, François I, "Eldest Son of the Church," was forming alliances with Lutheran princes in Germany against the Emperor, who was defending the unity of Catholic Europe. The last of the Renaissance popes, Clement VII, was succeeded by Paul III, marking the start of the Counter Reformation, a movement which was to be Jeanne's chief enemy when she was the mother of a Protestant heir to the French throne. Across the channel, another princess, Elizabeth of England, was beginning a similarly difficult childhood, with religious and political issues entangled with family relationships.

Closer to home, Marguerite's activities often involved persons important in Jeanne's later life. The child presumably attended the marriage of her aunt, Isabeau d'Albret, to René de Rohan, the occasion of Marguerite's visit to Alençon in August 1534. A daughter of the marriage became Jeanne's playmate, and in later years Jeanne protected her as Marguerite had protected Isabeau. During a triumphal tour of southern France (1535), Marguerite was met in Albi by Georges d'Armagnac, Bishop of Rodez and later Cardinal, who conducted her to the cathedral to the sound of silver trumpets and crowned her Comtesse de Rodez. Subsequently, he obtained the Abbaye de Séez through her influence. Twenty-eight years later, when he led the papal offensive against Jeanne, she was to remind D'Armagnac that he owed his rise to her mother.

In 1536, Marguerite was at the height of her power at court, temporarily in Lyons. The papal Nuncio reported to the Pope, "the Queen of Navarre attends the King's *levée* every morning and is a member of his inner council." He urged Paul III to extend his protection to Renée

la feü roine de nauaere
marguerite

MARGUERITE D'ANGOULÊME, QUEEN OF NAVARRE

of Ferrara,* whom Marguerite was defending against the brutal attacks of her husband.[16] In espousing the cause of Renée, Marguerite was defending not only a kinswoman but also the ideas they shared. One of her own protégés, Clément Marot, had been offered refuge by the Duchess when he fled France; his presence was one pretext for the Duke's attack on Renée.[17] Relations between the daughter of Louis XII and Jeanne became strained in later years, and the Duchess sometimes had to remind herself of her debt to Jeanne's mother. Jeanne may have heard that the Emperor was invading Provence and that her parents were attempting to mediate between him and the French king, although she certainly would not have learned until years later that in 1536 a Spanish spy named Juan Martinez Descurra first took a hand in the tangled intrigues of the Navarre princes with the Hapsburgs.[18] Twenty-seven years later the reports of this same Descurra to his Spanish masters would disclose details of Jeanne's political philosophy and tactics, at the same time providing one of the few revealing character sketches we possess.

Shortly before Jeanne's eighth birthday the succession to the throne was altered by the sudden death of her cousin the Dauphin, making Henri, Duc d'Orléans, who was married to Catherine de Medici, the heir apparent. The court poets vied with each other in expressing the general mourning. Marguerite was much affected, but she replied to a letter of condolence from Renée, "Do we not still have the King's other children, and the noble example of [his] brave Christian bearing . . . not to mention the victory over his enemies which the Lord has granted him?"[19]

Jeanne's absentee mother was the most prominent "career-woman" in Europe; much admired by her contemporaries, she retains to this day a hold over the imagination and affections of the French people, while her daughter is just a name. Even a brief account of Marguerite's activities explains the intermittent contact in Jeanne's childhood. Prior to 1537, there are only two references to Jeanne in Marguerite's letters. Scant and

* Renée de France, 1510–1575, daughter of Louis XII and wife of Hercule d'Este, Duke of Ferrara, was much influenced by Marguerite in her youth, as her correspondence of later years shows. Eighteen years younger than Marguerite and eighteen years older than Jeanne, Renée's religious position may also have been at a midpoint between them. Her extensive correspondence with Calvin, her protection of many Huguenots, and the presence in her household of a Calvinist chaplain, François de Morel, show that her connection with the reform was much stronger than Marguerite's; but she never became a public convert, like Jeanne after 1560.

tantalizing, they give a glimpse of the Queen's feelings about her small daughter. The first mention is in a letter to Montmorency, written from Lonray in 1532 (probably in March), when Jeanne was a little more than three years old. The purpose of the letter is to enclose one for the King; she charges the Grand Master with its delivery. By way of personal news she says that she arrived the day before at Lonray and is just leaving for the chateau of Alençon, where she will sleep that night. She is suffering from a pain in her shoulder and needs to rest, "away from my daughter, who is too noisy and boisterous."[20]

Marguerite could not have been more than twenty-four hours at Lonray, and presumably she spent some time conferring with Aymée and receiving the homage of the servants, many of whom had formerly been in her own household. One wonders whether Jeanne was brought to her mother or whether Marguerite went to the child's quarters, and whether she was awake when the Queen arrived. There would have been considerable bustle in the household at the arrival of the King's sister, who was also the ultimate employer. Jeanne had undoubtedly been told that her mother was coming to see her. Possibly her day's routine was changed for the occasion; almost certainly she would be "dressed up" for it. It is not unlikely that she was instructed about the proper way to greet the Queen who was also her mother. An intelligent child surrounded by adults of inferior station might well be imperious as well as articulate, and everything known of Jeanne in later years shows that she had a strong independent will. What did she do in this short visit that caused her mother to refer to her only as *trop bruyante?* Was she put out by the arrival of the only person (other than the King) who could displace her from the center of attention in that particular chateau with those particular people?

Marguerite does not mention Jeanne in her letters again until the summer of 1533, a year and four months later. Writing to Montmorency to thank him for sending news of the King, she says, "If only I could do something for you to give you the pleasure you give me." The letter incidentally informs him that Jeanne, approaching her fifth birthday, is visiting her mother at court, in Paris. She has not been well but is recovering, and her mother is planning to take her to St. Cloud or Suresnes, for a change of air.[21] This is the first of many mentions of Jeanne's health, which was always frail. Indeed, the known facts of

Jeanne's childhood relate principally to a series of illnesses. Only in the first years of her marriage (1548–1553) was she free from this handicap.

Opportunities for Jeanne to become intimate with her father were even fewer; Henri d'Albret is known to have visited Alençon only twice, briefly, during her childhood. Nor did he reside regularly at court; when not at war he spent most of his time in his own domains in the south of France. Jeanne's early contacts with her father took place when they were both visiting Marguerite at court. The position of the D'Albrets there was not very comfortable; they were poor relations and Henri d'Albret was an object of suspicion because of the Navarre question. Jeanne, a temporary resident in the royal nursery, had little chance to see her parents together in private. The only such occasion she herself mentions—in the 1555 letter to Gourdon—records friction between them. From other sources, chiefly the poems of Marot, we know that in these years both Henri d'Albret and Marguerite were exceedingly anxious to have a son. It could almost be described as an obsession, lasting for Henri until shortly before his death.

A NORMAN CHILDHOOD

Far from her well-known mother, in the center of the brightly lighted stage, Jeanne was growing from infancy to her ninth year in the Norman countryside. Aymée and Jeanne probably lived on the former's estate, Lonray, and visited in the larger chateau of Alençon, which Marguerite had inherited from her first husband, on such occasions as the Rohan wedding. The two residences were only about a mile apart. Lonray is bounded on the north by a line of thickly wooded hills about four kilometers from the chateau, the forest of Ecouves. On the west, this forest adjoins a cliff called the Butte de Chaumont, about six kilometers from the chateau. The orientation of the property is, therefore, south and east, with farmlands extending to within two kilometers of the town of Alençon. In the early fifteenth century Lonray passed into the Silly family, its owners in Jeanne's period, through the marriage of Guillaumette de Neuilly to Robert de Silly, who rendered homage to the Duc d'Alençon for the fief in 1407.[22] In 1450, Jacques de Silly obtained permission from Charles VII to fortify Lonray and he acquired the titles of *Maître de l'Hôtel du Roi* and Chamberlain in 1479. From then on the family was to figure in the ranks of French nobles who had rather close relations with the crown but who lived on their own estates rather than at court (for the most part), retaining a good deal of local power. François de Silly, *bailli** and Governor of Caen, fought "gloriously" at Pavia, where he simultaneously lost his life and gained for his widow, Aymée, the gratitude of François I and the friendship of Marguerite.

The medieval chateau had been sacked and burned on various occasions during the Hundred Years War. The chateau in which Jeanne grew up, constructed by Jacques de Silly and embellished by François in the early sixteenth century, was more elegant than the average Norman manor house, to judge from old drawings in the Archives and descriptions written before its destruction sometime early in the nineteenth century. It had a peristyle adorned with classic columns and sculptures in what was then the latest Renaissance fashion. Its large park, enclosed by a high stone wall, was subdivided into sections by *allées* of trees and adorned with fountains and statuary. Except for her brief visits to court, Jeanne's first eight years were spent in this environment, privileged, to be sure, but far from royal. Most girls growing up on an estate like Lonray were destined to marry owners of similar properties and devote their lives to their management and the raising of another generation of local nobility. But Jeanne was a child from the great world of the court, exiled until she was old enough to be important.

After she was widowed, Aymée became one of Marguerite's ladies-in-waiting and accompanied the Duchesse d'Alençon, as Marguerite then was, to Spain on the difficult mission to negotiate the King's release. As a sign of his gratitude, François I rewarded Aymée with the barony of Laigle, confiscated from one of the supporters of the Constable of Bourbon. Although Aymée lived more in the style of the country gentry than of the great nobles, she evidently had some wealth at her disposal, for in 1527 "a magnificent tomb, made of marble and gypsum" was erected in the village church, a few steps from the chateau, to house the remains of her husband, which had been brought back from Italy. It bore the inscription, *viva moriens amata amatissimo conjugi continuiis cum lachrymis construxit* (built for her most beloved husband, with unceasing tears, by her who was loved, and who, alive, is dying). The Latinizing tendency and somewhat pretentious style fashionable in the educated class is manifested especially in the rendering of Aymée's name into Latin, *amata*.[23] In the list of Marguerite's retainers, Aymée is described as

* *Bailli,* a ranking officer in the royal administration of the provinces since the reign of Philip Augustus, 1180–1223.

Dame d'honeur et gouvernante de Madame la princesse, and she was allotted fifty livres tournois a month as a salary. In addition, she was often granted extra money for Jeanne's expenses.[24]

Brantôme, chief reporter of the spicy side of the Valois court, whose grandmother was also one of Marguerite's intimates, tells a story in *Des Dames,* which involves Aymée.

When Pope Clément [VII] came to Marseille [1533] for the wedding of his niece [Catherine de Medici] with M. d'Orléans [later Henri II], three fine young widows found themselves so low in spirits and so full of sadness from the loss of their marital pleasures . . . that they asked M. d'Albany [John Stuart, Duke of Albany], cousin of the Pope and in his good graces, to ask [the Pope] for dispensations which would allow them to eat meat on fast days. The Duke agreed and arranged for them to come informally to the Pope's lodging. He also invited the King [François I] thinking to amuse him. . . . When they were all three kneeling before His Holiness, M. d'Albany began to speak in low tones and in Italian, which the ladies did not understand.
"Holy Father, here are three beautiful widows, good women, as you can see, who for nothing in the world would marry again . . . and because they are sometimes troubled by the desires of the flesh, they humbly beg Your Holiness for permission to have relations with men outside of the bonds of matrimony. . . ." "But," said the Pope, "that would be against the laws of God, I have no power to dispense!" "Here they are, Holy Father," said the Duke, "please listen to what they have to say." Then one [of the widows] began to speak: "Holy Father, we have asked M. d'Albany to present a very humble request for all of us and we show you, as proof of our need, our pale and emaciated complexions." "My daughters," said the Pope, "the request is unreasonable because it is against God's own ordinance." The widows, not knowing what the Duke had said, replied, "Holy Father, please at least give us leave for three times a week." The Pope repeated, "I cannot do it, to allow you the sin of voluptuousness would be to damn myself." The ladies then realized that M. d'Albany had played a joke on them, and another one of them spoke up: "Holy Father, we are asking only for permission to eat flesh on fast days." To this M. d'Albany said, "I thought you meant live flesh." The Pope then understood the joke and smiled, but he reproached M. d'Albany for bringing a blush to the cheeks of honest women. The King later had a good laugh over it with the Pope, who granted their request and gave them his blessing.[25]

Brantôme names Aymée as one of the three widows, but the story tells more about the Duke, the King, and the Pope than it does about Jeanne's gouvernante.

Fortunately, a much fuller portrait of Aymée exists, albeit a fictional one; it comes from no less an authority than Marguerite herself, in her most important work, the *Heptameron.* The character Longarine is believed to represent Aymée, and Jourda points out that her fictional name scarcely conceals the name of her estate.[26] Marguerite's characters are real, although not fully developed. She gives the reader a vivid impression of the personality and philosophy of life of each of the *devisants,* through their comments rather than through the tales themselves. These conversational interludes are sometimes humorous, but often dramatic in their suggestion of tensions in the group.

Longarine is the *femme raisonable,* full of common sense, realistic about human nature but not soured by her disappointments. Gay and forthright, she has a reputation for making people laugh and for telling the truth. She has high standards of fidelity, and she says at one time that if her husband were unfaithful she would kill him and herself. Yet Longarine is much less absorbed in romantic love than the other women of the group, in that she not only shows disdain for the pleasures of love but says, "the best course of all would be not to love, because it surely leads only to unhappiness and death" (LXX). Jourda says of Longarine, "life had tested her but she knew how to avoid pessimism and keep her gaiety; she reminds us a bit of the Marquise de Sévigné."

Although it is far from a three-dimensional portrait, a few of Longarine's traits come out clearly in Marguerite's characterization. Commenting on Tale XIX, Parlemente (Marguerite) makes a long speech about intellectual or spiritual love, illustrating the Platonic doctrine of a "ladder" of love which mounts steadily from lower to higher forms. Longarine agrees with the general theory, but emphasizes rather the continuity between the levels: "A man who has no love for carnal things will never attain to the love of God, since the soil of his heart is barren." In her comment on Tale XXV, Longarine insists that one can push too far the identification of evil thoughts with sin, "God will not condemn us if we do not put our evil thoughts into action," and later she says, "Whoever can do evil but does not is to be accounted blessed." She does not carry this tolerance to the point of condoning self-indulgence, however, for she places a high value on self-control. Commenting on Tale XLII she says, "Of all the virtues self-mastery is the greatest, and mortification of self can be used as the measure of virtue." Pride she considers a sin, "as when one esteems oneself wiser than others" (LI), but, "when virtue fails, we must call hypocrisy to our aid as we use

La Balliue de Cam

AYMÉE DE LAFAYETTE, BAILLIVE OF CAEN

high heels to make us taller. It is no small thing to be able to hide imperfections" (XLII).

Longarine's sound insights into human nature are shown in her comments on self-deception and on the egotism of men in relation to women. She has especially acute perceptions about the weaknesses of women, which lead them to put up with anything in the name of "love": "Your wives love you so that if you were to give them horns as big as stags' they would willing persuade themselves and others that they were garlands of roses" (VIII). "I believe that many a women hath loved unto death; love is so powerful that when hope of its success is lost it brings [women] to the worst despair" (XLIX). "To win back a lover a woman will do all things" (LXIII). Aymée also understands the intimate connection between love and anger in women: "Without sparing our sex, I wish to make plain to husbands that women of great heart are more often overcome by the fire of revenge than by the gentleness of loving forgiveness" (XV).

Although Aymée's own marital experience is not on the record, a good deal is known about Marguerite's disappointment and humiliation at the hands of Henri d'Albret. Marguerite depicts herself (Parlemente), as intensely sensitive to rejection and humiliation, and Jourda's comprehensive study bears this out. Her high ideal of Christian humility kept Marguerite from giving rein to that fire of vengeance characteristic of women with strong feelings; instead she retreated into melancholy and mysticism.

Aymée was deeply devoted to Marguerite. She may not have been impressed by Henri d'Albret, for in the *Heptameron* Longarine does not hesitate to make some sharp verbal thrusts at Hircan, his fictional counterpart (VIII). Aymée was tougher than Marguerite, assuming the character of Longarine to be essentially accurate. If she was determined to implant in Jeanne a realistic attitude toward life, she achieved some success. On the other hand, the correspondence between Jeanne as a young married woman and her husband, Antoine de Bourbon, contains some allusions to Aymée which indicate that the relation between Jeanne and her foster-mother was not a happy one.[27]

The staff provided by Marguerite to take care of Jeanne consisted of about twenty persons under Aymée's direction. Nicolas Bourbon, tutor, heads the list, followed by Nicolas Jouanne, business manager. René Perault, master of the stables, was assisted by a groom and three footmen.

Four women are mentioned, two of whom are described as "nurse and chambermaid" and one as *mère de la folle de Madame la princesse.* There were also two bakers and a pastry-maker, two furriers, two lackeys, a chaplain, and a serving-man "for the women."[28] Although there must have been other household servants, especially in the kitchen, who were retained by Aymée and not by Marguerite, as well as hands on the estate, this is a simple household. Marguerite's own establishment, for instance, included five grooms with half a dozen assistants, seven bakers with fourteen assistants, eighteen furriers, and about twenty servants in the kitchen. No private household would include more than fifty *gens de finance,* twenty-five secretaries, and seven physicians, as Marguerite's did, and of course there is no real comparison between the requirements of the King's sister, hostess to ambassadors, and those of a child-princess, living in the country.[29]

Two persons, important in Jeanne's childhood, are not listed in her household but in that of Marguerite: Jean or Gaston de Bourbon, Vicomte de Lavedan, Marguerite's first Chamberlain, and his wife, who was Aymée's second daughter, Françoise. Lavedan belonged to the Constable's branch of the Bourbon family; it is likely that Marguerite had taken him under her protection when the crown was punishing many of the Constable's relations. At a certain critical point in Jeanne's life, the Lavedans were with Aymée, although it is clear that their regular residence was elsewhere. They must have been considerably older than Jeanne. Aymée and Marguerite were contemporaries, but Marguerite was thirty-six when Jeanne was born in 1528, and Aymée's first grandson, Jacques (II) de Mattignon, was born less than three years later.

Despite her connections with royalty, Aymée's household may appropriately be compared with that of the Sieur de Gouberville, a sixteenth-century Norman gentleman of modest circumstances.[30] Gouberville's family (a sister and several illegitimate half-brothers) numbered eight, and there were fourteen servants, whereas the ratio of those served to those serving at Lonray was about five to fifteen. The Princesse de Navarre grew up in a rural atmosphere very different from the Valois court, where she was never at ease, and in later years when Jeanne had the responsibility of bringing up an heir to the throne, she did everything in her power to protect him from its "corruption."

Thanks to the existence of a good many sources like Gouberville's *Journal,* life in sixteenth-century Normandy can be reconstructed in

considerable detail.[31] The chateau of Lonray, with its recent embellishments, was considerably grander than Gouberville's manor house, which
corresponds closely to the model in Charles d'Etienne's *Agriculture et
maison rustique* (1564). At Lonray, some of the functional parts of a
manor, such as stables and storage-bins, might be removed from the
seigneurial residence, instead of surrounding it on all sides. Entrance to
the chateau may have been through a great hall with antlers and other
trophies on the walls, instead of through the unpretentious vestibule of a
working manor, but the kitchen was probably the center of life for
most of the household, if not for the chatelaine herself.

Olivier de Serres, in *Le Théâtre d'agriculture et mesnage des champs*
(1600), remarks that "the Constable of France no longer knows what
it is to eat well, [because he now eats] in the great room at the mercy
of his cook, where before he took his meals in the kitchen and had what
he wanted." Most rural nobles in the sixteenth century still used the
kitchen as the living-room, except for special occasions. The Sieur de
Gouberville not only ate there but spent his evenings beside the great
fireplace, writing in his *Journal*, working on his accounts or reading the
Amadis des Gaulles aloud to the household. When he had recovered from
an illness he reports with satisfaction that he has been able "to go down
to the kitchen again." The kitchen was sometimes on the ground floor,
to the right of the entrance, and sometimes on the first floor across the
hall from the *grande salle*, near the master's bedroom, so that he "can
control the laziness, blasphemy, and quarreling of the servants . . . in
the night when they stay late in the kitchen disporting themselves, under
the pretext of cleaning the vessels, washing, and preparing for the next
day." The kitchen was the most completely furnished room in a country
house, with different kinds of benches, stools, tables, and chests, as well
as utensils of all sorts. It often contained one or more beds for servants,
and easy chairs near the fire for the seigneur and his wife.

The *grande salle*, on the other hand, was reserved for the seigneurial
family and guests. It usually had a large dresser on which would stand
candlesticks, salt-cellars, and other objects which combined utility with
beauty, as well as books—the *Roman de la Rose, Amadis des Gaulles*,
and, in Protestant or humanist families, the Bible. A sophisticated
chatelaine like Aymée might keep her books in her own room, which in
a chateau of more than average luxury would have its own fireplace,
a large canopied bed, and chests and wardrobes for clothing and personal

effects. The master bedroom and the great room habitually had the best view, overlooking the garden, river, or woods, away from the noise of the farmyard and the servants' quarters. Unlike those of the kitchen, the windows of these rooms were curtained and tapestries adorned the walls.

France in the sixteenth century already had a reputation for good food—and Normans are notoriously big eaters. When the Sieur de Gouberville entertained the prior of the Abbaye de Lessay he offered him "larded chickens, capons, two partridges, one hare . . . and a venison-pasty that my cousin De Tocqueville sent me." The usual weekly purchases for his household included half a veal, half a sheep, a quarter of beef, and a whole pig. It was the custom, even at court, for the entire household to eat the chief meal of the day in the late afternoon, and the royal children of France sat at table even on some state occasions. Presumably, on ordinary days in Aymée's house, Jeanne would sit next to the Baillive "above the great salt," with guests, if any, in the kitchen. On the rare occasions of Marguerite's visits, one imagines dinner being served in the *grande salle* to the Queen of Navarre and the Princess, Aymée, and the principal members of Marguerite's suite, with the rest of her retinue joining the Lonray servants in the kitchen.

In addition to supervising routine household activities, as a widow Aymée must have spent a good deal of time on her seigneurial duties, such as arbitrating disputes on the estates, visiting the sick, fulfilling the obligations of her station to the local church, and taking part in the social and administrative life of the region. Her position was important, both because of the prominence of her husband's family and because of her own connections with royalty.

Since there was no male seigneur either at Lonray or in Alençon, Jeanne was probably deprived of the ritual of the hunt experienced by most noble children growing up in the French countryside. Similarly, her exposure to jousting, the *jeu de paume,* running, wrestling, the "manipulation of horses and arms," and all of the other two hundred and seventeen games Rabelais mentions as Gargantua's pastimes, probably came chiefly during her visits to the court. Quieter forms of diversion must have been available. In the evening, when the work of the day was done, Aymée might sit by the fire reading or telling stories to Jeanne, perhaps while doing needlepoint, or she and Lavedan or other guests might play cards, or backgammon. Sometimes after dinner there would be amateur music in an upper-class Renaissance household, especially singing of familiar songs, but also performance on lutes or recorders.

Jeanne's childhood, like that of children in all ages, was probably punctuated by special occasions: weddings, christenings, and funerals on the estate; visits of important guests; and morality and miracle plays and processions in the village. When plays were performed, usually in the church itself, the inhabitants of all the neighboring estates, nobility and peasantry, old and young, would attend. The Sieur de Gouberville tells that a morality play was performed in the church at Digonville every Christmas Eve after Midnight Mass, and that his entire household attended, returning to Mesnil-au-Val just in time for the *reveillon* before dawn. On many special days during the year processions and ceremonies combined revelry with religious observance: on Corpus Christi the Host was carried "through the greenwood to the chapel," its path strewn with flowers and herbs; on St. John's Eve fires were lighted on all the hilltops of the region; on the *Fête des Rois* a special giant cake was cut by the head of the household and distributed to all the residents of the estate.

If Aymée was really like Madame de Sévigné, as Jourda suggests, she may have been bored with these rustic pastimes and longed for the sophisticated pleasures of the court. It might be useful to know whether she made a point of taking Jeanne to see the processions in the village. Speculation on Jeanne's exposure to such events in her childhood is unavoidable because her first act toward the establishment of Calvinism in Béarn, in 1563, was the prohibition of similar ceremonies. Jeanne may not have had an aversion to quasi-religious ceremonies as a child, however. One entry in the *Registre* of Frotté, in 1542, notes that Marguerite's expenses include "one hundred écus given to the Baillive de Caen to repay the gift made by Madame la Princesse to the players of the Passion for their staging."[32]

Jeanne was isolated in her early years, having no children of her own rank to play with and few contacts with men, other than servants. She was intelligent and sensitive and must have observed many things on the estate which contributed to the formation of her character. In assessing the influence of the circumstances on her development, it is important to avoid, as far as possible, anachronistic conclusions based on twentieth-century attitudes toward children and the family. Philippe Ariès, in *Centuries of Childhood,* shows that the modern concept only began to emerge in the seventeenth century. Drawing upon the iconography of the fifteenth and sixteenth centuries, he demonstrates that childhood was not then regarded as a distinctive period of life.[33] "Children mixed with adults in everyday life and any gathering for work, relaxation, sport, or public affairs, brought together both children and adults." Even infants were dressed like adults. Their pastimes and games also were not differentiated. Louis XIII, Jeanne's grandson (born in 1601), took part in court dances and played tennis at the age of three, although he still slept in a cradle. At the same time he was taught to read and to play chess. By the age of seven, his education was entirely in the hands of men, and once when he was being punished, his tutor said, "you are no longer a child." Curiously, when distinctions began to be made between children and adults, they applied mostly to males. Little girls continued to be dressed like grown women and they were depicted in adult female activities, "as if childhood separated girls from adult life less than it did boys."

The concept of children's "innocence," so important later, was non-existent. Children attended the coarse farces which constituted the chief theatrical fare at court and in the village. References by Louis XIII as a very young child to sexual organs and activity—his own and others' —were reported with delight. Another attitude is what appears to us as shocking callousness toward the death of children. Ariès explains it as "a direct and inevitable consequence of demography." Parents "could not allow themselves to become too attached to something regarded as a probable loss." Citing Montaigne's belief that "children had neither mental activities nor recognizable bodily shape," Ariès considers the sixteenth-century indifference a natural, healthy defense-mechanism of parents in an age when the chances for survival of any given child were slight.

Jeanne had virtually no experience of family life, a circumstance which twentieth-century psychology considers dangerous for a child's development. The effect on Jeanne of her "emotionally deprived" childhood should be evaluated in the historical context, however—the normal expectations of a little girl of the high nobility in sixteenth-century France. Ariès shows that the concept of the family as a social cell, which eventually gave it a place of honor along with God and the King, was only beginning to emerge at the end of the century, together with that of childhood. Formerly, emphasis was on the "line," the continuity of the name—an attitude evident in many actions and statements of Jeanne's mature life.

EDUCATION OF A PRINCESS

Among other reasons for regretting the lack of information about Aymée is that she was probably responsible for the early stages of Jeanne's formal education as well as for her upbringing. In theory, Jeanne was educated by the humanist Nicolas Bourbon, and such was Marguerite's original intention.[34] The fact is, however, that Bourbon was in trouble with the authorities in 1533 because in the first edition of his *Nugae* he had referred to the Catholic Church as "the Roman Wolf" and attacked the cult of "images" and the saints. He spent some time in prison, despite Marguerite's efforts to procure his release. The Cardinal de Lorraine was more successful, and in May 1534, Bourbon prudently decided to absent himself. He spent the next two years in England, as a member of Ann Boleyn's circle, probably thanks to letters from Marguerite. There he admired Thomas Cranmer and Thomas Cromwell and had his portrait painted by Holbein. When he returned to France in the autumn of 1536 he joined the court in Lyons, center of the "new thinking," where Marguerite was at the height of her career.[35] In 1538, the second and much enlarged edition of the *Nugae* was published by Sébastien Gryphe, and Bourbon became embroiled in a series of pedantic squabbles with fellow-scholars, which took up most of his energies for several years.[36]

Since Jeanne was in Normandy until 1538—except for brief visits at court—she could not have been consistently under Bourbon's guidance until she was ten years old, despite his listing as her *pédagogue* since 1532. After 1538 Jeanne and Aymée were residing at Plessis-les-Tours, with longer and more frequent sojourns at court, where Bourbon was a member of Marguerite's entourage before he retired to a benefice in Condé (Maine-et-Loire) on the borders of Touraine and Anjou.* In the absence of any reference to other tutors in Jeanne's household, one

---

* Bourbon wrote a *poème d'occasion* for Jeanne when she was married. *Conjugium illustrissimum, A. Borboni et Janae Navarrorum, principiis,* Paris, 1549. Its style, characteristic of the somewhat mediocre group of humanists of which Bourbon was a member, is scarcely more banal than that of Ronsard, published by De Ruble in *Le Mariage de Jeanne d'Albret,* pp. 263–265.

assumes that she was taught to read and write by the Baillive. Even in the 1540's Bourbon must have been supervisor of Jeanne's education rather than her regular teacher. He probably planned the curriculum, instructed Aymée in its application, and checked up on his pupil during her sojourns at her uncle's court. There is no doubt that Marguerite's daughter was given an education designed to implement the humanist ideal, that is, the development of both character and intellect through absorption of the classic writings which were the models of the Renaissance.

Despite his somewhat indirect connection with Jeanne, it is worth while to consider Bourbon's educational philosophy, because he was officially responsible for the instruction of the Princesse de Navarre. In common with the rest of his group, his chosen language was Latin, and his literary output was characterized by rhetoric rather than by substance. As Joachim du Bellay says,

> Bourbon dans ses oeuvres nouvelles
> Ne montre pas un grand talent,
> Mais, en les nommant *Bagatelles,*
> Il fait preuve de jugement.[37]

Bourbon was the author of a great many dedications, ranging in tone from the obsequious to the vindictive, and he frequently transferred them from one person to another. He was involved in a number of acrimonious disputes with other poets, with whom he was alternately on intimate terms and at swords' points. When he returned from England in 1536, he believed that another poet, Jean Visagier, had plagiarized the *Nugae* in his *Epigrams,* and there was a lively feud between them for several years. His judgment of the brighter literary lights of the period sometimes diverges sharply from that of posterity: he says of Marot, "his poems will live as long as Virgil's," and he sees in Rabelais only a "debauched monk."

As befits a humanist, Bourbon's works show him to be above all a didactic moralist. He applauds moderation in all things, deplores the corruption of the times, laments the evils of human nature, and sees man's only solace in religion or in literature, "letters, which set an example for the young, provide consolation for the old and a refuge for the poor." Of Virgil he says, *il a mon amour et mon culte plus que tout autre.* Although he has momentary bursts of patriotic pride—in the *Eloge de la France* he says that France has an abundance of genius unknown in Greece or Italy—he once apologized to Marguerite in Latin for having dedicated another work to her in their native tongue.

In the *Bagatelles* we learn that the teacher's responsibility is a serious one and that it extends beyond intellectual training to manners and character-building, *la bonne morale*, "a burden heavier than Aetna." A young person should bend the knee to older persons of rank, address them in proper form, and express himself with modesty and respect. The teacher has a patriotic duty because "France needs cultivation" and because "mastery of language leads to diplomatic victories." Leaders need to be able to exercise moderation in the indulgence of pleasure and to discriminate between healthy recreation or exercise and "corrupting vices" or "vain waste of energy." Books are not to be swallowed un-critically, they are not all equal either in intellectual or in moral worth, "all that is bound in gold is not golden." The educated person has a moral obligation "to share his knowledge with the ignorant" and to excel the unprivileged in following Christ's example "so that those who say the pursuit of letters is but vanity will be confounded."

Bourbon's pedagogical method emphasizes mastery of the craft and having the right tools: "well-turned phrases and exactness in use of words are rare birds." Intellectual work should be done with great care and thoroughness, "any difficulty can be overcome by careful work," *faute de conscience pieuse, tout reste aveugle.* Repetition is essential for the development of an accurate memory and "only constant revision produces perfection" in writing. The good student learns "the arts of silence"—intensive listening and physical repose—which develop con-centration. When the time comes to recite, it is important "to think before you speak, enunciate clearly, and answer exactly the question asked." When reciting, "the book should be closed, the student should hold himself well and look the teacher in the eye."

Knowledge of the particular books Bourbon chose for Jeanne is lacking, but the general pattern of education in the French upper class suggests that they were mainly those of Latin authors, especially the poets, but also including Plutarch and Livy. Jeanne probably absorbed French literature from the atmosphere; she moved in circles where books were important and many contemporary works were dedicated to her mother or their authors subsidized by her. There is no evidence that she studied either Greek or Italian. The same is true of Spanish, although she undoubtedly understood that language. She had frequent contacts with Spaniards and many of her subjects had regular commercial dealings with that lost Navarre which was the object of her father's—and her husband's—diplomacy.

Nicolas Bourbon never turned Protestant, although he suffered persecution and exile for ideas which, if consistently followed, led in that direction. Like his patron Marguerite and the greater humanists Erasmus and Lefèvre d'Etaples, he may have been interested only in reform within the Roman church. He was probably not of the stuff of which innovators are made. During Jeanne's lessons with him, did he ever refer to the situation in England—to the ideas of Cranmer, for instance?— and if so, with what attitude? We have Jeanne's own word, in the letter to Gourdon, that as a child she was conscious of the danger inherent in the new opinions, and of her father's disapproval. She implies that her mother "dropped" the reform, and states that she herself waited until after the death of both parents to espouse it. Was Jeanne, who found it difficult to compromise, disappointed by Bourbon's change from his earlier bold stand to one of cautious conformity? If so, it may have contributed to the feeling that she could rely only on herself.

LA MIGNONNE DE DEUX ROIS?

More information about Jeanne is available for the year 1537 than for former years, because the Norman childhood was drawing to a close. The following year she and her household were moved to the chateau of Plessis-les-Tours, at the insistence of her uncle, François I, who wanted her nearer the court. His reasons stemmed from his own foreign policy and from the King's desire to thwart the plans Henri d'Albret was making for Jeanne's future, rather than from any sudden avuncular affection. D'Albret's plans in fact precipitated the King's decision to take over the supervision of his niece. This hitherto neglected princess suddenly became important because her father sought to use her as a means to the restitution of the kingdom of Navarre.[38]

Henri d'Albret was not prepared to relinquish his dream just because François I did not see fit to make the recovery of Navarre an object of royal policy. His attempt to act as mediator between his brother-in-law and the Emperor in 1536 was only a pretext to re-establish relations with Charles V, in the hope that if it was not worth the French King's while to aid the King of Navarre it would be worth something to the Emperor to do so in his consistent policy of making trouble for France.

In the opening months of 1537 D'Albret went to court one last time to try to engage François' cooperation; again it was in vain. He and Marguerite were both indignant at the King's indifference. Thereupon, Henri d'Albret decided to act on his own; without the King's knowledge he entered into new contacts with the Emperor through the spy Descurra.

The principal asset of the self-styled "King" of Navarre was his daughter Jeanne. He thought that if her hand were offered in marriage to Charles' son, later Philip II, the Emperor might be persuaded to restore Spanish Navarre to the young couple in the hope that the purely French domains Jeanne would inherit would thus also come under Hapsburg control. This was an understandable gamble in an ambitious man of feudal mentality in an age when our concept of the nation and the corollary ideas of patriotism and treason were just emerging. If Charles V and later Philip had become overlords of a large section of southwestern France, it would have enabled the Hapsburgs to score heavily against the French crown. In reality, however, Charles V was not prepared to take the risks of such a bargain and never seems to have considered it seriously. To keep Henri d'Albret dangling and hopeful, and France in a state of apprehension, on the other hand, served his purpose very well.

Although the means by which Henri d'Albret hoped to attain his object was his daughter, the person immediately affected was his wife. Marguerite was party to her husband's negotiations with the Emperor in the early months of 1537, but she came under increasing pressure from her brother, who knew how to exploit her extreme devotion. In the spring, François went so far as to suggest that he might, after all, lend his aid—money and men—for the reconquest of Navarre by force. This was probably a maneuver to outbid the Emperor with Henri d'Albret, since it would obviously be more advantageous to the latter for Navarre to be regained with the aid of François than in secret or open opposition to him. Henri d'Albret did not trust his brother-in-law, however, and with good reason. As early as the Treaty of Madrid (1526) the King had promised the Emperor that he would drop the demand for the restitution of Navarre, and despite many half-promises to the contrary (to Marguerite) in the intervening years, there was little realistic likelihood that he would add Navarre to the other sources of friction with the Hapsburgs. In 1531 Marguerite had reproached her brother for caring more about Milan than Navarre, and by 1537 she had been drawn in —to some extent—to her husband's dealings with the Emperor. As

Jourda says, "there were wrongs on both sides. If one can reproach the sovereigns of Navarre for a questionable attitude and diplomatic activities threatening to France, they had justifiable provocation. The notion of France's territorial unity was not yet established . . . and Henri d'Albret, an independent sovereign tied to France by loose feudal obligations, could very well, in view of François' evasions, look for support for his interests wherever he could find it."[39] The consequence for Marguerite was a conflict of loyalties with no easy solution. By the middle of the summer she had rallied to her brother's side, with the result that from then on Henri d'Albret was to carry on his intrigues without his wife's explicit knowledge, although she was uncomfortably aware of them at times.

The year 1537, then, was the most important so far in the life of Jeanne d'Albret. She began to be important to her father; she was involved in the increasing estrangement of her parents; and she became an instrument of her uncle's policy. In consequence, within a year her residence was changed and she spent considerable time at court. She had become the object of rival intrigues and the members of her household were subject to rival pressures. To become a pawn in the power-struggle of two such men as Henri d'Albret and François I was to acquire an uncomfortable kind of importance—as an instrument rather than a human being.

There is a certain irony in Marot's famous epigram to Jeanne,[40] addressing her as *la mignonne de deux rois*.* She was never really a favorite of either her father or her uncle, who found her stubborn resistance to their wills a great irritation. Eventually she would defy both of them. A further irony stems from the fact that the real point of the epigram is Marguerite's passionate desire for a son throughout the childhood of her only child, of whose female sex she had been "sure" in advance.

In the months before Marguerite had resolved her dilemma, Jeanne had a severe bout of dysentery. In March, Marguerite wrote Montmorency that she had had to renounce a planned visit to her daughter because the King required her presence at court.[41] Jourda says that François did not trust Marguerite, and in fact, it was not until late spring that she finally chose her brother's side over her husband's. In one letter to François she says, "all my life I have wanted to serve you not as a sister but as a

* La Mignonne de deux rois/Je voudrois/Qu'eussiez un beau petit frère/Et deux ans de votre mère,/Voire trois.

brother," and she assures him that no financial hardship would keep her from doing whatever she can for him, "I would sooner sell the furniture . . . than burden you with further expense." In the same letter she refers to what must have been a reproach from the King: "As for what you say . . . that the desire to see my daughter would make me set out sooner, you do me a great wrong, Monseigneur, if you think that, compared to the desire I have to see you, either husband or child would count at all."[42]

A reader of Marguerite's letters to her brother cannot escape awareness of her extraordinary devotion to him. Although the style and idiom of the period decreed the use of what we regard as uncomfortably self-deprecating language when addressing the king, in Marguerite's case it was sincere. Her actions bore out her words. This was one of the few occasions when she appears to have suffered any conflict when the interests of either her husband or her child were contrary to her brother's. A woman who had scarcely known her father, who experienced two disappointing marriages, whose longing for a son was repeatedly frustrated, Marguerite's identification with her brother was such that she considered her *raison d'être* to be a sort of second self to him, in accordance with the role created for her by their mother.

In the summer of 1537 Jeanne was well enough to travel. The King commanded her to come to Blois. En route she stopped at Vanves (outside of Sceaux, 10 kilometers from Paris) where Marguerite was nursing Henri d'Albret back to health after an illness. Marot celebrated the reunion with another poem.[43] By September, Jeanne was at Blois, while Marguerite had returned to Fontainebleau with Queen Eleanor and Princess Marguerite, who in turn had fallen sick and required nursing. She wrote at that time to Montmorency that the Queen and the Dauphine had recovered and that she was about to leave for Blois to see Jeanne.[44]

But Jeanne's own health had taken another turn for the worse. When Marguerite arrived in Blois, in October, she found her daughter desperately ill with fever, diarrhea, and hemorrhages. She wrote to François:

Monseigneur:

Not for so small a matter as the illness of my daughter would I give you the trouble of reading a letter, for I have [already] survived the hour when I would have imposed on you—for you are, after God, my sole consolation—that is, [at] the beginning of her fever and looseness of bowels with blood, which was so fast and furious that if God had not brought down her fever after twenty-four hours her little body would have had more than it could stand. Tomorrow will be the fifth day . . . this morning she took some rhubarb and I find that it has helped . . . I hope that He who put her in this world to be of service to you will give her grace to fulfill the desire of mother, father, and herself, which is rather to see her dead than [commit] any deed against your intention. . . . On this I base my hope of her recovery, because I have a firm faith that those who love you . . . cannot perish.

She closes by expressing anxiety for her brother's health and asks him to send news at once.[45]

Jeanne was convalescing, but Marguerite thought that there were not enough "galleries" at Blois for the girl to "take her exercise under cover," so she took her to Tours before returning to Fontainebleau. They traveled down the Loire from Blois to Tours by boat. Marot and Des Périers were in the Queen's suite and it was probably then that Marot wrote *The Epistle to Madame Marguerite,* a letter in verse, supposedly from Jeanne to her cousin Marguerite, whom the Queen and the poet expected to see shortly at court. From it we learn that Jeanne had a parrot and a pet squirrel, and that she was being taught to dance by Etienne, *un plaisant mignon.* The style combines the deliberate simplicity an adult would assume when writing as if from one little girl to another, with an elegance characteristic of Marot.[46]

Either during the trip or upon arrival in Tours, Marguerite received news that her sister-in-law, Isabeau d'Albret and her husband René, Vicomte de Rohan, had suffered financial losses and faced ruin. Marguerite's tender heart and strong family feeling, always especially responsive to Isabeau's many misfortunes, prompted her to make a quick trip to Brittany to take a hand in the situation and lend her prestige to keep the Rohan creditors from ruining them entirely. From her own account, Marguerite left Jeanne in Tours, was away three weeks, and, when she returned, brought Isabeau (and her daughter Françoise) back with her. She then discovered, from Montmorency, that the King was annoyed with her for having gone to Brittany. She had to justify herself to the Grand Master and to François I. In letters written from Tours in December, she explains her actions and, by way of appeal to her brother's sympathy, says more about Jeanne, or at least about her health, than at any previous time in her nine years of motherhood. In one letter to the King she says that just as she was preparing to start back to court, "your [sic] little girl took a turn for the worse . . . but after your letter her health returned. Although she is still in bed I do not think it dangerous to leave her, and I shall tomorrow . . . I had another burden heavier to bear than my child's illness, which only your letter could cure, as it did."[47]

The burden was her brother's displeasure. The full explanation is given to Montmorency, probably in the hope that the Grand Master could help persuade the King that not only had she done nothing to deserve his wrath but, on the contrary, had merely fulfilled several conflicting duties: "I stayed with Her Majesty the Queen because [François] commanded it, despite the fact that my daughter had twice been seriously ill. Nor was I willing to ask for leave until the Queen was rid of her fever. Then, at the King's command, I went to see my child, hoping to be allowed to stay until I received new instructions. In the meanwhile, hearing of the extreme straits in which my sister Madame de Rohan found herself and [knowing] that without me she and her husband and children were in danger of becoming the poorest gentlefolk in France . . . my obligation arising both from nature and from honor . . . I left my daughter to go and take care of my poor sister. . . . The time I spent coming and going was no longer than the time I would have spent in Blois, to which place I had permission to return with my daughter, whom I had brought by water to this town of Tours, so that with the coming and going I would be able to spend eight or ten days with her in all."[48]

Marguerite took Jeanne back to Blois and then set out to join the King in the south of France. She was in Limoges on December 19, where she stopped for twenty-four hours, at her brother's request, to wait for Madame d'Etampes, the King's *maîtresse-en-titre*, to join the party. Henri d'Albret also met her during the trip and Marot celebrated the reunion by inviting him to give Marguerite the son they both desired.[49] By early January 1538, the sovereigns of Navarre had arrived in Montpellier and Marguerite was reunited with her beloved brother after a year's separation. If there had been any strain on their intimacy in recent months— and Marguerite's letters leave little doubt that she feared so—it was not evident on the surface after the reunion. François was lavish in his attentions to his sister and she accompanied him to Moulins. At the ceremony in which Montmorency was made Constable of France, February 10, 1538, the Queen of Navarre escorted him from the King's private rooms to the great hall where he received the sword.

Jeanne's move to Plessis took place no later than the summer of 1538, when Jeanne, or Marguerite in her name, made provision for "six turkey cocks and six hens, to which the Princess is much attached," in the park of the chateau at Alençon. Pierre Beauschune, caretaker of Marguerite's property, was to receive an annual fee of 31 livres, 8 sous, and 6 deniers to care for the birds. One half of their eggs was to go to the Ave Maria convent in Alençon, founded by Marguerite.[50] These unusual birds (often thought to have been introduced into France by Jesuit missionaries returning from America in the seventeenth century) seem to have been pets of the solitary Princess. She could not take them with her as she entered the second phase of her life, a painful one. Marguerite's support of her brother's policy meant that she had not only ceased to abet the "King of Navarre" in his intrigues, but that she had resigned herself to the fact that Jeanne's fate was no longer in their hands but in those of the all-powerful King of France.

II

ADOLESCENT PAWN

1538–1548

P LESSIS-LES-TOURS was Jeanne's home between her tenth and twentieth years. Some writers have emphasized the forbidding appearance of the chateau and its macabre associations with Louis XI, calling it a "sad prison" for the little Princess. It is true that Plessis was not a Renaissance pleasure house, built to grace the Loire Valley in the sixteenth century. It had been constructed for Louis XI between 1453 and 1472, before Italian influence made itself felt in French architecture, when royal residences were still designed partially in terms of defense. In the fifteenth century Comines had described it as "fortified with large barriers in the form of iron *grilles,* with four stout bastions at its corners, the whole surrounded by a moat and thick walls."[1] The central part of the building, which is still standing, with its façade of pink brick and white stone and its rows of slate-covered dormer windows, is a characteristic French chateau of the fifteenth century. In the words of Gaston Paris, "the thick walls, rare windows, and massive pile of stone [of the Middle Ages] had given way to galleries and elegant little towers . . . the forms [of the feudal age] still dominate the conception . . . but the execution shows accommodation to new needs and new tastes. . . . Severity is coupled with grace to form an ensemble that delights the eye."[2]

The present building was formerly flanked by two wings, forming a court of honor, surrounded on three sides by an arcaded gallery ornamented with sculpture, similar to the galleries in the house of Jacques Coeur in Bourges and to the section of Blois built by Louis XII, which

41

was probably modeled on Plessis. These must have been the galleries *pour se promener au couvert* Marguerite thought preferable to Blois for Jeanne after her serious illness in 1537. The rooms are handsome and elegant, with large, richly decorated fireplaces. The fortifications, which have disappeared, undoubtedly gave the chateau a closed appearance compared to the wide park at Alençon, but it would be an error to attribute to Jeanne the sentiments of nineteenth-century writers imbued with the myth of Louis XI as a monster.

According to legend, Jeanne was desperately unhappy at Plessis. On this point the nineteenth-century writers follow Pierre Olhagaray, who wrote in 1609, "she filled the house with her cries and the air of her room with sighs, giving way to floods of tears. Her face—she was one of the most beautiful princesses in Europe—was distorted by the abundance of her tears."[3] In the opinion of Charles Dartigue, an authority on Béarn in the sixteenth century, Olhagaray's *Histoire des Comtes de Foix et de Navarre* is "mediocre and confused."[4] Olhagaray was a Protestant minister who had been a student at the Academy in Orthez founded by Jeanne. Sometimes he follows Nicolas Bordenave, whom Jeanne herself commissioned to write the history of Béarn and Navarre, but on this point he does not. In fact, Jeanne's official historian does not mention her feelings about Plessis, her residence there, or anything at all personal before the Cleves marriage. Jeanne was not known for her beauty, and it is possible that Olhagaray was merely trying to put a little human interest into his history.

With or without the evidence of tears, it is not improbable that Jeanne was unhappy at Plessis-les-Tours. Aside from the pressures that caused her transfer there and the increasing tension between the important adults in her life, no ten-year-old likes to be uprooted and torn from familiar surroundings. She must have known that the move had been ordered by the King to the extreme displeasure of her parents, and members of her household probably resented the move. If she had the painful memories attributed to her in later years, they were justified by the facts.

PARENTAL AMBITIONS AND FRUSTRATIONS

During the first year of her residence in Tours, Jeanne hardly saw her parents. Marguerite was following the court in the summer of 1538.[5] On June 15, she shared ceremonial honors with Queen Eleanor at Aigues-Mortes, where François I and Charles V met to put the finishing

La roine ihanne de nauare
petite

JEANNE D'ALBRET, ABOUT 1537

touches on a truce drawn up in Nice a few days earlier. Neither the King nor the Emperor showed the slightest interest in the Navarre question, and Jourda pictures Marguerite as very much disheartened. "One after another she saw her dreams collapse. Had she hoped to marry Jeanne to the Dauphin of France? It is possible. . . . She had hoped for the Spanish heir, in vain." Commenting on the fact that it was probably at this period that Jeanne was ordered to Plessis, he continues, "one can imagine the effect of this move on Marguerite. If up to then she had little time or means to enjoy her child, at least she could see her freely at those infrequent times, take her from Blois to Tours, send for her to come to Vanves, for instance. The King's act, making a semi-prisoner of the little princess, wounded Marguerite deeply. To be deprived of her child and have Jeanne under surveillance and possibly mistreated, was a severe emotional trial of the kind that hurts deeply and leaves lasting scars."[6] Marguerite tended to blame Montmorency for the failure of her hopes, and the cooling of relations between the King's sister and the Constable dates from this time.

In the meantime, Henri d'Albret was continuing his intrigues with the Emperor for the restitution of Navarre and the marriage of Jeanne to Philip. Jourda believes that he was acting without Marguerite's knowledge, and dispatches in the Simancas archives show that he had misrepresented Marguerite's position to the Spaniards, by implying that she was ready to betray her brother. She remained on friendly terms with the Emperor, however, and wrote him a letter, echoing one from François I, inviting him to visit the French Court.[7] The Emperor accepted, and when Marguerite met him at Loches on December 10, 1539, she was attended by Jeanne as well as by the King's children and much of the court. The royal party then followed the Loire Valley to Orléans, via Chenonceaux, Amboise, Blois, and Chambord, reaching Paris on New Year's Eve.[8]

Jeanne may not have taken part in this royal progress, and if she returned to Tours after a visit with her mother at Loches, it is possible that an episode featured in Charles de Ste. Marthe's* Funeral Oration for Marguerite took place in January 1540.

> Word arrived at court, then in Paris, that the good Princess [Jeanne] was at death's door. Marguerite, virtuous mother that she was, declared that she would go at once to her daughter and ordered her litter. . . . It was already

---

* Charles de Ste. Marthe, 1512–1555, poet. Accused of heresy in 1541, he spent over a year in prison before Marguerite secured his release and supported him.

dark (this was on one of the shortest days of the year) and it had begun to rain. Neither her litter nor the mules ... were at hand. The courageous Queen ... borrowed the litter of her niece, Marguerite, and, taking only a small retinue, left Paris at once. ... On arrival at Bourg-la-Reine ... she went straight into the church ... remarking to her companions that her intuition told her something—I do not know what—about her child's death. Only the Sénéchale de Poitou [Brantôme's grandmother], a very faithful and intimate friend, accompanied her. ...

[Later] when she had dined ... she sent for the Bible and knelt on a little bench before it ... a messenger was heard approaching. ... While she remained there, between fear and hope, Nicolas Dangu, Bishop of Séez at the time and now of Mende, to whose lodging the courier had gone ... knocked on the door. ... He found the good Queen on her knees, her face touching the floor, intent on her prayers.

When she rose ... she asked, "M. de Séez, have you come to tell a sorrowing woman that her only child is dead? I well understand that she is now with God." The prudent Bishop, who combined ... great learning and good judgment, did not wish to upset the Queen with too much sudden joy. He replied gently that indeed [Jeanne] was with God ... but that she was still in this world, that she had stopped losing blood, and that the doctors had sent good and happy news.

When [Marguerite] heard this she did not express wild and uncontrolled joy (as many others would have) but lifted her hands to Heaven and loudly praised God's goodness.[9]

In spite of her strained relations with Montmorency, Marguerite immediately shared her relief with him. "I hasten to tell you because you have shared so much in my anxiety that I would wrong you if I did not now share my comfort. I beg you to tell the King ... if she had belonged only to me, death would have taken her—like the others—but death did not dare to touch one whom it pleases the King to call his child."[10] By a process of elimination, Jourda places this episode in 1540, in spite of the fact that Marguerite addresses Montmorency as Grand Master, when he had been Constable for nearly two years. Jourda assumes that this was a slip of the pen in a moment of fatigue and extreme emotion.

The episode reflects Jeanne's precarious health and shows that Marguerite was not as indifferent to Jeanne as would appear from the over-all picture. It is possible that she generally held her maternal feelings in check in the interests of self-preservation, knowing that she and Jeanne were both in the King's hands. Ariès' thesis about the indifference of sixteenth-century parents may be relevant here. Another explanation for Marguerite's extreme agitation might be guilt.

THE CLEVES MARRIAGE, 1540–1541

The year between July 1540 and June 1541 witnessed feverish diplomatic activity centering about the marriage of Jeanne d'Albret.[11] Her father tried in vain to marry Jeanne to Philip, while François I successfully checkmated his brother-in-law and carried out his own plan to marry her to the Duke of Cleves. The full story of these intrigues is found in De Ruble's *Mariage de Jeanne d'Albret*. Only a summary of the main moves will be given here, as background for Jeanne's position in this critical year and her protests against the marriage, the first "historical" acts of her life.

The Duchy of Cleves, strategically located in the Rhine Valley, already had diplomatic ties with France, which served the consistent Valois policy of building alliances in the Germanies to weaken the Hapsburgs. Twenty-four-year-old William de la Marck, Duke of Cleves in 1540, was eager to cement the diplomatic advantage by a family alliance with the Valois, and in January of that year he asked François I for Jeanne's hand in marriage. The King took the occasion to bind Cleves more firmly by requiring the Duke to furnish him troops. The marriage contract was drawn up and dated July 16, 1540.[12] Not long afterward François I sent for Jeanne and informed her of his plans, at Fontainebleau, in the presence of Marguerite. On this occasion Jeanne declared herself "content" to carry out her uncle's wishes, according to the report of the secret agent Descurra, written the following June, which summarizes for his master (Charles V) the entire story of the Cleves marriage.[13]

The same source tells that a few days later, in early August, Henri d'Albret—without Marguerite's knowledge—sent Descurra to the Imperial ambassador Bonvalot, to propose again the marriage of Jeanne to Philip. Both swore to keep the new negotiations secret from Marguerite. Henri d'Albret's latest scheme was to have Jeanne kidnaped by the Spaniards. She and Marguerite were briefly in Abbeville in August, near the Flemish frontier. The ambassador thought it dangerous and impractical, and the Emperor, cautious as always, feared that Marguerite would discover the plot and reveal it to the French King, so that the ultimate result would be only to provide François with a new *casus belli*.

Marguerite was having difficulties of her own in the summer of 1540. Montmorency, trying to bolster his failing influence with the King, played on François' fear of "subversive ideas" when he showed the King sonnets Vittoria Colonna* had sent Marguerite. The Queen of Navarre was able to turn the episode to her own advantage, against the Constable, but she was in no position to take further risks.[14] In the autumn of the year, when all three D'Albrets were at Fontainebleau, she seemed reconciled to the Cleves marriage, and in January 1541, she joined the King in a cordial invitation to the Duke of Cleves to spend Easter at Amboise.

Henri d'Albret continued to importune the Emperor, who in turn continued to stall. Marguerite and Henri departed from Fontainebleau in February with Jeanne, left her in Tours, and returned to Béarn—Marguerite to take the cure for her rheumatism at Cauterets and Henri to pursue his objectives in the relative security of his own domains, where he could hope to escape royal surveillance. Distance did indeed make it easier for the D'Albrets to delay committing themselves. François I became increasingly irritated, and accused his sister of going back on her word and his brother-in-law of playing a double game. Descurra reports that Marguerite, severely pressed by both men, wept copiously and tried to plead the cause of each with the other. She even attempted to enlist the aid of the Duke of Cleves, asking him to consent to a delay because Jeanne was not ready for marriage.

In a letter of early April, signed, *la humble et bonne mère,* she complains that the Duke's ambassador, "instead of persuading the King of Navarre to approve of the marriage, has done just the opposite, as if you sought to have our daughter without wishing our friendship or alliance." She asks him to send instead "someone who is entirely devoted to your interests, even if he cannot speak French." She refers to the poor state of her own health, "the best the doctors can promise me is that if I take the natural waters in this country [Béarn] they hope I shall recover. I cannot carry out their instructions until the end of May. I have such confidence in you, Monsieur, mon fils, that—even though I am told the contrary—I do not believe that you would shorten my days by precipitating a marriage which is not yet ripe according to God and nature."[15]

Duke William, while conceding that the marriage should not be consummated immediately because of Jeanne's age and frail health, called upon François I to fulfill the contract, whereupon the King ordered Henri d'Albret to come at once to court, bringing Jeanne with him.

---

* Vittoria Colonna, 1490–1547, member of the great Roman family and wife of the Marquis of Pescara, an outstanding example of the Italian noblewomen prominent in the Renaissance, and interested in the reform. The first edition of her poems was published in 1538.

When the King of Navarre offered as an excuse for disobedience the refusal of the Estates of Béarn (Appendix A) to consent and their request that the Princess be married to a French prince, François threatened to carry through the Cleves marriage without the consent of the bride's parents.[16] Henri d'Albret still refused to bring Jeanne to court and the disagreeable task fell to Marguerite, who left Béarn in early May, still sick and apprehensive. Just as she was setting out, her husband received a letter from William of Cleves saying that he did not want to marry Jeanne without her parents' consent and proposing a two-year delay. With unusual candor for him, D'Albret replied that his desire to avoid a firm commitment was as much in Cleves's interest as in his own: should a turn of events make it desirable for François to make a deal with the Emperor, he was only too likely to desert them both.[17] Meanwhile the Duke had arrived at Amboise, and François began entertaining him lavishly with balls, banquets, and jousts designed to impress the German visitors, pending the arrival of the bride's family.

Since her return from court in February, Jeanne had been at Plessis. Aymée was in charge of the household, as usual, and the Vicomte de Lavedan, her son-in-law, was also there, sent by the D'Albrets in the hope that they could gain further time by persuading Jeanne to protest the marriage herself. Unfortunately from the historian's point of view, the greatest secrecy was maintained in these intrigues. The story that follows is found only in Descurra's report of June 1541; no hint of it occurs in Marguerite's correspondence or any other reliable source.

When the King's unequivocal command, with its declaration of intent to push the marriage through, arrived in Béarn, Marguerite was so distraught that she fell ill and the household feared for her life. Her lamentations irritated Henri d'Albret, who said, "Don't cry, Madame, this is all your fault. If it had not been for you, I would have been able to arrange matters so that they would not have come to this point." Marguerite admitted that by bowing to the King's will she "had brought misfortune on the House of Albret," but what was the use of recriminations? No remedy could be found for the past, but one must be found for the future. She proposed to have the Princess protest the marriage before witnesses to this effect: "I here protest before you that I do not wish, that I have no desire to marry the Duke of Cleves, and, as of now, I swear that I will never be his wife. If by chance [*par hasard*] I should promise to be his wife it would be because I fear that the King will otherwise do harm to my father the King. I make this protest in your presence so that you will be my witnesses. I sign this written protest and I beg you to sign it as witnesses."

"This idea pleased the prince," says Descurra, "but he said to his wife, 'what good will that do? You will tell the King as you always do.' 'Sire,' she replied, 'I swear to you never to reveal it to the King or anyone else in the world. I give you my word and this assurance, and I ask you to draw up the protest. I shall arrange with the King and the Duke to celebrate only the betrothal. Having done this, in three or four years we can marry our daughter to the Duc d'Orléans.* In the meanwhile, as soon as the betrothal is over I'll bring our daughter back to Béarn. I shall arrange this with the Duke himself and I shall use him to help me secure the King's permission to conduct her [to Béarn where she will be] in the midst of her subjects.' These words were not reassuring to the King of Navarre, nevertheless he said to the Queen, 'since you wish it, let it be done, but take note that if the King finds out, I shall hold it against you and in that case I shall see that you have as bad an old age as any wife or woman ever had.'"

Thereupon, Descurra reports, a secret agent was despatched to Plessis-les-Tours and "the protest [was] signed by the Princess and witnessed by her gouvernante, Aymée de Lafayette; the Vicomtesse de Lavedan, her daughter; and the Vicomte de Lavedan, her son-in-law."

Marguerite had started on her trip to court—she was in Bordeaux on May 8—but François I was impatient. On May 9 the court took a barge from Amboise to Tours and the King told the Duke "to take a look at the beautiful and renowned city of Tours," while he went to Plessis to prepare Jeanne to meet her fiancé, "by greatly praising the Duke's virtues."

The Princess, who was ill, listened to what the King had to say and replied that she kissed his hands for his kindness in coming to see her but that she was sure he loved her too much to give her to the Duke of Cleves. For her part she loved the King too much to accept the hand of any foreign prince, which would mean that she would never see [the King]. The King replied that they could both live at his court, but the Princess said that even so, she would not marry him.

Descurra reports what followed in dialogue form.

FRANÇOIS: You told me at Fontainebleau, in your mother's presence, that you were satisfied to marry the Duke of Cleves. Why do you refuse now? Who has told [conseiller] you to refuse?

* One of the sons of François I.

49

JEANNE: When I replied to Your Majesty at Fontainebleau that I would gladly marry him, I did not foresee all the harm that could result for my father. If Your Majesty wants me to marry, let me marry in France. I would enter a convent rather than marry the Duke of Cleves.

FRANÇOIS: I see clearly that you have been instructed what to say. Who told you of this harm to your father?

JEANNE: A gentleman sent to Your Majesty by my father's subjects.

FRANÇOIS: My girl, you will do what the King and Queen your parents command, and what you have promised to do you will carry out.

JEANNE: Sire, my father the King will not order me to marry the Duke of Cleves except to obey Your Majesty.

FRANÇOIS: Yes, they shall do it. This marriage will take place in spite of everyone [*qui que ce soit*], and if you will not marry the Duke I will never speak to you again.

At this point Descurra reports that Jeanne was sobbing and shouting so loudly that those in the next room could hear, "I will throw myself down a well rather than marry the Duke of Cleves."

At these words the King got to his feet in a fury and addressed Aymée de Lafayette, governess of the Princess.*

FRANÇOIS: Madame, madame, I see your hand in this. You have taught my niece well, but your efforts will not succeed.

La Dame de Lafayette, terrified, answered, "I do not know why Your Majesty is angry with me." The King shouted, "That's enough! Be quiet! I swear to God, heads will fall for this!"

AYMÉE: I beg Your Majesty to tell me why he is angry with me.

FRANÇOIS: Because you have advised my niece to refuse to marry the Duke of Cleves.

AYMÉE: Never in the world have I done that. What I advised her was to obey all the wishes of Your Majesty and of the King her father and of the Queen her mother. I beg Your Majesty to ask her yourself if I have ever advised her otherwise.

FRANÇOIS: That is as it should be, and the marriage shall take place.

Then, turning to the Vicomte, son-in-law of the Dame de Lafayette, he added, "M. le Vicomte, I swear you shall be punished." "I have committed no offense against Your Majesty," replied Lavedan, "rather I have been a good subject and a good servant, and if anybody cares to bring charges to the contrary against me, I shall reply in the usual way, with Your Majesty's permission."

FRANÇOIS: Go on [*allez, allez*], I know your armor well.†

---

* We do not know whether she had been in the room all the time or whether she burst in when Jeanne began to shout.

† The King was referring to Lavedan's connection with the Constable de Bourbon.

Later in the day the Duke of Cleves paid a fifteen-minute call on his bride-to-be. Unfortunately, Descurra gives us no hint of this conversation between the distracted twelve-year-old and the unwanted suitor twice her age.

The King left Tours without seeing Jeanne again but he sent the Cardinal de Tournon, a few hours later, to threaten her—as well as Aymée and Lavedan. According to Descurra, "the Cardinal said to the Princess, 'If you repeat a single word the King has said he will shut you up in a tower,' and to the others, 'the penalty will be death.' The Princess replied that '. . . she would rather die than marry the Duke of Cleves.'" When another royal emissary asked Jeanne the next morning whether she had not changed her mind overnight, she replied that, if she had formerly been somewhat unwilling, now she hated the thought. She told him to tell the King that she would kill herself rather than consent. "Without making any further effort to soften her resolution, he said to the Dame de Lafayette and the Vicomte, 'I am your friend . . . so I am warning you. If you cannot bring the Princess around to accepting the Duke, I can assure you that the King will do you harm.' Aymée replied, 'The King can do with us as he pleases, but it is not our fault if the Princess, our mistress, told the King she would not marry the Duke. We did not advise her to do so. We have always heard her say that she did not want to nor would she ever marry the Duke of Cleves.'"

Despite the King's explicit command, Descurra continues, Lavedan left Tours immediately to report the King's visit and his threats to Henri d'Albret and Marguerite. He met them near Bordeaux, where Descurra himself had just delivered another brusque letter to Henri d'Albret from the Emperor. The bad news brought by Lavedan and the evident futility of expecting any action from Charles V left no further room at the moment for the D'Albrets to maneuver. They did the only thing they could do, give in with what grace they could muster, in hopes of being able to take Jeanne to Béarn after the betrothal.

As usual the role of peacemaker was assigned to Marguerite, who wrote a courteous letter to the Duke, referring to the approaching marriage as an accepted fact, and then sent the following abject submission to the King.

Monseigneur:

In my extreme desolation I have only one comfort, that is the knowledge that neither the King of Navarre nor I have ever had any intention or desire except to obey you, not only concerning a marriage, but in whatever disposal you wish to make of our lives. Just now, Monseigneur, having learned that my daughter, appreciating neither the great honor you conferred upon her by condescending to visit her nor realizing that a good daughter has no right to have a will of her own, has been so foolish as to beg you not to marry her to the Duke of Cleves, I do not know what to think of it nor what to say to you. I am beside myself with grief [*oultrée de douleur*] and there is no friend or kinsman in the world from whom I can ask advice or comfort. The King of Navarre, for his part, is so astonished and put out that I have never seen him so upset. I cannot think where she gets such boldness as she has never shown. She excuses herself to us by saying that she will be more deprived of you than of us [that to lose you is a greater loss than to lose us] but this deprivation should not excuse such insolence, *without her having been so counseled by anyone, so far as I know.* Because if I knew any creature who had put such an idea into her head I would deal with [him or her] in such a way that you, Monseigneur, would know that this folly was committed against the will of her father and mother, who have never had any [will] but yours.

Knowing that your habit is rather to excuse than to punish faults, especially when judgment is lacking as with my poor daughter, I beg you very humbly, Monseigneur, not to forget the fatherly goodness you have always shown to her and to us, because of this unjust request she has made, and which is the first wrong she has ever done you. I beg you, by the perfection God gave you, to tolerate our imperfections and not to be angry. If your anger frightens all your subjects, Monseigneur, believe me when I say that to us it means death. You could inflict no greater punishment than to deprive us of your grace, which has always been our kingdom and our treasure, as we have shown all our lives. I beg you, Monseigneur, do not take from us the good you have bestowed upon us for so long, compared to which all other goods are as nothing to us. If we lost it, there would be nothing for which we care left to us. After the loss of your favor, we would lose possessions, the honors of this world, and life itself—because their only use is to serve you. . . .

I beg [God] to grant you very good health and long life, and that you may not remove from your good graces,

Your very humble and very obedient subject,
Marguerite[18]

Descurra's long dispatch mentions various spies, intermediaries, and ways and means of continuing the intrigues between Henri d'Albret and Charles V. He makes perfectly clear that Jeanne's father was insincere in his apparent submission. The King and Queen of Navarre never trusted each other again. The Spaniard concludes by reporting a conversation between the Cardinal de Lorraine and the King on the issues raised by Jeanne's protest. The Cardinal's opinion was that François should drop the Cleves marriage: "Not only is it not suitable to marry her against her will, but the Cleves alliance could be a nuisance if [François makes] peace with the Emperor." Descurra reports that others, including Madame d'Etampes, shared this opinion—an item of news which cheered Henri d'Albret when it came to his ears. The King replied that he did not wish to anger the Duke, and that it was an awkward situation. To this they answered: "marry him to one of your own daughters. The only safe thing for the Princesse de Navarre is to marry her to one of your sons, otherwise her father will never cease to use whatever husband she has against the interests of the crown."

By the end of May 1541 matters stood as follows: Marguerite had capitulated to her brother's will and was cooperating, however sadly or resentfully, in his policy; Henri d'Albret had been obliged to bow to superior force—without in the least relinquishing his long-range ambitions; François I was preparing impressive festivities for the wedding —a few days off, and Jeanne and her threatened entourage were waiting, helpless, in the chateau of Louis XI, for the inevitable.

On Wednesday, June 13, at seven in the evening, the King and the entire court made a solemn entry into the chateau of Châtellerault (32 kilometers northeast of Poitiers), whose façade was lighted for the occasion. A large pavilion adorned with chandeliers and tapestries had been built in front of the main entrance and the niches around its walls held the arms of the King, the House of Albret, and the Duke of Cleves, who was the center of attention in the dancing which opened the evening.[19] "When the ball was over, the King and Queen of Navarre, the Princess their daughter, and a great number of princes, lords, and ladies arrived. The King then took the hands of the Duke of Cleves and the Princesse de Navarre, his niece, and, after having spoken to them for a few moments privately, he presented them to the Most Reverend Cardinal de Tournon, who performed the betrothal ceremony. The King gave them several light, affectionate pats on the shoulder, as is the custom."

The Duke's chancellor, Olisleger, who was one of his principal advisers and had accompanied him to France, has left an account which adds further details.[20] Jeanne was escorted by the King, the Duke of Cleves by the Dauphin. "The Cardinal de Tournon asked each in turn if they were willing to marry each other and when each had replied in the affirmative, the Duke kissed his fiancée." Nicolas Bordenave, Jeanne's historian, says, "when the Cardinal de Tournon asked [Jeanne] for the third time whether she would marry the Duke, she never replied either yes or no, but said, 'Don't press me,' as Her Majesty herself told me."[21]

Sometime previous to this moment, on the day preceding "the pretended betrothal and ceremony," Jeanne had written a fuller and more explicit protest than the original, secret one of the previous month.

I, Jehanne de Navarre, continuing my protests already made, in which I persist, say and declare and protest again by these presents that the marriage proposed between me and the Duke of Cleves is against my will, that I never have consented to it, and that I never will. Anything that I may say or do after this because of which it could be said that I have given my consent, will have been because of force, against my will, out of fear of the King, of my father the King, and of my mother the Queen, who had me threatened and beaten by the Baillive de Caen, my governess. [She] has several times brought pressure on me at the command of the Queen my mother, threatening that if I did not do everything the King wished . . . I would be so beaten and maltreated that I would die, and that I would be the cause of the ruin and destruction of my mother and father and of their house. Therefore I became so frightened and afraid [crainte et peur] . . . that I do not know to whom to appeal [avoir recours] except to God, when I see that my mother and father have abandoned me. They know full well . . . and I have told them, that I would never love the Duke of Cleves and [that] I do not want anything to do with him. Therefore, I am protesting anew, that, if it should happen that I should be betrothed or married to the said Duke . . . in whatever manner it might come about, it will have been against my desire [coeur] and will, that he will never be my husband, that I will never consider him so, and that the marriage will be null and void. I call on God and on you as my witnesses, and [ask] that you sign with me [and show] that you know [d'avoir souvenance] the force, violence, and constraint which has been used against me to make me enter [pour le fait dudit] the said marriage.[22]

The witnesses to this document were Jean d'Arros, member of a leading Béarnais family, of which we shall hear much in later years, Francesque Navarre or Navarro, Jeanne's personal physician, and Arnauld Duquesse, a member of Jeanne's household at Plessis. The next morning she signed still another protest, briefer but to the same effect, which was witnessed by the same persons. In this second document she affirms specifically, "I persevere in my said protest made before you the day of the pretended betrothal and ceremony between the Duke of Cleves and me," and repudiates "the solemnity of marriage . . . which will be performed against my will."[23]

In the meantime, Olisleger tells us, "in the pavilion where the ball had been held the night before, a rich altar had been erected, draped with cloth of gold, bearing the arms of the Duke and the Princess . . . over the altar was a canopy of blue velvet. At eleven o'clock the King entered, followed by all the court. Marguerite escorted her daughter, the Dauphin [escorted] the Duke." The ambassadors of the Papacy, England, Portugal, Venice, Saxony, Ferrara, and Mantua were present. The Emperor's ambassador Bonvalot, who had been given a special invitation, found a pretext to excuse himself.

The Princess wore a golden crown, a cloak of crimson satin trimmed with ermine, and a gold and silver skirt trimmed with precious stones. When she entered the Duke greeted her and put a diamond ring on her finger. Jeanne did not take a step toward the altar. "Whether," in Brantôme's words, "because she could not move under the weight of her costume, or whether she wished to protest to the last minute, she refused to walk to the altar." The King then commanded the Constable of France to take Jeanne by the collar and carry her to the altar. "The court was struck dumb with amazement to see the ranking dignitary of the realm carrying out a task so far below his rank." Brantôme reports that Marguerite took satisfaction in his humiliation, "Look at the man who wished to discredit me in the eyes of my brother the King, now forced to carry my daughter to the altar." Montmorency, too, knew that the dreaded blow had fallen. Turning to his friends he said, "This is the end of my favor, I am saying goodbye to it."[24]

The bridal couple took their places under the velvet canopy and the Nuptial Mass was celebrated by the Bishop of Sisteron. The chronicler adds, "it was a melodious thing to hear the music during this mass." Immediately following the ceremony, the Duke's herald cried, *Largesse!* and threw a quantity of gold and silver into the crowd, "which was very well received." Then dinner was served in the great hall of the chateau, "entirely hung with cloth of gold and decorated with magnificent vases of gilded silver, the wedding gift of the King." Jeanne sat in the center of one of the two head tables, while François I presided over the other. A ball and a series of masquerades followed, lasting until late in the evening.

While it was still going on, the bridal couple was escorted to the nuptial chamber. Despite the agreement between Henri d'Albret and the Duke that the marriage would not be consummated, François I was determined that all the conventional forms would be observed. In the words of Bordenave, "the bridegroom was led to the bride's bed, into which he put only one foot, in the presence of the uncle, the father, and the mother of the bride—and all the greatest lords and ladies of the court, who stood rooted to their places until the poor groom was put out of the room, to sleep elsewhere. Thus the only issue of this marriage was wind and some matrimonial ceremonies with no result or consummation."[25]

Olisleger adds some homely details with what De Ruble calls his "German naïveté": "In the chamber that was usually the King's, were the Duke and the Princess, in their night clothes, side by side in bed. The King made everyone leave the room except the King and Queen of Navarre, Madame d'Etampes (the great mistress of the court), Louis, M. de Nevers, and two of the Duke's gentlemen, including myself. The King had pulled the curtains, and he withdrew into an alcove near the window with the others. There they chatted merrily until one in the morning. Then the King and Queen of Navarre conducted the Duke to his own room. The King took the Duke by the arm and called him 'my son.' After the King had gone to bed, the King and Queen of Navarre went to the Duke's bedside and talked to him for a long time in a friendly way."[26]

The celebrations, jousts every day and balls and masquerades at night, continued until June 20, with various members of the court taking turns as hosts. Then the Duke left for Cleves, which was threatened by the Emperor's troops. The court moved to Moulins and then to Lyons. Before rejoining it Marguerite went with Jeanne and her suite, headed by Aymée and Lavedan, for a brief stay at Plessis-les-Tours. Not surprisingly, Jeanne had fallen seriously ill again and Marguerite sent donations to all the religious houses of which she was a patron, asking that special prayers be said for her daughter.[27]

What was Jeanne's real role in this extraordinary story, with the fury of Henri d'Albret, the anguish of Marguerite, the grim determination of François I, ill-concealed beneath the cloth of gold? Knowing that her parents had originally opposed the marriage, one cannot help wondering whether her protests were as independent as the sources indicate. Jourda, the only modern historian to inquire into the matter, devotes two pages to the justification of Marguerite—for her reluctance to support the King wholeheartedly. Of her obligation to Jeanne he says only, "she could not help but be indignant that her only child should be no more than a tool of policy to her brother." Jourda concludes, in fact, that Marguerite preferred, "to the extent that she could do so, *to assure the happiness of Jeanne d'Albret*. If from the political point of view, she may seem somewhat guilty [of disloyalty to the King], her conduct is explained by sentiment."[28] But Marguerite's definition of happiness was her brother's service, and from Jourda we get no suspicion of connivance on her part, nor any suggestion that she had a moral obligation to support Jeanne. Granted that royal daughters were political instruments at the time, and that little attention was paid to personal feelings in dynastic questions, a Marguerite who connived with Jeanne in the protests, then let her daughter bear the consequences alone, is hard to reconcile with the accepted image of the woman who exposed herself to danger for the sake of Clément Marot, Isabeau d'Albret, and others. Such ruthlessness would be out of character for the tender mother depicted by Sainte-Marthe.

De Ruble, in the nineteenth century, believes that "The King and Queen of Navarre had the wisdom to give in . . . on condition that it would be a marriage in name only . . . easy to break, but as it was impossible to let the Princess in on the game because of her tender age, she endured the ordeal of seeing herself 'abandoned by all but God . . .' Prayers and threats proved useless to subdue her firm character, and resort was had to violence. She was frightened that she would be put to death. This was the price Marguerite had to pay for her daughter's consent."[29] The word "consent" hardly seems justified by the texts.

Aside from skepticism about the likelihood of a child carrying stubbornness to such a point in face of the pressures brought to bear, the question of connivance persists, because of the account of Bordenave, who was writing under Jeanne's orders: "The marriage was performed . . . against the will of the bride and of her father, who endured it rather than consented, in order not to anger the King. The daughter did not dare to oppose [it] openly, as much out of fear and respect for her uncle and for her mother (whom her brother had won over) as because of the embarrassment and simplicity of her age and sex. She had not yet reached the age when the law allows girls the right to consent to marriage. Nevertheless, *whether she was advised to do so or*

whether she did it on her own initiative, she secretly drew up a protest."[30]
If there was an "inside story," Jeanne did not choose to disclose it to her
official historian, many years later.

It is impossible to be certain that Jeanne was not acting with the
secret approval of one or both of her parents, although some documents
make clear that after May 21, at least outwardly, Henri d'Albret and
Marguerite accepted the marriage and Jeanne's protests assert that very
severe pressure was applied to make her give in. There are two possible
hypotheses. The first is that Jeanne never had any real opinion of her
own, and was obeying her parents all along. At Fontainebleau, in the
summer of 1540, she expressed herself as "content" to marry the Duke, in
conformity with the wishes of her uncle—and her mother. In the spring
of 1541, when Marguerite sent secret instructions for the original protest
(known only from Descurra), she obeyed. Aymée and Lavedan clearly
were acting on instructions from Marguerite. It is possible that in the
later protests, at the time of the wedding, Jeanne was also acting on
instructions, and that her parents, no longer daring to oppose the King
openly, wished to have the protests on the record so that the Pope could
someday annul the marriage. Such an explanation assumes connivance by
her parents and raises the further question, did Jeanne know of their
secret approval or not? If they did take Jeanne into their confidence,
despite her age, then the horror-tale of intimidation was a fabrication
—with some members of Jeanne's household participating in the pretense
—and Jeanne was a very good actress. A corollary conclusion is that
Marguerite was as much the King's pawn as Jeanne.

Another hypothesis is more easily reconciled with the evidence that
the King and Queen of Navarre had sacrificed their daughter, and that
the protests were really Jeanne's own. It may be that up to and including
the original, secret protest, Jeanne was following her parents' wishes, but
that in late April or early May she became seriously—and permanently
—convinced by the arguments first presented by Aymée and Lavedan.
Jeanne had great pride, not only personal, but pride of family and position. We know that the Estates of Béarn, no doubt with considerable
assistance from Henri d'Albret, objected to the Cleves marriage on the
grounds that marriage with a German prince would prevent their future
queen from living among her subjects and would seriously jeopardize
the continued existence of the "kingdom." Jean Sleidan, writing in 1564,
says that Jeanne's protests stemmed "not so much from scorn [of the

Duke] as from the whisperings in her ear that compared Germany, crude and uncivilized, to the delights and pleasures of France, and the position of a petty duchess to that of queen."[31]

Given this pride and Jeanne's willfulness, it is conceivable that she found it impossible to back down once she had taken a stand on an important matter, and that her self-esteem was at stake. In later years she repeatedly risked abandonment by those to whom she looked for authority and even annihilation by superior force in support of her own opinions. Is it not possible that the experience of the Cleves marriage impressed her with the feeling that the price of safety was distrust of others?

DENOUEMENT OF THE CLEVES MARRIAGE, 1541–1545

Events were to rescue Jeanne from the dreaded fate, but this was not evident for the next two years. If Marguerite had any afterthoughts in the months following the ceremony, they do not appear in her correspondence. On July 25, 1541, she wrote to Calvin, "You will have heard by now of the marriage between M. de Clèves and my daughter. The King of Navarre and I are so happy in this marriage because we think that God has given us a son after our own heart and mind, through whom we hope to give [God] honor and glory."[32]

A number of letters written by Marguerite to her son-in-law in the autumn and winter of 1541–2, and signed *la votre toute bonne mère et leale amye,* indicate a relaxed and affectionate attitude toward him. One of them, probably written in November 1541, accompanies a gift from Jeanne: "Upon receiving news of your wife, I hasten to send off the present bearer, who brings you a banner she has made for you . . . I very much want the love, so well launched in your marriage, to increase." There follows some information about Jeanne's health, cast in terms that anticipate a real marriage. "She is well but still very thin, and for two months she has been poorly. . . . We are doing everything to fatten her up, but she does not gain weight. She should be better now, because winter agrees with her better than summer. I am concerned for her health [because I wish her] soon to be able to give to you the pleasure a husband should expect, and to the King of Navarre the joy [heir] he desires. . . . The King wants her to go to Fontainebleau, but twice she has fallen seriously ill there; it is a very damp place . . . I await the time, devoutly wished for, when I can send her to you, but only God can give her health and strength, which I pray He may give you also."[33] On the same day Marguerite wrote the Chancellor of Cleves that "Jeanne was worried about the Duke's safety." "When she heard that treason had been committed in some of [the Duke's] towns she feared that it might also be attempted against his person, and wrote me that she would not be easy in her mind until she was reassured by someone in his own household."[34]

Not long after the wedding, Jeanne herself wrote the Duke in a tone hard to reconcile with the protests of a few days before:

Monsieur:

The bearer will give you the news in detail, but I did not wish to let him go without telling you that I hope to leave for Tours tomorrow . . . to carry out the doctor's orders. I beg you to send me your news, for there is no medicine in the world which could do so much for my health as knowing that yours is good . . . .

Your humble and obedient wife,
Jeanne de Navarre[35]

Two letters were written the following November. In the first she says,

I have been slightly ill with jaundice for about two months. I did not wish the Queen my mother to know that I had not yet recovered—as I now have. I beg you, Monsieur, be on guard against your enemies . . . . Since God is our Guardian, I am sending you a banner [bearing] the image of Him who is our hope, begging you to accept it. I am also sending two hour-books to [William's sister] Mademoiselle de Clèves, which I ask you to give her for me. . . . Begging you to give my respectful greetings to Madame, your mother . . . I pray, Monsieur, that our Lord will keep you in good health until I see you, which I hope will be soon.

Your very humble and very obedient wife.[36]

In the second letter she reports, "I have seen a beautiful performance of the passion, very well played . . . I was much relieved to know of your good health. . . . My mother has been very ill."[37]

Later in November, Marguerite wrote the Duke that Henri d'Albret had rejoined the court. "Passing through Tours he saw your wife, and found her much thinner than she used to be. Since his departure she has had a serious spell of vomiting blood, which troubled me so much that it gave me a fever that lasted until I knew she was better. I had asked the King for permission to go to see her and he granted it, but your father [in-law] did not wish it, saying that we should forget children . . . in the King's service."[38]

As the months went by the Duke became impatient and suspicious of François' intentions. Early in 1542 Marguerite found it necessary to reassure him. She urges him not to pay any attention

to those who do not know how to do anything but make up lies, and are not ashamed to spread them abroad when all the world knows the contrary. I am sure that you have such confidence in the King and such respect for his word and good faith . . . that you will reject the suggestions of the wicked, who judge others by their own malice. There have been some who tried to frighten me with tales of German marriage customs . . . but I would no more listen to them than believe them, knowing that the displeasure our alliance gives them makes them invent such wicked lies. I would gladly cut two years off my life and give them to your wife, if I could bring her to you. She is yours and I have nothing left. In the meanwhile, my son, I beg you not to suspect so wicked a thing [as that France would not keep to her agreement with the Duke] because, beyond the assurance you have from the King, I beg you to remember that the King of Navarre and I have never done, or had done in our house . . . anything which would justify such a suspicion.[39]

Jeanne's health improved and she was able to visit her parents at court in 1542, but she had probably returned to Plessis when François I visited Marguerite in Nérac in October. There was a lessening of tension between the King and his sister at this time, and also a relaxation of the pressure on Jeanne, because Marguerite believed herself to be pregnant again and the D'Albrets could once more hope for a son to inherit their domains. Even another daughter would offer Henri d'Albret an opportunity to negotiate further with the Emperor. Marguerite took very good care of herself and spent considerable time, including the Christmas season, in bed. Her letters show a return of some of her old gaiety. After François' visit she wrote him that she hoped soon to hear that the Queen was "in the same condition" and that the offspring would "bear the characteristics of Angoulême."[40] Henri d'Albret had been appointed the King's lieutenant in Guyenne, Languedoc, Poitou, and Provence; Marguerite was pleased that her husband seemed to be reinstated in the King's favor. François wrote her affectionate letters and gave her generous presents. He also contributed to Jeanne's expenses, a heavy drain on Marguerite's resources. But this improved situation did not last. In the spring of 1543 Marguerite had a miscarriage, which left her physically depleted and deeply depressed.

Charles V, meanwhile, had managed to turn the situation in the Germanies more to his advantage, so that François had greater need than ever of the Duke of Cleves. Pressure therefore increased on the French King to deliver the bride. Cardinal Jean du Bellay was instructed to escort the Princess to Germany.[41] Jeanne and Du Bellay were traveling east with the court, in late September 1543, when it became known that a dramatic reversal in the position of the Duke of Cleves had changed François' plans. The King expected to join his own army with another, in Germany, to force the Imperial troops back and to deliver the Princesse de Navarre to her husband in person. He had reached the frontier of Luxembourg when he learned, on September 15, that the Emperor had won a decisive victory and that the Duke had signed a capitulation (Treaty of Venloo) in which he surrendered his lands to Charles V, receiving some of them back as a fief of the Holy Roman Empire, renounced the French alliance, and promised to return to the Catholic faith, from which he had temporarily strayed.[42]

The court, which moved more slowly than the King, received the news at Soissons and paused there, awaiting developments at the front and instructions from François I. Presumably it was at Soissons that Jeanne had the first inkling that the God who was her "only recourse" might answer her prayers. Yet one obstacle remained. The Duke of Cleves wrote François a letter in which he justified his action on the grounds that he had been overwhelmed by superior force and stated that, although he had had to renounce the French alliance, he would not renounce Jeanne d'Albret, his lawfully wedded wife. He proposed to send a delegation worthy of her rank to escort his Duchess to Cleves.

François I was extremely irritated at this development and the French court resounded with accusations of betrayal against the Duke. Marguerite's reaction was so strong as to raise again the question of her real feelings about the marriage. She thanks her brother

for not having forgotten us in the midst of your affairs . . . and for giving the King of Navarre and me permission to say what we know about the marriage before God and our consciences. But if the said Cleves had behaved to you as he should have and as I hoped, we would never have entertained such a thought and would have *preferred to see our daughter die,* as she said she would, rather than lift a finger to prevent her going to any place . . . where . . . she could serve you. Since he is so infamous, we no longer fear to speak the truth and break the tie which binds [Jeanne to the Duke] no more than I bound to the Emperor.* . . . Just as in the beginning I ignor-

* A reference to a plan of many years before to marry Marguerite to Charles V.

antly begged you to make this marriage, *hiding from you my daughter's will,*
now I humbly beg you to help us free her in the eyes of men and the Church
as I know she is [free] before God. For I would rather see her dead than
in the hands of a man who has done you such a bad turn. . . . Neither the
daughter nor the father and mother have any wish to live in this world except
to serve you, on whom our lives depend.[43]

Letters and verses Marguerite wrote at this time show extreme concern for her brother's safety, transports of joy when he gains a victory,
and a firm conviction that his enemies are God's enemies. In one letter in
verse she refers to her son-in-law in terms quite different from those
of the letter to Calvin two years earlier:

> One can see by Count [sic] William
> Who, while serving the King and the kingdom
> Became rich, feared, and respected,
> But now is defeated, poor, and deposed . . .
> How God in Heaven curses the King's enemies.[44]

About mid-October 1543, Jeanne herself wrote a letter to Alexander
of Drimborn, charged by the Duke with the negotiations. "I cannot
deny the ceremonies which took place and the honor which the King
conferred on [the Duke] at Châtellerault. Even less can I deny [that it
was done] by the said King and by the King and Queen of Navarre, my
father and mother. But, seeing that the King had determined to give me to
him without being willing to listen to me, and that when I tried to speak
of it to the King and Queen of Navarre they were even less willing to
hear me, using the strangest pressures in the world against me, because
of my opinion, which was against their will, and feeling myself abandoned
by the King and my father and mother, I decided to turn to God—my
only recourse—who has granted me the boon that the said Duke has
committed against God Himself crimes which relieve the King and
my mother and father of the necessity to discharge the obligation [they]
formerly had to him. There is nothing more to say . . . except that if
you ask M. de Clèves about [my feelings] he will know very well what
to say."[45] This is quite a change from the "humble and obedient wife"
of the 1541 letters.

Charles V found that this letter "clearly shows insincerity," and
concluded that Jeanne had been prompted by advisers of the King of
France. "The Princesse de Navarre declares that everything that she has
done and promised was done by force . . . 'under the strangest pressures

in the world,' and that her uncle, father, and mother are discharged of their obligations . . . and in conclusion she holds herself free but claims to keep the Duke in suspense and uncertain." De Ruble comments, "The King of France, having lost the support of the Duchy of Cleves, claims at the same time that he is no longer bound to the Duke and that the Duke must keep his contract—in order to prevent him from contracting new alliances."[46]

What was bad news for François' diplomacy was good news for Jeanne, although some time was still to elapse before the marriage was annulled. In the Treaty of Crépy (September 18, 1544) between François and Charles, there was a clause demanding that "the King deliver within six weeks the protests of the Princesse de Navarre against the marriage, in authentic form, exactly as they took place, with the exact declaration of the said Princess, to explain to the Duke of Cleves, who, in the absence of such documents, considers her his legal wife." Antoine Perrenot, Bishop of Arras, better known by his later title, Cardinal Granvella, one of the Emperor's chief advisers, came to France in the autumn of 1544 to attend to the execution of the treaty. On September 27, Guillaume Bochetel gave him Jeanne's two known protests. But Granvella was not satisfied, and he told the Chancellor of Alençon, Olivier, that Jeanne must sign a notarized declaration in the presence of witnesses. This she did in Alençon on October 11, 1544.[47]

When this affirmation of the former protests was delivered to the Emperor and the Duke they were still not satisfied. The Emperor wrote to his ambassador in France, Jean de St. Mauris, on January 7, 1545, "Our cousin the Duke . . . has informed us . . . that he does not find the protests and renunciations of the Princesse d'Albret sufficient . . . so he desires, for his greater security and satisfaction, that another be drawn up in the presence of some Cardinal and qualified bishops."[48] Cleves was then making new marital and diplomatic plans; he wished to marry one of the Emperor's nieces. It was therefore to the interest of both parties to have the marriage annulled, and the purpose of the final protest was to make it easy for the Pope.[49]

On Easter Day, April 5, 1545, immediately after High Mass in the cathedral of Tours,

the most high and most powerful lady, Jeanne de Navarre . . . in the presence of Monseigneur, the most reverend François, Cardinal de Tournon, of M. Jean de St. Mauris, ambassador of the Emperor, and of the very reverend

Pierre Palmier, Archbishop of Vienne, Philippe de Cossé, Bishop of Coutances, Philibert de Babou, Bishop of Angoulême, Pierre du Chastel, Bishop of Mâcon, and others said and declared the following in the presence of the above named and of us, as notaries:

"Messieurs: I have formerly made declarations and protests about the marriage which it was desired to make between the Duke of Cleves and me. I declare again now to you, Monseigneur Cardinal and Messieurs Archbishops and Bishops here assembled, that I wish and intend to persevere in my said declarations and protests, and that I will never do otherwise. Because I cannot say it as well as I would like, I have written it out and signed it. I shall read it to you. I swear and affirm to you Messieurs, by my Lord, whose body I have just received, that these documents contain the truth." Whereupon the said lady read from the paper she held in her hands.

Jeanne affirmed the existence and the substance of the two protests of June 1541, referring to the circumstances under which they were made. She continues,

"I swear and affirm that they tell the truth, that such was my will and intention in which I had steadily persisted up to the declaration that I made in October of last year in Alençon. I swear and affirm that it also contains the truth. Furthermore, I swear that since then I have remained of the same will and that I do so at present and wish to continue so, and that I do not now and never have felt myself bound or obligated to the said Sieur de Clèves in lawful marriage nor [do I wish] to take him as my husband. I swear that what was done at the time of the pretended betrothal and ceremony was done in the way described in my said protests. I ask that the notaries who are present take note of this declaration."

When the said lady had finished reading the said document she was handed the Holy Gospel. She placed her hand on the open [Bible] and swore and affirmed that the content and declarations of all the protests were true, that she persisted in them and intended to persist. This done, the said lady presented two sheets of paper and a half-sheet, which she said had been written by her hand, and she swore that they contained the said declarations and protests.[50]

Bernardo de Medici wrote Duke Cosimo that he had witnessed this occasion and adds, "the Princess said that it had never been the intention of either her mother or her father that she be the wife of Duke William, it had all been done to please and obey the King."[51]

Even after this ceremony there was a good deal of hesitation and equivocation in the papal Curia. Some of the learned doctors did not think the case strong enough to warrant annulment, and it was necessary to remind the Pope that a refusal might cause the Duke to leave the Catholic fold again.[52] Marguerite, begging Paul III to grant the annulment, confessed that she had forgotten maternal feeling at the time of the marriage (*oubliée toute douceur maternelle*).[53] It was even necessary for Jeanne to address him a personal letter. Its key sentence carries overtones important to the relations between Jeanne and Marguerite: "My mother, the Queen, preferred obedience to the King to her own life, and to mine."[54] Despite the wording, *alla vita sua e alla mia,* Jeanne cannot have meant life in the sense of survival, because in that sense Marguerite could be said to have obeyed the King in order to *save* Jeanne's life. What was sacrificed was her liberty.

Finally, on October 12, 1545, Paul III dissolved the marriage on the grounds that Jeanne had consented only because of the violence applied, that she had never ceased protesting, and that the marriage had never been consummated.[55] Those whom policy had joined, policy had —at last—put asunder.

The hardened tone of her final statement suggests that Jeanne's position was probably consistent throughout the affair, from the spring of 1541 to the end, and that in her letters to the Duke in the months after the marriage she was concealing her true feelings, hoping that the wheel of fortune would turn up more favorable circumstances. Throughout her life she showed a masterful sense of timing and, when necessary, was adept at dissimulation. After the annullment she became reconciled with François I. In an unpublished letter she thanks him "for your affectionate remembrance of me as well as for the beautiful watch," and assures him of her desire to render him service, describing herself as "she who wishes to remain forever your very humble and very obedient subject, daughter, and niece."[56]

The helplessness of Marguerite in her brother's hands is evident in her correspondence in the years of the denouement. She admitted to the King that she had concealed Jeanne's real feelings and to the Pope that she had sacrificed her daughter. We must conclude that Marguerite, having initiated the idea of a protest, dropped it under royal pressure and allowed Jeanne to be subjected to "the strangest pressures in the world" and to the ceremonies of betrothal and marriage. Later, when it suited her brother's policy, she reverted to her former position. She could then make good use of Jeanne's consistent stand, on record in the protests. Henri d'Albret, as might be expected, resumed negotiations with the Emperor immediately after the annulment. In the changed circumstances, he could temporarily correspond with Charles V through his ambassador in France and avoid the indignity and risks of dealing with such questionable characters as Descurra—temporarily, but not for long.[57]

ADOLESCENT REBELLION, 1540–1548

Dartigue asserts that Jeanne "never forgave her mother for wanting to marry her to the Duke of Cleves," or rather, as the facts indicate, for being willing to sacrifice her in the interests of French diplomacy.[58] He may be right; forgiveness was never Jeanne's strong point, as her later years abundantly demonstrate. Quite aside from any strain in the relationship resulting from the Cleves marriage, there is evidence that her daughter was a problem to Marguerite in the 1540's. For one thing, she was a source of heavy expense.

In his *Registre,* Jehan Frotté, Marguerite's chief accountant, reveals that Jeanne's household was a drain on Marguerite's resources and that the mother incurred large debts as a result. In 1541, Marguerite asked her Receiver-General in the Duchy of Berry to remit to Mathurien Javelle, Treasurer in Alençon, "six times twenty livres tournois as reimbursement for sums he had advanced at the Queen's instruction to Madame de Lafayette, governess, for the small pleasures of the Princess."[59] In the three months of March, April, and May 1541, the "extraordinary" charges for Jeanne's household (outside the budget) rose to 1,335 livres, but they are not itemized. Since this was the time when Marguerite was instigating Jeanne's original protest and sending Lavedan to Tours, it is possible that this large amount was for his expenses and a bonus to him. It is hard to see how Jeanne's age and circumstances would permit her to spend so much money, even if she had wanted to; moreover, the mature Jeanne was seldom extravagant.

That the expenses of the Cleves wedding were very high is obvious from the *Chronique du Roy François I.* The Duchy of Berry alone contributed 40,000 livres tournois toward the cost of the trousseau, including 15,000 paid "to Claude Reynault, silk merchant dwelling at the Exchange in Lyons."[60] In view of Jeanne's attitude toward the marriage, this expense may be less attributable to Jeanne's extravagant tastes than to Marguerite's desire to do her part in providing the display, which was one of François' principal ways of impressing the Duke of Cleves with the advantages of an alliance with the French crown. Similarly, the 100 écus Jeanne drew for pocket money when she visited the court at

Amboise some months later was probably necessary if she were to maintain her position as a Princess of the Blood.[61]

As long as François lived and she basked in his favor, Marguerite could tolerate any burden. So great had been her agitation during his illness, that when he died her household tried to conceal the fact from her. Marguerite never recovered from the loss, and her own health deteriorated rapidly. The terrible blow brought lesser troubles in its train, including a worsening of her financial situation. In the spring of 1547, when her nephew Henri II had just succeeded to the throne, Marguerite tried—unsuccessfully—to negotiate loans so that she could pay her debts. The new King then assigned his aunt a pension of 25,000 livres tournois, which relieved her acute financial embarrassment. Javelle was reimbursed 2,167 livres at this time ("for the amusements and charities of the Princess"), and Aymée was granted 50,000 livres for the maintenance of the household.[62]

To Guillaume Faen, Sieur d'Izernay, who supervised Jeanne's accounts, Marguerite wrote, "I have studied the expenses of my daughter, which you say cannot be reduced. [You also say] that my daughter cannot do with fewer officers . . . this the King of Navarre and I find intolerable [*insupportable*] and it must be discontinued . . . because we simply do not have the means to meet it." She says that several people have remarked on Jeanne's retinue, *merveilleusement grande,* and she begs him "to hold my daughter in check, because with the other expenses, I really cannot afford it."[63] Jeanne was at court for an extended visit at this time, but she had gone at Marguerite's insistence, to accompany Henri d'Albret to the coronation of the new King. The Queen had excused herself because of poor health and mourning for her brother. She had also requested that Jeanne be allowed to represent her as godmother to the new Valois princess, Claude de France, whose christening took place "on Saturday, November 11, 1547, between seven and eight in the morning, in the chateau of Fontainebleau."[64]

Jeanne was not the only source of Marguerite's difficulties. The Queen's generosity and the many obligations of her position are evident in the *Registre.* She spent 100 gold écus and 1,300 livres tournois on entertaining the King in his Nérac visit of 1542. When her chief baker was married, she gave him 500 écus and furnished the bride's trousseau. The cloth of gold came from Toulouse and the silk from Lyons. Among the items listed are lengths of cloth of gold and silver, purple and crimson velvet, taffeta "for linings," black velvet "for hats," nine ounces of gold thread and crimson satin "to make a canopy for the nuptial bed." The trousseau alone cost 995 livres. In addition, there was a wedding present of two enamels ordered from Léonard Limousin in Limoges, at a cost of 67 livres and 10 sous. There were also heavy expenses in Alençon, including repairs to the chateau; Marguerite's over-all expenses for the second half of the year 1544 reached 16,160 livres tournois.[65]

Jeanne's extravagance is therefore not in itself sufficient to explain Marguerite's irritation with her daughter. Probably expense was only one of several factors in their uncomfortable relationship. At Henri II's accession Jeanne was no longer a child. She was eighteen years old and a member of the court. Marguerite, for the first time since her marriage, was living in her husband's domains. She suffered from increasingly bad health and from her adored brother's death. Out of favor with the new King, she was forced to crawl to Montmorency, returned to power as Henri II's chief adviser and confidant.[66]

Marguerite undoubtedly needed the affection and companionship of a daughter. They were separated for the greater part of the years 1547 and 1548, yet no letters have been found, which is surprising as far as Marguerite is concerned. Jeanne, for her part, may have drawn the conclusion from earlier events that her mother did not really care about her and could not be depended upon to defend her interests. Writers in the sixteenth century and since have dwelt on Jeanne's indifference to her mother.[67] Now that she was in a position to evaluate power as she witnessed the intrigues of the court, Jeanne may have misunderstood Marguerite's submission to the Cleves marriage and attributed it to ambition rather than to the all-consuming devotion to her brother. Possibly Jeanne was temperamentally incapable of understanding such devotion.

Jeanne's life history could be told in terms of the causes she espoused —always to redress some injustice—and it is plausible to assume that this tendency was rooted in a feeling that she had accounts of her own to settle. Aside from the specific conflict over the Cleves marriage, there was Marguerite's lifelong pattern of attention to the King's children while neglecting her own daughter. Jeanne's feelings toward her father may have been more ambivalent. For two known reasons she must have felt a degree of sympathy for him: his disagreement with Marguerite at the time of the marriage, mentioned by Bordenave, and her resentment of the inferior position of her father's family and of her own relatively insecure position within the most privileged environment in France. Jean Sleidan's comparison of a "petty German duchess" with a queen reflects this, as does Jeanne's later insistence on her royal prerogatives and intransigence in the Bourbon cause.

On the surface, relations between Marguerite and Jeanne in the 1540's do not seem to have impressed observers as especially difficult. The Queen and her suite made several stops at Plessis, traveling between the court and Béarn. In a *poème d'occasion,** Marguerite has given a glimpse of attitudes toward Jeanne, including her own.[68] Each of the ladies in the Queen's retinue takes leave of Jeanne. Françoise de Rohan, Jeanne's first cousin, who made long visits at Plessis, says:

> The more I am beaten
> The more my love grows, and the more
> I regret the hand that beats me,
> For the pain was pleasurable.
> So farewell hand, whose rigor
> I prefer to wealth and honor.

It is possible that Marguerite has imposed on Françoise the statement that pleasure outweighs the pain. It must be a fact that Jeanne tyrannized over Françoise. Why, if it were not known to all the company, would Marguerite mention such behavior in stylized verse on a conventional occasion?

In her own farewell, Marguerite suggests that her feelings are too strong to be expressed:

> If these [other] farewells
> Make the reader weep,
> What if I should add my own?
> It is better to say nothing. . . .

De Ruble, who follows the tradition (formulated by Sainte-Marthe) of Marguerite as a tender mother, says that in this poem Marguerite "speaks her whole heart." A reader may wonder whether Marguerite did not have mixed feelings on these occasions. Jeanne was hard to love and Marguerite was a generous person with strong affections and loyalties.

---

* *Les Adieux des dames de chez la Royne de Navarre, allant en Gascogne, à Madame la princesse de Navarre.* Jourda places it in 1546, after the papal annulment of the Cleves marriage, because of an allusion by the Sénéchale de Poitou to the fact that Jeanne may soon be a bride.

If exasperation overcame sympathy, her biographers could be right in assuming that she found much pain and little satisfaction in the relationship.[69]

CONTENTED PAWN, 1548

At court with her father, Jeanne again was a pawn in the hands of a King of France (her cousin, Henri II) in 1547, but there was an important difference—she was delighted with the choice of Antoine de Bourbon, Duc de Vendôme, as her bridegroom. Again, Marguerite and Henri d'Albret were opposed. The King of Navarre, in fact, was actively pursuing the familiar phantom of an alliance with the Hapsburgs. He employed his usual tactics of delay in consenting to the King's plan, and made a long sojourn in Béarn on the pretext that administrative affairs required his presence. The trip was slow and painful because he was suffering so much from gout that observers thought him "not long for this world."

Henri II at first had been disinclined to the Bourbon marriage for Jeanne, according to the Emperor's ambassador, Jean de St. Mauris, and he seriously considered marrying Jeanne to François d'Aumale, eldest son of Claude de Lorraine, Duc de Guise. "The King would have been glad to oblige the Seigneur d'Aumale," says St. Mauris, "except for two facts. The first was that [Antoine] complained that it was not right to award the Princess to a lesser House than his own, the second [was] that the girl much preferred [Antoine]."[70] Jeanne's pride in her royal status partly explains her preference. D'Aumale's youngest brother, Claude, Marquis de Mayenne, was married to Diane de Poitiers' daughter, and Jeanne is supposed to have said to Henri II, "Do you wish someone who should be carrying my train to be my sister-in-law, on terms of intimacy with me?"[71] Furthermore, Charles V was at the time advising Philip to marry Jeanne, and there was no comparison whatever between the position of a Comtesse d'Aumale and that of a Queen of Spain.[72] These are negative factors, against D'Aumale, but Antoine de Bourbon also had a positive attraction for Jeanne: a political appeal since he was in line for the throne of France, and an emotional, personal appeal.

Nobody familiar with the history of France in the second half of the sixteenth century can help wondering what might have happened if Henri II had married Jeanne to the man who was only Comte d'Aumale in 1547, but who became the great Duc de Guise in 1550, and later leader of that ultra-Catholic party which—as events turned out—was the chief enemy of Jeanne d'Albret, the Calvinist Queen of Navarre. Jeanne's life would have been very different with a strong husband instead of a weak one; and it is hard to imagine how she could have become a Calvinist, unless she had separated from Guise. One thing is certain: she would never have had the son we know as Henri de Navarre.

Henri II demanded an answer from the D'Albrets, and sent the Sieur d'Estrées to Béarn to force their hand in December 1547. Henri d'Albret excused himself, "not so much because of the bad condition of the roads, as because of my illness. I beg you to allow me time . . . and to listen to my remonstrances about the marriage in connection with the welfare of my House, for the assurance of which I can only look to you."[73] Marguerite wrote to the King also: "Please be so gracious as not to remove your favor from us, owing to the absence which is against our will. As to the marriage . . . you wrong the father and mother if you do not firmly believe that their fortunes, their daughter and their very lives are dedicated to your service . . . do not doubt that we have no will but yours."[74]

Henri II was not reassured. He knew that the King of Navarre was negotiating with the Spaniards, and he did not trust Marguerite's assurances of loyalty. Even if he did not know in detail about all the earlier intrigues between Henri d'Albret and the Emperor, the royal resources were considerable, and Montmorency, *brouillé* for years with Marguerite, was at the King's right hand. For a period of months in 1547–8, at the explicit command of the King,[75] Montmorency's agents intercepted all letters addressed to either of the D'Albrets.

The court moved to Lyons in the summer of 1548, and Marguerite finally brought herself to pay her respects to her nephew as King. It must have been a painful experience for the failing Queen—she had only fourteen months to live—to be forced to frequent the scene of her greatest triumphs as a mere relic of a bygone era, to see another in her brother's place, and to know that her opposition to the marriage did not influence the outcome—or even seem to bother her daughter. During the brilliant and much-celebrated festivities accompanying Henri II's entry into Lyons, September 23, 1548, Marguerite was more or less relegated to the train of Catherine de Medici, the only person who paid any attention to her. "I feel for you in your trouble," Catherine wrote, "as I always knew you [felt] for me in mine."[76]

Henri d'Albret was feverishly corresponding with the Emperor's ambassador, and the King of France was very much aware of the fact. Henri II wrote Montmorency at the end of September, that the King and Queen of Navarre "want very much to prevent the marriage." He refers to Marguerite in condescending tones as *ma bonne tante* and states that she detests her prospective son-in-law. He adds, "I will do what I can to see that the marriage, or at least the betrothal, takes place at Moulins, and I assure you that it will take place, whether by love or by force."[77] The King arrived in Moulins on October 8, and was shortly thereafter joined by Henri d'Albret, who had been delayed by a revolt in Guyenne. Henri II sent the following report of their interview to Montmorency:

What has delayed my writing was the late arrival of the King of Navarre, who has finally met me here. His anger had cooled and he spoke to me in the gentlest possible way about other things. I asked him in so many words whether he would carry through what he had promised me, that is, the marriage of his daughter. He did what he could to evade the issue and to delay further, but I told him he must give his consent by Sunday—which he agreed to do. The contracts are ready; the marriage will take place on Sunday. I am getting out of it cheaply, I only have to give him 15,000 francs a year toward the expenses of his kingdom. It is true that my good old aunt and her husband are on the worst possible terms [*se veulent le plus grand mal du monde*] and already she has no use for her son-in-law. The King of Navarre does nothing but swear by the faith he has in me, and I trust him as much as I should."[78]

The wedding itself, October 20, 1548, was evidently not much of a spectacle. The Emperor's ambassador comments that very little was made of it "because the King's haste did not allow time enough to organize the usual festivities."[79] It was a great contrast in this respect to the Cleves wedding. Another contrast is of particular interest: the bride was happy. The King wrote to Montmorency, "I have never seen a happier bride than this one, she did nothing but laugh. I think that she did not mind it very much." He goes on to say that Henri d'Albret has asked permission to take Jeanne to Nevers, and that he has decided to grant it: "having his daughter safely married, I have a hold on him." He expresses the opinion that Henri has "no other thought in the world now but to pile up money and have a good time."[80]

A letter to D'Aumale—soon to be married to Renée's daughter, Anne d'Este—from a mutual friend, shows the impression of Jeanne's wedding night that Antoine was spreading abroad. "The Duc de Vendôme performs his marital duties very well both day and night. He says that

JEANNE D'ALBRET, ABOUT 1548

the six couplings went off very gaily [*les six couplements se sont passés bien gayement*]. I wonder if you will do as well by your bride?"[81]

If the absence of ceremony and Jeanne's delight present a contrast to the earlier wedding, there is one familiar feature: the annoyance of the bride's parents. Marguerite wept copiously and said that she had little left to live for. This disappointment was worse than the earlier one in that it was irrevocable and that it had been rather brutally imposed by her nephew, while the former blow could be softened by the thought that it was in her brother's interests. Henri d'Albret took out his anger on Antoine, who was known for his extravagance. The morning after the wedding the King of Navarre stormed into the newlyweds' lodgings and dismissed most of Antoine's servants. Henri II wrote to the Constable, "The said King told me that he would soon trim [Antoine's] feathers and he has made a good start . . . I believe he has not left them ten gentlemen . . . the others have to pack up and go home."[82]

The King's letter of October 24 (to Montmorency) refers again to Jeanne and her mother, "The Queen of Navarre is at swords' points with her husband, out of love for her daughter, who does not care about her mother [*ne tient compte de sa mère*]. You have never seen anyone cry as much as my aunt did on leaving, and if it had not been for [my insistence] she would never have gone with her husband."[83] Brantôme, not always reliable, was probably right when he said that Henri d'Albret treated Marguerite badly, "and would have behaved even worse without the intervention of her brother."[84] In 1548 Marguerite was deprived of her brother's protection. Victim of a vain and insensitive husband, pushed aside by the new regime, treated with indifference by her daughter, her health gone, Marguerite had only her religion and the memories of a glorious past to console her.

III

BRIDE AND DAUGHTER

1548–1555

ANTOINE de Bourbon, Duc de Vendôme, directly descended from Robert, sixth son of St. Louis, was "First Prince of the Blood," that is, next in line to the succession of the French throne after the sons of Henri II if they had no male heirs.[1] His father, Charles de Bourbon, had distinguished himself in the wars against the Hapsburgs in the early sixteenth century, and had been rewarded in 1515 when François I raised him to the highest rank of the French nobility (duke and peer). He and his children escaped the disgrace which fell on the Bourbons generally after the Constable's treason. Jeanne's senior by ten years, Antoine was born in the chateau of La Fère (about twenty-five kilometers northwest of Laon) on April 22, 1518, the eldest of thirteen children. He was educated at the Collège de Navarre in Paris, and in 1537, when his father died, was named Governor of Picardy. He campaigned extensively in the next few years against Charles V, sometimes under the command of the Dauphin, the future Henri II, and acquired a brilliant military reputation.

Not even Antoine's detractors begrudge him credit for his military achievements, which were recognized when François I gave him the rank of peer in 1544, when he was twenty-six years old. Brantôme says that in war, Antoine was *fort animé, brave, vaillant, courageux, eschauffé, colleré, prompt à faire prendre.* The Venetian ambassador Mihieli says that he was "famed for his courage in battle, though rather as a fine

76

soldier than as a great commander. He is nevertheless regarded as one of the ablest princes in the kingdom, as good as M. de Guise or the Constable." Another Venetian thought that neither Antoine nor Montmorency "can hold a candle to M. de Guise." De Ruble, the only modern historian who has concerned himself with Antoine other than as an actor in the tragicomedy of court intrigue, thinks him a greater military man than the Constable, on a level with Guise and Monluc: "he showed a natural bravery under fire which became the patrimony of his family."[2]

Objectively, royalist historians can find little to admire except Antoine's military gifts—but he was the father of Henri IV. Brantôme, writing during the son's reign, and reflecting the national gratitude for a strong ruler after a generation of chaos and civil war (as well as flattery), says, "he was very brave, because in the House of Bourbon there are none who are not." His last word on Antoine is telling: "If in his time he had done nothing but procreate our great King of today he would have done much and is worthy of great and incomparable praise. To him France owes all her good fortune."

Later writers have also tended to gloss over Antoine's defects or to praise extravagantly the father of Henri IV because of his paternal role. Henri IV had some striking faults, but even modern historians have difficulty in dealing with his reign objectively. The moral behavior of both father and son, especially their sexual promiscuity, poses a problem. Brantôme says of Antoine, "he was much given to love affairs, but which of our great kings has not loved women? Those who did not were unnatural men and given instead to great and monstrous vices." This expresses both admiration of Henri IV and disgust with Henri III, whose effeminacy was distasteful to his contemporaries and has continued to plague historians. De Ruble dismisses Antoine's morals in a single sentence: "he had regrettable habits [*moeurs*], but they were no worse than others."[3]

The only reliable contemporary opinions of Jeanne's husband are those of foreigners whose observations were recorded before the outbreak of civil war. After March 1562, even foreigners judged Antoine in terms of their own interests; both Catholics and Protestants could find grounds on which to condemn him, so that they too are biased—but against him. The Venetian ambassadors were accurate reporters, and the Most Serene Republic had no direct stake in the course of events in France. Three different *Relazioni* describe the King of Navarre in 1561–1562, the final

ANTOINE DE BOURBON, DUC DE VENDÔME

and most important year of Antoine's career and a critical moment in French history.* The fullest account is that of Mihieli.

The King of Navarre . . . presents a much more impressive appearance than his brothers, who are short and not very well-formed. He is tall, handsome, strong, animated. . . . friendly with all the world, without arrogance and without standing on ceremony. His manner is open and outgoing, in a truly French way. His spendthrift habits are such that he is always in debt. Because of his agreeable manners and generosity [*largesse*] he has won over everyone, especially the nobility, who like and honor him greatly. He is a good speaker, but he is vain, imprudent, and shifting in his aims and actions. He willingly undertakes important matters but it is to be feared that he lacks force proportionate to his great schemes.

Brantôme also comments on Antoine's ambition: *les desseins de ce roy n'estaient pas petitz*. Impressions of Antoine are as consistent as the man was inconsistent: attractiveness of appearance, affability and charm of manner, persuasiveness, personal vanity and susceptibility to flattery, addiction to women and to luxurious living, carelessness with money. Beneath the surface, observers quickly discerned his ambition coupled with a lack of firmness which marked his entire career with "great schemes," pursued first by one means and then by another, but always without long-range vision, realism, or sufficient self-discipline to subordinate any immediate advantage or pleasure to greater ends. Montaigne's word *ondoyant* is the most succinct description. Agrippa d'Aubigné, Henri IV's childhood friend, puts it more delicately, "he erred more through lack of brain than lack of goodwill."[4]

Antoine resembled his father-in-law both in his assets and in his liabilities, and he reinforced the similarity by fixing his ambition on the lost kingdom of Navarre. Like Henri d'Albret, he was obsessed with the injustice of Ferdinand's "theft" of Navarre, and would never admit that its recovery was not worth any risk to the French crown. Like Henri d'Albret, he insisted upon maintaining the symbols of royalty, especially the title of King. Whereas Henri d'Albret had inherited the mirage, and, from a feudal point of view, might conceive of the restitution of the kingdom as his mission in life, Antoine de Bourbon chose it. If there were such a kingdom, incontestably it belonged to Jeanne d'Albret. As some ambitious, luxury-loving men marry for money, Antoine married Jeanne

* Antoine died in November 1562. On the importance of the year 1561–1562, see Chapters VI and VII.

for the title of King and the chance to play the role of ruler, rather than merely First Prince of the Blood, at the mercy of the French crown.

An incident reported in November 1547 bears out the point. Catherine de Medici was expecting a child, and one of the court ladies asked Antoine if he would prefer the King of France to have a son or the King of Navarre to have one. This question was intentionally provocative, because at the time Henri II had only one son, the future François II, whose health was frail, and if the King had no others Antoine would stand closer to the throne. Antoine is said to have replied without hesitation that he would prefer the King of France to have a dozen, because if the King of Navarre had even one, the Princesse de Navarre would not inherit her father's kingdom.[5] Antoine was a pragmatist; Jeanne was a bird in the hand, while the throne of France was but a remote possibility.

Any reader of his letters to Jeanne can obtain a fuller understanding of Antoine than even the most astute contemporary observers. His correspondence, edited by the Marquis de Rochambeau, contains more than two hundred fifty letters. More than half are addressed to officers under his command and deal with military or administrative matters. The other half includes letters to Montmorency, Guise, Henri II, Catherine de Medici, and, most important, Jeanne d'Albret. In letters to his equals or superiors the themes of his ambition and the many difficulties of his situation predominate. His correspondence with his wife, especially in the early years of their marriage, shows Antoine at his most appealing. Like those of his son, Antoine's letters are characterized by an earthy humor and a lively style. This is the husband who aroused Jeanne's passion and who showed some fondness for her, before his *ondoyant* tendency in relations with women humiliated his wife and before his politico-religious shifts led him in paths where she could not follow. Antoine cut a fine figure at court when Jeanne first met him, and it is easy to understand his personal appeal, "in a truly French way."

In the Rochambeau collection, of eighteen letters written by Jeanne before Antoine's death, only one is addressed to him. We are therefore dependent upon a study of his letters to her for impressions of their feelings. Information about Jeanne's attitude toward their infant children can only be drawn from Antoine's correspondence. Certain personal themes predominate: pleasure in a mutually satisfactory sexual relationship; concern for the image they present to the world; Jeanne's emotional insecurity, her dependence on her husband, and his constant reassurance. His wife's tendency to quarrel with people and to get upset elicited many admonitions from Antoine, ranging from humorous teasing to annoyed scolding in a quasi-parental tone.

THE BRIDE AND HER MOTHER, 1549

Shortly after their wedding, Antoine and Jeanne paid a visit to his mother, Françoise d'Alençon, Duchesse de Vendôme. She must have heard about Jeanne's protests against the Cleves marriage and may have wondered whether such independence would be a useful trait or a handicap to her son. She might have welcomed the match because it would bring Antoine, with his claim to the throne, into closer alliance with its current occupant, Henri II. History does not record her reactions. There is a hint of Jeanne's feelings toward her mother-in-law in a letter of Antoine's the following summer (August 1549), in which he says that his mother wishes Jeanne to stay with her while he is off at war. The impression given is that Jeanne would be reluctant: "I beg you to go, since she wants it so much, and when you get bored [*quand il vous ennuyera avecq elle*], you can make an excuse to go and look after our affairs."[6]

The honeymoon visit, described as "ten days of festivities" was, in any case, a mere stopover, since Jeanne and Antoine were on their way to Béarn with Marguerite.[7] By early December they had arrived in Tours, where they spent the Christmas season. There is no evidence for the interpretation of nineteenth-century writers that they stopped at Plessis because Jeanne wished to visit her former "prison," a visit more easily explained by the fact that Jeanne's household there was being broken up. The *Registre* of Frotté shows that at this time new positions were found for some members of the staff. There was cause for rejoicing in the chateau at Plessis during this visit; Jeanne was pleased with her marriage and members of the household must have been relieved when they remembered the difficult days of the Cleves "marriage."

The Queen of Navarre, her son-in-law, and the new Duchesse de Vendôme resumed their journey south early in the new year. On January 16, 1549, they arrived in Casteljaloux, and shortly thereafter reached Pau. Twenty-year-old Jeanne was making her first extensive visit to her future domains, with her dashing husband at her side. "What joy for the people of Foix and Béarn," says Olhagaray, "who had until recently suffered the imprisonment of their Princess. They hoped from her no less than from Marguerite, who was the most precious flower in the garden of their house."[8]

Antoine remained in Béarn until June 1549, participating in negotiations for the restitution of Navarre, reopened by Henri d'Albret. That tireless intriguer had made an excuse to leave court as soon as the wedding was over (October 1548), and his actions of recent months were causing alarm in Spain.[9] A belligerent thirty-year-old King of France and the presence in the south of Antoine de Bourbon—who had commanded some successful campaigns against Spain in the north—posed a more serious threat to the aging Emperor than had Henri d'Albret's unsupported intrigues. Simon Renard, Charles V's new ambassador (since January 1549), and other Spanish agents reported that a quantity of arms had been collected and that the citadel of Navarrenx had been reinforced to a point where it could hold out for a year. Henri d'Albret had mobilized the support of certain lords in Basse-Navarre, including the Comte de Gramont and the Baron de Luxe, who promised to provide 3000 mountain fighters accustomed to guerrilla warfare. The slightest movement of the Béarnais ruling family was interpreted as a military maneuver by the Spaniards, and in February 1549 the Viceroy of Navarre (the Duke of Maqueda) asked the Emperor for 2000 additional soldiers to protect the frontier.

It is probable that the four principals in the "royal" family were not united in this renewed Navarrese ambition, and that, while Antoine enthusiastically supported his father-in-law, Jeanne and her mother were opposed. One of the Spanish agents writes, "Madame d'Alençon and the wife of Vendôme are very pleasant in their manner, but there is reason to fear that underneath they do not feel as they act." As in the past, Henri d'Albret paid little attention to Marguerite's opposition. In March, he recalled Descurra into his service and secret meetings took place between the Spaniard and the Bishop of Lescar, Jacques de Foix, in which the latter gave the Spaniards to understand that Henri d'Albret, furious at Henri II for marrying Jeanne to Antoine, was bent on vengeance. Charles V, wearied by the Navarre question, turned the matter over to Philip, who instructed his agents to get all the information they could without making any promises. Hapsburg policy was consistent: to use Henri d'Albret, and later Antoine, in every possible way, and to keep their hopes up, without ever conceding any concrete advantage.

Antoine threw himself into the intrigues and rushed about Henri d'Albret's domains accepting homage and promises of support in his future kingdom. Toward the end of March he entered the Basque country, accompanied by 2000 men in native costume wearing red berets, to be received by the Comte de Gramont at the head of an equal number of vassals wearing black berets. He made a triumphant tour of the area, and it was rumored that he would make a secret visit to Pampeluna. Henri d'Albret was no doubt glad to be able to put on such a show, but he had no confidence in Antoine. To the Bishop of Lescar's comment "Sire, it seems to me that in your son-in-law you have acquired a useful helper for what you wish to do," he replied: "You do not know him very well."

Antoine had been summoned to take part in the solemn entry into Paris Henri II was planning for the month of June 1549. Some weeks before he left Béarn, Marguerite went to Cauterets to take the waters. Jeanne joined her briefly, toward the end of May, but she was restless and her mother realized that she was not happy apart from her husband, whose departure had been delayed. A letter from Marguerite to Antoine reveals Jeanne's discontent.[10] She begins by describing the grandeur of the Pyrenees, which declare the glory of God, "in whose hand rests the earth and all it contains," and the rushing *gave* (river), "whose depths reveal the depths of our sins."[11] She sums up the lesson and gives the exact date in these lines: "Thus, my son, the sight of Cauterets on this Ascension Day shows us the greatness of God in the high mountains and our own baseness in the Gave far below, as well as God's goodness, quick to rescue us, in these baths where health is found." Of Jeanne she says, "Your wife has no pleasure or occupation except in talking about or writing to you. She does it in company and in private . . . the waters cannot quench the flame of her love." Marguerite says she would be willing to let Jeanne go to him, that she would be consoled in her loneliness because "nothing but your presence can help her, we watch her perish from day to day, without you, my son, she is not alive," but that a better solution would be for Antoine to come to Cauterets, "so that the love in your hearts will triumph and be fulfilled in the sweet fruit of a fine child." She concludes with a plea that Antoine join in her prayer that before her death she will see Jeanne pregnant by Antoine in Cauterets.*

* *Avecques moy supplyez ce bon Dieu/Que mère grande par vous soye en ce lieu.*

Her wish was never granted. Not long afterward Antoine started north and Jeanne left Marguerite with the intention of joining him en route to Paris. Although the Queen's health was failing rapidly, she urged her daughter to go. Jeanne was unable to catch up with her husband, however, for he was suddenly recalled to military service by Henri II, who judged the moment propitious for the recapture of Boulogne from the English, because Somerset, regent of the young king Edward VI, had his hands full putting down a rebellion at home.

A series of stylized letters in verse, exchanged between mother and daughter in the following weeks, gives us an inkling of their relationship at the end of Marguerite's life. The first is from Marguerite to Jeanne, shortly after the latter's departure, in which the lonely Queen gives way to her sense of desolation, kept under control at the time of parting. She feels that nature shares her sorrow, "The sky . . . grants me thunder to echo my cries, my sighs move the winds, my lamentations bring hail . . . it is the weeper who brings on the rain." Jeanne responds that she is crying also, no longer able to master her emotions, and that her pain will not cease until she is reunited with her husband, her mother, and her father. "Then, forgetting the too painful absence, joy and pleasure will return and I shall have my complete desire."

Marguerite's next letter says that she can bear her sorrow only if Jeanne and Antoine are reunited. "As soon as you are eye to eye with him I will no longer mourn, because I believe your hearts to be so united by true love and virtue that they are but one." She expresses herself "content to place my heart near yours, without ever separating [you] from each other." Jourda comments on Marguerite's use of the pathetic fallacy here, "Romanticism before the Romantics." He compares Marguerite to Madame de Sévigné (*j'ai mal à votre poitrine*), and Jeanne to Madame de Grignan—"she reasons, she does not feel."[12] Such an identification with her daughter's feelings may have seemed a way for Marguerite to get close to Jeanne—at last. Jeanne's answer, although it seems somewhat forced, *manièrée,* shows that her heart, or at least her conscience, had been touched. She expresses concern, and, echoing Marguerite's vocabulary, calls upon the wind to be her messenger and carry her prayers for her mother's recovery. She begs God "to let me see your hundredth year."

Marguerite's third letter was written upon her return to Pau, after a dream in which Love appeared and charged her to write constantly to

Jeanne, "until the poor Princess achieves her desire." Marguerite arose at once from her bed, took pen and paper, and "sat beside the open window, listening to the voice of the Gave, which . . . in its sweet sounds" reminded her of Jeanne. If Jeanne answered, the letter has disappeared, because another from Marguerite follows, expressing her renewed distress about Jeanne's plight and blaming herself for having added to her daughter's suffering by an excess of maternal feeling. She should rather submit to God's will and pray that He will be "father, mother, and husband" to Jeanne. She also prays for an end to the painful separation: "By His crucifixion I ask Him to send back my daughter with my son to me, so that I may see them both, with these two eyes, full of health and joy before I die."

The last letter in the series is Jeanne's answer. The opening theme is that, by definition, love brings pain, and that this is true of the affection between parents and children, as she, Jeanne, knows from experience:

> Amour ne peult, selon son naturel,
> Se demonstrer autre que très cruel.
> D'en bien parler je doilz avoir puyssance
> Puisque j'en ay tant faict d'experience.
> Or, si voullez dire l'affection
> De père et filz estre sans passion,
> Je dis que non. . . .*

She speaks of her present anguish, "endless days and wearisome nights," in contrast to "the happy times when I rid myself of sorrow." The time remembered with longing was probably the first few months of her marriage, between October 1548, and April or May 1549. Finally, she determines not to add to her mother's sorrow, and falls back on "the proverbs of the ancients," which tell us that "after the rain the dear sun shines again,"† and that "one month of happiness makes us forget one hundred thousand years of torment." In advising her mother to expect the future to be better, she excuses her audacity with another old proverb, *vrayment, un fol conseille bien un saige.*

In this letter, with its consciously optimistic message, there is an

---

* It is of the nature of love to be very cruel, I speak from much experience of it. So, if you wish to say that affection between father and son is without passion, I say no . . .

† Curiously, this well-worn "lesson of nature" later provided the motto of the Huguenot movement, *Post Tenebras Lux,* or, *Après les ténèbres, la lumière.*

interesting slip of the pen. When Jeanne is speaking of the black present and of her hopes for the future she writes:

> Et le présent me monstre triste face
> Où je ne scay trouver plaisir ni grâce,
> Car l'advenir, duquel *malheur* j'espère,
> Me promet bien faire meilleure chair.*

The editors of the poem have firmly changed the *malheur* of the manuscript to *bonheur,* on the grounds that she had to mean happiness in the general context of the letter, whose entire message is Jeanne's determination to be courageous and to accept the wisdom of the ancients and the lessons of nature. But Jeanne wrote *malheur* and did not catch the slip if she reread the letter. Does the slip reflect a deep unconscious disbelief, formed in her unhappy childhood, that anything could have a "happy ending"?

This correspondence in the last year of Marguerite's life, the first of Jeanne's marriage, raises questions about their feelings. Their uneasy relationship must have been partly the result of guilt on both sides. Its roots lay buried in the past, but the present situation compounded it. Marguerite was facing death; she had given up the world but she was lonely and yearning for intimacy with her daughter. To see Jeanne happy and to share in her life was her only remaining—expressed—wish. Jeanne attempted to respond to her mother's need, but her own emotional security was tied up with Antoine, and she seemed more upset by her failure to meet him than a realistic consideration of the facts warrants. She was tortured by anxiety and seeking reassurance—but not from Marguerite. Antoine's letters to his wife show Jeanne's need explicitly. In the letters between mother and daughter it is veiled by the conventions of the verse form as well as by the lack of intimacy.

As poetry these letters are not very impressive. Jourda claims that the verses "are often heavy and prosaic, occasionally moving. The tormented affection of the Queen manifests itself constantly. The Queen's letters are certainly not masterpieces, but they speak from the heart." He has little use for Jeanne as a daughter, in whose letters "one feels nothing but effort, often an awkward effort." Of Jeanne as a poet he thinks even less, *des vers de Jeanne d'Albret mieux vaut ne pas parler.*[13]

---

* The present shows me a sad face and I know not where to find pleasure or grace. For (because) the future, from which I hope for unhappiness, promises me much greater ease.

We must concede that her verses are conventional in content, stiff in expression, and derivative in style.

Antoine had arrived in Paris in time for the King's ceremonial entry on June 10. A letter he wrote soon afterward to Jeanne shows that he did not yet know of her departure from Béarn to join him. It also shows his desire to be treated as a partner by his father-in-law.

My dear,

Although I wrote at length two days ago . . . I did not want to lose the occasion of the King's sending . . . the present bearer, to tell you that I am in as good health as possible. For it to be perfect I would have to spend a little time with you. If you think well of it, sound out your father the King as to whether you and he are coming or not and let me know at once. I can hardly wait because of the desire I have to see you. I am off to La Fère, our home [*notre chez nous*], to wait patiently for news. I would never have thought that I would love you as I do. I intend another time, when I have to take a long trip, to have you with me, for all alone I am discontented [*je m'ennuye*] . . . I beg you, make yourself as helpful to the King, our father, as you can. If he would like me to return there let me know and I will hasten to join him, or, if he wants you to come, leave as soon as you can and travel as fast as possible. . . .

I would never have thought it possible that I would be so indifferent to the ladies of the court. They seem all to have become ugly and boring. I do not know whether the sweet breeze that blows from Béarn is the cause or whether my perception is so changed that it can no longer be deceived as it formerly was.

In conclusion Antoine asks "humbly to be remembered to the King and Queen our father and mother," and prays God to give Jeanne a long, happy and healthy life. He signs himself, *vostre très affectioné mary, Antoine*.[14]

Another letter was written in haste from Mouschy on August 8. His return to the front is taken for granted; it must have been the subject of an earlier, missing letter. Antoine explains that he arrived in the nick of time to join the King: "We leave this morning on our trip which I think will not be either long or dangerous." He now knows that Jeanne is on her way to Vendôme and says that he is sending his brother, the Cardinal de Bourbon, to keep her company "until I can come myself, which God willing, will be soon, although not as soon as I want." He urges Jeanne to join his mother at La Flêche, a favorite estate of the Vendôme family near Angers. The Boulogne campaign was not only short, but successful. Antoine left camp sometime in September, and he and Jeanne were finally reunited in the late fall, probably in Vendôme.[15]

Henri d'Albret left Pau about the middle of December in answer to a summons from Henri II. Almost immediately Marguerite's health took a turn for the worse, and messengers caught up with her husband before he had left his own domains. He turned back at once and reached Pau on December 21, a few hours after Marguerite's death in Odos-en-Bigorre, a few miles to the east. Jeanne and Antoine had returned to Béarn early in the new year and were present at Marguerite's funeral in the cathedral of Lescar on February 10, 1550.[16]

No direct evidence is available on Jeanne's feelings about her mother's death. Did she grieve—or feel relieved of a burden? Several years later, in 1555, when she had borne three sons, lost one of them, and had some dealings with her father, Jeanne may have developed some belated devotion to her mother's memory. In a letter of condolence to the wife of the Constable (Madelaine de Savoie), whose mother died in that year, Jeanne says, "I assure you, cousin, that I have deep sympathy for you, having suffered the ordeal of losing such a mother as I had."[17] No conclusion can be based on this fragment, which may be merely a dramatic phrasing of conventional sentiments. (Jeanne's other references to Marguerite occur in polemics dealing with the reform movement.) There is no evidence that Marguerite was really mourned by either her husband or her daughter—in marked contrast to the desolation of the poets, the humanists, and her many devoted retainers.

A SOLDIER'S WIFE, 1550–1553

In 1550 Henri d'Albret was again called to court by the King. He seems to have left in March and to have remained away from his own domains for about a year. Henri II was making preparations for a resumption of the war with the Emperor and he wished to make it difficult for the King of Navarre to carry on his intrigues with Spain. Henri d'Albret took no important part in the royal counsels; an English observer reports with astonishment that he ranked below the representative of the King of Bohemia at the baptism of Prince Charles-Maximilien de Valois (later Charles IX) on September 10. Jeanne had probably accompanied her father to court. She and her husband were both there on September 14, when news came of the death of Antoine's mother, the old Duchesse de Vendôme. But Antoine had been at court only intermittently, as much of his time was spent at the front or in Amiens, discharging his functions as Governor of Picardy.[18]

War between France and the Emperor broke out again (in Italy) in the spring of 1551. Henri d'Albret and Antoine de Bourbon, who had returned to Béarn, took advantage of the situation to resume threats against Spanish Navarre, and the Duke of Maqueda renewed his demands for help, asserting that he had insufficient forces to repel the invasion he felt to be imminent. This threat of military action had no more substance than any of Henri d'Albret's earlier bellicose gestures, however. By midsummer Antoine was back in Picardy, and Henri d'Albret had started another round of negotiations with Charles V. The King of Navarre was now a widower. His new proposal was that he should marry Charles V's niece, the Duchesse de Lorraine, and that Spanish Navarre be restored to him as her dowry. In exchange, he promised that any sons of this marriage would reign in Béarn instead of Jeanne, and that he would aid the Emperor in an invasion of France. These negotiations, unknown to Jeanne and Antoine, were conducted by Jacques de Foix, Bishop of Lescar, for Henri d'Albret, and by Descurra for the Emperor. But that autumn Henri d'Albret fell seriously ill—to the point where his death was rumored in Spain—and the negotiations were dropped.[19]

Jeanne was not in Béarn in early April 1551 when she sent word to her father that she was expecting a child. Henri d'Albret gave 400 livres tournois to the messenger who brought the good news. Since there are no letters to Jeanne from Antoine in the first half-year, we can assume that she was with him.[20] Upon his return to the front in July, she went to Coucy, a feudal fortress near Compiègne belonging to the crown, to which Antoine could come easily when he had leave and where Jeanne would be safer than at La Fère. In the chateau of Coucy, "about five o'clock in the morning of September 21, 1551," Jeanne "was delivered of a beautiful son, named Henri for his grandfather and given the title Duc de Beaumont. He was baptized the following February in Coucy by the Archbishop of Sens, his great-uncle. The King of France and the King of Navarre were his godfathers and his godmother was the Princesse Marguerite de France"—sister of Henri II, who had been brought up by Jeanne's own mother.[21] Responsibility for the Prince was given to Aymée de Lafayette.

Antoine was present at his son's birth but he left Coucy four days later and was constantly on the move for the next fifteen months. In

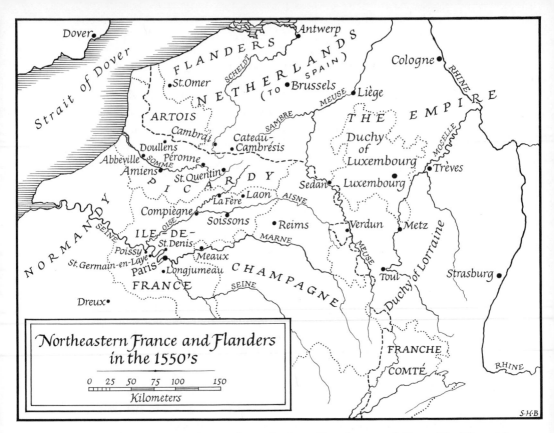

Northeastern France and Flanders in the 1550's

0   25   50   75   100   150

Kilometers

S·H·B

October, he wrote letters from Amiens, Doullens, and Chantilly. He paid occasional overnight visits to his wife and child; there are letters written from Coucy on November 4 and December 24, but between those two dates he had been to Abbeville, Amiens, and La Fère.[22] This activity was part of the preparation for the French attack on Metz, which succeeded when the Constable triumphantly entered the city, on April 10, 1552, with his chief officers, including Antoine de Bourbon. The Duc de Vendôme subsequently was given the task of defending Therouanne (suburb of St. Omer), the most exposed position on the northern line. Between May and late summer he struggled to discipline his men, extend the area of French control, and offset the ambitious schemes of the Duc de Guise. He had also to surmount the obstacles of inadequate supplies, changing orders, and floods of rain which washed out the roads. His success was recognized in June, when Henri II gave him the revenues of the county of Charolais, and in August, when he was named chief of all the armies in Artois.[23]

In a series of striking victories, Antoine later established winter quarters and assured the food supply by arranging for the storage of grain in important garrisons. Officers who exploited the situation for personal profit were severely punished, as Antoine moved constantly up and down the front to enforce discipline.[24] His greatest triumph was the capture of Hesdin (suburb of Abbeville) on December 19, 1552, which so alarmed Charles V that he got out of bed and retreated in the midst of disorder so great that he could not assemble his personal baggage. The Duke of Alva, commanding the Hapsburg forces, broke camp at dawn and led the army in retreat, following his sovereign.

The Artois campaign reflects the public image of Antoine at his best, and his letters to Jeanne at the time show that the private image was not yet at variance with it. From the front he wrote his wife that he had been ill but had recovered sufficiently so that her messenger found him in the woods, "marking the trees." As soon as possible, "I will come to you, with as great anticipation of pleasure as I have ever had in my life. You and our son had better be in good form to welcome me or else I shall make a face and say 'a pu' just as he does. In the meantime, my dear, I beg you to see to the burial of my late mother, because when I was sick I had the feeling that it might bring bad luck to some of the rest of us, her children, to have left her so long above ground." Jeanne had evidently asked for instructions about dealings with some of their vassals, and her husband says, "it would be well for me to be present . . . for the fear of the prince is an important factor with such people." He instructs her to keep the revenues from Mondonbleau (27 kilometers from Vendôme) in her coffers, as he intends to use them for improvements in the park and buildings at La Flèche.[25]

Jeanne too was leading an itinerant life, although she stayed longer in one place than her soldier-husband. Unfortunately none of her letters of this period have survived, but we learn certain facts from Antoine. In 1552 he asks that she request her father either to escort her to meet Antoine or to allow him to come "there," which implies that Jeanne was briefly in Béarn, saying, "I must see you, either here or there, as I cannot live any longer without you." He suggests that they meet in Poitiers and go from there to Vendôme and then to La Fère. He will send someone with a supply of money, so that her trip will not be hampered by the lack of it. "When you are with me you shall lack neither money nor anything else that lies in my power, for no husband ever loved a wife as I love you. I hope, my dear, that in time you will realize it, more than you have up to now. This is all, except to assure you that no lady—of the court or otherwise—has any power over me, unless to make me hate

and not love her, but that, on the contrary, I am saving everything I
have for my spouse, praying her to do the same. In closing, I pray God
to allow us both to remain in this good intention . . . your very good and
affectionate husband."[26]

Occasionally, Antoine and Jeanne were able to arrange meetings
despite his military activity. In one letter he says, "I know now for certain that I can live without you as little as the body without the soul, so
I beg you with all my might to come straight to Cognac."[27] Another
time he rejoices in the news that she and their son are well and assures
her that he is just as anxious to see her as she is to see him, "but I do
not think it advisable for me to come to Paris. It will be easier here in
Picardy. I beg you to go where I instructed you via Nicolas and we will
have as good a time as possible in secret."[28]

In one rather long letter Antoine shares his military and political
triumphs with his wife: "I could ask no greater satisfaction than what
the King said to the Constable, 'If I had followed the advice of M. de
Vendôme and left the troops under his command [an unfortunate turn
of the war] would never have happened,' and he added '*mon compère*,
I have never known him to deceive me, but always to tell me the truth.' "
Antoine then had the further satisfaction of hearing the Constable tell
the King, "that I both knew the country and understood the men in
service better than he did."[29]

Throughout Antoine's correspondence with Jeanne there are references to his hunting birds. At the end of this letter he says, "please spare
nothing in the care of my birds so that when I come you can offer me the
enjoyment of them." Another time he sends her "a pair of small grey-
hounds, the prettiest possible, and a linnet which kept me company during my illness, the prettiest and the best talker you've ever seen. I rec-
ommend her to you because she loves me so that when I speak she
answers, as she does not to others, that is why I love her."

As for the coming battle, there is nothing to fear—we are in no danger,
the enemy is retreating. If we do anything it will be to lay siege to some little
place so that we can say we've done something. This hypocrisy annoys me, if
we are not really doing anything I want to be near you. . . . As for my health,
thank God it is good except for the slight cough you know of which has not
left me and is waiting until I am near you to bid me goodbye. Furthermore,
I assure you that you are more beloved than you have ever been and more in
my good graces, which makes me say, "to the devil with war."[30]

After Hesdin was taken (December 1552) Antoine and Jeanne had a few months together at La Flèche, in the chateau built by Antoine's mother. Henri IV (born December 1553), was conceived during this period, and it is probable that these months were the happiest of Jeanne's life. She was twenty-four years old, happily married, had a son, and was expecting another child.

By early summer Antoine had returned to the front. Despite several courageous and ingenious maneuvers on his part, Therouanne fell to the Emperor on June 20, and by mid-July Hesdin—hard-won the year before —also had been taken. There seemed nothing to prevent the enemy from marching into the heart of Picardy. The French army had to retreat, but the King rewarded Antoine with revenues in the county of Armagnac and an outright gift of 20,000 ducats.[31]

Jeanne knew she was pregnant before her husband's departure, and during the summer she felt ill and restless. Antoine's first letter (written during the fighting over Therouanne, therefore before June 20) deals with the question of where she should go for the birth of the expected child.

My dear, I understand that you want to have the baby in Mont-de-Marsan, but if you do it will inconvenience me a great deal because I will not be able to leave this region until near the end of October and I cannot get from here to there in less than a month . . . which would be well past the time when the baby is due. Not to be there would greatly displease me . . . I beg you to go to La Flèche or Vendôme, whichever you prefer. I am sure that if you tell your father the King that you cannot travel without risking great danger and that you had set out with the intention of joining him but on the road you found yourself so uncomfortably pregnant and sick that you could not go further . . . [he will understand. If he allows you to stay] ask him humbly to do you the honor of coming . . . at the time of the delivery and [tell him] that in return you and your husband will take pains to give him as much pleasure as possible, and that in Vendôme . . . there is very good hunting.

News from camp is that the enemy has made an attack on Therouanne and lost between 1800 and 2000 men "without being able to set foot in the town. Our people are disregarding [French losses] and have so astonished the enemy that they do not know what to do . . . we are in very good shape after nearly two months in camp."[32]

In contrast to the idyllic first half, the second half of the year 1553 was a time of emotional turmoil for Jeanne. Antoine's reply to a lost letter of hers shows that she had begun to be disturbed on three counts: Antoine's feelings toward her, his health, and whether he was being sexually faithful during the separation. He takes them up in that order.

On the first point, I assure you, my dear, that you have never been higher in my good graces than you are at present, and believe me, if you continue as you are, this will steadily increase. For the second, I would say that I have never felt better. . . .

As for the third, I have offended neither God nor you, and have no desire to begin now. I am surrounded by trotting horses every day, I feel fine and feel no need for a mare. [I suggest that you go to] St. Maur-des-Fossés to enjoy the good air for three weeks or a month . . . and when you are sufficiently rested, take the road for La Flèche, where I wish the child to be born.[33]

Jeanne may have been soothed by his reply, but a severe blow fell the following month. In the words of Claude Régin, Bishop of Oloron, "On August 20, 1553, in the chateau of La Flèche in Anjou, died the young prince, aged twenty-three months. His body was taken to Vendôme, escorted by me. On September 21 of the same year his funeral services were held at the same time as those of the late Madame Françoise d'Alençon, Duchesse de Beaumont and Vendôme, his grandmother."[34] The Duke of Albuquerque (who had succeeded Maqueda as Viceroy of Navarre for Charles V) states that the Duc de Beaumont died in the chateau of Gaillon, near Rouen, but he must have been misinformed, for Régin, a retainer who kept records for Jeanne, was there.[35]

No documentary source deals with the cause of the Duc de Beaumont's death. The explanation current in Henri IV's reign was that Aymée took exaggerated precautions against drafts and cold. Believing that "it is better to sweat than to shiver," she kept the child in an airless, overheated room, until he died of suffocation. This traditional account appears in Palma Cayet's *Chronologie Novenaire*, published in 1608.[36] The author was a former Huguenot pastor who had served both Henri de Navarre and his sister, Catherine de Bourbon. Cayet's position and the publication of his book in Henri's reign means that his was the family version. If Jeanne believed that Aymée was responsible for her son's death, it would certainly explain the strained relations between them in the summer of 1553.

Again, we can only infer Jeanne's feelings from Antoine's letters. Immediately after receiving the news of the baby's death Antoine wrote her a long but rather conventional letter of condolence, "we must not rebel against God's will, but pray that He will be as ready to help us in our need as [He was] to rescue the children of Israel in the flight from Egypt, when they had to cross the desert and the Red Sea, pursued by the fury of Pharaoh and his army . . . I beg you, my dear, not to take this visitation other than as an obedient child. . . . I am sure that the Lord will send his angel as he did to stop the sacrifice Abraham was making of his son, Isaac, in obedience to God's will. . . . We are in His power and we must offend Him as little as possible." The only personal note in this labored letter occurs toward the end. "Meanwhile, believe me that neither this nor anything else, more important, would have the power to diminish the love and true affection I bear you."[37]

Jeanne's anxiety grew more acute, and Antoine continued to reassure her—until finally, in exasperation, he scolds his wife for being immature. Her reaction to her first son's death does not conform to Ariès' theory of indifference to the loss of children. The importance of an heir to royal families is undoubtedly a factor, but Jeanne's own unresolved inner conflicts must also be taken into account. The trouble with Aymée seems to have been uppermost in her mind. "I see by your last letter how Madame la Vicomtesse [Aymée's daughter, Françoise, wife of Lavedan] has turned Madame la Baillive against you and that she wants to go home. My dear, you know how often I have told you that *it is your natural tendency to torment your husband and all who love you.* It seems to me that from now on you should try to overcome it, because it will bring nothing but shame to your servants and pain to your husband. I am sure that if you will believe me, you will lessen your own pain and mine also. . . . I assure you that I have never wanted to see you more than I do now . . . if the King did not hold me here by force I would be on the road already."[38]

Aymée may not have been responsible for the tragedy, but Jeanne believed she was and never forgave her foster-mother, although she did not dismiss her until two years later. Immediately after she became Queen, Jeanne revised her household staff and corrected the record in the Archives with her own hand.[39] At the head of the list stands the name of Aymée de Lafayette, "first lady-in-waiting and gouvernante to the children of Madame la Princesse," at a salary of 500 livres a year; it is crossed out with a heavy black line.

Following the spate of letters about her difficulty with Aymée, there seems to have been a period when Jeanne did not write Antoine at all.

He writes, "it is so long since I have had news from you that I fear the next will bring distress. If there is bad news, I beg you to let me bear it alone and not to torment yourself with it." Fearing that she is brooding over the loss of their son, he offers consolation, "For one that God takes from us He can give us a dozen. Remember your condition, which should give you great comfort. . . . We are both young enough to have many more. Let us put ourselves and our affairs in God's hands, you will see that good will come of it."[40] This must have elicited a reply to the effect that the pregnancy was progressing satisfactorily, because Antoine's response, "From the camp, in haste," says, "I am especially pleased to hear that [the unborn child] is full of life and moving about. I promise you, my dear, that nothing could make me more content than your last letter."[41]

Antoine's tone becomes more relaxed, typical of a soldier's communication with his wife. "Despite the enemy, I was able to put 2000 men into René [probably Rainecourt, 20 kilometers from Péronne] last night . . . we slept within earshot of their drums and they of ours. . . . I received the shirt you sent me and I will bring it back still clean because it is no fun for a man who sleeps fully dressed in this cold weather to change his shirt in the morning."[42]

At some time in September or October 1553, Antoine urged Jeanne to go to court, at Compiègne, to join the Queen, Catherine de Medici, "so that I will be better able to send you news, and more frequently." We do not know whether she followed this suggestion or not, but during her wanderings of this period she went at least briefly to Tours. Her only surviving letter to Antoine was written from there. It deals with impersonal matters and gives no evidence of a disturbed state of mind.[43] She begs "Him who can do all to send peace, and may He send you back in good health to see your park at Plessis where your deer fell the forest, but, Monseigneur, I cannot tell you how many horns they have. I will do so as soon as I can." She signs it, "your very humble and very obedient daughter and *mignonne,* wife and mistress, Jehanne de Navarre."

Jeanne must have written at least one other letter to her husband from Tours, because he says, "My dear, I have received your letter from Tours asking about my health. I can assure you that it has not been so good for a long time as it now is and I don't see how it could be better . . . unless you were with me . . . I beg you, my companion, don't worry about me. I have hopes of bringing a whole skin back to you soon. I am sending word by the courier for you to go to La Flèche."[44] Jeanne

96

is evidently still upset and her husband is becoming impatient. He refers to "another letter . . . in which you are suffering from the torment caused you by the Baillive and the Vicomtesse. I shall write them about it as you ask and I assure you that I will not support them or any others against you, but on the contrary, will side with you as the mistress. In return, I beg you to control yourself wisely, as you promised me. You are no longer a child but a woman, and old enough to have good discretion. You are capable of good sense and of managing yourself and our affairs so that I should not have to worry about anything."

Jeanne's state of mind was worrying her husband. He was also insistent that she should not do anything which might jeopardize the safe, normal birth of the expected child. Her father was entirely concerned with his grandchild-to-be. Family legend, elaborated by the eulogistic "historians" of the seventeenth century like Palma Cayet and Olhagaray, describes him as intensely irritated by the death of the Duc de Beaumont, and says that he held Jeanne responsible because she had turned the baby over to Aymée. He disapproved of Jeanne's wandering somewhat aimlessly around France in the final months of her pregnancy and wanted her to come home and let him take charge. For a while he had hoped to remarry and have a son himself, thus assuring the succession and bypassing Jeanne, but his failing health had forced him to give up the scheme. No documentary evidence supports the frequently repeated statement that Henri d'Albret "ordered" Jeanne to return to Béarn in the autumn of 1553, but a letter written about this time urges her to be careful and states that he wishes her "as much happiness as any good father could wish for his child." He would like to go to her but it is far, "nevertheless, if my health can stand it, after I have taken the waters I shall not fail to come to you."[45]

Jeanne was more interested in the company of her husband than of her father. Antoine writes, at about the same time, "My dear, I have just received, by your *valet-de-chambre,* your letter saying that you want to come and meet me. I beg you to believe that you cannot want it any more than I do, but what I wrote [discouraging the plan] was not without reason because the host . . . cannot lodge you well here. . . . As soon as the King is better I will set off to meet you and it cannot be soon enough to suit me. . . . I think it would be best for you to come in this direction and I like the idea of Pontoise, as you suggest." In a postscript he reports that his brother, Louis de Bourbon, Prince de Condé, has recently become a father. "M. le Prince received news yesterday that my sister [-in-law], the Princess, has been delivered of a daughter. May God deal with us differently!"[46]

Jeanne's health continued to be a cause of anxiety. Antoine says, "I have received your letter describing how your illness continues to torment you, which worries me a great deal. I assure you, my dear, that had it not been for the postscript in Raphael's* letter saying, 'Since my last Madame has been well, I hope she will have no more trouble,' I was of a good mind to come to you at once and be your doctor."[47]

Antoine's last letter to Jeanne at this time tells her that the camp is about to be broken up and that he has leave to depart and join her, "which I hope to do about the end of this month of September in which we are. I urge you, my dear, don't lose an hour in preparing to go to your father the King. I shall make as great haste as possible to overtake you."[48] Antoine had made up his mind to a long visit in Béarn, and a portion of this letter is devoted to instructions about the transport of his hunting dogs and birds. He gives Jeanne a choice of coming to meet him or waiting "for me to join you at La Flêche, so that we can set out together. . . . Let me know which of the two you prefer so that I can plan my route. I think I shall prove to be a good doctor when I am with you . . . my cough has left me and I feel as well as I ever have."

Whether the deciding factor was Henri d'Albret's health, or the imposition of his will on Jeanne and Antoine as tradition says, is not clear, but it is a matter of record that sometime after the middle of October 1553, Antoine and Jeanne had met—some say at Compiègne, others at La Flêche—and were on their way to Béarn. Traveling very slowly because of Jeanne's condition, they reached Poitou on October 29. Henri d'Albret met them in Mont-de-Marsan, and the city fathers presented their King with a barrel of wine to welcome him and his daughter.[49] On December 4 they arrived in Pau; ten days later the future Henri IV was born.

BITTERSWEET MOTHERHOOD, 1553

According to family legend, as recorded by Palma Cayet, Jeanne was settled in the chateau at Pau and her father stationed a faithful old servant, Cotin, in her quarters for the sole purpose of notifying him at

---

* Raphael de Taillevis, Antoine's personal physician, was traveling with Jeanne.

the first sign of labor pains. Sometime in the next few days, the legend continues, Henri d'Albret showed Jeanne his will, "fully made out in her favor, which he kept in a golden coffer covered with a great golden chain that would go around a man's neck twenty-five or thirty times." He promised to give it to her on two conditions: first, that while giving birth, she sing a song popular in the region, invoking the aid of the Virgin (represented by a statue at the end of the bridge over the Gave just below the chateau), and, second, that the child be a son, born without a cry, "so that you will not present me with a crying child or a complaining mother."[50] Jeanne accepted the bargain. In the early hours of December 14, her labor began and her father was summoned. When she heard his footsteps she began to sing, "Our Lady at the end of the bridge, help me at this hour." Before she had finished the verse the child was born without uttering a sound. The King handed her the golden coffer containing the will (but without the key) and took the infant, wrapping him in a corner of his night robe, saying, "That is for you, my girl, but *this* is for me." He rubbed Henri's lips with a bit of garlic and the baby began to suck it. Then he administered several drops of the noted local wine of Jurançon, which Henri swallowed easily. Thereupon the grandfather exclaimed, triumphantly, "You're a real Béarnais!" Later in the day, many of the local nobles assembled on the terrace of the chateau, and lesser folk on the lawns, below a window where the proud King of Navarre held up the infant prince for all to see, saying, "Look! the lamb has given birth to a lion!" This was a moment of sweet revenge for Henri d'Albret in his eternal feud with the Spaniards, who had said derisively when Jeanne was born, "the bull has sired a lamb."

Legend aside, the Bishop of Oloron's official account states: "On December 14, 1553, Madame Lady Jeanne, Princesse de Navarre, gave birth to her second son at Pau in Béarn, between one and two hours after midnight. He was baptized on Tuesday, March 6, [1554], in the said city of Pau. His godfathers were his grandfather the King of Navarre, who named him Henri, and Monseigneur the Cardinal de Bourbon-Vendôme, his paternal uncle. His godmother was the sister of the said King of Navarre, widow of the late Duc de Rohan."[51] It can be assumed that the midwife and physicians whose salaries are listed in the Chambre des Comptes, were in attendance on Jeanne, although neither Régin nor any other source says so. The traditional account may not have been documentary truth, but it was the official version promulgated in Henri's reign and constitutes the opening scene of a rich legend concerning France's most popular king, which has persisted to this day.[52]

When the story of Henri's birth is considered from Jeanne's viewpoint it loses the picturesque quality appropriate to the birth of a folk-hero. Even at this moment the "King of Navarre" was determined to use his daughter for his own ends. As the Vicomte's historian says, "he never gave Jeanne a thought except to the extent that she could contribute . . . to the reacquisition of Pampeluna, by no matter what means."[53]

Jeanne and Antoine spent the rest of the winter in Pau. Antoine divided his time between hunting and visiting the local nobles, trying to ingratiate himself. He was as extravagant as ever and made many demands on the treasury of Henri d'Albret, who was frequently irritated with his son-in-law and somewhat resentful of what he regarded as usurpations of his own authority. The Spaniards also inform us that when the King of Navarre renewed his intrigues with them, hoping this time to marry Princess Juana,* Antoine refused to take any part in them.[54] When Antoine was recalled to the royal army in Flanders in the spring of 1554, Henri d'Albret advised him to seize the opportunity to communicate with the Emperor's government in Brussels, "but the Duke replied that he had nothing to communicate to the King's enemies except with a sword or a gun in his hand." Since the Spaniards were interested in a new deal with Henri d'Albret only if Antoine were party to it, nothing came of this scheme.

Throughout the summer and early autumn of 1554 Antoine was campaigning in Flanders, maintaining his reputation as a soldier, and Jeanne stayed as near him as possible. She spent most of the time at Gaillon, near Rouen, but went on occasion to Coucy and La Fère when it seemed possible that Antoine might meet her. These meetings were often hastily arranged and usually kept secret from Henri II, because the King regarded such leaves as desertion. On one occasion Antoine told his wife to meet him "ten leagues from Abbeville, but with the smallest retinue possible. Bring only the Baillive or the Victomtesse and two *femmes-de chambre,* leave the rest with our son."[55] On December 30, 1554, he urges her to come to some village near Beauvais, "but not one belonging to the Cardinal Châtillon or any other of the great lords, so that the court will know nothing about it, because if the King knew that I had gone to meet you, he would send me right back to the front."

* Daughter of Charles V, widow of King John of Portugal (died January 1554).

The need for secrecy causes him to add in a postscript, "send a man to the Hostellerie Sauvage in Beauvais to tell me where you are."[56]

Jeanne's preoccupation with Antoine is reflected in one of the few known letters from this period of her life. It is addressed to the Duchesse de Guise (Anne d'Este), whose husband also was active on the Flemish front during the campaign of 1554.

My cousin:

I beg you to send news by the bearer . . . I hear that Contet* has arrived from camp. You would do me a great favor by letting me know what he says . . . by the bearer, who is sure . . . [and] what he has heard about the return of our husbands. . . . If there is news that you fear to have known, rest assured that I will keep it as secret as any friend you have. Knowing that you are a little lazy about writing, I would be perfectly happy to receive [a letter] by your secretary . . . and especially if you know anything about M. my husband, to whom I have written a letter I am sending you, and beg you to keep it [until it can be delivered].[57]

An undated letter of Antoine's shows that he still reciprocated his wife's affection. "I have a good mind to send for you and the little one, for I do not wish to be without you any more. Believe me, I am wretched without you, more than you might think. You will feel sorry for me when you see me as I am very thin and have no real hope of gaining until I see you and can come to life again in your hands."[58]

Jeanne was expecting another child. Her third son, the Comte de Marle, was born at a quarter past five in the morning of February 19, 1555, in the chateau of Gaillon in Normandy. Claude Régin records the fact and says that he performed the baptismal service.[59] The Comte de Marle died in infancy, the death, according to family tradition, caused by his nurse's irresponsibility. Palma Cayet tells the story:

When M. de Vendôme and the Princess his wife . . . went to visit the King of Navarre in Béarn . . . the Prince was a very fine baby and everyone wanted to hold him. . . . One of the gentlemen-in-waiting and the nurse who was taking care of him amused themselves by tossing him back and forth across the sill of an open window. . . . Sometimes they would pretend not to catch him . . . which was the cause of the tragedy that resulted, because the nurse, expecting that the gentleman would catch him, although he pretended that he would not, let [the baby] go and the little Comte de Marle fell and hit a stone step below, on which he broke some ribs. The gentleman . . . rescued the Prince and brought him back to the weeping

* Louis d'Humières, Sieur de Contay, son of Jean d'Humières, Governor of Péronne under Antoine.

nurse. . . . The King, M. de Vendôme, and the Princess were out hunting at the time and this accident was kept secret from them. I have heard some of the old family servants say that if they had been told, [the baby] could have been saved . . . but he died, to the great regret of the King, M. de Vendôme, and the Princess. . . . Later, when [the facts were] disclosed, the King became very angry with his daughter, the Princess."[60]

The Comte de Marle has left no mark on history, as far as documentary evidence goes, and Palma Cayet erred in placing the episode —if it ever occurred—in the lifetime of Henri d'Albret, who died on May 24, 1555. As late as the autumn of 1557 Spanish documents refer either to the sons of the Duc de Vendôme or to his "eldest" son. On March 21, 1557, Antoine announces proudly to his sister that Henri II intends to marry his daughter, Marguerite, "to my eldest son."[61] A Spanish report, dated November 23, 1557, quotes Antoine (in an interview) as referring to "his only son that he would not lose for all the wealth in the world . . . his only heir," although Descurra, in a letter dated November 30 of the same year, still speaks of "the sons of Vendôme." De Ruble concludes, plausibly, that the Comte de Marle died in the middle of November 1557. The November 23 letter was written by an agent (Don Sancho), who had talked with Antoine in person, while Descurra, who was not in Béarn at the time, might not have learned by November 30 of the child's death ten days or two weeks earlier.[62] The spurious references to Henri d'Albret are important because Palma Cayet's book bore the imprimatur of Henri IV. The King of France and Navarre permitted the family chronicler to depict each of her three sons as a cause of antagonism and trouble between Jeanne d'Albret and her father.

FATHER AND DAUGHTER

Although few details are known, it is easy to believe that the antagonism between Jeanne and her father indicated in family legend might have existed in reality. During her childhood, Jeanne saw Henri only at intervals, principally at court, where the D'Albrets' only claim to importance was François' affection for his sister. Self-centered and self-indulgent, Henri d'Albret can hardly have been at his best when visiting his egotistical brother-in-law's court. Jeanne's only personal reference to her father —as distinct from allusions in official documents—is her report to the Vicomte de Gourdon that he had forbidden her mother "to meddle in matters of doctrine," with the result that Jeanne feared him and waited to become a Protestant until after his death.

In the first great crisis of her life, the Cleves marriage, her father was at least partly responsible for the pressures brought to bear, although Jeanne's resistance served his interests better than compliance would have. When she was grown up and married Henri d'Albret made no effort to conceal his dislike and distrust of her adored husband. Even after the birth of Henri IV, he entered into negotiations with Spain, which, had they been successful, would have disinherited her and her children. To these indisputable facts tradition adds his anger on two tragic occasions, and includes no compensating note of sympathy for his daughter in the loss of her sons. In the 1550's, when it became clear that Jeanne's marriage to Antoine would not further the restoration of Navarre, Henri d'Albret dropped what interest he had had in his daughter's future. He insisted upon having absolute control over his grandson, down to the most minute detail, but his promises to the Spaniards would have deprived that grandson of his inheritance. Jeanne must have felt a good deal of resentment toward her father at this time, and the account she had to settle *with* him must have loomed larger than the account she had to settle *for* him.

The King of Navarre's health had been steadily deteriorating for about eight years. In the spring of 1555, after visiting Casteljaloux, he stopped to visit the Comte de Gramont, and died in the chateau at Hagetmau on May 24 or 25.[63] Outwardly, Jeanne's mourning for her father was conventional. Her husband had more than sufficient reason to welcome his death; Antoine was "King of Navarre"—at last. D'Albret's death had been expected for some years, and an undated letter of Antoine's shows apprehension about Jeanne's reaction and tries to comfort her in advance:

in these circumstances, my dear, it is necessary to rely upon the Great Physician . . . and beg him to grant [the King] renewed life. . . . [Knowing that] you love him more than anyone in the world after me and that you would regard it as the greatest loss you ever had, . . . I fear that your temperament will cause you to give way to lamentation [*que vostre nature ne vous constraigne de faire une demonstration*] and I beg you to keep calm. I assure you that [if need be] you have a husband who will be father, mother, brother, and husband to you.

As to the other news, that you are not pregnant, thank God. It means that I will see you sooner. It seems to me that you would do wrong to feel badly about it, in view of the satisfaction we have in our fine handsome [son] who gives us as much pleasure as others would have from a dozen.[64]

HENRI D'ALBRET, KING OF NAVARRE

Jeanne had just turned twenty-one when her mother died; when she became Queen in her own right she was twenty-seven. She had never been close to either of her parents, and tended to react strongly against weaknesses they exhibited, especially submission to others and lack of independence. Her life pattern shows a consistent determination to be free of any authority outside herself. Her anxiety to avoid being a weakling, a pawn, and, above all, a dupe, may explain Jeanne's tendency to become *brouillée* with her associates and her almost pathological suspicion and distrust.

In the eyes of the world, and in the external circumstances of Jeanne's life as a child, Marguerite was the more influential of her parents. The daughter was blamed for being cold to and unworthy of her mother, which is a heavy burden for a child to bear.[65] It seems likely that Jeanne despised Marguerite's vacillation in religion, and determined to outdo her in firmness, even while admiring her successes. She used Marguerite's weapon of dissimulation effectively and repeated her mother's behavior in bringing up her own children.

Henri d'Albret was an effective ruler in his own domains and Jeanne as Queen accepted him as a model. But in her childhood, spent in "France," she had no exposure to this side of his character, and at court Henri exemplified the disadvantages of dependence, even more than Marguerite. Moreover, he was gullible and unrealistic, and his flamboyant personality did not inspire respect. Given Jeanne's intense pride, she probably could not easily identify with him and therefore found it more difficult to sort out the aggressive and submissive elements in her own nature than had Marguerite, with her strong attachment to her brother. Jeanne sought, successfully, to realize her "masculine" side for her own ends—to eliminate weakness and vulnerability. This does not imply mannishness, which was quite alien to Jeanne's personality, but the qualities of initiative and energy often designated as "masculine" in contrast to the "feminine" quality of passivity. Jeanne always hoped that some man would take the lead, but, when she was disappointed, she was capable (unlike Marguerite) of self-reliance. When her mature character emerged, after later crises, involving her conversion and the disintegration of her marriage, it incorporated traits of both Henri d'Albret and Marguerite, and was consistent with the character of the twelve-year-old who had defied François I.

IV

KING AND QUEEN

1555–1558

ANTOINE, returning from court, received news of Henri d'Albret's death in Poitou; Jeanne, at the chateau of Baran in Braine, near Soissons, on May 29, 1555.[1] By the middle of June they had met in Saintonge and made a triumphal entry into their "kingdom." In a letter to Prince Philip, the Duke of Albuquerque describes their reception as "transports of enthusiasm," which bears out the Béarnais historians, whom we might otherwise suspect of exaggeration.[2]

The first task of the new King and Queen of Navarre was to hold funeral services for Henri d'Albret. These took place on July 25 with many of the vassals of the House of Albret paying their final respects, although the Comte de Gramont and the Baron de Luxe were not present. Nor did anyone represent the King of France.[3] Henri II had recently tried —in vain—to persuade Antoine to exchange Béarn for territories in the center of France. He had then suborned Nicolas Dangu, Bishop of Mende, to lure from his post the Governor of the fortress of Navarrenx, so that royal forces might take it by surprise attack. If this maneuver had succeeded, Béarn would have lost its most important citadel. But the Governor foiled the plot, and throughout the Vicomté demonstrations of Béarnais patriotism resounded, accompanied by outspoken hostility to the crown of France.[4] Although the attempt failed, the episode reveals the real conflicts between Antoine and Henri II, masked by the courteous letters exchanged. (In the very week he was plotting to take Navarrenx the King bestowed upon Antoine the administration of Guyenne, formerly held by Henri d'Albret.) It also foreshadows the problems Jeanne was to face during the civil wars, when the crown undermined the allegiance of some of her chief vassals by promising rewards she could not match.

As soon as their duty to the late King had been discharged, the new sovereigns called the Estates of Béarn (see Appendix A) into session, to accept them as rulers in the coronation ceremony. Composed of two bodies—the clergy and nobility in one and representatives of the Third Estate in the other—the Estates had important privileges and jealously guarded prerogatives. Their protest against the Cleves marriage had been typical of their habit of keeping a close eye on the vicomtes' government and dynastic decisions. The session was scheduled to open on August 13, but there was a delay of five days because the Estates were reluctant to recognize the Duc de Vendôme as joint sovereign with Jeanne. She told the delegation that brought the protest that "if she, who was their Queen and sovereign lady, regarded him as her lord, they should do the same, because the husband is lord of the person and property of his wife." They objected that sovereign power was not in the class with private property and said that if she were to die they would regard Antoine as a mere foreigner. They wished to make sure that only Jeanne's children would inherit Béarn. "After long altercation," in Bordenave's words, the Estates agreed to accept Antoine as joint sovereign and on August 18 he and Jeanne took the oath.[5] Among the prominent persons who took the corresponding oath of homage and fealty was Nicolas Dangu, Bishop of Mende. The new King and Queen made no changes in administration at the start of their reign; it is probable that they retained in office even those whose loyalty they suspected in the hope that this would offset the influence of Henri II, while dismissal might have the opposite effect.

The Estates then presented their grievances and obtained confirmation of their established privileges. Jeanne and Antoine avoided several pitfalls by promising that "they would always follow the course of justice"; they issued ordinances (see Chapter X) on a variety of subjects, such as the punishment of vagabonds, the rights of shepherds to pasture their flocks, and the regulation of the coinage.[6]

Jeanne did make changes in her household, as distinct from the government. She appointed Claude Régin, Bishop of Oloron, whose *Mémoire* gives the vital statistics of her children, to the position of *maître des requêtes,* at an annual salary of 100 livres, and two stewards, each of whom received 300 livres. She added six new grooms to the stables, and three new employees to the bakery. There were to be four secretaries, including Victor Brodeau—entrusted with many delicate missions—three physicians, and three chaplains. Counting the stable hands, the retainers numbered about one hundred, including Jeanne Gilbert, "the Queen's midwife," and fourteen ladies-in-waiting, with salaries ranging from 25 to 300 livres per year, among whom were the Vicomtesse de Lavedan (at a reduced salary) and Suzanne de Bourbon-Miossens, gouvernante of Henri de Béarn, and their daughters. The deletion of Aymée's name was perhaps the most important change.[7]

The records of the Chambre des Comptes in Pau show that Jeanne was generous; she made outright gifts amounting to 2403 livres and 11 sous between her accession and the end of 1555. Antoine's love of hunting and interest in animals generally is evident in the records: he bought many horses, falcons, and "rare beasts for the menagerie," and sent *isards* (chamois) of the Pyrenees as presents to Montmorency and Diane de Poitiers. He supported a number of musicians, both for the royal chapel and for secular purposes—he loved to dance. Gambling was another expense; he once lost 4 livres to his brother the Cardinal de Bourbon, in a game of darts.[8]

In secret, Antoine was playing a far more dangerous game with Charles V, in which the stakes were crowns, kingdoms—and the fate of his wife and children. This was a game with few rules, and Antoine held no important cards. His attempt to play off the Emperor against the King of France will be discussed later because it is impossible to follow Antoine's secret game at the same time as his public actions.

Antoine left Béarn in September 1555 to attend court on legitimate business. The properties of the Duchy of Alençon were being distributed among a number of claimants. As Marguerite's heir, Jeanne was among them, and Antoine went to Paris to represent her interests. Jeanne remained at home with the two Princes, Henri, who would be two years old in December, and the eight-month-old Comte de Marle. During Antoine's absence she made a visit to the County of Bigorre and seems to have taken some important steps toward becoming a Calvinist. By December, shortly after Jeanne's twenty-seventh birthday and her first as Queen of Navarre, Antoine had returned to Pau. Relations between Jeanne and her husband were still close, judging by a letter Antoine wrote from Paris, probably about the middle of October.

My dear,

I cannot tell you how grateful I am to you for sending your news and that of the children so often, you cannot imagine how much good it does me . . . [The reason I have not written lately is] that I had a passing fever at Villers-Cotterêts which lasted twenty hours, so I went back to Juilly to stay with M. de Mende, where I took pills which were too feeble [to do any good]. Then I came here to meet the King . . . and came down with a severe colic . . . with a fever that lasted eight days and the greatest pain that can be endured. They gave me pills twice and a liquid medicine made of rhubarb and other poisons, with the result, my dear, that I am purged enough for a lifetime and these drugs have so extracted the humors from my body that nothing is left but the good, which is being kept in reserve for you and no other, I promise you. . . .

You say you want to wear a coiffe next summer and I think you could not do better, it became you very well last year. I am sending by the bearer a golden chain . . . worth less than I would like, but please value it in accordance with the affection it brings. I have ordered a coach for you and today I plan to buy horses, white or grey. I have one for myself, red-and-white piebald. You shall choose the ones you want.

The postscript to this letter reads: "Please send news of our children as often as you can."[9]

Another possible reason for Antoine's trip to Paris without Jeanne in the autumn of 1555 is revealed in a letter he wrote to Montmorency the following spring, on April 26, 1556: "to give you my personal news, God today took a little girl to whom my wife gave birth two weeks ago tomorrow. He will make up the loss when and as He pleases."[10] There is no record of Jeanne's feelings about the loss of this daughter who has not left even a name to history. She and Antoine were together in Nérac between early April and late June 1556, so no correspondence was exchanged between them, and he does not mention the matter in any of his other letters.

Antoine went to Paris again in the summer of 1556. He must have been there very briefly, for he was still in Nérac on June 23 and had returned to Pau for the opening of the Estates on July 15. Henri II had recently become aware of new intrigues between the King of Navarre and the Emperor. In letters written to the King and the Constable in the spring, Antoine had attempted to put a totally different interpretation on certain facts uncovered by some of the crown's agents.[11] It is possible that one purpose of this hasty trip was to prevent the situation from becoming even more dangerous. Financial necessity may also have played a part, because letters to Jeanne at this time refer to the difficulties of borrowing money. In one of these he remarks on the high cost of living in Paris. The tone is gay. "We set out tomorrow to rejoin you . . . each with the intention to do his duty in the appropriate place, on the field of honor or in the beds of our wives. [We have proved] to be good businessmen, getting out of Paris with some money still unspent. This is no easy accomplishment and it is the truth about Paris, record it in your journal. I am sending you a melon that seems ripe. I hope it is good and I shall be annoyed if it is not because I want anything that comes from me to match my feelings."[12] In another letter he speaks as a doting father: "I have plucked up my courage to ask the King for a company of fifty armed men [to be under the command of] our son. . . . When you say that he is blooming I do not doubt it, nor that as long as . . . he is in your hands, he'll be the healthiest in the world."[13]

This correspondence shows evidence of Antoine's ambition, so often remarked upon. "My dear, I have received two letters which show me your great desire to see me . . . mine is no less . . . but the desire to be in the ranks of those who leave behind when they die a memory of great deeds, keeps me here longer than I wish . . . there is also the ingratitude of those who are in our debt. . . . I await the hour when I can mount my horse to come to you."[14] As a good wife, Jeanne was trying to help him in his career. When Antoine was put in a bad light by the revelation of his Spanish intrigues, she wrote to the Constable asking him to continue his favor and friendship to her husband.[15]

After the Estates had adjourned, July 29, 1556, Antoine and Jeanne spent some time visiting their towns in Basse-Navarre. In St. Jean-Pied-de-Port and Sauveterre they were greeted outside the city by delegations of notables, who presented them with the keys to the city, and by girls offering flowers. Antoine's charm and gallant bearing made a favorable impression on the populace, as did the fact that both he and Jeanne took part in the Basque ceremonies, including dances put on in their honor, according to a report from the Duke of Albuquerque to Princess Juana, Regent of Spain.[16]

The Spaniards were worried by Antoine's activity. Charles V, who had abdicated in January 1556, was expected to arrive in Spain by sea and the Duke of Albuquerque, as Viceroy of Spanish Navarre, feared that Antoine was planning an attack. The Spaniards would have been less fearful if they had known that Antoine's performance was mostly bluff, but it cannot be denied that it was impressive. In late September, after Jeanne had returned to Pau, he covered the ground strenuously, visiting many of the remote villages to reinforce their loyalty. He was averaging 32 kilometers a day. One hasty note to Jeanne says, "This will not be long because I have one foot in the saddle and am not very well set for writing. . . . We are today, Sunday, at St. Justin [Landes], tomorrow we'll be at Haire [Aire-sur-l'Adour], Tuesday, Arzacq [Basses-Pyrénées], Wednesday, Morlaas. I do not know whether we can get to Pau to surprise you that day. . . . Take care of yourself." A few days later he says that he plans " to be in Pau the day after tomorrow, where I hope to find you as gay as your letters. As for us, we are in fine form . . . from morning to night on horseback . . . but it does not make me as happy as lying warmly beside you, which—God willing—I shall do on Saturday."[17]

About the middle of November, Jeanne, her husband, and Henri de Béarn left Pau for an extended journey whose ultimate purpose was Antoine's "solemn entry" into the capital as King of Navarre and the presentation of their son to Henri II, their suspicious sovereign. The would-be royal family traveled in short stages with a large retinue in order to impress their vassals along the way, as well as the court. They had so many armed retainers that both the English ambassador and the Duke of Albuquerque reported that it seemed like an army.[18]

The first big event was the reception of their new sovereigns by the magistrates of the city of Limoges. They organized an escort of more than seven hundred men, "representing all the crafts of the town," and a large number of young people to take part "in the said glorious entry and happy event." On December 20, in the Château d'Isle outside Limoges, Antoine and Jeanne were presented with the keys to the city. The next morning, seated beneath a canopy on a dais, Antoine received the homage of the four mendicant orders, the local clergy, the royal officers, and the city fathers. The president of each incorporated body made a speech "which the said lord heard graciously and accepted with great pleasure, as was obvious by his happy smile and the courteous responses he made." Then the King of Navarre made his solemn entry "dressed in a rich tunic with sleeves of cloth of silver . . . and gold buttons. . . . He rode a beautiful white horse, the handsomest ever seen . . . caparisoned in the same way." He was accompanied by the Bishops of Mende and Oloron and a number of lords. Later in the day the ceremony was repeated for the Queen of Navarre, "dressed in cloth of gold trimmed with ermine . . .

and stones of inestimable value . . . also riding a white horse." Among
the tributes paid to Jeanne were verses honoring her mother. The authors
were conscious that poetry was not their particular gift, "our poor songs
cannot sufficiently praise the flower of flowers and her excellent daughter,
for that we would need Virgil or Homer." That evening in the Château
de Breuil the city fathers gave a dinner and ball in honor of their visiting
sovereigns and the next day they presented gifts, which included a
statue of Minerva for Jeanne.[19]

After spending Christmas in Limoges, Jeanne and her family traveled
through Angoulême—the native heath of François I and Marguerite—
to Vendôme, arriving there on February 4. This was young Henri's first
visit to the principal fief of his father's family. Henri II sent a guard of
honor to escort them to Paris. No documentary account of the effect,
if any, they made on the populace or on the court exists, but there is
the traditional account of the meeting of the two Henris, formulated
(in print) by Palma Cayet in 1608. The King is said to have taken
Henri de Navarre (who had celebrated his third birthday during the
trip) on his lap, and to have asked whether he would like to be his son.
The child, pointing to Antoine, said, "No, that is my father," in the
dialect of Béarn. Henri II then said, "Well then, how would you like
to be my son-in-law?" "Yes, I would like that," the Prince replied.[20]

Legend presents the episode as an official initiative of the Valois to
secure an alliance with the Bourbon heir. The result, fifteen years and
many events later, was the marriage of Henri de Navarre and Marguerite
de Valois. Letters of both Jeanne and Antoine show that the alliance
was indeed conceived at this time, but their allusions indicate that the
initiative came from Antoine. In a letter to one of her ladies, Brantôme's
mother, Jeanne says, "I write to gladden your heart . . . my dear friend,
with the good news that my husband, having mustered up the courage
to ask the King for his daughter for my son . . . the King honored us
by granting it. I want you to know how pleased I am." Antoine's
expression of satisfaction goes even further. On March 21, from Chantilly,
he wrote to his sister, Marguerite de Bourbon, Duchesse de Nevers,

My sister,

They say one should keep nothing from friends, and since I have none
better or closer than you . . . I want you to be the first to know my good
news . . . the boon and favor it has pleased the King to show me by his

agreement to marry Madame Marguerite, his daughter, to my eldest son, which I take as a particular sign of his good grace. I find myself today at peace and satisfied, with everything I could ask for in this world.[21]

Antoine's reference to the King's "agreement" is less specific than Jeanne's statement that her husband had "mustered up courage to ask," but it does not contradict it. Attribution of the initiative to the Valois King by later chroniclers is, however, more flattering to the House of Bourbon, whose glory they sought to enhance.

Still in this euphoric mood, Antoine was sent to the northeastern front, while Jeanne and Henri returned to Béarn.[22] They were not reunited for several months, until Antoine met Jeanne in Saintonge prior to their official entry into Bordeaux on August 22.[23] Another separation followed shortly, when Antoine went on a tour of inspection of fortifications in the vicinity of Bayonne, during which he was quite ill. Antoine de Noailles* reported to Henri II, on October 19, that the King of Navarre had "a serious dysentery which has kept him in bed. . . . He sent to Auch for a doctor, who gave him rhubarb, with some effect."[24]

The next time Antoine and Jeanne took the road to Paris, in January 1558, they traveled with a small retinue and were in no hurry to reach the capital. This was partly because Antoine had lost his secret game with the Spaniards, but also because they were most reluctant to obey the King's command to attend the wedding of the Dauphin, François, with Mary Stuart, niece of the Guises. The eclipse of the King of Navarre was a subject of gossip, and his mood was much changed from the day when he could tell his sister that he had everything he wanted in this world.[25]

Recalled to the front in June, Antoine hoped to regain his former position by new military exploits, and he was also anxious to avenge the death of his brother, the Duc d'Enghien, who had recently been killed in the war. He wrote Jeanne that he hoped Philip would appear on the battlefield, "because I need no other prisoner to ransom our kingdom."[26] The Hapsburg forces had the upper hand in the fighting, but Spain was bankrupt and needed peace. France needed it no less; by October the negotiations leading to the Peace of Cateau-Cambrésis (signed in April 1559) had begun. It was obvious from the start that France would not

---

* Antoine de Noailles, 1504–1562, Governor of Bordeaux, Admiral of France after 1559.

demand the restitution of Navarre. Antoine had failed to obtain the support of the King of France, his official policy during these three years. The alternative, secret, policy had fared no better.

ANTOINE AND THE HAPSBURGS, 1555–1558

Ready and willing to embrace the cause of *Navarra Irridenta* before he married Jeanne, Antoine had become Henri d'Albret's enthusiastic collaborator in the early years of his marriage—often too eager to suit his father-in-law. Within a month of the latter's death he was in direct contact with the Spaniards through Descurra.[27] The new intrigues would have begun even sooner had it not been for a familiar obstacle: the letters of the Duke of Albuquerque introducing Descurra were addressed to the *Duc de Vendôme et Prince de Béarn*. Antoine declared that in future he would accept none unless they were addressed to the King of Navarre.[28]

When Antoine received Descurra in Pau, in early July 1555, the Spaniard summarized the last proposals of Henri d'Albret as the Emperor understood them, that is, that the Vicomte would aid Spain to conquer Guyenne if Spanish Navarre were restored to him. Antoine declared himself ready to accept the same terms, but Descurra persuaded him that it would be even more glorious to be King of France. They outlined a plan for the division of the spoils. Descurra demanded for the Emperor territory south of a line from Bordeaux to Aix-en-Provence and some fortresses on the Flemish frontier, as well as the surrender of Piedmont to the Duke of Savoy and part of Champagne to the Duc de Lorraine. In order to deceive the King of France about the military preparations, Antoine would pretend to be preparing an attack on Spain to retake Navarre. Instead of resisting, Spanish troops, under the command of the Emperor or Philip, would join forces with Antoine and invade France. Henri de Béarn, aged one and one-half, would be held at the Imperial Court as a hostage until the plan was carried out. Antoine asked for a reply before Christmas.[29]

A month later, in August 1555, Descurra returned to Béarn without an answer but with additional clauses concerning possible marriages between the Hapsburgs and the children of Antoine and Jeanne. Antoine also modified the original proposition by signifying that if Navarre were refused he would content himself with Milan. These meetings were held in the greatest secrecy, sometimes deep in the woods when Antoine was hunting, sometimes in the middle of the night, in the royal bedchamber, with only Jeanne present as a witness. As far as we know, Jeanne was independently involved only to the extent that she sent a message to the Emperor (without Antoine's knowledge) asking protection for herself and her children if they were threatened by the King of France.[30]

Charles V was preparing to abandon the world and to retire to the monastery of Yuste in Spain. He declared that he had turned the Navarre question over to Philip; but the latter was delayed in England until late autumn, so that Antoine had left for court (to participate in the settlement of the Alençon inheritance) without receiving an answer. Antoine was said to have boasted that he would soon be crowned in the cathedral of the ancient capital, Pampeluna, and the Duke of Albuquerque was suspicious of his movements.[31] Spanish dispatches in 1556 stressed Antoine's military reputation and described Jeanne as "Vendôme's bellicose wife," who was urging him to undertake a foreign war to divert him from his intended treason to France.[32] The Spaniards feared that Antoine would try to capture the Emperor when he landed in Spain, and we know that he and Jeanne were enthusiastically received by the Basques in the late summer of the year. Spanish fears were not eased until after September 28, when the Emperor landed at Laredo. He received Descurra on October 13, at Burgos, and repeated in person what he had already written—that Philip would make the decision.[33]

Antoine flew into a temper when he found Charles V still procrastinating. He accused the Spaniards of evasiveness and declared that he "did not intend to wait longer with his tongue hanging out."[34] A year and four months had gone by since he had asked for an answer by Christmas 1555. Aside from the strain of so risky a plan, he had had a bad scare in the early months of 1556, when Lagebaston, Premier Président of the Parlement of Bordeaux, had alerted Henri II to the existence of intrigues between the new King of Navarre and the Hapsburgs. Antoine had taken pains to depict Lagebaston as a troublemaker and had apparently succeeded in his attempt to maneuver between his two powerful adversaries. The French King did not know the full scope of the plot, but Antoine lived in dread of further revelations.[35]

For various reasons Philip was inclined to conciliate Antoine and to deal with him favorably at the close of 1556: the French were in the strongest military position since early in the century; Hapsburg prestige was adversely affected by the Emperor's abdication; the Reform movement was spreading rapidly in Antoine's domains. It seemed to Philip that any arrangement which would make Antoine dependent on Spain would reduce his own difficulties. Accordingly, Philip advised the Duke of Albuquerque that he would agree to the exchange of Milan for Navarre, requiring only that Spanish officers should supervise the exchange.[36] The cautious Emperor revised his son's message before it reached Antoine, to the effect that the Navarrese fortresses must be delivered before Milan was yielded.

Antoine was apprised of this development by Descurra in Vendôme on January 30, 1557—during the trip to Paris with Jeanne and Henri. He complained bitterly that the Emperor was playing with him and alluded to the ultimate disaster that overtook the Constable of Bourbon and others who had trusted Charles V. His reasoning was sound in that by the Emperor's proposal Antoine stood to be exposed as a traitor to France and might also be abandoned by Charles V. Descurra objected that nothing could be accomplished if Antoine would not trust the Emperor, to which Antoine angrily replied that the Emperor should also show some confidence in him. After several meetings—in some of which Victor Brodeau represented Antoine— the King of Navarre put his response in writing.[37]

In the first months of 1557 Antoine was aware of the difficulties of the Spaniards. Philip's willingness to concede Milan confirmed his impression that it would be worthwhile for the Hapsburgs to meet his conditions. The encounter with Henri II, with the result optimistically reported to his sister, also made Antoine believe that he had been reinstated in the good graces of the French King.[38] The sources show that, despite his repeated insistence that the Navarre negotiations were in Philip's hands, the Emperor continued to make the ultimate decisions and to insist on his former terms. This fact, often overlooked, accounts for the outcome of the Hapsburg-Navarre negotiations at this time.

Philip made concessions to Antoine in a letter to the Duke of Albuquerque from London, in April 1557.

> You will send word to Vendôme that I consent to have Milan handed over to him first. You will ask him by what means . . . he expects to keep [Milan] from falling into the hands of the King of France, in which case we would both lose it. . . . I expect of such a gentleman that he would keep to his word under all circumstances . . . but I ask that he put his two sons in our hands, as he has promised . . . and that he apply himself to the

planned enterprise against the King of France as soon as we have turned over Milan.[39]

Philip was in London, but when Victor Brodeau was dispatched to negotiate details, he went to Spain, under pretext of an errand to Queen Eleanor, the Emperor's sister. Brodeau returned to Béarn with a treaty dictated by Charles V which the Emperor said was his final word on the matter.[40]

The first article ignores Antoine's demands and Philip's concessions: Milan will be turned over to Antoine three months after Spanish armies cross the Pyrenees and enter Guyenne. Other important articles promise military aid to help Antoine hold Milan effectively and recognize the sovereignty of Jeanne d'Albret over the counties of Armagnac, Foix, Périgord, Limousin, Comminges, and Gaure, the vicomtés of Marsan, Tursan, Gavardan, Nebousan, Bigorre [sic], and Condom and Bazas, claimed by the crown of France. Marriages between the Houses of Castille and Albret are also stipulated. The Imperial Council fully expected Antoine to accept this treaty; on the very day that Brodeau and Descurra left Spain (July 19, 1557), Princess Juana set in motion the military preparations for the invasion of Guyenne.[41] The document was delivered to Antoine in early August when he was returning to Béarn from court. There is no firsthand account of his immediate reaction, but his long delay in answering—as well as the reply in November—showed his dissatisfaction that after two years of negotiations no progress had been made. Antoine's long silence astonished and disturbed the Duke of Albuquerque, who complained of it to Princess Juana.[42]

While matters were thus suspended, a dramatic change on the international scene altered Antoine's position: the French defeat at St. Quentin (August 10, 1557) resulted in the capture of many important officers by the enemy, including the Constable himself. Antoine thereupon stiffened his demands to the Emperor, believing that Henri II would be so preoccupied and weakened that he would not be able to take action against the Navarre-Hapsburg coalition. This was a serious miscalculation. It was only Philip who had granted the concessions of the previous spring; the Emperor had canceled them, and now the former military disadvantage of Spain, which was the reason for Philip's conciliatory attitude, had been reversed: the Hapsburgs had the upper hand of France and no longer needed the self-styled King of Navarre. The sacrifice of Milan was not necessary. After an exchange of letters with Philip, the

Emperor wrote to Albuquerque, on October 24, that "in view of the fact that Vendôme has not accepted the offer we have made, my son and I consider ourselves released from our promises."[43]

Antoine, overconfident and unrealistic, countered with a new version of his original demands. On November 23 he told Don Sancho of Pampeluna (who had replaced Descurra after Antoine said that he no longer trusted him) that he wished to have Navarre, and, to fool France, he wanted to appear to conquer it. Afterward he would exchange it for Milan, and also yield French Navarre and the whole of Guyenne to the Hapsburgs. As a token of good faith he would hand over "his only son, whom he would not lose for all the wealth in the world . . . his only heir."[44] (The infant Comte de Marle had just died.) This is the period when Antoine de Noailles reported that Antoine was seriously ill, and the strain of waiting must have been torture. Charles V, cautious and procrastinating, was probably aware that time was on his side in the war of nerves.

Significantly, Antoine's connection with the Reform movement dates from this period. The Calvinist minister Boisnormand entered his service in October, and in December, Calvin wrote his first letter to the King of Navarre, urging him to assume leadership of the movement in France. Toward the end of 1557 Antoine was still hoping to conclude an alliance with the Hapsburgs, but he was also encouraging the Protestant movement as an alternative source of support.

The final blow to Antoine's hope of obtaining the restitution of Navarre with aid from the Emperor came in a letter from the Duke of Albuquerque, delivered in late January 1558, during the trip to court for Mary Stuart's wedding. The Emperor's instructions conclude, that the Duke is to "notify Vendôme . . . that the Council reaffirms what I recently wrote him, that is, my son and I consider ourselves released from our offers, since he has not accepted them and now makes new demands."[45] Antoine replied verbally that he had gone as far as he could and that if Charles wished to continue serious negotiations he must write in his own hand, "to the King of Navarre"; otherwise, Antoine would accept no further communications.[46] Despite this haughty tone he left an agent in Angoulême to wait for a reply, but none ever came.

Larger considerations had made "the Navarre question" pale into insignificance for France and Spain. Bankruptcy threatened both monarchies and serious negotiations were under way to end sixty-five years of war. The King and Queen of Navarre therefore continued their journey to Paris in a strikingly different mood from the year before. In La Rochelle, on February 4, they attended a Calvinist service in public for the first time.[47] The *ondoyant* Antoine, although furious and disheartened, had found another vehicle for his ambition, which had the added appeal that it would avenge his "wrongs" at the hands of both France and Spain.

V

THE PATH TO CONVERSION

1555–1560

THE evolution of the religious posture of the King and Queen of Navarre can only be understood in the context of the course of the Reformation in France before 1555. After *l'affaire des placards* (1534) François I had turned against the "new thinking," so flourishing in the 1520's. With royal policy reinforcing that of the Sorbonne, outright heretics were forced to flee while their sympathizers, like Lefèvre, Briçonnet, and Marguerite herself came to a crossroads (although they did not realize it until later). Either they could persist in advocating reform, outside the Roman fold, or they could content themselves with independent inner belief while outwardly conforming. Erasmus, Marguerite, and most of the humanists chose not to make an irrevocable decision which would have altered the course of their lives. Calvin did so. Luther had faced the same choice, but he had the backing of his immediate sovereign, the Elector of Saxony, when he made the break. In France, to choose the Reformation was to defy the state as well as the Church.[1]

The reasons lie in the historical relations between the Roman Church and the French crown. Over the centuries the church in France had developed considerable independence and a claim to be autonomous (except in matters of doctrine), expressed in numerous references to "the Liberties of the Gallican Church." François I had reached the height of "political" Gallicanism* when, through the Concordat of Bologna, concluded with Pope Leo X in 1516, he gained even greater control than former kings over appointments of French bishops. As a result of the special relationship, the offices and revenues of the church provided the king with his greatest source of patronage. François I therefore already possessed most of the national and political advantages for which Henry VIII had to break with Rome, although of course he recognized the Pope as head of the church and had nothing to gain by challenging the title. An important consequence for the fate of the Reform movement was that any new religious institutions—as distinct from doctrinal reforms—inevitably were seen as threats to royal power and to the status quo, especially if the leadership came from outside France.

The spiritual and moral aspects of the reform, on the other hand, had considerable appeal for Frenchmen. The increasing availability of the Bible in the vernacular helped convince many that the reformers were justified both when they claimed to be resurrecting the true church and when they attacked many of the features of Catholicism not found in the Gospels as man-made corruptions. Furthermore, John Calvin was a Frenchman—with the humanist and legal training customary for French leaders—and appealed to them in their own language, of which he was a master.

In his native land some followed Calvin spiritually and intellectually, if not physically, to Geneva, and from the mid-1530's to the 1550's their numbers increased. In many sections of France they went beyond mere belief to action. They met secretly to worship in a way very different from the traditional Catholic way, often under the courageous leadership of ministers sent from Geneva. Calvin created a new and strong establishment there and Geneva was becoming a Protestant Rome. Robert M. Kingdon has shown how many important lines of communication developed between the exiles in Geneva, who remained French in their orientation, and the new Calvinist communities in France. The most important of Calvin's colleagues was another Frenchman, Theodore Beza, whose particular concern was the encouragement of the movement in France. His success is reflected in the records of all eight Parlements

* Scholars distinguish between "ecclesiastical" Gallicanism, which grants the liberties to French bishops, and "political" or "royal" Gallicanism, which emphasizes the prerogatives of the crown. The highest point of the former was reached in the Pragmatic Sanction of Bourges, 1438; later developments favored the crown.

in the early 1550's, which show a mounting tide of heresy in spite of denunciations, persecutions, new legislation, and severe penalties. The domains of Henri d'Albret, later Jeanne's, were the most seriously affected. Kingdon's analysis of the assignments of the first eighty-eight pastors sent to France from Geneva (by 1558) reveal that sixteen were sent to Guyenne, Gascony, and Béarn, where there were twelve churches, eight were assigned to neighboring Poitou, and five to Aunis and Saintonge.[2] He points out that the southwest was the "unquestioned stronghold" of the Protestant movement and that it was the only region where there was a serious attempt to establish rural churches. In general, Calvinism was an urban movement, but the towns in which it was centered were not the leading cities, such as Bordeaux, but places like Bergerac (three churches) and Nérac, site of Marguerite's court, where Marot, Calvin, and Roussel had all found asylum. Although there was a growing Huguenot movement in the capital, the Paris church, fully organized by 1557, was never able to play a role commensurate with the importance of the city as few members of the leading classes joined it. Later in the century Paris became the headquarters of the Holy League —the French arm of the Counter Reformation—and even under the Edict of Nantes, Paris Huguenots found their position precarious.[3]

Another reason for the importance of the southwest is the role of the nobility. Calvin himself gave priority to the conversion of seigneurs. Noble adherence could do more than anything else to spread the movement. In 1555, the year that Calvin finally achieved supremacy in Geneva, Antoine de Bourbon's brothers, the Duc de Condé (Louis I) and the Duc d'Enghien, paid a visit there and were given a warm welcome.

Some Frenchmen converted to Calvinism in the mid-1550's actually emigrated to Geneva. The *Livre des Bourgeois,* in which are inscribed citizens—residents possessed of sufficient wealth to pay the initiation fee —shows that while only six foreigners were registered in 1554, the number jumps to one hundred and nineteen in 1555. One hundred and seven came in 1556, one hundred and three in 1557. The majority of the new names are French.[4] A letter from the Parlement of Bordeaux to Montmorency in 1554 says: "Since Easter many persons, both men and women, of different ranks, in several towns of this jurisdiction, have sold all their goods . . . have retired with their family and fortunes to Geneva. More leave every day . . . in spite of the fact that we have done our full duty . . . and decreed that [those guilty of heresy] be seized and their goods confiscated . . . we have not been able to stamp out the contagion."[5]

As the years went on it became easier—because safer—for Huguenots to stay at home, especially in the jurisdictions of the Parlements of Bordeaux and Toulouse. This was possible because the King and Queen of Navarre were attending sermons delivered by pastors from Geneva —beginning in 1557—while still officially Roman Catholic. Calvin's first official liaison in France was with the court of Navarre. This was not evident, however, until Jeanne had been Queen for two years. When she and Antoine took the oath as sovereigns in 1555, they confirmed Henri d'Albret's ordinance of 1546 designed "for the conservation of the Catholic faith and the extirpation of all heretical sects."[6] Henri d'Albret had opposed the reform since the mid-1530's; nevertheless, he had allowed Roussel to remain Bishop of Oloron after Marguerite died, and even after his *Exposition Familiale* was condemned by the Sorbonne. Among the salient points of Roussel's thought are the right of the priest to interpret scripture, that is, to preach; the doctrine of salvation by faith; and the beliefs that Jesus Christ is the only mediator, that communion should be administered in both kinds to laymen, and that Peter was not placed above the other Apostles. Henri d'Albret had not enforced his own legislation against heresy. Dartigue explains his leniency in political terms: the Vicomte needed the support of members of the clergy, merchants, and his own officers who admired Roussel. It is also possible that he wished to show his independence of the French crown in religious policy.[7] With the rise of Calvinism, Roussel's ideas seemed more moderate than formerly, and during the 1550's he was attacked by Geneva on the Left as well as by the Sorbonne on the Right.[8]

Nonenforcement of the legislation against heresy favored the spread of Calvinist ideas, even as it protected Roussel. Dartigue believes that officers who were charged with suppressing heresy constituted the group most favorable to it. The reform was also spread by shepherds who spent the winter in the plains of Guyenne and the summer in the mountains of Béarn. The very places riddled with heresy according to the Parlement records were those most frequented by Béarnais. Dartigue concludes, however, that only in Oloron was radical Protestantism really significant before 1555, and that, "for the Reform movement to be seriously launched, it was necessary for the sovereign to set an example and to create the cadres. This was to be the role of Jeanne d'Albret."[9]

ANTOINE, JEANNE, AND THE REFORM, 1555–JULY 1559

In public acts and statements in 1555 and 1556, Antoine and Jeanne gave no sign of diverging from past policy or from Catholic worship. Although there is evidence that Jeanne was drawn to Calvinism before Antoine was, she did not reveal her conversion until Christmas Day 1560. After that day she never wavered, and she took great pains to give her children a Calvinist upbringing. Antoine showed no interest in the reform until he began to despair of realizing his ambitions by exploiting Spanish designs on France in the autumn of 1557. His relation to Calvinism changed with the winds of favor from Madrid and Paris, until he turned against it in January 1562 and joined the advocates of persecution. Even then, had he not died later the same year, there might have been another shift. Some sources report that on his deathbed he embraced Lutheranism.

To establish the probable chronology of Jeanne's conversion, relating it to Antoine's moves and disentangling as far as possible her motives from his, is a task complicated by the scarcity of firsthand evidence and by the necessity to isolate for analytical purposes threads which are inextricably intertwined in the sources. Probably because of these difficulties, historians disagree about whether Antoine's clearly political interest in Calvinism came first, or whether Jeanne led the way and Antoine followed—until it no longer served his ambition.

One school of thought maintains that when Antoine first took up the reform Jeanne was not in agreement. Brantôme's famous comment is that Jeanne "loved a dance more than a sermon. I have it on good authority that she reproached the King her husband for his interest in the new religion, saying that if he wanted to ruin himself, she did not wish to lose her possessions." De Ruble and other nineteenth-century writers incline to this view, and some of the evidence bears them out.[10] On the other side, Dartigue points out that most commentators of the latter part of the sixteenth century believed that Jeanne was converted earlier than Antoine, and then endeavored unsuccessfully to carry her husband along. This belief is often expressed in connection with their daughter, Catherine de Bourbon, who remained a devout Calvinist despite severe pressures from her brother to follow his lead in abandoning their mother's faith. When Catherine was forced to marry into the Lorraine family, in 1599, the Venetian ambassador, for example, reported that it was generally feared she would have a pernicious influence on her husband's religious views, like her mother's influence on her father.[11]

It is possible to make out a case for either interpretation. On the one hand, all known negotiations between the House of Navarre and Geneva were handled by Antoine from 1557 until his desertion in 1562. During these years Calvin and Beza corresponded with Antoine and the Huguenots looked to him for leadership, albeit with diminishing confidence because his sincerity was in question. At first Jeanne was in the background, and even after her conversion, until the autumn of 1561, she ostensibly followed the lead of her husband. Having only this evidence, one could conclude that while Antoine toyed with the movement Jeanne became gradually and seriously converted, but that she concealed their growing disagreement as long as it seemed possible that Antoine might become a real convert—and a real leader. The argument for Jeanne's primacy, on the other hand, depends in part on psychological factors and in part on documentary evidence which has come to light in the twentieth century.

Bordenave, Jeanne's official historian, makes no mention of a separate religious development on her part in the 1550's and he specifically places Antoine's initial interest in 1557.

At that time the Reformed Religion was increasing greatly in all parts of France and was being practiced secretly in many sizable towns. A considerable proportion of the gentlemen and officers of the said King and Queen, having forsworn the Roman faith, professed the new one and wished to be able to practice it in the household of their master and mistress. Since they had not been able to secure a minister in Paris . . . the Seigneur de St. Martin was sent by the others to get one from Geneva, where many . . . [people from the region] had withdrawn to escape the fires which had been lighted in France against all those who spoke against the papal traditions or departed from them. On October 14 [St. Martin] returned to Pau, where the court of Navarre was sojourning, with François Le-Gay, called Boisnormand, a learned man, a specialist in the Hebrew language, who was then appointed minister in charge of the chapel in the household of the said King and Queen.

He comments on the great crowds that came to hear Boisnormand preach and the agitated protests of the Catholics against him.

Although the King, Antoine, regarded the minister with favor and often discussed with him points of difference between the two religions in a friendly way, he did not forswear his own nor adopt the new one. This did not prevent people from suspecting him of being a Lutheran* . . . and

* Bordenave is being a good reporter here. In the early stages of the French Reformation anyone who deviated from Catholicism was described as Lutheran. Himself a Calvinist minister, Bordenave certainly knew the difference.

rumors to this effect reached Rome, where Georges, Cardinal d'Armagnac was stationed.

Jeanne's historian next refers to the messages of censure sent by the Pope and the King of France to Antoine.

These letters so intimidated the Prince (who was of a fearful and irreso-lute character) that he dismissed the said minister, who returned to Geneva. Somewhat later he was recalled, however, and joined the King and his wife when they were . . . on their way to court [February 1558] . . . having left their son, Henri, only four years old, as their lieutenant in Béarn. [Henri] was in the charge of Suzanne de Bourbon, wife of Jean d'Albret, Sieur de Miossens, and Louis d'Albret, Bishop of Lescar. These counsellors exercised their power in such a way that, under the government . . . of a child, a woman, and a priest . . . all of whom professed the Roman faith in public, the chief foundations of the reformed religion were laid and the Roman greatly weakened.[12]

The so-called *Mémoires de Jeanne d'Albret*—a political manifesto justifying her joining Condé's rebellion against the crown in September 1568—also makes no suggestion that Jeanne acted separately or even felt differently from Antoine in the 1550's. The weight of the *Mémoires* derives from the fact that, like Bordenave's history, they were written at her command by a member of Jeanne's staff. Apparently she did not choose to cast any further light on the details of her conversion nor to increase public knowledge of her differences with Antoine. Near the opening of the *Mémoires* Jeanne says: "Since 1560 everyone knows that it pleased God by His grace to rescue me from idolatry, to which I had been too long given, and to receive me in His church. Since then, by the same grace, He has allowed me to persevere. . . . Even during the life-time of my husband, the late King (who, withdrawing from his first zeal, put a thorn not in my foot but in my heart . . .) neither favor nor hard-ship turned me to the right or to the left . . . I have always followed the straight path."[13]

Antoine's first known interest in Calvinism resulted from the necessity to develop a new strategy. The officers of the court of Navarre could hardly have sent to Geneva for a preacher who later officiated in the royal chapel without the knowledge and implied approval of their King. De Ruble goes so far as to state that the Sieur de St. Martin "was sent to Geneva by Antoine de Bourbon."[14]

Jeanne had made no statements in public, but as early as August 1555, shortly after her father's funeral, she had written an important letter to the Vicomte de Gourdon.

M. le Vicomte:

I am writing to tell you that up to now I have followed in the footsteps of the deceased Queen, my most honored mother—whom God forgive—in the matter of hesitation between the two religions. The said Queen [was] warned by her late brother the King, François I of good and glorious memory, my much honored uncle, not to get new doctrines in her head [*mettre en cervelle dogmes nouveaux*] so that from then on she confined herself to amusing stories [*romans jovials*]. Besides, I well remember how long ago, the late King, my most honored father . . . surprised the said Queen when she was praying in her rooms with the ministers Roussel and Farel, and how with great annoyance he slapped her right cheek and forbade her sharply to meddle in matters of doctrine. He shook a stick at me which cost me many bitter tears and has kept me fearful and compliant until after they had both died. Now that I am freed by the death of my said father two months ago . . . *a reform seems so right and so necessary that, for my part, I consider that it would be disloyalty and cowardice to God, to my conscience and to my people to remain any longer in a state of suspense and indecision.* . . . It is necessary for sincere persons to take counsel together to decide how to proceed, both now and in the future. Knowing that you are noble and courageous and that you have learned persons about you, I beg you to meet me in the chateau of Odos-en-Bigorre at the end of this coming September.

Hoping that you will come, I pray God, M. le Vicomte, to guard you in His holy keeping.

Written at Pau, August 22, 1555.
Jeanne, Queen[15]

It is interesting to learn that Marguerite's own daughter thought she had hesitated between the two religions, but even more important are the italicized passage and the fact that Jeanne was planning a meeting of Calvinist sympathizers in the obscurity of Bigorre when Antoine was due to absent himself from Béarn, more than two years before he showed any inclination to the reform.

During this same autumn, in her husband's absence, Jeanne spent much energy to secure for her great-uncle, Louis d'Albret, the Bishopric of Lescar, one of two sees in Béarn. Shortly before he died, Henri d'Albret had asked the Pope's authorization to name his illegitimate uncle to the Bishopric of Lescar, but it had been refused. In October 1555, Jeanne wrote to Pius IV, and to the Cardinals Georges d'Armagnac and Jean du Bellay, urging her great-uncle's candidacy.[16] Her appeals were successful.

This correspondence and other relevant matters are revealed in *L'Histoire de l'herésie en Béarn,* written in the middle of the seventeenth century but unpublished until the 1920's and unknown to De Ruble and other nineteenth-century scholars. What makes this source important is that the author, Pierre de Salefranque,* includes copies of many documents—he calls them *Preuves*—from the Archives of the Parlement of Navarre. Because the Archives were destroyed by fire in 1716, our only access to the documents is through Salefranque's history. If one accepts them as genuine, as Dartigue does, there is sound evidence that Jeanne took up the reform considerably earlier than Antoine, and without his knowledge, when he was at court in the autumn of 1555 and the summer of 1556. This would justify those who believe that Jeanne was converted first. Yet nineteenth-century historians, using only sources available to them, quite properly and logically attributed the initiative to Antoine. In other words, it would explain away the conflict of opinion mentioned above.

In 1555 an ex-monk named David, who had been attached to the suite of the Maréchal de St. André, was recommended to Antoine by the noted physician and scholar Julius Caesar Scaliger. Condemned by his Bishop for causing a public disturbance with his sermons attacking the abuses of the Roman Church, David seems to have been taken under the protection of the court of Navarre by Jeanne in Antoine's absence.[17] Nevertheless, Salefranque states positively that Jeanne was not a heretic until she returned to Pau in August 1556, after several months in Nérac with Antoine earlier in the year.

> When she returned . . . in 1556, she introduced heresy . . . by bringing four heretics named David, Pierre Henry de Barran, Solon, and Lemée. They were called ministers, a title with which the people were not yet familiar. They believed them to be orthodox Catholics. [David] was destined for the Queen's household and the three others were to preach outside. The Queen concealed from her subjects the novelty she was introducing, and obliged the Bishop of Lescar, Louis d'Albret, to give his approval. . . . By this means the heresies of Calvin were preached in the churches of Béarn. . . . The Queen even declared herself to be . . . "his chief parishioner," subject to the Bishop's discipline . . . By this ruse and hypocritical submission she was able to establish heresy without the people knowing what was happening and without their having an opportunity to protest and rise up against it.[18]

* Salefranque, 1600–1687, belonged to an important family of the *noblesse de la robe* in Béarn. He abjured Calvinism in 1631, and seems to have written his history as part of the preparation for the revocation of the Edict of Nantes (1685).

The specific reference to Jeanne's *soumission hypocrite* is based on a letter from Jeanne to the Bishop, which resulted in his granting permission for Henry de Barran to preach in public.[19] Salefranque places part of the blame on Louis d'Albret himself: "The Pope prophesied well when he judged this man unworthy of being a bishop." Salefranque's *Preuves* include three letters from Cardinal d'Armagnac to Louis d'Albret in the latter months of 1556, warning him that he risked a summons before the Inquisition if he did not dismiss Barran.[20] He was also under attack in Béarn itself, for "in addition to heresy, which he favored, he was full of vice, and his chapter was forced to remonstrate with him . . . to see that the word of God was sincerely preached, to use his pastoral staff to defend his flock and to drive out heretics . . . to abandon his riotous living, to visit his diocese . . . and [they said] that they were reporting his behavior to the Queen."[21]

Salefranque is in no doubt, however, that it was Jeanne who was chiefly responsible, and that the weak Louis d'Albret was following his niece's lead. "He had a blind admiration for the Queen, which made him criminally lenient to heresy . . . the Queen even thought that he belonged to the Pretended Reformed Religion himself." When attempts were made to remonstrate with him, he excused himself by saying that he had acted as he had because he feared falling into Jeanne's bad graces. "He feared the Queen's wrath more than that of God." When a delegation of Catholic officials waited upon him and asked him to make a straightforward declaration as to which religion he favored, he replied "somewhat uncertainly . . . that he had chosen that of his predecessors."[22] Later history shows that Louis d'Albret remained in the Roman church—and in office—for the rest of his life.

Antoine was absent several times while these events were taking place, and when he was in Béarn, his attention was directed to his intrigue with the Spaniards. The Vicomté was administered principally by Jeanne. Antoine had given no sign that he was interested in Calvinism. In fact, on his return from court in 1556, he led an impressive Catholic procession carrying an enormous candle.[23] But the Protestant movement was gaining strength elsewhere in France, and within a year he was associated with it. François d'Andelot turned Calvinist at this time, the first of the Constable's three nephews to do so. The Paris Huguenots, now fully organized, had their first clash with the authorities in September 1557. *L'Affaire de la rue St. Jacques* was a riot by some Sorbonne students around the house where the Huguenots were holding their secret worship, resulting in the arrest of a number of Calvinists. Bordenave and the Spanish reports on Antoine show that at the time the King of Navarre first allowed, or sponsored, the preaching of Boisnormand in the chateau at Pau. From then on, he openly tolerated heresy—and to tolerate it was to encourage it.[24]

The most striking proof of Antoine's shift in religious direction is Calvin's first letter to him, dated December 14, 1557. It was natural for Antoine to regard Calvinism as a possible vehicle for the fulfillment of his ambition; it was equally plausible for Calvin to concentrate his hopes on the King of Navarre. The tone of the letter, which flatters Antoine, indicates that it is the beginning of a correspondence. Calvin, assuming that Antoine has "seen the light," urges him to come into the open and take the secular lead of the French reform movement:

Sire:

Having heard of the grace God has shown by approaching you more familiarly than ever, to show you the pure doctrine of His son Jesus Christ, I am presuming to write. . . . I have also heard that you do me the honor to hold me in good affection, which has emboldened me to believe that I would find a welcome. Furthermore, I am sure that when you see that I desire nothing else than that God should be glorified in you, for your good and salvation, you will gladly be exhorted by me in the name of Him who has authority over you. [Kings are God's lieutenants] and this is the time, when all is corrupt and perverted with detestable falsehoods forged by the devil. . . . If men of low condition . . . can sacrifice themselves so that God may be purely worshiped, the great should do so all the more. God, who has pulled [you] from the shadows of superstition . . . and illumined [your] understanding of the Gospel, which is not given to all, does not want this light hidden, but rather [wishes] you to be a burning lamp to lighten the way of great and small. . . . If you, the organ of the children of God, keep your mouth closed, who will dare to open his to say a word?

Calvin refers to the proposed meeting of the Estates-General (see Appendix A) and warns that the enemy will try to charge the reformers with sedition. He emphasizes the distinction between troublemakers and sincere Christian reformers, and encloses a pamphlet he wrote in 1543 for the edification of the German princes, although he would not presume "to tell you what to do."[25]

Whether because she had made no public move or because of her reputed interest in worldly matters, Jeanne was thought to be out of sympathy with Antoine's interest in Calvinism. Since the letter to Gourdon shows that she had in fact been seriously interested in the reform for over two years, her silence seems contradictory. Jeanne may not have made up her mind. If, on the other hand, she had been fully converted, she may have thought that she had but to bide her time until Antoine truly embraced the movement. In that case, no independent stand on her part would be required; she would be expected to follow her husband as a matter of course.

Historians such as De Ruble and Romier agree that Antoine's connections with Calvinism were directly related to his presumed political advantage. It is much more difficult to determine Jeanne's motives, or even her beliefs, until the announcement of her conversion in December 1560. Such uncertainty was not shared by Salefranque, however: "The Queen did what she could to turn the people to heresy without a murmur." Jeanne supported the Bishop's authority against her own Sovereign Council when it protested the preaching of Henry de Barran, as well as against the Pope's agent, Cardinal d'Armagnac. If there was need for discipline of the Bishops or if they needed reinforcement, this was the business of the "secular arm," Jeanne wrote from La Rochelle in February 1558.[26] She was standing on her sovereign power: "those of the Reformed Religion believed that the ultimate authority over the church in Béarn was the Queen . . . just as in England they recognize the King as the head of their Anglican church."[27]

When Antoine and Jeanne went to court in 1558, David, who was traveling with them, preached in public and was accorded the title, "preacher to the King and Queen of Navarre."[28] After they reached Paris, Antoine, at least, attended Calvinist services at the Pré-aux-Clercs; moreover, when Antoine de La Roche-Chandieu, a leading Huguenot minister, was arrested, the King of Navarre used his influence to obtain his release. D'Andelot was imprisoned for heresy; his brother, Gaspard de Coligny, Admiral of France, was converted. These signs of growth in the movement took place just when the Guise faction was benefiting from the marriage of Mary Stuart to the Dauphin. Calvin himself tried to assist the Huguenots by asking the German princes to send ambassadors to Henry II, urging an end to the persecution of his French followers.[29]

Geneva understandably was taking an increasingly active part in French affairs. One of Calvin's letters undertook to instruct Antoine about the quarrel which had developed between David and Boisnormand. (Some historians maintain that David had been bribed by the Guises to bring the King of Navarre back to the Catholic fold, but, in any case, he was not trained in Geneva like Boisnormand, and it was natural for Calvin to support the latter.) Calvin's letter of June 8 refers to the example of D'Andelot and urges Antoine to be "the standard-bearer of God. I know many will advise you to dissimulate, but listen, rather, to the counsel of God . . . which is to testify for Him before kings. . . . Take courage, trust Him whose fight you wage." Calvin realistically reminds Antoine that the King and the Guises will blame him whatever he does and that he has less to lose by taking a bold stand than by vacillating.[30]

Calvinism was making great headway in Béarn in 1558, during the absence of the King and Queen. The activities of Boisnormand and Henry de Barran vividly illustrate the growth of the movement. Under attack from D'Armagnac, who had a specific assignment to suppress heresy, and from local Catholics, the Calvinist ministers were often hounded out of town and had to hide and change their names frequently. In a report to Calvin, September 10, 1558, Boisnormand clarifies the general situation. He had attracted great crowds in Nérac and eventually the Bishop had forbidden him to preach. Then he went to Béarn, and worked with Barran, for whom he expresses great admiration. After a while he returned to Nérac with great acclaim; when interrogated by officers of the Parlement of Bordeaux, he claimed that "three out of four magistrates and the majority of the people were of our opinion."[31]

The Reformation was gaining throughout France, especially in the domains of the King and Queen of Navarre.[32] Despite pressure from the Papacy and the crown of France, Antoine and Jeanne were encouraging it. Antoine was doing so to strengthen his position *vis-à-vis* Henri II and Philip II. Either they might listen to his claims, hoping thereby to divert him from heresy, or they might yield to his importuning because they feared the spread of heresy if they did not. In 1558 Antoine stood to gain in either case.

With Jeanne one cannot be sure. Her motives may still have been identical with Antoine's. In early November she wrote to the King and the Constable urging consideration of her claims to Spanish Navarre at the peace conference. She even asked the Constable to speak to the Cardinal de Lorraine in her behalf.[33] One would never guess from the tone of these letters that she and Antoine were among the chief promoters of heresy in France. She may have been dissembling her true sentiments, for a letter to the Vicomte de Gourdon provides a curious contrast by alluding to the bad state of the kingdom from the Protestant point of view. "The terrible cruelties perpetrated under the Edict of Chateaubriand [June 1551] sadden my heart . . . The peace to be made between King Henry and Spain has no other purpose than to overcome with fire, flame, and other calamities those who are followers of the reform . . . in spite of the embassies sent to King Henry, (at our secret instigation) by the cities of Zurich and Berne, the Elector Palatine, Duke Christopher of Wurtemberg, and the Landgrave of Hesse, asking that the persecutions be modified."[34]

Salefranque poses the question of Jeanne's sincerity. Considering the events of the years 1558 and 1559, he asks when she left the church, and draws up a balance sheet of facts supporting the view that she had become a Protestant as opposed to facts indicating that she was still a Roman Catholic. In the first column he places her patronage of the Calvinist ministers and her opposition to the power of the Guises; in the second, her apparent cooperation with D'Armagnac and her continuation of Henri d'Albret's legislation against heresy and orders to the Council to enforce it. To the question "How do we explain the contradictions?" he answers:

Some assert that in the early days the heretics intended to stay in the church and work for the reform of the abuses they claim to have been insinuated in the church . . . and that they were constrained to schism so as not to participate in the filth [ordures] of our pretended Babylon. . . . The real reason for the pretended submission of the Queen and her ministers (to the authority of the church) was none other than to deceive the people and persuade them to adopt heresy without knowing it and without being able to defend themselves. . . . [The Calvinists] wished to copy the example of the perfidious laborers in the vineyard, who were . . . supposed to give the fruits of their labors to their lord, but instead, took over the vineyard and chased the lord out. . . . Everyone knows that the heretics of today [1660's] claim to have an extraordinary vocation, straight from God. We think it probable that the Queen exercised this prudence out of fear of arousing the people and also out of fear of her husband, *who was Catholic and would not have tolerated such a change* . . . this became evident after his death, when she declared herself fully in favor of the heretics and opposed to the church.[35]

Salefranque obviously believes that Jeanne was a Protestant in these years, cleverly pretending otherwise, and that Antoine was still a Catholic, despite his overt activity favoring the movement. Jeanne *may* have been converted already, but recorded events of the first months of 1559 do not support such a conclusion. She was in Paris until April, and the fact that she allowed members of her household to attend Calvinist services at the house of Michel Gaillard, Seigneur de Longjumeau, is her only known connection with the reform.[36]

Antoine had been in the south of France since autumn. He had continued the war with Spain on his own for a few weeks after the fighting had officially stopped and negotiations of the Treaty of Cateau-Cambrésis had begun. This campaign, a total fiasco from the military point of view and called "the wet war" because Antoine's army was defeated as much by torrential rains as by the enemy, was probably undertaken to strengthen his claims at the peace conference. It certainly did nothing for his military reputation and all commentators report it in satirical terms.[37]

After the failure of his attempted invasion of Spain, Antoine had spent several months in Pau, where he devoted at least a part of his time supervising improvements in the chateau. He employed a mason, Thomas Forgue, to enclose the garden with a stone wall, and a carpenter, Augier Bardon, to build a covered gallery. The public rooms of the chateau were also repaired.[38] During these months, unlike Jeanne, in Paris, he was reported to be attending Protestant services, in defiance of the wishes of Henri II. On Easter Sunday, March 26, 1559, he took part in the services in the Pau church and two days later attended Calvinist worship in a private house. He was supporting a second regular preacher, Arnaud Guillaume Barbaste, in addition to Boisnormand.[39]

The world believed Antoine had turned Protestant, although he had not said so. As usual, he was playing a double game. The patron of Calvinist ministers in Béarn posed as the determined foe of heresy to Henri II. In June 1559, after he and Jeanne had been reunited in Poitou, he wrote to the King, apropos of a disturbance in the Ile d'Oléron off La Rochelle, "I have stayed longer than I intended in this region . . . but it has not been without use to your service . . . a fair number of people are holding assemblies, posting placards, and [behaving] with brashness and insolence that speaks more of sedition than of religion, although their pretext is to hold religious services." Antoine assures the King that he will see to it that the situation is taken in hand, although his health prevents him from going to the islands in person.[40] Both Antoine and Jeanne were playing ambiguous roles in 1559 in terms of religion, but it is not clear whether it was the same game or a slightly different one.

Henri II wished to seal the peace of Cateau-Cambrésis with a lasting alliance between France and Spain. The marriages of his daughter Elizabeth to Phillip II (recently widowed by the death of Mary Tudor) and of his sister Marguerite to Philip's ally, the Duke of Savoy, were occasions of great celebration in Paris in July 1559. During the jousts the King was fatally wounded; he died on July 10. The sudden death of the King produced drastic changes in the power structure at the French court. Montmorency and Diane de Poitiers "fell from the heights with the King's last breath." Catherine de Medici could hope eventually to emerge from the obscurity of a *mère de famille*. But the new King, sixteen-year-old François II, had two able and ambitious uncles by marriage, the Duc de Guise and the Cardinal de Lorraine, who saw the opportunity for which they had been preparing. In the months that followed they exploited the situation to the disadvantage, not only of the Queen Mother, but also of Antoine de Bourbon, First Prince of the Blood.

ANTOINE, JEANNE, AND THE REFORM, JULY 1559–DECEMBER 1560

For about a month after the death of Henri II, Antoine seemed to be the arbiter of the situation in France. This prospect was welcomed by some, feared by others. The factions were jockeying for position and hoping to turn the course of events to their own advantage. The English ambassador, Nicholas Throckmorton, hoped that an alliance based on their common Protestantism could be established between England and France, and William Cecil advised Queen Elizabeth to write to Antoine and Jeanne. The letter to Antoine is formal and obsequious in tone, Elizabeth expresses herself as "anxious to please and to serve" him. Her letter to Jeanne begins with an encouraging Latin phrase, *si Deus nobiscum quis contra nos?* The Queen of England says that she has been anxious to have the pleasure of Jeanne's acquaintance, but, since distance forbids, it may be done in spirit and good will, a sentiment she will always entertain toward Jeanne. She has instructed Throckmorton to express her feeling "not only for [your] rank in the world but even more for the true profession and sincerity of your Christian religion, in which [I] pray the Creator may keep [you] by His grace, and that [you] may continue a supporter of His Holy Word."[41]

Antoine assembled his close advisers* and decided to go to court with a numerous escort.[42] This was an error in judgment. The Guises were

* Aymery Bouchard, Chancellor of Navarre; Nicholas Dangu; François d'Escars; Guy Chabot de Jarnac.

fully prepared to take advantage of the fact that they were on the scene while Antoine was away. Under the direction of his uncles, the young King moved the court to St. Germain and reissued an old Edict forbidding anyone, "even the gentlemen of my house," to approach the court under arms. This Edict, formerly unenforced, was revived with new and severe penalties. The Guises made elaborate preparations for armed defense, should it be necessary, and assigned Blaise de Monluc to keep an eye on Antoine's movements in Guyenne. Philip II sent to France a new and astute ambassador, Perrenot de Chantonay, brother of Cardinal Granvella, whose dispatches are among our most important sources for the next five years. Catherine de Medici, unable to resist the Guise leadership, was cooperating with it, and seems to have been instrumental in bribing Antoine's advisers as the King of Navarre and his party made their uncertain way to court. The first object of the Guises was to delay Antoine's progress so that they could entrench themselves in power before his arrival.

During the course of the voyage people with all sorts of motives flocked to Antoine urging their own cause. In Vendôme there was a meeting of disaffected nobles: Condé, the three Châtillons, François de Vendôme (Vidame de Chartres), Antoine de Croy (Prince de Porcien, just twenty years old), and François de La Rochefoucauld. They constituted the nucleus of the emerging Huguenot party. The Constable was represented by a secretary. Those present agreed on opposition to the Guises but on little else. Delegations of Calvinist ministers, constantly arriving, thought the time ripe to come out into the open, and demanded that Antoine "purge the court of idolatry." When he replied that he should continue to attend Mass so as not to offend the King, they accused him of using religion for petty bargaining. Thus began the disillusionment of the more astute Huguenots in Antoine; they were to shift gradually to Condé and then to Coligny, reluctantly at first, because they had counted heavily on Antoine's superior rank.

Antoine was making so many contradictory promises that it was difficult to know where he stood. By not pursuing any single consistent course, he lost the opportunity to lead those who would have followed him and made it easier for the opposition to consolidate itself against him. The Guises pointed to the gatherings of malcontents as evidence that Antoine posed a threat to the peace of the kingdom. He played into their hands at every turn. In Vendôme, on August 8, he even received Killigrew,

Throckmorton's secretary, in secret audience; like all of Antoine's moves, this was reported to the Guises.

Consequently, when Antoine finally arrived at court, on August 18, he met with a very cold reception. Not only was no official escort sent to meet him, as was customary for members of the royal family, but proper lodgings had not been prepared for him and his suite. The King kept him waiting for two days before granting him audience, and the manner of the Guises was glacial. When the King did receive him he said that he had entrusted the government to his uncles and wished all his subjects to obey them as they would obey him personally. He spoke of his concern over the growth of heresy, and, when Antoine assured him of his loyalty and orthodoxy, replied that he was glad to hear it because if Antoine wished to follow any other course, especially in regard to religion, he would not tolerate it. The Spanish ambassador did not pay his respects until Monday, August 21, after agreement with the Guises. He too spoke threateningly, declaring that "a remedy for the sad state of religion would be found by the Kings of France and Spain, who were much concerned about it."[43]

At the coronation of François II on September 18 the triumph of the Guises and the disgrace of the Bourbons were obvious: "The King of Navarre and the Prince de Condé, modestly equipped, followed the [Guises'] cortege like prisoners in a Roman triumph."[44] Some historians claim that proud Jeanne, stung in her royal pride when she heard of Antoine's humiliation, urged him to leave court, but there is no evidence for the assertion. Jeanne had remained in Béarn, devoting herself to administration and the education of her son. By the time full reports of events at court reached her, it was probably too late for her to change their course. Not until the following year (1560) did it become evident how serious was the damage to her husband's prestige. A leading scholar of the period has recently said: "Navarre was then [July 1559] in a stronger position than he appears to have realized. . . . Many would have thought him worth serving if, together with the Queen-Mother, he had sought a political alliance of all anti-Guisard elements. . . . One is forced to conclude that he lacked the vision, ability and constancy of purpose to seize the initiative and claim his rightful position."[45]

In order to keep Antoine occupied, the King gave him the assignment of escorting the Princess Elizabeth to Spain, a journey which took place during the last two months of the year. Antoine was pleased to undertake it, hoping at last to negotiate with Philip face to face. As usual, he was to be disappointed. Jeanne, accompanied by Henri, joined him at La Flêche in mid-October, and they met Philip's bride in Angoulême in early December.[46] On December 6 they were given a magnificent reception in Bordeaux. Antoine had commanded that the streets leading to the cathedral be covered with red carpet and that members of the Parlement kneel to the Queen of Spain. This they refused to do, reminding him that they had not even done so for Charles V. When the Valois princess received them, Jeanne stood at her right hand, Antoine and Antoine de Noailles at her left.[47]

If Antoine's insistence on ceremonial in order to impress the Spaniards was evident in Bordeaux, he and Jeanne were no less conscious of protocol in their own domains. When they passed "from France into Béarn," they asserted their royal prerogatives by taking the best lodgings for their own retainers, those of the Valois Princess were given second best. Both the Frenchmen and the Spaniards in the party objected, but Antoine was adamant.[48] They arrived in Pau on December 21 and entertained Elizabeth in the chateau during the week of Christmas. An English agent reports that she was nobly served and feted. "The King and Queen of Navarre have done their part with great magnificence, their house being richly decorated."[49]

The day after Christmas, Elizabeth and her suite left for the Spanish frontier, escorted by Antoine. The ceremony of delivering the French Princess to her husband's representatives was carried out in the first days of January, not without several minor crises over precedence. Antoine became a figure of ridicule because of the degree to which he stood on ceremony and his apparent unawareness of the disdain of the Spaniards.[50] Jeanne's opinion of Antoine's gullibility in his dealings with the Spaniards —not only at this time but for the rest of his life—is well summed up in the early pages of the *Mémoires:* "It is almost unbelievable that this Prince, who was possessed of good judgment, could ever have had any confidence in them." She emphasizes it a few paragraphs later: "I am obliged to say again that it is almost too incredible that the Prince allowed himself to be so bewitched by them. They were like the painter who covers the picture with whitewash and wipes out what was there in order to put something else on the canvas . . . they whitewashed all the evil turns they had done him, in order to superimpose their new stratagems."[51]

By December 1559 the Protestant movement was growing rapidly in France.[52] Even in the Parlement of Paris, the highest court in the realm, there were some Huguenots and sympathizers. The most courageous of them, the Conseiller Anne du Bourg, had dared to protest the persecutions and to say in a loud clear voice, "It is no small thing to condemn those who, amid the flames, call on the name of Jesus Christ." This was said on June 10, 1559, in the presence of the King, Henri II, accompanied by the Cardinals Lorraine and Guise, the Constable, and the Duc de Guise. Four members of the court were arrested the same day, Henri II angrily declaring that he would see Du Bourg burn before his own eyes. By what the Huguenots regarded as God's justice, the King had died, exactly a month later, pierced in the eye by a lance of Montgomery. Du Bourg had remained in prison between July and December, the center of rising tension between the Guise faction and those opposed to it. On December 23, 1559, he was burned at the stake in the Place de Grève in Paris. His steadfastness and courage were said to have converted more young men—especially students—than all the books of Calvin. The Protestants also gained support from many moderate Catholics, the kind who would later be called *politiques* (see Appendix B) because of the mounting fear and increasing dislike of the government of the Guises.

The extravagance, arrogance, and semiforeign origin of the King's uncles made it possible to organize a party directly opposed to them. They were accused of exploiting their position for their own advantage and of consuming the wealth of the kingdom. There was a widespread demand for a meeting of the Estates-General to curb their power. The Guises countered by playing on the fear of civil war, for it was generally believed that the Huguenots were about to resort to arms. This fear was partly justified.

Although the Huguenots profited from the hostility to the Guises, their cause was weakened by internal dissension. The moderate faction, following the lead of Calvin and Beza (at least in their public statements), believed that only spiritual and intellectual weapons could legitimately be used to resist tyranny and to further true doctrine. Beza puts it succinctly in a letter to Bullinger, on September 12, 1559: "We are frequently asked if it is permitted to take arms, especially against a King who is a minor. Up to this time our answer has always been that this enemy is to be confronted armed only with prayers and patience."[53]

François Hotman,* on the contrary, was probably the author of a pamphlet, the *Livret de Strasbourg,* justifying resistance to tyranny; he was also active in the intellectual preparation of the Conspiracy of Amboise. Kingdon points to another division: while the majority of Calvinists in France followed the moderate counsel of Calvin and Beza, the exiles in Geneva favored a resort to arms.[54] The Florentine ambassador Nicolò Tornabuoni claims that only the "little Huguenots," of humble origin were persecuted, while *les grands* escaped with mere reprimands.[55]

Huguenot extremists planned a coup d'état by which the King would be rescued from the domination of the Guises and Calvinism made respectable—if not dominant—under the protecting wing of the House of Bourbon. In February 1560 they held a secret meeting in Nantes to make final plans. The Bourbon princes took no active part in the conspiracy, but the Prince de Condé, who was in contact with the conspirators, is often referred to as "the silent chief."

The result of the conspiracy was an attack, on March 16, 1560, on the chateau of Amboise, temporary residence of the court. It was led by the Sieur de La Renaudie, a zealous Calvinist of the lesser nobility who had been exiled to Geneva. In addition to its poor organization and inadequate force, the conspiracy suffered from many betrayals in the weeks preceding the attack, so that the Guises were fully prepared and able easily to assure its failure. The next day the Duc de Guise became Lieutenant-General of the kingdom. In the following weeks the government took drastic reprisals on many of the "little Huguenots." A considerable number of them seems to have believed naïvely that all that was intended was to see the King and tell him of the oppression of his advisers. Under torture some of the victims implicated the Prince de Condé.[56]

Despite its failure, the Conspiracy of Amboise is important in the history of French Protestantism because it was the first resort to arms and because it brought the Prince de Condé to the fore of the movement. It also raised the question of Antoine's complicity. A number of his vassals and retainers were among the victims, although the painstaking investigations of the Guises were unable to pin any direct responsibility on the King of Navarre himself. Antoine expressed indignation and offered his services, with the aid of 5000 men, to the King. François' only

* François Hotman, 1524–1590, Professor at the University of Strasbourg and well-known Calvinist publicist, author of the *Franco-Gallia,* 1573.

response was to ask that David and Boisnormand be imprisoned, to which Antoine replied that they were no longer in his service.[57]

Queen Elizabeth was thought to have supported the conspirators and her ambassador was *persona non grata* at court. On March 24 she issued a manifesto, which was shown to Antoine in advance, condemning anyone who threatened the government of François II. This disclaimer was intended to help the Huguenots but it came too late and was interpreted as evidence of complicity. The King asked Antoine for an explanation. He pretended that he had been taken entirely by surprise, "he was not the serf of the Queen of England and she should not expect to peddle her wares to him."[58] De Ruble thinks it impossible that Antoine was ignorant of the conspiracy, given his many connections with those known to be responsible, and concludes that only he was in a position to finance it. Kingdon, however, shows that, according to the sources, Condé had refused to take an active part and Antoine was ignorant of the plot. Moreover, when the Company of Pastors was later accused of complicity, Calvin testified that he would not have been opposed if the movement had been led by the man "who ought to be chief of the King's Council, according to the laws of France," that is, Antoine, as First Prince of the Blood.

If the King of Navarre had no direct connection with the attack on Amboise, he may have known that such enterprise was likely and deliberately refused to accept any information because of the risks involved. If it had been successful, he could have come forward as the "protector" of the kingdom, but when it failed it was equally in character for him to assert his innocence, his ignorance, and his indignation. The Prince de Condé, accused of being the secret leader of the plot, defended himself with bravado in April 1560 and then left court. In May he was in Bordeaux with Antoine, and in June he retired to his brother's court at Nérac.

Despite their apparent triumph, the summer of 1560 was an anxious time for the Guises. The Catholic forces had lost control in Scotland, where John Knox and the Lords of the Congregation had gained the upper hand and concluded the Treaty of Edinburgh with England. This reversed a centuries-old pattern of alliance between France and the Scots against England and it greatly strengthened international Protestantism. At home in France, a moderate, Michel de L'Hôpital, had been appointed chancellor, and François Hotman from Strasbourg and Theodore Beza from Geneva were in Nérac, at the court of Antoine and Jeanne. At Antoine's request, the Company of Pastors had sent Beza, in Calvin's words, "to the King and Queen of Navarre to teach them the word of God."[59]

The atmosphere in Nérac is depicted in a letter from the Calvinist minister La Motte to Calvin in late July. "I was in Nérac two weeks ago and saw a spectacle which greatly surpassed my expectations. Preaching is open—in public. The streets resound to the chanting of the Psalms. Religious books are sold as freely and openly as at home [Geneva] . . . this excitement is caused by the impending arrival of Théodore de Bèze, he is expected at any moment."[60] Scholars have not been able to discover exactly what happened in Nérac between July and October 1560. The spies of the Guises were everywhere and great secrecy was observed. Because of Beza's long visit to her court, Jeanne's definitive and public conversion, announced the following Christmas Day, is attributed to his influence by Weiss and Geisendorf.[61] Beza was a powerful personality and there is little doubt that it was hoped in Geneva that his visit would result in the open espousal of the reform by both the King and Queen. At no time does Beza claim that he was responsible for Jeanne's conversion, however, and the *Histoire Ecclésiastique,* long attributed to him and certainly written by close associates, not only does not credit Beza with Jeanne's conversion but reports that she was "cold" to the movement.[62] On the other hand, Jeanne must have been receptive in the summer of 1560, since a letter of Beza's to Calvin of August 25 (dealing with other matters) concludes, "the ladies commend themselves warmly to you and asked me to write to you especially for that purpose."[63]

Regardless of his progress with Jeanne, Beza had reason to be optimistic. François II had agreed to call the Estates-General—as the Huguenots (especially) had been demanding—and opposition to the Guises, as reflected in the war of the pamphlets, had reached a new high. Gaspard de Coligny was emerging as one of the chiefs of the Huguenot party. While not of royal blood, he was the Constable's nephew and a man of force and ability, who, with Jeanne d'Albret, would become the most effective Huguenot leader. Nothing reflects the growth of the Protestant movement more clearly than the actions taken by the Guises, in concert with Philip II, to discredit anyone who leaned toward the reform and their treatment of the Bourbons as virtual traitors. Locally in Béarn, the Counter Reformation was taking the offensive also. Cardinal d'Armagnac threatened Antoine with loss of his kingdom if he persisted in sponsoring heretics and he excommunicated Henry de Barran, Boisnormand, and La Gaucherie.[64]

While the growth of heresy was definitely encouraged by Jeanne and Antoine, at the same time they were sending assurances of their orthodoxy to the Pope. Their emissary was as bizarre as his mission: Pedro d'Albret, bastard son of Jeanne's grandfather, whose ambition was to obtain the Priory of Roncevaux. His niece helped him, as she had earlier helped her other uncle of the bar sinister, Louis d'Albret, to obtain the Bishopric of Lescar. In both cases, they assisted her in carrying out her policies, as a *quid pro quo.*[65]

The King and Queen of Navarre were acting with extreme caution, as was prudent under the circumstances. When the Estates of Béarn earlier in the year had demanded of their sovereigns "measures to suppress the daily scandals and dangers to the church," Antoine and Jeanne had responded in terms which could apply equally to Catholic or to Protestant discipline. The bishops were to "instruct the conscience of the people with pure doctrine" and "oppose all errors so that God would be . . . honored and served in the vicomté. If the said bishops need the aid of Their Majesties, all aid would be provided by the said Majesties for the preservation of religion and maintenance of order." Forissier comments, "We are faced with a very special royal policy. If it does not surprise us coming from Antoine, we understand it less in the Queen. We should remember, however, that until her final conversion she continued to play a sort of double game, justified in her eyes by the danger which threatened from the crowns of France and Spain and the Vatican. She did not follow the dictates of her conscience in making this sacrifice to opportunism that made her oscillate between Geneva and Rome, according to the supposed interests of her husband and her dynasty. . . . She feared . . . that her alleged heresy would serve as a pretext to the Pope and the King of Spain to rob her of her crown. Had not Haute-Navarre been taken from her grandfather, Jean d'Albret, by collusion between Madrid and the Vatican?"[66] Bordenave reports that this same sobering historical allusion was made by D'Armagnac in his attempt to persuade Antoine and Jeanne to cease favoring the reformers.

Antoine's part in the double game caused him further trouble. Some compromising letters he wrote during the summer of 1560 fell into the hands of the Guises and a number of his presumed fellow-conspirators were arrested, notably the Vidame de Chartres. Catherine and the Guises were determined to prevent an uprising led by the Bourbons because it would be much harder to justify the measures necessary to repress it than the Conspiracy of Amboise, with its unimpressive leadership.[67]

François II sent the Cardinal de Bourbon to Nérac in early September to persuade his brothers (Antoine and Condé) to go to court. They had refused to attend the Assembly of Notables at Fontainebleau in August, and they were implicated in violent episodes in Provence and in the abortive uprising in Lyons. The kingdom was torn with rumors and deluged with pamphlets attacking the Guises. Catherine de Medici appealed to Philip for aid, and the Duke of Albuquerque mobilized all able-bodied men between the ages of twenty and sixty in Haute-Navarre. The Cardinal having failed in his mission, François II sent the Seigneur de Crussol to Antoine with the express command to come to court without further delay, bringing with him Condé, who had for six months been avoiding responsibility for the Conspiracy of Amboise while accusations against him multiplied. Faced with this ultimatum, delivered on September 9, Antoine had to choose between obedience and open defiance of the crown. Contradictory advice poured in from all sides. It has frequently been stated that Jeanne was among those who favored disobedience—at least as far as the journey to Orléans was concerned—but there is no reliable evidence to prove it. It is quite possible that this opinion is attributed to her—like the opposite opinion of the previous year, when she is said to have urged him to go to court—on the basis of her own firmness in defense of her rights in later years. It does not seem to fit in with her extreme caution, or dissimulation, on this period. I do not feel justified in assuming, as do the Protestant historians, that she had definitely made up her mind. It seems much more likely that she and Antoine were still playing the same game, although Jeanne was more skilled at it and she had the advantage of being in the background as long as both the Guises and the Huguenots were uncertain as to which way Antoine would ultimately jump.

Condé's wife, Eléonore de Roye, on the other hand, had definitely cast her lot for Calvinism and for the Bourbon leadership. She warned her husband and his brother not to come to court without an army at their back. Some historians think that she was representing the interests of Catherine de Medici as well as her own. The Queen Mother was also finding the power of the Guises oppressive.[68]

After a great deal of hesitation, Antoine decided to obey the King's command. His correspondence shows that he and Condé left Nérac after September 17 and did not reach Orléans until October 30. The Guises had taken every precaution to prevent his gathering an armed force as he advanced, although they did not know his exact route. Royal officials in Guyenne were given orders to oppose by force any attempt on his part to enter a town with an armed escort. When he reached Poitiers, the first week in October, a great gathering of people was prepared to rally to him —adventurers, unemployed men-at-arms, and Calvinists. The Maréchal de Termes was given the assignment of keeping order and watching his movements. There was a bitter quarrel between them because Antoine was insulted by the Maréchal's attitude. He claimed that the latter's orders (from the crown) were not genuine because they contradicted assurances he had been given by Catherine herself, and he insisted upon sending an emissary of his own to the Queen. Catherine sent back a flattering and reassuring reply, in effect denying her orders to the Maréchal and sacrificing her subordinates to the policy of luring the Bourbons to Orléans. The episode caused a ten-day delay in Poitiers, during which Antoine was assailed by fanatical Protestants who accused him of betraying the cause and adventurers offering advice that would serve their own ulterior interests. The King had commanded Antoine to bring his preachers with him. Beza had set out with the Bourbon princes from Nérac, but in the course of the trip he prudently disappeared. Calvin and the Company of Pastors were very anxious until he suddenly reappeared in Geneva in the first days of November.[69]

The Guises had succeeded in preventing Antoine from collecting an army and he made his way up the Loire Valley the last week in October with a small escort, arriving in Orléans at five o'clock in the afternoon of Thursday, October 30. If his reception in August 1559, before the Guises were fully in control, had been humiliating, this one was infinitely more so. Again, no ceremonial welcome was tendered him and as he crossed the courtyard and climbed the stairs he had to push his way through armed guards and a crowd of curious courtiers making disrespectful remarks and gestures. The King, flanked by the Guises, the Cardinal de Tournon, and St. André, scarcely greeted him. Antoine kept his *sang-froid* and declared that he had come in obedience to the King's command and brought his brother, the Prince de Condé, who wished to clear himself of false accusations. François II commented dryly that he had done well to obey and commanded Antoine not to leave the court without permission, so that he could justify himself when his turn came.

The Prince de Condé, kept waiting outside at first, received no greeting at all when he entered a few moments later; when he repeated his brother's assurances of loyalty and obedience, the King replied that he had chosen appropriate persons to pass judgment on Condé's conduct. The King then withdrew to the private quarters of the Queen Mother, accompanied only by the Cardinal de Bourbon and the Chancellor. Shortly he sent for the Bourbon brothers and accused Condé of complicity in the Conspiracy of Amboise and in uprisings in Bordeaux and Lyons. The Prince categorically denied that he was in any way responsible and in turn made accusations against the Guises: that they had invented the charges against him, that their ambition and avarice had ruined France. The Guises prudently absented themselves from this confrontation—who could tell when the Bourbons might be in power? Catherine also took no active part, although she was present and weeping copiously, observers report. Despite Antoine's plea that his brother should be heard and offer to guarantee Condé's innocence with his own life, the King ordered the Prince's arrest.

After his brother was led off to prison Antoine was so upset that he withdrew without speaking to anyone for the rest of the day, and refused to eat. He did not appear at a session of the Council of State (to which his rank admitted him) until two days later. After that he attended every day and affected a servile manner toward the Guises and their partisans. He urged that investigations of sedition be pushed forward and that no mercy be shown to the guilty. He was under no physical restraint but was so closely watched by the Guises that Throckmorton told Queen Elizabeth he was as much a prisoner as his brother.[70] He resumed his usual practice of receiving foreign ambassadors and urged them not to believe the charges against Condé. Chantonay reports that he went so far as to declare "that if it were proved that his brother had intended anything against the person of the King, he, Antoine, wished no pardon . . . for if anyone deserved death in such a case—as they would—a Prince of the Blood would deserve a thousand."[71]

The Guises seemed stunned by the ease of their victory, and for two weeks no further legal action was taken against Condé, although a number of important people were arrested, including his wife, Eléonore. Condé was forbidden any communication with the outside world, and one hundred armed men were stationed outside his door. He expressed confidence in the King's justice, but challenged the competence of most of the King's counsellors on the grounds that they were in the service of his bitterest enemies. He repeatedly denounced the Guises in the same terms as had the pamphlets of recent months and demanded that judges be chosen from his peers and the Parlement of Paris. Speculations of foreign observers varied greatly, and the Venetian ambassador Mihieli wrote the Most Serene Republic on November 10, "God knows how this will come out."[72]

On November 13 Condé was interrogated by the Chancellor, the Premier Président, Christophe de Thou, and three other members of the Parlement of Paris. The Prince refused to answer and appealed to the King and a full session of the Parlement. This and several other appeals were denied, and it became clear that he would receive no mercy, especially after various adventurers and agents arrested in recent months were brought to Orléans for the announced purpose of testifying at the trial. The royal prisoner continued to attack the Guises in ever more violent terms, and it was rumored that he expected to be rescued by another uprising, similar to the Conspiracy of Amboise, on the occasion of the opening of the Estates-General the following month.

Condé's wife, who had been released by Catherine and allowed to come to Orléans, was fearless in her husband's behalf, but no one at court dared to help her (if they had cared to do so). Since the start of the legal proceedings Antoine also had spoken courageously in Condé's defense. In this he had the cooperation of Catherine de Medici, who had found that joining forces with the Guises against the Bourbons had delivered her into the hands of the former. What she needed was continued rivalry between them, as evenly balanced as possible.

Protestant historians, at the time and since, have claimed that the Guises planned to assassinate Antoine in November 1560. (They had no basis for bringing legal charges against him as they had against Condé.) Bordenave, La Planche, La Popelinière, D'Aubigné, Palma Cayet, and the *Histoire Ecclésiastique* develop this theme in virtually the same words. Their source is Jeanne's so-called *Mémoires*. She claims that the Guises enlisted the aid of the King himself in a plot to kill Antoine.[73] François II was supposed to send for Antoine to come to his bedroom, where the King would receive him all alone in his nightshirt, and accuse him of plotting to overthrow the government. If Antoine replied boldly, the King would threaten him with his dagger and, if Antoine tried to defend himself, would call for help. Guise, St. André, and some others, waiting for the cue, would rush in and kill Antoine. It would be announced that he had attempted to take the King's life. François II was not capable of murder, however. He was disturbed by this suggestion and asked his mother's advice. This gave Catherine an opportunity to intervene against the Guises and she warned Antoine through the Duchesse de Montpensier, Jacqueline de Longwy.

When Antoine was first summoned he made an excuse not to obey. When the order was repeated, he asked two faithful servants, Captain Ranty, lieutenant of his private bodyguard, and Cotin, the old servant whom Henri d'Albret had stationed in Jeanne's quarters before Henri de Béarn was born, to go with him. As he approached the King's chamber he met a gentleman who said, " 'Sire, why do you go where you are sure to lose all?' The Prince, turning to Ranty and Cotin, said, 'I go to a place where they have sworn to kill me, but never will a skin have been sold as dearly as I will sell mine. If God wills, He will save me. But, I beg you, by the loyalty you have always shown me . . . do me this last service. If I die, get my shirt and take it, all bloody, to my wife and my son, and get my wife to swear, for the great love she has always borne me and for her duty (because my son is still too young to avenge my death), that she will send my shirt, pierced, torn, and blood-stained, to the Christian princes outside of France so that they will avenge my cruel and traitorous death.' And he entered boldly into the royal chamber." The Cardinal de Lorraine accused Antoine of being the moving spirit behind the recent disturbances in the kingdom, from the attack on Amboise to the latest pamphlets against the "Tiger of France," as the Cardinal de Lorraine was called by his enemies. The young King echoed his uncle's sentiments. Antoine replied firmly but gently that he was not guilty and then retired —without the King's giving any signal. Antoine was saved and allegedly the Guises said of their royal nephew in exasperation: "there is the most cowardly soul [coeur] there ever was!"

The Guises, in league with the Spaniards, had planned to seize Jeanne and Henri de Béarn at this same time, but Jeanne outwitted them by visiting her fortresses. She and her children were safely inside the citadel of Navarrenx, defended by faithful armed retainers, during the first two weeks of November 1560.[74]

François II had decided that the court would spend two weeks hunting before the resumption of official business—that is, the trial of Condé and the opening of the Estates-General. On Saturday, November 16, after a hunt in the woods near Orléans, he was stricken with a violent headache. The next day he complained of a severe earache and took to his bed with a high fever. Catherine de Medici and the Guises scarcely left his room, each fearing the influence of the other. The uncles hid the seriousness of their royal nephew's illness from the court and announced that he had an ear infection. They gave secret orders for the postal service between France and neighboring realms to be suspended —and they put severe pressure on Condé's judges to give a decision. These were much too astute to fall into any such trap, however, and used the King's illness as a pretext for delay. On November 26 a group of Guise partisans, acting in the King's name, in the absence of the accused and of witnesses for either side, condemned the Prince de Condé to death for treason and announced the execution for December 10 in the principal square of Orléans.[75] This was the day the meeting of the Estates-General was scheduled to open. The Guises undoubtedly thought that the execution of Condé would effectively prevent the Estates from demanding that the Princes of the Blood be given power.

To borrow the language of the Protestant historians, a greater power than that of the Cardinal de Lorraine was to cancel out this verdict. The King's fever mounted, he grew delirious, and he could keep neither food nor medicine down. On December 1 the Venetian ambassador reported that he was not expected to live. Prayers and processions were held throughout the kingdom, and the King himself, in one of his lucid intervals, prayed that he might be spared to purge the kingdom of heresy.[76] The Cardinal de Lorraine and the Duc de Guise, seemingly on the point of crowning their triumph and ridding themselves of the enemy, trembled at the prospect of the King's death; without him they were powerless. Antoine de Bourbon, on the other hand, insulted and mocked by the lowliest courtier a few days before, so impotent that he could not protect his own brother from being condemned to a traitor's death, now appeared to many as the rising sun. If François II died he would be succeeded by his brother Charles (IX), aged ten, and one tradition of the Capetian monarchy held that the regency in such cases belonged to the Princes of the Blood.

According to another tradition, the regency belonged to the Queen Mother. Catherine saw in the situation a chance to equalize the power of the two rival factions and to assert her own authority. She let it be known that she was planning to assume power if the King died, and Antoine was given to understand that he was in danger of his life. She sent for him on December 2, when she thought he was sufficiently frightened. As he entered the room the Duchesse de Montpensier warned him to agree to everything if he wished to live. Attended by the Guises and members of the royal council, Catherine began the interview by having a secretary read the historical precedents for the regency of the Queen Mother. Then she repeated the accusations against the Bourbon princes and demanded that Antoine renounce his claims to the regency. If the King died, he must also promise not to allow the Estates-General to urge his claim. Heeding the warning of the Duchess, Antoine replied that he had never conspired against the crown, that his only demand was for a fair trial to clear himself of false accusations, and that he renounced the regency, not because he could not back up his claim but because he preferred to retire to his own domains. As for the Guises, he would forgive them for the Queen's sake.

Catherine had gained what she wanted. She then appeased Antoine's vanity by repeating the proposal that her daughter Marguerite should marry Henri de Navarre, in order to unite the two families even more closely. At her request, Antoine and the Guises embraced in apparent reconciliation. Historians are agreed that this was the first important manifestation of Catherine's political ability. Her triumph was made easier by Antoine's deficiency of the same quality. The Queen Mother had acted swiftly, anticipating not only the death of François II but the arrival of Montmorency, who was advancing with a large armed force. She did not wish to risk the possibility that he would inspire Antoine with courage.[77] De Ruble stresses the significance of this interview between Catherine and Antoine, "in this scene was cast the religious destiny of France. The false indifference of Antoine ruined the hopes of the Calvinist party and condemned it to rebellion."[78] I would place the turning point for the Huguenot cause about a year later, after the Colloquy of Poissy; this, however, clearly was Jeanne's own turning point.

François II died in the evening of Thursday, December 5, 1560. Only his young wife, Mary Stuart, attended his body during the next hectic days. Catherine was giving orders and sending out messages far and wide; the Guise uncles were trying to salvage what they could of their power. Denied even a proper royal funeral on the grounds of economy, the body of François II was conveyed to St. Denis by a small company of subordinate lords and prelates, without a single important personage in the escort. Foreign observers remarked especially upon the absence of the Duc de Guise and the Cardinal de Lorraine. Catherine later realized that the prestige of the crown had been lowered by this neglect; on the first anniversary of her son's death she held a state funeral with full honors, including belated eulogies.[79]

In the absence of documentation, we can only imagine Jeanne's feelings when she learned of Antoine's humiliation, but her public reaction speaks loudly. On Christmas Day 1560 she became a Calvinist. In Bordenave's words,

> The Queen of Navarre had always looked with disfavor rather than with favor on the Reformed Religion and had done everything in her power to draw her husband away from it, but at the time when her husband was most helpless and when the danger of the ruin of her house was greatest, she put everything in God's hands, against the advice of many of her advisers, and openly declared herself to belong to the said Reformed Religion, with such constancy that never again could she be turned from her course, no matter what assaults Satan and the world made upon her. In the year 1560, therefore, at the Christmas communion, she foreswore the Roman religion at Pau in Béarn and, having made a confession of faith, partook of Holy Communion according to the rites of the said Reformed Religion.[80]

Since Bordenave's history was written at Jeanne's command, we are obliged to accept the statement that she had not embraced the reform until 1560 as an expression of what she wished the world to believe, even if one suspects, with Salefranque, that she had been converted some years earlier. The assertion that "she had done everything in her power to draw her husband away from it" is harder to accept. If it is true, her actions during the remaining months of their marriage represent a drastic change of attitude. If the time of her conversion is uncertain, its motivation is complicated. It is impossible to be sure that she embraced Calvinism from spiritual conviction rather than because it offered a vehicle for her dynastic ambition and political rights. Indeed, both Bordenave and the *Mémoires* imply that political factors—especially opposition to the Guises—changed her from the "cold prospect" described by Beza and Brantôme to the dedicated Calvinist leader of later years. But, this is probably only part of the explanation.

There is no sign of a religious or mystic "experience" as a turning point in Jeanne's writings (including letters, or any other source). But this does not impugn the sincerity of her conversion, or convict her of indifference in religious matters. Her subsequent career testifies to a Calvinist "high seriousness." Even less does it imply the sort of cynicism which employs religion as a cloak for conscious, ulterior motives. The evidence suggests that the moral climate and authority of Calvinism held a strong appeal and motivated Jeanne's conversion.

Among adherents of any religious faith there are not only differences in degree but in the kind of commitment; and where persecution is the price of adherence, the numbers are likely to be smaller and the intensity greater. The nature of French Calvinism reflects its minority status. In such circumstances, even the layman must have a strong motivation for his conviction, whether primarily spiritual or not. The positive appeal of a new faith probably reflects the relevance of some of its important characteristics (doctrine, ritual, morality, or a combination of elements) to the personal needs of the convert, conscious or otherwise, better than the corresponding characteristics of the old faith. A new commitment is sought because the old one does not fulfill its function.

In French aristocratic families who converted to Calvinism the leadership of women is striking. Laurence Stone comments on the appeal (of Protestantism in general) "to aristocratic wives tormented by the futility of their idle and neglected lives, for whom the new doctrine at last seemed to offer some explanation for their existence."[81] Jeanne's position as Queen in her own right set her apart from most aristocratic wives, but it made a strong ideological orientation especially important. Furthermore, Calvinism offered fulfillment of Jeanne's basic emotional needs: the simple and forthright Calvinist style of life, with its emphasis on consistency and logic, suited her temperament, and Calvinist insistence on strong, direct authority was more congenial to her inflexible mind than the complex structure of the Roman church. Jeanne had found individuals to whom she looked for authority weak—and in conflict with each other. In the God of Calvinism, Jeanne could draw upon a trustworthy authority outside herself, which at the same time allowed her to assert and strengthen her own authority and identity, thus freeing her from some conflicts that had divided her energies and some compromises that had threatened her integrity.

Salefranque's documents and the letters to Gourdon show that Jeanne had responded to the appeal of Calvinism as early as 1555, but the inclination did not crystallize into conviction until 1560, when the outer circumstances of her life reinforced it and precipitated a decision. The Catholic Valois court had corrupted Antoine and brought out in him elements that Jeanne had despised since her childhood: weakness, gullibility, compromise, hypocrisy. When his humiliation at Catherine's hands proved that he would not assume the necessary initiative and that the only chance for Bourbon leadership and the survival of Jeanne's kingdom lay in the possibility that the powerful Catholic faction would be challenged by the Calvinist faction, Jeanne had no choice but to take the lead herself.

She could henceforth stand on her own. Bordenave's account reflects the speed and directness characteristic of Jeanne when her mind was made up. Nor is there any subsequent regret or wavering: her Calvinist belief affected every important decision of later years. Jeanne's conversion enabled her to outshine Marguerite, who had never dared risk bold leadership; it gave ideological content to the Bourbon cause; it freed Jeanne from an outgrown dependence on Antoine. Linked with the Bourbon cause, Calvinism galvanized her energies and provided the unifying focus of Jeanne's life.

The adherence of the Queen of Navarre was immediately welcomed by the two most influential Protestants in western Europe. In mid-January 1561, Calvin wrote his first letter to Jeanne, in which he salutes her courage: "I know that you do not need my advice . . . to take arms and do battle against . . . the difficulties that will assail you." He rejoices in the role of Beza, "who long ago sowed good seed in you . . . although it was almost choked by the thorns of worldliness . . . God in His infinite goodness has prevented it . . . from disappearing altogether." Calvin then begins to outline her future duty, but cuts himself off, "when I see how the spirit of God rules you I have more occasion to give thanks than to exhort you." He refers, gently, to his disappointment in Antoine, "for a long time we have tried to do our duty by the King, your husband . . . as you will see again from the enclosed copy of a letter we have sent him."[82]

Queen Elizabeth, through Throckmorton, also expressed satisfaction. After a tantalizing reference to an unexplained promise given Jeanne, he says that he has been instructed to congratulate the Queen of Navarre on her "affection for the true religion." The English Queen reminds Jeanne that "the present offers great opportunities to encourage those well-disposed," and that "the enemy should not be aided by the indifference or lukewarm attitude of its professors."[83] This last is undoubtedly an allusion to Antoine. Throckmorton must have resented the time spent and risks incurred in his dealings with Antoine, which had caused the Ambassador to fall from favor at the French court, and thus become less useful to his own government.

Whatever the reasons for Jeanne's conversion, her courage cannot be underestimated. For the remaining twelve years of her life she would be singled out as an enemy by the most powerful movement in Europe, the Counter Reformation. The Papacy, Philip of Spain, and the Guises challenged her title and threatened her domains and at times her person; the French crown exploited her difficulties. Because of her religion also, these enemies made every effort to thwart Jeanne's greatest ambition— the strengthening of her son's position as an heir to the throne of France.

VI

A HUSBAND LOST,
A PARTY GAINED

JANUARY 1561–FEBRUARY 1562

ALTHOUGH six months were to pass before her departure from Béarn, Jeanne apparently decided to go to court about the time of her conversion. Antoine refers to her forthcoming arrival as early as January 21, 1561, and on March 29 the Venetian ambassador reports that she is expected. There were good reasons for this decision. The first was public: having officially espoused Calvinism, with all the risks implied, Jeanne had decided to participate actively in the movement on the national scene, no longer confining herself to the domains where she was sovereign. This meant entering into the struggle of the factions at court to strengthen the Protestants and to cooperate with such Catholics as were willing to make concessions. She may have been influenced by the letters from Calvin and Queen Elizabeth, who had interpreted her announcement as a signal that she was prepared to implement her convictions by action.

Conditions were increasingly favorable and it was time to throw her weight into the balance. The Estates-General met in Orléans between mid-December 1560 and the end of January 1561, and Catherine was obviously trying to change the situation of the former reign by reconciling the Guises and the Bourbons in a "union of the princes." To reduce the power of the former was inevitably to build up the latter. If some commentators have overestimated the liberalism of Michel de L'Hôpital,* nevertheless the speeches of the new Chancellor did reflect Catherine's desire to shift the balance of power, and the necessity to reckon with the demands of the Huguenot nobles meant that any shift was likely to be an improvement from the anti-Guise point of view. Even if the toleration implied was only a matter of tactics, it still provided an opportunity for the Huguenot leaders.[1]

They were not slow to exploit it. By March, Coligny had resumed his seat in the King's council and there were rumors that he would be made the "governor" of Charles IX. In early April he installed a Calvinist minister in his apartments at Fontainebleau and invited members of the court to attend the sermons. Chantonay, scandalized, reported to Philip on April 9 that Catherine had accepted the invitation, accompanied by the royal children.[2] The Paris Huguenots were resuming their services at the Pré-aux-Clercs. In the same week Odet de Châtillon† made a public announcement of his conversion, which, though no surprise, provoked a riot in his episcopal city of Beauvais and a scandal in Catholic circles throughout Europe. Condé had been released from prison and declared innocent of the charges against him by the royal council (March 13) with the cooperation of the Duc de Guise, who threw all the blame on François II.[3]

The alarm of the Spaniards at this turn of events, reflected in Chantonay's dispatches in these months, had already caused Philip to send a special envoy to counteract the Huguenot offensive. Don Juan Mauriquez de Lara had arrived on January 4.[4] His immediate objectives were to reduce the influence of the Châtillons by persuading Catherine to send them away from court, and to keep her from calling a "national council," in which Huguenot ministers would confront Roman Catholic prelates on equal terms. Catherine was considering this move as part of her *politique de bascule,* using as her pretext the fact that the Council of Trent

---

* Michel de L'Hôpital, 1507–1573, had been Chancellor of Marguerite de France (Duchess of Savoy), sister of Henri II. He had a distinguished legal career, and was the outstanding lay advocate of religious toleration in Catherine's service. In 1568 he fell from power.

† Odet de Coligny, Cardinal de Châtillon, 1515–1571. Brother of Coligny and D'Andelot, the Cardinal-Bishop of Beauvais was the last of the three to embrace Calvinism. Despite the scandal, he was not excommunicated until 1563, when he married Elizabeth de Hauteville (who had influenced his conversion) and called himself Comte de Beauvais. Later he fled to England, where he took an active part in negotiations between the Huguenots and Queen Elizabeth. He died just as he was preparing to return to France after the signing of the Treaty of St. Germain.

had not produced solutions adequate to the religious problems of France. As she wrote to the French ambassador in Vienna on March 29, "if no results are obtained . . . we will be forced to resort to a national [council]." When she had definitely decided upon it, she instructed her ambassador in Madrid to make Philip understand that it was not like Spain, "where the evil is just beginning to appear . . . here it is so entrenched that it is impossible to eliminate it without resorting to the remedy of a national council."[5]

If the general situation in the early months of 1561 indicated that the moment had come for the Huguenots to strike, the actions of Antoine de Bourbon were not reassuring to those who looked to him for leadership. Antoine "passed for the chief of the reformers" and was "surrounded by heretics," but at the same time he kept protesting his orthodoxy and attended Mass alternately with Protestant services.[6] So undermined was Calvinist confidence in the King of Navarre that both Francis Hotman and Calvin had written to urge him to take a decisive stand.[7] On February 18 he received the Earl of Bedford, sent by Queen Elizabeth, who was hoping to use Antoine as "an ally at the foot of the throne," but a week later he withdrew his support from Françoise de Rohan, Jeanne's cousin, in her lawsuit against the Duc de Nemours. Court circles were divided into two camps by this notorious case, and to support Nemours, intimate friend of the Duc de Guise, was a gesture of solidarity with the ultra-Catholic party. Antoine was also stressing his allegiance to the Papacy through his ambassador, Pedro d'Albret, who had succeeded in persuading the Pope to recognize him as a royal ambassador, over the objections of both the French and Spaniards.[8]

Catherine's policy of uniting the princes had caused her to grant Antoine the title of Lieutenant-General of the Kingdom (March 24), which the Duc de Guise had held in the former reign. But, as she wrote to Philip on March 27, he "is willing that I should command everywhere and absolutely. I have made him Lieutenant-General under me, in whose hands rests the supreme authority, just as in the past." Catherine wanted the Spaniards to believe that she was neutralizing Antoine by giving him the form without the substance of power, but foreign observers interpreted it as a defeat for the Queen Mother and the recovery of the initiative by the King of Navarre. Chantonay was depressed by the prospect, and the Florentine ambassador told the Grand Duke of Tuscany that Catherine had "finally proven that she is only a woman."[9]

It is not necessary to decide between the interpretation of historians who regard this as a manifestation of Catherine's political genius and those who think she acted out of weakness—only mitigated by Antoine's greater weakness. Did Jeanne believe that Antoine finally was in a position to lead the Huguenot party and that therefore she must go to support him, or did she think he was losing the initiative to Coligny and Condé and that she must impel him into the leadership? Either way the Protestant cause stood to gain by her presence. As the Venetian ambassador wrote on March 29, "It was she who had imbued her husband with these opinions and who might also be able to hold him to them."[10]

The formation in early April of the Catholic Triumvirate by the Constable, the Duc de Guise, and the Maréchal de St. André showed how strong was opposition to the rising Huguenot party. It also had the effect of swinging Catherine even more to the Huguenot side, as her chief object was to escape domination by any faction; since the Catholic party remained stronger she needed the Huguenots to balance the scale.[11]

Jeanne's other reason for going to court had a public aspect—to reaffirm a façade of solidarity between the King and Queen of Navarre —but she may have been merely trying to save her marriage. Now that he had attained the second position in France, Antoine's ambition might be sufficiently appeased so that he could accept Jeanne and agree to reunite their lives and policies. Antoine encouraged such a hope in a letter written from Orléans on January 21, after asking for seeds of melons, cucumbers, and sweet onions, "a leather bag about one foot high of each . . . in tightly made packages, as you always do, as soon as possible . . . because we are approaching the season to sow seed," which he wants at once because he has promised them to Catherine. He says he has been visiting the Guises, "from whom God deliver us soon," and concludes, "I pray the Lord to give you and your little flock health as far as this court—where you will be so well entertained that you'll risk getting sick of it—and give you a long and happy life." It is signed, "your most affectionate friend and most faithful husband."[12]

A number of matters required her attention before Jeanne could depart. The Estates of Béarn met from February 23 to March 10, and it was necessary for Jeanne to assure her revenues for the coming months and respond to certain demands in order to leave the kingdom sufficiently well-ordered to withstand predictable difficulties for her deputies.

For this task she chose Louis d'Albret, Bishop of Lescar, and Armand de Gontaut, Seigneur d'Audaux, who were to share the duties of Lieutenant-General.[13] Both were local notables, the Bishop was her great-uncle and Audaux was a seasoned military man, a necessity if Béarn needed to be defended in her absence. In April she took the waters in Eaux-Chaudes.[14] This was to become a habit, for Jeanne's tuberculosis, described as "galloping" in later years, began to be noticed at this time.

To strengthen her Calvinist ministers—Jeanne did not "establish" the reform until 1563—she ordered her council to protect them, and warned that she expected others she would send during her absence to be "made welcome." The following October she was obliged to write to the Bishop of Lescar ordering him to enforce this policy, complaints of ministers who had been molested having reached her at court.[15] After leaving Béarn for Nérac in early July, she took similar steps to advance Calvinism in the Duchy of Albret. She was undoubtedly encouraged by the crown's announcement (June 12) of the coming "national council," known in French history as *le Colloque de Poissy*.[16] Theodore Beza had been invited to attend, and Jeanne's hopes for the colloquy are revealed in a letter to the Vicomte de Gourdon from Nérac.

Since the coronation of the new young King [May 15] a halt has been called to persecution, pending a free council . . . to take place in Poissy . . . a debate on disputed matters of religion between ministers, bishops, and cardinals before the King and his council. Theodore Beza, whom you know, will be there as spokesman with twelve ministers and many deputies. I pray God he will fortify them with the force of pure truth.[17]

While Jeanne was traveling to court, the Edict of July was issued on the religious question. Because of its mutually contradictory clauses, Romier describes it as "a marvel of calculated incoherence and, it must be said, of deception." While it forbade the adherents of the reform to assemble in public or to hold service even in private," in any other form than that of the Catholic Church, under pain of bodily punishment and confiscation of goods," it also stipulated that the ruling was only temporary, pending the "determination" of the religious question. It declared a "general amnesty for all crimes touching religion," so that the royal authorities could not undertake any new prosecutions and had to release Protestants presently detained. The Protestant leadership had been advised in advance that they did not have to fear the Edict. One Huguenot minister wrote to Beza, "we know for certain that the whole purpose is to appease King Philip and the Pope and to extract some money from the clergy."[18] Jeanne's actions on her journey show that she understood this and it is probable that she also had been informed.

As she made her way up the Loire Valley, the havoc wrought to the status quo was reported to his master by Chantonay. In Tours, "she preached firmness to the Protestants and intimidated the royal officers." At Notre Dame de Cléry, near Orléans, one of her ministers, Jean de La Tour, preached to great crowds, "everywhere the heretics await her coming as if she were the Messiah, because they are certain that she will perform miracles in their behalf. Personally, I do not doubt it, for wherever she goes she meets with no resistance." One senses the regret of the Spanish ambassador when he reports that in one place, as she was entering a house, the floor collapsed just as she crossed the threshold, leaving a yawning abyss at her feet.[19] A lighter note is struck in a letter from the English ambassador Throckmorton to Cecil later in the year. Commenting on the rash of disturbances in Jeanne's wake, he says, "At the convent of Ste. Madelaine [near Orléans], twenty-five religious ladies, the fairest of sixty, threw aside their habits and scaled the walls . . . such was their abhorrence of the superstitions of the cloister, or rather, so much did they prefer profane company."[20]

On August 20 Jeanne had reached Longjumeau, long an important Huguenot center in the Paris region. Crowds came to greet her, but she was tired and she deputed seven-year-old Henri (who had come to meet her) to address them. The next day she entered the capital quietly—the ceremonial entry took place a week later—and withdrew to private quarters. For the next few days she received none but "the faithful of her own church." These privileged visitors almost certainly included Beza when he arrived on August 23.[21]

The prospect of Antoine's leading the movement Jeanne had come to encourage had declined considerably in recent months. On May 14 the Venetian ambassador reported that he seemed increasingly inclined to the Catholic side, even boasting that he would carry his brother and his wife along with him. By mid-July the loud displeasure of the Huguenots with Antoine is recorded by the same observer. Chantonay told Philip that Antoine "never stops begging the Nuncio to testify to his orthodoxy," and that he considered himself "the arbiter of religion in France."[22] The Spaniards had long ago ceased to take Antoine seriously, but as usual they played on his weakness, while reserving their real pressure for Catherine.

Determined to go ahead with the Colloquy and obliged to appease Philip, the Queen Mother had been trying to effect a "grand and public reconciliation" between Guise and Condé. She finally accomplished this on August 24, after Jeanne had arrived in Paris but before her official entry. That day the Venetian ambassador noted that it was fortunate Catherine had succeeded before Jeanne's arrival, "because if that Princess had been at court, many people think that, with her hatred of the house of Guise, she would have upset everything, "being a woman with a frightening brain" (*essendo dona di terribile cervello*).[23]

The personal relationship between Antoine and Jeanne had also deteriorated in recent months. The King of Navarre's liaison with one of Catherine's "flying squadron"* was a matter of gossip; he was also considered the chief playboy of the court. Chantonay remarks:

It would seem that Vendôme is not much troubled by his wife's absence. When they are together she dominates and he lacks the freedom to call on the ladies and pass the night enjoying himself as he does now. He is often indisposed as a result, like this morning, when neither the council nor the Parlement could meet because of his absence.[24]

Calvin had already admonished Antoine, with evident embarrassment, in May.

Sometimes we are forced to displease those whom we would please, which will eventually give them one hundred times more contentment than if we left them in repose. . . . I have heard that you have been won by evil means to yield . . . many things . . . you should resist strongly and firmly . . . [I have also heard] that foolish love affairs are preventing or at least cooling your interest in doing your duty.[25]

In August, when Calvin heard that Antoine had gone so far as to make fun of Jeanne's religion ("You'll see," he said to a group of court ladies, "she'll convert you all") Calvin wrote again, more sternly: "God will punish those who have not done their duty according to the place and degree He has given them. If we speak sharply, Sire, it is because it is now or never."[26]

* Louise de La Beraudière, known as *la belle Rouet,* because her father was seigneur de la Rouet. Antoine had a son by her.

If Jeanne was not fully informed of court gossip by her own agents, she learned of Antoine's peccadillos in the most unpleasant way, by an anonymous letter, dated July 2, from Strasbourg.

The Bishop of Auxerre,* his sublime pimp, the wife of a well-known Maréchal . . . [and others] lead this poor blind King as they please, to his shame. . . . To keep still is worse than to speak of this . . . in order that he may be brought to a better life, and you, Madame, to tranquillity . . . I pray the good Lord . . . to separate His Majesty from this scum [*canaille*] and that you, Madame, will accept this [information] as you would wish if you were in my place.[27]

Since this document has remained in the Pau archives, Jeanne may have received it before her departure from Béarn.

On the occasion of Jeanne's official entry into Paris, August 29, she was escorted through the capital and out to St. Germain by Antoine, Condé, Coligny, and other Huguenot nobles. The best apartments in the chateau at St. Germain had been prepared for her and she was treated according to the etiquette reserved for foreign royalty. That night there were fireworks and entertainment in her honor, following a dinner tendered by Catherine to the whole court. Jeanne sat on the Queen's right and Henri de Béarn sat between the King and his sister, Henri's future bride, Marguerite de Valois. Chantonay says that the marriage was referred to in terms flattering to the Béarnais, and that "Madame de Vendôme radiated pride in her son."[28] The Spanish ambassador feared the worst: "She comes resolved to do all the harm she can to religion, and even to her husband, because he goes to Mass. I am convinced the Queen will have a hard time living with her."[29]

Almost a full year had elapsed since Antoine had left Jeanne in Béarn, a year of crisis and conflict for both. Whatever resolution of the religious and political problems lay ahead, the prospects were not bright for the marriage of the King and Queen of Navarre. Everybody knew that Antoine had been acting and speaking in ways humiliating to Jeanne, as his wife and as a Queen. And Jeanne was angry. She had written a menacing letter to the Cardinal d'Armagnac, accusing him of leading Antoine astray. Shortly after their reunion, Chantonay wrote, "His wife says openly how much she detests [Vendôme], even to the point of

---

* Only the last part of the letter has survived. The Bishop of Auxerre was Philippe de Lenoncourt, a member of Chantonay's cabal. The woman was probably the wife of the Maréchal de St. André.

having no regrets at losing him, either for herself or for her religion. For this reason, although she has little power, I fear her anger."[30]

THE FLOOD TIDE OF CALVINISM,
SEPTEMBER 1561–JANUARY 1562

To summarize the important debates of the *Colloque de Poissy* (September 8–October 3) would unbalance Jeanne's biography, since she was only a spectator at the sessions. Like the earlier confrontation of Protestants (Lutheran) and Roman Catholics at Ratisbon in 1541, the Colloquy showed how great was the abyss separating them in matters of theology, church discipline, and the application of the Christian ethic. The leading participants included Beza and the Italian Peter Martyr on the Calvinist side, the Cardinal de Lorraine and various papal representatives on the other. Prominent among the latter was Hippolyte d'Este, Cardinal of Ferrara, sent by Pius IV to assure the failure of the Colloquy, partly by charming the ladies, including Jeanne d'Albret. No religious settlement was achieved, but the Colloquy was an important factor in precipitating the civil wars.[31] By the mere fact that it was held, the Colloquy unleashed the full force of the Calvinist movement in France. What Romier calls "Protestant boldness" was stimulated by the very procedure, which "implied a decisive change in the official attitude of the crown toward the dissenters. . . . In the King's own presence . . . Calvin's vicar had solemnly set forth the reformed doctrine . . . of what use from then on was censure [of it], since the King's own ear had not been shocked?" *Le Harangue de M. de Bèze devant le Roy* was much in demand by Parisians at the end of September.[32]

Manifestations of this boldness were occurring throughout France in the autumn of 1561. In the southwest, where the movement was already well-launched, the Huguenot party was forming a sort of military republic, with a captain for each church and a colonel for each local group of churches under a general in each of the two regions, Guyenne and Languedoc. In the southeast, crowds were invading the churches to break the "images" and attacking members of the clergy. A Spanish bishop traveling across France to Trent said that the only tranquil diocese he saw was that of Narbonne. In Lyons, Calvinist services were celebrated in the center of the city and attended by many leading citizens. Even in the eastern provinces, strongholds of the Guises, heresy was spreading and the Bishop of Troyes became a convert.[33] The growth of the movement could be illustrated by thousands of incidents, but none is more telling than the fact that Blaise de Monluc,* before and afterward known as the most militant of Catholics, considered changing sides in 1561. Courteault, an authority on him, says "there is no doubt that Monluc, on the one hand informed by his brother† of what was happening at court, and on the other much impressed by the considerable progress of the reform in the Agenais, at this moment seriously thought that the Huguenot party was on the eve of triumph in Guyenne and that if he joined it he would have a better chance of the obtaining the [royal] lieutenancy which he yearned for."[34]

Of these two factors the first was undoubtedly the more important. The vogue of Calvinism at court in these months was a source of amazement—delighted or horrified—to all observers. Before Jeanne's arrival the allied families of Coligny and Condé constituted the nucleus of the Huguenot party at court: the Admiral's wife, Charlotte de Laval; her sister Madelaine de Mailly, Comtesse de Roye; the latter's two daughters, Eléonore, Princesse de Condé, and Charlotte, Comtesse de La Rochefoucauld, and their nephew and niece, the Prince and Princesse de Porcien. The Marquise de Rothelin, the Crussol ladies,‡ and Renée of Ferrara also belonged to the inner circle. The preponderant role of women at the Valois court is striking—and not only among the Huguenots. The Constable's wife and the Duc de Guise's widowed mother were among the leaders of the Catholic party and, of course, the royal power was in the hands of Catherine de Medici.

In the apartments of the Huguenot ladies Protestant services were conducted daily by their own ministers, a sizable group of whom Claude Hatton, an ardent Catholic, said in astonished indignation, "they were better welcomed than would have been the Pope of Rome if he had

---

* Blaise de Monluc, 1501–1567, made his military reputation in the Italian wars. For his relations with Jeanne, see Chapters VII, XI, XII.

† Jean de Monluc, Bishop of Valence, 1508–1579, one of Catherine's principal advisers and most conspicuous of the French bishops lenient to the reform.

‡ There is considerable confusion, even in some of the contemporary sources, between three different Crussol ladies at the French court. The eldest, Jeanne de Gourdon de Genouillac, wife of Charles de Crussol, Sieur de St. Astier, was a practicing Calvinist. Her two daughters-in-law (Louise de Clermont-Tonnere, wife of Antoine de Crussol, who became Duc d'Uzès in 1562, and her sister or niece Hélène, wife of Jacques de Crussol, Sieur de Baudiné) figure among the political Huguenots in this period. Jeanne's reference to the Duchesse d'Uzès in 1572 (see Chapter XIII) demonstrates the transient nature of her association with the reform. See *Correspondance de Bèze*, IV, 200, note 1.

come."[35] Among the Catholic ladies there was a fad of reading pamphlets imported from Geneva or Germany which the Paris bookstores could not keep in stock.[36] The center of attention was Theodore Beza, whose sermons were preached to overflowing audiences. In Hatton's words,

mounted in the pulpit, he spoke fine appropriate French in a fluent, un-hesitating style and triumphed over the cackle, having the manner and gestures that attract the sympathy and command the will of his auditors . . . [Catherine] and the King of Navarre found it much to their taste, although they did not wish to declare themselves Huguenots because of their positions.[37]

Beza's letter to Calvin shows that, although pleased, he was not so flattered as to be distracted from his mission.[38]

The height of the "Huguenot fashion" at court was reached on the occasion of the marriage of Jeanne's cousin Jean de Rohan (brother of Françoise) and Diane de Barbançon, niece of a former mistress of François I. It was held at Argenteuil on September 29, a date chosen by Jeanne and Coligny so that the Admiral and other Huguenot nobles could avoid attending the mandatory Mass of the Order of St. Michael scheduled for the same day. Beza officiated, *à la mode de Genève,* which caused a scandal in ultra-Catholic circles, but, as Pasquier pointed out, the crown made no attempt to stop it.[39]

On the contrary, some of Catherine's most influential advisers, including L'Hôpital and Jean de Monluc, were so sympathetic to the Calvinists and so critical of the Roman church that they were suspected of heresy. Indeed, the Queen Mother herself seemed to favor Calvinism. In addition to the permission she granted the Huguenot nobles to "live after their own fashion" (as Chantonay said of Jeanne), she permitted the royal children to pray in the vernacular and to sing the Psalms of Marot. In the royal chapel Protestant services alternated with Masses.[40] Marguerite de Valois, the King's sister and later wife of Henri de Navarre, says in her *Mémoires,* that she had a hard time defending her Catholic allegiance. "In order to keep my religion at the time of the Synod at Poissy, when all the court was infected by heresy, I had to resist the powerful persuasion of several lords and ladies of the court, even my brother Anjou, who has since become King of France. . . . Being a child he had been impressed by that regrettable *Huguenoterie* and never left off shouting at me to change my religion. He threw my Hour Books in the fire and forced me to carry Huguenot Psalms and prayers in their place." Marguerite reported these matters to her ardently Catholic governess, Madame de Curton, who took her to Cardinal Tournon. The Cardinal "advised and fortified me . . . and gave me books to replace those that had been burned. . . . My brother Anjou . . . insulted me, saying that it was obvious that I had no understanding, that all intelligent people of whatever age and sex, having heard the truth preached, had withdrawn from such bigotry . . . he added that my mother would have me beaten. But he said this on his own; the Queen my mother did not know that he had fallen into error, and as soon as she found out she punished him and those in charge of him."[41]

The *Mémoires* were written many years later when Marguerite was a member of the ultra-Catholic party, *brouillée* with her brother Henri III (formerly Anjou). Even if one suspects Marguerite of exaggerating, there is much evidence that many people were expecting Catherine to join the Huguenot camp at any moment. Those who feared it and most opposed it, the agents of Spain and the Pope, were ignored. When Chantonay warned Catherine that he could no longer forbear to report to his master what he saw "with his own eyes," she dismissed it, saying that "he could write whatever he pleased." The permissive attitude toward criticism of the Church was reflected even in the games of the royal children. A conference between Catherine and the Cardinal of Ferrara was interrupted one day by a procession of mock prelates led by Henri de Béarn in a red cape and homemade Cardinal's hat and including Charles IX (a mere bishop with his make-believe miter). The Queen and Cardinal burst out laughing, but Catherine quickly recovered her parental mien, scolded the offenders, and sent them from the room, remarking that somebody at court was sure to report them. (She was right. The Spanish ambassador treated it in exactly the same tone as news from Trent, in no less than three dispatches.) Other adults at court were amused and made the children repeat the performance. The newly arrived papal Nuncio, Prospero di Santa Croce, then made a special appointment with Catherine in order to complain, only to have her dismiss the subject: "all these things [are] merely the jokes of little children."[42]

Chantonay's rising alarm reflects the influence of the Huguenot leaders in the royal council, as does Beza's elation. He dared to hope that the royal family would turn Calvinist and his letters in the late autumn are those of a man who believes he is about to realize his greatest ambition.[43] Some leading members of the French clergy also considered conversion.

The case of Antonio Caraciollo, Bishop of Troyes,* who had been drawn to Calvinism by Peter Martyr, illustrates one reason for the failure of Protestantism in France at the very moment that it seemed about to triumph. He and other bishops who had been "converted" in the spiritual sense, at least to the point of seriously considering a change, hesitated because they feared that they would be unable to keep their titles and benefices. Asked for a clarifying statement, Beza felt it was too vital a matter for him to decide and referred it to Calvin. The answer was that such a person could not keep his special position but would become a minister like any other. As to the temporal wealth of the bishopric, Calvin made an exception to his usual stand—a categorical refusal—for Caraciollo, saying that he might keep it on condition that it was used for the relief of the poor. This meant that a bishop who became a Calvinist must do so as a private individual and lose his titles, his special position, and his wealth. Caraciollo managed to reap the advantages of both sides; and, while abandoning some of his benefices (receiving a compensating 2000 livres tournois from the crown), he kept the title, styling himself, "Antoine, Bishop and Minister of the Holy Gospel."[44]

It is not surprising that French bishops, cultivated aristocrats to whom the Roman Church offered a career, chose not to renounce it. Beza's biographer Geisendorf comments on the probable significance of Calvin's intransigence, and speculates that had he been more flexible, "a kind of French Anglicanism, which would have changed the course of history, might have come into being."[45] Caraciollo's question and Calvin's answer postulate a France in which Calvinism would be the established religion, with a Calvinist royal family; otherwise the benefices (given by the crown as a result of the Concordat of Bologna, 1516) would not be available. The relatively easy establishment of Anglicanism under Henry VIII derived from the fact that the sovereign took the initiative, and under the Church of England bishops who bowed to the royal will kept the estates and ecclesiastical titles obtained under the Church of Rome.

No one person, if one excepts Beza himself, was more conspicuous or influential in the brief season of the Protestant flood than Jeanne d'Albret. The Queen of Navarre was one of the highest ranking persons in France to be a convinced Calvinist. Although she was not in line for the throne,

---

* Antonio Caraciollo, Prince of Melfi, 1515(?)–1570, was the son of an Italian who first came to France as a prisoner in the armies of Charles VIII. The Caraciolli were typical of the Italians who rose in the service of the crown in the early sixteenth century and became the target of much criticism, especially during Catherine's rule.

as Condé was (after Antoine and his son), she was a sovereign ruler in the feudal sense still prevailing, and the niece of François I. The fact that Throckmorton was more and more dealing directly with Jeanne, ignoring Antoine, reveals how Europe's leading Protestant power assessed the situation. Dispatches of foreign agents mention Jeanne almost daily. She exploited her position in the service of *la cause* in two principal ways, as an organizer and as a proselytizer.

In late October she and Beza, with the cooperation of other Huguenot nobles, formed a unified Calvinist consistory out of what had been separate services, each with its own chaplain. Calvinism at court was thus organized under one director—Beza himself. In a letter to Calvin on October 30, he expresses regret that he cannot yet return to Geneva because he must "work out the constitution of a single church for the three families of the Queen of Navarre, the Prince de Condé, and the Admiral." During November all three wrote to Geneva asking for Beza's services a few months longer.[46] The Huguenot leaders hoped that a new church, begun in their small but powerful circle, would gradually become a more inclusive one. Such had been the regional pattern of Calvinist growth. If the crown were to break from Rome, as Henry VIII had, the dream of a national church would not be beyond realization.

Pending the conversion of the royal family, if Beza had succeeded in working out the constitution of a single church for the three ranking families, an organization quite different from the one that actually exists would have been formed. If the Calvinist churches in the widespread domains of Jeanne, the Condés, and the Châtillons had been subordinated to a single direction, outside the region, the nucleus of a national church would have existed. Since such a pattern did not develop—owing to the change of Huguenot fortunes in 1562—one can only speculate what its structure might have been.

Jeanne's regular attendance at Protestant services—"with all the doors open," as exasperated observers pointed out—had the effect of creating good publicity (*foyers de propagande*) for Calvinism. The Venetian ambassador says, "The Queen of Navarre's residence was a public school for the new doctrine. It was a refuge for the new evangelists, who received there a very kind and honorable welcome. The example of highly-placed persons emboldened the new sectarians, who began to rise against the Catholic party throughout the kingdom." Hubert Languet, a Lutheran who was trying to aid the Huguenots, says, "the cause is greatly advanced by the Queen of Navarre . . . since her arrival it has taken a leap forward."[47]

Contemporary enemies of the reformers often insisted that many of the large numbers who attended Calvinist services did so out of curiosity to see the colorful and controversial Queen of Navarre. The largest gathering at St. Germain was an open-air service in the park of the chateau on December 1, at which Beza preached and administered communion to a congregation of seven hundred. The crowds in Paris were naturally much bigger. Both Chantonay and Beza himself estimated that six thousand attended a service he conducted when he accompanied Jeanne to the capital in mid-December.[48]

It did no harm to attract the crowds and it was always possible that some who came from curiosity would prove to be fertile ground for the good seed. Much more important, however, was to counteract prejudice and build sympathy in the powerful, such as the Cardinal of Ferrara. A man of luxurious tastes, who probably would have found the atmosphere of the Roman curia a half-century earlier much more congenial, he played a somewhat ambiguous role at the French court. He was one of several representatives of the Papacy, but regarded with suspicion by his colleagues. Brother-in-law of Renée and friendly with Condé and Coligny, he was hostile to the Guises. Jeanne evidently thought it worth while to cultivate him.

On November 12, the Cardinals of Ferrara and Armagnac accepted an invitation to dine with Jeanne, on condition that she return the visit the following day. At the beginning and end of the meal one of Jeanne's preachers said Calvinist prayers. When the tables had been cleared, a dais was brought in and members of Jeanne's household arrived and seated themselves. Then Jean de La Tour—an unfrocked Franciscan—preached a sermon, "so moderate and well-spoken," says Chantonay, "that the two prelates did not disapprove anything he said." Armagnac declared that St. Paul himself could do no better. The evening ended with a concert of Psalms by a children's choir which included Henri de Béarn and his cousin Henri de Condé. The two prelates seem to have taken the entire performance in stride and there is no record of any objections on their part, but the Protestants criticized the fact that they had remained covered and had not genuflected at the name of Jesus Christ.

Two or three days later—the return engagement was postponed on account of Jeanne's health—the Queen of Navarre, accompanied by

QUEEN OF NAVARRE Jeanne d'Albret

Condé and Coligny, dined with the Cardinal. Jeanne had brought her own food, possibly because there recently had been an attempt to poison her and Antoine. Afterward, when they were taking seats in the chapel, she said, "loud enough for all to hear, that, since they had been foolish enough to come they must see it through, but 'let us show by our attitude that we are here against our better judgment.'" At one point Jeanne and Jean de La Tour went up to a gallery and the guest of honor turned her back on the Cordelier who was preaching the sermon. This particular instance of rudeness may have been provoked by the fact that the sermon was full of satirical allusions to monks who had deserted their calling, but Jeanne's bad manners were undoubtedly deliberate. It was in character for her to feel no obligation to be polite merely because she was a guest, and she probably thought the Cardinal's good manners an expression of hypocrisy rather than of tolerance.[49]

Jeanne was capable of subtlety when she chose, and with no hoped-for convert was this so necessary as with the eleven-year-old King of France who called Jeanne "aunt." (She was his father's first cousin.) In a long dispatch of November 26, Throckmorton reports to Queen Elizabeth two interviews he and Thomas Challoner, newly appointed ambassador to Spain, have recently had, one with the King and the other with the Queen of Navarre. Antoine's comment was characteristic:

> The King then desired that the Queen would by her Ambassador request the King of Spain to have consideration of him and his wife for the kingdom of Navarre being wrongfully withholden from them. His wife, to whom it belongs, reposes more trust in the amity of the Queen than in any other. And he thereupon desired Challoner to have his case recommended to the King of Spain, when it pleases the Queen to give him charge to do so.[50]

The conversation of the two Englishmen with Jeanne is one of the most curious episodes that has come down to us.

> They then went to the Queen of Navarre, unto whom Challoner used good words from the Queen, for which the Queen of Navarre thanked her, . . . The Queen [of Navarre] then took him by the hand and made him sit by her, and said to him the Queen [Elizabeth]'s credit is great, and the more so for standing so firmly in God's cause. [Jeanne] was glad to hear that the candles and candlesticks were removed from the Queen's chapel. The Queen of Navarre then said she would tell him a secret, but she must not be made the author of it, and desired him to write to [Elizabeth] that it may not be used thereafter.

Within the last few days the King [Charles IX] visited her, and walking aside to talk of things meet for his age, he said, Good aunt, I pray you tell me what doth this mean, that the King my uncle, your husband, doth every day go to Mass, and you come not there, nor my cousin your son, the Prince of Navarre? I answered (quoth the Queen), Sire, the King, my husband, doth so because you go thither, to wait upon you and to obey your order and commandment. Nay, aunt (quoth he), I do neither command him nor desire him to do so. But if it be naught (as I do hear say it is) he might well enough forbear to be at it, and offend me nothing at all; for if I might as well as he, and did believe of it as he doth, I would not be at it myself. The Queen said, Why Sire, what do you believe of it? The King answered, The Queen, my mother [Catherine de Medici] and my schoolmaster, M. de Cipière, doth tell me, that it is very good, and that I do there daily see God; but (said the King), I do hear by others that neither God is there nor anything very good. And surely, aunt, to be plain with you (quoth he), if it were not for the Queen my mother's pleasure, I would not be there myself. And therefore you may boldly continue and do as you do, and so may the King my uncle, your husband, use the matter according to his conscience [without regard] for any displeasure he shall do unto me. And surely, aunt (quoth he), when I shall be at my own rule I mean to quit the matter. But I pray you (said the King), keep this matter to yourself, and use it so that it come not to my mother's ears.[51]

Aside from the fact that Charles IX is known to have been a very impressionable child, it is hard to interpret this incident. The young King was not in a position to take independent action in 1561 even if he had wanted to.

With other young people of Protestant inclination, especially if she outranked their parents, Jeanne's proselytizing was more successful. It came to her attention that Catherine du Bellay, daughter of Elisabeth d'Yvetot and Martin du Bellay, had refused to accompany her mother to Mass and was being punished for it. On October 3, 1561 Jeanne initiated a correspondence with the mother, who is called Madame de Langey, from the name of her fief. Referring to the fact that Madame de Langey's late husband had grown up in Antoine's household, Jeanne says that she wishes to honor and continue the affectionate relations between their families. Coming to the point,

I cannot think that, as the mother of so good and virtuous a girl, daughter of so fine a man, it would be possible for you to treat her with such inhumanity and cruelty as . . . they say, greatly damaging your reputation. To remedy this I have wished to persuade you, cousin, and say frankly that if her religious views are the reason . . . you must realize that God's word separates fathers from children and husbands from wives. It recognizes nothing else in the world but serving purely the glory of Him who told us that anyone who loved his father and mother more than Him was not worthy of Him. . . . I pray you, be better advised. . . . Even if her opinion were not good, which I do not believe, reason would be a better way to bring her back than the violence you are using . . . especially in this time when the King does not wish the consciences of his subjects to be forced.[52]

Madame de Langey's reaction was to give up the struggle and turn her daughter over to Jeanne. The Queen of Navarre expresses her approval of this decision in a letter dated only November 1561. "I pray you send her soon, outfitted in a manner worthy of her family, with dresses and jewels, but you know what is needed, having been married from our house yourself."[53] Jeanne's dealings with Madame de Langey illustrate the power of the great nobles over those dependent on them. Highly placed persons, even members of the royal family, needed protection, and they paid for it by submitting to interference in their private lives. The girl, Catherine, remained a member of Jeanne's household for over two years, when she was married off to another of Jeanne's vassals. That the arrangement worked out well, at least from Jeanne's point of view, we know from a letter written the following May, when Catherine was to pay a short visit to her mother. "I have no girl in my service with whom I have greater reason to be satisfied . . . send her back soon. . . . I only wish her companions shared her habits."[54]

The unremitting pressure of the Huguenots in the autumn of 1561 made it necessary for the crown to provide them with a new statute or legal framework defining their rights. In a speech on January 3, 1562, Michel de L'Hôpital asked for full religious toleration. He was also the principal author of the document known as the Edict of January. While it fell far short of full toleration—the preamble specified that it was not to be construed as sanctioning the new religion—its concrete terms constituted the most liberal conditions French Protestantism had ever known or was to know again until the Edict of Nantes (1598), for which it was the model. The great new gain was that for the first time Calvinist worship *in public* was authorized, although qualified by hampering regulations.[55]

Beza and Coligny collaborated with the Chancellor in working it out and never was Huguenot optimism greater. The Protestant flood reached its high-water mark in the weeks of its preparation. Hubert Languet tells of public assemblies in the Paris region, attended "not by two or three hundred, but by two thousand, three thousand, and sometimes nine or ten thousand; today I estimate no less than fifteen thousand." In addition to many women, these crowds included officers of the crown, whose presence testifies to the indulgence of the royal authorities, despite frantic protests from the clergy and the agents of foreign Catholic powers.[56]

Catholic testimony is found in the letters of Santa Croce to Borromeo. As early as November 15 he comments on the Protestant assemblies and records his protests to Catherine, who responded evasively. By early January he is saying that if he were to be recalled from the French court the Huguenots would get the upper hand because the Catholic leaders would also retire in discouragement. At the same time he tries to mitigate the alarm in Rome. "I am told on reliable authority that only one-eighth, possibly only one-tenth, have left [the Roman church] contrary to what is generally said." In a less optimistic mood, he referred in another letter, to "this kingdom, half-Huguenot."[57]

The Cardinal was unduly alarmed. By the time the Edict was submitted to Parlement and the losing fight against registration had begun (January 17, 1562), the tide had begun to recede. By mid-February nobody could any longer look upon Calvinism as the wave of the future in France. It was doomed to remain the creed of a minority party, on the defensive against a formidable multipronged attack from the Counter-Reformation forces at home and abroad.*

COUNTEROFFENSIVE, NOVEMBER 1561–FEBRUARY 1562

Huguenot successes and the likelihood of further gains stimulated a Catholic counterattack, which gained momentum during November, December, and January. The French clergy, aided by outside reinforcements such as Father Laynez, General of the Jesuit Order, made a conscious evangelical effort, a counterreformation in the literal sense. From Parisian pulpits inflammatory sermons aroused the congregations against the royal family and the crown's officers as well as the Huguenots. As part of what they called the "reconquest," the Constable and the Bishop of

---

* E. Léonard, Le Protestant français (Paris, 1953), 16–18, summarizes estimates of Huguenot strength in this period. In 1561, Coligny claimed that there were 2,150 churches in France. The 1598 census estimated 1,250,000 souls, or 274,000 families, including 2,468 noble families. In Louis XIII's reign, that is, under the Edict of Nantes, about one-tenth of the population of Paris was Huguenot (30,000 out of 300,000), according to J. Pannier, historian of Huguenot Paris (L'Eglise Réformée de Paris sous Louis XIII (Paris, 1922).

Paris set up machinery for determining the number of heretics, parish by parish, and found that there were between four and five thousand declared Calvinists in the capital. Destruction of Huguenot property, assassinations, and other violent incidents were occurring all over France.[58]

On the international level, it was clear by late November that the Catholic powers, especially the King of Spain and the Duke of Savoy, might use armed intervention if necessary to keep France in the Roman camp. (Calvin feared that Geneva would be the first victim.) The threat of invasion was only one weapon in their arsenal. In order to solidify the Catholic faction and make Catherine entirely dependent upon it, their principal aim was to weaken the Huguenot party by separating its leaders. One way of bringing pressure to bear on Catherine was to gain Antoine for the Catholic party, and one way to weaken the Huguenots was to steal the first Prince of the Blood from them and exploit his position in the interests of resurgent Catholicism instead. A letter from Cardinal de Tournon to Cardinal Borromeo on February 4, 1562, makes the point in lucid terms. He reviews the policy of the Catholic party since the death of François II, as he sees it, "in short, to give [the Queen Mother] the benefit of all their help and advice so as to strengthen her courage and resolution." But, he continues, "They finally realized that, far from being cured, the evil in the kingdom was growing rapidly worse. They saw the Queen drawing the chiefs of the enemy more closely into her counsels. Consequently they decided, or rather came to understand, that it was necessary to win over the mind of the King of Navarre by playing upon his particular interests."[59]

Antoine thus became the focal point of the struggle for about three months. The Huguenots, especially Jeanne, made one last intensive drive to secure him as the leader of French Calvinism at exactly the time that the agents of Spain and the Papacy decided to do whatever was necessary to achieve the contrary result. The contest was very uneven. The correspondence of ambassadors and other agents of the interested parties, French, Spanish, Italian, German, and English, reveals a series of distinct but interrelated intrigues on the Catholic side, ranging from a plot to frighten Catherine by kidnaping the Duc d'Anjou to the Cardinal de Lorraine's efforts to exploit Protestant pluralism by bringing Lutheran theologians to the French court. Some of these illustrate only background aspects of the Spanish offensive against France or of the ultramontane offensive against Gallicanism; others relate to the struggle of the factions

Le Roy de nauarre Antoine de Bourbon

Antoine de Bourbon, Père de Henry IV.

ANTOINE DE BOURBON, KING OF NAVARRE

at court to dominate the crown; and still others revolve wholly around Antoine. The Catholic party knew that the price required to bring him definitely into their camp, if it were possible, was at least the promise of another kingdom in place of Navarre. So little did they trust him, however, that they determined to obtain prior concessions, abandonment of the Huguenots and separation from Jeanne if not repudiation of her as his wife, unless he could bring her with him back into the fold. In recent months it had been obvious to everyone that Antoine's only remaining interest in Jeanne lay in the "kingdom" and title that were his only because he was her husband. Thus the disintegration of their marriage was interwoven with Antoine's political interests, and both could be exploited by the Catholic party.

In Paris, Antoine's cronies who had been suborned by Chantonay, notably Lenoncourt and D'Escars, exerted their influence on the King of Navarre, while in Madrid a special envoy, the Seigneur d'Auzance, managed to persuade Philip to concede "in principle" that Antoine should be compensated for Navarre with another kingdom. It was made clear, however, that the implementation of the bargain on Philip's side would not take place until after Antoine had succeeded in abolishing Calvinist services, even in the private apartments of the Huguenot nobles, in expelling all the Calvinist ministers, and obtaining the restitution of all churches, chapels, and benefices that had been usurped. Sébastien de l'Aubespine, French ambassador to Spain, tried in vain to make Philip understand that the clock could not be turned back to 1559, but Elizabeth de Valois herself could get no further concessions.[60]

When D'Auzance arrived in St. Germain on January 2 he took the news of Philip's concession straight to Antoine, who gave him a hero's welcome and insisted that he repeat his message verbatim in the presence of friends called in to share his triumph. D'Auzance later had to repeat it a third time for Catherine and the King. Antoine then gave a great banquet and ball to celebrate. "This rejoicing," Chantonay wrote to Philip, "was so great and so extraordinary that everyone thought the fuss far greater than the news."[61]

About a month earlier Chantonay had told his master that the Huguenots were bidding in the same terms, and that Jeanne had promised her husband "the crown of a great kingdom, in three months," if he would declare decisively for Calvinism.[62] The kingdom of France is implied. This is probably a distortion of the Huguenot argument that Antoine stood to gain more by concerning himself with France—where he and his son had a legitimate claim to the throne—than by chasing after the will-o'-the-wisp of Tunis, Sardinia, and other places mentioned by the Spaniards. Antoine was thought to have "nothing but real women and imaginary crowns in his head." The *Histoire Ecclésiastique* reports him bedazzled with a vision of himself as "lord of the seas, with the galleys of France and Spain at his beck and call." Calvin wrote one last desperate letter to Antoine in January 1562, to give Jeanne every possible support. "Letters from the Queen, your wife, have emboldened us [to write]. God has touched her to the quick. . . . You are her chief . . . you should praise God that He has so disposed that instead, as formerly, of her not being an aid to you, now she applies herself . . . to her duty. Furthermore, Sire, since she is resolved to pay her back debts to God and make up for past faults, so it is up to you to hasten to march always first. It is the best of all your preeminences to behave so virtuously that she who wishes to please you has double reason for rejoicing in that, ranging herself with you, she also glorifies God. We cannot hide from you that up to now you have not acquitted yourself as God has a right to require of you."[63]

But the Huguenots could not offer the kingdom of France. In January 1562, Antoine took the irresistible Spanish bait, which carried with it the certainty of papal approval and the possibility—dangled by the Triumvirs—of the regency. Temporarily turning his back on hesitation, Antoine began furiously to carry out his side of the bargain. He spoke in Parlement against the Edict of January and insulted its liberal Catholic sponsors by calling them heretics and demanding their dismissal. He replaced his Huguenot preachers with conservative Roman Catholics. As one observer wrote, "The King of Navarre was never so earnest on the Protestant side as now zealous on the other."[64] He also tried to coerce Jeanne into following suit; when that proved impossible, he set about making her position at court untenable.

Antoine's change of direction had destroyed Catherine's carefully constructed balance of power. A Lieutenant-General who was also a leader of the Catholic party might attempt to take over the regency. He might even succeed. As Romier says, "after the King of Navarre's about-face . . . the superiority of the Catholic party was overwhelming."[65]

Antoine's lead was followed by some who had been considered firm Calvinists as well as many who had followed the movement only when the tide was rising. Now it was ebbing fast. On February 4, Catherine dismissed the liberal tutors of Charles IX and reinstated the former, conservative, ones. She forbade her ladies to discuss Calvinist doctrine or to read heretical books. At her command a number of men arrested in Paris for iconoclasm were hanged instead of released, as had been the recent practice. She decided to send an impressive delegation to the Council of Trent. By mid-February the Châtillons were leaving court and the Guises were expected to return. Santa Croce reflects the changed atmosphere in a letter to Cardinal Borromeo predicting that "the sect" will soon disappear in France and that "the faithful" have taken a new lease on life. "Even though there are today many Huguenots, I do not think there are more than three or four to each hundred Catholics and these seem to have much more devotion than was formerly to be found in this city." With Tournon and St. André advising the Queen and the Guises about to arrive, "one may expect that all the intentions [of members of the royal council] will be favorable to the Catholic religion."[66]

This time the papal Nuncio was right. When the crown ceased vacillating and the overwhelming majority of nobles closed ranks in support of the Roman church, the Calvinist movement was forced into the position of a dissident minority, which would soon resort to armed rebellion.

THE PARTING OF THE WAYS, JANUARY–MARCH 1562

Jeanne was by no means ignorant of the designs of the enemy. The chief reason for the intensity of Huguenot pressure on Antoine in the last months of 1561 was that the Spaniards were in a position to outbid the Huguenots with the King of Navarre. If it were possible to secure Antoine on the Huguenot side before Philip decided to gratify him, they reasoned, the party might be strengthened to the point where the royal family would change sides. The distribution of power made this hope unrealistic, but Huguenots do not easily retreat.

In addition to information provided by agents in the employ of the Huguenot leaders, Jeanne received valuable aid from those of Queen Elizabeth and from various mercenary secret agents indispensable to the conduct of sixteenth-century diplomacy. One of these, a member of the Estouteville family, was called the Vicomte de Gruz. Disgruntled because he had not been paid for former services to the French crown, he was looking for a new employer in the summer of 1561. In early August, he was approached by Chantonay.

The Spanish ambassador thought he had found his opportunity. After pointing out how badly the writer had been used . . . he offered him a large pension if he would enter into his master's service. The writer, feigning to agree and discoursing with him, learned much about the designs of Spain on France and their (sic) intrigues with the Pope . . . and other great lords comprised in their Holy League . . . together with many things concerning the Kings of France and Navarre. The writer took post to the Queen of Navarre at Blois, to whom he declared the whole matter, as she was much more discreet than her husband who is easy to be overreached by anyone cleverer than himself. The writer . . . informed her of the reply which the King of Spain and the Pope would make to her husband touching his kingdom . . . that meant . . . nothing less than the total ruin of his family [and told her that Philip] was plotting to deprive him of the succession to the French crown. . . . The writer begged the Queen of Navarre to inform her husband . . . but to do this with great caution.[67]

De Gruz asked to be taken into Elizabeth's service, but presumably was refused since there are no further dispatches of his in the Calendars of State Papers. Throckmorton probably thought that he was too well known to the other side to be useful, but the episode proves that Jeanne was alerted to some aspects of Spanish strategy even before she arrived at court.

Chantonay's dispatches of succeeding months reflect Jeanne's unrelenting pressure on Antoine. On November 18 he wrote, "every day the Queen of Navarre renews her efforts to make her husband declare for the reform"; other letters repeat the theme.[68] One should not underestimate the concerted pressure of three such personalities as Beza, Coligny, and Jeanne. The new Venetian ambassador, Marc-Antonio Barbaro, though he mistakenly thought that Antoine was "persuaded that Calvinism was the path to salvation" and that he "much loved" his wife, reported accurately that "she had a very clever and penetrating mind, harasses him night and day, and strengthens his opinions every time anything occurs which might weaken them."[69] Nor did she give up in January, when D'Auzance brought Philip's reply from Spain. According to Throckmorton, as late as March 6, just before she was forced to flee, the Queen of Navarre with Coligny and Condé was standing more firmly in defense of the cause than ever.[70]

This was not without some effect on Antoine, as long as Philip procrastinated, and until the end of the year, his counterthrusts were more or less perfunctory. But when the Spaniards made it clear that he would have to prove himself, Antoine began a brutal onslaught on Jeanne.

At first he attempted to "convert" her, in the sense of external conformity to the Roman church. Jeanne's response is summarized in the *Histoire Ecclésiastique:* "The Queen of Navarre, a very wise and virtuous princess, tried to soften her husband . . . in vain . . . with tears and prayers . . . moving everyone to pity her. When the Queen Mother tried to persuade her to accommodate her husband, she finally replied that, rather than ever go to Mass, if she held her kingdom and her son in her hand, she would throw them both to the bottom of the sea. This was the reason they then left her in peace on this matter."[71]

Antoine was forced to abandon his first objective—to lead Jeanne to Mass—but his second one provided her with very little "peace": Calvinist services in her apartments must cease and she must not attend them elsewhere. In the second stage of the struggle Jeanne resorted, not to tears but to argument, using what Chantonay describes as "inflexible logic" and "throwing her husband's inconsistencies in his teeth."[72] She finally relinquished her own services, but attended those in Condé's quarters. This continued for some days until Chantonay reminded Antoine that total dissociation from Calvinism was Philip's primary condition, which obliged the King of Navarre to confront his wife. The carriage Jeanne had ordered and the members of her household who were to accompany her waited while the King and Queen of Navarre exchanged bitter recriminations "so loud that everyone in the chateau could hear." Jeanne finally dismissed the carriage. When Antoine and Jeanne spent some time in Paris at the house of the Bishop of Auxerre, she was able to escape surveillance and attend the Calvinist services at Popincourt once or twice, but more often she was constrained. The quarrels of the King and Queen of Navarre are remarked upon with increasing frequency.[73] If there had been a time for reconciliation and compromise, it had passed.

Observers dwell on the precarious state of Jeanne's health. On November 21, Antoine told Chantonay that she was so ill he did not dare use physical force to bring Jeanne to Mass. The ambassador adds, "Madame de Vendôme is really ill and the doctors are certain that she cannot recover." He predicts that she will soon leave court to take the baths in her own country. The Cardinal of Ferrara says that Antoine was postponing his command for her departure, "either because of the harsh winter season or because of the indisposition of the Princess." On January 10, an English agent in Paris reports, "the Queen of Navarre is very sick and in danger."[74]

Jeanne's stubbornness had made it as impossible for Antoine to fulfill Philip's second condition as the first. He therefore shifted his tactics again: he would disassociate himself from Jeanne and drive her from the court. Bordenave states that his Catholic "seducers so incensed the King of Navarre against his wife that he sought to obtain a divorce from her in the court of Rome [on the grounds] of manifest heresy." The Cardinal of Ferarra is alleged to have promised a papal dispensation and the Cardinal de Lorraine to have persuaded Antoine to imprison Jeanne. Davila and Brantôme say so too, and there is no doubt that Jeanne herself believed it, although there is no documentary proof that legal steps toward divorce were ever initiated.[75]

Of repudiation and separation in the personal sense there is a great deal of evidence. After the failure of Antoine's first two efforts, he asked Philip to accept Jeanne's exile from the court and personal separation from himself as sufficient fulfillment of his side of the bargain. On January 29 the Duke of Alva notified Chantonay that the King of Spain had agreed.[76] At the same time it was rumored that the Guises were spurring Antoine on by holding out the lure of a young and ardently Catholic bride—their niece Mary Stuart—to be his queen in the new kingdom. It is doubtful if anyone, with the possible exception of the gullible Antoine, took this proposition very seriously, but it shows what was being said of Jeanne's marriage. The Spanish party was simultaneously trying to drive away Coligny, Jeanne's strongest ally. As Chantonay noted on February 11, "with the Châtillons chased out, it should not be hard to get rid of Madame de Vendôme."[77]

Catherine was reluctant to see them go, leaving her with nobody but Condé—and him not for long as it turned out—to balance the increasing power of the Catholic party. She told Throckmorton that she had asked the Huguenot leaders not to leave, but swore him to secrecy in the hope that the other side would not have their suspicions confirmed. Because of the pressures on herself, Catherine was cultivating Jeanne to a marked degree in the final days before Jeanne's departure. When Catherine received foreign ambassadors, the Queen of Navarre sat so close to the sovereigns that nothing could be said to them without her overhearing it, a source of embarrassment to those, like Chantonay, who often came to complain of the crown's indulgence to the Huguenots.[78] On February 19 the two queens spent a day in Paris, ostensibly shopping, "disguised as bourgeois ladies in simple headdress. They visited the boutiques around the Palais de Justice and on the Pont St. Michel, where they heard many murmurings against the great of the realm, even against the Queen of Navarre, in her presence."[79] In later correspondence with Catherine, Jeanne sometimes appeals to the memory of their friendly association at this time, when their respective predicaments brought them into close cooperation, and in the *Mémoires* she says that the Queen Mother was even considering placing herself and the King under the protection of Condé.

The Queen of Navarre had other defenders in court circles, more sincere if less powerful. They too had an ulterior motive—the defense of Calvinism—but this was shared by Jeanne herself. When Antoine first spoke of expelling his wife from court, Madame de Crussol, as spokesman for the Huguenot leaders, made so eloquent a plea in her defense that the Spanish ambassador credited it with delaying Jeanne's exile.[80] Queen Elizabeth's agents in Paris were sympathetic bystanders, and Throckmorton's dispatches reflect indignation at Jeanne's treatment and admiration for her courage. Their position did not permit them to intervene directly, but their reports made a sufficient impression on their Queen for her to instruct Throckmorton "to encourage the Queen Mother, the Queen of Navarre, and the Prince of Condé to show their constancy [and to convey] her intention to stand by them."[81] (This letter, dated March 31, arrived too late to affect the immediate situation for Jeanne, who was then in flight somewhere between Meaux and Vendôme.)

In Geneva, Jeanne's plight, indicative as it was of the danger to the cause, provoked an expression of sympathy, support, and encouragement from Calvin.

> Your husband the King has long been attacked by two horns of the devil, D'Escars and the Bishop of Auxerre. Not only has he allowed himself to be overcome, but he himself takes arms against God and His people. I mention only what everybody knows. I know, Madame, that you are the prime target of his arts. But even if the difficulties were one hundred times worse, God's virtue will be triumphant when we shall [be able to] take refuge in it. . . . In the meanwhile, Madame, do not fail to stand firm.[82]

Jeanne's retainers, who shared her sufferings and her dangers, also supported her. One of her young ladies-in-waiting, Georgette de Montenay, expressed her admiration in a sonnet dedicated to the Queen of Navarre, in which she assures Jeanne that God will soon avenge her "in a wondrous fashion, in spite of Satan's rage. Console yourself, then, O Queen with

your God, who hates lies . . . if the wicked are against you it only re-
dounds to your honor, on earth [it earns you] a bright light and in
Heaven an angel's glory."[83]

A trivial pretext was found to force Catherine's hand so that she gave
in to Antoine's insistence that Jeanne be sent away. Chantonay's son was
baptized on Thursday, March 6, with the Kings of France and Navarre
serving as godfathers. Jeanne had not only refused to attend but she
had prevented Henri from going. Throckmorton told Cecil on March 14,
"The King of Navarre has lately tormented his wife because she would
not suffer the Prince, her son, to go to Mass nor to be present at the
christening of the Spanish ambassador's son." Chantonay seized the
occasion to demand Jeanne's immediate expulsion, even threatening to
depart himself if the Queen of Navarre did not.[84]

The importance the opposite party attached to Jeanne's removal can
be measured by their insistence upon it. Chantonay wrote to Philip on
March 25, "It is true that if the court goes to Blois Madame de Vendôme
will be separated from it by only 13 or 14 leagues [in Vendôme], but if
only she is not present at court religious affairs would go better, given
time." The Cardinal of Ferrara congratulated himself on obtaining a
promise from Catherine that no Protestant services would be permitted at
court after Jeanne's departure.[85]

Antoine finally issued a direct command by letter for Jeanne to
leave. We know of this through Chantonay's dispatch and cannot be sure
of the exact day. Whether he feared that he would give in again if
obliged to confront Jeanne in person or merely wanted to avoid another
scene, he gave as his reason that he had no time to take the trip to court
from Paris, where he was staying.[86] Antoine already had removed Henri
from Jeanne's household to his own, and he subsequently dismissed the
Prince's Huguenot tutor, La Gaucherie, and his *gouverneur,* Beauvoir,
replacing them with conservative Catholics. He allowed Jeanne to say
goodbye to her son. The Cardinal of Ferrara says that she addressed him
"a long and severe remonstrance, to persuade him never to go to Mass,
in any guise whatever, even going so far as to say that if he disobeyed
her in this, he could be sure that she would disinherit him and would not
be known in the future as his mother."[87]

Bordenave is silent about this farewell scene. The Cardinal's source
was probably one of the servants Antoine had placed in Henri's entourage.
Jeanne, in the *Mémoires,* merely mentions as an instance of God's grace

that "miraculously, my son has been preserved in the purity of his religion, amid so many assaults [on it]."[88] She said this six and one half years later, in November 1568. In fact, Henri had held out with amazing stubbornness, for about four months, but in the end he had attended Mass with his father and, later, with the rest of the royal family. His mother's remark must refer to the fact that she had been able to bring him back to the Calvinist fold after several years as a practicing Catholic. His future life would show that Henri had a flexibility in religion which differed from his father's *ondoyance* in that it was a function of realistic political aims and not mere whim or pursuit of ephemeral advantage.

Concern for the religious aspects of his upbringing was not the only reason Jeanne feared to leave Henri with his father. Not long before their households had been separated, she had been obliged to discharge a family of Portuguese servants because of Antoine's (unsuccessful) attempt to seduce the daughter. We learn from Antoine's correspondence, what Jeanne probably did not know, that on March 8 he asked Artus de Cossé, Seigneur de Gonor, for a loan "of at least 6000 francs to meet the obligation of my son for an assignation which was arranged for him."[89] Henri had just turned eight years old. (Antoine's unwillingness to face the consequences of his own vices is among the characteristics that embarrass those who, like the royalist historians, wish to find virtue in him.)

The Châtillons had left court in February. On March 1, Huguenots holding services in Vassy were massacred by the Duc de Guise. Shortly thereafter Catherine moved the court to Fontainebleau, more remote from the turbulent capital than St. Germain. Paris gave Guise a hero's welcome on March 16—foreshadowing its role as the stronghold of the Holy League in later years. Condé left court on March 23 for Meaux, and began to mold the seigneurs who came from all directions into a Huguenot army. Civil war, so long dreaded, was becoming a reality. The air was full of rumors, including the intention of the King of Navarre to imprison his wife. On March 27 or 28 Jeanne fled Fontainebleau as secretly as possible. She went first to Meaux, but remained only long enough for an interview with her brother-in-law before continuing her flight southward.[90]

Jeanne's decision to cast her lot with Calvinism had withstood its first severe test. Her faith had not only survived, it had grown stronger, probably for reasons that had little to do with doctrine. In the words of one commentator, a moderate Catholic whose objectivity makes him reliable,

It must be confessed that [the King of Navarre] did not take the best means of winning [Jeanne] back to the true religion by using force, by showing his disgust with her, while at the same time entertaining propositions of another marriage and taking a mistress at court. [He gave] the Huguenots the opportunity to speak adversely of his behavior, which was even more displeasing to a high-minded woman. [She] could not do other than belong to the party which pitied her the most and from which, outwardly, she received the most comfort and support.[91]

It was the end of an era, for Jeanne and for the Huguenot cause. Although Antoine lived another eight months and no legal separation took place, their marriage was destroyed beyond repair in the opening weeks of 1562. It had disintegrated during the previous year, but, as long as Antoine still hesitated, conceivably it could be salvaged, at least in the sense of a conventional façade, together with Antoine's association with Calvinism. Henceforth neither was possible. Jeanne's career as a wife—in name—had only a few months of denouement to run, but her career as a leader in the losing cause of French Protestantism was just beginning.

VII

STRATEGIC NEUTRALITY:
THE FIRST CIVIL WAR

MARCH 1562 – MARCH 1563

JEANNE would probably have returned to her own domains in the spring of 1562 in any case, but the coincidence of the disintegration of her marriage with the outbreak of civil war, Antoine having gone over to the other side, created special problems and dangers. She faced a number of choices. One possibility was to join the Cardinal de Bourbon, who was attempting to mediate; another, at the opposite extreme, was to rally to her other brother-in-law, the Prince de Condé, leader of the militant Huguenots. Still another possibility was behind-the-scene cooperation with Catherine.

When Jeanne left the court, she went first to Meaux, where Condé was gathering the Huguenot army. In the *Mémoires,* written six years later, she says that Catherine had expressed a wish to escape the domination of the Triumvirate and place herself (and the King) under the protection of Condé,[1] and that Coligny and Condé should be warned not to trust any royal command until then because it would have been issued under pressure from the ultra-Catholic party. Jeanne also claims that after her arrival in Vendôme, a few weeks later, Catherine, while ostensibly asking her to persuade Condé to lay down his arms, really desired exactly the opposite and so informed Jeanne by a confidential messenger. She further alleges that Catherine urged her to kidnap the Queen's two youngest children (from Amboise) and conduct them to Condé. Although un-

186

confirmed, this is not impossible, given Catherine's dilemma at the time, her willingness to exploit any situation, and her skill at playing a double game.

Whatever Catherine's intentions, Jeanne avoided committing herself. Somewhat later in the spring, when Catherine was herself negotiating with Condé, she wrote the Queen Mother in a rather aloof tone: "I am not in touch with them [Condé and Coligny] and it would be unfitting for me to advise so many people who know more than I. I hope you will excuse me. All I was able to do was send a messenger . . . as you requested, and from [Condé's] reply I conclude that he has no other desire but to obey and serve you."[2] Only at the end of the letter does she show real feeling, "I remind you of your promise not to ask my son to do anything contrary to what I have taught him."

Jeanne thus refused either to mediate openly or to help Catherine; neither did she officially join Condé—until more than six years later. This was probably a disappointment to the Prince and others who had grown accustomed to her active participation in the movement during the previous months. Her brief visit to Meaux may, nevertheless, have affected the Huguenot leadership. De Ruble, without giving any evidence, declares that it was she who worked out the plan for the seizure of Orléans by Condé on April 1—within forty-eight hours of Jeanne's interview with him. "It was to the Queen of Navarre that the Huguenot party owed this act of boldness, even of genius, the only one in the First Civil War [see Appendix B]. After the arrival of his sister-in-law, Condé seemed transformed, his indecisive ambition gave way to firm courage."[3] Jeanne's presence had this galvanizing effect on later occasions, which makes De Ruble's speculation plausible. That her "neutrality" in the spring of 1562 was but another example of her skill at dissimulation, is even more likely.

Jeanne's correspondence at this time with the Vicomte de Gourdon and her actions as soon as she reached the safety of her own domains, show beyond doubt her loyalty to Calvinism.[4] The course she chose was a bold one, because she had to pursue it alone: a policy of disengagement from all factions, although she shared with the court party a desire for peace and with Condé the advocacy of Huguenot privileges and a sense of injustices to be redressed. She decided to concentrate her efforts in her own domains, to assert her sovereignty and to strengthen her authority, while preparing to defend herself and her lands in every way possible.

An expression she used several times in later years reflects her aims: "God . . . has always granted me the grace to preserve this little corner of Béarn, where, little by little, good increases and evil diminishes."[5]

Although in the long run neutrality proved impossible, Jeanne had a great deal to gain by maintaining her strategic neutrality, including time—six years—and by any other choice she stood to lose things she could not afford to lose. Antoine, backed by the Catholic party, was preparing not only to repudiate, but, according to some, to capture and imprison her.[6] The military forces of the Huguenots would prove no match for the royal armies. Condé was impulsive, inexperienced, and not in a position to take on the defense of Jeanne's widespread domains, encompassing all of southwestern France, against a concerted move by Philip from across the Pyrenees and the royal forces from the north. If Jeanne yielded to Catherine's wishes, she would not only sacrifice her convictions and lose her independence—and the chance to establish Calvinism in her own lands—but she would also expose these to the ravages of German mercenaries for whose services the Huguenot leaders were already negotiating, with the financial aid of Queen Elizabeth.* Most important of all, by any other course she would further jeopardize her son's position and his inheritance. Henri was already a hostage in the hands of Antoine and Catherine; by refusing to join Condé, Jeanne kept open, on reasonably amicable terms, avenues of communication with the Queen Mother, through which she could oblige Catherine to keep her informed. She exploited this conventional civility to her own advantage. By refusing to condemn Condé, on the other hand, she maintained relations with the Huguenot party, the Calvinist movement, and the Bourbon family—in order of ascending importance—against the day when she (and Henri) would find it possible, desirable, or necessary to join them openly.

In the weeks of her flight at the start of the civil wars Jeanne had only a small suite of personal retainers and no competent adviser. Under pressure from Antoine, she had left her able secretary, Victor Brodeau, at court, which had the advantage that he could supply her with reliable

---

* These negotiations culminated in the Treaty of Hampton Court, signed on September 10, by which Queen Elizabeth undertook to help the Huguenots in exchange for Le Havre, pending the return of Calais. There is considerable controversial literature on this point, and some French historians have accused Coligny and Condé of treason. Jeanne was not involved in the negotiations, although she was undoubtedly informed of and probably in favor of them.

information. She had great confidence in Brodeau and often entrusted him with important missions, but he was less an adviser than an employee. Louis de Goulard, Sieur de Beauvoir, *gouverneur* of Henri de Béarn and a real friend and counselor to Jeanne in later years, had been a member of her entourage in the previous months at court; it is possible that Jeanne's reliance on him dates from this anguished period.

Jeanne's isolation is shown in a letter written to Gourdon shortly before she left Paris. After deploring the "discord prevailing in the kingdom" and the loss of influence of "those known to be most expert in matters of doctrine and government," she says, "In such times I am in perplexity and need the comfort and advice of a loyal friend. Please come, or at least write and tell me what you think should be done and your opinion of all that has happened since Guise's outrage at Vassy [massacre of Huguenots] and other infractions of the Edicts."[7] Gourdon's reply approves Jeanne's course: "since you are deprived of your husband's support and threatened with the loss of your lands, you should do nothing whatever openly contrary to his wishes. As far as religion is concerned, everybody knows and nobody doubts that Your Majesty, so enlightened and virtuously steadfast, follows the reform and supports it. It is not necessary to furnish your enemies with any further acts or declarations." He promises to stop and see her, "to receive instructions" in April, when he plans to join Condé.[8]

Further evidence that prudence rather than indecision was the ruling consideration lies in Jeanne's correspondence with the authorities in Geneva during these difficult weeks. On March 10 she had asked permission to retain in her service the Sieur de St. Germier* who had been "loaned" to the court of Navarre in April 1561. He was undoubtedly the bearer of verbal messages and questions as well as the letter.[9] Even more important was Jeanne's meeting during her flight with Theodore Beza, chief spiritual counselor of the Huguenots, who had been opposed to resistance by force. In the spring of 1562 he was with Condé, first at Meaux and then at Orléans. Sometime before April 5, at Olivet, a village near Orléans in the direction of Jeanne's immediate destination, Vendôme, Jeanne met again with Beza, "to whom I told everything."[10] Jeanne was indeed "between two fires," to use her own expression, or

---

* Antoine de Lutrec, Sieur de St. Germier, a well-known jurisconsultist and native of Navarre, was condemned for heresy and took refuge in Geneva in 1555. The City Council had granted him permission to "visit" Jeanne on April 3, 1561.

possibly three, with Antoine issuing orders in apparent contradiction to Catherine, and Condé suspicious of her intentions. She was also in very poor health and had to stop several times and take to her bed, thus increasing the risk of capture.

The enforced secrecy of the trip makes it hard to know exactly when Jeanne reached Vendôme, but it was certainly before May 3, when she wrote letters from there which have survived. She dared stay only a short time. Vendôme was the seat of Antoine's family, and she was warned repeatedly that he intended to imprison her there. The only known event of her stay in Vendôme is a subject of controversy. Shortly after her arrival, a band of Calvinists sacked the churches of the town and the chapel of the ducal chateau, and then violated the tombs of the Bourbons. The publicists of the Guise party were quick to exploit the episode; it is brought up endlessly in pamphlets throughout the civil wars. In succeeding centuries it has been cited by some Catholic historians as an example of Huguenot atrocities—and as proof of Jeanne's fanaticism, although the exact identity of the vandals and whether they acted with Jeanne's approval, explicit or implicit, is not known. (The question of Jeanne's tolerance is dealt with in Chapter X.)

Ever since Antoine's subjects in Vendôme had learned of his abandonment of Calvinism, persecution of the Huguenot minority had increased. It is possible that the May outrages were perpetrated by local Huguenots who dared to take vengeance because of Jeanne's presence, in which case she could not be held directly responsible and may not even have known about it until too late. On the other hand, there were some rabid Calvinists among the Gascons in her suite and it is possible that they may have joined in, or even initiated, the sack. It still could be conceivable that it was done without Jeanne's knowledge, not to mention her approval. In the absence of certainty, the spectrum of opinion ranges from belief that, although Jeanne knew about it and did nothing to stop it, she took no initiative ("she allowed her soldiers to vent their fury"), through a belief that she "encouraged" or "condoned" it, to a belief that she commanded and even witnessed and "gloated over" it.[11] This last, most unfavorable, interpretation, is that of Chantonay, an excellent source for Spanish opinion and a good one for events at court which he witnessed, but hardly reliable in the present instance. Partly because Jeanne subsequently sent coin obtained by melting down some of the Vendôme treasures to Condé, De Ruble accepts this last view, and, without excusing Jeanne, attempts to explain it as a natural reaction to the painful and humiliating events of recent months: "sacrificed to unworthy rivals, violently separated from her son, expelled from court under threat, repudiated in fact and soon to be repudiated by law . . . chased through the countryside . . . what woman's heart, wife, mother, and queen, would not be ulcerated by such outrages? Jeanne could not withstand the passion of vengeance."[12] He cites Beza's letter of May 23 to Jeanne as evidence that she had a guilty conscience. This long letter answers one from Jeanne, unfortunately lost, in sufficient detail for us to be sure that she had sought his reaction to the episode.

On the first point you mention, all I can say of the destruction of images is what I have always felt and preached, namely that this kind of behavior does not please me at all, especially as it has no sanction [in the Bible] and it speaks more of impetuosity than of zeal. Nevertheless, idols and idolatry are against God's will, and it seems that in so widespread a movement there may be some secret action of God, who by this means chooses the humble to shame the great and the proud. I confine myself to reproving that which should be reproved and to moderating such impetuosity as much as possible. The destruction of the tombs is wholly inexcusable, and I can assure you, Madame, that M. le Prince [Condé] is not only resolved to investigate it down to the last detail but to punish those responsible so as to make an example of them. . . . For my part I shall look into it and let us hope that we will see some results from my efforts [esperons que nous verrons l'effet de ma diligence].[13]

The tone of Beza's reply implies that he and Jeanne agree in disapproval. Condé opposed iconoclasm and had recently sent Beza to Angers to restrain the faithful.[14] Jeanne may have mentioned the episode in order to assure her brother-in-law that she supported party discipline while remaining aloof from active participation. In any case, Beza's letter is not a reproach to Jeanne, but an assurance of support.

Jeanne had evidently asked Condé for an armed escort to accompany her through Guyenne to Béarn, and Beza transmits the answer: "As to your departure, it seems to us that much the best thing would be for you to escape as quietly as possible, partly so that you could be sooner in your own domains where I assume you would be much safer . . . and partly because you could take advantage of the bands coming from your lands who will not only have cleared the way, but also can serve as your escort." After stating that Condé cannot spare the men, Beza points out that for Jeanne to move with even a small army would increase her danger by "irritating you know who" [*ceux qui scavés*]. This is a clear reference to Catherine and Antoine.

News of the outrages in Vendôme reached the court on May 21, and observers report that the "King of Navarre" was furious. Chantonay wrote Philip that Antoine swore vengeance on Jeanne, that he planned to get the King to sequester Jeanne's lands, turning the administration over to him, and condemn her to life imprisonment. The approving comment of the Spanish ambassador is, "this would provide a fine example for the great of this kingdom."[15] If any concrete implementation of Antoine's proposal was undertaken at this time we do not know of it, although eventually the Spaniards pursued just such a policy.

Antoine, who was enjoying popularity in court circles as a result of his recent adherence to the Catholic party, had begun to treat his wife as an acknowledged enemy in the late spring of 1562. It did not suit Jeanne's policy to reciprocate, however. Beza's letter deals at great length with her inquiry about why she and Antoine were no longer mentioned by name in the public prayers at Condé's headquarters. We infer that she was indignant from the amount of persuasive detail in Beza's reply and from the fact that he says, "I think the only person to whom I have communicated your wishes has already written you."[16] This could only mean Calvin himself, or Condé. Beza assures Jeanne that he shares her anguish on the subject, but shows that the facts of the situation make it necessary to refuse her request that the prayers be restored. "As long as your husband the King gave some appearance of the fear of God, he was named in the prayers with you—in the hope that he would gradually benefit from it, as he has so often protested he would." Even "after he joined God's enemies, we nevertheless continued . . . still more ardently," but now that "he has declared himself the leader and protector of those whose hands are stained with the blood of the children of God . . . and who have always been their desperate enemies and persecutors . . . consider, Madame, what the effect would be if we pray [for God's help] against His enemies and those of His Church while at the same time naming one of their chiefs as our own?" Beza tries to soften this straightforward statement by saying that he personally has not given up praying in private that Antoine may return to the fold, and that in the meanwhile he and Jeanne can be considered to be included in the collective public prayers for all the Princes of the Blood. Not even the King of

France or Condé himself is named in the public prayers in Orléans, *pour evitter à toutte jallousie*. Beza urges her to overcome the temptation of adding omission of the prayers to her sorrows, assuring her that he would sooner forget himself than Jeanne and those close to her in his own prayers.

Whether or not Jeanne was mollified by Beza's response on other matters, she followed his advice about her departure, possibly because there was no viable alternative. Sometime in the early part of June she left Vendôme and headed for Béarn by rapid and exhausting marches on a circuitous route, never knowing when she might be overtaken or captured in ambush.

JEANNE AND MONLUC: THE INITIAL CONFLICT

Between Vendôme and the safety of Béarn lay Guyenne, where Jeanne held in fief lands and titles (inherited from her mother) much less under her control than the smaller domains of her father, where she claimed sovereignty. In Guyenne, civil war had broken out in 1561 and Blaise de Monluc had been put in command by Catherine as deputy for Antoine, the King's Lieutenant-Governor. Monluc's appointment had been hailed by the Spaniards somewhat optimistically—"Guyenne has found its savior."[17] With very little money and not much substantial backing from the crown, Monluc and his deputy, Charles de Coucy, Sieur de Burie, had been trying for several months to "restore order," that is, to suppress the Calvinists, since, as Monluc reported to Catherine, "all Guyenne is aflame under the banner of the reform."[18] The news of Condé's seizure of Orléans, April 1, 1562, had complicated Monluc's problem and he was trying to secure Toulouse and Bordeaux, seats of Parlements and the two chief cities of the region. In June, after Jeanne's departure from Vendôme, still another task had been imposed upon him by Antoine—to prevent Jeanne's escape into Béarn and perhaps, to capture her. Although there is no evidence of definite orders for her capture, Jeanne, among others, believed the repeated rumors and warnings.[19] Thus in the early summer of 1562 a series of bitter clashes was initiated between the fierce Monluc and the intransigent Jeanne, in which neither would give quarter.

On June 4, an emissary sent by Jeanne caught up with Monluc on his way to aid Burie, who was experiencing difficulty in holding Bordeaux. His mission was to assure Monluc that "there was no need to proceed since the Queen of Navarre and M. de Burie had arranged everything and she had left France (sic) especially to appease the troubles, and see to it that those of the Religion [Calvinists] were allowed to keep their arms."[20] This posed a dilemma for Monluc, who well knew, after a lifetime in the service of the French crown, how rapidly things changed at court and how risky it was to err in the direction of too much zeal. To oppose Jeanne might be to disregard the real wishes of Catherine as opposed to her expressed wishes. Moreover, Jeanne had recently sent messages to the Parlement of Bordeaux, which, despite strong anti-Huguenot sentiments, had responded by sending a delegation to pay her homage.[21]

Jeanne's strategy is clear: to separate Burie from Monluc (there was considerable rivalry between them), and to neutralize as far as possible the influence of both with the Parlement of Bordeaux. To Catherine she could write that she had tried to pacify Guyenne by advising the Protestant leader Duras* to retire to Orléans. This was a clever move. Protestant strategy was precisely to gather their forces in Orléans; what Jeanne claimed as an act of "pacification" conformed to Condé's policy rather than to Catherine's, but the Queen Mother could hardly object to anything done in the name of peace. In the *Mémoires* Jeanne claims that Catherine "approved everything I had done and made an infinity of complaints against my husband and of the fact that she lacked the means to do what she really wished."[22]

We have the words of one reliable witness, a moderate Catholic, that he at least believed in Jeanne's sincerity. Berenger de Portal, Sieur de La Pradalle, royal administrator of finances in Guyenne, who had several times acted as intermediary between Jeanne and Monluc, wrote to the King on August 17: "The Queen of Navarre, greatly and ardently desiring [*desirant d'une très grande et ardente affection*] the end of the disturbances, murders, sacks, and lawlessness of Guyenne, has often written to MMs. de Burie and Monluc, and to the Parlement of Bordeaux, begging them to send [envoys] to her for this purpose . . . but the outcome could not be favorable as long as MMs. de Burie and Monluc were not willing to carry out or even to consider the two points [of the Edict of January] assuring liberty of conscience and the [Protestant] right to be left in peace."[23]

* Symphorien de Durfort, Seigneur de Duras, leading Huguenot commander of the region.

Monluc's hesitation was not to last long and Jeanne did not count on it. She feared that she would be caught in an indefensible place or that her strength would give out and she would be unable to travel fast enough to escape. She had sent word to Armand de Gontaut, Sieur d'Audaux, one of her lieutenants in Béarn, to assemble an army and clear a path for her between Périgord and Béarn. Starting with a mere handful, he went from town to town and from chateau to chateau, collecting recruits and equipping them at his own expense, without stripping the Béarnais garrisons, until he had gathered about five hundred knights. Jeanne later reimbursed him for this loyal and generous response.[24]

Jeanne meanwhile was following a roundabout route, avoiding fortified towns and hoping the royal authorities would not know exactly where she was. Repeated warnings that orders had been issued for her arrest increased her anxiety to keep on the move, but the critical state of her health forced her to call a temporary halt.[25] She chose as her refuge, in late July, the chateau of Caumont (Lot-et-Garonne), property of an important noble family, Huguenot but ardently royalist. The chateau was almost impregnable; Monluc himself says so. Even so, she stayed only a few days and would have left sooner had she not been confined to her bed.[26] As soon as possible she continued her journey by boat, down the Garonne to Bordeaux, where she was received with civility although some elements of the population murmured against her.[27] Again she moved on quickly, crossing the deserted plain of the Landes to Béarn. The immediate danger was now behind and she arrived in Pau about mid-August.[28] From there she went almost immediately, with an armed escort of loyal Béarnais, to the small health resort of Eaux-Chaudes that she favored over the better-known Cauterets, preferred by Marguerite. There she could at last draw breath—but not for long.

The struggle with Monluc had only begun. Jeanne had escaped for the moment, but the Protestants, under Duras (who instead of going to Orléans had made an unsuccessful attempt to take Bordeaux), suffered a series of grave defeats. Monluc's victorious men terrorized the countryside. He boasted that "one could follow my trail . . . by the corpses hanging from the trees along the road; one hanging makes a greater impression than one hundred killed in battle."[29] Bergerac, Sainte-Foy, Agen, Lectoure—all the principal towns of Guyenne were experiencing conquest by Catholic armies in the late summer and early fall of 1562. Catholic, but not exclusively French, for since mid-July the royal armies had been reinforced by Spanish units, the first to fight in the French Wars of Religion.*

Duras, commanding the weakened Protestant forces, could bolster up Montauban, the only fortified city in Guyenne still in Huguenot hands, but he was unsuccessful in his most important assignment: to march with his reassembled army of 8000 to the side of Condé. By defeating Duras at the battle of Vergt (between Bergerac and Périgueux) on October 9, Monluc won the first round for the control of Guyenne by preventing the two Protestant armies from joining forces.[30]

Monluc had acquired great fame as a shrewd and imaginative captain as well as an unenviable reputation for atrocities. He had admirers and defenders, but his enemies were even more impassioned. Not the least of these was the Queen of Navarre. "God knows she hates me," he wrote, "and she has baptized me a tyrant, with all the insults known to man."[31] The antagonism was mutual. Not only did Monluc correspond with Philip in the hope that the Spanish King would commission him to invade Béarn (which the French crown was unwilling to do as long as Jeanne remained "neutral"), but he went so far as to say in public that he hoped to be sent to Béarn because he was "very eager to find out if it was as much fun to sleep with queens as with other women."[32] This remark, which created a scandal when it was repeated at court and something of an international incident between France and England, was typical of Monluc after the victory of Vergt.[33] Although gratified by the extravagant praise of the courtiers, who dubbed him "hero," "liberator," and "pillar of the crown," he was too realistic to be taken in by it.

In Guyenne, all was quiet on the surface in late autumn. Monluc said, "nobody dares admit that he had been of the Religion, but there is fire in the ashes."[34] Jeanne was the principal manipulator of the bellows which rekindled the flame. As De Ruble says, "The victor of Vergt was keeping watch on the frontiers of Béarn. [Monluc] realized that the Queen of Navarre was his real opponent, the only one worthy of him. . . . He had surrounded Béarn with a network of zealous observers, constantly on the alert so that the slightest move of the Princess could be spied upon. . . . Monluc was determined to prevent the execution of her plans."[35] To this end he took up residence in Agen, about equidistant from Montauban, the headquarters of Protestant resistance, Toulouse and

---

* The last Spanish forces left France after the Treaty of Vervins, 1598, ending the war between Philip II and Henri IV.

Bordeaux, both recently conquered but seething under the surface, and Périgord and Béarn. A state of potential civil war prevailed, with abortive uprisings and reprisals, especially in Bordeaux. Behind each Huguenot move Monluc (rightly) saw the hand of the Queen of Navarre. Without money, without a real army, she had only her partisan passion and verbal encouragement to offer, but they were supplemented by daring exploits that made up in panache for what they lacked in practical military value. Some of the outstanding Huguenot captains, important in the wars to come, established their reputations at this time —men such as Armand de Clermont de Pilles, whose capture of Mussidan, in January 1563, and Bergerac, in March, figure among the legendary feats of the Gascon Huguenots. On the Catholic side too, the First Civil War in Guyenne foreshadowed the future; Monluc began to organize one of the earliest "leagues" of loyal Catholics against the "fomenters of sedition."[36]

The crowning satisfaction for Monluc was his designation by the crown as the King's lieutenant in Haute-Guyenne, from Bigorre to Péri-gord and from Languedoc to Béarn. This occurred after the death of Antoine in November, and was a temporary appointment, until Henri de Navarre should come of age.[37] The title made the soldier of fortune, risen out of the local nobility, superior in rank to all the greater nobles of the area. For Jeanne, conversely, his appointment was a staggering blow. That the man who had massacred her subjects, undermined her authority, and insulted her personally should rule in some of her domains and in her son's name was more than she could tolerate, and she protested the appointment to Catherine with as much guile as possible, pretending not to believe the news. Meanwhile, her struggle with Monluc was destined to last eight more years, with mounting bitterness on both sides.

JEANNE AND ANTOINE: THE FINAL PHASE

Jeanne had been absent for more than a year when she returned to Béarn in mid-August 1562. Two matters claimed her immediate attention as Queen: the first, imposed by the circumstances, was to tighten the controls and prepare the military defense of her domains. To this end, she took steps to increase the isolation of her subjects and to combat infiltration of elements that might undermine her authority, by imposing severe penalties on natives leaving the country and by issuing regulations enabling the authorities to keep a careful check on outsiders. The possession and use of arms was strictly controlled. Garrisons were reinforced and the chief citadel, Navarrenx—where she took refuge at critical moments—was stocked with supplies necessary to withstand a siege.[38] The second important matter was the establishment of Calvinism. Certain preliminary measures were taken in this direction immediately, although the full implementation of her religious policy was to begin only a few months later, in the early months of 1563. This delay probably resulted from the necessity to deal first with new problems created by Antoine, who was anxious to convince the Catholic leaders of his cooperation and to overcome his reputation for unreliability. According to Jeanne, he wrote to her court of Parlement in Pau "ordering them to stop immediately all exercises of the Reformed Religion, which I had introduced with his consent . . . and to remove all those who were not of the Roman [faith] from office, even to the point of exiling them from the country. . . . The emissary [Jean de Lescripvain, Seigneur de Boulogne, Antoine's secretary] had instructions not to mention this to me. When I learned this, I used the natural sovereign power God had given me over my subjects (which I had yielded to my husband) . . . to imprison the said Boulogne, and kept the dispatch."[39]

Boulogne had a second mission, which might well have constituted a still more compelling reason for his arrest, although Jeanne does not mention it. Antoine, more than ever "under the spell of a painted kingdom," as Bordenave puts it, now that he was accepted by the Catholic party, was determined to force Philip to deliver a kingdom—at last.[40] But the price was the relinquishment of Navarre. Since he had no claim whatever to Navarre in his own right, it was necessary to act in Jeanne's name, and even if he could coerce or trick her into cooperating in her own ruin, he still had to persuade Philip that it was legal. He sent Boulogne with a procuration for Jeanne to sign, authorizing Antoine to negotiate freely. So hard-pressed was the Queen—it was within a few days of her arrival—that she did sign it.[41] Bordenave adds, "but to preserve her children's rights, if God were to favor them with a more peaceful time when justice would be stronger than force, she made a solemn revocation of this procuration in the presence of the Sénéchal de Béarn, swearing that she had been forced to sign it and had not dared to refuse."[42] This disclaimer—which has never been found in the Archives—attests to an admirable prudence. But Jeanne need not have bothered. The original procuration, signed on August 25, is still in the Pau Archives; it was never delivered, and within three months Antoine de Bourbon was dead.

In the autumn of 1562 the royal Catholic army was attempting to subdue the Protestants and their English allies in Normandy. The most important event of the campaign was the siege of Rouen, begun on September 27 under Antoine's command. The city fell a month later, under that of the Constable. The fighting was furious on both sides, and the leaders took unreasonable risks; the Spanish ambassador wrote Philip, "it is to be feared that some disaster will result."[43] Antoine was particularly foolhardy, appearing in the front lines with his head uncovered. On October 16 he was shot in the shoulder and removed to a camp some distance away, where he lingered for a month. At first his wound was not considered serious, although the fact that the bullet had not been found was a cause of anxiety, and he was well enough to be carried in the triumphal procession of the royal army after the capture of the city. Chantonay reported to Philip on October 19 that, despite a slight fever, he looked healthy and that the infection was draining.[44] On the 22nd the papal Nuncio reported that he looked better.[45] But the Huguenots foresaw doom—the hand of God striking down the traitor. A report to Queen Elizabeth says, "even if he lingers he cannot recover because the wound will not heal with the bullet still in his body."[46] By the end of the first week in November his condition had worsened, and the Venetian ambassador reported to the *Signoria* that he could not sleep, that he had lost a lot of blood, and that he could not be saved.[47] Within three days the infection had spread through the whole upper part of his body and the courts of Europe were abuzz with intrigue, each trying to procure for its own candidate the succession as Lieutenant-General. Catherine, no doubt deliberately, encouraged each faction in turn. Because Antoine had lacked any consistent policy—except to acquire a kingdom for himself—attention during the last days of his life centered largely on his rivals. Everyone was speculating on which of them would succeed in rushing into the political vacuum.[48]

Allusions in diplomatic dispatches to Antoine himself, aside from the imminence of his death, deal with matters long familiar to reporters of the Valois court, his love affairs and his religion.[49] After he was wounded, Antoine had sent for Mademoiselle de Rouet to keep him company during what he hoped would be his convalescence. While he lingered, observers merely note the fact in passing, but after his death "amorous excesses" were alleged to have hastened the end. Since there was scarcely an important man in the sixteenth century whose death did not occasion similar rumors, it is not worth while to attempt to prove or disprove these insinuations.

It seemed hardly possible for Antoine to add further to the reputation for *ondoyance* in religion he had acquired in recent months, but, as Bordenave says, "he gave no less evidence of inconsistency when he was dying than during his life."[50] Reportedly as the result of a conversation with Catherine, the Catholic party sent Vincent Lauro, a retainer of the Cardinal de Tournon who had influenced Antoine during the Colloquy, to persuade him to confess and receive the last rites in the Roman manner. This he did on November 9, and subsequently made an addition to his will, naming among others the Duc de Guise, to whom he left some horses.[51] A few days later, however, on a barge bringing him to Paris, he asked his Huguenot physician, Raphael de Taillevis, to read the Bible aloud. A passage from St. Paul (Ephesians 5:22, 25) made him exclaim, "You see, Raphael, how God wishes wives to obey their husbands." "That is true," replied Raphael, according to his own account, "but Scripture also says, 'Husbands, love your wives.'" Raphael took this opportunity to lecture Antoine about his lapses from Christian marriage. "Ah, Raphael," sighed Antoine, "after twenty-seven years in my service you see only the worst days of my life." Then he said that if God granted him the grace to live he would have the Gospel preached throughout the kingdom—according to the Confession of Augsburg![52] The next morning, when the barge docked at Les Andelys, the Cardinal de Bourbon came aboard to see his brother, accompanied by a Jacobin who addressed Antoine in a way calculated to please the Cardinal. Antoine made no reply and signaled Raphael to continue his reading. Antoine later fell into a coma, but at nine in the evening, he roused himself, called a favorite servant, an Italian, and grabbed him by the beard, saying, "Serve my son well and see that he serves the King well." Thereupon he died.

In a *Relazione* that concludes with the outbreak of the civil war the Venetian ambassador, Marc-Antonio Barbaro, makes an astute comment on Antoine: "He is a man lacking in stability, who has already changed three or four times, and he never considers anything but his own ulterior interests [*attende solamente all'interesse suo*]. He uses religion as a means [*usando la religione per mezzana*], and if he thought he could better advance himself in the opposite [religion] would throw himself into it with all his heart, even if he had already received the indemnity he is demanding."[53] Barbaro did not believe Philip would carry out his promises any more than he had in the seven previous years during which Antoine had pursued the phantom kingdom and title. The day after Antoine's death, his latest envoy to Philip, a Portuguese named Antonio d'Almeida, arrived in France bearing what would have been still another disappointment. As Santa Croce wrote to Cardinal Borromeo, "I think it very fortunate that he found the King of Navarre dead . . . I believe this refusal would have brought about another great change, since he was already disposed to make one."[54]

It is not surprising that Antoine was little regretted at court, where he had been chiefly a nuisance and a laughingstock; the indifference is thinly disguised by the conventional mourning. De Ruble goes even further. Speaking of the letters of condolence written to Jeanne, he says, "a note of congratulation is discernible in this funereal vocabulary."[55] In writings that survive, Jeanne herself never referred to Antoine's death except in the context of its effect on her position and that of her son or on the status of her lands. In the *Ample Déclaration* or *Mémoires* she merely says, following the episode of Boulogne and the procuration, "Soon after this I lost the said lord, my husband . . . and I shall restrain myself from saying anything more about the disadvantages of all kinds this brought about for me and my son."[56] Reference to her own disillusionment with Antoine and suffering at his hands occurs in the context of his desertion of Calvinism, which "put a thorn not in my foot but in my heart."

As long as he lived, whatever her private feelings, Jeanne maintained a façade of dignified solidarity with Antoine. She had asked that his name be restored in the Huguenot prayers—along with her own, to be sure—at the moment that Antoine was proclaiming to all his plan to deprive Jeanne not only of her lands but also of her liberty. Personal emotions were simply not relevant when sovereign rights were at stake. As soon as she received word that Antoine had been wounded, Jeanne sent one of her gentlemen-in-waiting to offer her help in any way possible; without waiting for his return she made preparations to go to Normandy herself if necessary.[57] She had an inventory of the treasure of the chateau of Pau drawn up by the bishops of Oloron and Lescar,[58] and she reopened direct negotiations with the Spaniards, expressing annoyance that she had not been party to their recent dealings with Antoine.[59] These were preliminary steps to resuming the reins of government, when and if she could. It was altogether possible that Jeanne's situation would be even worse if Antoine were to die and if either Philip or Catherine should decide to attack her.

Local legend has it that Jeanne received the news of Antoine's death at Navarrenx; this seems probable, since she often prudently retired there at times of crisis. A dispatch sent by the Duke of Albuquerque to Philip conveys a striking impression of her state of mind: "This morning I received a visit from a secretary of Madame de Vendôme, called Colon, whom she sent to inform Your Majesty, through me, of her husband's death and of her sincere desire to serve Your Majesty and to possess your friendship. He left this afternoon in great haste, because in my opinion his mistress is much more afraid than he is saying and she does not feel safe in any direction."[60] From the same source we learn that Jeanne "seemed in a trance" in the first days of her widowhood. This could mean stunned, as by a blow, or preoccupied, as when every bit of energy must be mobilized to meet the kind of challenge that isolates one from others.

Personal considerations aside, the death of Antoine profoundly affected not only Jeanne's official position but her relations with her subjects, her adversaries, including Monluc, and her Protestant allies, in France and elsewhere. She had really been alone for some time; as a widow, though hard-pressed, she was free. The fundamental gain was freedom to negotiate with Catherine, now deprived of the opportunity to play Jeanne off against Antoine or to pretend that in dealing with Antoine she was also dealing with Jeanne. The first important aspect of the change concerned the upbringing and education of Henri de Béarn. When Jeanne had fled leaving her son at court, Antoine replaced Jeanne's Protestant tutors with those of his own choosing, notably Jean de Losses. Bordenave says that soon after Antoine's death Catherine allowed Jeanne to resume control of her son's education. The faithful Beauvoir was reinstated as *gouverneur,* assisted by La Caze, and La Gaucherie, "a learned man and very zealous in the reformed religion," as his tutor.[61] Henri nevertheless remained a hostage at court during the next four years, until his mother, after spending some months there herself, was able to flee Paris a second time, taking Henri with her.

Antoine's last act regarding his son, just before he went to the front in September, was to escort him to visit Renée, Duchess of Ferrara, at

Montargis. The ostensible reason was Henri's health; he had the measles and needed a change of air. Given Renée's known sponsorship of Calvinism, her absolute unwillingness to live at court, as well as her friendly relations with Jeanne, however, several other reasons are possible. One wonders whether he felt some twinges of conscience at having brutally separated Henri from his mother, or whether even Antoine thought it desirable for Henri to experience some atmosphere other than that of the Valois court. He may have had a premonition that he would not, this time, return from the wars and wished to leave Henri with somebody he and Jeanne could both trust. But rumors that the Prince de Condé might attempt to kidnap Henri and demands of the Spanish negotiators that he be turned over as a hostage are more probable explanations—especially of Catherine's willingness to permit it.[62] A letter to Antoine from a physician whose signature has been erased reports, "Your son has much improved, thanks to God he has only a little fever, which I hope will entirely disappear after the dose of rhubarb he took this morning with no difficulty. . . . [He] slept very quietly [*fort doucement*] last night . . . and is beginning to resume his natural habits in every way."[63]

Henri must have made a rapid recovery because he was back in Paris on September 26, when he wrote one of the earliest letters that has survived in his own hand. Its purpose was to ask news of his mother. Everyone knew that Jeanne's health was precarious, and nobody at court could avoid awareness of the dangers of her position, not even a child who was still three months short of his ninth birthday, especially not one who already had the reputation of having *un esprit vif et subtil*."[64] The letter, addressed to one Larchant,* is short and to the point:

> Write me to relieve my anxiety [*pour me mettre hors de peine*] about the Queen, my mother; because I am so afraid that some evil will befall her in this trip you are taking, that the greatest pleasure anyone could give me is to send me news often. May God lead you there and back safely. Praying God to keep you, from Paris, this 26th of September,
>
> Henry[65]

---

* The editor of Henri's letters identifies this person as Nicolas de Grémonville, Seigneur de Larchant, who later became an officer in Henri IV's army. The letter was found in the archives of the chateau at Caumont, which raises the question as to whether Jeanne made another visit there in September. We are sure only of the one in July, but there are many gaps in accounts of her movements at this period, when every effort was made to conceal them.

Jeanne's concern for her son, her feelings toward Monluc, and the direction of her new relationship with Catherine after the death of Antoine are revealed in a letter she wrote to the Queen Mother in late February or early March 1563. It is undated but can be placed by her allusions to the recent assassination of the Duc de Guise (February 18) and to Catherine's negotiations with the Protestants, which led to the Pacification of Amboise (March 19). De Ruble says, "Of all the monuments of her epistolatory style, it is perhaps the one in which she reveals herself most frankly."[66]

Madame:

I do not know by which end to begin my letter, whether with the reply it pleased you to write and send me by M. de Beauvoir, or by the unwelcome news he brought of what has happened since his departure from court. But first, Madame, I thank you very humbly for the continual remembrance you are kind enough to have of me and mine. . . . I have known you for so long a time, Madame, that I would never doubt it.

One thing I very much desire: that your kindness to me and mine should not be turned aside by those who show sufficiently in their actions what they have in their hearts against our House. I well know, Madame, that there is nothing you wish less and that you wish, indeed, to show us the means to render you service, but the fact is, Madame, that I see the results as quite the contrary.

Before going any further, Madame, I beg you to forgive me if anger makes me forget myself and write too boldly, and I protest that concern for your service spurs me on more than my own private interest.

Since God has granted me the grace to purge my heart of avarice and ambition, you might never realize, Madame, that neither the one nor the other causes me to complain or to importune you. Insofar as I am removed from these two vices, and since I have such an open heart, I take special plans, Madame, to conserve the honor, authority, and grandeur of my son, with God's grace. I desire him to be such, Madame, that those to whom he has the honor to belong will recognize that in what I do for him I am raising a faithful servant for them. Knowing well, Madame, that not all my powers can accomplish this without your favor and good grace, I asked for it in my affliction. Moreover, I have found it efficacious in achieving the results which I recognize I could never deserve.*

As you had done my son the honor of allowing him to keep the estates of him [Antoine] who lost his life in the service of his master—a service so well-known that you will be pleased to recognize it as the basis of this just plea—and since the survivor [Henri], into whom God has already put the will, the fidelity, and the obedience for your service, is too young to do all

---

* A reference to Catherine's reinstatement of Jeanne's tutors for Henri.

that is required, I hoped that my chief desire would be accomplished when I sent the Sieur de Rostaing* to request that you give [Henri] a deputy for the government of our Guyenne who would be entirely devoted to you.

Although I am sure that the Sieur de Rostaing would not forget anything I told him, since the matter touches me so closely, I do not hesitate to ask you to take the trouble to read my long and wearisome letter, which reminds you of what I told him. First, about the government of Guyenne . . . I asked you to do me the honor of appointing a lieutenant who is not attached to my husband's enemies, those I consider responsible for his death—a thing I cannot pass over in silence, Madame, or easily bear in my heart. Because it was rumored that the Maréchal de St. André might be appointed, I made so bold as to request that you not do so, for several reasons. One was that he has not been a friend to our House, even though he pretended that he was. Another was that Monluc hoped for his appointment, which put me in a fever of fear of worse things to come.

Subsequently, I asked the Sieur d'Audaux to talk to you further on this matter . . . to demonstrate that it would be the best way to ruin entirely what Monluc has already spoiled, and to put me, Madame, into perpetual torment. Then I learned, before either Rostaing or Audaux could reach you, that [the appointment] had already been made, but only until my son comes of age. But as I have had an excess of honor in association with you, Madame, and only too much experience with the network of intrigue at court, I could not approve . . . and I trust, Madame, that you will not find that I have exceeded my duty by addressing myself to you on wings that fly above the heads of others.

I am fully aware, Madame, of your perfect good will and friendship, and of your desire to further my son's welfare and my own, and I cannot ignore your acts, so praiseworthy that I kiss the ground where you walk. But forgive me, Madame, if I write as I spoke to you at St. Germain, where you did not seem to mind. Your good intentions are obstructed by the interference of those whom you know too well for me to describe them. I tell you frankly, Madame, that whoever persuaded you to do this wrong to my son [the appointment of St. André] is no good servant of yours or the King's. As for his sentiments toward me, the facts speak for themselves—that he, or they, willfully and maliciously disregarded the faithful service my son and I perform in the said Guyenne. Our devotion to you was too strong to be set aside, however, as long as we knew our hearts to be pure. . . .

And now, Madame, it has pleased God to remove this injury to my son, because the Maréchal de St. André is dead.

I trust, Madame, that no matter how strongly others may urge you, that this time it will please you to lean as far in the direction of my son as you formerly allowed yourself to be pushed in the other. I implore you humbly,

* Tristan de Rostaing, Sieur de Thieux, *Grand Maître des Eaux et Forêts,* bearer of Jeanne's first message on this subject.

Madame, do not let foreigners see my son shamed, so that my enemies can laugh and my friends weep.

In conformity with your pleasure that [Henri] succeed to his father's honors and estates, I ask again, very humbly, Madame, that you give my son a lieutenant who is your faithful servant and who will recognize that you are his only master. If such is the case, he will be my friend. Otherwise, I am too closely bound [to the crown] by natural ties to be able to agree with anyone who is unfaithful to you. Consider also, Madame, that in so doing you will be assuring the greatness of my son and the relief of the lands we hold in obedience to you.

As for this land of Béarn, where God gives me the grace to see the benefits of his blessings, you will always find here a handful of souls faithful to the King's service and to you. I shall never be ashamed to offer you both the sovereign lady and her subjects. I assure you, Madame, that it would distress me greatly to have to endure again, as I have up to the present, a governor of Guyenne who defies me under cover of your service, for which I shall always bow my head and render the obedience due from a faithful subject.

These are the considerations which make me humbly beg you to place someone in Guyenne who understands your will and who will make my vassals understand it. This will be no small gain . . . for this devastated Guyenne. . . .

I have learned from the Sieur de Beauvoir of the pitiful event that has happened* and it seems to me, Madame, that it should now be easy to make peace, for which I pray God unceasingly. I beg you, pursue it without cessation . . . the said Beauvoir tells me that you have already begun.† I can say nothing more about this than that if you do not succeed, it is because our sins are so great that it does not please the good Lord to withdraw His punishing hand in order to extend the hand of mercy.

Since I shall wait to hear the reply you give Audaux before I send Beauvoir again, I beg you, Madame, not to disapprove my keeping [Beauvoir] here. I desire, Madame, to be in your good graces and to preserve the honor you have done me until such time as my affairs, which hold me here, will permit me to come and render you most humble service, in person. You have my son as a testimonial of my wholehearted devotion. I beg you, Madame, to hold him in your protection and good grace, in which I myself wish to remain forever.

Praying God, Madame, to give you as many blessings as you have had difficulties, with a very long and happy life, from your very humble and very obedient sister and subject,

Jeanne[67]

* The assassination of Guise.
† Parleys which led to the Pacification of Amboise.

Another letter, written about the same time but to a very different correspondent, the Vicomte de Gourdon, is equally revealing—of a different Jeanne. The first part is a list of her sorrows.

> I have suffered so much, first through the death . . . of my very honored lord and husband, whom God keep in glory, and then through the loss of the ill-fated battle of Dreux,* gained and lost in the same day [and] the capture of the Prince . . . still more by the things M. the King and Madame the Queen Mother oblige my son, the Prince de Béarn, to do. They are detaining him and they make him sign and give his approval to requests false in the light of truth and of his upbringing, reflecting hatred of the Reformed Religion and of its adherents. . . . I am anxious and so distressed and sad at heart that I can find no joy or peace of mind.

At the end Jeanne expresses her opinion of a matter that everyone in France was discussing, the responsibility, if any, of Admiral Coligny in the assassination of the Duc de Guise: "he is falsely accused . . . I cannot believe anything so vicious of a man so upright and straightforward as the said Admiral is recognized by everyone to be."[68]

To Catherine, Jeanne showed the diplomat and the vigilant sovereign, to Gourdon, the Huguenot partisan and a lonely woman, recently widowed, deprived of her son and helpless to prevent him being turned against her. Rarely did Jeanne permit herself to express self-pity or plead for sympathy in this way. She tended more and more to use her widowed state as a positive asset rather than a weakness. Thus turned, it reinforced the independence of the sovereign and the flexibility of the diplomat. The Calvinist convert could add another facet to the triple role Jeanne played as she turned her energies to the establishment of the reform in Béarn. One important source of weakness—Henri's growing up in the enemy's camp—had to be endured for the time being, until she could contrive a way to remove it.

---

* The Battle of Dreux, December 19, 1562, was the most important military engagement of the First Civil War, in which both Guise and Coligny added to their military reputations. Condé was captured; on the Catholic side, the Maréchal de St. André was killed.

VIII

PRECARIOUS INDEPENDENCE

1 5 6 3 – 1 5 6 7

I N the four years following the end of the First Civil War Jeanne pursued a number of policies, some of her own choosing and some imposed by the actions of others. Her first goal was to increase the autonomy of Béarn while remaining on as good terms as possible with Catherine de Medici. Aside from administrative and military precautions, the principal form of her independence was the establishment of Calvinism in 1563, followed in 1564–5 by certain modifications necessitated by opposition from her own subjects and by a series of attacks by the Counter Reformation party. These same factors also required her to compromise with regard to the second goal—to get her son back—not merely in the sense of reasserting her authority over his education, but literally, to bring him away from the court, back to his native kingdom, under her control. To achieve both goals she had to fight off enemies, play on their divisions, and resort to guile and dissimulation. In the process she became involved in many feuds, even with some of her own vassals and coreligionists.

REFORM AND SELF-DEFENSE, MARCH 1563–MARCH 1564

On January 20, 1563, Calvin write Jeanne a letter which begins as a conventional expression of condolence. His real purpose was to urge her to carry through the establishment of Calvinism in Béarn. "Now that the government is in your hands, God will test your zeal and fidelity." He speaks of "an obligation to purge your lands of idolatry," and shows that he is aware of some of the obstacles. "I take into consideration the difficulties which can hold you back, the fears and doubts which can sap courage, and I do not doubt that your advisers, if they look to this world, will try to stop you . . . I know the arguments advanced to prove that princes should not force their subjects to lead a Christian life . . . but, all kingdoms which do not serve that of Jesus Christ are ruined, so judge for yourself." He refers to the fact that she is constantly "spied on by a neighbor" (Monluc), and warns that it is a long task, "I do not say that all can be done in a day."[1] Because "paper cannot include everything," he is entrusting the details of his advice "to the present bearer, whom I chose because he is the best I have on hand." The letter offers only one concrete suggestion: "begin in the places that are most difficult because they are most conspicuous, and when you have gained one it will bring others in its train." The bearer named was Jean-Raymond Merlin. A native of Dauphiné, Merlin probably went to Switzerland about 1540. He was a friend of Calvin, Farel, and Viret, who considered him very able. He had been in Poissy during the Colloquy but had not played an important part. Although Calvin told Jeanne he was sending him on January 20, he did not arrive in Béarn until early March, and the letter may have been delivered by someone else.[2]

In France during these weeks the First Civil War was petering out. Catherine was preparing the Pacification of Amboise and Jeanne was moving about her domains. At court Jeanne's every movement was interpreted in terms of the military situation—on February 3 she was reported to be on her way to join Coligny with 4000 mercenaries—but her real object was to pave the way for her reforms by building morale and securing loyalty among her subjects. One means to this end was magnanimity. She saw to it that officers received their back wages, even if they had fought against the Huguenots, and went out of her way to overlook disloyalty of vassals such as Jacques de St. Astier, Sieur de Bories, who had been lured away from the traditional devotion of his family to the house of Albret.[3] In the spring of 1563, Jeanne could hope that the end of civil war and concessions gained at Amboise for *hauts justiciers** would provide an atmosphere favorable to the imple-

---

* *Haute justice:* one of the most important remnants of feudalism in sixteenth-century France was the right of the landed nobility to have their own courts. Whereas the two lower degrees, *basse* and *moyenne justice,* were widely held, only the greatest nobles could dispense *haute justice,* which made them independent of the crown in many ways.

mentation of the plans she and Merlin were preparing in Béarn. On the other hand, a papal bull condemning heretics regardless of rank (April 1) was not reassuring. If France needed a breathing spell, the international Catholic party was not disposed to grant one.

Some of Jeanne's first religious measures applied only to certain localities; others were the foundation-stones of a general politico-religious establishment which was not completed until 1571. The earliest ruling to provoke wide repercussions was the abolition of customary public processions on Corpus Christi (in 1563, May 30). Soon afterward the "images" were removed from the churches of Lescar and Pau.[4] Concurrently, Merlin was creating an administrative structure to provide Geneva-style discipline. He had started by convoking an assembly of ecclesiastics, and Jeanne had asked Calvin to send her more ministers. On June 1, Calvin wrote, "finally, we have found you a dozen men. If they are not as perfect as could be desired, I pray you, Madame, have patience. . . . Put them to work and keep a firm hand on them, your authority will be needed to arm and defend them. . . . When you have [achieved] some order I pray you to return our brother Merlin."[5]

Merlin was already being assisted by "various other learned persons, mostly native Basques and Béarnais, to preach to the people in their own language."[6] By September a full-blown synod had come into existence. It met on the 20th day of that month in Pau. Merlin was elected as the presiding officer, and in the final session it was voted to ask the Geneva authorities for his services for another year.[7] Included in the ambitious scheme was the establishment of a Protestant academy, modeled on that of Geneva. This did not become a reality—the college at Orthez—until several years later, after many vicissitudes. The achievement of these few months nevertheless surpassed in scale any Calvinist organization that had been undertaken so far in France. On October 3, Francis Hotman could write to the Duke of Wurtemberg: "The Queen of Navarre has banished all idolatry from her domains and sets an example of virtue with incredible firmness and courage."[8]

Resistance to the new religious policy appeared at the very start. The Parlement of Bordeaux had condemned Jeanne for abolishing the processions and for licensing Calvinist preaching. The Estates of Béarn (June) were profoundly agitated by the former, and on June 27, the nobles, by a small majority, and the Third Estate, by a large majority, protested Jeanne's ruling eliminating "the accustomed procession, in which the Host is carried and said . . . to be God [as] proof of idolatry and an offense to Almighty God." They asked her to reverse it, "in the name of custom, tradition, and the ancient liberties of the realm, as well as to preserve the peace." Perhaps because of the threat implied in the last phrase, Jeanne chose to exert her authority by insisting on the letter of the law. The protest had not been submitted three days in advance as prescribed by the regulations, and she would therefore not accept it. She assured them that she was "always willing to do whatever was necessary for the salvation of their souls" and would receive any grievances "concerning the public welfare" if they observed the rule, but that in the matter of the processions they must content themselves with her first decision.[9] Some of her subjects also maintained their position. This clash was a faint foreshadowing of what would happen as Jeanne continued to purge her lands of "idolatry" and establish religion *à la mode de Genève.*

While far-off Calvinists like Hotman were expressing optimism and the people affected were beginning to resist, Merlin himself was far from satisfied with the accomplishment. In two long letters written to Calvin on July 23 and December 25, he reports the situation in considerable detail.[10] He says that he has so many irritations (*fascheries*) that his health is affected. He is anxious to impress Calvin with his admiration for Jeanne and wants her to be aware of it. "These annoyances are not caused by the Queen, for I can assure you that I hold her constancy in admiration, and I pray you confirm this more and more in your letters."

In the July letter he dwells chiefly on the obstacles to the reform. Most of Jeanne's advisers are opposed to it, and unfavorable propaganda excites unrealistic fears among the people, "as if we wished to create bishops and popes or overthrow the authority of the magistrates." Such opposition is to be expected, however; more discouraging is the fact that "those who profess the Gospel hamper its progress more than its enemies. Those who have most power in the country after the Queen, and without whom nothing can be accomplished, are those who most retard the reform by speaking of awesome dangers, sometimes from the Spaniard, or Monluc, or even [the crown of] France." They dwell on the inadequacy of the means or they insist that nothing should be done without consulting Coligny and Condé, ". . . uniquely to hold things up." Many of the nobles have the right to confer benefices and think that they should either be compensated in money for the loss or have the right to choose the Prot-

estant ministers. More than once Merlin alludes to the intractable nature of the Béarnais: "heads in this country are so hot and so stubborn
that it is very hard to get rid of any fancy they have in them."

Weaknesses in Jeanne compound the difficulties: "she is inexperienced
. . . having always been either under a father who managed affairs, or
under a husband who neglected them." Her financial position is desperate:
"she spends more than her income and her affairs are in a state of confusion, partly because she is cheated by some of her own officers and servants. Her own household is in disarray "as she has no man whom she can
trust." The inadequacy of her advisers makes it easy to understand why
the religious program does not progress more rapidly "since some are
open enemies, others fear to get involved, and still others are incapable."

Despite Merlin's awareness of her difficulties and his reiterated praise
of Jeanne's intentions, the fact was that he wanted to go much further and
faster than Jeanne. Even in the July letter he mentions suggestions that
she would not accept, notably a complete inventory of ecclesiastical wealth
as a first step toward confiscation, or at least partial diversion, for support
of the reform. "I could never persuade her, which is why some [treasures]
have disappeared that cannot now be found." The Queen also refused
to allow Merlin to confront Roman Catholic priests in public debate—
in the Swiss style.* On his own word, it was Merlin who pushed Jeanne
into prohibiting the Mass at Lescar in July. "When [Jeanne] gave orders
for the idols to be removed from the Temple, which was done, not without difficulty, she had not thought to do anything more at the time. But
I begged her, as long as she was there, to assemble the priests and the
town authorities and forbid them to say or hear the Mass or to celebrate
in future any papal superstitions anywhere in the town, which she did."

The rift is more obvious in the second letter, written five months
later, and Merlin's tone betrays greater frustration with than admiration
for Jeanne. "I saw that there was no way to obtain the total abolition of
idolatry in this country from the Queen of Navarre, or rather from those
who obstruct God's work . . . Even though the Queen continues to display great zeal, what I feared has come about and I fear still worse. The
ardor to repudiate the Papacy, with which she burned, has cooled since
news has come that the Spaniards are standing on the frontier ready to

---

* The Swiss cities which adopted the reform generally did so after a public
"disputation" between reformers and members of the Catholic clergy, authorized by
the secular authorities: Zurich, 1523; Berne, 1528; Geneva, 1535; Lausanne, 1536.

throw themselves into this country . . . she is so aghast [*épouvantée*] that she is much less confident and I have not been able to get her to surmount it . . . she is paralyzed by fear, which has not been lessened by the Pope's postponement [soon to be discussed] even though she pretends otherwise."

Merlin complains that Jeanne's other advisers "consider that I want to go too far in wishing to overthrow the Papacy [*m'estiment trop violent à abbatre la papauté*] although they are forced to admit that without me things would be worse than they are." When Merlin tried to persuade the Queen that it was illogical to abandon what she had undertaken, "she presented me with a difficulty by saying that she did not believe you or M. de Bèze . . . would agree with me, in view of the conditions of this country. She thinks all the other ministers are merely following me and she says that . . . her people are really opposed to the Gospel, so that if [Catholicism] were wholly taken away they would be left without religion, because even if the Gospel were preached . . . they would not receive it." Jeanne was thus caught between her subjects, who found the new legislation too radical, and her minister, who thought it too half-hearted.

Merlin correctly perceived that since the late summer Jeanne had not been following the most direct route to their common goal; he even shows the reason for the apparent cooling off, but he does not appear to recognize it as such nor to appreciate its significance. For about six months after his arrival there had been no threat of alarming proportions to Jeanne's domains or to her person and she had profited from the interval to launch the reform. As far as the French crown was concerned, the lull was the fruit of the Pacification of Amboise, and the Papacy did not initiate direct action until the King of Spain had failed in an attempt to lure Jeanne off her course.

In the opening months of 1563 Philip hoped to exploit Jeanne's recent widowhood by persuading her to marry into the Spanish royal family. If it had succeeded, this maneuver would have resulted in the alliance Henri d'Albret had worked so hard to achieve—but without the benefit for which he had sought it. If Jeanne had married Philip in the 1540's her father would still have pursued the phantom of the lost kingdom, but if Jeanne married one of Philip's sons in the 1560's she stood to lose what was left of it, as well as her independence and her Protestant faith. Philip could not count on cooperation from Catherine, given the indulgence toward Calvinism that followed the peace of Amboise, so he decided to trap Jeanne by employing the same techniques which had worked so well on Antoine. As his agent, he chose the man most experienced for the task, who knew from his part in earlier intrigues the entire history of the Navarre question. Don Juan Martinez Descurra had many contacts in Jeanne's domains and knew how stubborn she could be. He reported to his master through Philip's Secretary of State, Don Francisco di Erasso, and dealt with Jeanne chiefly through two of her secretaries, Armand de Colon and Gensanna, although at a certain critical moment he talked with the Queen of Navarre herself. The greatest secrecy was observed in these transactions, of which Merlin and her other advisers were probably ignorant. The documents have been studied and their most important parts translated and interpreted by the distinguished Béarnais historian Raymond Ritter.[11]

When Jeanne reopened negotiations after Antoine's death, Philip had an opportunity to offer the bait. The correspondence between Jeanne's agents and Descurra, on the one hand, and between Descurra and Erasso, on the other, show that Jeanne was evasive. To Philip's demand that she abandon her religious policy so that they could come to an agreement, she replied that she would submit to a "good, free, and holy council." In April and May she held up negotiations for several weeks while she took her spring cure at Eaux-Chaudes. Descurra had been instructed to make clear that "everything could be arranged once she had come back into the bosom of the church." As late as June, Jeanne managed to conceal the extent of the reform in progress. "Vendôme's wife has made no innovations in religion. She has given everyone freedom to act as he chooses." She countered Philip's accusations by retorting that she had it "on the highest authority that [Philip] had promised her Basque subjects arms to rebel against her," and swore that "for nothing in the world" would she behave so in regard to *his* subjects, believing that "each should rule on his own, without interfering with others." A dispatch from Gensanna to Descurra (July 11), after the stormy session of the Estates, reveals that Jeanne's secretary had been in touch with Armand de Gontaut, Seigneur d'Audaux, who, though a Huguenot, did not hesitate to express doubts about the Queen's religious policy. When he forwarded Gensanna's letter to Spain, Descurra added a postscript, "so that she will have no excuse, send the present bearer to her to repeat that the King [Philip] will tolerate no preaching or exercise of the new religion . . . and send this letter so she will see that I have said it." After showing the documents to Philip, Erasso reports, "His Majesty must find a remedy, but he would much rather the initiative came from her."

Thus far Descurra had been operating from Pampeluna, by correspondence; in late July, Philip sent him to Béarn to talk to Audaux (among others) to increase pressure on Jeanne. When she learned of his arrival, Jeanne insisted that he talk to her first. On August 14, Descurra sent a long letter to Erasso reporting verbatim his interviews with the Queen of Navarre. Its first-hand impression of her personality contrasts with that given in Merlin's letters.[12] Descurra reports that when he arrived in Lescar on August 2 he found the churches devastated there, as well as in Pau: "She had sent members of the accursed sect to burn the statues and the crucifixes and had ordained that Mass could not be said, on pain of death, and that ecclesiastical goods be confiscated." He claims that Jeanne supervised the execution of the destruction in person, and that she had proclaimed her intention of doing likewise throughout Béarn. To assure the execution of her orders she had mobilized six companies, a total of two thousand soldiers, and he reports a heated exchange when Jeanne told the Catholic governor of Oloron, "I commanded you to enlist only soldiers of my religion," who replied, "In all Béarn there are not a thousand persons of your religion and in my company there are not fifty." Descurra adds that there were not fifty Calvinists in all the companies together.

The heart of the report is Descurra's account of his confrontation with Jeanne on August 3, in the garden of the chateau of Pau, where they could not be overheard. "More than ten heretic captains were stationed within sight but out of earshot." From what follows, in Descurra's own words, much of Jeanne's political and religious philosophy emerges, including the original Protestant claim that they were not innovators, but restorers of the ancestral faith.

Descurra began by telling the Queen how shocked he was by what she had done to the churches: " 'no baptized Christian has ever committed such an enormity . . . the Pope and all the Catholic princes must be your enemies, to the point where you will be completely destroyed, to avenge this injury to the Most High.' All this time she was looking at me most intently and she grew very pale. Somewhat troubled, she asked, 'How can it matter to the princes . . . what I do in my own domain, as they do what they wish in theirs? All the more so as I do what the Gospel teaches. . . .' I replied, 'Your error lies in what you have just said. You think to do good but it is evil. Take care, Madame, from Perpignan to Roncevaux, your lands border on Spain. The Most Catholic King will not tolerate your religion so near to his subjects, as you will see by this letter.' " Descurra then handed her Erasso's letter of July 17, which Jeanne began to read. After a moment she said, " 'The Most Catholic King guessed what I was doing, because at the very moment this letter was written I began the purification of the church at Lescar . . . but I desire very much to show him that I do not deserve what he says . . . because I was born in this religion and instructed in it from my birth. My mother, my father, and my husband died in it. Although I am just a little princess, God has given me the government of this country so that I may rule it according to His Gospel and teach it His laws. I rely on God, who is more powerful than the King of Spain . . . but if he threatens me because I am his neighbor, why does he not do the same to the Queen of England, who is of my religion and who has dealt with her churches . . . in the same way?' I answered that if two men kill a third, one may get off in court, but eventually both will pay, adding, 'it is easier for the Catholic King to punish you than the Queen of England. Rest assured that if he but gives the signal . . . within a month you will lose all your possessions this side of the Garonne . . . I warn you that [if you keep on the present course] the House of Navarre and Foix will disappear.' " Descurra then remarked that he did not know who had advised her to adopt such a policy, " 'but whoever it was did not consider, aside from the offense to God . . . the danger that could result for you.' To which she replied, 'You have been engaged in this matter for many years . . . I wish you would tell me what I ought to do.' " Descurra's answer was that she should "arrest those who had advised her and burn them at the stake, restore the churches, call together her subjects and 'in their presence, implore God's forgiveness . . . in a solemn process, restore what had been destroyed. Thus might you appease the anger of the Catholic princes.' She replied that she had no intention of doing this."

Jeanne said that she had consulted many learned men, and that she thought she had served God well. She then dismissed him until the next day and sent for Audaux, instructing him to report to her after talking with Descurra. Audaux asked, still according to the Spaniard, "Is there no remedy for this evil?" Descurra repeated his conversation with the Queen, and Audaux gave him the impression that they were in agreement. "You must know that I am out of favor because I tried to stop her . . .

I told her what would happen but to no avail. I fear our total ruin, because if the Catholic King makes war on us the King of France will defend us but he will keep what he takes . . . thus we cannot fail to fall prey to one or the other." Audaux also blamed Coligny for encouraging Jeanne and Catherine for her policy of laissez faire. "Madame de Vendôme can do as she pleases in her own domains."

When Jeanne summoned Descurra the next day, she had passed to the offensive. She claimed that "everything that we proposed was like the propositions Your Majesty made to her late husband . . . and she suspected that the object was likewise the same." Descurra tried to get her to speak of the marriage proposal, but she refused to be pinned down [*elle traitait de façon très générale et de rien en particulier*]. In conclusion she said, "You must know in Spain as they do in France that I am thirty-four years old. It is customary for a widowed princess to wait a year before she remarries. I might change my mind between now and the end of the year. In the meanwhile, if [Philip] is willing, let us continue to be good neighbors." When the King of Spain had read this report he sent it back to Erasso with a notation in his own hand: "This is quite too much of a woman to have as a daughter-in-law. I would much prefer to destroy her and treat her as such an evil woman deserves."[13] This is an accurate description of the policy Philip adopted in the next few months, Descurra's mission having failed.

Meanwhile Jeanne was attacked by the Papacy itself. Pius IV was much displeased with events in France. After making peace with the Huguenots in March, Catherine had gone out of her way to appease them; by midsummer she had succeeded (temporarily) in unifying Protestant and Catholic leaders in a joint assault to capture Le Havre from the English. To Jeanne in particular she had been generous: Henri de Béarn had been granted some of the titles and perquisites formerly held by his father, and Monluc had been made to apologize.[14] The papal attack was launched by Georges, Cardinal d'Armagnac, who had known Jeanne all her life. Their relationship had been troubled by his arrest of Barran and La Gaucherie in 1560, but there had been no open break between them. On August 18, 1563 he wrote Jeanne a letter, in which, under the guise of friendly advice, loomed the prospect of total condemnation by the Roman church.

After referring to his past connections with her family and expressing the hope that she "will take in good part what your old, devoted, and very faithful servant has to say," he speaks of his distress that the "recent horrible events at Lescar were done in your presence, Madame, and I hear, at your command." He foresees dire consequences if Jeanne follows the advice of evil counselors, whom he calls wolves in sheep's clothing. The attempt "to plant a new religion in your domains . . . according to their plan . . . will never succeed because your subjects will never consent, as they already have given you to understand, during the last session of the Estates." He warns that "if you undertake to force their consciences . . . really, Madame, there is nothing so likely to cause a rebellion," and that "the King of Spain will not tolerate [heretics] as neighbors," since Jeanne's domains "lack the great rampart of the ocean" that shields England. Anticipating the argument that she would lose all her worldly goods rather than abandon her faith, he pleads for her children's rights to inherit their kingdom intact and invokes respect for her ancestors. Shifting from the political to the religious, he stresses that difficulties in interpreting scripture make it impossible to confine oneself to the Gospel alone: "nothing is clearer and less confusing than Jesus Christ's words at the Last Supper, 'this is my body,' nevertheless, today we see all Christendom in an uproar over the meaning of these three [sic] words." He attacks Protestant pluralism, in contrast to the Roman church, where differences are reconciled over the centuries by the Church fathers and the councils, "being always one and the same everywhere, it is the true church." Expressions of devotion and affection multiply toward the end. "As your oldest servant, and it is certain that you have none more faithful, I beg you very humbly, with tears in my eyes . . . to return to the true Christian fold and abandon the wolves." He specifies what he means by this last: restore the churches and banish the Protestant ministers.[15]

Tradition has it that Jeanne was so incensed by this communication that she made the courier wait while she withdrew to her study to write an answer to be delivered at once.[16] If this is true it shows a considerable command of debating skills on Jeanne's part; her reply is a point by point refutation of Armagnac's arguments. Acknowledging their long connection, she comments, "I could nevertheless have desired that this good and faithful friendship on your part had not been lessened, or rather adulterated, by what I scarcely know whether to call religion or superstition. . . . As to the reformation . . . in religion, which I have begun at Pau and Lescar, I am most earnestly resolved, by the grace of God, to continue [it] throughout my land of Béarn. . . . I have learned from my Bible (which

I read more than the works of your doctors) in the Book of Chronicles
. . . that I might be reproached if, professing myself a servant of God,
I did not destroy idols in consecrated places." Though the Cardinal expects
her ruin because she is surrounded by evil counselors, "I am not yet so
forsaken by God as not to have good men about me, who not only parade
the garments of religion but practice its teachings, for as the head is,
so are the members." Jeanne spells out—as she had not for Descurra—
the Protestant position, "neither have I undertaken, as you assert, to
implant a new religion, but only to restore the ruins of the ancient faith."
She claims further that no consciences are coerced: "I do nothing by force,
nobody is condemned to death or imprisonment."

Alluding to her powerful neighbors, "I know them better than you
do. The one hates my faith and I abhor his, even so, I feel sure that we
shall continue to live peacefully together . . . the other, who is the root
of my race . . . does not hate the reformed faith, as you say, but permits
its exercise by nobles and princes about his person, amongst whom my
son is fortunate to be included . . . I well know that I am serving God,
whose grace surrounds my lands more surely than the great ocean England." Jeanne denies that furthering the reform jeopardizes her worldly
interests. "On the contrary, instead of lessening my son's heritage, I increase it by the means appropriate to a true Christian. . . . If God's spirit
did not instruct me, my common sense would do so, having before my eyes
an infinite number of examples, the main one, to my great regret, being
that of the late King, my husband, which sorry tale you know from the
beginning, through the middle, to the end . . . where are the fine crowns
you promised him . . . if he would fight against the true religion and
against his conscience, as his last words prove?"

Indignation mounts when she takes up Armagnac's reference to
Huguenot atrocities. "Pull the mote out of your own eye so that you can
see clearly enough to cast out the beam in your neighbor's! First cleanse
the earth of the blood of just men shed by your [party]." Jeanne then
states that she does not believe that the end justifies the means: "I do not
mean that I approve or excuse the evil done in some places under cover
of the true religion, to the great regret of its ministers and good men.
I am the first to demand that [evildoers] be punished, as polluters of the
true religion. From this pestilence Béarn by the grace of God shall be
preserved."

Following the order of Armagnac's points, Jeanne then takes up religious matters. "I perceive by your description of our ministers that you do not know them and have never heard them, or you would know that they never cease preaching patience and humility . . . and the duty to obey temporal rulers. . . . When you say that we abandon the ancient doctrine to follow apostates, take a look in the mirror [*prenez vous-même par le nez*], you who renounced and rejected the blessed milk on which the late Queen, my mother, nourished you before Roman blandishments poisoned your understanding." The corruption of the early church was "a slight injury which your [party] has turned into a cancer. I agree with what you say about the Prince of Darkness, and you and those like you are his disciples."

Jeanne's irony reaches a climax when she takes up Armagnac's allusions to the Last Supper. "As to the three words . . . St. Augustine resolved this difficulty, as I have learned from our ministers . . . [who] I believe, have better noted the passage than you . . . because they do not make the mistake you made . . . [when you said that] Jesus Christ said before the Last Supper that he would speak no more in parables, whereas it is clear in the 13th chapter of St. John that it was *after* the Last Supper . . . read also St. Luke, chapter 22, again, before misquoting it. This kind of mistake might be forgiven me, a mere woman, but for a Cardinal to be so old and yet so ignorant, really Cousin, I am ashamed for you."

Armagnac had expressed the wish that Calvin and Beza would submit their ideas to a council. Jeanne says that the desire is shared by the Geneva leaders themselves, "on condition that the council be a free one and that their safety be guaranteed, having John Huss and Jerome of Prague in mind as examples of the liberty and safety of your councils." So much for rebuttal. Jeanne then takes the offensive.

You say that you are astonished that intelligent people can be so misled, so am I. If you lose patience . . . I have even less. I am very much annoyed that you, to whom God gave the grace of hearing the truth, should reject it and hold to such infamous idolatry . . . if you do not sin against the Holy Ghost, you come very close. I pray you hasten to repent before your sins close the door to God's mercy. . . . Keep the names "heretic," "seditious" . . . for you and yours. . . . I thank God that I know how to serve and please Him without your teaching. . . . I also know how my son should grow up and live in the true church, outside of which is no salvation.

You ask me not to find what you say either strange or evil. Strange, no, given your position, but as evil as anything on earth, especially when you excuse yourself as legate of the Pope. I have seen the price France paid for accepting a legate.* In Béarn I recognize only God, to whom I must account for the rule he has given me over His people. . . . Keep your tears for yourself . . . out of charity I will join mine to them . . . that you may return to the fold and become a true shepherd and not a hireling.

If you can find no stronger arguments . . . you cannot convince me . . . and please stop annoying me . . . let this useless letter be the last of its kind. . . . I see that you are determined to let loose on this little land of Béarn that flood of misfortune in which you recently attempted to drown France . . . I pray God to pardon you, trembling as I pray lest I be reproached as Samuel was when he wept for Saul.

From her who knows not how to describe herself, being unable to say "friend" and doubting our relationship until the day of your repentance, when she will be your cousin and friend,

Jehanne[17]

Both letters were printed and widely circulated in a little brochure.[18] If the contest had really been between Jeanne and Armagnac, the Queen of Navarre might have enjoyed at least a debater's victory, but the Cardinal's place was soon filled by a more formidable opponent. On September 28, Pius IV condemned Jeanne for heresy and summoned her to appear before the Inquisition in Rome within six months. This is called a *monitoire*, being put on notice. It is the "postponement" referred to by Merlin. If she failed to comply she faced excommunication and confiscation of her goods, while her lands would be declared "open to the first-comer who had the will and the force to take them."[19]

The papal warning illustrates the tendency of the Counter Reformation party to overplay its hand. The presumption of the Papacy to discipline Jeanne, as a ruler, over the head of the King of France, provoked a strong reaction at court and added fuel to the Gallican flames which were already feeding on articles being prepared at the Council of Trent, one of which declared Henri de Navarre a bastard. On October 18, Catherine de Medici wrote to her ambassador in Spain, Jean d'Ebrard, Seigneur de St. Sulpice, that the Council was proposing decrees which infringed upon the prerogatives of the French crown, including one depriving princes who tolerated heretics in their domains and another invalidating the rights of Henri.

As a result of such action the French delegation had been withdrawn from the Council and the Pope's ambassador to the French court had

---

* A reference to Hippolyte d'Este, Cardinal of Ferrara, whom the Huguenots blamed for the failure of the Colloquy and the extent to which the Edict of January limited Huguenot worship.

been sent back to Rome.[20] A letter from Charles IX to St. Sulpice on November 30 says, "The Pope has cited the Queen of Navarre in a warning posted on the crossroads . . . summoning her to appear in person,* failing which he arrogates to himself the right to give her kingdom to whomever he pleases. Since this is a strange act of great consequence for me and for my whole kingdom, I do not propose to let him do her wrong [je ne me delibère pas qu'il lui fasse tort]." The King asks St. Sulpice to "keep your eyes open and see if you can penetrate their intentions."[21] As early as the last week in November, observers were concluding that, because the crown was interposing itself between Jeanne and Rome, "the Pope will not proceed against the Queen of Navarre."[22] In December, Catherine sent one special agent, the Seigneur de Lansac, to Spain, and another, the Seigneur d'Oysel, to Rome, to protest the Pope's action, "which is against the ancient rights and privileges of the Gallican Church." (Pius also began proceedings against the Cardinal de Châtillon and eight French bishops.) Lansac was instructed to assure Philip that the King of France was satisfied with Jeanne's conduct, "since she had reinstated the Mass everywhere and was about to come to court in accordance with the King's request."[23]

Catherine was obliged to carry on intense diplomatic activity in Jeanne's behalf for many months to come, but by the end of the year 1563 everyone understood that the Queen of Navarre was under the King's protection. In return, Jeanne was required to modify her religious policy and agree to go to court. Catherine was always optimistic about her power to handle people if only she could keep them close to her.

The King of Spain was the first to understand that the papal attack was a failure, and he was ready with a new offensive of his own against Jeanne, while sending conventional messages of sympathy to Catherine through Lansac. As early as September 20, Throckmorton had told Cecil, "The King of Spain makes show to trouble the Queen of Navarre's country, and [he] will crown Don Carlos King of Navarre." The usually shrewd English ambassador was mistaken. Rather than open invasion —which would have met French resistance—Philip was planning to kidnap Jeanne and deliver her to the Inquisition in Spain. This was a highly complicated plot involving Monluc and a number of secret agents. It began in the autumn of 1563 and was not abandoned until Jeanne had

* It was usual for important persons to be allowed to be represented before the Inquisition.

actually reached court the following June. Several times plans had to be changed when information leaked out to agents of the other side—or those who were playing both sides. At the end of November, for example, an embroiderer in the employ of the Queen of Spain, Elizabeth de Valois, learned of the plot (through the indiscretion of one of the conspirators when drunk) and told his mistress, who in turn told the French ambassador. St. Sulpice wrote thanking the embroiderer, as well as the Queen, in the name of the King of France.[24] Catherine's agents and Jeanne herself received a steady stream of information and warnings in these months and Jeanne took care to conceal her moves, but of course it was impossible to know everything or to identify all the persons in the pay of the conspirators.

Surrounded by a network of spies and potential kidnapers, with the Pope's ultimatum and the threat to her son's rights hanging over her head, it is not surprising that Jeanne gave Merlin the impression that she was "paralyzed with fear," and that her ardor to "overthrow the Pope" had cooled. Moreover, the first organized rebellion in her domains broke out in Oloron in December 1563. Fortunately she was able to "pacify" the town in a few days and the sedition did not spread. The coincidence of all these dangers explains why Jeanne spent some time in her citadel of Navarrenx at the end of the year. While there she received word that Pius IV had excommunicated her, although only three of the six months mentioned in the *monitoire* had expired.[25]

Greatly in Catherine's debt for the crown's firm stand in her defense, Jeanne expressed her appreciation in an obsequious letter. "Your bounty has anticipated the very humble request I was going to make . . . to take my cause in hand . . . the only thing left is to bow my head, confessing that I can never sufficiently acknowledge this most recent favor . . . I put myself wholly under the wing of your powerful protection. . . . I will go to find you wherever you may be and shall kiss your feet more willingly than the Pope's."[26] But verbal assurance, however effusive, was not enough. She was obliged to obey the summons to court, but she could not do so until a trustworthy deputy was found to govern in her absence. For this task she asked Catherine to grant her the services of Antoine d'Aure, Comte de Gramont,* one of the leading seigneurs of Béarn,

---

* Gramont was considered a Huguenot in 1563, and he was undoubtedly sympathetic to the reform, but it is hard to be certain of his real convictions. When the test came, during the invasion of Jeanne's domains in 1569, he played a very equivocal role.

allied to the Châtillons and respected by all. Bordenave says of him, "a man of fine mind and excellent judgment, open-minded, most accessible, and possessed of this grace: that without discontenting one religious faction he satisfied the other. He was liked and respected by both sides."[27]

Pending her departure, it was necessary for Jeanne to convince Catherine that she intended to cooperate. For this she turned to Montmorency. In a letter to the Constable she explains that she must have Gramont on the spot before she can leave, chiefly because of Monluc's machinations. "I would have gone to court long ago except for the new obstacles which arise, every time I am on the point of departing, through the agency of Monluc, who never stops creating all the disturbances he can, such as seizing my property at Nérac, Mont-de-Marsan, Lectoure, Casteljaloux. . . ."[28]

The Queen of Navarre was reported on her way to court as early as December 19, and Merlin's letter of Christmas Day says gloomily that "the Estates will be held in a few days and I fear we will encounter more obstacles . . . the sole reason for holding them is to get money for the trip the Queen wishes to make to court. . . . May God will it to be for her welfare." He says that he will accompany her and urges Calvin to write because Jeanne "wants your opinion, not so much because she does not know it, but in order to have a further pretext for delay [in the reform] until she arrives at court, where excuses will not be lacking."[29]

Jeanne was obliged to modify her religious policy in the direction desired by Catherine. The Queen Mother wrote Gramont that "His Majesty so loves and respects the Queen of Navarre that he is resolved to move Heaven and earth [*employer le vert et le sec*] to protect her from whoever might attack her . . . in order to avoid new problems [we] have given her to understand that she must conduct [affairs] in such a way that her subjects will not be led to rebel nor her neighbors to support them. . . . She could do no better than what the King himself does, that is, to let them all live in freedom of conscience and in the exercise of their own religion without forcing [the conscience] of any."[30]

Some formula had to be found which would minimize Catholic resistance but also provide sufficient leeway for the increasing number of Calvinists, whom Descurra had described as "growing like weeds." They were undoubtedly a minority, but they were highly placed: nobles, magistrates, merchants, and Jeanne's entourage. By an Edict of February 2, 1564, Jeanne permitted Mass to be celebrated in places where it was currently authorized, but not where it had been suppressed. The movable wealth (chalices, crosses, ornaments) of the churches and the religious orders was liquidated and the money distributed to the poor by secular authorities. Calvinists might hold services wherever they were presently permitted and in others the Queen chose to add. All crimes committed under the pretext of religion were pardoned unless lese majesty were involved.[31] Dartigue notes that this was the first official proclamation of religious toleration within a single kingdom in European history.*

In addition to Gramont, Jeanne took into her service at this time the most colorful of all the ministers from Geneva who figure in her story, Jacques de Spifâme, Sieur de Passy. His family was among the Italians who rose in the service of the French crown early in the century and he had held important posts, including the bishopric of Nevers, during the reign of Henri II. After the King's death he turned Calvinist and went to Geneva. He had served the Prince de Condé as ambassador to the German princes and helped to promote Calvinism in Lyons. In January 1564, Jeanne asked the Geneva authorities for the loan of Spifâme, because she knew no one better qualified to meet her "need for some virtuous and excellent person with integrity in religious matters, piety, and sound morals; learned, experienced, and gifted in advising and conducting affairs of state, justice, and law enforcement."[32] Immediately upon his arrival in Pau, Spifâme became Jeanne's chancellor and general supervisor of her affairs. In addition, he took a prominent part in the Synod that met on March 14. Merlin was elected to preside, in spite of the rule that nobody should hold that position twice, but the assembly charged M. de Passy with a number of important duties, including "to urge the Queen, before her departure, to establish the Protestant college at Orthez and to draw up the oath to be sworn by the teachers."[33]

Before her departure Jeanne reorganized the Sovereign Council and established another to handle ecclesiastical affairs. Gramont, who pre-

---

* Exception must be made for certain free cities. The Peace of Augsburg (1555) allowed the princes of Germany to choose (between Catholicism and Lutheranism only) but gave no freedom to individuals. In England the Act of Uniformity (1559) authorized only Anglican services, although it can be argued that the administration of the act provided a good measure of de facto toleration under the Elizabethan settlement. In France, even under the Edict of Nantes (1598), Calvinist worship was much more restricted than Roman Catholic worship. Whatever the statutes said, her opponents did not consider Jeanne's policy tolerant.

sided at its first meeting on March 20, sent a glowing report to Catherine the following day. He states that the crown may take satisfaction in the state of affairs in Jeanne's absence, "even in matters of religion, which are so well arranged that all her subjects express satisfaction. . . . [In achieving this] the arrival of M. de Passy, who has been here for three weeks or a month, has greatly helped us. I only wish he had been here six months ago . . . [if he had] religious affairs would have been conducted more quietly and with less exaggeration. He does not favor the haste with which things have been done." Indeed, Spifâme's criticism of Merlin's policy was one cause of the feud that later developed between him and Jeanne, during the course of which sensational charges were made on both sides. But this was the honeymoon period. Gramont continues, "knowing how much Your Majesty desires not only the conservation of the Queen of Navarre's domains but also the good management of her household, [you will be pleased that] the said Queen has put it entirely in the hands of the said Sieur de Passy . . . one realizes how much such a person was needed . . . I beg Your Majesty to write [and tell Jeanne] to believe in him."[34]

Gramont says that Jeanne is writing a letter thanking Philip for the expression of good will transmitted by Lansac, in the hope of restoring at least the outward forms of civility between them—one of Catherine's goals. This (undated) letter does not seem to have been dispatched until the following month. It was never answered because Philip refused to use the title "Queen of Navarre" and Jeanne would accept no communications addressed to "Madame de Vendôme."[35] Earlier Jeanne had appointed Savary d'Aure, Baron de Larboust, a cousin of Gramont's, as her envoy to Philip. In a letter of introduction for Larboust to St. Sulpice, she says that she wishes the French ambassador to add to or revise the instructions as he sees fit, "so that they will advance the King's affairs, which I do not wish to separate from my own." Among other things, Larboust's instructions said that, "although there were differences of religion, she had never believed that on that account [Philip] wished to quarrel or stir up trouble in her country" and that she considered each to be sovereign in his own country, "free to maintain his people in such religion as seemed best to him. . . . Differences in religion are no excuse for war in Christendom."[36]

Even if Jeanne was as frightened as Merlin thought, she never betrayed it to the enemy.

JEANNE AND THE CROWN, 1564–1566

Nearly six months had elapsed since Catherine had undertaken Jeanne's defense and summoned her to court. Jeanne had given signs of accommodation and made arrangements to be absent from her domains, but she still procrastinated, even after leaving Béarn in late March. The fact that Catherine was taking the young King on a tour of the realm provided an excuse. "I assure you Madame," Jeanne wrote, probably in early May, "that if I had been sure of your departure, I would have been ready sooner to go and receive the honor of kissing your hands. . . . I am off to Limoges and if I am informed of your route I will meet you before you arrive in Lyons."[37]

Catherine had two objectives in taking the King and court on the tour, which was to last two years (March 1564–May 1566). The first was to "pacify" the troubles and unify the King's subjects by exposing them to his presence and by rallying their leaders to the crown. The second was to meet in person with the King of Spain. Relations with her most powerful neighbor had become increasingly strained; their exchanges about Jeanne are typical. Chantonay was no longer effective and Philip appointed a new ambassador, Don Francis d'Alava, early in 1564. As with lesser adversaries, Catherine felt that if she could only talk to Philip "everything could be arranged" with her son-in-law. Her emphasis on the relationship is consistent with her policy of seeking solutions by exploiting family ties and arranging alliances through marriage. Philip made this difficult by not committing himself until the very last minute.

As the court traveled, Catherine extended the royal favor now to one faction and now to the other. The first spring was spent in the eastern provinces. First, Champagne, in April, where the Treaty of Troyes with England was signed. By regaining Le Havre from England for only 120,000 gold crowns and by evading the question of Calais, this treaty embodied the success of Catherine's recent military and diplomatic policy. In early May, the court honored the Guise-Lorraine family, by attending a christening (immortalized by Ronsard) in Bar-le-Duc. During the court's stay in Dijon, the next major stop, the chief subject of conversation was the birth of a son to Mademoiselle de Limeuil, a cousin of Catherine's and a member of her flying squadron, mistress of the Prince de Condé. This occurred shortly before Jeanne's arrival, and one can imagine that her reluctance to join the court was not lessened by the prospect of seeing her brother-in-law made a fool of as her husband had been.[38]

A more important occurrence, the death of Calvin on May 27, although ignored at court, was important to Jeanne, as well as to Renée of Ferrara, who was also traveling to meet Catherine when she learned of it. Some weeks earlier, after Jeanne had visited the Duchess at Montargis, Renée recounted their principal differences to the Geneva reformer. As the climax of a very long letter justifying her own ambiguous position, Renée complains that some of Calvin's ministers, who have been trying to persuade her to take a definite stand, seem to sanction lies, if they will further the cause, and to advocate total condemnation of those of the opposite party, even if one has family ties with them. "I must tell you that I do not believe such lying words come from God." Since the ministers apply their arguments specifically to the Duc de Guise, her murdered son-in-law, she also focuses on his case. "I know that he was guilty of persecution, but I do not believe God holds it against him, frankly, because before he died he gave signs of repenting, but nobody wants to admit it and they try to close the mouths of those who know it. . . . I know that I was hated . . . by many, because he was my son-in-law . . . they want to blame him for the faults of all of us." Renée is particularly offended that these accusations are made against a dead man. When this line of argument was presented "one day, in this place, to the Queen of Navarre and myself, and all possible evil was being said of him," the Duchess continues, "I asked [the speaker], in her presence, to say under oath whether he was telling the truth or not.

> He confessed that he was not . . . but claimed that it was necessary [to lie] for the preservation of the Religion, an opinion approved by the said lady [Jeanne], who added that any means was legitimate in defense of religion and that lying was good and holy in such a case [*la mensonge estoit bonne et saincte en telle endroit*] . . . I cannot believe this, since Satan is the father of lies and God of the truth. . . . Nevertheless, the said lady has so much zeal and such good judgment in many things that I should like to be able to follow her example. Her mother . . . was the first [French] princess to sponsor the Gospel and it could be that her daughter will succeed in establishing it. It seems to me that she is as well-suited . . . as any woman I know. I love her with a mother's love and praise all the graces God has bestowed upon her.[39]

Renée obviously did not believe that the furtherance of the true religion justified the use of lies. In an exchange of letters on the question, "Did Jeanne d'Albret approve of lies?," one editor of Calvin's letters, Jules Bonnet, defended Jeanne on the ground that Renée's praise of her in the latter part of the letter reduces the importance of the statement in question, "which appears more an offhand expression of annoyance than an opinion arrived at by reflection." He adds, "Let us not be more severe on the Queen than Renée de France."[40] But the problem can be resolved, if at all, only in the context of the general question of Jeanne's tolerance, or lack of it. Significantly, this conversation concerned the Duc de Guise, and Jeanne was never objective about the Guises, as she was about some other opponents.

Jeanne too was in contact with Geneva during the spring of 1564. From St. Léonard, near Limoges, she wrote on May 16 to the Council to say that she was sending with Spifâme "my nephew Nemours . . . to be well instructed in his youth, so that his life may from the beginning be regulated by good and honest discipline . . . as it is in your city." The "nephew," Henri de Savoie, Comte de Genevois, was the illegitimate son of Jeanne's cousin Françoise de Rohan and the Duc de Nemours. He had been born in Jeanne's household and she undertook responsibility for his support and education. He was placed in the care of Laurent de Normandie, one of the most respected Genevan publishers.[41]

Jeanne joined the court at Mâcon on June 3rd. Observers' reports reflect the incongruity of her personality in that milieu. After Antoine's death Jeanne never wore anything but heavy mourning; in her train were eight Calvinist ministers, including Spifâme, also somberly dressed, singing psalms and reciting long prayers. An escort of three hundred cavalry accompanied her, necessitated, she claimed, by the plots of Monluc and the Spaniards. The day after her arrival, the Corpus Christi procession passed under windows either tightly shuttered or occupied by "heretics shouting insolent and obscene remarks" in the lodgings of the Queen of Navarre and her suite.[42] Santa Croce had told Borromeo that neither Jeanne nor Renée was *persona grata* at court but that the former's presence could be very useful for the policy of pacification.[43] This judgment was predicated on the assumption that the Queen of Navarre would be cooperative, which turned out to be wishful thinking. It was awkward for the crown, to say the least, to have Jeanne reasserting her Calvinist leadership while Catherine continued to reassure Philip and the Pope that she had complied with her request and no longer deserved punishment.

French diplomacy had been so successful in recent months that even the Emperor was supporting Jeanne against the Pope, but, as Catherine's ambassador in Rome complained on the very day of Corpus Christi, "His Holiness always comes back to the fact that the said lady forces the consciences of her subjects and will not confine herself to the liberty allowed in your edicts."[44] When a special procession, described as "so devout one would have thought oneself in Spain," took place on June 8, Jeanne and her followers did not dare to protest disrespectfully in the King's own presence, but as soon as the court reached Lyons, where there was an active Huguenot community, she attended the public sermons and took Henri with her. This greatly irritated Catherine, who stopped Calvinist services within the city, removed Henri from under Jeanne's roof (where he had been allowed to stay as a favor), and snapped at Madame de Crussol, "I will cut off the head of anyone who does not attend Mass." She forbade her ladies to visit Jeanne's apartments "for any reason," on pain of exile from the court.[45]

Jeanne was not without allies, however. Pierre Viret, one of Calvin's most important lieutenants, was the leader of the Lyons Huguenots at this time. According to Santa Croce, when news of Calvin's death arrived, Viret "left for Geneva to be elected in [Calvin's] place, but, having learned en route that it had been given to Beza, he returned." The Nuncio's report of his own dealings with the Calvinist preacher testifies to Viret's reputation.

> I tried to win over Viret, the most famous of the Huguenot preachers. . . . He came first to see me, complaining that he was dying of hunger. He also said that, if he were convinced that he was in error, he would change his opinion. . . . When the Queen Mother heard that I had talked to him, she asked . . . me to follow it up (as I was not so extreme in my opinions as others and he might listen to me). [Catherine] greatly desires to reconcile the conflicting opinions and she suggested that I offer [Viret] money, . . . saying that if he would preach the opposite of what he now says . . . all the other Huguenots would follow him.[46]

Santa Croce then arranged for a confrontation in his private apartments between Viret and an Italian Jesuit, Possovino. "They argued for a long time and finally Viret said that it was enough for one day, but that he would continue another time if he could be joined by others of his opinion. It seems to me that another colloquy may be in the offing, and I hope for some favorable result. . . . I do not wish Your Holiness to be too hopeful, however, for much evil might result instead." There was no real sequel to this intriguing episode because the plague had broken out in Lyons and within a month the court had moved on, but Viret's battle of words with Possovino and other Catholic polemicists had marked him as dangerous and he was later banished from France. It is possible that Jeanne decided as a result of the 1564 events to procure the services of Viret. Four years later she appointed him director of the Academy at Orthez and he played a leading role in Béarnais Protestantism until his death.

Although she was out of favor and restricted in the exercise of her rights, the Queen of Navarre still had influence. A well-known humanist jurist, Charles du Moulin, who held the office of *conseiller et Maître des Requêtes de l'hôtel de la Reine de Navarre,* had been condemned on June 5 by the Parlement of Paris for a book on the Council of Trent that outdid in Gallicanism even that Gallican stronghold. The crown at first supported the judgment (June 15), but less than a week later Charles wrote to the Parlement requesting Du Moulin's release, "because certain considerations make it desirable that he be more gently treated." The considerations were the intervention of the Queen of Navarre and the Duchess of Ferrara.[47]

It was at Crémieu (Isère), on July 9, that Jeanne finally obtained an official audience to present her two requests: to return to her own domains and to take her son with her. Both were refused. Henri would continue to accompany the King and Jeanne was instructed to take up residence in Vendôme, where she would be much farther from the Spanish frontier— and much less independent.[48] Vendôme was held in fief of the crown; there, Jeanne was merely Duchess.

The Queen of Navarre did not leave until some time after her dismissal; she was still at court during part of its sojourn in Roussillon, from mid-July to mid-September. From there Jeanne wrote a letter of condolence to the Comtesse de La Rochefoucauld (whose sister, the Princesse de Condé, had died in July) in which she says that she is going to Vendôme for reasons of health. She left on August 14, "little satisfied," according to Santa Croce, who also says, "it is believed she spits blood regularly."[49] Henri continued to travel with the court, and within a few weeks Nostradamus, the famous astrologer, prophesied that he would become King of France.

In Vendôme, Jeanne came into conflict with the crown once again. "Disorders" were occurring because, according to the Protestants, the agent [Miron] sent by Catherine to administer the Edict of Amboise was persecuting them. On the other hand, Jeanne had appointed two ardent Calvinists as Governor and Lieutenant-Governor of the duchy. The murder of the latter officer, Philibert de La Curée, Sieur de La Roche-Turpin, precipitated an open clash between Jeanne and the crown's agents, including the Duc de Montpensier, Prince of the Blood and ranking royal officer in Anjou. In the words of an anonymous contemporary English reporter,

> Some of those which slew de la Curea (sic) were in a place not far from Vendôme, where the Queen of Navarre lies. She caused a number of men to be raised, took them, and laid them in prison in Vendôme. The Duke of Montpensier sent to have them out, but she would not deliver them. Another sort of these which slew [De la Curée] got into a house which belonged to one of the archers of the King's guard and would not suffer her officers . . . to come in, nor deliver the malefactors. [Jeanne's officers] then burned the house and all in it.[50]

In the long run, the King supported Jeanne and Montpensier was relieved of his command after a stream of violent protests from the Duchesse de Vendôme, but the conflict lasted many months. One of Jeanne's unpublished letters to Catherine deals with this episode.

Madame:

> I am no less distressed by the necessity to importune you than the occasion for it is annoying . . . but it is my duty . . . I have summoned . . . Miron several times to see for himself . . . how those guilty of the murder of La Curée are escaping justice, but he would not listen. . . . The consequence, Madame, is that . . . the murderers have taken refuge in a fortress . . . belonging to the King . . . I sent to M. de Montpensier at once, since it is in his government. . . . You can judge all the facts for yourself, Madame, since copies of all the letters I have written and received on this matter [are available]. I pray you, Madame, take pity on the poor domains of Touraine, Maine, and Vendômois, and send a *commissaire* who is *homme de bien* and who has enough force to see that Your Majesties are obeyed.[51]

Little else is known about Jeanne's activities during these months after her departure from court. She was supposed to confine herself to the duchy but does not appear to have done so. Her correspondence shows that she spent some time at La Flèche and that at least one of several meetings with the Châtillons took place in their fief, in November 1564, when "the Scot who slew the King" was also present. This was Gabriel de Lorges, Comte de Montgomery, Captain of the royal Scottish Guard (until his lance accidentally caused the death of Henri II), and later Jeanne's commander-in-chief in Béarn.[52]

All Huguenot leaders were apprehensive about the approaching interview at Bayonne, where Catherine encountered the Queen of Spain and the Duke of Alva, whom Philip allowed to go to France although he refused to go himself. The dispatches of St. Sulpice from Madrid show how Catherine's defense of the Queen of Navarre and Jeanne's own actions contributed to Philip's alibi. The French ambassador had protested the violation of Jeanne's county of Foix by Spanish forces in November 1564 because the crown took the position that Jeanne's sovereign rights and her religious policy were two separate matters. For Philip, heretics had no rights, especially if they were sovereigns, and he recognized no "Queen of Navarre" except one of his own making. In a letter to Philip's wife, Elizabeth de Valois, who was acting as intermediary, St. Sulpice pleads, in March 1565, that "the variety of humors in our kingdom and the necessity and evils of the times oblige us to be patient." He asks the Spanish Queen to persuade her husband not to treat Jeanne so differently from all the others. A week later he explained in a secret letter to Catherine that the Queen of Spain had been delayed in setting out because Philip "understood that the Queen of Navarre, whom he calls Madame de Vendôme, and the Prince de Condé would accompany the King [of France] . . . the Queen of Spain cannot give the title of Queen to Madame de Vendôme because it would prejudice her own rights [to Navarre] and [Philip] does not wish her to meet with rebels and fomenters of sedition." A few days later he informed Catherine that Philip would permit no Spanish representatives to attend any meeting if Jeanne and Condé were to be present. St. Sulpice advised Catherine to take Philip at his word and renounce the unrealistic plan to bring the Spaniards and the Huguenots together. He appeals to Catherine's pride of family by emphasizing the pleasure it would give her to meet Elizabeth de Valois and the opportunity to arrange royal marriages, her favorite form of diplomacy.

About April 15, Catherine told St. Sulpice that Jeanne and Condé would not join the court until after the Bayonne meeting, yet she still hoped to change Philip's mind. St. Sulpice wearily made another assault on the Spanish King, but on May 7 he wrote, "Far from changing his mind . . . the King declares that he would never give his consent . . .

[because] among other reasons, his subjects would be scandalized and would no longer regard his wife as Queen if she were to frequent such company." He added that if Elizabeth were only half a league from Bayonne and found out that Jeanne and Condé were there, "she would turn right around and go home."[53]

The interview at Bayonne looms large in Huguenot history because contemporary Protestants and many historians before the twentieth century saw in it the origins of the Massacre of St. Bartholomew. Although modern scholars are agreed that there was no specific "premeditation" of the massacre, at Bayonne or elsewhere, the interview was an important link in the chain of events during which developed the alliance between the ultra-Catholic party in France and Spain, known later as the Holy League. St. Sulpice predicted the reaction of the Huguenots to the Bayonne meeting and warned Catherine that to exclude Jeanne and Condé was to confirm their suspicions.[54]

Huguenot fears would have been justified by the Duke of Alva's instructions: to secure Catherine's promise that Protestant worship would be wholly suppressed in France, Calvinist ministers banished, and judges and other important officers required to take an oath of Catholic orthodoxy. The declaration issued at the end of the conference (July 27, 1565), as vague as most statements of agreement in principle, gave an impression that everyone was satisfied, but Alva confided to Philip the fear that "the heretics at court and others about to arrive will change the Queen's mind."[55] Catherine did in fact turn to a policy of appeasing Calvinist leaders as soon as she left Bayonne. She gave Jeanne permission to go to Nérac and paid her the honor of a state visit at the end of July.

When the court traveled it required about eight thousand horses, "like an army on the march." The royal family, with one hundred gentlemen-in-waiting and as many pages, was flanked by a Swiss guard and the Scottish guard. Then came stewards, officers, and servants of the crown, as well as such necessary attendants as surgeons and lawyers. To this must be added the suites of the foreign ambassadors and the flying squadron (eighty girls and as many servants). Moreover, each Prince of the Blood, with his own retainers, swelled the mainstream of the royal party. There were also many wagons full of clothing and equipment. What the Venetian ambassador called a "nomad city" of persons who supplied necessities to supplement provisions that could be commandeered locally must also be mentioned.[56] It must have been difficult to accommodate such an influx even in sizable towns like Lyons or Bordeaux. In Nérac it is hard to imagine; one is obliged to assume that all except the most important persons were housed in tents.

The chateau, built by Marguerite in pure French Renaissance style, was in those days approached by a drawbridge over the Baïse. From the modern bridge which has replaced it, the royal park is immediately below on the left; to the right, upstream, one sees a curiously shaped medieval stone bridge and the roofs of the town. Directly ahead is a high terrace dominated by the remains of a great fountain. Only one wing of the chateau survived an eighteenth-century fire, which also destroyed the communal archives of Jeanne's period. To reconstruct the court's visit to Nérac, therefore, one must draw heavily on the historical imagination and it is tantalizing to have no details of what Abel Jouan calls *quatre jours de gala.*

Historians of the Bourbon family say that Charles and Catherine tried to persuade Jeanne to restore Catholicism in Béarn during this visit. If so—and it is likely—they were obviously unsuccessful, although she did ease the situation of Roman Catholics in the Duchy of Albret, of which Nérac is the capital. Catherine nevertheless allowed Henri to stay with his mother for some time after the court moved on, making its way through Angoulême, Saintonge, and Anjou in the late summer and autumn. Jeanne meanwhile received Condé, and accompanied him to a meeting of Huguenot leaders in Cognac.[57] She also spent some time at La Flèche before rejoining the court.

On December 8 Charles IX wrote his new ambassador to Spain, Raymond de Rouer, Sieur de Fourqueveux, that he had reached Blois the day before and that his aunt, the Queen of Navarre, her son, and the Prince de Condé had arrived to pay their respects. He added that he was expecting Coligny, the Cardinal de Lorraine, and the Constable at any minute.[58] This turn of the year 1565–6 was marked by another of Catherine's many "reconciliations," which was no more substantial than earlier ones. By February new quarrels had dispelled the illusory harmony.

In addition, new dangers had appeared on the further horizon. One, relatively minor, was the clash of Frenchmen and Spaniards in Florida. In spite of some fairly sharp protests and demands for reparations for the massacre of a colony there in September 1565, the French did not really fight for Florida. One explanation may be that a majority of the

235

Frenchmen involved were Huguenots, and to expend energies on their defense would be to strengthen Coligny and exacerbate the conflict with Spain.[59] A more serious problem developing closer to home would offer Coligny a greater opportunity, present Philip with a greater challenge, and pose new complications to Catherine de Medici: the Netherlands revolt was taking shape and the Huguenot leaders were preparing to support it on a big scale.

With these added to older dissensions, the court atmosphere did not reflect the harmony Catherine sought. Sir Thomas Smith wrote to William Cecil on December 10, "The Huguenots look that the Edict of Pacification should forthwith be broken and they to have no other remedy but to take themselves to their weapons. The Papists also look for no less than that the King and Queen should openly declare . . . that they would have but one [Catholic] religion in France." The next day he reports further agitation because of preaching at court, sponsored by the Queen of Navarre, the Prince de Condé, and the Duchess of Ferrara. "The Cardinal de Bourbon charged the Queen of Navarre that she did contrary to the edicts. She replied that she did none other than as she was licensed by the King in Lyons. These three were licensed to have preaching and exercise of the [Calvinist] religion in their chambers in the court, but to their domestics only and [with] the doors shut."[60] This was the first mention of a falling out between Jeanne and her brother-in-law, the Cardinal de Bourbon, one of Jeanne's many quarrels at court.

Moulins was the last long stopping place on the tour. The Queen of Navarre was a member of the royal caravan as it inched its way toward Paris between late March and May 1, 1566. The Spanish ambassador expressed anxiety that under her influence the Duc d'Anjou was moderating his opposition to the Huguenots and exasperation that she continued to hold Protestant services—with all the doors open.[61]

JEANNE IN PARIS, 1566

It has not yet been possible to establish where Jeanne stayed in Paris in 1566, the longest visit she ever made to the capital. (In earlier years, she probably stayed at court.) The eighteenth-century historians of Paris claim that Jeanne and Antoine possessed two town houses, one on the Ile de la Cité (on the site of the Hôtel-Dieu), and the other in the Marais, on the rue du Roi-de-Sicile (4th *arrondissement*). The latter, best-known as the Hôtel de St. Paul (from its owner in the early seven-teenth century, François d'Orléans-Longueville, Comte de St. Paul), was an imposing residence covering the ground bounded by the rue Pavée, the rue des Francs-Bourgeois, the rue de Sévigné, and the rue du Roi-de-Sicile. M. Jean-Pierre Babelon, Director of the Museum at the Archives Nationales and an authority on Renaissance Paris, doubts that Jeanne owned either of these establishments, but he thinks it quite possible that she and Henri may have rented the latter.* It was owned by Marguerite de Valois (first wife of Henri IV) between 1582 and 1601, and therefore called *l'Hôtel de la Reine de Navarre* for a few years, which may account for the confusion,—between Jeanne and her daughter-in-law.[62]

The most agreeable known event of Jeanne's eight-month sojourn, otherwise so fraught with crises and feuds, was her visit to the Estienne† printing establishment on May 21, 1566. While she was inspecting the presses, Estienne asked her to compose something he could print to commemorate the occasion. The result was a somewhat stiff quatrain:

> Art singulier, d'ici aux derniers ans
> Representez aux enfans de ma race,
> Que j'ai suivi des Craignans-Dieu la trace
> Afin qu'ils soient des mêmes pas suivans.

A few copies of Jeanne's verse and Estienne's response—allegedly also written on the spur of the moment—were set in type with the date and distributed (probably) to members of Jeanne's suite.[63]

Since her espousal of Calvinism and consequent isolation in court circles, Jeanne had had much less contact with writers and artists. When she and Antoine enjoyed royal favor, verses or prose *encomia* had been addressed to her by, among others, Charles de Fontaine and Joachim du Bellay. Jacques Pelletier, who had planned to dedicate his *Dialogue de*

---

* M. Babelon is currently working on sixteenth-century Parisian dwellings and it is to be hoped that he will solve the mystery of Jeanne's town residence. The so-called Hôtel d'Albret, 31 rue des Francs-Bourgeois, built by the Montmorencys in the 1550's, was reconstructed by Mansart in the seventeenth century before coming into the possession of César-Phoebus d'Albret in 1648. Descended from a collateral branch of Jeanne's family, César-Phoebus, who maintained a very grand household, is responsible for the association of the house with the name, Albret. It is also adjacent to the site of the former Hôtel du Roi-de-Sicile or St. Paul, which probably compounded the confusion.

† Robert (II) Estienne, 1528–1592, of the third generation of the great family of printers, known for his fine Greek and Hebrew texts, was her host. The response he wrote to Jeanne's verse appears at the end of this chapter.

l'autographe (Lyons, 1551) to Marguerite, honored her daughter instead, since it was not actually published until after Marguerite's death. Jeanne was included, with other ranking ladies, in François Billon's *Le fort inexpugnable du sexe feminin* (Paris, 1555). Other dedications in earlier years included two translations from the Italian.[64] After 1561 there was a dearth of such tributes, except for a few written by young, female, Huguenot admirers.[65] A Basque translation of the New Testament, by Jean de Liçarrague, which Jeanne herself had commissioned, was dedicated to her in 1571, at La Rochelle, but it is in a different category. Apart from the fact that the French Renaissance was fading out in the chilling atmosphere of the Wars of Religion, her concerns were far removed from the world of courtly letters.

Much of Jeanne's time and energy in Paris was consumed in dealing with thorny situations in her various domains. This had been difficult enough in the duchy of Vendôme, when she was on the spot. With other lands held in fief from the crown she had to cope at long distance. In some regions, local leaders exploited Jeanne's religious differences with the King and the weakness of her position to free themselves of inherited obligations. In Limoges, for instance, the town fathers and their Vicomtesse came into conflict over three basic powers of government— justice, taxation, and the control of the military. The challenge to her authority originated in resistance to the establishment of Calvinism in 1563 and 1564. Jeanne had thought it important enough to go to Limoges in person in the spring of the latter year, thereby delaying her arrival at court. The town sent four separate delegations to negotiate with the Sovereign Lady in the next two years. Eventually she yielded the right to raise arms and some financial prerogatives, but clung stubbornly to the rights of *haut justicier*.

This was fundamentally a struggle in the classic pattern, whereby towns strengthened their autonomy at the expense of the feudal class by exploiting conflicts of the latter with the crown; but it was compounded by the religious issue. The opposition was led by ultra-Catholics and the faction loyal to Jeanne was largely made up of Calvinists. Moreover, the majority of the population could be swung against Jeanne by playing on fears which arose directly out of the politico-religious tension. One was the fear of being on the losing side; since the crown was stronger than the Vicomtesse, Limoges would eventually pay the price of disobedience if it followed her wishes. Another was the fear of social upheaval. Huguenots confiscated church property and introduced innovations in marriages, wills, and education, among other things, so that the traditional order would be weakened and perhaps destroyed if Jeanne had her way.[66]

More dramatic was the situation in the county of Foix, at the opposite end of Jeanne's domains from Limoges. Foix, in the central Pyrenees, was the fief of Jeanne's most distinguished ancestors on the paternal side. Throughout the county and especially in its capital, Pamiers, small but zealous Calvinist congregations had grown up since Jeanne's conversion, while the bishop took advantage of her difficulties to enlist royal support in restoring church property which had been taken over by the reformers. The King's council issued no less than seven rulings on this matter between 1563 and 1567—all against Jeanne.[67] By the most important of these, on February 20, 1566, Calvinist worship was abolished in Pamiers on the grounds that it had not been established before March 7, 1563, and therefore violated the terms of the Pacification of Amboise. (The Calvinists asserted that it was established long before but had been suspended in March 1563 because of the plague.) As a result of the suppression of the reform, the situation in Pamiers burst into flames in May 1566. The Parlement of Toulouse undertook to repress the sedition and succeeded only in intensifying the conflict, which became a civil war on a local scale. In her *Mémoires,* Jeanne refers bitterly to "the wrong done me in my county of Foix and my towns of Pamiers and Foix, which at this time were pillaged, sacked, and consumed by garrisons and commissions, in which I was denied all justice and had to suffer the annulment of the privileges given by former kings to my ancestors."[68] The county was not "pacified," and continuing conflict there was one reason for Jeanne's return to the south a few months later.

Even where she was "sovereign" all was not serene in Jeanne's absence. The legislation of 1564, for all its embodiment of tolerance, had provoked resistance from both Catholics and Protestants in Béarn, and Gramont's considerable talents were not sufficient to prevent many violent incidents. At their meeting of September 1565, the Estates protested strongly against being "constrained to furnish lodgings for [Calvinist] ministers" and against the requirement "that all teachers must be equipped with a certificate of Protestant orthodoxy." The Roman Catholic clergy flatly refused to attend the session held in May 1566.[69]

A few days after the adjournment of the Estates, a Calvinist synod

was held in the town of Nay. Jeanne had convoked the ministers by letter (in April) in which she urged the "continuation of the purification of
doctrine [as well as] of the discipline of the churches." In conclusion she
asked them "not to fail to keep her apprised of what was done in the said
assembly." Accordingly, the presiding officer, Michel Vigneau, was sent
to report to the Queen at court and to request her "to carry out the suppression of all vestiges of idolatry." In response, Jeanne issued the Ordinances of July 1566, which renewed and extended the prohibitions
against Catholic ceremonies and instituted the first "puritan" laws against
blasphemy, drunkenness, gambling, and prostitution. Pierre Viret was
appointed to direct the College at Orthez and turn it into a Calvinist
academy on the Geneva model. Most serious of all, the procedure for
the bestowal of benefices was altered, antagonizing virtually the entire
nobility. Gramont decided to suspend the enforcement of these ordinances
temporarily, because, in Bordenave's words, "not a few of the Reformed
religion and all those of the Catholic [religion] said that only angels
and not men could live according to them."[70] Protests poured in declaring
that the new regulations not only set aside time-honored custom but also
violated Jeanne's own legislation of 1564. Isolated instances of resistance
and violence gave way to more organized local action. It was only a
matter of time before widespread rebellion would explode.

The necessity to bolster her crumbling authority, and royal confirmation of Henri's rights to some of his father's lands gave Jeanne an excuse
to absent herself from court—with Henri—for weeks at a time. She
asked permission, first, to take him to the county of Marle in Picardy,
later, to Vendôme. Each time she was allowed to go "only to visit her
domains," after pleading the necessity to introduce her son to his subjects. Each time she stayed away a bit longer. Catherine may have been
under the delusion that Jeanne had been intimidated into submission. The
Queen Mother, moreover, had bigger worries, for Pius V, the new Pope,
had recently aimed a whole series of bulls at the French crown,* and
Philip II was requesting permission for a Spanish army to cross French

---

* June 16, 1566, urging greater severity toward heretics; June 20, urging acceptance of the Trent decrees; June 27, urging extermination of the Huguenots; October
17, condemnation of the reformers in general terms; December 11, condemnation of
six French bishops for heresy: Jean de St. Gelais, Bishop of Uzès; Antoine Caracciolo,
Bishop of Troyes; Charles Guillart, Bishop of Chartres; Jean de Monluc, Bishop of
Valence; Louis d'Albret, Bishop of Lescar; Claude Régin, Bishop of Oloron. This last
was the climax of proceedings brought against them by Pius IV in 1563. For details,
see C. Hirschauer, *La Politique de St. Pie V en France* (Paris, 1922), 17–19.

territory on its way to suppress the Dutch Revolt. The request was de-nied and the bulls ignored, but both added fuel to the explosive situa-tion in France. Catherine was apparently taken by surprise when the Spanish ambassador told her, in mid-February 1567, that he thought the Queen of Navarre had made her escape from "France" altogether, taking her son and all her retainers with her. She was still in Paris on January 23, when Sir Henry Norris mentions that Henri, with the King and his brothers, took part in a game of charging the barrier, but on January 26 the same Englishman reports, "The Queen of Navarre, the Prince de Condé, and the Admiral are departed. The Queen is in some sort discon-tented, that having a preacher at her house in Paris, the King had com-manded the Provost-Marshal to hang him on her gates; but the preacher being conveyed away, she thereupon took her leave."[71]

Jeanne went first to La Flèche, for which she had permission, in the last days of January. From there, after she had received news of the smouldering crisis in Béarn, she crossed into Poitou and thence, in secrecy and great haste, into her own domains, "carrying her son to safety across the Garonne, which had been her principal object in going to the court three years before," as Palma Cayet says in his *Chronologie Novenaire.* In the *Mémoires,* Jeanne merely says that she had permission (*par leur congé*) and that she retired because she knew the "troubles" were about to begin again.[72] In fact, the Second Civil War did not break out until September 1567, and the Huguenots took the offensive. Jeanne must have been anticipating her return and trying to decide what to do about the religious situation in Béarn for some weeks. She concluded a long letter to Beza on December 6, "since I am thinking of returning some day to my sovereign estates, I pray you to advise me how I should proceed in religious matters so as to abolish idolatry entirely. . . . I do not ask whether I should do it, for God's command is sufficiently clear, but what means should be used, given the backwardness [*rudesse*] of my people. I have in mind one way to make the truth known . . . by [holding] public debates, almost like a little national council . . . I beg you, in God's name, M. de Bèze, send me your opinion and pray for me."[73]

The letter of the Spanish ambassador gives her enemies' view of the Queen of Navarre at the time of her flight; we can imagine Jeanne's satisfaction that she had escaped the hostile court once again, and that this time Henri was with her. "The Duchesse de Vendôme left here a few days ago. I have it on absolutely reliable authority that she seeks only to fool the King and his mother . . . and that she has taken both her children and all her retainers. I thought it advisable to inform the Queen Mother, who thanked me a great deal, but was very much surprised. She assured me that she would do something about it . . . in order to avoid serious consequences. She said she was all the angrier [*d'autant plus faschée*] because she had just loaned the Duchess 2000 écus because she was pleading poverty! . . . This woman is the most corrupt [*dévergondée*] and passionate creature in the world . . . even though she pretends to stand aloof from the Admiral, he is so adroit that he knows how to use her . . . and I know for a fact that he encouraged her in this enterprise . . . [The Huguenots] are beside themselves from fear that Your Majesty will march and they are trying to raise money from their churches. They get some, but not as much as they want."[74]

Reponse en Forme de Sonnet au Nom
de l'Imprimerie a la Dite Dame Royne

Princesse que le ciel de grâces favorise,
A qui les Craignans-Dieu souhaitent tout bonheur,
A qui les grands ésprits ont donné tout honneur,
Pour avoir doctement la science conquise.

S'il est vrai que du temps la plus brave enterprise,
Au devant des vertus abbaise sa grandeur,
S'il est vrai que les ans n'offusquent la splendeur
Qui fait luire partout les enfans de l'Eglise.

Le ciel, les Craignans-Dieu et les hommes savants
Me feront raconter aux peuples survivans,
Vos grâces, et votre heure et louange notoire.
Et puisque vos vertus ne peuvent prendre fin
Par vous je demeurerai vivante, à cette fin
Qu'aux peuples à venir j'en porte la mémoire.

IX

JEANNE *BROUILLÉE*

AS some people are accident-prone, Jeanne d'Albret was prone to feuds and strained human relations, to becoming what the French call *brouillé*. The dictionary translation of the noun *brouille* is "quarrel," "falling out," of the verb *se brouiller*, "to be on bad terms with," "to disagree with animosity." Laurence Wylie, in *Village in the Vaucluse*, provides vivid insight into this phenomenon as it operates in a Provençal village in the twentieth century. "If you are *brouillé* with someone it means literally that you have been mixed up with him; your mutual relationship has become confused. You have quarreled and are "on the outs." . . . You threaten physical or legal action. . . . In reality you know that your loss of rational control is not so complete as it seems. You have tried to frighten your opponent and to dramatize the situation. . . . Oral aggression is socially acceptable and it may sometimes be even more effective than other types of aggression." When themes on this subject were assigned to children in the village, repeated reference was made to the fact that their own *brouilles* were brief—a day or two—but "when grown-ups get angry they stay *brouillés* for a year or sometimes for their whole life."[1]

What is significant is not that Jeanne frequently disagreed with others but that she dealt with differences aggressively, turning them into bitter quarrels. Some people can disagree with a minimum of personal hostility; Marguerite d'Angoulême and Renée de France, for instance, did not as a general rule react by becoming *brouillées* with their opponents. Marguerite's falling out with Montmorency and Renée's temporary quarrel with Jeanne stand out as exceptions. Jeanne, on the other hand, had re-

243

sorted to oral aggression in self-defense as a child, as is evident in the story of the Cleves marriage. She had quarreled with her parents, her uncle, and her foster-mother. As a young married woman she required constant soothing from Antoine. After the disintegration of her marriage this tendency became more pronounced, especially in the period of the tour of France. During her months in Paris, in 1566, Jeanne was *brouillée* on all sides, with Catherine and the court, with a number of officers of the crown, with her in-laws, with members of her own family, and even with some of her leading vassals and Huguenot allies.

Catherine de Medici exerted all her skill in dealing with the Queen of Navarre. So many matters of real substance separated them that she took pains to overlook provocation on Jeanne's part and to emphasize their mutual interests. Her correspondence with her agents and ambassadors is studded with explanations of the need to handle (*ménager*) the Queen of Navarre and suggestions of ways and means to do it. She made many moves to accommodate Jeanne, which she was obliged to justify to the Catholic party. But Jeanne, although she had written effusively of willingness to kiss Catherine's feet, in fact refused to cooperate in the "reconciliations" on which Catherine's policy depended. Chantonay's prediction in 1561 that Catherine would find Jeanne "hard to live with" proved accurate. Jeanne continually violated royal prohibitions against public preaching at court; she would not modify her attitude toward, for instance, Montpensier or Monluc, although Catherine supported her against them; she capitalized on episodes like Du Moulin's arrest to add to the crown's difficulties.

Jeanne's distrust of Catherine was not unwarranted, but she was unwilling—or unable—to achieve smooth surface relations. She was easily offended, regarding all who crossed her as personal enemies. Always suspecting betrayal, her pursuit of vengeance was relentless. She sensed injustice on all sides and embraced any cause which offered a chance to fight it. Her role in the Rohan case, a *cause célèbre* which lasted many years at the Valois court, is a striking instance of this facet of her character.[2]

Françoise de Rohan, about seven years younger than Jeanne and her first cousin, had been taken under Marguerite's protection as a very young child, in 1537, when the Rohans had been threatened with financial ruin. In the Plessis years Françoise had been a semi-permanent member of Jeanne's household and suffered the domination referred to in Marguerite's poem. By the time Jeanne became Queen of Navarre, in 1555, Françoise was one of Catherine de Medici's ladies-in-waiting and the handsome Jacques de Savoie, Duc de Nemours, was supposed to be her cavalier. He had given her to understand that he wished to marry her, but the amount of time he spent in the company of Anne d'Este, wife of the Duc de Guise, his close friend and companion in arms, was court gossip. Even when Françoise became obviously pregnant in the summer of 1556, Nemours would not respond to her tearful pleas. Catherine mitigated her humiliation by sending her to visit Jeanne in far-off Béarn. Under Jeanne's roof, in the chateau of Pau, Françoise was delivered of a son on March 24, 1557. She returned to court in 1558 and, when repeated appeals both to Nemours and the King brought no result, instituted a suit for breach of promise against Nemours before a special commission of *parlementaires,* under the direction of the Bishop of Paris. She took this step when Jeanne was in Paris, in the period of Catherine de Bourbon's birth. In the struggle that followed the death of Henri II, members of the court sided with Françoise or Nemours, according to their allegiance to the Bourbons or the Guises. Up to February 1561, Antoine de Bourbon was the official protector of Françoise, but when he abandoned her there was nobody to take his place. During the period of the Colloquy, Antoine's repudiation of Jeanne, and the beginning of the civil wars, no action was taken one way or the other. The assassination of the Duc de Guise (February 1563) reopened the question because Anne d'Este and Nemours wished to marry. Jeanne, under attack from the Papacy and Spain and in need of protection from the crown, was in no position to counter the influence of the Guise faction, although she had continued to sponsor Françoise and had assumed responsibility for her son's education.

The crisis occurred during Jeanne's stay in Paris in 1566. Some months before, a judgment against Françoise had been issued by the Archbishop of Lyons, Primate of Gaul, a Guise partisan. On April 28, 1566 the King's Council confirmed the Archbishop's ruling. Jeanne threw all her energies into Françoise's defense. She challenged the competence of each member of the King's Council by name (except the members of the immediate royal family), some because they were related by blood or marriage to Nemours, others because they were "notoriously *inféodés"* to the Guises or in their service, and still others because they were partisans or retainers of the House of Bourbon. Jeanne demanded, "in the name of God, that justice be administered by impartial judges . . . in the Parlement of Paris."[3] Neither at this time nor on several occasions in later years would the Parlement accept the case, because it had been evoked to the royal council.

Jeanne's personal hostility to Anne d'Este, which had been mounting for several years, burst through the façade of her dignity. On one occasion they are described as "shouting at each other like fishwives." The Seigneur de Lansac says that, when he reproached Jeanne for speaking "in the dry impertinent tone which she alone can command," in the presence of the King's mother, she retorted, "You are a rude, bold man to dare to come between me and the King's mother, for this, someday you will be obliged to draw your sword." Turning to Catherine, Jeanne said, "I am astounded that you do not punish him for such audacity."[4]

The greatest secrecy surrounded the preparations for the wedding of Anne d'Este and Nemours in the chapel of the Abbaye de St. Maur-des-Fossés on May 5, but, "at the moment [the Cardinal de Lorraine] was about to pronounce the sacramental words, an officer [of the Parlement] rose to his feet and said, loud and clear, that he represented *la dame de Rohan* and that she forbade [the marriage] to proceed." The Cardinal hesitated and the assembly gasped, but in a few seconds he recovered himself and the ceremony continued to the end. Françoise's emissary was beaten up and imprisoned.[5] An anonymous, unpublished *Chronique* says that Jeanne had planted this individual, "an evangelical notary," in the congregation.[6] Françoise, with the encouragement of Jeanne, then appealed to the Pope, although she had been considered at least *demi-huguenotte* for several years.

Jeanne refers to the state of the case in her letter to Beza at the end of the year, "even the Pope does not approve the iniquitous sentence of the Bishop [sic] of Lyons . . . nevertheless the others are now procreating children. I do not know what will happen."[7] The cause was lost but the struggle continued—as far as Françoise and Jeanne were concerned. The Pope delayed his response during the period of the Second and Third Civil Wars. In March 1571, he pronounced in favor of Nemours, who had, by then, been married to Anne d'Este for nearly five years. Whereupon Françoise, who was at La Rochelle with Jeanne, officially embraced Calvinism. Françoise, known in later years as the Duchesse de Laudun, outlived Jeanne by nineteen years. Her life was turbulent to the end, as was her son's, and both were the cause of no little embarrassment to Henri de Navarre when he inherited the role of protector.[8]

One result of Jeanne's role as avenging fury in the Rohan case was that she became *brouillée* with her one real friend in the royal family, Renée de France. A close friend of Marguerite's, the only surviving member of the older generation, a sponsor of the reform but not a militant convert, Renée was in a unique position to mediate between Jeanne and the crown. We have already seen how different was Renée's approach to religion from Jeanne's, and the fact that her every mention of Jeanne is in the context of her admiration for Marguerite suggests that the relationship was not easy for the Duchess. The strain reached the breaking point in the spring of 1566, because Renée was the mother of Anne d'Este, Nemours' bride.

The Ferrarese ambassador reported to his master in a letter of June 2, 1566, "sharp words were exchanged between Madama [Renée] and the Queen of Navarre, when she was visiting the Duchess, on account of some uncomplimentary remarks the said Queen had made about Madame de Nemours. . . . When she started to kiss her, as was her custom . . . Madama [refused] saying that she would never again allow lips as poisoned as [Jeanne's] to approach her . . . but the said Queen burst out in anger and departed to tell [Catherine], who only laughed at her. Many think that it is the Queen Mother who keeps them thus at odds."[9]

Relations between Jeanne and her in-laws were beset with quarrels and lawsuits. When Antoine married Jeanne, his brother, the Cardinal de Bourbon, had waived his own rights over certain lands of the Bourbon-Vendôme branch of the royal family. Since Antoine's death Jeanne had exercised these rights, pending the coming of age of Henri de Béarn. In 1566, however, the Cardinal attempted to annul his action of eighteen years earlier. In his formal petition to the crown and Parlement for restitution he accused Jeanne of fomenting trouble in the kingdom. Catherine, once more, supported Jeanne, and the prerogatives of the Bourbon-Vendômes stood in the name of Henri. The Queen Mother certainly had no reason to do Jeanne a favor at this time, but the Cardinal was a satellite of the Cardinal de Lorraine and the balancing of the factions required Catherine to support Henri's rights against him.[10] Jeanne and her brother-in-law had in common the Bourbon cause and, although they remained at cross-purposes on the most effective way to further it, the Cardinal defended his nephew's rights to the royal succession in 1572 and Jeanne made him an executor of her will.

No such mixed feelings had characterized Jeanne's relations with her sister-in-law, Marguerite de Bourbon, Duchesse de Nevers. Their feud reached its climax in 1559 over the *Heptameron* of Marguerite de Navarre. The Duchesse de Nevers had allowed a certain Boaistuau to publish and dedicate to her (1558) a collection of tales called *Histoire des amans fortunez,* which was a truncated plagiarization of the *Heptameron.* Boaistuau claimed that he had "corrected and improved" the work of an anonymous author. The book was enjoying a certain popularity when Jeanne came to Paris in January 1559. "To avenge the memory of her mother, [Jeanne] showed an almost superhuman energy."[11] She bought up every available copy and succeeded in destroying virtually the entire edition. She then commissioned Claude Gruget, who, like Boaistuau, had been among Marguerite de Navarre's retainers, to edit and publish an authentic edition, *Le Heptameron des Nouvelles, remis en son vray ordre, confus auparavant en son première edition, et dedié à la très illustre princesse Jeanne de Foix, Reine de Navarre, par Claude Gruget, parisien, 1559.* The preface includes a sarcastic reference to Marguerite de Bourbon, who is accused of usurping the honor of being "the second Marguerite de France." The Duchesse de Nevers died a few months later, leaving three daughters. The eldest, Henriette, carried on her mother's quarrel with Jeanne and they were known to hate each other, but Jeanne adopted Marie, the youngest, who turned Calvinist. Marie was a member of Jeanne's household at La Rochelle and Jeanne later arranged her marriage to young Henri de Condé.

During these years Jeanne was also *brouillée* with her own great-uncle on the paternal side, Pedro d'Albret. She had helped him to acquire the bishopric of Comminges in 1561 as a reward for his services as Antoine's ambassador to the Pope, but he had since conspired against her with Monluc and Philip II. St. Sulpice's dispatches in 1564 and 1565 contain many allusions to Pedro's activities, which were conducted with such guile and duplicity that it was never possible to bring specific charges against him. Jeanne reciprocated by depriving him of the bishopric—in favor of one of Antoine's bastards—and by charging him, as well as Monluc, with treason. Pedro seems to have been the shiftiest of the D'Albrets—no small achievement. In one letter St. Sulpice begs Elizabeth de Valois to keep her husband "from employing such shady characters."[12] Both her Albret uncles, Pedro and Louis, Bishop of Lescar, were undoubtedly disloyal to Jeanne, but the intensity of her reaction and the extent of her personal vindictiveness seem excessive. I believe these emotions have sometimes been mistaken for religious fanaticism, by both her attackers and her defenders. Even such valuable officers and deputies as Audaux and Gramont fell under Jeanne's suspicions and displeasure. Whenever they ventured to disagree with her she was inclined to regard them as traitors. The most striking recorded instance of Jeanne's vindictiveness alleges that she ripped out the head of a priest in one of Marguerite de Navarre's most skillfully done tapestries and substituted the head of a grimacing fox. Possibly this is merely one more example of the many libels produced in the civil wars,[13] yet Marguerite and Jeanne were both skilled needlewomen and it is not impossible to imagine Jeanne expressing her feelings in this way in an hour of intense frustration and rage.

Jeanne had brushed aside Cardinal d'Armagnac's allusion to divisions among Calvinists, but no objective reporter can deny them. Nor is it surprising that a movement comprising so many intensely aggressive and egotistical personalities should be characterized by feuds, on theological and other matters. Among the most notorious was Jeanne's feud with Spifâme.[14] By 1565 Jeanne's transports of enthusiasm for Spifâme, in which Gramont had joined, were a thing of the past. After the trip to Geneva with young Nemours the previous summer, Spifâme may have spent another few months in Pau while Jeanne was in Vendôme. Parts of the story are confused and contradictory in the sources. Some say that Jeanne became angry and dismissed him for "betraying her interests" in January 1565. In any case, he had returned to Geneva for good in March of that year and was expressing dissatisfaction with Jeanne, whose court he claimed to be "under the domination of Merlin." At the same time Jeanne sent an envoy to complain of him to the Geneva authorities.

For a year thereafter there was an extraordinarily bitter and complicated series of charges and countercharges, involving not only the Queen and Spifâme but also Jacques Servin, Controller of Navarre and one of the bearers of Jeanne's messages. Spifâme's most important charge was that Merlin was Jeanne's lover and that Henri de Béarn was illegitimate. In March 1566, Beza revealed to the Council that he had been apprised by the Queen of Spifâme's calumny against her and of her suspicions that his own marriage was not legal. Even more important was the disclosure of secret negotiations between Spifâme and certain highly placed persons in France, in which he promised Catholic leaders to reconvert to Catholicism if he obtained the bishopric of Toul, while to Coligny he promised to establish Calvinism there. The status of the case changed at once from civil to criminal. Spifâme was tried, condemned, and executed within two weeks, every day of which brought a new sensation. The climax of this *brouille* and that of the Rohan case occurred at the same time. A historian of the Spifâme feud remarks on "the implacable enmity Jeanne suddenly conceived for her former adviser. . . . What pressures did she bring to bear on the ministers and, consequently, on the Geneva magistrates?"

Although Spifâme was executed for crimes that had nothing to do with Jeanne's original charges, his real offense came to light as the result of pressure applied by her. The Geneva authorities agreed with Catherine de Medici that the Queen of Navarre must be *menagée,* and she did not even hesitate to disagree with Theodore Beza himself.

Jean-Baptiste Morély, one of the most controversial and mysterious figures of the French Reformation, was serving as Henri de Béarn's tutor in Paris in the last months of 1566, after the death of La Gaucherie. Morély's book, *Traicté de la discipline et police chrêtienne* (Lyons, 1562), criticizing the organization of the Reformed Church, had been condemned by national synods at Orléans and Paris (1565). The Geneva authorities had excommunicated the author and ordered the book burned publicly in 1563, but he had nevertheless retained the favor of the Huguenot nobility. The alarm of the pastors rose to fever pitch when Jeanne put Henri in Morély's charge, and fear that "his corruption [will] spread now that he has become the tutor of M. le Prince" was the subject of several letters to Beza in the late summer of 1566.[15] They had complained directly to Jeanne also, and she had reproached Morély, but retained him in her service.

The Calvinist leaders then sent a prominent Huguenot scholar, François Béroald (or Bérauld) on a special trip to Paris (from Orléans) to present evidence of Morély's errors and "make the Queen understand what kind of man he is . . . and that he is not what she thought." Bérauld urged her to dismiss Morély so that "M. le Prince, so well-launched in the true faith by the late M. de La Gaucherie, known for the possession of all the virtues, may not be corrupted by such a teacher, who has insinuated himself into this important position by clever ruses and calculated guile."

Jeanne was sufficiently impressed to hold hearings on the accusations against Morély and she invited Coligny and the Cardinal de Châtillon as well as leading Calvinist ministers (L'Espine, Holbrac, Pierre Merlin, and La Roche-Chandieu are named), to attend. Several accounts of the sessions, held in the last week of November, were sent to Beza. Jeanne's chaplain, Pierre Hespérien, reported that in the final one Morély was condemned on several counts, after which Jeanne "dismissed him, but in the gentlest way."

Morély was probably fortified by Jeanne's attitude. In any case he was not a man to submit passively. He apologized to Beza for "things said in anger for which I am now ashamed," while pleading to retain the post; he asked Laurent de Normandie to intercede for him, using as an argument his success with Henri, "who never before knew how to profit from letters and science." Jeanne's own letter to Beza (December 6) shows that this was no idle boast. After remarking indulgently, "it seemed right not to be so harsh as to crush him, but to give him time to recognize his errors," Jeanne admits, "I wish him well on account of the grace God has given him to teach my son so well and with such learning; in passing I must tell you that the seven years my son spent with the late M. de La Gaucherie were so much time lost, because he only learned a few rules, by rote, without understanding. The result was, that without foundations, the building fell in ruins. He has learned more in three or four months in Morély's hands than in those seven years, although good old La Gaucherie [*vieux bonhomme*] was a man of conscience and my son owes to him the roots of piety . . . for which I thank God."

Jeanne still hoped that Morély could "regularize" his standing with Geneva. She was planning to send a messenger to deal directly with Beza when royal displeasure fell upon her and the orthodox ministers together, so that *l'affaire* Morély was temporarily pushed into the background. As reported to Beza by La Mare on January 5, "the voyage of the Queen's spokesman to Geneva . . . has been delayed because of the sudden departure of the Queen's two preachers,* who were obliged to flee before they were apprehended in the Queen's own house by the King's explicit command. The explanation is that there had been a great crowd when Hespérien preached two days before. Since then, a real bellows-of-Satan,

* Almost certainly Hespérien and Barbaste, although no document I have seen states their names. They were the regular chaplains in Jeanne's household at the time.

from the Sorbonne, preached at the Temple of Notre Dame, in the King's presence, that 'it was a mockery of the royal authority to permit such a scandal as the gathering of more than 3000 persons at the house of the Queen of Navarre.' The result of this beautiful sermon was the attempted arrest . . . we are all included in the wrath that has fallen on her . . . but we hope that the smoke will soon be cleared away with God's help."

Even these dramatic events did not cause his enemies to neglect Morély, however.* On January 5, La Mare says that because he is still in Jeanne's household, six weeks after the supposed dismissal, the ministers have asked Coligny's chaplain, Pierre Merlin, to protest anew to Jeanne. Merlin's own report to Beza (January 10) gives his version of the hearing and spells out what Hespérien had called Jeanne's "gentle" dismissal:

promising him that when he had regained good standing in the church and become reconciled with those whom he had offended, he would always be welcome in her house. Up to now he is still there. When the said lady's ministers were leaving the city (because the Provost was on their heels to hang them forthwith) they begged me to urge her to follow the ruling and to dismiss [Morély] in fact. When I did so, a week ago, she replied that she was obliged to keep Morély so that M. le Prince would not lose time . . . she claimed that she could not find anyone else so well-qualified . . . and that she did not intend to change tutors until the court left the city. She added that she was very much annoyed that Morély should be out of line with the church because he is the most gifted and skillful man she has ever seen, and that her son has learned more from him in three months than in eight [sic] years from the late M. de La Gaucherie . . . which makes me fear that unless we find her a man who suits her, it will not be easy to make her forget Morély, no matter how strongly she is pressed to do so.

On the same day, Morély wrote Beza: "I beg you, if you think I have any ability to teach M. le Prince, my master, as experience leads me to hope, God having blessed my work thus far, please help me to keep the position."

Whether Jeanne's respect for Beza was the determining factor, or whether she merely felt it necessary for Henri's tutor to stand well with the establishment, the pastors were victorious. When Jeanne left Paris

---

* Jeanne's emissary arrived in Geneva in February to present her arguments, but she had by then returned to Béarn, leaving Morély behind. The episode only hardened the attitude of the Calvinist authorities toward Morély, who was repeatedly condemned, both in Geneva and in French national synods. See R. M. Kingdon, *Geneva and Consolidation* . . . , 92–99, 107–111.

in late January, "with all her retainers," Morély was not among them, and she subsequently appointed only tutors of undisputed orthodoxy. Before the appointment of Florent Chrêtien, who became Henri's tutor in 1567, after Jeanne's return to Béarn, two other tutors were proposed to Jeanne after Morély's dismissal. The first was Martinius, whom Jeanne turned down as "too simple and uncivil," the second a Lyonnais named Massaillan, who does not seem to have been appointed either.[16]

Jeanne was undoubtedly aware that she was being manipulated during her months at court. Hemmed in on all sides, she was not really free to do as she wished in any matter. Frustration was compounded by apprehension over the accelerated Counter Reformation offensive and tension as she prepared her escape, dreading what would happen if she failed. Difficult as they were, she could at least make alternative plans to deal with these matters, but her rapidly deteriorating health and the unmistakable signs that she had not long to live, must have increased the pressure still further. In the *Mémoires,* Jeanne draws up a catalogue of the injustices she suffered in these months. In addition to those already mentioned, she refers to accusations that she had conspired to kill the Queen Mother and to kidnap the Duc d'Anjou. She includes a long digression about the murder of one Savigny, "said to be a bastard of my late husband," which she lays at the door of the Cardinal de Lorraine, along with all the other ills of the kingdom and the renewal of civil war. She says that she wrote "an infinity of letters" but that she never obtained satisfaction.[17]

It is perhaps not surprising that Jeanne was *brouillée* with more people during her stay in Paris in 1566 than at any other time of her stormy life. Explaining the psychological functions of the French *brouille,* in theory alien to Anglo-Saxons, Wylie says, "A *brouille* may cause the blood pressure to go up. It may cause unhappiness. At the same time, it is exciting. It gives a person an opportunity to dramatize himself and his situation . . . the frustration of desires, the worries about health, about the family, about the future, would at times be almost unbearable if one were not able to find release in the excitement and drama of a *brouille.*"[18]

X

QUEEN AND ADMINISTRATOR

1555–1572

JEANNE was *haut justicier* and feudal lord of more than twenty fiefs held of the French crown,* but the "kingdom" or *souveraineté* where she styled herself *Jehanne, par la grâce de Dieu Reine et dame souveraine,* meant Béarn, Soule, and (Basse) Navarre.[1] There she recognized no earthly power but her own. It is about eighty kilometers from the northern limit of Béarn to the Spanish frontier at its farthest point, and about sixty from east to west. The two Basque provinces, Soule and Basse-Navarre together, are only about one-third as large. Within this small kingdom, however, there is considerable topographical variety.

The northern edge of Béarn is a plain, easily accessible from the Gascon country contiguous with it. Entering Béarn from the north, there is no sudden change of landscape to mark the traveler's arrival in the former vicomté, unless he has come across the strange expanse of the Landes, with its sand dunes and scrubby pines, in which case the cultivated fields and populous villages resemble those found on emerging from the Landes into Gascony. Whatever the approach, one quickly comes upon the *gaves* (Béarnais for rivers) along which the important towns are located; then, suddenly, the atmosphere becomes Béarnais, and no mere local

---

* The exact number depends on whether one counts all the smaller ones apart from the larger ones in which they were sub-fiefs. The most important were: those inherited from Henri d'Albret, the counties of Foix, Bigorre, and the duchy of Albret; those from Marguerite, the counties of Armagnac, Rodez, and Périgord, and the vicomtés of Limoges, Quercy, and Marsan; those from Antoine, the duchies of Vendôme and Beaumont and the county of Marle.

variant of rural France. The Gave de Pau, swiftly flowing from south-east to northwest, is the northernmost of these rivers; running through Orthez and Lescar as well as Pau itself, it marks the edge of the plain. Immediately to the south are rolling hills covered with vineyards or pastures filled with cattle and sheep, but the eye tends at first to leap over them to the Pyrenees, with their sharp peaks, snow-covered most of the year, punctuating the horizon. Smaller rushing gaves flow out of the mountains, due north, emptying into the larger rivers. Each forms a distinct valley, closed at the southern end by the mountain mass, with a single pass leading to the Spanish side, more open and flattening out at the northern end, on the edge of the plain.

There are several villages in each valley, nestled by the river or perched on the foothills, all clean and very neatly kept. The white buildings are large, but rather low, with steep slate roofs and walls often made of boulders polished by the rushing waters. Characteristically, a large door permits wagons to enter the part that serves as a barn, and an inside stairway leads to rooms above, occupied by the family. The traditional costume, still worn on such occasions as the procession of August 15, consists of short black pants and a red jacket with wide lapels over a high-necked white shirt for the men, while women wear volumi-nous pleated skirts, red or black, with a white lace apron. The upper part of their bodies is enveloped in a richly embroidered black shawl, fastened at the waist. Over the white bonnet, close to the head, is draped a red hood which falls over the shoulders. On ordinary days, in the twentieth century, only the ubiquitous beret* worn by men in Béarn and throughout the Basque country, distinguishes the descendants of Jeanne's subjects from inhabitants of other regions. Each valley has a sense of identity, expressed in the organization of local government; loyalty is to the valley rather than the village. In sixteenth-century docu-ments, the geographical regions of the vicomté are designated as *les bourgs,* the towns of the plain, and *les vallées.*

In Soule and Basse-Navarre, the soil is stonier, the mountains steeper, the roads more tortuous, and the villages less open, less prosperous. The most important town in Basse-Navarre, St. Jean-Pied-de-Port, at the foot of the famous pass of Roncevaux, is cramped within its old fortifications. A medieval village whose fortune was made by pilgrims going to

---

* The beret is found in nearby Gascony also. Nearly all French berets are manu-factured in the towns of Oloron or Nay in Béarn.

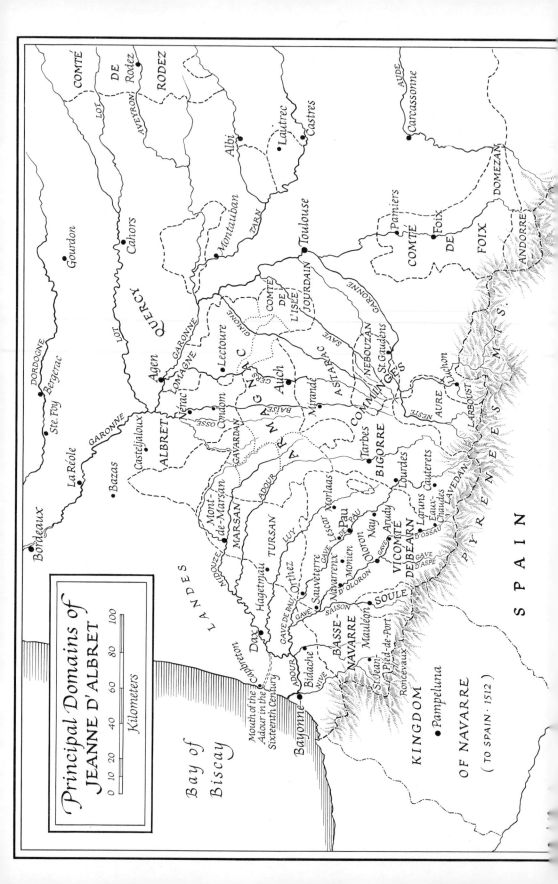

Principal Domains of JEANNE D'ALBRET

Kilometers
0 10 20 40 60 80 100

Bay of Biscay

SPAIN

KINGDOM OF NAVARRE
(TO SPAIN · 1512)

PYRÉNÉES MTS.

ANDORRE

COMTÉ DE FOIX

FOIX

DOMEZAN

Pamiers

Foix

Carcassonne

AUDE

COMTÉ DE RODEZ

RODEZ

Rodez

AVEYRON

LOT

Castres

Lautrec

Albi

TARN

Montauban

Toulouse

JOURDAIN

COMTÉ DE L'ISLE

GARONNE

SAVE

NEBOUZAN

St. Gaudens

COMMINGES

AURE

NESTE

Luchon

LARBOUST

GAVARDAN

ASTARAC

GERS

Mirandé

Auch

ARMAGNAC

LOMAGNE

Lectoure

Condom

Nérac

ALBRET

Agen

QUERCY

Cahors

LOT

Gourdon

Bergerac

DORDOGNE

Ste. Foy

La Réole

GARONNE

Bazas

Casteljaloux

Bordeaux

LANDES

Dax

Capbreton

Mouth of the Adour in the Sixteenth Century

ADOUR

Bayonne

NIVE

Bidache

Mont-de-Marsan

MARSAN

TURSAN

Hagetmau

MIDOUZE

ADOUR

LUY

Orthez

GAVE DE PAU

Sauveterre

Orthez

GAVE

Navarrenx

GAVE

SAISON

BASSE-NAVARRE

Mauléon

SOULE

St. Jean-Pied-de-Port

Roncevaux

Pampeluna

Lescar

Morlaas

Pau

PAU

GAVE

D'OSSAU

Nay

Arudy

Oloron

Monien

D. Monien

GAVE D'ASPE

Laruns

Eaux-Chaudes

VICOMTÉ DE BÉARN

GAVE

D'OSSAU

Cauterets

Lourdes

LAVEDAN

BIGORRE

Tarbes

BAÏSE

OSSE

GIMONE

BAÏSE

DORDOGNE

Compostela, in the mid-twentieth century St. Jean is enjoying an economic revival, thanks to tourists motoring between France and Spain. Basque houses are made of wood, painted in bright colors, with balconies running around the upper storeys. The name of the family and the date of the house are usually to be found over the doorway, framed in borders which display the skill and imagination of the artist. Traditional costume and patois are still prevalent in the Basque country and in the high valleys of both Béarn and Basse-Navarre holidays are celebrated with stylized local dances centuries old.

Mountain regions throughout the world tend to form a subculture different from that of the plain, but not many happen to be located athwart such important arteries of commerce and migration as those of Jeanne's kingdom since early medieval times. Alongside the basic pastoral economy, similar to that of the interior of Spain or the Peloponnesus, a varied commerce and considerable industry developed in the towns where the valleys empty into the plain. Spain's acquisition of an empire in America had greatly stimulated trade through Béarn since the fifteenth century, and caravans of products from the New World, as well as Spanish leather and metal products, from one direction, and salt, wine, grain, and textiles, from the other, provided a prosperous living for legitimate merchants, as well as for the smugglers for which the region is legendary. In the east-west trade, Béarnais handled such products as the dyes of Languedoc, the perfumes of Provence, and fish from Bayonne. As a consequence, markets and fairs which offered quantities of nonlocal goods were more numerous than in most regions of Europe as small as Béarn.

Béarn swelled this commerce with its own animals and animal products, especially meat, dairy products, and wool, but also including horses and mules, which were much in demand. Rights, privileges, and penalties in the valleys were reckoned in terms of grazing or other aspects of animal husbandry, reflecting its importance in the economy. Native grains were naturally scarce, only the coarser ones like barley and rye really flourished, until the introduction of corn in the eighteenth century. Wheat was a luxury imported from Bigorre or Armagnac, and to this day Béarnais bread is notably less fine and white than most French bread. Among agricultural products, only certain fruits flourish in the vicomté, apples, pears, cherries, and nuts, and, of course, some varieties of the grape.

There are still sizable forests in some parts of Béarn and wood remains an important product, as it was in the sixteenth century, when Béarnais timber was to be found in the ships of England, France, and the Low Countries. A number of quarries* and some extractive industry—salt and iron—existed. In Henri d'Albret's reign, his mercantilist policies resulted in the development of textile manufacture (at Oloron and Nay) and tanneries (at Orthez). They greatly enlarged Béarnais industry, formerly restricted to pottery and other articles for domestic consumption.

Mineral springs, located at the extreme southern tip of the valleys, were reputed to be beneficial for the relief or cure of arthritis, tuberculosis, digestive and nervous complaints, and sterility. Marguerite went regularly to Cauterets (in Bigorre). Jeanne's preference was for Eaux-Chaudes, in the Ossau Valley, where she habitually spent a week or two every spring and every autumn that she was in Béarn. Henri and Catherine continued to take the cure until 1590. The renown of Eaux-Chaudes was at its height in the 1570's and 1580's, when the Calvinist nobility patronized it, following the lead of the Béarnais royal family. A bell in the *maison du roi*—the most important building and for some years the only one built of stone—called the clients to the regular Bible readings, prayers, and sermons that Jeanne had decreed in 1571.

The natives of the village of Laruns, closest to the springs and the last town on the French side of the frontier, naturally exploited the clients. In 1576, Henri was forced to issue a set of regulations restricting what they might charge for lodging, food, and transport. The owners were required to provide a fireplace and a latrine for each of the nineteen cabins. In return, the King gave in to their insistence on regulations prohibiting the guests from doing laundry or keeping animals, and he allowed them to charge "a reasonable supplement" for damage done to the furniture.

During the season in the years of this fashion, the inhabitants of the valley undoubtedly added to their income, but after 1590 the Béarnais royal family, become the French royal family, no longer went to Eaux-Chaudes, which lapsed into its primitive state, except for a brief revival just before the Revolution. Today, the springs bubble in the wilderness

---

* The eighteenth-century statues representing French cities in the Place de la Concorde and the Church of the Madelaine in Paris are made of marble from the Ossau Valley.

and the only buildings are a small power-station and an abandoned pavilion.

Jeanne spent much of her time in Pau, in the chateau which had been enlarged and embellished by her parents. Surrounded by its small park, it has a striking site, on the top of a steep cliff, overlooking the river immediately below, the vineyards of Jurançon in the foreground, and, in the distance, the entire range of the Pyrenees. Since Napoleon created the Boulevard des Pyrénées along the whole length of the cliff above the river, the chateau is at the extreme western end of the promenade, separated from a string of luxury hotels by the former Parlement building (eighteenth-century) now occupied by the Archives des Basses-Pyrénées.

In Jeanne's reign the chateau was a royal residence as richly furnished as Fontainebleau, according to the scholars who studied and published the Inventory Jeanne had made in the autumn of 1562.[2] The collection of solid gold- and silverplate (kept apart in the Tower of the Treasury) is not included, although a set of gold forks and several hundred *vases* with gold or silver mountings are mentioned. These are containers of all kinds; cups, goblets, pitchers, decanters, bottles, saltcellars, cruets, flagons, jars for medicines and perfumes, cases for such items as eyeglasses, and equipment for sewing and writing. They are made of materials like crystal, ivory, jade, ebony, jasper, porphyry, and alabaster. Jewels, tapestries, and precious embroideries figure prominently, but there is much less armor than one would expect and there are few religious objects—they had probably been sold or melted down in 1561. Equipment for hunting, including jeweled birdcages and hoods for falcons, is plentiful, and there are many luxurious toilet articles, combs, mirrors, manicure articles, toothpicks—and an impressive number of clocks.

The editors draw attention to a considerable number of portraits and to the finest known collection of elaborate enameled objects (Jeanne was Vicomtesse of Limoges). Although some are also useful, most of these are ingenious decorative pieces, chiefly statuettes made of enameled gold set with precious stones. In addition to numerous birds, there are animals including a bear tied to a tree, a camel, and a monkey. Among the human figures are a chambermaid whose arms and legs move, a woman holding a mirror bathing in a fountain, and a golden goddess rising from a sea of pearl—a gift to Jeanne from the city of La Rochelle.

The most unusual feature of all is a collection of gold and silver toys —unique according to the editors—some enameled and studded with gems. Nearly one hundred and fifty articles (nos. 616–724 and 754– 790) of the Inventory describe a set of miniature furniture and other objects known as *le petit ménage.* In addition to tables, chairs, beds, lamps, clocks, fire-screens, stove, kitchen utensils, and table settings, this includes a *"pot de chambre* the size of a child's fingernail," a cradle with the arms of Navarre, musical instruments, birds and birdcages, hunting equipment, a coach and horses, a fountain, a cannon "with a little man to fire it," a complete set of barber's equipment, and many objects for personal use such as eyeglasses and gloves.

A human touch occasionally creeps into the Inventory. A notation in the margin of no. 754, "a small green velvet coffer with silver mountings, with the little silver dishes it contains," reads "Given to Madame [Catherine de Bourbon] at the Queen's command." In the margin next to no. 113, a Book of Hours bound in blue damask stitched with pearls, is written, "the Queen has taken it for herself." Some of the enamels, tapestries, and jewels have been identified in the French royal collections, the Louvre, for instance, but there is no trace of *le petit ménage,* which was probably melted down to meet expenses by Catherine later in the century.

Jeanne's financial records enable us to imagine her life in Pau even better than the Inventory. On the payroll were architects, painters, jewelers, masons, lapidaries, embroiderers, many musicians, one fool (female), one dwarf (male), one Spanish spy, one midwife—in addi- tion to the expected physicians, secretaries, and different categories of servants. Entries detailing money given to the nurses of Jeanne's children and widows of household domestics and dowries and wedding presents to their children are numerous. Jeanne's property was kept in good con- dition, judging from the amount of repairs, not only to buildings, but to coaches, tapestries, and "the watch and the eyeglasses of the Queen." The stable, the hunting-birds, and the menagerie cost a great deal of money in Antoine's lifetime, as did his indulgence in gambling. In the later years charitable gifts, scholarships, and traveling expenses of Calvinist ministers figure more prominently, though worldly concerns are not wholly abandoned. We find, for instance, "the mounting of twenty-nine emeralds" at 1086 livres, a watch studded with diamonds and rubies at

308 livres, a Spanish horse for Henri, and 200 livres for the *menus plaisirs* of Catherine. Jeanne authorized 326 livres for the printing of a New Testament in Basque by P. Haultain of La Rochelle in 1571, and added to her library complete new editions of Froissart, Pliny, and Guicciardini. Dresses of black silk and mantles of black velvet for Jeanne and Catherine figure among the expenses of that year, as does the cost of Jeanne's own personal laundry (not itemized) 35 livres, and that of her dwarf on one occasion—four shirts, twelve handkerchiefs, and six pairs of socks. A particularly intriguing item (no. 311) is a fine of 500 livres Jeanne imposed on herself in 1563—for neglecting her prayers.

It would be interesting to know the exact date of this negligence. In 1563 Merlin was pushing her toward drastic reform while Philip was threatening invasion, the Pope was declaring Henri's claims invalid and Catherine de Medici was forcing Jeanne to change her policy, leave Béarn, and join the court. Jeanne may have neglected her prayers simply because she felt too sick and worn out by the thorny problems of ruling the kingdom she had inherited from her father.

HENRI D'ALBRET'S SUCCESSOR

At the court of France, Henri d'Albret, with his royal pretensions, often appeared to be a fool. To the King and Montmorency, who had to take him seriously, he was a dangerous troublemaker. Both opinions were justified by his behavior, which displayed only two facets of his character—his Gascon temperament and his obsession with the lost kingdom, a flamboyant combination. The court gossips would probably not have believed that behind the façade of the ridiculous—or pathetic— "King of Navarre" was a shrewd and highly gifted Vicomte of Béarn.[3] Beginning as a young man, he had consistently imposed a clearly articulated political philosophy on the Vicomté, increasing his own power at the expense of the Estates and the many particularisms of his small domain. At the outset of his long reign, in 1519, he created the nucleus of the Conseil Souverain, which became his main administrative instrument (and Jeanne's), consisting of the Chancellor, three prelates, and three laymen. Despite a few inevitable conflicts between the Conseil and the Estates, the Vicomte's authority had been firmly established. Dartigue finds that Henri d'Albret had worked out "a kind of concordat of his own interests with those of the people, by use of power, strong but supple enough to collaborate with and use the Estates, so that he kept resistance at a minimum while successfully undermining local authority."[4] It is significant, the same author adds, that by the end of his reign there had been no rebellion in the name of "ancient liberties" for many years.

The seven members of the council charged with civil matters were to be supplemented by a criminal court. This was a delicate matter— justice being the touchstone of medieval government—and the Vicomte had created it in stages over a long period, 1526–1552. The latter year was the climactic one of Henri's administration, with the establishment of the *nouveau fors,* which consolidated his judicial system, and the *foraine,** incorporating new import duties by which he had increased his revenues. An active legislator, Henri d'Albret left a large body of coher- ent written law. He even employed two nomadic printers, Jean de Vingles and Henry Poyvre, to print 2000 copies of the *Nouveau Fors*—the first book ever printed in Béarn.[5]

Henri d'Albret was extremely popular with his subjects. He kept them from realizing the extent of their loss of power by such means as never attempting to raise money without consent, making local notables his chief officers in the towns and valleys, controlling abuses, and above all, being receptive to grievances which he handled with the kind of skill his grandson was to display in a much larger kingdom.

Although Jeanne had spent little time in Béarn prior to her accession, she had observed enough of her father's political techniques—and in- herited enough of his skill—to handle the crisis precipitated by the French crown at her father's death. Henri II, having failed to persuade Antoine, then at court, to relinquish Béarn in exchange for lands in the center of France, corrupted some of the leading Béarnais seigneurs, notably Nicolas Dangu, Bishop of Mende, to attempt a military coup whereby the crown would take over Béarn. The attempt was foiled in military terms by Bernard, Baron d'Arros, but it was Jeanne's skill in handling the after- math that prevented a general defection of the nobility, which would otherwise probably have attempted to reassert its power, according to the classic pattern at the start of a new reign, particularly when the late King had increased the central power and when the new ruler was a woman. In the summer of 1555, Jeanne rapidly reconstituted her authority by rewarding the faithful and by retaining the would-be traitors in their offices, with the result that her father's system continued intact. Dartigue

* *Fors,* the Béarnais charter of traditional rights. *Foraine,* body of laws governing relations with foreigners.

believes that, because of her skillful management, the episode in fact served to strengthen Jeanne's position. Public opinion turned against the rebels—Dangu in particular "had no political future"—and the nobility rallied strongly to the Vicomtesse, "who showed herself able to evade the gravest problems . . . to redress legitimate grievances and to say 'no' when her authority was challenged."[6]

Until Antoine's death in 1562, Jeanne, as ruler, was occupied with three sets of problems—administrative, judicial, and fiscal.[7] A situation demanding immediate attention was the financial corruption of the purveyors of supplies to the palace. Those who supplied wine and provisions for the royal falconry were especially notorious for excessive demands on the treasury and for lining their own pockets. Jeanne tightened the supervision of accounts and promised the Estates that she would dismiss any malefactors. She requested that they bring any suspicion of abuse to her personally. This weakness was never completely eliminated because Jeanne's officers were able to exploit her frequent, long absences from Béarn. The Third Estate was agitating for repeal of Henri d'Albret's ordinance requiring local officers in charge of public works and markets to procure authorization from the Conseil Souverain before each expenditure of money and to present an itemized account to the Chambre des Comptes every two months. Failure to do so was punishable by a stiff fine. This had been among the most necessary of Henri d'Albret's reforms, but the localities resented it and hoped to force the new vicomtesse to repeal it. Jeanne refused to cede on the principle, declaring that she could not depart from her father's will. Nevertheless, she promised immediate action on requests for funds and excepted urgent repairs to roads and bridges from the procedure, "so that the traffic indispensable to the prosperity of the country would not be interrupted."

The new criminal court had deprived the Sénéchal de Béarn and the local magistrates of much of their old judicial power. At the beginning of Jeanne's reign they instigated complaints in the Estates, alleging that the court exceeded its just powers and was careless in respect to the rules of the *fors*. Jeanne stood firmly on her prerogatives, while promising to punish all abuses. In this she showed awareness of the concordat between the central power and the people, who, under Henri d'Albret's system, had acquired advantages never enjoyed when they had been at the mercy of the notables, in such matters as the rights of an accused person pending and during trial. Public opinion was, therefore, favorable to the new

system, and opposition to it rapidly diminished after Jeanne refused
to capitulate. She also announced her intention of supplementing Henri
d'Albret's code of justice with another, to regularize procedures not
included in his. She worked on this matter with a committee of jurists
in 1563 and the *styl de la justicy de la Reine Jehanne* went into effect
in March 1564. A related decision, widely acclaimed, that the *styl* and
all future legal and judicial acts would be written exclusively in Béarnais,
added to her popularity.[8]

The Estates had protested in vain against Henri d'Albret's tax on
goods passing between France and Spain through Béarn (1553), and
they revived the attack at the beginning of Jeanne's reign. In reply she
pointed out that the necessities of life were not affected by the tax. It did
not apply to wheat from Armagnac or fish from Bayonne, for instance,
which were consumed in Béarn, but primarily to such luxuries as Spanish
oranges and Moroccan leather. Therefore, only a few Béarnais, merchants
in the prosperous towns, suffered from it. This being the case, she turned
a deaf ear to the protests and continued to collect the considerable
revenue, which had the advantage of being regular and certain. At the
same time she showed herself sensitive to the problem, and at the outset
of her reign requested the King of France to reduce taxes on Gascon wine
exported to Béarn. Her "pressing and repeated actions" were successful
during the first dozen years of her reign. (Cooperation with the Vicomtesse of Béarn in such ways was part of the crown's attempt to hold the
loyalty of the "Queen of Navarre" and keep her from Henri d'Albret's
kind of intrigue.) Jeanne also permitted textiles of better quality than
those of the royal factory of Nay to enter Béarn from Bigorre untaxed,
and decreed the free circulation of cattle and sheep, so that, "apart from
the established taxes of markets and fairs, no Béarnais would be subject
to internal taxation."[9]

The depreciation of both French and Spanish coin during the last
years of the war (1555–1559) had an adverse effect on the money of
Béarn, caught between the two large adversaries. French provinces
bordering on Béarn were turning out counterfeit Béarnais coin, and in
retaliation the natives were manufacturing substandard coin. Jeanne met
this problem by assuring that the new mint in Pau, under strict supervision, would turn out only coin "of irreproachable content"—on pain
of death. As a result, parity in weight and in value between French and
Béarnais coin was restored in 1557, over the protest of the Cour des

Monnaies in Paris and despite an edict of Henri II that Béarnais coin would be accepted in France only at a value less than its face value.[10]

In the first seven years of her reign Jeanne went beyond the mere preservation of her father's achievement. She consolidated it and gained for herself the same kind of respect and loyalty he had enjoyed. The traditional attempt to resist centralization had been held in check and Béarnais independence reinforced. After the break with Antoine and the flight from Monluc, her people rallied strongly to her. Antoine had never been popular in Béarn, where he was often referred to as *le mari de la vicomtesse,* and, if it had not been for the religious issue, Jeanne might have achieved a harmony with her subjects surpassing her father's.

THE RELIGIOUS ESTABLISHMENT

Béarnais separatism,* already intensified as a reaction to the attempt of the French crown to take over the Vicomté, was exacerbated by the religious issue. Ever since Marguerite had justified her right to give asylum to Protestants persecuted in "France" by the independence of Béarn, "a tight relationship had grown up between Béarnais sovereignty and the defense of the Reform movement; under Jeanne d'Albret these two causes became one."[11] This development was fostered by Henri d'Albret's laissez-faire religious policy in the last years of his reign. The Vicomte, a religious conservative, whose ordinance of 1564 inveighed against all innovations in religion as a threat to law and order, had yet permitted Gerard Roussel to hold the Bishopric of Oloron until his death, and the "new thinking," stimulated by Marguerite earlier, had spread —and strengthened—in his later years, especially among the upper class, merchants, clergy, and officials of the government.[12]

Jeanne maintained her father's policy in this as in other respects, as far as legislation or official action was concerned, until after the announcement of her conversion, December 25, 1560. Antoine's open sponsorship of the reform and the preaching of David, Boisnormand, and others, beginning in 1557, had raised questions about the real intentions of the vicomtes in the minds of their own subjects (as for observers then and since). As late as May 1560, however, Jeanne had expressed herself

---

* Because of the intensity of particularism in the valleys, it is not possible to use that term for the jealous pride in their independence shared by all Béarnais. The valleys were also the stronghold of separatism. Ossau, in particular, stayed loyal to Jeanne in the Third Civil War when most of the Vicomté defected.

in terms consistent with Roman Catholic belief and promised that the "secular arm" would support the bishops in enforcing discipline.[13] Her statements were ambiguous in that they could apply to any church organized in episcopal form and did not touch on matters of substance. On the other hand, Louis d'Albret, the ranking bishop, was under fire from Rome and we have ascertained the plausibility of Salefranque's thesis—that Jeanne was insinuating the new doctrine into her domains under a mask of Catholic orthodoxy. Yet no doctrinal change whatsoever was introduced.

In preparation for her absence to attend the Colloquy in 1561, the Vicomtesse, newly turned Calvinist, commanded her officers to welcome and support the ministers already in Béarn "and others she would send." Her first religious ordinance, July 19, 1561, decreed that oaths could be taken only on the Bible, that teachers had to be approved by the ministers, and that the pulpits were closed to "idolaters." The faithful (Protestants) were authorized to hold public prayers in the absence of a minister, since there were so few available.[14] These first official steps taken by Jeanne, which made Calvinism legal rather than "establishing" it, reflect her caution—or dissimulation.

Because of the pressing problems of personal and political survival which kept Jeanne neutral during the First Civil War, the real launching of her religious program was delayed until the Pacification of Amboise (March 1563), by which time Merlin had been sent by Calvin to help her accomplish the task. The measures of 1563 and 1564, enacted with the aid of Calvin's two emissaries, first Merlin and then Spifâme, constitute the first phase of Jeanne's reformed establishment. The strength of Béarnais separatist sentiment—and Jeanne's popularity—undoubtedly account for the fact that they were accepted with relatively little resistance. In this respect Béarn's separation from Rome resembled that of England. The association of Roman Catholicism with menacing foreign power enabled Jeanne, like Henry VIII, to rally important elements of the population as much or more on political grounds as on religious grounds. Until 1566 resistance to Jeanne's policy was not important enough to stimulate the organization of a real rebellion against it. One reason was probably the moderate nature of the measures enacted, much less radical than Merlin wished, although drastic enough to horrify Philip of Spain and the Pope. As one historian says, "The reform in Béarn was much less aggressive and more conciliatory than in France."[15]

Until 1563, Béarnais Protestantism had flourished and spread where conditions were favorable but it was totally unorganized. Merlin's real accomplishment was to change this situation. Through three synods held within a twelve-month period, consistories and colloquies (periodic assemblies of ministers in regional groups) and other features of *la discipline de Genève* were set up so that Béarnais Calvinism acquired a rational structure. Although it was not completed until eight years later, with Jeanne's Ecclesiastical Ordinances of 1571, the framework of an established church was in existence by the autumn of 1563.

The strong reaction of Spain and the Papacy suggests that they were fully aware of the long-range significance of Jeanne's first major moves. It was disturbing enough that John Knox had created a Calvinist establishment in Scotland, but if one were allowed to develop in Béarn it might spread throughout France, a far more serious challenge to the church. The alarm of some of Jeanne's subjects, however, was caused more by the surface changes in their everyday life, such as the prohibition of processions (protested by the Estates), the removal of "images," attacks on the Mass (emphasized by Descurra), and the requirement to attend public sermons, first applied in Sauveterre. Two other policies, announced at this time, were not implemented until much later: the confiscation of ecclesiastical wealth and the foundation of a Calvinist Academy.[16]

Since the Catholic powers applied pressure not only to Jeanne but also to the French crown on her account, Catherine de Medici, while protesting their interference, also made clear to Jeanne that the price of protection was modification of her religious policy. Merlin's letter to Calvin on Christmas Day, 1563, has shown how much Jeanne was already holding back, from his point of view, and with the arrival of Spifâme the reform was curtailed still further. In February 1564, Jeanne issued a declaration of liberty of conscience for all her subjects, which regularized the practice, prevailing in some Béarnais communities, of coexistence between the two sects. They shared the same buildings, and equality in such matters as baptism, marriages, and funerals was made official. This is called the *simultaneum*.

It is our pleasure that the state of religion remain as it is at present. ... All our subjects, of whatever religion and station, may live in liberty of conscience, that is, those of the Roman religion shall go freely and openly to the places where the exercise of their religion was taking place at the time of the last assembly of our Estates, without, however, their attempting to repair, change, or restore [it] in places where the Mass has been suppressed and other ceremonies forbidden. . . . Likewise, those of the Reformed religion shall live in the same liberty . . . and perform their services in the places which we have or shall establish.[17]

In the historical controversy over Jeanne's toleration, or lack of it, the *simultaneum* is regarded as proof of her moderation and fairness by her apologists and dismissed as insincere, an unavoidable concession to pressure, by her critics. For whichever reason, it was a freezing of the status quo in order to retain the support of the crown, appease the Catholic powers, and leave Béarn as tranquil as possible while Jeanne was absent on the royal tour. The Ecclesiastical Council, established at the same time, was intended to furnish an instrument by which Gramont could control the situation. Extremists on both sides were dissatisfied, naturally, and two years of uneasy equilibrium followed. Jeanne was forbidden by Catherine to reside in the Vicomté.

The second phase of the reform went much further. On June 5, 1566, the Synod at Nay voted to request the Sovereign Lady to carry out "the total suppression of idolatry." The Calvinist ministers were supported by the Conseil Souverain and Gramont was having great difficulty restraining them, while the forces of resistance were growing louder, particularly as a result of the requirement to provide lodging for the ministers as they went from one small community to another strengthening the congregations. There had been many protests in the Estates of 1565, and in 1566 the clergy was so incensed that they refused to attend at all.[18]

In 1566, when Jeanne was residing in Paris but absenting herself for weeks at a time with Henri, to prepare their escape, civil war had already broken out over the religious issue in her county of Foix. Jeanne's response to the news from Béarn, brought by Michel Vigneau representing the Synod, was to grant the request to "purify" Béarn. Although "the total extirpation of the Roman religion" would have to wait until her return, she expressed the hope that "by then all of our subjects will have been gained to the cause of the Gospel."[19] The ordinances of July 1566, went beyond mere restatement and extension of the legislation of 1563 in two ways. First, they embodied a puritan code for the reform of morals. Dancing, various popular games, gambling, drunkenness, prostitution, and "debauchery of all kinds" were proscribed and severe penalties, usually banishment, established for disobedience. Second, changes in nomination to benefices alienated the leading seigneurs.[20] The syndics and *jurats,* who represented the Estates between sessions, protested to the Conseil Souverain, pointing out that the ordinances were "in flagrant contradiction, not only to the custom and privileges of the country, but to [Jeanne's] own legislation of 1564, which specified that neither religious group was to infringe upon the rights of the other."[21] Agitation against the new regulations was such that Gramont suspended their enforcement, pending the Queen's return. This did not prevent the organization of a conspiracy against Jeanne on their account, in Oloron, led by Gabriel de Béarn, Baron de Gerderest, in which the two Bishops were also involved. The plan included the abolition of Calvinism in Béarn, the expulsion of all foreigners (non-Béarnais), and the capture of Jeanne and her children.

The conspiracy was fully organized when Jeanne returned in early February 1567. She was able to circumvent it, thanks to warnings by and cooperation of loyal subjects, including many Catholics, who out-numbered the rebels.[22] Especially helpful was Jean de Belzunce, Seigneur de Monein, a Catholic and brother-in-law of Charles, Comte de Luxe, stubbornest of the rebels. Yet the 1567 session of the Estates, over which she presided in person (July–August), was a stormy one. All aspects of the 1566 ordinances were challenged. In the upper House, forty-nine representatives demanded their retraction and only forty-two supported them. In the Third Estate, only the representatives of Pau and its surrounding villages stood with their Sovereign Lady.[23]

Bordenave says of Jeanne at this time, "if it had been possible to do it without displeasing God, she would have given in to the will of her subjects, but since she could not . . . without offending God . . . she took a firm resolution to disregard their request . . . whatever might be the consequences, and prayed the Lord to fortify her in her intentions."[24] Dartigue interprets this statement as evidence of a severe *crise de con-science* on her part, believing that, whereas she had hoped Calvinist preaching and the spread of Protestant instruction would result in "the protestantization of Béarn by persuasion," in the summer of 1567 she was obliged to recognize that this was impossible.[25] From a somewhat different point of view, one might interpret this turn toward greater authoritarianism as one manifestation of the over-all hardening of Jeanne's character at this time. During her absence she had encountered opposition and betrayal; she returned home only to find them again—in those who had the greatest obligation of loyalty and obedience. Jeanne believed in Divine Right. God had given her the task, and she would shoulder the responsibility. Moreover, the situation probably served to demonstrate once more the lesson she had drawn from the disillusionments of earlier years—she could trust nobody but herself.

The outcome of the second phase of the reform, therefore, was quite different from the equilibrium of the initial phase. Whereas the religious toleration of 1564, however tentative, had forestalled civil war, the decision to "suppress idolatry" of 1566 made it inevitable. Even so, Jeanne might have been able to keep the upper hand if the rebellion had been confined to Oloron. The rebellion in Basse-Navarre, which broke out almost immediately after the Estates had disbanded, presented a much graver challenge. During the last four months of 1567 and the first six of 1568 there was no possibility of proceeding with the reform or anything else Jeanne might have wished. All her attention was required by the Navarre rebellion and the problems posed by the interference of the French crown in it.

As part of the "pacification" of Basse-Navarre, after the rebellion had been put down by force, she was obliged to make concessions to the Catholics: the public exercise of the Roman faith was permitted where there were still Catholic majorities, which meant, for instance, that one might legally call a priest to a sickbed. Those Roman Catholic nobles who formerly had possessed the right to give benefices might do so as before. Both sects were allowed to give elementary instruction, although Catholic teachers were to be examined by the Protestant Conseil Souverain. The ordinance requiring local support of itinerant Calvinist ministers was revoked.[26]

These concessions came too late to prevent a much more inclusive rebellion which was coordinated with the Third War of Religion in "France," 1569–70.[27] After Jeanne had joined Condé and Coligny in La Rochelle, in September 1568, the crown, declaring that she and Henri were prisoners, sent an army under the command of Antoine de Lomagne, Seigneur de Terride, to reconquer Béarn for Catholicism. It was called *l'armée de protection* in conformity with the royal claim that the purpose was to "protect" Henri de Navarre's inheritance until he was free and of age. In the spring of 1569, Terride's army with the collaboration of local rebels took over all of Béarn except the fortress of Navarrenx, where a small troop loyal to Jeanne, under command of her Lieutenant-General

Bernard d'Arros,* withstood a siege from May 27 to August 8. Terride's campaign was marked by many incidents of violence against Protestants and by illegal procedures, including a session of the Estates (July 8–15) packed with defectors, which undid all Jeanne's religious legislation and reestablished Catholicism.[28]

The very week that Terride was holding his illegal Estates, Jeanne in La Rochelle commissioned Gabriel de Lorges, Comte de Montgomery, commander of an *armée de secours*. Incorporating the guerrilla forces of several Gascon vicomtes, Montgomery struck swiftly and hard.† As a result of his lightning two-week campaign, admired even by Monluc, Béarn was completely reconquered by August 22. Every act of Terride's was annulled and those who had collaborated with the enemy were punished.[29]

The historical controversy over Jeanne's responsibility for the reprisals that accompanied Montgomery's triumph is discussed in the next section of this chapter. The fact that the events had occurred is mentioned to explain that Jeanne could complete her reform program with a much freer hand than she had begun it because the rebels had retreated to the mountains of Navarre, the French crown was forced to sue for peace in the national war, and "the faithful" had the upper hand in Béarn. Since the restored Estates were wholly Calvinist in sentiment—no others might hold office—Jeanne could claim that she was merely acquiescing in the requests of her subjects when she completed her Calvinist system. Moreover, Dartigue remarks that if she "ever had wished to practice toleration . . . this notion was from now on totally alien to her thinking."[30]

The first step had been taken by D'Arros' ordinance of January 1570, banishing Roman Catholic clergy from the country and requiring all Jeanne's subjects to attend public (Calvinist) prayers and to have their children baptized within ten days. Other edicts enforcing this, especially on officers of the government, were issued later.[31] The completed religious establishment is embodied in the Ecclesiastical Ordinances, issued on

---

* One of the "twelve barons," D'Arros came from a family outstanding for its unswerving loyalty to the D'Albrets. Bernard, who had played an important role in preventing the betrayal of Béarn to Henri II in 1555, was incorruptible. He was also content to be a mere servant of Jeanne's, standing aside and cooperating with Montgomery when the latter was in command and then assuming responsibility again.

† Montgomery's *armée de secours* is often called the Army of the Vicomtes because these hitherto independent Gascon captains formed its best regiments. Among the most important were: Bruniquel (Bernard de Comminges), Montclar (Antoine de Rabastens), Paulin (Bertrand de Rabastens), Gourdon (Nicolas de Flotard), and Sérignac (Gerard de Lomagne, Terride's brother).

November 26, 1571,[32] the most important legislation of her reign and the last.* Many articles merely restate more clearly earlier practices and rulings, organized as parts of a coherent system. Others implement programs which had been blocked by resistance and about which nothing could be done during the "troubles," as Jeanne called the civil wars.

The strictly religious content of Béarnais Calvinism was realigned to conform to the Confession of Faith of La Rochelle, drawn up the previous spring. Its *saine doctrine* recognized only two sacraments, baptism and communion, with the requirement of a "confidential interview" with a minister before receiving the sacraments—in both kinds. Since all spiritual matters are spelled out in the Confession, to be observed on pain of banishment, the Ecclesiastical Ordinances are confined to matters of administration, the rights and duties of Calvinist ministers in the education and discipline of the faithful—all modeled on Geneva. While the clergy is given great scope to perform their many functions, the secular authority is explicitly declared to be supreme. In the Preamble to the Ordinances, citing Biblical and historical precedents, Jeanne sets forth the theory that rulers have a vocation from God to assure the eternal salvation of their subjects. Accordingly, all members of the clergy are under the secular arm and must take an oath in the presence of one of its magistrates. The Confession of La Rochelle and implementing ordinances are imposed by edict of the Vicomtesse and disobedience is punished by her officers. Legal problems arising from the enforcement of Calvinism, particularly with regard to marriages and inheritance, are to be handled by the Conseil Souverain.

The chief problem outstanding from the earlier phases of the reform was the matter of financing the Calvinist ministry. The decisions to take inventory of movable ecclesiastical wealth and to use revenues from vacant benefices had been the only practical steps taken in this direction before the Civil War. Afterward, ordinances confiscating the property of traitors—many were ecclesiastics—made it possible for the first time seriously to take over the wealth of the old church for the use of the new. On the other hand, Jeanne issued many pardons to suppliants, whose lands and goods were restored on condition that their owners convert to

---

* As part of the Ecclesiastical Ordinances, Jeanne decreed that the year should henceforth begin on January 1 instead of on March 25. This preceded by eleven years the reform for all Catholic Europe, decreed by Pope Gregory XIII in 1582, but it was not original with Jeanne. Charles IX had instituted the change for the French court in 1565, although it was not consistently observed.

Calvinism. In each case the loss in revenue had to be weighed against the gain in loyalty. Special commissions took inventory and special officers collected revenue from those who did not convert.

This procedure was followed until October 1571, when Jeanne announced to the Synod of Pau that, as her conscience would not allow her to collect "God's wealth," she was "emptying her hands" of all ecclesiastical revenues and turning them over to the church "for the support of the evangelical ministry, the schools, and the relief of the poor." She forbade her officers in future to touch the ecclesiastical revenues. The finances of the Béarnais church from then on were controlled by a special council and fourteen auditors, all chosen annually by the synod, that is by the Calvinist clergy itself.[33]

To designate education as one of the chief duties of the church is characteristically Calvinist, following the example of Geneva and carrying out the belief that only with proper instruction can one do God's work, whatever the station of life to which one has been called. At the very outset of Jeanne's reform program, she and Merlin had planned to transform the *collège* Marguerite had founded at Lescar into a Protestant institution.[34] Partly as a result of local protests in Lescar, in 1564 Jeanne ordered the Jacobins of Orthez to vacate their large building so that the new school could be installed, giving them the smaller premises of the Cordeliers in exchange. Two years passed before Jeanne issued letters patent from Paris, designating it as an "academy like the one in Geneva," and the opening was delayed until 1567, after her return. Meanwhile, the most important Calvinist minister ever to be associated with the Béarnais church arrived to serve as director of the Academy.* This was Pierre Viret, whom Jeanne had met in Lyons in 1564. By 1568, fifty young men, subsidized by Jeanne, were preparing for the ministry. In the spring of that year she issued the *Lois Collegiales,* which spell out in detail the organization, curriculum, discipline, and daily routine. Jeanne's hopes for the Academy were not fully realized until after the Civil War, however, Terride's conquest having suspended its operation. In 1570, despite protests from Orthez, it opened in Lescar, and remained there until Henri moved it back to Orthez in 1579.

By the end of Jeanne's reign nearly two hundred pensionnaires were preparing for the ministry, half on full scholarship, and about two hun-

---

* Beza, although Jeanne's advisor from afar, was never affiliated with the Béarnais church as such.

dred commuters attended. Professorial chairs were established in Latin, Greek, Hebrew, mathematics, philosophy, and theology, as well as a singing master who taught the students Marot's Psalms for an hour each day. The over-all direction was in the hands of a committee chosen by the synod, and expenses were met by revenues confiscated from the Roman Catholic church, as were those of the elementary schools. These were greatly increased in number after the Civil War, so that free public instruction was available to all Béarnais boys by the end of the sixteenth century, in striking contrast to the rest of France—or Europe. As in Geneva, the chief duty of the deacons was to interview children regularly to see that they attended school and did their lessons. When the time came, the deacons also decided whether a boy would go on to the Academy or learn a trade; in the latter case they were responsible for placing the boy as an apprentice. Even more unusual, regular instruction at the elementary level was provided for Béarnais girls, although it was not mandatory, in a separate school. A brief experiment in coeducation at the Academy (1570) was abandoned on the grounds that "it could lead to many inconveniences and scandals."

Jeanne intended Viret to be director of the Academy, and he himself wrote in March 1567 that he had been "charged with the preparation of young men for the Holy Ministry."[35] But since he spent the years 1567–1569 in Pau, while the Academy was in Orthez, and his health was frail, it seems unlikely that he ever taught regular classes until the institution returned to Lescar, after the Civil War. We know that he taught theology there in the last year of his life. Viret's importance to the success of Jeanne's religious establishment should not be underestimated, however. In addition to his academic functions, he served as over-all guiding spirit of the Béarnais church and presided over the synods as long as he lived. He was among the pastors held as hostages in Pau during the Civil War, and it is believed that he escaped execution only because of his value as a possible exchange prisoner.

Viret died in Orthez, ironically, en route to attend the Synod of La Rochelle, in April 1571. It was a dreadful blow to Jeanne. As she wrote to the Council of Geneva, "Among the great losses I have suffered during and since the war, I count the loss of M. Viret, whom God has called to Himself, as the greatest."[36] Viret, who has been called "the gentlest and most moderate of the reformers," was one of two important collaborators with whom Jeanne never became *brouillée*. The letter indicates her esteem for him, as does the fact that he was buried in the ancient crypt of the vicomtes of Béarn with near-royal honors.

Comparisons can be made between the Reformed Church of Béarn and the Church of England under Elizabeth, as well as with the Genevan church. While much of the ecclesiastical organization copies the latter, Béarn's monarchical form of government makes Jeanne's in some respects an Erastian* church also. Like citizens of all republics, the citizens of Geneva were subject to the struggle of various bodies for supremacy, a situation that can sometimes be exploited by playing them off against each other. In a divine-right monarchy, on the contrary, the subject is at the mercy of the sovereign's policy in the application of the law. Because of Jeanne's theory of secular supremacy, her Ecclesiastical Ordinances created a Calvinist church quite different in its relation to the state from that of Geneva. It differed also from Beza's abortive attempt of 1561 to form a united Calvinist organization for the lands of the Bourbons, Condés, and Châtillons, since it was highly centralized and restricted to Béarn. Had it endured it would probably have offered parallels and comparisons to the Kirk in Scotland and to the Calvinist establishments in Germany. But Jeanne died about six months after creating it and Henri was forced to repeal her legislation. Although revived after his escape from Paris in 1576, the Béarnais church never developed as fully as Jeanne had planned. During the civil wars Henri was not present to supply the strong royal leadership presupposed; after his conversion to Roman Catholicism in 1593, there was no possibility of its functioning according to her intentions. In the reign of Louis XIII, as a result of Richelieu's policies, Béarn suffered the same curtailment of its privileges, religious and otherwise, as other Calvinist strongholds.

On paper, Elizabeth's Act of Uniformity (1559) reads much like some articles of Jeanne's Ecclesiastical Ordinances a dozen years later, but in practice, prominent Roman Catholics who held services in their own houses were merely fined in England, whereas in Béarn they might lose their titles and lands. The historical circumstances of Jeanne's reign made her record in regard to toleration less consistent than Elizabeth's. Events corresponding to the stages of Jeanne's evolution had taken place under Elizabeth's predecessors. In England there had been reversals of policy

---

* Erastianism is the theory that the secular power is supreme in ecclesiastical affairs. For Jeanne's views as expressed in the Preamble to the Ecclesiastical Ordinances, see Appendix C.

and rebellion, but they were spread over a period of thirty years under four different monarchs,* as compared to the eight years of Jeanne's reform program (1563–1571). Because of the relatively small size and vulnerability of Jeanne's kingdom, pressure from the French crown could force Jeanne to permit a remarkable degree of toleration at the time of the *simultaneum* in 1564, and to make similar concessions in 1568. However, when she had the upper hand, after Montgomery's victory, Jeanne pursued the "suppression of idolatry" with every legal means at her command.

Much heat was generated in nineteenth-century polemical articles as Huguenot writers tried to refute the charges of Catholic writers who depict Jeanne as the incarnation of Calvinist bigotry.[37] The few who were scholarly enough to go to the sources tend to fall victim to the anachronistic fallacy. In the sixteenth century very few private individuals believed in religious toleration in the modern sense or considered it a positive good in itself. Among European rulers I know of none. Since God held kings responsible for their subjects in religion as in other respects, the desirable situation was for them to belong to the same sect, a notion expressed in Latin by the phrase *cuius regio, eius religio,* and in French, *un roi, une loi, une foi.* Each ruler was free to deal with dissenting subjects according to particular circumstances, hence French toleration usually varied according to the relative strength of the crown and the dissenters. François I, a strong monarch, was intolerant; Catherine de Medici, faced with a militant Huguenot party and handicapped by the weakness of the crown, was relatively tolerant. Where attempts to enforce conformity as an aspect of obedience had proven futile, farsighted rulers like Elizabeth or Henri IV decided that some degree of toleration was a lesser evil than civil war. Both were strong and popular monarchs, but both believed the price of total conformity too great.

Jeanne d'Albret stood in the mainstream of her times. She believed in her absolute right over her subjects, responsible only to God, as she stated repeatedly in correspondence with Cardinal d'Armagnac, Philip II,

---

* Henry VIII separated from Rome and confiscated church property in the 1530's, but he retained Catholic dogma except for the primacy of Peter. Under Edward VI (1547–1553) the Church of England became a (moderate) Protestant church, but returned to Rome, officially at least, in 1553, when Mary Tudor became Queen. There were martyrdoms in each reign. Conflicting religious legislation on the books was among the problems facing Elizabeth when she came to the throne in 1558. Her solution was the Elizabethan Settlement, a national church, with internal leeway for differences on controversial points.

and spokesmen for the French crown. Obligatory membership in the Calvinist church and punishment for disobedience were logical consequences of this belief. There were degrees of disobedience, however, and different forms and degrees of punishment.

Jeanne certainly exerted pressure on her Catholic subjects to convert. She made it worth their while to do so and disadvantageous not to. Her confirmation of D'Arros' edict of January 1570, which closed Catholic churches and required attendance at Calvinist prayers, shows intolerance. At the same time, she did not intend to persecute her Catholic subjects—unless they were guilty of lese majesty. She repeats endlessly that she has not and will not "force the consciences" of her subjects. She tried to close loopholes for disobedience without using force to compel obedience. The wording of an open letter to the Catholic seigneurs who were protesting—and disobeying—the ordinances of D'Arros clarifies her position and their dilemma.

Everyone knows with what ardor we have always sought the advancement of God's glory and the repose of our subjects by every legitimate means. . . . We know, nevertheless, that, in great defiance of God's will . . . and our ordinances . . . a number of our subjects have been taking the liberty to depart from the true path and to persist stubbornly in their idolatries and superstitions . . . on the false pretext that they would be forced by beatings [*à coups de baston*] to attend public prayers conducted by our ministers. . . . We do not intend that anyone should be thus constrained in matters of conscience. . . . If such violence has occurred it was against our will . . . but to those who are seeking to disregard the edict of the Seigneur d'Arros . . . we say now that we have approved, confirmed, and established it . . . on every point. . . . We desire that the said edict be observed entirely and everywhere [*en tout et par tout*] . . . we have never intended to alter it in any respect . . . still less have we intended to allow our subjects to return to their idolatries and superstitions or to dispense them from observation of the said edict, whereby it is decreed that [everyone] must attend the public prayers and exhortations . . . in fear and in reverence for God. . . . Nevertheless, our intention has never been and is not now that they should be constrained by open force and violence to join the said Religion [*constraictz par force et violence ouverte à se ranger à la dite religion*].[38]

Catholic subjects who were not guilty of treason were not subject to banishment or loss of property—unless it was attached to public office. The nineteenth-century writers on Jeanne's religious policy confused punishment of traitors with lack of religious toleration even more than the entanglement of these two matters in the sixteenth century warrants. The conception of *cuius regio* meant that it was possible for a religious minority to attribute punishment of its members to their religious opinions, even when they were guilty of flagrant treason. Jesuit writings against Elizabeth are a striking instance, and modern scholars are still struggling to ascertain the true role of religion in the English Queen's policy.[39] With Jeanne also, a study of punishment meted out to the rebels after Montgomery's victory is necessary, if we are to disentangle—as far as possible —the religious issue from that of rebellion.

VENGEANCE OR JUSTICE?

Between the spring of 1567 and the summer of 1569, Jeanne's authority was challenged in three organized rebellions. Even a general account of them would require a book in itself, because there is an abundance of documentation.[40] My purpose is to assess Jeanne's concept of justice by examining her treatment of the rebels after her authority had been restored, as it was in all three cases. Resistance to the religious program of their Sovereign Lady was the alleged cause of each rebellion, and unresolved grievances from the Oloron uprising of 1567 and that of Basse-Navarre which followed it—as well as continuity of leadership from both—enabled the greater rebellion of 1569 to develop very fast, once the royal armies were known to be on the way to support it.

Jeanne's techniques form a consistent pattern: first, military suppression; then, when she had regained the upper hand, replacement of brute force by political pressure and legal action, accompanied by concessions, compromises, and general pardons for the "little people." Pardons for the leaders were granted with discrimination, depending on the willingness of the rebels to humble themselves, beg for mercy, "return to their obedience," and remain in it. All the leaders of the Oloron uprising of 1567 were pardoned in the official sense; that is, the sentence of execution which hung over them was revoked and they kept their offices and property. (Jeanne had reason later to regret this clemency, when they rebelled again in 1569, with the backing of the King of France.) Her treatment of Charles, Comte de Luxe, and Valentin Domezain, leaders of the rebellion in Basse-Navarre, 1567–1568, cannot be taken as a reflection of Jeanne's own policy because pressure from the French crown forced her to pardon them. In a speech addressed to them on this occasion, she said that "wicked subjects who rebel against their prince cannot be held as nobles, but rather as traitors, deserving no grace before God's justice, still less before that of men," but that "God's High Providence has inspired [me] to extend clemency to those who are remorseful . . . and desirous of mending their ways. . . . On this assurance I forgive you the past, hoping that my clemency will produce fruits worthy of good and faithful subjects. May God will it."[41] The fact that they rebelled again, a year later, showed that they were unrepentant; De Luxe was rewarded by Charles IX with membership in the royal order of St. Michael.[42] Only after Montgomery's victory had restored her authority can one safely balance Jeanne's policy of pardon against that of reprisal, and even then it is not easy to disentangle her personal responsibility for the latter from that of her lieutenants.

Jeanne's commission to Montgomery endowed him with virtually unlimited powers (*plein pouvoir . . . pour reduire et remettre toutes choses en notre obéissance . . . pour chasser et defaire les dits enemies . . . et pour chastier tous rebelles*).[43] This broad mandate, which shows that Jeanne trusted Montgomery's judgment, is always cited by those who wish to hold her responsible for his acts. Quite aside from the brutalities characteristic of sixteenth-century armies, Catholic or Protestant, Terride had completely reversed the status quo in Béarn, through his use of the Estates, so that equally drastic and highhanded action was required to undo his accomplishment. The rebels to be chastized were highly placed and degrees of disobedience had to be taken into account. Apart from the active leaders, who had coordinated the political and military experience gained in the earlier uprisings,* the three men on whom Jeanne had chiefly depended had also defected in one degree or another.

Claude Régin, Bishop of Oloron and "second baron of Béarn," had been intriguing with the rebels since 1567. Terride made him superintendent of finances, from which position he rewarded the rebels and prevented Jeanne's officers from exercising their charges. He fled after Mont-

---

* From the Oloron rebellion: Jacques de Ste. Colomme, Seigneur d'Esgoarrabaque; Gabriel de Béarn, Sieur de Gerderest; Jean, Sieur d'Armendaritz; François de Béarn, Sieur de Bonasse; a lawyer, Jean de Supersantis; Henri de Navailles, Sieur de Peyre; and his son-in-law, Guy de Biran, Sieur de Gohas. From Basse-Navarre, Charles, Comte de Luxe, and Domezain. The demands of the second group are embodied in *Manifeste des gentilhommes de la Basse-Navarre et du peuple, qui ont pris les armes pour la défense de la réligion Catholique* . . . , published in *Mémoires*, 147–164. The points made are almost identical to those made in De Luxe's letters to Jeanne, cited below.

gomery's arrival and appealed—in vain—to Monluc to revive the war against Jeanne.[44] Armand de Gontaut, Seigneur d'Audaux and Sénéchal de Béarn, also cooperated with Terride. Both Régin and Audaux were deprived of their offices and property by Jeanne after the war and neither was ever pardoned by her. Régin died in 1580, still in exile. Audaux was reinstated by Henri that year and assisted Catherine de Bourbon as his regent in Béarn for some years.[45] Antoine de Gramont had been even more closely associated with Jeanne's rule, but in the Civil War he withdrew to his own estates at Bidache and refused to cooperate with D'Arros or Montgomery. The fact that he took no active part in the rebellion spared him punishment after the war ended.[46]

Jeanne's deputy-governor of the fortress of Navarrenx, Armand de Gachissans, Sieur de Salles, had reported to her as early as April, when Terride was just arriving in the Vicomté, "I do not know how to begin, Madame, as I have nothing to say that could please you. Affairs here are in such a state that three out of four have turned their backs on you, some openly and others in secret." After a careful listing of the most striking acts of treason so far committed, he says, "It is to be feared that the good men will be overcome by the wicked . . . money is in such short supply that we have had to have recourse to your plate."[47]

Henri de Navailles, Seigneur de Peyre, one of the twelve barons, was governor of Pau for Terride.[48] On the day Montgomery's army entered the Vicomté (August 8), Peyre executed eight (out of a dozen) Calvinist pastors he was holding as hostages and Terride abandoned the siege of Navarrenx and retreated to Orthez, where Montgomery caught up with him on August 10. All accounts, regardless of the bias of their authors, agree that the fighting of the next four days, which resulted in Montgomery's capture of Orthez on August 15, was the bloodiest episode of the entire Third Civil War, in Béarn or elsewhere.[49] A group of Terride's lieutenants, captured by Montgomery, were sent to Navarrenx pending exchange with prominent Protestants taken prisoner in battles outside Béarn, or, in the case of native Béarnais, pending trial by the Conseil Souverain.

The fall of Orthez proved to be the last military engagement of the war in Béarn because the aid Terride was expecting from Monluc did not materialize. Local leaders, loyal to Jeanne, took over in all the important towns and hastened to rally to Montgomery as representative of their *dame souveraine,* while the rebels fled to strongholds in the mountains.

Peyre left Pau on August 19.* The official end of the war and the restoration of Jeanne's authority were celebrated in the chateau of Pau on August 22 by Montgomery, his lieutenants, and loyal Béarnais nobles, with Viret officiating in the name of the restored Calvinist church.[50]

Montgomery's task of "pacification" proved much more difficult than the "liberation." The episode which became the focus of controversy over Jeanne's reprisals—or Montgomery's in her name—occurred in Navarrenx the night before the ceremony in Pau. Six of the thirty-four prisoners taken at Orthez were killed, including three of the well-known Béarnais rebels, Gerderest, Ste. Colomme, and Gohas. After nearly four hundred years, it is still not reliably known whether they were "massacred," as Catholic polemicists believe, or whether they were shot trying to escape, as Jeanne explained to the Duc d'Anjou a few weeks later.[51] D'Arros was in charge at Navarrenx and the sources tell nothing of his part in the affair or his later reactions. Montgomery was in Pau. The case for clearing him of personal responsibility rests less on that fact than on an order, issued on August 23, for the Conseil Souverain to move to Navarrenx to try the prisoners.[52] This was consistent with Jeanne's general policy of observing legal forms, but it seems unlikely that the matter will ever be definitively settled, since the sources leave room for conflicting interpretations. On the other hand, Montgomery almost certainly was responsible for the death of Bertrand de Gabaston, Sieur de Bassillon, governor of Navarrenx, in that town a few days later. Bassillon was suspected of collaborating with the enemy, although the charge has never been substantiated.[53]

It is not certain when Jeanne learned about these incidents, but it is known that her lieutenants had not received any orders from her since their departure from Castres, on July 27, to liberate Béarn. Bernard d'Astarac, Baron de Montamat, famed Gascon captain and zealous Huguenot, who shared the administration of Béarn with D'Arros after Montgomery's departure, wrote Jeanne on August 23,† that they were awaiting word from her, "we have had no commands since our departure."[54] Mont-

* Like most of the rebel leaders who were not killed in subsequent battles outside Béarn, Peyre took refuge in "France." His goods were sequestered and Jeanne never lifted his sentence of banishment.

† Letters from both Montamat and Montgomery on this date inform Jeanne of the death of Louis d'Albret, Bishop of Lescar and her great-uncle, two days before. Montamat mentions that no money was found in his house. This is not surprising since it had been sacked (and the old man beaten up) by Terride's troops a few days earlier.

gomery himself refers in several letters to lack of communications from Jeanne, and he keeps repeating the same items of news. On September 11 he says that the present messenger is the fifteenth he has sent and that only the minister Hespérien and the treasurer La Rose have succeeded in crossing enemy territory to Béarn. They arrived on September 4.[55] This means that Montgomery had only Jeanne's initial commission to guide him until that date—well after the executions at Navarrenx. Hespérien and La Rose must have brought some word from their mistress, but not what Montgomery wanted, for he says on September 28, "more than ever I need instructions and beg you to send them."[56]

In the meanwhile, Montgomery went ahead on the basis of Jeanne's original instructions. On September 16, he canceled Terride's changes with one stroke, by revoking all his acts and declaring guilty of lese majesty the native Béarnais who had enacted his orders in the Estates. The latter edict was softened, however, by a general amnesty, declared on September 22, which decreed that no inhabitant of the Vicomté was to be molested in his person or in his property, regardless of religion. An ordinance of September 24 singled out three rebel leaders for punishment, as exceptions to the amnesty: Audaux was deprived of his office of sénéchal; Ste. Colomme was removed (posthumously) from the governorship of Oloron; and a captain Du Tilh was punished, as the chief adjutant of Ste. Colomme.[57]

Montgomery was a rough man of war and it is worth remembering that he won Monluc's admiration, but an objective examination of the facts does not reveal him to have resorted to violence outside of battle, with the single exception of Bassillon. In any case, he left Béarn in early October, his task done, to return to the "Army of the Princes" leaving any remaining problems to D'Arros and Montamat. Jeanne's first directive since the liberation, issued in St. Maxient on September 22, must have arrived about this time to guide them. In the opening clause, all Jeanne's subjects are forbidden on pain of death to have any dealings with banished persons, and the policy is announced of punishing the rebels, "by pursuit if necessary," and selling their goods to the highest bidder. The rest of the ordinance lays the basis for the restoration of Calvinism.[58]

The accomplishment of this program in Béarn took two years. In Basse-Navarre it was never possible to execute it, since the rebel leaders had found asylum there and were supported by the population. The reform had never been popular with the Basques. De Luxe, Domezain, and such of the Béarnais rebels as had been able to flee with them encouraged further resistance by exploiting the fear that Jeanne would succeed in imposing Calvinism in Navarre as in Béarn. If their appeals for French support had met with positive response, the rebels probably would have descended on Béarn and undone Montgomery's accomplishment. "Only the rivalry between Monluc and Damville," says Dartigue, "saved the vicomté from what would undoubtedly have been even worse ravages. This is why [D'Arros and Montamat] could not, even if they wished, show clemency. . . . In applying edicts with the exact wording of those of Charles IX against the Huguenots, except that the terms used for Catholics and Protestants were transposed, and in excepting the rebel leaders from the amnesty . . . the Princess was only trying to conserve her authority in line with all the sovereigns of her time."[59]

In the autumn of 1569, rebel leaders were punished by confiscation of their wealth and inclusion in the Proscription List posted throughout the Vicomté. (This was later revised, with provision for trial within fifteen days.) The final list contained about eighty-five names;* it included some persons already dead, indicating that their heirs would suffer the punishment—loss of offices and property. A few leaders of the rebellion were also banished. Nobody suffered the death penalty, or even imprisonment.[60]

Jeanne insisted on severe punishment for the syndic Luger, who had expedited Terride's illegal legislation; he was stripped of his office in a special ceremony in the Estates.[61] She banished Peyre, Domezain, De Luxe, and Armendaritz. Bonasse almost certainly would have been banished had he not been killed at the siege of Tarbes. A number of prominent Catholics left Béarn for France or Spain voluntarily, without trying to soften their fate, even though their names were not on the list. On the other hand, Jeanne pardoned a considerable number of lesser traitors, after they had humbled themselves, and allowed some Catholics of proven ability to hold office, as exceptions to her edicts. After the Peace of St. Germain ended the national war, a conciliatory policy became the rule. Those who "made their submission" had their names struck off the list and their property restored.[62]

---

* The living included Régin, Jean de Bordenave (President of the Conseil under Terride), Audaux, Domezain, De Luxe, Armendaritz, members of the Ste. Colomme family, Peyre, Bonasse, and Luger. The elder St. Colomme, Gerderest, and Gohas (killed at Navarrenx) were listed. As in all civil wars, families were split. Jean de Bordenave was a cousin of Nicolas, and Terride's brother was Montgomery's first lieutenant, for instance.

That Jeanne was troubled about whether a good Calvinist ruler might in conscience retain in her service officers who had deserted "the Religion" during Terride's domination, is known because she sought advice on the matter from the Synod at La Rochelle in April 1571. Article XLVII records:

> The Queen of Navarre asked whether she might, in conscience, employ as officers Roman Catholics, when there were not enough of the Religion, and whether she could keep them as members of her household. Whereupon Her Majesty was requested to scrutinize very carefully the record of each one and to use, as far as possible, God-fearing members of our Religion. Catholics who are law-abiding and of good morals should be instructed [in Calvinist doctrine]. But as for traitors, who had abandoned her in her necessity and had committed great cruelties during the troubles, she should never allow them to exercise any public office, nor receive them at her court or in her household.[63]

This advice is consistent with a general decision, taken the following day, "concerning the censure of those who had abandoned the Religion."

> Those who did so during the troubles and are now deeply repentant [*touchés au vif de leur révolte*] should be consoled and exhorted by the Consistory, where their misdeeds will be examined. . . . For the unrepentant [*obstinés*] who have left and are living in the communion of the idolaters, it is declared that they no longer belong to us . . . but we will go no further [*ne passerons pas plus outre*].[64]

After she had returned to her own domains, this problem was still on Jeanne's mind. In the minutes of the Synod of Pau (October 1571) we find, under the heading Other Private Matters:

> Her Majesty asked if she should dismiss Papist officers of her household who did not wish to convert to the true religion. She was advised that they could be kept on, provided that they were repentant [*pas obstinez, debordez ou dogmatisans pour desbaucher les austres*] and willing to listen to the word of God.[65]

With the most powerful of the Catholic rebels, Charles de Luxe, Jeanne carried on an extensive correspondence between August and December 1571. De Luxe was physically out of her reach and politically under the protection of the French crown. As in earlier clashes between Jeanne and Monluc, neither would yield. De Luxe began the correspondence in the name of all the rebels who had gathered around him in the mountain strongholds of Basse-Navarre and Soule (which had been given to him as a reward by Charles IX) in August 1571.[66] "Having heard that it pleases Your Majesty to reinstate in your good graces those who humbly request it, we are trying to obtain freedom of our consciences, the exercise of our religion, and the restitution of our goods, honors, and estates." He claims that he would rather be dead than have his name stained with the infamy of treason, "having never thought that I had failed in my duty. Nevertheless, Madame, if you have judged otherwise . . . I most humbly pray that it will please Your Majesty to forget all things past and to receive us in your favor as your very humble and very obedient subjects." Jeanne replied on August 29 from Quistres, in Guyenne, during her trip home from La Rochelle. The tone is conciliatory: "the affection I naturally bear all my subjects . . . makes me easily forget and bury . . . the past, when they recognize me . . . as their sovereign and princess."

The tone of De Luxe's second letter is more importunate: "I make so bold as to claim that I merit [your good graces] as much as any man in the world"; he concludes by asking her to "send word establishing liberty of conscience, and the exercise of our religion in your kingdom [as well as] the restitution of our honors, prerogatives, property, and privileges, with commands to your officers to annul all sentences and edicts to the contrary." Jeanne's response was written on September 11, from Arudy, a village on her regular route to Eaux-Chaudes. "I can give you no other answer except to repeat that if you recognize my authority as you should, I will always be glad to accord what you ask, and on this condition I now concede the substance of your request."

The arrogance of De Luxe's next letter, the longest in the series, is such that Communay, no apologist for Jeanne, says, "we think there exist very few examples of a vassal using such language to his suzerain." In the first part of the document (which he entitled "the Request"), De Luxe presents his view of past events.

In the name of a large number of gentlemen and others of your subjects, whose goods were seized at Your Majesty's command about three years ago . . . and against whose honor and good name . . . certain orders were issued in your town of Pau. Moreover, for about two years past, the Roman, Catholic, and Apostolic Religion has been obstructed and forbidden in your kingdom . . . although [the said gentlemen] have never thought they had said or done anything to displease Your Majesty . . . and cannot imagine what has irritated and embittered Your Majesty against them, unless it be that when Your Majesty was absent . . . three years ago, they took arms at the King's command . . . for the protection [of your lands] . . . during your absence. . . . In accepting the said orders from the King [they] never understood that they were being separated or distracted from . . . obedience to you . . . on the contrary, . . . they thought . . . to be saving your crown.

The particular items of the "very humble request" follow:

(1) that Your Majesty shall approve, avow, and hold all your subjects, of whatever quality and condition, who bore arms in these past years for the said protection, as your very humble servants, your very loyal, very faithful, and very obedient subjects. . . . (2) that Your Majesty shall forget the past and in token thereof shall send letters patent by which it shall please Your Majesty to cancel and annul all orders, commissions, and decrees [of your officers] to the contrary . . . in order that everything to the prejudice of the honor, good name, reputation, integrity, fidelity, and loyalty [of the said gentlemen] shall be pulled out by the root, removed, struck off, and broken so that the memory of them shall be forever erased. . . . (3) that Your Majesty shall promise that [the said gentlemen] shall live in freedom of conscience and the full exercise of their religion, that it shall be reestablished . . . in all places where it has been abolished . . . and that its adherents shall not be obstructed or molested in any way. . . . (4) that it shall be your good pleasure . . . to restore all their estates, rights, franchises, liberties, privileges, and pensions with the unrestricted use which [the said gentlemen] enjoyed under [Jeanne's predecessors]. . . . (5) shall command by letters patent that the estates, dignities, offices, benefices, revenues, and other goods of the [Catholic] church shall be restored as they were before.

Jeanne replied from Pau, on September 25.

I have seen the request you sent, which is more worthy of a man who chooses to continue to offend me than of a chastened subject who wishes to acknowledge his faults. To tell you what I really think, I am very much surprised at the tone you have used throughout this affair, and still more that you should pretend to think, in order to justify your past actions—which can be neither disguised nor excused—that I should condemn those who saved my kingdom in my absence. If I were to declare that you were serving me and had remained faithful, what could I say to those who resisted you to protect my welfare and who truly served me? So that you will not have any doubt, accept this as final: if you will not recognize my authority, as I have previously said, and place yourself in dependence on my mercy, you will try in vain to obtain anything whatever from me, for I would as soon abandon my crown itself as this resolution. And do not think that time will change my mind. It will rather, if you continue as at present, give me occasion for bitterness than for clemency toward you, which would, nevertheless, much distress me.

The correspondence continues in the same vein for several months more. Jeanne's letters to Charles IX and Catherine de Medici in this period often refer to De Luxe and to the crown's intervention on his behalf. To them also she explained her position, "I require, first, satisfaction for the crimes and faults of the past and that my mercy be implored . . . which grace I shall grant as freely as I already have to all those who implored it as they should." De Luxe was never "pacified" in the sense that Jeanne hoped. On the other hand, he reaped a rich reward from the French king for his part in the "Protection," an outright gift of 20,000 livres and an annual pension of 800 livres in addition to the vicomté of Soule. In the 1580's, Henri lifted the sentence against him, but he never played an important role again.

The Simancas Archives contain about seventy-five letters and several hundred orders of Jeanne's for the year 1571, only a handful of which have been published.[67] Analysis of these documents, which reveal many difficulties and complications inevitable in the wake of civil war, enables us to classify them into four main categories. Most numerous are letters of thanks and orders which reward the faithful by restoring or giving them offices or property. There are also pardons for particular *un*faithful subjects, with Jeanne's reasons for excepting them from the general ordinances. The third and most general category could be described as "picking up the pieces" of her authority, including many financial matters. Dispensation of justice through the courts occurs so often that it constitutes a category in itself. Almost all the documents of the latter type render judgment in disputes or annul specific acts or appointments by rebels during the war.

In one of several letters to her most important lieutenant, D'Arros, Jeanne wrote, on April 1, 1571, "I can never thank you enough. I beg you to continue your precious service despite my long absence, which I hope soon to remedy. In no way do I disapprove of the measures of amnesty you have accorded some of my rebellious subjects in Béarn. If they frankly ask my forgiveness, I will grant it, with no hard feelings for the past." Bertrand de Gachissans, Sieur de Salles, also received special thanks, and the office of governor of Navarrenx. "I will never forget your service, and hope soon to restore order completely. I need your help." Jeanne's secretaries Enecot de Sponde and Jean Pelletier, who had done their best to carry out her orders under virtually impossible circumstances, were given offices and incomes for life, as well as lodgings in the chateau of

Pau. Michel Beranger, treasurer, was reconfirmed in his office. Jeanne writes, "I know that the many iniquities are not caused by malice on your part and I consider you one of my best officers." A series of letters and commands involves one Captain Moreau, who resisted attempts by the Bishop of Rodez to coerce or bribe him into deserting Jeanne. He was rewarded with a personal letter and the payment of his wages retroactive to the start of the "troubles." Concierges, ushers in the chateau, even *valets-de-chambre,* who had stood fast under pressure, received letters and gifts from their grateful mistress, whom some knew as Comtesse de Rodez, d'Armagnac, de Bigorre, Vicomtesse de Limoges, Duchesse de Vendôme—and others simply as *la Reine.*

Some of the pardons are general in wording, "those for whom representatives of our Estates have requested indulgence." Others are specific, such as that of the Baron du Hart, for whom a member of Henri's household had asked Jeanne's forgiveness. She replied, "I have ordered the dispatch to be drawn up. It should be ready by the time he is willing to admit his errors and come to find me." To Madame de Montoye she wrote, "because you were brought up under my protection I choose to forget the rebellion and offenses of your late husband . . . to this effect I have ordered his goods restored to you." In the case of two widows named Carsusan, each with several children, whose husbands' property had been confiscated because they had been involved in one of Terride's illegal acts, Jeanne said, "it is our pleasure to take pity on them. Following our natural inclination, we ordain that they should be accorded one half of their late husbands' goods."

In Béarn, the situation was chaotic, but Jeanne's authority had also been challenged or overthrown in all her other domains. The phrases *mettre ordre, remettre ordre,* or *donner ordre* occur in virtually every command, on matters ranging from the Collège de Périgord at the University of Toulouse, where the Parlement had usurped her right to name the scholars, to the distant country of Marle on the Flemish frontier, where revenues were being withheld from her agents. Jeanne badly needed income. She had been sinking deeper into debt since Antoine's death. The extravagant King of Navarre had left many creditors, whom she had paid off with difficulty in 1563, after a search was made "for the money that the late King had hidden in one of the lower rooms of the chateau of Nérac, whose keys had been lost."[68] Monluc's activities had deprived her of valuable rents and property in Guyenne during the First and Second Civil Wars. In the Third, she had mortgaged her jewels for *la cause* and her officers in Béarn had melted down most of her plate. In 1571, none of her officers or servants had been paid in full and some not at all for two years. Extensive repairs were needed not only to most of her chateaux and fortifications but also to income-bearing property. There is a correspondence about the repair of mills in Rodez, another about the management of the forest in Vendôme, among letters to agents in every one of her fiefs, urging them to collect money due her as soon as possible. To meet expenses she was forced to sell some of her feudal rights; for instance, "the necessity to raise a notable sum immediately and to avoid total ruin . . . because of losses during the recent troubles . . . and the impossibility of establishing any kind of order without alienating some of our lands and rights" obliged her to sell *haute, moyenne, et basse justice* in the lesser fief of Auberchy (Guyenne). The Comtesse d'Armagnac was so hard up that she went to considerable pains to recover a silver platter that had been stolen from her in Agen.

Financial hardship did not keep Jeanne from being generous to those in need, like the eighty-year-old widow of the night watchman at the chateau of Nérac and a young minister who had accompanied her to La Rochelle, who needed money to visit his dying mother in Sauveterre. Nor did she wish Henri to be deprived of healthy recreation when they finally returned home. An order of May 1571, several months before they left La Rochelle, concerns repairs to "the wall of our tennis court in Pau, on the side where it adjoins the chateau, which was destroyed during the late troubles . . . so that when our very dearly beloved son is in residence he may take pleasure in . . . the most honest exercise in which one can pass the time." Jeanne's renunciation of the former church wealth, in October 1571, which put it entirely at the disposal of the Calvinist clergy for evangelical, educational, and charitable purposes, is an impressive testimonial to her own commitment to these matters, when one considers her financial predicament. It would have been easy to justify the application of these resources to her debts, at least in part.

Jeanne's attitude had hardened in the face of continuing rebellion. She required those known to have been involved to humble themselves before reinstatement, but if they did so, punishment ceased. This is not to say that she "forgave" them. Even when treason was not involved, she seems never to have forgiven what she considered "wrongs" nor to have trusted those she believed responsible. (The repeated disobedience of some of her subjects shows that this instinct was sometimes sound.) But justice should not be confused with forgiveness. As sovereign, she did not continue to punish those who had submitted and sued for mercy. She also drew a sharp distinction between the lesser folk, who had been coerced or swept along on the tide, and men of rank, who had used their position and privileges in treasonable ways. The balance between pardon and vindictiveness shows more of the former than of the latter.

In this respect Jeanne can stand comparison with Elizabeth, although it must be remembered that her position was much weaker than the English Queen's and it is impossible to know whether greater power would have made Jeanne more merciful, or less. Her son leaned more heavily in the direction of mercy, and in addition he forgave his enemies. Ironically, it was one of his chief weaknesses, and at least one writer believes that his assassination was planned by those whom he had trusted too much and too often.[69] Henri's resilience derived partly from his Gascon lightheartedness and toughness, inherited from Henri d'Albret, characteristics that skipped the generation of the woman who linked them, for whom everything, at least in the latter years of her life, was *serieux.*

If Jeanne as a young woman had really "enjoyed a dance more than a sermon," there is no doubt that she had been sobered by the vicissitudes of her life since the conversion and the break with Antoine, and even embittered by the rebellions of her subjects. Throughout her reign, however, she was a conscientious ruler, with a paternalistic concept of her duty to her subjects. Even under the extreme handicaps of enforced absence, failing health, and civil war, she never failed to respond to their appeals for justice, mercy, or aid. Her popularity was adversely affected among the Basques by the repressive features of the religious policy; but it was reinforced, along with Béarnais separatism, in the Vicomté because of the punitive measures of the French crown against her. After her death Henri, and Catherine de Bourbon as his regent, reaped the benefits of her administrative and judicial system, which had given Béarn a government outstanding for its rational structure and its inclusion of the education and welfare of the people.

XI

PARTY LEADER
AND DIPLOMAT

1568–1570

IN order to consider all the significant aspects of Jeanne's record
as sovereign together, the controversy over reprisals after the end
of the Civil War in Béarn and the legislation of 1570–1571 were included
in the last chapter, violating chronology. The circumstances which led
to Jeanne's abandonment of neutrality for active leadership in the
Huguenot party must now be examined.

THE GREAT DECISION, MARCH–SEPTEMBER, 1568

Once Jeanne had "pacified" the Oloron rebels in September 1567,
the Navarre rebellion broke out and, simultaneously, the Second Civil
War began in the north of France. The Queen of Navarre, fully occupied
in her own domains, continued her policy of neutrality. The fighting
lasted only six months and the war was officially terminated by the Peace
of Longjumeau (March 23, 1568), but, unlike the Pacification of Amboise, which had provided a breathing spell of four years after the First
Civil War, it is probably the most artificial of all the traditional divisions
in the Wars of Religion. The Peace of Longjumeau scarcely existed,
except on paper. It was trusted by neither side—nor was it observed,
because the forces favoring war were considerably stronger than those
favoring peace; the latter had been fatally weakened, while the former
were gathering momentum.

Anne de Montmorency, Constable of France, adviser to four kings, had lost his life in the Battle of St. Denis (November 10, 1567). Unquestionably Catholic and royalist, yet uncle to the Châtillons, Montmorency had been able to serve as an intermediary on many occasions. The "first seigneur of France" had provided a balance within Catholic ranks to the Guise faction. After his death the old third force disintegrated: his eldest son conferred with Huguenot leaders in Chantilly, while his second son was included in the councils of the Guises.[1] Gradually a new and more effective third force, the *politique* party, would take shape. At the same time (May 1568) Michel de L'Hôpital, leading advocate of coexistence of the two religions, failed to temper the action of the extreme Catholic faction in the King's Council and withdrew from court in discouragement. He held the office of chancellor for six more months, but his influence on royal policy had ended.[2]

As the moderate party disintegrated, a marked acceleration was taking place in the ultra-Catholic camp. On March 29, six days after the peace was signed, leaders of the Guise faction agreed in a secret meeting to observe the peace only until the Huguenots were disarmed and then to seize Orléans, La Rochelle, and other Huguenot centers.[3] They could count on the support of the Parisians (whose ultra-Catholic sentiments had been fanned anew when the Battle of St. Denis brought the war to their doorstep), the Papacy, and, of course, the King of Spain. Pius V had resolved to prevent in future the French policy of playing off Rome against Madrid. He appointed Fabio Mirto Frangipani, Bishop of Caiazzo, as nuncio, and sent him to France with the specific assignment to unite the French and Spanish courts. The Pope and Philip began their cooperation when each promised money to the French crown if it would pursue a policy of exterminating the Huguenots instead of compromising with them.[4] The near bankruptcy of the royal treasury was one of the most compelling reasons for making peace. Another foreign factor favoring war was the intensified conflict in the Netherlands. The Duke of Alva had arrived in Brussels to implement a new policy—the "Spanish fury." Alva's replacement of Philip's sister Margaret, his agent in the moderate phase, signalized total war in the Low Countries. This in turn led to greater aggressiveness on the part of the Huguenot leaders, especially Coligny, who believed that the only hope for French Protestantism lay in active cooperation with the Dutch rebels, military as well as diplomatic.[5]

Violations of the agreement of Longjumeau throughout France

proved that the people, Catholic and Protestant alike, no more desired peace than did their leaders. In Normandy, the populace forced its way into the Parlement of Rouen on the day the peace was registered (causing the *parlementaires* to flee) prior to killing many Huguenots and destroying their property. In Toulouse, the Parlement beheaded the bearer of the King's instructions to proclaim the Edict, disregarding a royal safe-conduct. Catholics everywhere rejected the mere idea of an armistice. On the Huguenot side, many captains refused to disarm, the city of La Rochelle was in open rebellion, and arsenals there and in other Protestant strongholds were being restocked. The reiters, German mercenaries hired by Condé in the recent war, had not been paid off, and continued to ravage the eastern provinces.[6] In the words of a Florentine observer, *tutti stanno di mala voglia* (everybody hates everybody else).[7]

Most serious of the obstacles to the acceptance of peace was probably the intensified aggressiveness of the Catholic "leagues." They now embraced a much greater proportion of the population than before and had begun to coordinate their activities. In 1568 "a process of federation is to be observed by which the provincial leagues are gradually welded into one whole—in a word, the mighty *Sainte Ligue* of 1576 exists now, potentially."[8] The two most important leagues were that of Maréchal de Tavannes, in Burgundy, and the one in Guyenne, under Monluc. The King of Spain had long been in correspondence with Monluc. Part of his new drive was to unify into a single policy his dealings with the Guises on the one hand and with Monluc on the other. "Monluc was the military, the Cardinal de Lorraine the diplomatic agent of Philip's purposes."[9]

The Queen of Navarre had managed to stay out of the Second Civil War, but the key role of Monluc and Guyenne in the new Counter Reformation strategy greatly worsened her position. Nobody needed peace as much as Jeanne—except Catherine. In 1568 each took considerable pains to preserve it, but, paradoxically, neither could avoid adding to the likelihood of war because neither could afford peace at any price. Catherine's problem was on a larger scale, commensurate with her kingdom, but Jeanne's was a matter of life and death.

As a result of the Navarre rebellion, Jeanne appealed to the Parlement of Bordeaux to support the reinforcement of her authority, in the hope that if they cooperated, which would imply at least a measure of royal support, she would be secure enough to prevent further uprisings. In late January 1568, the Parlement held hearings on Jeanne's complaints that

Monluc was obstructing the exercise of her sovereign powers and Monluc's countercharges. She argued, through a representative, that it was necessary for her to recruit men to bear arms for the enforcement of peace. Charging that she had held illegal assemblies of seven or eight hundred armed men, Monluc wrote that Jeanne's policy "to exterminate the Catholic religion" made for bad blood between the crowns of France and Spain, and that she herself was responsible for the rebellion in Basse-Navarre. Jeanne claimed she had the King's permission to raise arms in her own defense, but Monluc denied this, saying that the King had expressly forbidden it. The court ruled that nobody could raise arms without the specific permission of the King or his Lieutenant-General —Monluc.[10]

To resolve the impasse Catherine sent a skilled diplomat, Bertrand de Salignac, Seigneur de La Mothe-Fénelon, to Jeanne, on what turned out to be the first of several missions. The ostensible object of the first visit (February 1568) was to persuade her to pardon the leaders of the Navarre rebellion. Jeanne suspected at the time, and later firmly believed, that his real assignment was to encourage the rebels. (Subsequent events were to confirm this belief.) In the *Mémoires* Jeanne says of this first exchange with La Mothe-Fénelon, "[I] threw back at him the words 'rebel' and 'seditious' that came frequently to his lips, applied to those who bear arms in the service of God and the King." Here Jeanne is stating the Huguenot claim that they were the defenders of the royal power against those (the Guise-Spanish party) who wished to overthrow it.[11]

Later, when Fénelon passed through Bordeaux, he reported to the Parlement that the Queen was very angry because, in its decision of January 26, "it had forbidden her subjects to go to her aid in putting down rebellions, as if she had not offered all her worldly goods, including her rings, to the crown [to aid] against its enemies." She also claimed that the King had "begged her to continue to exercise justice as he does in the Parlement of Paris." Fénelon then produced a letter from the King reprimanding the Parlement for its treatment "of *nostre très chère et très aymée tante, la Royne de Navarre,* who . . . had always tried to keep the peace and never approved those who, under the pretext of religion, had taken arms to trouble the peace. . . . She complains that your Edict of January 26 prevents men from entering her service . . . but does not prevent [others from] rebelling against her. . . . We find it very strange

that you should act thus, without informing us."[12] This verbal support
of Jeanne's position was the crown's reward for the cooperation she had
promised Fénelon; it did not express Catherine's real sentiments. Jeanne
was also dissimulating and exempted from the amnesty in Basse-Navarre
the individuals with whom the crown was most concerned.

Jeanne and Monluc continued to work at cross-purposes. In April
they clashed directly, outside Parlement, and each appealed to the crown.
On April 2 Monluc wrote a plaintive eight-page letter to the King accusing Jeanne of stealing some horses (and protecting from punishment the
agent who had actually executed the act) and other injuries. Toward the
end he says, "I beg you very humbly, Sire, just because she is a very great
lady, do not take her word for it. . . . I would rather retire to Italy . . . or
anywhere else outside of France . . . than suffer such offense . . . or, what
is more, to lose my wife, my children, and all my possessions. . . . And so
that Your Majesty cannot think that she had reason to do it, I assure you
that in all these years . . . she has never asked me for anything in which
I have not obliged her."[13] About the same time Jeanne wrote to Catherine,
listing outrages committed against her with his complicity, "I beg you
very humbly, Madame, may it please you to give orders to M. de Monluc
so that he may live in peace with me and I with him."[14] Once again
Jeanne was *menagée,* as is evident from Catherine's response to Monluc:
"Please watch yourself and avoid doing anything to my sister, the Queen
of Navarre, that could harm her. . . . If anything irritates her . . . we may
never be able to arrange things in such a way that her kingdom will
remain peaceful. . . . I beg you particularly, M. de Monluc, not to do anything in regard to the said lady, nor to [her partisans] that could obstruct
the will of the King, my son, who wishes to embrace them, now that
peace is made. Believe me, this is of great consequence to his service."[15]

In May, Fénelon was again sent to Jeanne, to express the King's
distress that, despite her repeated declarations of peaceful intentions, she
continued to persecute the Catholics. The King is said to be very much
displeased, and, while he will not abandon his aunt, he must require her
to respect the Roman, Catholic, and Apostolic religion and reinstate the
officers she has punished. It is in order to help her that he has again sent
Fénelon.[16] The real object of the second mission was to lure Jeanne to
court, for, even more than in 1564, Catherine felt it imperative to draw
her away from her domains. Since she no longer was supported by the

moderate faction, Catherine might not be able to prevent the Spanish-Guise faction from attacking Jeanne, which would weaken her own position.

In the *Mémoires* Jeanne emphasizes her efforts to promote peace, "During this turbulent time, I sent again and again to Their Majesties and to my brother-in-law, M. le Prince . . . to cry 'peace! peace!' Everyone knows how I wished it and how I rejoiced each time its shadow appeared."[17] The bait held out by Fénelon was therefore well-chosen—the opportunity to play mediator on a national scale—but Jeanne regarded it as a trap.

I discovered that they wished to draw me to court, and my son too, under the pretext of doing me the honor of making me the mediator between the King and his subjects of the Reformed religion, assuring me that peace would never be well-secured [otherwise] . . . that I alone was qualified to conduct such negotiations, since I had the honor of being so close to Their Majesties . . . that whatever I proposed on behalf of [the Huguenots] would be above suspicion, and, on the other hand, that I was so well thought of by those of the [Protestant] religion that they would really trust me.

Such were the sugar-coated treacherous words by which the said La Mothe tried to trap me. I found them very strange . . . because the scorn and offenses that I had suffered made it clear that these good opinions of me had never crossed their minds. . . . My reply to this long elaborate speech was brief, namely, that I could not believe that they would wish to use me in a matter of such great importance. . . .

He added that Madame de Savoye* and Madame de Ferrare had also been suggested, but that [Catherine] . . . had chosen me. . . . [This was] an invention intended to draw me to court. . . . The only other thing I said . . . was that I would never negotiate anything at the court so long as the Cardinal de Lorraine was there. He replied that for me to go there was the best way to drive [the Cardinal] away.[18]

There follows Jeanne's version of the events of July and August 1568 which affected her directly: how she sent Antoine Martel, Sieur de Vaupilière, to the King with *Articles envoiez par la Royne Jeanne de Navarre au Roy tant sur l'observation de l'Edit de Pacification que pour le Gouvernement de Guyenne* and how all her requests were denied or ignored.[19] She says that she carried out her promise to pardon the Navarre rebels "to my great disadvantage," but that the crown perfidiously sent

---

* Madame de Savoye was Marguerite de France, sister of Henri II and wife of the Duke of Savoy, who had been brought up by Marguerite de Navarre, for whom she was named. The Duchess was highly esteemed by all factions.

the Sieur de Losses to capture her (and Henri) with the aid of Monluc, a plan foiled "when by God's hand the said seigneur was stopped by a hemorrhage in the stomach, which gave me time to prepare my defense." She also defends her communications with Condé, "what could be more natural than to be on friendly terms with my brother-in-law, my son's uncle, who stood in his father's place?"[20]

The mention of Condé is the link between Jeanne and the coming of the Third Civil War. In late July the Duke of Alva decisively defeated Louis of Nassau at Jemmingen and shortly thereafter executed Egmont and Hoorn, the Dutch patriots. For the moment the Counter Reformation forces had the upper hand in the Netherlands and sought to follow up their advantage in France. The two immediate objectives were the reduction of La Rochelle and the capture of the Huguenot leaders. These were scattered: Condé at Noyers, Coligny at Tanlay, and Jeanne, with Henri, in Béarn. Condé and Coligny were warned and departed on August 23 to take refuge in La Rochelle. When she learned this, Jeanne decided to abandon neutrality and go to La Rochelle herself, with her children.

The renewal of war was now a certainty. The conditions which had permitted Jeanne to stand aside in the First and Second Civil Wars had changed: without an influential moderate faction to balance the ultras, Catherine would not be able to protect Jeanne; without Protestant armies between Béarn and the Ile de France, Jeanne would be at the mercy of the French and Spanish Catholic armies, allied to the rebels in her own domains. In order to join forces with Condé, Jeanne was obliged to undertake still another flight, to run a race against time, and to match wits with a whole series of clever adversaries.

In the latter part of August, Jeanne went to Nérac. As she explained with characteristic irony, "knowing that the Sieur de Losses was on his way to do me a good turn and being certain that if he wished to resort to force, I would be better able to stop him there [Nérac]." Relatives, neighbors, and subjects flocked to her side in the duchy of Albret, many of whom Jeanne claims to have sent home again, "so that ours [the Protestant army] would not be the first to assemble." When Vaupilière returned with the King's unsatisfactory reply, described by Jeanne as "forged in the workshop of the Cardinal [de Lorraine]," she prepared for either peace or war, fearing the latter, because "Their Majesties were in the hands of false and traitorous pilots," a situation which "would force the Princes of the Blood . . . virtuously to put their hand to the task."

She mentions the peace messages she sent to Monluc, to the King and Catherine, and to the other Huguenot leaders from Nérac, which "give the lie to those who say and write every day that we took arms first. . . . We did indeed resort to them, but at first it was in order to interpose them between those of the enemy and our lives and later it was in order to use both life and arms in the service of God and our King." She had heard that Condé and Coligny were also in danger of being captured and in fact her messenger had found them gone on August 23. The progress of their train across central France is dramatically described by the contemporary Protestant historians, who compare it to the departure of Israel out of Egypt. They crossed the Loire singing Marot's translation of Psalm 114, *Quand Isreal hors d'Egypte sortit* . . . Upon receiving news of their escape, which filled her with mixed feelings, "joy that God had delivered them and pain to see the Princes of the Blood traveling across France like vagabonds," Jeanne resolved to join her brother-in-law. She did so gladly on account of her son, "it pained me to have him surrounded by women at his age." She wished him to bear his first arms for God and his King.[21]

Unlike other turning points in her life, the agony of the decision is fully described by Jeanne herself.

Do not think . . . that I undertook this journey lightly. Believe me, it was not without conflict, with others and with myself. For Satan, who always sets himself against the good instruments God creates by His grace, did not sleep while the holy zeal was needling me [*aiguilloner*]. This enemy drew on the help of promises and flattery by the great, but in vain, since I am sufficiently accustomed to such traps to resist things so vile and unworthy of a generous heart as ambition and avarice.

My enemy, seeing that he was losing time in that direction, aroused a number of my own retainers of different temperaments, some clever, others worldly-wise, still others wholly naïve, animated by foolish zeal. Nor were the timid left out. In brief [Satan] overlooked nothing he thought would serve to dissuade me from my Christian enterprise. The boldest tried to make me doubt the justice of the cause, alleging arguments everyone knows, that are not worth repeating. But what good did it do to listen to them? as if a young person twenty years old could use the glasses of an old man in his sixties . . . for they only made me see everything so small and confused that I could not recognize the things they claimed to point out. Thinking to cause my ruin, they ruined themselves and fell into the ditch they dug for me (unless God then raised them up). To my great regret . . . they changed the minds of not a few, but my opinion of the matter has remained firmer than ever, primarily because of the prodding of my conscience, informed by the word of God. . . .

During this dialogue in my mind I not only had to fight outside enemies, I had a war in my entrails. Even my will was in league against me. The flesh assailed me and the spirit defended me. If I felt better one hour, I felt worse the next. In short, because these passions are hard to describe and can only be judged emotionally [*par sentiment*], I would beg those who have been through it and whose hearts have been tried like gold in the furnace to spend their efforts in imagining my torment rather than in reading about it, and to believe that Satan, the old enemy, who has perfected his arts better than any man, did not forget either solemn rhetoric, persuasive eloquence, sweet flattery, or outright lies to achieve his ends. And he well knew how to choose the means best suited to their attainment . . . even the temptations of the soul . . . he had won over half of my will to conquer the other half. Nevertheless, I was finally victorious, by the grace of my God.[22]

This is excerpted from a much longer account. Among the tempters Jeanne counts those who accused her of having abandoned her kingdom and left it "prey to the foreigner," Philip II, who was threatening invasion. Her answer is that she committed Béarn to God, "without whom not a hair of our heads can fall," and to *gens de bien,* whom she could trust to preserve it as best they could. On August 30 she had appointed Bernard d'Arros as her Lieutenant-General.

Jeanne did not wait for Condé's message (received Friday, September 3), informing her of his departure and his route, to make the decision, but only to plan the details of her escape.[23] The first problem was to avoid capture by Monluc, both at Nérac and in crossing the Garonne, which ran between Nérac and Bergerac, where she could be met by an armed force sufficient to protect her the rest of the way. Monluc had given orders that every crossing be guarded to prevent her escape, but Jeanne outwitted him. She invited him to send his wife and children (as playmates for Henri and Catherine) for a visit to Nérac. Just as they were about to set out, on Monday, September 6, a messenger announced the Queen's regrets that she had been obliged to depart.[24] Only fifty men, including servants, accompanied her. The immediate destination was Casteljaloux, where Jeanne had prepared for her arrival by removing the keys of the town gates and the chateau from the officials to whom Monluc had given them.[25] She was delayed there for an extra day by the illness of Marie de Clèves, whom she then decided to send back to Nérac, with some of the other ladies.

The next stop was Tonneins, where Fénelon met her in a final attempt to persuade her to go to court. The letters he brought from Catherine have been lost, but Jeanne claims that they spoke of Condé as the prisoner of a rebellious Coligny, which is plausible because it is precisely the line later applied to Henri. In the *Mémoires,* Jeanne spends some time reporting the discomfiture of Fénelon as she pointed out the inconsistencies between the crown's actions and the crown's words, and she dwells with obvious satisfaction on some witty and pertinent remarks of Henri's to the crown's envoy. Because she spent two days at Tonneins waiting for her vassals in the county of Armagnac, led by the brothers Astarac, the Barons de Fontrailles and Montamat, Monluc had another chance to capture her—he was at Agen, only a few kilometers away. Again luck was on her side, and, as Olhagaray says, "The Queen of Navarre crossed the Garonne three fingers away from the nose of Monluc."[26]

Minor discrepancies aside, Monluc's account of these days bears out Jeanne's, as far as the facts are concerned. The important difference is in the interpretation. Jeanne exaggerates her danger by overestimating Monluc's efforts, while he justifies his lack of action and slowness in comprehending what was happening. Jeanne did everything possible to quiet his suspicions and mislead him. When Monluc read letters Condé had written to the King assuring that he was only going to visit his brother-in-law, the Comte de La Rochefoucauld, as well as Jeanne's repeated peace messages, what was he to think? Remembering his past experiences, and especially Catherine's recent letter warning him to do nothing to "irritate" Jeanne, he hesitated to use force against a Princess of the Blood. He had not received any explicit instructions from the crown. As he explained to the Parlement of Bordeaux the following December, "I confess that she took me by surprise, having assured me many times that she would never take arms against the King . . . if I had made the slightest move she would have said that she was being unjustly attacked."[27] No doubt he thought that he could excuse himself, if necessary, by quoting the statements of peaceful intentions issued by Jeanne and Condé. In this he was mistaken. He was severely reproached for negligence and said bitterly, on more than one occasion, "the little guy is always wrong."

The first fighting of the Third Civil War occurred en route to Bergerac, when Jeanne's escort was fired on from the chateau of Eymet (Dordogne). At Bergerac, on September 13, the Queen was met by much of the nobility of Périgord, "who had come of their own free will to expose life and goods for the general cause," to the visible surprise of Fénelon, who was still traveling with the Queen's suite. Consequently, Bergerac was the first place where it was safe to pause and transact some necessary business. From there Jeanne wrote letters justifying her conduct to be delivered by Fénelon when he returned to court. On the 16th she went to Mussidan, where she was met by an important Huguenot noble, François de Briquemault,* whom Condé had sent to command her escort. A few days later (September 24) Jeanne's party met Condé's near Cognac. "It is hard to say who was most joyous, he to see us or we to have found him." Together they were welcomed into the fortified city of La Rochelle on September 28, "with all signs and acclamations of joy and contentment."[28]

The *Mémoires* were written about two months after Jeanne's arrival at La Rochelle. Her tone in the conclusion is that of a woman who has accomplished a difficult and dangerous job and is glad to relinquish responsibility into the rightful (masculine) hands. "I delivered my son [to] M. his uncle, so that, under the tutelage of the latter's prudence and valor, he would learn the task to which God has called him, and in order that later, when his age and means permit, he will be able to use them, and his life, in the service of God, of his King, and of his blood." Of herself she says that she is living in La Rochelle, "deprived of the pleasure of my own houses, but only too happy to suffer for my God," as if she were simply to wait quietly in semi-retirement until the outcome was decided by the war—between the men on either side.

MINISTER OF PROPAGANDA AND FOREIGN AFFAIRS

Jeanne made her headquarters in La Rochelle for nearly three years. From the embattled Huguenot port she kept in touch as best she could with her own domains and served "the general cause" in several vital capacities. For the first few months she fought principally with the written word. Like many dispensers of propaganda, Jeanne had relatively few arguments, which she could elaborate at great length and with varying emphasis for different audiences. The themes appear in her requests to foreign princes for aid as well as in her manifestoes, since it was necessary to refute the arguments of Catherine's agents and to convince potential

* Briquemault played an important role as one of Coligny's chief aides. He escaped the Massacre of St. Bartholomew, but met a horrible death a few weeks later, when fires were lighted around the scaffold on which he and Cavagnes were executed, so that the spectators could see more clearly their dying agony (Haag, II, 134).

allies that the Huguenots were justified in resisting the crown. (They refused to call it "rebellion.") The first statement of Jeanne's "war aims" can be found in four letters she wrote in Bergerac on September 16, 1568, which were delivered a few days later (by Fénelon) to the King, the Queen Mother, the Duc d'Anjou, and the Cardinal de Bourbon. Shortly thereafter, they were printed. Together with similar statements from Condé, they were widely circulated and became important in the ideological struggles of this phase of the religious wars.[29]

The letters express certain basic themes with slight variations in phrasing. First (from the letter to Charles IX), the crown is guilty of bad faith because it has broken agreements with the Huguenots embodied in the Edicts of Pacification (Amboise and Longjumeau), thus "disappointing the hopes raised by the promises it has always pleased you to give your poor subjects of the Reformed Religion in letters to the Parlements." Second, the Huguenots believe that the King and his mother would never go back on their word, but, since they are surrounded by "evil counselors," they must be "rescued" by those who have the greatest obligation because they stand closest to the throne, namely, the Princes of the Blood. A corollary theme is the enormity of the crimes of the Cardinal de Lorraine. Even though he has many accomplices and agents, in Jeanne's eyes the Cardinal is directly responsible for every evil that has befallen France since the death of Henri II, nine years earlier. Most vicious, to Jeanne, are his attacks on the royal blood, aimed at the destruction, first, of Antoine and now of Condé and Henri de Navarre. "By his damnable cleverness," she wrote Catherine, the Cardinal "has already too much exploited the place, which does not belong to him, closest to our King and to you [and he has] blocked your ears so that you cannot hear our cries."

The third theme is justification of Huguenot reaction to these wrongs. Despite the crown's bad faith and the impending ruin of the kingdom and the princes, they and the Huguenots have shown infinite patience and Christian forbearance. They have continued to respect the law and have not stooped to retaliate with the same weapons; they have made every effort to keep the peace. "If you will believe your obedient servant," Jeanne told the King, "and weigh my fidelity against the infidelity of the Cardinal and his accomplices . . . you will find more truth in my acts than in their words." If Condé and Jeanne have finally resorted to arms, it is because their duty commands it, in defense of God and the King—and in self-defense. They can no longer turn the other cheek when to do so would result in the extinction of the House of Bourbon and possibly of France herself.

Each of these points embodies a particular aspect of the underlying argument that the Huguenots are defenders of the law and the traditional order. Just as they claimed to be "restoring" the old religion, so were they fighting in order to restore the "natural" hierarchy, in which the Princes of the Blood shared leadership with the King. This can be regarded as a resurgence of feudal thinking or as a rudimentary form of constitutionalism. Interpretations exemplifying both views, and a whole spectrum between them, are not lacking. The legalistic orientation of Huguenot propaganda in this phase of the wars—in Condé's manifestoes as well as Jeanne's—explains the amount of space devoted to specific violations of the Edicts by the other side.

The main themes are expressed so as to make the strongest appeal to a particular correspondent. Jeanne knew what chords to strike. She plays on the King's resentment at not being master in his own house ("we know your good will and what we owe you . . . and that these evils are done without your approval") and on her loyalty to him as her sovereign. The resort to violence—as in the plot to capture Henri—was quite unnecessary, "as if your simple command were not sufficient to bring both the mother and the son to your side." Finally, she underlines her total devotion, claiming that she would sacrifice anything to fulfill her duty to the King. Jeanne flatters Anjou's self-importance by referring to his supposed special power and influence with the King. She may not have been aware (in September 1568) of the growing antagonism between Charles IX and Henri d'Anjou, who was his mother's favorite. When their mutual antipathy became general knowledge (it figures regularly in the dispatches of foreign observers after the spring of 1571) it was often treated as an aspect of the King's restlessness under his mother's tutelage. If she had known about it, Jeanne would probably not have used this ironic flattery, which could not win Anjou to her side. She also points out that Condé had "retired" rather than take arms against the royal army, that is, against Henri d'Anjou himself.

The letter to Catherine, the longest of the four, is in many ways the most interesting. Jeanne reminds the Queen Mother of their past relationship and of their mutual suffering at the hands of the Guises. "Forgive me, Madame, if I begin with the time when they corrupted the late King, my husband . . . and remind you of the fidelity you found in me . . . and of what you said just before I left Fontainebleau." She points out that if the Bourbons fall the crown is endangered, and she strips away the pretense that she and Condé are under fire because of their religious beliefs: "it is not zeal for religion that animates them . . . it is the royal blood of France that makes them sick to their stomachs." She makes clear that one of the enemy's most potent weapons is the separation between herself and Catherine, "I well know, Madame . . . how you have been turned against us. . . . For the conservation of your authority it is necessary [for you] to separate from those who would do you harm and therefore would ruin those who wish to save you." The tone is at times intimate, "my feelings have not changed in spite of time and distance," and at times imperious, "make sure that you distinguish between good and evil."

The Cardinal de Bourbon received a different kind of letter, loaded as it inevitably was, with Jeanne's resentment that he, the eldest Prince of the Blood, should have sold out to the enemy. There is a heavy emphasis on the supreme importance of the Bourbon family. Jeanne charges him with desertion, "Will the Cardinal de Lorraine always hold you in thrall? . . . against your own brother, sister, and nephews?"—and with cowardice, "the task of women and of men who do not bear arms, like you, is to fight for peace . . . do your part, for God's sake. As for me, I will spare nothing." She sweeps aside the religious differences between them with a pragmatic argument, "if religion separates us, does our common blood then separate? do friendship and natural duty cease to exist? *Non, mon frère.*"

A fifth letter belongs with this group, although it was written a month later and to a foreign ruler—Queen Elizabeth of England—because what Jeanne always calls *les trois occasions* (her three grounds for taking arms) are stated with particular succinctness and effectiveness, as was desirable for a correspondent outside the family and outside France, to whom it was appropriate to present an over-all picture.

The first is the Cause of the Religion . . . which was so oppressed and afflicted by the inveterate and barbarous tyranny of the Cardinal de Lorraine . . . that I would never have been able to bear the shame to my honor . . . if my son and I had not joined the numerous blessed company . . . resolved to spare neither blood, life, nor goods [in its defense]. . . .

The second reason, Madame, which follows from the first, is the service of the King . . . since my son and I have the honor to be closest to him in blood . . . we hastened to oppose those, who, abusing the great goodness of our King, were making him the author of his own ruin . . . betrayer of his promises . . . to keep the peace made between him and his faithful subjects. . . .

The third reason is particular to my son and myself . . . seeing that the ancient enemies of our House . . . had determined to ruin it entirely . . . and that my brother-in-law, the Prince de Condé, had been obliged to seek safety (since he did not wish to resort to arms) . . . and also because I had been warned that the enemy would attempt to kidnap my son. . . .

These, Madame, are the three reasons . . . I have taken to arms, any one of which would have been sufficient. . . . We are not guilty of lese majesty against God or our King . . . as I very humbly beseech you to believe . . . and to give us aid . . . which God will reward with His holy grace and the preservation of your land. . . .

The *Mémoires* or *Ample Déclaration* is Jeanne's *apologia pro vita sua*. It contains no new themes, but rather much more detailed and verbose statement of the same ones, in a style that is both rambling and jerky. About twenty-five main "wrongs" done to Jeanne or other members of the Bourbon family are mentioned, some of them inclusive acts, like subversion of her authority at different times and places, and others specific, like the mission of De Losses to kidnap Henri. An exact list of her charges would number in the hundreds. Jeanne's obsession with the villainy of *ceux de Guise,* and of the Cardinal de Lorraine in particular, is echoed throughout Huguenot propaganda.

It would not be appropriate here to analyze the career of the Cardinal in detail sufficient to place it in proper perspective; suffice it to say that he had no such power, for instance in the royal Council, as Jeanne attributes to him.[30] Nevertheless, one does not have to be a partisan of the Bourbons to recognize that he was a key figure in the ultra-Catholic party and therefore justifiably feared by the Huguenots.[31] It is also true that the Guises had "usurped" the position of the Bourbons in that they had built up a party to counter the influence of the Princes of the Blood, which, for a variety of reasons, was considerably stronger and closer to the crown under the last Valois kings than that of the Princes.

By the nature of their respective positions Jeanne had few dealings with the Cardinal; what she says about him is largely myth. The crown and many of its agents, on the other hand, were well known to her. In the case of La Mothe-Fénelon, who appears in the *Mémoires* in a role reminiscent of the serpent in Eden, a brief statement of his shows the other side of the coin. In a dispatch of December 5, 1568, from London, where he had become ambassador shortly after his last mission to Jeanne, Fénelon throws all the blame for the renewal of the war on the Huguenots. "There are only too many proofs that for the least thing in the world and the most trivial occasion . . . they rush immediately to arms, without one being able to divert them by any means, as I can testify myself, having been sent for this purpose to the Queen of Navarre and the Prince of Condé."[32]

For an historian, the responsibility is not so easily placed. On September 25, 1568, the crown rescinded the Edict of January, which left the Huguenots with no legal protection whatever. If it is argued that this royal action was in retaliation for the move to La Rochelle, it is also arguable that the Huguenot leaders had not as yet committed any aggressive act, merely the defensive withdrawal to the security of La Rochelle. The fact that in the course of the religious wars political theories passed from the Huguenot to the Catholic side (and vice versa) indicates that ideas figured more generally as means rather than as ends.[33] Each faction found plenty of material for polemics and undoubtedly there were many on both sides who believed their own propaganda. Jeanne should be classed among them. Her tendency to see all things as black or white makes it unlikely that she could have experienced the inner conflict she describes or played her subsequent role in the war unless completely convinced she was "justified."

Nearly two-thirds of the one hundred and twenty pages of the *Mémoires* are devoted to Jeanne's charges against the opposite party. The remainder is divided about equally among appeals to the crown, accounts of Jeanne's movements, efforts to uphold the law by promoting peace or defending it, and digressions. Some of the latter are of considerable interest although—or because—they deal with unimportant matters blown up out of all proportion in incoherent or irrational terms, but they are not really germane to the present theme of the ideology of *la cause,* and will therefore be considered elsewhere.

Within a month of Fénelon's assumption in mid-November of his new responsibilities in London, his dispatches reflect the success of a very different Frenchman at Elizabeth's court. By favor shown to Odet, Cardinal de Châtillon, the Queen of England maintained contact with her fellow-Protestants in France and kept the French crown worrying about her intentions. Elizabeth herself had spoken to the Spanish ambassador, "of the Guises as her enemies and the Châtillons as her friends," Fénelon wrote on December 28. When Fénelon subsequently reproached her, as he reported to Charles IX, "that she should concern herself with neither the one nor the other, except as Your Majesty's subjects," she claimed that she had not named either family, while admitting that it was possible for the Spanish ambassador thus to interpret what she had said. In the same week, she was giving audience to representatives of William of Orange and the Lutheran Princes. She gave Fénelon to understand "that although she would not declare herself against either Your Majesty or the Catholic King, if there should be a league against her religion, she would willingly go to its defense."[34]

Fénelon's dispatches and Catherine de Medici's correspondence display increasing anxiety about Elizabeth's relations with La Rochelle in the winter of 1568–9, understandably in the context of a flow of letters between Cecil and the English Queen, on the one hand, and Condé, Jeanne, and Henri, on the other. Jeanne's letter to Cecil on January 16 expresses warm appreciation of favors received and hopes of more to come. "I cannot tell you the relief, joy, and contentment that we find in the news from you." She is thankful "that you should employ yourself for the aid and defense of the cause of religion we sustain . . . I beg you to believe that God will recompense you. . . . I will spare nothing to show you how dear I hold those who work for God's cause . . . we pray you to exert your good will to us in the hearing of your mistress." On February 1 she wrote to Elizabeth, "your favor is so important and conspicuous [remarquée] not only to the churches in all France, but everywhere, Madame, that I am moved to beg you very humbly, to continue your good will."[35]

So substantial and conspicuous were the arrangements between the . Huguenots and the English Queen at this time that some commentators call them a "treaty." Arcère, an eighteenth-century royalist historian of La Rochelle, considered that the concessions made to English merchants and shippers (especially exemption from certain taxes) were treasonable and that Jeanne was largely to blame. Such conduct "infringed upon the sovereign majesty of the King and would leave a humiliating mark on the memory of the Rochelais if one does not take into account that it was entirely the doing of the chiefs . . . the Queen of Navarre in particular. . . . In a town where she enjoyed the highest consideration the ill-informed people . . . were incapable of conceiving that a princess so full of virtues could commit wrong, so they followed her blindly in a step she . . . advocated to everyone."[36] Arcère exaggerates when he implies that Jeanne gave Elizabeth, or anyone else, sovereign powers over La Rochelle, but the contemporary accounts of friend and foe are unanimous in representing her as the most zealous of the "chiefs."

The Huguenot leaders were also negotiating for men and money with the Prince of Orange, the Dukes of Wurtemburg and Bavaria, the Elector of Brandenburg, and the Swiss Cantons. The Duke of Wurtemburg received four letters written by them within twenty-four hours (January 31–February 1, 1569). Jeanne's version of the common message—the introduction of an envoy who was to present the case for aiding La Rochelle—assures the Duke that "we have in hand the means to block a conspiracy of the greatest potentates . . . to annihilate those who follow pure doctrine." She begs him "to take your part as we expect of you as a true Christian prince." Letters from Condé and Coligny (also signed by Henri de Navarre) to Wolfgang of Bavaria, Duc de Deux-Ponts (or Zweibrücken), urged him to cross the Loire to join forces with them as soon as possible.[37] He did so, but three months elapsed before the meeting took place and in the meanwhile a drastic change had occurred in the Huguenot command.

On March 13, in the Battle of Jarnac (about halfway between Saintes and Angoulême), the Prince de Condé was taken prisoner and then treacherously shot by an officer of the victorious Duc d'Anjou.[38] Among the papers found on his body was a bloodstained letter from Jeanne, asking for information from the front and thanking him for sending word that Henri was in good health. "I am happy to hear it, and also to know that he serves you as he would his own father."[39] The titular command was inherited by the two Bourbon princes, Henri de Navarre, aged fifteen years and three months, and his cousin Henri de Condé, a few months older, in a scene which was possibly the proudest moment of Jeanne's life. Actually the real responsibility passed to Coligny, who exercised it for the remainder of the Third Civil War and until his own assassination three and a half years later.

During the spring of 1569, the chief task of the mother and aunt of the two boy commanders was to avoid losing the hard-won foreign allies by assuring them that the fight would continue, that the cause was in good hands, and that Catholic rejoicing over the victory was not justified. On March 21 Jeanne sent Puch de Pardaillan to Cecil "to inform the Queen [Elizabeth] of the truth, since the enemy is sure to make the most of the late battle." She pleads "that you will continue the affection you bear to so just and legitimate a cause, and that you will not fail to do everything possible to promote [continued aid] by all the means I know to be at your disposal. . . . Amongst us, great and small are resolved to spare neither our lives nor our fortunes in the service of God's quarrel . . . against . . . the enemies of the Right and of peace."[40]

Jeanne must have been relieved to receive within a few days a memorandum from Odet de Châtillon assuring her of English sympathy and intention to carry out the "treaty" arrangements. He reports that the English Vice-Admiral Winter, who had recently returned from La Rochelle, "told everyone of the fine treatment he had received from the Queen and was loud in her praises, which serves to encourage the Queen of England and her Council to favor our cause." Even more significant was an acid letter from Queen Elizabeth to the victor of Jarnac on April 17: "it appears that we are expected to rejoice . . . but we cannot refrain from expressing our regret to see our brother's affairs [Charles IX] conducted in such a way that it is necessary for him to risk his closest and most precious brother [for a victory] that results in loss, ruin, and the spilling of his own people's blood . . . we would much rather hear of a generous peace." The lesser Protestant allies also sent assurances of continued support to the Huguenots.[41]

Jeanne's letter to Beza served the purpose of reassuring the Calvinist leadership; but it is also a letter of a friend, revealing personal concerns, and is couched in more informal terms. She says that she is happy to have the occasion to write, "because I consider you one of my best friends."

First, I want to inform you of the profound suffering the shameful murder of . . . the Prince de Condé has caused me. . . . It must be admitted that excessive license prevails in our armies . . . which is the reason God inflicted this loss upon us. . . . [Our] leaders did my son the honor of giving him the supreme command . . . he is committed to sharing their fortunes in life and in death, and has promised never to abandon them until it has pleased God to grant the churches of France . . . some assurance of liberty.

She then tells him about the councils established and the hoped-for German aid. She insists that Huguenot losses have been slight, "except that some mercenaries have passed to the enemy [since Condé's death], thus little by little does the Lord winnow out the good grain . . . although there is still plenty of chaff." She reports that Viret is in Pau and is well, and that she is residing in La Rochelle. "My health, damaged by continuous harassments, is fairly good." The letter, closing with greetings to "my nephew"—the son of Françoise—was written on April 19, 1571, just as Terride's army was entering Béarn. Jeanne either did not know the invasion had begun or she was hoping for the best, as she merely says, "the King has taken all my lands, except Béarn, which, up to now, has resisted the enemy's threats."[42]

Fénelon's testimony to the continued vitality of the Huguenot party in a dispatch of May 19 shows that Jeanne's claims were not just propaganda. He says that Pardaillan has persuaded Elizabeth that "notwithstanding the loss of the Prince, they remain as strong and well-led as before." He warns Catherine that English assistance to the Huguenots will continue because feeling is running high.[43] It was a fortunate moment for Jeanne to receive good news from some direction. After her arrival in La Rochelle, Philip had threatened to invade Béarn, the crown had declared that she and Henri were prisoners in the hands of rebels, and the Parlement of Bordeaux had officially stripped Jeanne of her titles and prerogatives. By the end of May 1569, Terride's army had overrun every town and fortress in Béarn except Navarrenx, where the small force faithful to Jeanne was besieged.

Catholic Europe, including Catherine de Medici, had expected the collapse of the Huguenot party after Jarnac. By June, the accumulating evidence that she was mistaken caused the Queen Mother to shift her tactics in a way that eventually changed the entire situation. If the Huguenots could not be defeated in the field, perhaps their strength could be drained by drawing them to the conference table in such a way as to separate them from each other. As early as June 3 Sir Henry Norris told Queen Elizabeth, "The Queen minds . . . to practise to withdraw the Queen of Navarre, offering Madame Margaret in marriage to the Prince her son," and Alava wrote Philip a few days later, "The Queen is resolved to embrace La Vendôme and her son."[44] Coligny's bait was to be an alliance with the Dutch and command of the royal army. Throughout the summer, however, this plan was still in embryo and the Huguenots remained on the offensive. The Duc de Deux-Ponts successfully joined the Army of the Princes in mid-June and the Huguenot leaders issued a new manifesto demanding the restitution of all their rights and the full exercise of their religion.[45]

In July, Fénelon informed Catherine that the Huguenots were seeking to raise a sizable loan (200,000 écus) in England, for which Jeanne's jewels were the principal collateral. Later dispatches give further details. Elizabeth was curious to see the jewels and had them appraised. On August 3, the English Queen acknowledged that she was holding them in security for a loan of 20,000 livres. A month later, however, she swore to Fénelon that she had nothing to do with the loan. This secretiveness —or duplicity—characteristic of Elizabeth's policy, was often complained of by her own ministers.* Most of the loan was put up by private individuals in England, "for it is not possible to prevent those who wish from coming to the rescue of their coreligionists," as Fénelon wrote Catherine de Medici.[46] In a letter to Elizabeth on July 19, Jeanne predicts three different kinds of reward for English support of the Huguenot cause: "in Heaven, for the protection of God's church, in the hearts of Protestant Princes, and in glory and fame to the ends of the earth."[47]

Adding to the Huguenot advantage was the virtual disintegration of the royal army under Anjou through famine, fever, and inability to capture the initiative. Peace rumors were frequent at this time, on this account and because of the crown's financial and psychological plight.[48] It is not surprising, therefore, that Catherine determined to pursue her new policy with all her might. "On the first instant [August 1569] there departed hence one Chassetière, alias Brodeau, secretary to the Queen of Navarre . . . with letters from the King, the Queen-Mother, and the Cardinal de Lorraine to persuade the Queen of Navarre to lay down arms, offering great conditions and amongst others Madame Margaret in marriage for the Prince, whom they must practise to mount on a Spanish horse, and so bring him to the place of rendezvous."[49] Thus did Sir Henry Norris succinctly sum up the plan for Cecil. To execute it would require two and a half years of hard work on Catherine's part.

ACTIVE LEADERSHIP

Even in the early months of the war and apart from her service to the Cause with her pen, Jeanne stood out from the rest of the noble Huguenot women who had taken refuge at La Rochelle, some of whom were also

---

* Jeanne was not satisfied either. On September 26, 1571, Walsingham wrote Burghley that Coligny wished to exchange the receipt the English Queen had given Odet for the jewels "for another, signed and sealed . . . in order to content the Queen of Navarre." Coligny thought that Jeanne suspected "the Cardinal used some negligence in her behalf." Since Jeanne and the Admiral had parted company by September 1571, it is natural that he should interpret her concern as a criticism of his brother, rather than of Elizabeth. Cited by E. G. Atkinson, "The Cardinal of Châtillon in England, 1568–1571," in *Proc. Huguenot Soc. of London*, III, 258.

widows, although none was a "sovereign." As the Spanish ambassador reported to Philip on December 10, 1568, "The Duchesse de Vendôme is coming to share the leadership of the rebels with the Prince de Condé."[50] He may have been alluding to Jeanne's role as Minister of Propaganda, but he must also have heard that she was the "chairman" of a supervisory committee that undertook the general administration of La Rochelle and all aspects of the war that were not strictly military, including finances, fortifications, discipline (except in the army), and, in part, intelligence. This body, usually called the Council of the Queen of Navarre, was somewhat fluid in membership and seems to have come into existence informally to meet obvious needs. The document which contains its significant but incomplete minutes is called *Registre des Ordonnances et Délibérations du Conseil estably près de la Royne de Navarre, 1569–1570*.[51] Many of its members bore names synonymous with the Huguenot movement: La Noue, La Rochefoucauld, Soubise, Rohan, and Rosny (François de Béthune, father of Henri's companion who became the statesman Sully). Some were members of Jeanne's staff, already veterans in her service, like her secretary, Victor Brodeau, and Barbier de Francourt, Chancellor of Navarre. Some were her vassals, like Michel d'Astarac, Baron de Fontrailles, who had often escorted her, most recently from Tonneins to La Rochelle. Not a few would lose their lives in the Massacre of St. Bartholomew.

The Council's activities consisted of enacting and then enforcing regulations to implement policy, especially the concessions made to the English and financial policy. Local officers of the Ile de Ré, Oléron, and the other islands were forbidden to charge English merchants for salt, and customs officials might not collect taxes on provisions for English ships. The officials of the Admiralty were required to give an accounting every Saturday of moneys collected for the Cause; when merchants complained that this was bad for business they were threatened with punishment. Dealers in wood were ordered to deliver fifteen wagons full, to mount cannon on the new fortifications; they were to be reimbursed "after the troubles." Private ships were commandeered with their crews to serve for the duration. The Queen's Council tried to protect its partisans by reimbursing persons who had traveled or incurred other necessary expense, by issuing passports and by handing down decisions favoring the faithful at the expense of the lukewarm. There were, in addition, regulations against blasphemy, drunkenness, and sexual offenses, as well as relief measures for the poor and for the refugees.

Some conflict developed in the summer of 1569 between this Council and that of the Princes, especially over authority in financial affairs. The Princes' Council accused that of the Queen—in her absence*—of creating "great confusion, disorder, and setback to the affairs of the Cause," and repeated their ruling prohibiting all other officers, including the Queen's Council, from meddling with money matters, "either of loans, or of financing the fortifications, or of any other kind whatever, on pain of having all their authority revoked."[52] One sound reason for strict financial controls was that money was in such short supply. Near the beginning of the war, in January–February 1569, after a conference at Niort, the Huguenot leaders announced that the ecclesiastical wealth in the region they controlled would be sold for the benefit of the war effort. Money was also raised through loans, and to inspire confidence the Queen of Navarre and the leading seigneurs of the party "engaged their own wealth as a guarantee." The promissory notes or bonds were issued in Jeanne's name, with all her titles. The good bourgeois of La Rochelle evidently were not sufficiently "inspired," because a system of quotas for forced loans was established:

> The Queen . . . undertook to raise money. She asked the citizens . . . for 184,000 livres tournois to meet expenses . . . but the impossibility of raising such a sum forced her to reduce it to 84,000. The imposition . . . fell first on 400 citizens who were regarded as comfortably off [aisés] . . . who were asked for 200 écus in the first week, as a first installment. . . . This tax was collected with such . . . disregard of ability to pay, that for the slightest delay one was sent to prison . . . the houses of fugitives were demolished . . . the zealous . . . served the cause less by real aid than by making a deafening noise, casting the heaviest charges on the least passionate. . . . There was also a graduated tax to pay the laborers on the fortifications.[53]

Not surprisingly, the forced loans were among the causes of friction between Jeanne and the Rochelais.

Without money, the Cause would eventually founder, but without a commander-in-chief, it risked a quick death. When she learned of the disaster at Jarnac and Condé's assassination, Jeanne rushed to the camp

---

* Jeanne was specifically exempted from responsibility; her Council is accused of taking advantage of her temporary absence, but it is more likely that the Council of the Princes was exploiting her absence to reduce her power.

to rally the troops. The messenger's identity and other details are missing, but the sources agree that she went at once and made an effective speech on the theme the Prince is dead, long live the Prince. The army, even without Condé, must remain that of the Bourbon family, with Henri de Navarre and Henri de Condé as the new chiefs. In De Thou's words,

> The Queen of Navarre, who had great courage and the mind of a man . . . made a speech designed to raise the spirits of the lords and troops standing in a circle around her. . . . First, she praised the Prince de Condé . . . who had shown as much fidelity as bravery in the just cause he had undertaken to defend, up to the moment of his death. . . . She exhorted them to imitate his courage and resolution . . . and to follow his example. . . . [She further said] that they must not think so good a cause could die with the Prince . . . that they should not despair . . . because God . . . could promptly and easily remedy the ills caused by the Prince's death. . . . Indeed, before them stood the Prince de Béarn and the son of the great Condé, who had inherited his valor as well as his name, and that she did not doubt that the two young Princes, aided by the lords in the present assembly, would be capable of sustaining so worthy a cause. In private, she spoke to her son words to inflame his young heart.* She then returned to La Rochelle to procure new aid for the party.[54]

The *nouveaux secours* meant specifically diplomatic negotiations with foreign Protestant powers, but for the duration of the war Jeanne also continued to share in the formation of policy. As legal guardian of the two Princes, she was able to support Coligny's authority and help maintain the morale of the army and the solidarity of the party. In May, when the German army was expected, "The opinion of the Queen of Navarre, who was urging the junction [of the two armies] they say, was that they should be employed either to reestablish her in the possession of Béarn, of which she had been almost wholly deprived, or [having left sufficient force to protect Guyenne] they should cross the Loire again . . . and risk a head-on battle, or . . . march straight to Paris and force the King to make peace on conditions as advantageous for them as shameful for him."[55]

On June 11 the "Army of the Princes" finally met that of Wolfgang of Bavaria. However, the Duke died within a few hours, from fever exacerbated by excessive drinking according to most contemporaries, although Fénelon says he was poisoned and points out that he had dined

---

* Alava was undoubtedly right when he reported that Henri was glad when his mother permitted him to bear arms.

with Jeanne the night before.[56] To celebrate the arrival of reinforcements, after her return to La Rochelle, Jeanne had gold medals struck off. On one side appears her head and Henri's, with their titles, and on the other the motto PAX CERTA, VICTORIA INTEGRA, MORS HONESTA (A firm peace and total victory or an honest death).[57] In this period of the war Catherine mentions that Jeanne is "marching with the Admiral."[58] It must have been a relief to accompany the army (temporarily) as well as to see her diplomatic efforts crowned with success at the height of her anxiety about the war in Béarn. The Germans were not sent there, as she had suggested. Instead, we remember that she commissioned Montgomery as leader of the "Army of Liberation," integrating in it the several semi-independent viscounts who had been resisting the royal Catholic armies in Guyenne.[59]

Communications between Béarn and La Rochelle were rare and risky. Among the few messages delivered to D'Arros from La Rochelle were two he received on July 1, 1569. One, dated June 10, was signed by Jeanne's secretary Enecot de Sponde. The bearer of the other, signed by Jeanne herself, must have broken all records for speed; it is dated June 28 and promises that help is on the way. The Béarnais historian Dubarat found documents in the Pau Archives which enabled him to work out the key to communications between La Rochelle and Béarn during the war.[60] Through Gramont, D'Arros sent money to one Etienne de Norton at Capbreton, "to reimburse him for expenses of the passage of those who were sent to the Queen by sea." Capbreton was a port of some importance in the sixteenth century,* from which one could reach La Rochelle much faster than by land. Norton, the local seigneur, was a known Huguenot and prosperous.

Concern for what was happening in the south did not prevent Jeanne from following closely the Huguenot armies outside her own lands. She rewarded at least one military exploit with personal letters of congratulation. This was the rescue of Niort in a daring attack by the Seigneur de Puyviaut, a member of Jeanne's Council. Striking at dawn with only eight hundred men, he outmaneuvered the force of seven thousand Catholics which was besieging the town. Fine speeches and heroic acts abounded in this episode. The man who carried the Huguenot standard

---

* Owing to a change in the course of Adour River, Capbreton has since declined as a port.

through the breach had been run through with a cutlass. He died as he stepped inside the walls.[61] To Puyviaut and to the Protestant governor of the town, De La Brosse, Jeanne wrote that "she could not fail to add her own joy and gratitude for their fine and praiseworthy actions, which she held in such esteem that whenever she had the means to do anything for them, she would spare nothing to do so, as if it were for herself."[62]

Fénelon reports that Huguenot morale continued high in the late summer. This is confirmed by a letter from Sir Henry Norris to Cecil saying that the Queen of Navarre, "with twelve ensigns and 600 horse, has visited the camp and banqueted the Count of Mansfield."* He adds, "The Princes' army is very powerful and much redoubted of its enemies."[63] One reason was the close collaboration between Jeanne and Coligny. In the first week of September, Alava noted that the Prince of Orange and his two brothers had been to visit Jeanne, "who cannot say one word without consulting the Admiral." He also says that Henri de Béarn "sucks the Admiral's milk" and that Coligny has "filled his young head with dreams of a hundred kingdoms." At least the real "kingdom" he would inherit from his mother was now liberated. Alava was aware that Jeanne was not free from anxiety: "The Queen of Navarre has neither money nor health."[64]

The most important battle of the Third Civil War, Moncontour (about 40 kilometers northwest of Poitiers), fought on October 3, was the first of many reversals to strike the Huguenot party after its brief (post-Jarnac) heyday. Henri d'Anjou's military reputation, of which much was to be made when he reigned as Henri III, last of the Valois, was based on this decisive defeat of Coligny at Moncontour. The Admiral fell back on Niort, then made a long retreat to the south, known as "the voyage of the Princes" because the two young Henris were taken along for morale purposes. D'Aubigné's vivid picture of Coligny's plight after Moncontour includes an allusion to Jeanne often cited by French historians. The Admiral, "with the blame for all the disasters on his head while his merits were passed over in silence, was burdened with the responsibility for young princes, enfeebled towns, fallen garrisons, and ill-equipped foreigners." He was also racked with fever, without money, and "surrounded by powerful enemies without mercy, abandoned by the great, except for one woman, who, having but the name of one, had gone to Niort to succor the needy and to take charge."[65] Among the problems

* Mansfield, Commander of the German Army after the death of Deux-Ponts.

GASPARD DE COLIGNY, ADMIRAL OF FRANCE

needing Jeanne's attention were the thousands of Protestant refugees who were pouring into La Rochelle and Niort as a result of the recent Catholic victories. A reliable source estimates their number to have been over sixty thousand.[66]

The absence of Coligny, Henri, and the armies for many months isolated Jeanne in fact and furthered Catherine's policy of isolating her in spirit. The Peace of St. Germain was not signed for ten months after Moncontour, but with the approach of winter Catherine began seriously to press her diplomatic offensive. Immediately after the battle Alava had written to Philip that Henri de Béarn must be brought to Catholicism. "At all costs his mother must be kept away, all she does is foment heresy."[67] Jeanne was increasingly alone in her zeal for continuing the fight. A letter she wrote the Princes on November 24 shows her fear that the enemy's maneuvers would succeed. She claims to have told one of Catherine's agents that she would die rather than make peace before the free exercise of her religion was granted. When he replied that there were many men in her own army who would not agree, she retorted that "even if they all consented, her signature and that of Henri would never be found attached to such a peace."[68] On the same day this letter was written, the Florentine ambassador, Petrucci, reports that Jeanne had been supervising the construction of new fortifications at La Rochelle in person, "to stir up the others." On one such risky sortie outside the walls she was nearly taken prisoner.[69]

Fearing a siege by royal forces, La Rochelle was more than ever dependent on communications by sea, and the winter of 1569–70 found Jeanne issuing letters of marque to numerous captains. One means to which she resorted in the desperate attempt to augment Huguenot sea-power was confiscation of a Venetian ship, which she renamed *La Huguenotte*. When another Venetian ship was captured by an enemy captain and anchored in the nearby harbor of Brouage, one of her agents, disguised as a fisherman, set fire to it in the night and killed six guards before he overcame the enemy and brought the ship back to La Rochelle.[70] By attacking Venetian ships Jeanne overplayed her hand and alienated the one ally who could really help—England. Queen Elizabeth complained of the violation of neutral shipping and demanded reparations on January 15, 1570. Another letter, with almost identical wording, was sent on March 23, which shows that Jeanne was not inclined to comply, although the letters were addressed to her personally.[71]

By the spring of 1570, Elizabeth and everybody else knew that the Huguenot will to resist had all but disappeared and that only Jeanne's intransigence was holding up the conclusion of peace, especially since Coligny had fallen seriously ill.[72] Diplomats' correspondence is increasingly taken up with the long-drawn-out negotiations and their concomitant intrigues. But Jeanne's martial spirit never flagged. When the great Huguenot captain La Noue hesitated to have his arm, crushed at the siege of Fontenay, amputated, "The Queen of Navarre greatly helped him to become resolved . . . and held his hand in the hour when [the arm] was cut off." The result was "prompt healing, and the skill of the good workmen who made him an iron arm . . . greatly diminished the inconvenience he suffered." La Noue was known for the rest of his life as Bras-de-Fer. One of the ministers also was loud in his praises of the care Jeanne took of him during a long illness.[73]

As late as July 7, 1570, one month before the peace was signed, the Protestants tried unsuccessfully to take Saintes by storm, "aroused by the Queen of Navarre, who would not let them long remain out of action, no matter how much they needed rest."[74] With even her fellow-Huguenots determined to make peace, Jeanne was forced to take up once again the weapons of diplomacy. This time, however, she was not to deal with friendly, if wary, foreigners, but with the most important and most dangerous adversary of her life—Catherine de Medici.

QUEEN OF HUGUENOT FRANCE: JEANNE AT LA ROCHELLE

La Rochelle has never been merely one port city among many.[75] In the high Middle Ages it was already conspicuous for its wealth and municipal pride. Both were expressed in the mighty wall, reinforced with earthworks, that completely encircled the city, even on the port side, so that citizens would not be prey to the sailors whose ships brought goods from every region of the world. Three protective towers have survived to our own day. The Tours de la Chaine and St. Nicolas flank the entrance; between them, until the seventeenth century, an enormous chain closed the passage every night. The size and weight of this chain were proverbial, as anyone can understand who has seen the links preserved. In the Fourth Book of *Pantagruel,* Rabelais tells how Gargantua was tied to his cradle, so that he could not hurt himself, with four great chains, one from La Rochelle, "which they raise in the evening between the two great towers of the port." The third tower, a fifteenth-century lighthouse (Tour

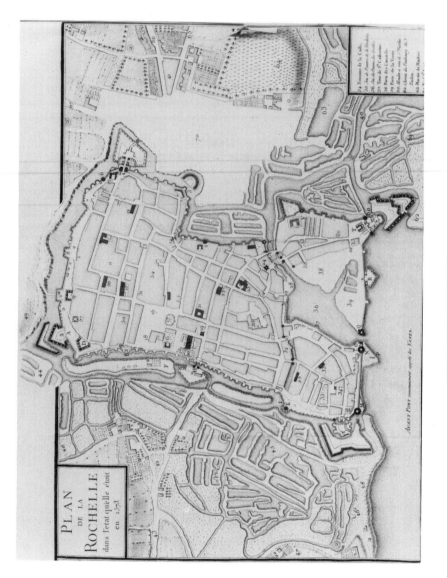

PLAN OF LA ROCHELLE IN 1573

de la Lanterne), is also mentioned by Rabelais (V, 32), when Pantagruel recognizes *"la lanterne de la Rochelle, laquelle nous fit bonne clarté."* Between the Tour de la Lanterne and the others stretches a bit of the old rampart. A steep flight of steps leads from the ground to a narrow street, which runs along the top of the wall, with old houses facing the sea from their perch on the dike. The light, "a massive torch, gave the signal of safety to those who might have lost their way . . . and also warned them of rocks and other dangers on this coast." The lantern itself was hexagonal in shape, made of marble, "with six panes of glass so that the wind would not blow out the flame."

The port is still full of craft in the twentieth century, although it cannot accommodate large vessels in the era of power-shipping. Small ships in the coastal trade and fishing boats are numerous; in summer they jostle pleasure boats. Sailors of the French Navy at all seasons and vacationing French families who swell the population (30,000) in summer are not unmindful of the past. They climb the towers, walk on the ramparts, and seem never to tire of hearing about the heroic exploits of the many sieges, which every true Rochelais knows by heart. Although no wall extends out on either side of the Tour de la Grosse Horloge in our day, one is still very conscious that in passing through its archway one has left the port for the town. The central streets of the town retain a good deal of their historic atmosphere. They are wide, for an old town, very straight, and for the most part *porchées,* that is, the sidewalks are covered by stone arcades, with low arches upheld by thick pillars. No two arches are exactly alike, but they all afford shelter from the rain and wind and they all frame the shops, buildings, and vignettes of town life in such a way that the simplest errand in La Rochelle has a flavor that distinguishes it from a similar errand elsewhere.

A few Renaissance buildings remain, including one that is a masterpiece of French fifteenth-century town architecture, the Hôtel de Ville. It stands two blocks off the rue Chaudrier, which runs from the Porte de la Grosse Horloge to the Place de Verdun (about a ten-minute walk). The Place, formerly Place d'Armes, was the site of the chateau—a medieval fortress. In the Place d'Armes the Peace of St. Germain was solemnly proclaimed on August 26, 1570, and there Jeanne greeted Coligny and the two Henris when they returned to La Rochelle two months later, after more than a year's absence.

During her nearly three years of residence in La Rochelle Jeanne almost certainly lived in an imposing town house sometimes called *l'Hôtellerie des rois et des princes,* but usually l'Hôtel d'Huré, because the prominent Mérichon family who owned it were also seigneurs d'Huré. It was situated between the present rue Bazoges and rue des Augustins, which parallel each other, and the rue Chaudrier. The Hôtel de Ville is about two blocks to the east. The Hôtel d'Huré seems to have been the most admired residence in town.[76] The Duc de Guyenne, brother of Louis XI, had used it as his headquarters in the late fifteenth century, as had both François I and Charles IX when visiting La Rochelle. Louis XI had tried in vain to buy it from Mayor Mérichon, and Henri IV succeeded only in renting it. In 1589, Henri's treasury paid "to Yves and Nicolas Bertinault and Jean Thevenin of La Rochelle, the sum of 110 écus as a year's rent on the house where the King is accustomed to stay in the said La Rochelle." This document was signed and registered in the Chambre des Comptes de Navarre on July 31, 1589, the day before the tenant of the Hotel became King of France. The Bertinault brothers and their brother-in-law Thevenin had bought the house in 1555, possibly as an investment, from Marguerite Mérichon.

Except in the most critical moments of the war, it would be a mistake to imagine Jeanne confined within the walls of the city for more than a few weeks at a time. We have seen that in 1569 she spent some time "marching with the Admiral" and making sorties in the region for inspection of defenses and reviews of the troops. In the summers, after the declaration of peace made it possible, she left the unhealthy atmosphere of the town for the purer air of the country, as did prosperous Rochelais, for in the sixteenth century La Rochelle was swept by disease in the hot months, owing to what is described as "the miasma arising from the marshes."[77] Jeanne's summer residences, of which no trace remains, were in the village of Roufflac, since absorbed in the suburbs, and at La Jarrie, a small town about 20 kilometers southeast of the city.[78]

Jeanne presided over a brilliant assemblage of Huguenot nobility, which included Françoise d'Orléans-Longueville, second wife and widow of the Prince de Condé, the Comte and Comtesse de La Rochefoucauld, Anne de Salm, widow of Coligny's brother D'Andelot, Jeanne's cousin Françoise de Rohan, François de Bethune, and many others. The most elegant social occasion at this court was the double wedding of Coligny to Jacqueline d'Entremonts, a widow from Savoy who had formed a romantic attachment to him from afar, and Coligny's daughter Louise (by his first wife, Charlotte de Laval) to Charles de Teligny, a heroic Huguenot captain, killed at St. Bartholomew.[79] Inevitably, conflicts between members of this court and their hosts, the Rochelais, strained the unity of the Cause and not only in relation to unavoidable bones of contention like financial policy. It would be hard to find a city prouder of its independence or more impassioned in defense of its privileges—and Jeanne regularly interfered with municipal elections.

La Rochelle had been granted the privileged status of *commune* by Eleanor of Aquitaine in the last year of the twelfth century and had possessed a highly developed urban government since the thirteenth (a mayor, twenty-four aldermen, and seventy-five notables). The role of the port during the Hundred Years War (1346–1453) had not only increased pride in the possession of *haute justice,* the right to coin money, and other privileges, but had grafted patriotic sentiment onto the municipal tradition—a combination that has persisted to our own day. The Peace of Brétigny (1360) gave La Rochelle to Edward III but the Rochelais conceded the English King lip service for only a few years before reasserting their loyalty to France. Jean Chaudrier, first of the series of heroic mayors in this double tradition, took the chateau by surprise in 1371 and turned it over to the French. The crown rewarded La Rochelle by adding further privileges, including the right to garrison itself (with the razing of the earlier chateau) and the automatic ennoblement of the mayor. This office was, therefore, the symbol of La Rochelle's autonomy. Upon the mayor, elected yearly, reposed the duty and privilege of upholding the honor of the city.

The two traditions, in harmony during wars with a foreign enemy, came into conflict in periods when the crown was asserting control (over all communes) by measures invariably seen by the Rochelais as infringements of their rights. Louis XI, for instance, after violating Charles V's promise never to alienate the city from the royal domain by giving it to his brother Charles de Valois, was obliged at the latter's death to swear on his knees, one hand on a crucifix and the other on the Bible, that in future he would uphold the municipal privileges to the letter. Rochelais played an important part in French exploration and colonization of the New World in the first half of the sixteenth century, and both François I and Henri II had to compromise with the proud city and rescind ordinances they could not enforce. By the 1560's there was a new element in the situation—the espousal of Calvinism by a majority of the powerful bourgeois families. Geography and political autonomy made La Rochelle the least vulnerable of the Huguenot towns and the logical refuge for the Bourbon princes and the Huguenot nobility.[80]

The Rochelais were undoubtedly not surprised, when it was time for the annual election of the mayor in the spring of 1569, to find themselves once more facing pressure from *les grands*. Moreover, the situation presented new complications. The Huguenot leaders had been declared rebels by the crown and to cooperate with them was to violate the royalist tradition. At the same time, Jeanne and Coligny were natural allies for the dominant Calvinist bourgeoisie. For a while the second consideration outweighed the first. In the words of one Rochelais historian, "Since it was of the greatest importance for the Huguenot leaders to have a mayor of La Rochelle who would cooperate with them . . . the Prince de Béarn asked the municipal corporation to continue in office the incumbent, Salebert [who technically could not be re-elected]. In order not to irritate a people always infuriated by the least novelty contrary to their privileges, he exercised diplomacy, insinuating that it was the town itself that was abrogating its law, because of the great necessity of the times . . . 'it seems to me that if the said continuation in office comes from yourselves, and is done by you, there will be no breach in your privileges, which you will conserve as much with a re-elected magistrate as with a new one.' "[81]

In 1570, Henri was not present to make an appeal and the commune did not choose to volunteer the surrender of its privileges. Jeanne had to act arbitrarily. Her choice for mayor was "one Guillaume Choisi. As the said lady did not wish that during the troubles there should be any mayor who was not wholly in accord with her desires . . . she carried this election by her own authority. . . . Members of the municipal corporation were thus not as free as they would have liked to be."[82] The Princes were not necessarily more zealous in the Cause than the citizens. When royal agents first made contact with Jeanne, some of the Rochelais feared that the Queen of Navarre and the Admiral would conclude a peace, abandoning both French Protestantism and its bastion.[83]

The reinforcement of the fortifications, necessitated by the threat of siege in the winter 1569–70, added to the hardship and resentment of the citizens, already suffering from supplementary taxes, food shortages, and overcrowding because of the refugees. Stones were taken from the church of Notre Dame, at Jeanne's command, and this offended the less "zealous." The arms of the King, the town, and the mayor were placed on a new gate, Porte de Cognes, "by the authority and command of the Queen and the princes, by whom the said fortifications and gate had been constructed, since they were all-powerful in the said town." They had decided not to place their own arms on the gate, the Rochelais chronicler adds, significantly, "on the advice of the mayor and aldermen."[84]

For good reasons of their own, the Huguenot leaders lingered on in La Rochelle for a year after the war was over, but the Rochelais saw no reason to endure in peacetime violations of their privileges they had tolerated only as a means to victory. The mayor and aldermen asked that the "foreign garrisons" (the armed forces of the princes) be removed and that the government be entirely restored to the commune. In a speech preceding the elections of 1571, the mayor asked the princes "to trust the town."[85] When Jeanne finally departed, in late August 1571, "the inhabitants of the town were greatly relieved . . . their liberties having been infringed upon in the three years that the Queen of Navarre had made her residence there . . . and their authority reduced."[86]

There were compensations, however. Nature had given La Rochelle a more advantageous position than other Protestant towns but "the princes," especially Jeanne, had made it the capital of Huguenot France. From the autumn of 1568 until Richelieu destroyed the "state within a state" in the greatest of all the sieges (1628), La Rochelle was the center of Huguenot activity, intellectual as well as political and military. In May 1571, during the term of Blandin, whom Jeanne had supported for the office of mayor, the former monastery of the Cordeliers was converted into a college* for instruction on the highest level, "which she took under her special protection. The Queen called to this town the most learned men of the *Religion Prétendue Reformée* to create a seminary of piety and a center for the education of the holy ministry of the said religion." She and Coligny created chairs in Greek, Latin, and Hebrew. The first occupant of the last-named was François Bérauld, brought from Orléans. The Latinist was Lefebvre, from Auvergne. Nicolas Grouchy was appointed as professor of Greek, but when he died, three or four days after his arrival, "the Queen replaced him with Pierre Martinius, of Navarre, trained under Ramus." The college "testified to the very evident piety and virtue of the Princess and to the affection she had for La Rochelle, maintaining such great men at her own expense . . . for the glory of God."

* Rue du Collège, off the Place de Verdun, site of the present *lycée*.

The professors of Greek and Hebrew each received a salary of 500 livres tournois a year, to which Jeanne contributed 400, Henri 300, and Coligny and young Condé 150 each.[87]

Thanks to the princes also, the first Protestant synod ever to be authorized by a King of France was held in La Rochelle, April 2–11, 1571.[88] At Jeanne's request, Theodore Beza himself came from Geneva to preside and many of the leading Calvinist ministers attended.* The document drawn up, still called the Confession of La Rochelle, constitutes a uniform credo of the French Reformed Church and remains in force today. Necessary clarifications and refinements of doctrine were made, certain "deviationists," including the famous Morély, were formally condemned, and a committee was established to undertake responsibility for refuting "the accusations and libels of our adversaries." The Synod was also concerned with the sphere where politics and religion overlap, advising Jeanne about the employment of apostate Calvinists and Roman Catholics. The assembled ministers showed a degree of political insight into another problem, which was to bedevil the kingdom of France down to the end of the old regime, when they advised her not to permit the sale of offices, most particularly not those of justice.[89]

Before her departure from La Rochelle, Jeanne made a speech of formal thanks to the inhabitants, "for their generous and devoted support, expressing her appreciation of the services they had rendered the party by offering their city as an asylum to the Huguenot leaders."[90] On the whole, there does not seem to have been any more friction between the Queen of Navarre and the Rochelais than inevitably arises in a municipality accustomed to autonomy when the great pay it the dangerous compliment of making it their headquarters. As for the Cause that had brought her there, Jeanne's diplomatic activities had been extremely successful and her ardor in the fight was greater and more consistent than that of any of her collaborators, both during the war and when the real test came—with the making of the peace.

* Nicolas de Gallars acted as secretary. La Roche-Chandieu and Holbrac from Paris, Merlin (Coligny's chaplain), and a sizable delegation from Béarn were among them.

XII

JEANNE AND CATHERINE
DE MEDICI

T HE frequent shifts in Catherine de Medici's short-term policy should not obscure the logical consistency of her long-range objectives: to keep France free from domination by Spain; to keep the factions within France sufficiently balanced so that none was stronger than the others with the crown; and to promote the interests and strength of the Valois family so that it would remain in control domestically and free to maneuver internationally. The Huguenot faction rarely presented as grave a threat to Catherine's balance of power as the Guises and usually offered the most effective means to offset the Counter Reformation party, which also threatened the Huguenots' foreign allies. Catherine's continuing aims and the peripheral conflict between Catholic and Protestant rulers outside France were important elements in her relationship to Jeanne, although at times they were overshadowed by the drama of the direct power-struggle between them.

With the exception of the promotion of the reform, Jeanne's own underlying aims were quite comparable to Catherine's: to assure the autonomy of her kingdom and her own independence as sovereign vis-à-vis powerful neighbors, and to secure her son's succession. Jeanne faced obstacles even more serious than Catherine's, since her "kingdom," a feudal remnant as opposed to an emerging nation-state, was menaced by two powerful neighbors instead of one, divisions among her allies limited their value to her, and the destiny she most desired for her son was only a remote possibility in Jeanne's lifetime, since Catherine had three young sons.

The outside forces that neither could control operated sometimes to bring the two queens together, for instance in 1563, when papal action against Jeanne infringed upon the liberties of the Gallican church. At other times they were driven apart, when Catherine was pressured into refusing concessions to the Huguenots. Both stood to gain by peace, but neither could avoid a resort to arms when the price of accommodation was too high. All these factors contributed to the complications of the struggle between them, a confrontation requiring the full use of their respective psychological and political weapons.

EARLIER CONTACTS, 1533–1569

Jeanne and Catherine had known each other in a general way at court since the daughter of the Medici married François I's second son in 1533. At that time nobody anticipated that she would so far surpass her family's greatest ambition as to become wife of a dauphin (by the death of the eldest son in 1536), let alone Queen Mother and real ruler of the kingdom (by the death of Henri II in 1559). In 1533, Catherine was fifteen years old and Jeanne was five. For the first dozen years of Catherine's residence at court, Jeanne was only an occasional visitor and it is improbable that Catherine had any reason to notice the child. Her position was notoriously humiliating in the early years, when she was handicapped by her status as a banker's daughter, neglected by her husband, and even threatened with repudiation, until 1543 when her first son was born. If Jeanne stood out from the other inmates of the royal nursery in Catherine's mind, it was probably because Jeanne's mother was among the few people at court who were kind to her. The circumstances and their respective ages make it likely that Jeanne and Catherine first came into significant contact when Jeanne was a marriageable cousin, aged nineteen, in the early months of Henri II's reign, and Catherine was the new reigning Queen. We know how great was Jeanne's pride in her royal blood and how she scorned a marriage which would have made her the sister-in-law of Diane de Poitiers' daughter. Reports of Jeanne's attitude toward proposed marriages between their children suggest that she scorned Catherine as a mere bourgeoise.

Chantonay told Philip in 1561 that Jeanne was offended when Catherine referred to Henri de Navarre as *mon fils* and would have preferred her to address him as Monseigneur.[1] On the other hand, Catherine envied the robust vitality and natural leadership of Jeanne's son as compared to her own, especially after Nostradamus' prediction (1564) that the Béarnais would be King of France. She made a number of attempts to arrange marriages for her daughter Marguerite which would have eliminated the Béarnais, and Jeanne did not strengthen his chances by demanding on several occasions that Marguerite be raised in the reformed faith.[2] For a while a marriage was contemplated between Catherine de Bourbon and Henri d'Anjou, but the Queen Mother disliked the idea and refused to take it seriously. These maternal rivalries provided the sole basis for any relationship, other than personal sympathy or antipathy between two members of the court. Until the disintegration of her marriage, Catherine as Queen Mother dealt with Antoine: as King of Navarre, as First Prince of the Blood, as Lieutenant-General of the kingdom, and even as presumed leader of the Huguenot party.

Any letters which may have been exchanged between Catherine and Jeanne in these years have not survived. Temperamentally they were very different. Catherine tended to weep and plead, giving each person the impression that she agreed with him. Jeanne was forthright, dogmatic, and sharp-tongued—which did not prevent her from being equally accomplished at dissimulation, in a different way. Scholars agree that Catherine's concerns were primarily dynastic and that she never understood the importance of religion to many of her contemporaries, Catholic and Protestant. Jeanne took her religion seriously; even if personal and political rather than spiritual considerations had led to her conversion, it figured in every major decision for the rest of her life. At least in February and March 1562, before Jeanne's flight from court, when the capture of Antoine by the ultra-Catholic faction made Catherine favor the Huguenot side, their relations were friendly enough for Jeanne to appeal to the memory of these days in later correspondence. Circumstances did not require the organization of these disparate elements into a definite relationship until Antoine's separation from Jeanne, which coincided with the First Civil War. Jeanne's "strategic neutrality" during that conflict was probably a boon to Catherine—the fewer the declared enemies of the crown, the better. Jeanne was not asserting her Protestant partisanship; Catherine's permission for her to resume charge of Henri's education after Antoine's death may have been a reward.

While Jeanne maintained a neutral position in regard to the national conflict for six years she was pursuing goals within her own domains that violated royal policy and frequently added to Catherine's problems with Philip; but Catherine defended her nevertheless, even supporting the Queen of Navarre against some of her own agents. Even after Jeanne had deceived Catherine and taken "French leave" (the French say *partir à l'anglaise*) from court, returning to Béarn with Henri in 1567, surface relations remained cordial. Jeanne's letters right down to the Third Civil War contain appeals to their mutual interests, as do Catherine's. Through Fénelon's several missions and in other ways Catherine continued to act —at least officially—as if Jeanne might stand aside from the developing conflict and come voluntarily to court. On her side Jeanne was writing "an infinity of letters" in an attempt to avoid a break with the crown.

Beneath the surface, Catherine was encouraging De Luxe and other Catholic seigneurs in Basse-Navarre to rebel against Jeanne's authority and Jeanne was interfering with the rights of her Catholic subjects under royal edicts in lands held in fief, yet each was still hoping to maintain friendly surface relations. Even after Jeanne had joined Condé in La Rochelle and the Prince had issued his call to arms, the crown resorted to the fiction that Jeanne and Henri were prisoners of the Huguenots, especially Coligny, rather than acknowledge a break. When the Parlements of Bordeaux and Toulouse took over Jeanne's lands at the King's command, it was made clear that the purpose was "to preserve her domains for the said lady and Queen, which shall hereafter descend . . . to the Prince, her son." A price was put on Coligny's head but not on those of the Princes of the Blood.[3]

But with Jeanne rallying the troops that fought against Henri d'Anjou in the hot war of 1569, it was impossible to maintain the fiction any longer—although Terride's army was called "the Army of Protection." For a year, October 1568–October 1569, communications between Jeanne and Catherine were suspended and when they resumed they were different. On both sides, surface cooperation was more strained and underlying hostility more evident. The blood spilled in the Third Civil War prevented the restoration of the unreal cordiality that had partially masked the basic conflict between them.

In the ensuing struggle, which was to last the rest of Jeanne's life, two and a half years, three phases are distinguishable (for purposes of analysis) because, despite many side issues and subplots, in each one principal matter was at stake. Throughout, the fulfillment of Jeanne's

JEANNE D'ALBRET, QUEEN OF NAVARRE, 1570

aims would mean the frustration of Catherine's—at least in part—and vice versa. The first phase comprised the negotiations of the Peace of St. Germain, begun at the turn of the year 1569–1570 and concluded the following August. Next came the struggle over the execution of the peace settlement, which began as soon as it was signed. In the absolute sense, this phase never had a chronological end, since Jeanne was still accusing the crown of defaulting on its obligations shortly before her death. This issue gradually gave way to the third one—the marriage between Marguerite and Henri. For about a year, until September 1571, conflict centered on the execution of the Edict, as Jeanne wished, and little progress was made toward the marriage, as Catherine wished. Then, as Jeanne's position became relatively weaker and Catherine's stronger, the focus shifted. In the last seven or eight months of Jeanne's life the marriage treaty dominated the concerns of both women.

NEGOTIATING THE PEACE, NOVEMBER 1569—AUGUST 1570

Catherine took the initiative in reopening communications for the good reason that in the autumn of 1569 the Huguenots, despite their defeat at Moncontour, needed peace less than did the crown. Recent events had shown that the royal armies could not crush the enemy by sheer military power. If it was also evident that the Huguenots could not win in the field either, and that their resources were inadequate, still their plight in respect to money did not compare to that of the crown. As the Florentine ambassador put it, the King was negotiating on account of "the total lack of money" (*la mancanza assoluta di denaro*).[4] Montgomery's victory had given the Protestant party momentum that not even Moncontour could slacken. In mid-January 1570, an observer remarked, "the army of the Princes joined with that of Montgomery is as firm and great a force as they have had during the whole war."[5] The Huguenot leaders were united and their morale was high, while Catherine, in addition to the usual factional strife, was troubled by two new rivalries within the royalist camp. The jealousy between Monluc and Damville, her commanders in the south, could be exploited by the Huguenots with deadly results for the royalist party. Even more awkward was the growing hostility between Charles IX and Henri d'Anjou, which could be exploited by every interested party from the Pope to William of Orange.[6] In 1569–70 such maneuvers hurt Catherine more than Jeanne. As a result, their relative powers were more evenly balanced in the first phase of the struggle than they were ever to be again. In each succeeding phase Jeanne's forces declined while Catherine's gained in strength.

Although Catherine's peace strategy had been detected by Sir Henry Norris as early as June 1569 and there had been a feeler in August, she did not begin to pursue it wholeheartedly until autumn, when the crown could no longer afford to fight, psychologically or financially, while the Protestants continued on the offensive. Immediately after Moncontour, Catherine sent Michel de Castelnau, Seigneur de Mauvissière, to Jeanne at La Rochelle, with a message that, "first, Her Majesty desired to be affectionately commended to the Queen of Navarre, and secondly, being well-disposed to promote her interest and repose . . . the Queen promised to obtain from the King her son, favorable terms of peace for the Queen of Navarre and her adherents, provided that they would petition His Majesty like good, loyal, and dutiful subjects, and present . . . reasonable articles of accommodation." After various conventional phrases to the effect that she was always at the service of Their Majesties, and that her party was extremely anxious for a good peace, Jeanne replied that she thought the crown's "real intentions were quite contrary," pointing to its relations with Spain. As evidence she produced a letter from the Duke of Alva to the Cardinal de Lorraine which had been intercepted by one of her own agents. She agreed, however, to ask the Princes "to draw up articles embodying their just demands."[7] Beauvoir was dispatched to the army, then in Toulouse, and Brodeau to court. This was the period when Jeanne wrote urging the Princes to continue fighting and when she herself was raising a fleet and supervising the new fortifications at La Rochelle. Her response to the message Catherine sent by Brodeau is striking evidence of Jeanne's position at the end of the year and helps to explain why it took another seven months to wear her down. She complains that the Crown has not replied to the Huguenot request,

that it would please the King to grant us liberty of conscience, the public exercise of our faith, with the restitution of our estates, honours, and dignities, we cannot proceed with this negotiation. For this cause, Madame, I again despatch . . . to be informed of Your Majesty's final intentions. Apprized . . . that we must make no demand respecting the exercise of our religion, I can scarcely persuade myself, having once had the honour to know Your Majesty's sentiments intimately, that you could wish to see us reduced to such an extremity as to profess ourselves of no religion whatever, which must be the case if we are denied the public exercise of our own ritual.

As you, moreover, assured [my agents], Madame, that you sincerely desired peace, I will state to you the only way to obtain this blessing: it is, Madame, to be achieved only by allaying the feuds and animosities which now exist amongst all classes in the realm; and to satisfy your humble subjects, of whatever degree and faith, who desire nothing so much as permission to worship God according to their conscience in obedience to their king. Madame, with tears in my eyes, and actuated by sentiments of affection and loyalty toward you, I solemnly assure Your Majesty, that if it will not please the King and you to condescend to our sorrowful demands, I see that nothing can result from this negotiation but a truce, to be followed by disastrous civil conflicts. We have come to the determination to die, all of us, rather than to abandon our God, and our religion, the which we cannot maintain unless permitted to worship publicly, any more than a human body can live without meat and drink.

I pray you, therefore, Madame, take gracious heed of my fervent and humble supplications, and grant peace, with tranquillity, to this realm. I have indicated to you the sole method of achieving this purpose; consider, more-over, Madame, the torrents of blood which must flow; and the iniquities certain to be committed during this cruel war, which one word from your royal lips can arrest.

You may perhaps suspect, Madame, that we ask much at first, in order to obtain concession the more readily on diverse points. Believe, Madame, however, that the affairs of the immortal soul admit not of the same latitude as temporal concerns. There is only one road to obtain eternal salvation. Therefore, what we propose for Your Majesty's acceptance, is all that we can concede, and neither more or less. I can, therefore, but implore for it Your Majesty's earnest attention. I know well, that if it pleases you, you can grant our demands to the full . . . of which legitimate influence and authority, if Your Majesty makes the use we trust in, all will doubtless be well.[8]

Articles were drawn up in the name of the Princes and sent to the King, after they had been approved by Jeanne. The principal Huguenot demands were for free exercise of their religion throughout the kingdom with no restriction whatever, restitution of goods, titles, and offices, cancellation of all sentences against them, admission on an equal basis to all royal offices, and the possession of fortified cities as a guarantee.[9]

Nothing came of the first attempts to negotiate (November 1569– February 1570) because the Huguenot demands were such that not even Catherine's predicament could justify conceding them. The crown could more easily carry on the war, difficult as that would be, than face the reaction of the Counter Reformation party to such weakness. Some of the agents involved in the long negotiations were significant actors in the national drama of the subsequent civil wars, and several later served Henri IV in positions of responsibility. For the Huguenots, most important were Beauvais La Nocle (Jean de La Fin) and Charles de Teligny, later Coligny's son-in-law. They were assisted by Briquemault, La Noue, Cavagnes, and Jeanne's own retainers, Brodeau and Beauvoir. The crown's principal agents were Biron (Armand de Gontaut) and Henri de Mesmes, except in the exploratory phase, when Castelnau and Cossé were active.[10]

Charles received the Huguenot demands on February 4, 1570. He sent Biron and De Mesmes to La Rochelle with his refusal,* the first of many trips. The Counter Reformation party was exerting all possible pressure to keep Catherine from making peace. For instance, Pius V bestowed a sword of honor on Henri d'Anjou, the victor of Moncontour being among the most vociferous opponents of an accommodation with the heretics.[11] Catherine, in the meanwhile, desperately trying to justify peace, wrote her ambassador in Madrid, "please make the Catholic King, my good son, believe that extreme necessity has obliged us to take the path of pacification, rather than that of force." The King's letter goes further. Even allowing for some exaggeration to make a point, it gives a vivid picture of the toll taken by civil war: "order and discipline have disappeared in our armies, gentlemen and soldiers are forming leagues to protect their own interests without regard for my service. . . . Churches have been sacked or destroyed by my rebellious subjects. . . . Moreover, so many buildings have been destroyed that I will be able to restore them only with much time and expense." He refers to the German armies that are still ravaging the kingdom and says that the burden of paying them off is more than the crown can stand, "my financial resources being completely exhausted." Of the proposed peace he says, "it is a beginning . . . after which I shall lead [the Huguenots] bit by bit . . . to the Catholic Religion."[12]

Jeanne's intransigence played into the hands of the real enemy—Catherine's as well as her own. On February 10, 1570 she wrote two long letters to the Queen Mother which brought the talks to a complete standstill for about a month. Jeanne told Catherine, "the nobles to whom I communicated the response . . . on the point of religion, found it so far

---

* In fact, the King's answer conceded much, and Catherine was severely criticized for it. Some Huguenot demands were simply unrealistic. If, for example, "free exercise of the religion with no restrictions" had been attempted in Paris, it would have been unenforceable, as the experience of the Paris Huguenots under the Edict of Nantes was to show.

from their hopes . . . that they were ready to refuse to hear talk of peace any longer, but because of my duty to Your Majesties, I pointed out that they must continue . . . and hope that the King will not hold to this first response . . . but will accord a better one." She begged the Queen Mother not to let herself be fooled "by those who do not wish the kingdom to be at peace . . . but wish instead civil war to continue until all is ruined." She urged her "to believe that it is not possible for us to live without the free exercise of our religion," adding, "it is by your wise prudence and mediation that we will obtain this grace from the King . . . which is no less important to him than to us, since, as I have so often written you, there is no other way to bring about equality between his subjects." She also asked Catherine to use her influence "to prevent cruelties against those of the Religion . . . because, much as we hold [violence] in horror, it is beyond anybody's power to stop [my people] from taking private vengeance." The first letter includes an angry reference to the threats of Philip to Béarn, "the Spaniards are already nibbling at my country; I assure you, Madame, that they will never swallow a bite that will make them as sick at their stomachs as this one, if they try it."

In the second letter, apologizing for its excessive length, Jeanne rehearsed the course of the negotiations since the previous autumn, when the crown first made overtures for peace ("with what joy I and all those of our party heard that good news!") through their disillusionment when they realized it was only a feeler "to see if we had been so weakened by losing the battle [Moncontour] that we would settle for a half-peace in which the principal point [religion] would be ignored or so feeble that it would be insufficient to nourish our souls." Her grievances are many. She accuses the King's advisers of deliberate deception ("a peace made of snow this winter that would melt in next summer's heat") and insists that their real aim is to exterminate the Huguenots. In the meanwhile, none of the various Protestant spokesmen have obtained a straight answer on any point, while the crown keeps falsely accusing them of procrastination and evasiveness. Announcements have been made that the peace is concluded so that foreign allies of the Huguenots would not deliver promised aid. The appeal for outside support was their only recourse, as the crown had done the same . . . first. If the Huguenots now wish peace, "it is not from weakness, still less because we are afraid . . . but only because of our concern, as faithful subjects . . . to prevent the ruin of the kingdom."

Jeanne dwells upon "the lying inventions originating in the hard, black heart of the Cardinal de Lorraine," which distort the facts of the situation in France to the Emperor and other foreign rulers, with the result that "they have lost faith in the word of Your Majesties." She insists on her belief that Catherine and the King are sincere in their dealings but that their wishes are disregarded and changed by the Cardinal, citing at great length letters and dispatches, intercepted by Huguenot agents. Furthermore, "I know for a fact that he sent three assassins to kill my son, my nephew, and the Admiral, and I do not doubt he has me marked out also, but we are all in the hand of God." Then Jeanne refers to her relations with Coligny. "I know some tell you that dissension will develop between me and M. l'Amiral . . . do not believe these people, Madame . . . your close relation and very humble and faithful servant, as I have the honor to be, will always be in accord* with a man so good and so Christian . . . who supports me in the said devotion to God's service and that of Your Majesties."[13] Sir Henry Norris was justified in warning Cecil, on February 17, not to expect peace in France as soon as Catherine's agents gave him to believe.[14]

In March, the military leaders of the Huguenots met at Montréal, near Marseilles, and issued a proclamation stating that the Princes would no longer negotiate unless the free exercise of Calvinism was conceded. Earlier, Cardinal de Châtillon had told Cecil that the Queen of Navarre was resolved never to settle without it.[15] A comparison of the wording of the Princes' several manifestoes with that of Jeanne's letters evinces her leadership. Her letters often antedate the proclamations by a few days or weeks, and Coligny sent his agents to court via La Rochelle—until he and Jeanne became *brouillés* in 1571.

Although the Huguenots were obviously resisting the royal initiative, and Jeanne in particular showed no serious interest in making peace, Biron told Charles in mid-March, "it can do no harm to listen to them and take what is good in what they say . . . also [we can] learn their intentions."[16] So the talks were officially resumed, but for four months they yielded no results. Many miles were covered by the various agents and many hours were spent in conference, including secret meetings between, among others, Teligny and the King; Brodeau and Beauvoir and Catherine; and Biron and Coligny. Jeanne's agents also met with the

---

* There was no rift at all between Jeanne and Coligny until the summer of 1570, and it did not become serious until a year later.

Cardinal de Bourbon and Henri d'Anjou. The permutations and combinations were almost infinite in number, but to little avail—as long as the Huguenot leaders were united. During these endless delays, as Petrucci called them, the Protestant English interpreted Biron's missions as espionage and the Huguenots repeatedly claimed that the negotiations were a trap. A letter of Jeanne's to the King in late April, mostly taken up with assurances of devotion and "confidence in Your Majesty's virtue, magnanimity, and good faith," comes to the point when she says that, if the King will not listen to the Huguenot deputies, "I greatly fear that the machinations of those I have mentioned often enough . . . not to offend either my hand or your ears [sic] by naming them again . . . will deceive you into making another false peace . . . like the others." From the other camp, at least one Spanish agent referred to Jeanne's as "the deputies of Satan."[17]

As late as May, Coligny was planning to carry the war to Paris, but after a serious illness in June he was described as weary of war, and he showed in a letter to Charles that he was ready to conclude an armistice, during which peace terms could be worked out.[18] This was the signal for serious peace talks to begin; it also marks the beginning of what was to become a deep rift between the Admiral and Jeanne.

Coligny's shift was probably the most important factor in ending the stalemate, but others were not lacking. Charles IX was beginning to assert his independence from his mother.[19] In July, he advocated a new policy: to draw Henri de Navarre to court with a concrete marriage proposal, which he claimed would be a more effective way than war to defeat the Huguenots.[20] As early as April the Spanish ambassador had told the Duke of Alva that Henri was being "dragged along" by Coligny;[21] by May there were rumors that he might flee the Huguenot camp, "return to his obedience," and convert to Catholicism.[22] For the next two years Jeanne was to fight against the realization of this policy—which was certainly adopted by Catherine if it did not originate with her—and she succeeded in keeping it from becoming inevitable until the autumn of 1571 and from happening until after her death.

Another factor that helped the parleys move to a swift conclusion was the state of the royal army after the June Huguenot victory at Arnay-le-Duc. Maréchal de Cossé confessed that he could not even keep up with the Princes' army, let alone fight and defeat it. On July 4 he warned

Catherine and the King that if peace were not concluded or reinforcements found, "I see this army disintegrating."[23] At the peace table the Huguenot deputies threatened to continue the war unless the Edict of January was restored. Fénelon wrote from London that the Huguenot leaders, as represented by Cardinal de Châtillon, were determined not to abandon their arms without a firm guarantee of their religion and their rights, but if the King would grant them a just and strong peace, they claimed to be "in a position to render the crown the most notable service it had had in two hundred years."[24]

The Peace of St. Germain favored the high nobility; only *hauts justiciers* were allowed free exercise of Calvinist worship, in their own houses, and never at court, or within two leagues of any royal dwelling, or within ten leagues of Paris.[25] Four strongholds were granted: La Rochelle, Montauban, Cognac, and La Charité. The crown agreed to pay off the reiters. The implementation of other points, less prominent during the negotiations, was to loom large in the next phase of the conflict between Catherine and Jeanne. The peace, christened *boiteuse et malassise** was indeed lame and uneasy, but, as a Florentine observer wrote on August 20, "if the war had lasted another six months, France would have been wholly lost and ruined."[26]

The ultra-Catholics were bitter. The Parisians offered to keep the war going at their own expense, and Monluc observed, "We defeat them again and again . . . but the edicts are always to their advantage. We win by arms and they by these devilish writings." The *politiques* were relieved but cynical. Pasquier wrote, "We ended where we should have begun, but such matters are like lawsuits. One should never speak of an agreement until one has exhausted all the money in one's purse."[27]

The Edict was signed in St. Germain on August 8, registered, reluctantly, by the Parlement of Paris on August 11, and announced with fanfare in La Rochelle on August 26. Jeanne had written two letters of thanks and devotion to Catherine and Charles on the 15th, but she had not concealed her apprehensions: "I thank God for the peace it has pleased Him and the King to make, and I pray him to strengthen His Majesty . . . to see that it is carried out, for I do not doubt that those . . . who have obstructed it thus far, will make every effort to bring it to

---

* Biron was lame (*boiteux*) and Henri de Mesmes was Seigneur de Malassise (uncomfortable).

CATHERINE DE MEDICI

nothing." Letters written exactly a week later provide a truer reflection of her sentiments. They were the first in a long series demanding her rights and accusing the crown of bad faith.[28]

IMPLEMENTING THE PEACE, AUGUST 1570—AUGUST 1571

Jeanne's motives in the peacemaking phase stand out even more clearly in the succeeding phase: to obtain for French Calvinists the greatest possible degree of religious liberty and full civil rights. Although in the minds of others the conditions of the peace were affected by her sovereignty and Henri's position as First Prince of the Blood, to Jeanne they were quite separate. Like Henri twenty years later, she regarded these rights as valid and indisputable, independent of religion. She believed that the Huguenot claims were, in themselves, a matter of justice, which should not be conceded as a favor. Whenever possible she opposed Catherine's policy of granting or withholding Calvinist rights as appeasement or punishment of the Bourbon family. The methods she employed in the earlier phase carried over—with embellishments—into the period when she fought for the full implementation of the peace. Under a veneer of friendly cooperation and respectful obedience, she drove a hard bargain, insisting on the letter of the law. When lesser issues were insinuated to obscure the points she considered essential, she ignored them, procrastinated, gave evasive replies, or made herself unavailable. When her back was to the wall, she fought, almost literally to the death.

Catherine's motives in the earlier phase were modified in the second by factors beyond her control. She had achieved her over-all objective— to stop the bloodletting and lessen the excuse for foreign intervention, from whatever source. But she had not yet weakened the Huguenot party, and, although military expenses were reduced, the crown's assumption of the obligation to pay off the reiters partly canceled out that advantage. The issues that loomed in the autumn of 1570 threatened to create even thornier—and no less expensive—problems than civil war.

All these issues were connected in one way or another with the war in the Netherlands and the growing involvement of the Huguenots and Queen Elizabeth on the Dutch side. Louis of Nassau was in France, and he became Jeanne's most valued adviser aside from her own retainers. Francis Walsingham was also in France, to support Franco-Dutch collaboration and to counteract Spanish influence. Coligny was interested in building a coalition which would be positively Protestant as well as negatively anti-Spanish. Charles IX, increasingly independent of his mother, was anxious to substitute a foreign war—against Spain—for civil war, in the interest of national unity. (He would fall more and more under the influence of the Admiral, no longer an enemy.) Henri d'Anjou, the favorite son, resented the loss of his military leadership and was easily played upon by the ultra-Catholic faction. Walsingham and Coligny thought that a marriage between Anjou and Queen Elizabeth would fulfill Catherine's ambition to find a kingdom for Anjou while canceling out his usefulness to the Counter Reformation party. As a result of all these factors, the leaders of the latter went into a veritable frenzy of activity to block a French alliance with England, the Franco-Dutch coalition, the Navarre marriage—and the implementation of the peace.

The tangle of intrigues resulting from these conflicting ambitions brought onto the French scene many new personalities, in addition to the familiar ones. In 1570–1572, France was the crucible in which all the conflicts of Western Europe, political, ideological, and dynastic, met and interacted. Catherine risked seeing the domestic balance of power destroyed by the influence of Coligny on the King, the international balance of power destroyed by the anti-Spanish coalition, and the pressure of both the Huguenots and the Counter Reformation party on the crown greater than ever. It was the worst dilemma she had yet faced. Her solutions to its interlocking aspects were evolved during the second phase of her struggle with Jeanne. Her primary aim was to weaken the Huguenot leaders by drawing them to court and sowing seeds of dissension between them. If the Huguenots were less powerful, Philip and the Pope would be appeased. Catherine could thus strengthen her position against both sides. Coligny was to be attracted by the French command in the Netherlands war, Jeanne by the marriage of Henri to Marguerite de Valois. The Queen Mother had to wait a considerable time before enjoying any success, however, since the Huguenot leaders were still united—and still in La Rochelle—for many months after the Peace of St. Germain. Their party remained on the offensive, while the Papacy was launching a new drive against them, and bringing pressure on Catherine. This left the Queen Mother with little room to maneuver.

As early as August 1570, Sir Henry Norris commented on Jeanne's determination to obtain every concession possible from a reluctant Catherine: "The Queen of Navarre has demanded the restoration of some small towns in Guyenne which are kept from her by Monluc."

Furthermore, an important "Occurrence in France" (in October) was the return to La Rochelle of Coligny and the Princes, resulting in the coordination of Huguenot demands.[29] English observers were sympathetic and Spaniards were alarmed, but their accounts of Huguenot boldness were almost identical. Among other manifestations, including threats to renew the war, Jeanne's steps toward completion of the reform program in Béarn drew special attention from the Spaniards. They also report her *très altérée* and anxious to go home.[30] Her intensified activities during the war probably had accelerated the deterioration of her health. Even so, she did not leave La Rochelle until late August 1571.

Between the signing of the peace and the end of the year (1570) Jeanne wrote nine letters to the King, Catherine, and the Duc d'Anjou, complaining that Catholics generally and the royal officers in particular, were ignoring the Edict. On August 22 she told Catherine that "enemies of the public tranquillity are still committing an infinity of evil acts . . . the Catholics have begun to renew their associations [leagues] in order to prevent those of the Reformed Religion from enjoying the fruits of your Edict of Pacification. I know that this is contrary to your intentions, which is why I cannot fail . . . to inform you, so that you can take matters in hand [and so that] people will obey better than in the past."[31] On August 25, she officially requested Charles IX to appoint royal commissioners to administer the Edict and investigate violations, offering to appoint an equal number of Huguenots.[32]

At least she was relieved of one long-standing source of trouble. Monluc had been seriously wounded at the siege of Rabastens in late July, and his removal was one of the first fruits of the Peace of St. Germain. He was replaced by Honorat de Savoie, Marquis de Villars (the Queen of Navarre complained to him too.) Monluc emphasized the difficulties of the task at the time of his replacement. "It is not an unalloyed privilege to have to deal with the Queen of Navarre and her son . . . who, now grown, and being what he is, is the greatest enemy of our religion. He lacks neither the courage nor the means to trouble us, both in Guyenne and in the royal council . . . I would have quit long ago on this account, except that I did not wish the King to be able to reproach me with abandoning him in his wars or in his needs."[33] One of Jeanne's most important letters of complaint to Charles (September 5) expresses her hope that Villars will be an improvement over Monluc. She also takes up two other specific matters, rumors that the King might not deliver the promised fortified towns and accusations of piracy against captains from La Rochelle, acting under Jeanne's orders, "fabricated by persons who care more about their own interests than about your service and the public tranquillity."[34]

A month later her tone is sharper: "would to God that your Edict of Pacification were observed as faithfully elsewhere as it is by us . . . I am beset by those of contrary inclination, who still retain my towns and my houses."[35] One clause of the Edict required the restitution of rights and several of Jeanne's letters deal with specific appointments and offices. She stood firmly on her prerogatives, insisting that Henri be given the administration of Vendôme and that officers appointed by the crown during the war resign in favor of her own appointees.[36]

After the return of Coligny and the Princes to La Rochelle (October 25), the Admiral's demands were coordinated with Jeanne's.[37] Having been declared a traitor with a price on his head, he had been more thoroughly stripped than Henri and Jeanne of his possessions and rights. In the autumn of 1570, he and Jeanne for the last time formed a strong team. Moreover, they had powerful outside support. Hubert Languet, representing the German Princes, was at court to further the Huguenot claims, and, even more important, Queen Elizabeth had instructed Walsingham to take special charge of "that party in France which hath professed reform in religion. We would have you at all times . . . let it appear to the King that we think nothing can procure more assurance of inward quietness in his realm than the observation [of the Edict]. . . . In any other things wherein you shall be able to further . . . the favor of those of the religion, we would you should endeavor yourself in such sort as may stand with our honour."[38] Still more advantageous was the fact that Charles IX was expressing increased sympathy with the Dutch. He had given Louis of Nassau a warm welcome and brushed aside the Spanish threats this provoked.[39]

The sustained Huguenot offensive gave the lie to Catherine's earlier assurances to the Pope that peace would weaken them and it caused Pius V to launch a new counteroffensive. Frangipani's dispatches in the late summer and autumn of 1570 show that he was applying unrelenting pressure on Catherine and Charles to assure that the peace would be "only an armistice" and to block its execution.[40] He feared that there were secret clauses even more damaging to the church and he was deeply pessimistic about the future because of the favor shown to the Montmorencys, the return to court of Renée of Ferrara, and, particularly, the influence of Louis of Nassau. He complained bitterly of the "softness" of the French cardinals, especially the Cardinal de Bourbon, to whom he attributed the initiative for the Navarre-Valois marriage. He failed to dissuade the King from restoring his benefices to Cardinal de Châtillon or from supporting Louis of Nassau. He failed to heal the growing rift between Charles and Anjou. He complained in vain of Jeanne's anti-Catholic measures in Béarn, and his request that France and Spain take joint action against her was ignored.[41] His only concrete success, reported to the papal Secretary of State on September 30, was Charles' promise— in violation of the Edict—not to allow Ramus, "or any other heretic," to teach at the Collège de France.[42]

So bad was the state of France from the papal point of view, that Pius sent the prothonotary Bramante as a special envoy to reinforce Frangipani in the last two months of the year. His official assignment was to persuade France to join in an international Catholic league against the Turks, but his concrete purposes were to block the Navarre marriage (by proposing one between Marguerite and King Sebastian of Portugal instead) and to keep the French from entering the Netherlands conflict on the side of William of Orange. In his first dispatch Bramante tried to mollify the Pope by assuring him that the real purpose of the Peace of St. Germain was to lull the Huguenots into a false sense of security and that the King was about to eliminate them. He quotes "excellent Catholics" as saying that it was necessary to move slowly in annulling the Edict.[43]

Bramante and Frangipani had a number of interviews with Catherine and the King, which is one reason that the progress of the Queen's own policy—to trap the Huguenot leaders instead of openly attacking them —was so slow as to be hardly perceptible until after Bramante's departure early in the new year. Although months before Alava had commented sourly that "there is lots of talk about the Navarre marriage," and had even told Philip, "the King and Queen have committed themselves to it in writing," actually little toward its realization had been done and Jeanne had consistently ignored it.[44]

The first meeting of royal and Huguenot commissioners* on the

---

* The commissioners appointed to administer the Peace of St. Germain included Briquemault, Cavagnes, and Brodeau, but the chief responsibility was borne by Teligny and Beauvais La Nocle.

execution of the Edict, at the beginning of 1571, gave Catherine her opportunity to force on Jeanne's attention the marriage proposal, and, as a first step, the crown's desire for her to come to court—bringing Henri. On January 3, 1571 Catherine sent a letter to Jeanne via Artus de Brissac-Cossé, assuring her of the intention of "the King, my son, to embrace the affairs of the Prince of Navarre, whom the King and I infinitely desire to see here, with you." Cossé had been instructed to make a specific proposal of marriage between Marguerite and Henri, orally. On the same day, Jeanne was writing to Catherine about the things on *her* mind:

> As I have already demonstrated at length, unless the King takes matters personally in hand, things will simply go from bad to worse. . . . There are too many matters to go into in the space of this letter, but I must bring to your attention my particular grievance of the treatment [by your officers] of me and my son in my towns, which have not yet been returned . . . and the denial of his rights and those of his bastard brother* . . . all of which actions are contrary to the terms of the Edict of Pacification. . . .
>
> I am assured . . . that if my son and I come to court we will receive the treatment we deserve, but I have a suspicious nature, Madame, as you well know, which makes me fear that, although your intentions are good —which I do not doubt—those who have been able in the past to alter them in regard to us . . . continue to have credit with you . . . and will succeed in blocking justice. . . . Believe me, Madame, I am not ignorant of the fact that we are entirely dependent upon Your Majesties' goodness . . . but I am a proud little woman [*je suis ung petitte glorieuse*] and I desire to receive at court the honor and favor I think I deserve more than those who receive better from you.
>
> I would fear to anger you by these words, Madame, if your kindness to me in my youth had not accustomed me to the privilege of speaking frankly and privately to you . . . in my old age. . . . Begging you to accept this letter as in the past, and to show me by your future actions that you honor me with your friendship.[45]

Jeanne also wrote to three of the King's officers, making further demands and complaints about specific violations of the Edict in her domains.[46] But Catherine was not to be stopped. Petrucci accurately noted on February 23, "everything possible is being done to separate the Huguenot leaders" [*si fa ogni opera di disunire questi capi ugonotti*].[47]

---

* Charles de Bourbon, 1563–1610, Antoine's son by Mademoiselle de Rouet. He later became Bishop of Comminges and Lectoure, and Archbishop of Rouen.

The royal initiative could no longer be ignored and in February Jeanne changed her tactics from ignoring Catherine's proposals to creating excuses for delay.

On February 4, acknowledging Cossé's message and other recent communications detailing "favors" accorded her, under cover of effusive expressions of devotion, she took the opportunity to accuse the crown of duplicity and to put off both her appearance at court and a definite reply to the proposal. Jeanne says that she has given "the present bearer [Masparault] documents which will testify to the rebellion and imposture perpetrated by my subjects, unfortunately with your support. I cannot conceal from you, Monseigneur, the annoyance I feel that the services of my grandfather, my father, and my husband remain so little in your memory that a handful of traitors can exceed me and my son in your favor. . . . If we . . . who stand so close . . . are thus forced to protest . . . what can others then hope for?" Turning to her handling of the Béarnais rebels, some of whom had asked the King to intercede for them, she says, "Masparault tells me that you have been given to understand that four thousand were banished, the truth is that eighty-four were exempted from the amnesty. . . . As for your message that you are waiting for my son and me to come to you, I beg you to believe that . . . I desire it more than you do, but our affairs are going so badly that they tie us here. . . . I am not enjoying the fruits of your Edict in the majority of my strongholds, Lectoure, Villemur, Pamiers . . . you can judge from this how well you are obeyed."[48] A letter of February 22 specifies other grievances but repeats the same underlying message—that Jeanne was more interested in the fulfillment of promises already made than in listening to new ones.[49]

In late February 1571, it seemed that Jeanne might succeed in avoiding the issue altogether and that the talks would be suspended, like the peace negotiations of the previous year. Catherine then made two moves which reversed this trend and enabled her to gain the initiative: she began to apply pressure on Coligny; and to deal with Jeanne she called again on the man who had succeeded in breaking the earlier deadlock—Armand de Gontaut, Seigneur de Biron.

In early March, Biron went to La Rochelle for the first of many interviews with Jeanne. We have the accounts he sent to Cossé, one of his fellow-negotiators, and to the King. The former contains more interesting detail.

I arrived here three hours ago with the Sieur de Quincé, who went to see the Queen of Navarre before taking off his boots. I later went myself, as did the Admiral. The said Queen retired into her study with the Prince her son, the Admiral, Quincé, and myself. After the said Quincé had delivered your message and pointed out how satisfied [the Queen] should be with the King's action, both on account of the general welfare and her own private interests, we fell into discussing details. Then the going became rough [*la fust le mauvais passage*]. To be brief, I forgot nothing you told me, in spite of the scowling face in front of me. I told her that one fortunate thing was that those involved were all her well-wishers and that you, Monsieur, only sought to be able to take an acceptable reply from her to the King, whereas others who might have come would have desired the contrary. Finally she calmed down and took a fairly reasonable line [*elle se modera et est venue en assez bon chemin*].The Admiral invited us to supper, over which we lingered three hours. M. de Teligny was the only other person present. I remonstrated with her again, very firmly, on the specific issues in Béarn and Navarre. You will find that things will work out much as you wish.[50]

The message to the King was briefer and a little more positively optimistic. "From what I have gathered . . . it should not be too difficult to lead them . . . on the path we decided upon." He adds that people in La Rochelle greatly desire peace, "all that is necessary is to administer strict justice."[51]

With this reassurance, Catherine left Biron to conduct the marriage negotiations as he saw fit, until midsummer. He traveled regularly back and forth between La Rochelle and the court, as did many couriers, as the worst winter on record finally gave way to spring. Jeanne continued to make demands.[52] The fact that Henri was in Béarn for some weeks and that she left La Rochelle on inspection trips herself assisted her Fabian policy. Michel de Castelnau, another member of the negotiating team, could report to Catherine on June 12 that he had found Jeanne and her entourage "full of honest desire to perform humble and faithful advice" to the King, and that "they speak of nothing but the great privilege it would be to kiss the hands of Your Majesties." "If there is no change of opinion," said Castelnau, Beauvoir would soon bring word of Jeanne's plans to go to court. He admitted, however, that Jeanne had made no reply to the King's inquiries about matters in Béarn, alleging that she had never received his written articles—which had been sent in January. In conclusion he said that there were so many intrigues afoot in Jeanne's entourage that "unless the King can impose order, he will have even more trouble with the Queen than in the past."[53]

Beauvoir was indeed assigned to go to court, although he did not carry the news for which Catherine was waiting, and he did not leave until many weeks later, because he was delayed by a bad attack of gout. On June 21, Jeanne wrote to the King, Catherine, and both of the King's brothers to say (in slightly different words to each) that she would send Beauvoir to explain once and for all her policies in her own domains "because I am still of the opinion that you have never understood them," and expressing a hope that when they knew, "from the lips of a man who was a leading member of our council in the days of my father and husband also . . . you will be satisfied and that my subjects will no longer be able to justify the wrong they do me under cover of your approval, as they have up to now."[54] On August 17, Jeanne was still assuring Charles that Beauvoir would come, "as soon as he is able to travel."[55] These and several other letters dispatched in the interval were delivered by couriers. None refers directly to the marriage proposal, or to any concrete plan to come to court, although several contain conventional assurances that she wishes she could.

While Catherine was trying to master her frustration with Jeanne, she could console herself with the first fruits of the "practices" on Coligny. It is not surprising that the first people to take seriously Catherine's policy of attracting the Admiral with promises were those most opposed to it. In mid-November 1570, Frangipani told Cardinal Rusticucci that the Admiral was to be drawn to court in order to neutralize his influence. Bramante went further: according to him, the King had promised Cardinal Pellevé to have Coligny assassinated.[56] By spring 1571, the Spanish ambassador reported that the Admiral was impatient and anxious about Jeanne's delaying tactics because, until the Navarre marriage was settled, he would not feel free—or safe—in going to court, "which he much desires to do."[57] Castelnau found him "very cooperative" and there are repeated references to a rapprochement between him and Catherine in July.[58] Catherine must have taken satisfaction in his letter of August 3, asking her to expedite certain matters so that he could come, and in reports from her agents that he was preparing to depart.[59] He had evidently been reassured by Louis of Nassau and Teligny, who had secretly been received by Charles IX (at Lumigny) in late July.

As Coligny drew closer to Catherine, anticipating in spirit his actual departure from La Rochelle, he and Jeanne grew apart and eventually became *brouillés*—as Catherine wished. Jeanne distrusted the crown's motives and thought that the Admiral was walking into a trap. She also understood that his departure would isolate her and offer new temptations to Henri. These considerations would have strained their relations, but what made their separation inevitable was that Coligny's desire to push the Franco-Dutch coalition drew him into intrigues with various foreigners concerning another possible marriage for Henri. The papal Nuncio was correct in reporting (August 31) that "there is great discord between them because the Queen wishes to conduct her own affairs by herself, without interference from the Admiral, while he seeks to make her obey the King."[60]

If it had been only the Admiral, Catherine's policy might have been less completely successful, but every political interest represented in France was seeking to exploit the position of the First Prince of the Blood to its own advantage. The ultra-Catholics, while doing their utmost to block Henri's marriage into the royal family, favored any other scheme to separate him from his mother, bring him to court, and, if possible, into the Roman church. This was to be expected, and Jeanne had a life-long habit of dealing with the Spanish-papal-Guise faction as the enemy. Much harder to counter were the intrigues of fellow-Protestants who thought the cause would be advanced by a marriage between Henri and Elizabeth of England. For a few weeks in the spring and summer of 1571 there was a temporary suspension of the continuous marriage talks between the English Queen and the Valois princes. Into this vacuum rushed an international cabal whose object, so far as it can be discerned from gossipy accounts of their secret meetings and multiple intrigues,* was an English-Navarre alliance to strengthen Coligny's position as leader of a Franco-Dutch coalition. Our source is the *Mémoires* of Michel de La Huguerye, a free-lance spy who entered the service of François de Beauvais, Sieur de Briquemault, in the autumn of 1570.[61] As Briquemault was one of Coligny's chief lieutenants, it must be assumed that the Admiral was party to the intrigue.

Nothing could have been more alien to Jeanne's real ambitions for

---

* By an unlikely and ephemeral concatenation of circumstances, the desire of the Grand Duke of Tuscany, among others, to offset Spanish influence led to the participation of his agent, Fregoso, in collaboration with a Dutch prince (Louis of Nassau), the English ambassador to France (Walsingham), and Huguenots (Briquemault and Teligny, especially). See Desjardins, III, 438-439, for a summary of the plan. No results had been obtained before the incipient coalition was doomed by Philip's victory at Lepanto in October 1571.

Henri. Her interests were centered entirely in France. She was not in the least interested in a foreign marriage for her son, even, or perhaps especially, with a reigning monarch, and Elizabeth was known for her capricious treatment of favorites and her canny way of keeping anybody else from real power. Jeanne was concerned to assure Henri's position as sovereign in Béarn and as an heir to the throne of St. Louis. As she had been unwilling to be banished from the center of power as a mere Duchess of Cleves, she was absolutely opposed to any plan that would deprive her son of his destiny and relegate him to the level of a pawn in other people's chess games. Her concern for the Cause, although secondary, was genuine; and it too was centered in France. She favored an international Protestant coalition, because it would offset Spanish power and strengthen the Huguenots against their domestic enemies, but to bargain away Henri's future in order to bolster Coligny's ambition or Dutch independence or Elizabeth's security was, to this Calvinist Cornelia, to mistake means for ends.

La Haguerye is not a trustworthy reporter.[62] Although they make lively reading, it is not worth while to cite the three alleged interviews between Jeanne and Louis of Nassau he describes, in which the Dutch prince tried to persuade her of the advantages of the English marriage.[63] La Huguerye's account of the falling out of Jeanne and Coligny, on the other hand, deserves consideration because, as in all propaganda, there is a kernel of fact. According to the statements he puts into the mouth of Coligny, the Admiral made several serious charges against Jeanne: first, that she undermined his authority and hounded him to retire after the war (*elle print plaisir de contredire depuis en toutes choses pour le desgouter et le faire retirer*);[64] second, that she would not cooperate with him and was more difficult to deal with than his worst enemies (*qu'il avoit plus de peine à se gouverner avec elle qu'au milieu des armes contre ses plus vigilans enemys*);[65] and finally, that she had deceived him by giving the impression that she agreed with the plan to marry Henri to Elizabeth and then doing just the opposite, "it being her nature to do the contrary of what she was advised or had promised and to throw all the blame on the other person."[66]

These statements are exaggerated, yet the record shows that Jeanne rarely cooperated with anybody for more than a short time, that she was accomplished at dissimulation, that she was jealous of her own authority, and that Henri's career—his "destiny"—was the all-absorbing passion of the final years of her life. The latter consideration is also relevant to Coligny's complaint that Jeanne was motivated by overweening ambition.[67] It is not surprising that the *brouille* between Jeanne and Coligny was marked by reciprocal charges that each had placed private ambition above the common cause. Aside from the fact that it is the usual fate of allies, it was precisely the result that Catherine had intended when she chose the marriage as the inducement for—or weapon against—Jeanne, and the Netherlands command to entice the Admiral.

When Coligny had been won over by the Queen Mother, Jeanne knew that the full force of royal pressure would fall on her. "Wishing to strike while the iron was hot, the Queen Mother sent the Sieur de Biron posthaste . . . to solicit the said lady anew and point out the great advantage [of the marriage] to the Kingdom in general and to her in particular."[68] This was in the third week of August 1571. Jeanne could no longer remain in La Rochelle and send an occasional evasive message to sweeten a stream of demands and complaints. Some gesture of accommodation was necessary, one which would also give her more time. Her failing health—ignored for the past two years spent in following the armies and supervising the fortifications—provided her with a convenient pretext. She decided to go home and take the cure at Eaux-Chaudes.

In a period of ten days she addressed several letters to the King on this subject. The first, written before she left La Jarrie, was hasty and to the point. "Monseigneur, if I do not go to drink the hot waters at once I will do great damage to my health. I am sending the present bearer to explain the urgency and to beg you humbly to approve it, because I well know, Monseigneur, that there is no lack of those who will try to make you disapprove."[69] She adds that her reason is in order to be "more healthy and better able to obey your commands." Another, more leisurely, was written on August 24, after she had set out for Béarn. "I can never thank you enough for the honor you do me in wishing to see me, which benefit I myself naturally wish even more than you do. But, to my great regret, Monseigneur, I have been obliged to yield to the exigencies of my health. . . . As soon as I have taken the hot waters I shall set out to obey your command, as I have notified you by the Sieur de Pardaillan, and since, by the Sieur de Beauvoir."[70]

By September 9 she had arrived home in Pau, after an absence of two years, tumultuous in Béarnais history. On that day she wrote another letter to the King, one of the very few in these last years to reflect any satisfaction: "I make so bold as to tell you that my homecoming was as happy as I could wish, having found all my subjects so united and so joyous in their welcome to me that I can say it is a long time since I have been so happy. I leave tomorrow to take the waters . . . and the weather is so favorable that I hope to recover health and strength . . . to use both for your service. As soon as I have put some order in my affairs, I am prepared to come in humble obedience and the fidelity you will always find in me, in all matters, everywhere. . . ."[71]

XIII

CONFRONTATION:
THE MARRIAGE TREATY

SEPTEMBER 1571—APRIL 1572

WHEN Jeanne returned to her own domains late in the summer
of 1571, most of the Catholics in Béarn rallied to their native
sovereign, as a reaction to civil war and "foreign" domination. Her
Calvinist subjects were, naturally, jubilant. She took advantage of the
favorable conditions to complete her legislative program with an energy
amounting almost to frenzy, as if she knew there was little time before
her health would give out or her political nemesis triumph.

CATHERINE'S OFFENSIVE

Catherine was drawing the net tighter every day. She had determined
to push through the Navarre marriage over opposition, not only from
the Counter Reformation party, but from many Huguenots as well.
Her allies were *politiques* (especially the Montmorencys) and such
Huguenots as agreed that "to marry the two religions" was the best
if not the only way to pacify the kingdom.[1] With Coligny's "nails clipped,"
in Jeanne's phrase, the Queen Mother worked out a three-pronged
strategy to do the same to Jeanne. First, Catherine insisted, steadily,
firmly, and openly, that Jeanne come to court. Her messages did not
mention the various issues raised by the marriage, but implied that only
details remained to be worked out. This obliged Jeanne to raise the
specific problems herself. Simultaneously, Catherine strengthened the

354

assumption that the marriage was a foregone conclusion in her dealings
with others, so that she could use public opinion as a source of indirect
pressure on Jeanne. Finally, she launched a campaign to obtain from
the Pope a dispensation for her daughter to marry a heretic.

Biron, Castelnau, and Cossé had not produced the desired result in
their frequent embassies to Jeanne. As soon as Catherine knew (in
August) that Coligny had capitulated, therefore, she suggested to the
King that it was time for the negotiations to produce concrete results.
From Paris, where she was purchasing jewels for Marguerite as a royal
bride, she wrote, "The Comte de Retz* and I are attending to it in such
a way that you will see her as honorably provided for as her sisters, and
with less expense. I am told that the Queen of Navarre is complaining
that you have only spoken of this marriage . . . through a third person.
. . . It seems to me that it would do no harm to send Maréchal de Cossé
to her with a letter in your own hand . . . requesting that she meet you
in Blois, bringing her son, in early September." Cossé was accordingly
sent, but, by the time he reached Béarn, Jeanne had retired to Eaux-
Chaudes to take the waters. Biron, who followed a few weeks later,
did not catch up with Jeanne until November. In the interval, her
response to all messages was that she could not hold further discussions
until Beauvoir returned with replies to her questions and requests. But
Jeanne's nerves were fraying. In a letter to Catherine before she left
La Rochelle she had said, "I cannot imagine why you should find it
necessary to say that you want to see me and my children, but not in order
to do us harm. Forgive me if I laugh when I read these letters, for you are
allaying a fear I have never had. I have never thought that you fed on
little children, as they say."[2]

During these same weeks, reports of foreign observers demonstrate
the success of the second prong of Catherine's policy. The Spanish ambassador told the Duke of Alva on September 12 that the marriage would
take place after the Queen of Navarre had finished the cure. Within a
few days Biron and Beauvais La Nocle were said to be "making final
arrangements," and even Walsingham described the negotiations as
"thoroughly concluded." Before the end of October, Catherine's preparations of the trousseau were mentioned as items of news, but without
surprise. To make the assumption plausible, the marriage had to appear

---

* Retz, Albert de Gondi, d. 1603, Comte and later Duc de Retz, Maréchal de
France and a member of Catherine de Medici's inner circle of advisers.

as merely one item, albeit the culminating one, in a general policy of pacification and national unity. Another was the well-publicized favor shown to Coligny after his arrival at court. As Alava remarked, "they are making such a fuss over him that it is clear they want to use him." One person they wanted to impress was Queen Elizabeth. Fénelon reports that she was "very curious" about the Admiral's welcome, wishing to know every word that was said. She was told that his reception was "as good as that of any man in twenty years," that he had been kissed by the Queen Mother and taken at once to the Duc d'Anjou's room (he was in bed with a slight illness) where the marriage of the Prince de Navarre with Madame had been "concluded," and that Henri and his Mother would soon come to court. Some people in England thought this good news, Fénelon said, but others feared that internal peace in France "would be a source of trouble for England" (*ne fût le travail et le trouble d'Angleterre*).[3]

An essential part of Catherine's plan was to persuade Coligny and Louis of Nassau to become her agents, by allaying Jeanne's fears, by urging her to court, and ultimately, by persuading her to approve the marriage on terms the crown was prepared to concede. The Florentine ambassador Petrucci, who was one of Catherine's confidants in these months, reported on September 29 that Coligny had undertaken to urge Count Louis to persuade Jeanne that the Huguenots should yield some of their strongholds to the crown. According to his dispatch of October 16, the Queen was developing a somewhat forced comradeship with the Admiral. When Coligny remarked that he understood the hesitations and suspicions that were keeping Jeanne from coming to court because he had felt the same way himself, Catherine is said to have replied, "We are both too old to fool one another, you and I . . . she has less reason to be suspicious than you had because she cannot believe the King would be trying to arrange a marriage of his sister with her son only to do him harm."[4]

The crown meanwhile took steps designed to satisfy Huguenots and *politiques* of every rank. The King sent letters patent to his officers throughout the country, instructing them to see that the Edict was strictly carried out. In order to dramatize his intentions, he attempted to redress a particular grievance. Members of a Parisian Protestant family named Gastines had been condemned for heresy by the Parlement of Paris and hastily executed. Some of their ultra-Catholic neighbors had then erected a monument (in the form of a pyramid surmounted by a cross) on the spot where their house had stood, inscribed with the full text of the Parlement's condemnation. *La croix de Gastines* had become a symbol of intolerance and injustice to the Huguenots and their supporters. It was relatively easy for Charles to order the Parlement to rescind its decision and his officers to remove the cross, but he could not enforce his will. Anti-Huguenot passion ran so high in the capital that the royal officers delayed obedience for many weeks—until the end of the year.[5]

At the other end of France, in the meantime, Jeanne seized upon the situation as evidence that the crown was not sincere and told Biron she would not go to court until the cross had been removed. The Spanish ambassador, Don Francis Alava, had been prominent in arousing the Parisians to resist the King's command, an activity that dramatized Spanish opposition to religious toleration in France. The French crown, which had already requested Alava's recall, began to insist upon it. He left France in November, just as Queen Elizabeth's new ambassador, Thomas Smith, arrived to relieve Walsingham during an illness and to assist him in the preparation of an alliance between England and France. The arrival of Smith, whom Alava described as "a violent heretic and evil man" [*hérétique acharné et très méchant*], and the Spaniard's departure indicate the direction of French foreign policy in 1571–72. The Navarre marriage was its domestic counterpart.[6]

Catherine needed support from the anti-Spanish Catholic camp outside France as well as from the *politiques*. The third prong of her offensive against Jeanne, indirect like the second, was pressure on Pius V to grant a dispensation for the marriage. Even if it could not be obtained, a dispensation must be sought if French Catholics were to accept the marriage of a daughter of France with Jeanne's son. In this Catherine could take advantage of the influential position of her cousin Cosimo de Medici, who had recently been granted the title of Grand Duke of Tuscany by Pius. Cosimo's response to Catherine's first request was that the best way to achieve her end was for Coligny and Jeanne and Henri to convert to Catholicism. The Grand Duke probably made this conventional observation for the record, and Catherine echoed it in her more urgent second appeal.[7]

In vain did French and Florentine diplomats importune the Pope on four separate occasions between the end of August and the middle of October, with the argument that the Catholic cause stood to gain from French national unity, especially because, as they claimed, Henri's eventual conversion was certain. The Pope declared that he would lose his last drop of blood rather than grant a dispensation *before* the conversion. Meanwhile, encouraged by the great victory of Lepanto against the Turks (October 7, 1571), the Pope made a counterassault, in the hope of so intimidating the Valois family that they would abandon the marriage altogether. He sent Bishop Salviati to the French court to urge the marriage of Marguerite with the King of Portugal instead; Salviati was followed by Cardinal Alexandrini, the Pope's nephew and legate in Spain. It was awkward for the Pope that Don Sebastian already had declined the honor of Marguerite's hand—an affront that contributed to Catherine's anti-Spanish policy—but Alexandrini persuaded him to change his mind. This was so much wasted effort, since the Navarre marriage "is a resolution I have taken with such careful consideration," Charles explained to his ambassador in Rome, "that I expect from it not only the peace and welfare of my kingdom . . . but also of Christendom in general, since the Prince is so young and so favored by inheritance that it should not be too hard to lead him in the path His Holiness desires, as was the case with his late father." Gallican support for the marriage and the long history of French resistance to papal interference in domestic affairs favored Catherine's plan. Frangipani reported in an exasperated tone that "most of those who call themselves Catholics approve and advocate the marriage . . . comparing it to that of Clovis and Clothilde,"* while Catherine referred pointedly to the right of three French archbishops to issue dispensations and to the example of Henry VIII forty years earlier.[8]

While Catherine was giving priority to the struggle with the Pope and Biron had another round of interviews with Jeanne, somebody, probably in the papal entourage, came up with an argument that provided the Queen Mother with the ultimate weapon against Jeanne.[9] It was suggested that the Pope, instead of granting a dispensation for the marriage, might declare Henri illegitimate on the grounds that the Cleves marriage invalidated Jeanne's marriage to Antoine. This threat had loomed distantly in 1563, at the time of Jeanne's excommunication, but the firm support of the crown had rendered it ineffective. In 1571, Catherine was willing to use this sophism against Jeanne. By so doing she shifted the balance of forces between them to her own advantage, irreversibly. Because

* Clovis, first king of the united (Merovingian) Franks, was converted to Roman Catholic Christianity by his wife Clothilde, who promised him victory over his enemies under the sign of the cross, c. 500 A.D.

of Gallican theory and sentiment, the crown might disregard papal un-willingness to grant a dispensation, and the stigma of Henri's illegitimacy, while affecting it adversely, could not destroy Catherine's scheme. For Jeanne, however, it was a fatal blow. If Henri was not the legitimate son of Antoine de Bourbon, he might marry into the Valois family and inherit his mother's domains, but he would lose his position as First Prince of the Blood and heir to the French throne. Catherine therefore had little to lose and much to gain by adopting the specious argument to force Jeanne's cooperation.

Jeanne's pessimistic tone whenever she mentioned the marriage (once she had accepted it as inevitable) and the intensity of her struggle over every detail with Catherine (when they finally met) led some contemporaries to conclude that she was entirely opposed to the marriage. To the extent that she would not freely have chosen it, this conclusion is inescapable, but as the only sure means to her ultimate end—the con-firmation of Henri's rights as First Prince of the Blood—she was, I believe, willing to accept it, despite her many fears and reservations. The prospect of Henri at the Valois court filled her with dread, but the reinforcement of his position was something she had always wanted.

We do not know exactly when the subject of Henri's illegitimacy was resurrected or by whom, or when and how Jeanne learned that the crown was prepared to use it. The Spanish dispatches, which provide so much detail of this kind, do not mention it, nor do Biron's letters. It was a closely guarded secret indeed if it was not confided to Biron and if Philip's agents did not discover it. It seems probable that Catherine mentioned it to Beauvoir in their private discussions at court in October, of which there is no record from either side. Catherine may have men-tioned it casually, seemingly in passing, as somebody else's idea, to which she was opposed. The slightest hint that the crown would act on it was probably sufficient. The argument itself was all too familiar to Jeanne. The purpose of the last two of her protests against the Cleves marriage, in the presence of cardinals, was to assure that the so-called marriage could never be used to disinherit children born to either Cleves or Jeanne in another, duly solemnized, union.

Beauvoir probably was the bearer of the fateful news because both La Huguerye and Bordenave, with their opposing prejudices, say that it was after his return from court in November that Jeanne agreed to accept the marriage. Moreover, it was then that she added a third tactical line to the two she had been pursuing for the past year. She began to prepare conditions which make sense only if she had accepted the inevitable, such as demanding Guyenne as Marguerite's dowry. In one of his last reports to Philip, Alava says, "the Duchesse de Vendôme has lost her head over the marriage of her son, proposing something new every day. Now she is demanding that the King promise to reconquer [Spanish] Navarre within two years, and they say they would, if she would abdicate at once in favor of her son, so that he could have the title of King when he marries the Princess . . . the Admiral says she is crazy and refuses to have anything to do with her."[10]

Of the two established tactical lines, one was defensive—stalling, procrastinating, and avoiding the real issues—the other offensive—pressing her own complaints and accusations of bad faith against the crown. Evidence of Jeanne's defensive tactics lies in Biron's letters to the King and Catherine in November. His letter of November 12 to Catherine is worth quoting at length because it illustrates a number of Jeanne's methods and their exasperating effect on the royal representatives.

On the 9th [the Queen] seemed very satisfied and we spoke pleasantly of affairs at court and of her trip there. She expressed an intention to set out as soon as possible . . . but the following day she imposed three conditions, saying that she could not leave until the 30th . . . and that she wished the Prince to remain in Béarn . . . until all the arrangements were completed. [The third point concerned the religious ceremony.] I explained at length that Your Majesties did not wish to force her in any respect . . . as tactfully as possible, to keep her from getting worked up, as I saw she was about to do [*le plus dextrement possible afin de ne l'eschauffer, comme voyais qu'elle y voulait entrer*]. . . . She replied that she would go no further than she had already decided, according to her conscience, and launched on other aspects . . . in a way quite contrary to my wishes. She said that the Cardinal de Bourbon [would marry Henri and Marguerite] not as a Cardinal but as her son's uncle. . . .

At supper she said that promises made to her had not been fulfilled. After supper, she called Count Louis and me aside and said that La Vallette had not yet surrendered Lectoure, nor had the garrison been removed . . . which was contrary to the Edict and to the King's direct promise . . . she said that [promises contained in] the dispatches brought back by Beauvoir were a mere mockery.

[There followed a long argument about Lectoure.] I did not succeed in removing her imagined grievance . . . and when I pressed her to tell me what else was on her mind . . . she said that the cross in Paris had not yet been torn down . . . and that she would not leave until these two things

were accomplished [the yielding of Lectoure and the removal of the cross].
She added that she refused to be deceived, like others who had gone to court.
. . . I saw that my reasoning and protests were only aggravating her . . . so I
possessed my soul in patience and in silence. . . . The next day there was
nothing but laughter and good humor . . . she says she is writing to my wife
and my sister. . . . She is also sending a messenger [to court] who can bring
letters patent from the King, returning her towns and chateaux, to her at
Nérac . . . I fear, Madame, that at this very hour she is writing a letter that
will cause you and the King pain . . . so I am sending this one secretly . . .
to reach you first. . . . I believe that she will be satisfied when Your Majesties
make a great show of annoyance [*feront grande demonstration d'etre marris*]
that Lectoure has not been put in her hand . . .[11]

By November 20, however, Jeanne's health had provided another—
genuine—opportunity for delay, and Biron had to inform the King of
another change in plans. "On the 18th she took pills for a cold that had
given her a bad toothache and pain in the entire right side of her head . . .
they did little good. . . . Yesterday she had dysentery and a high fever.
Today she is a little better. . . . She is distressed at the delay, fearing you
will take it amiss. She says that in two days she will either be cured or
much sicker . . . in the former case, I have persuaded her to set forth
as soon as possible." An additional excuse is revealed in an item of "News
from France," dated December 3: "The Prince of Navarre had lately a
great fall from his horse and was sorely bruised and has blemished his
face." At the end of the month, Killigrew mentions to Burghley the
suspicions and fears that explain Jeanne's procrastination. "The marriage
between the Prince of Navarre and Madame Margaret is doubtful. The
Admiral has had secret intelligence to look to himself, for all is not gold
that glistens. The wisest think that if he agree with the House of Guise*
it will be to his greatest danger. Upon this little broil at Paris about the
pulling down of the cross, divers things have broken out . . . these
suspicions keep the Queen of Navarre, Montmorency, and the Admiral
from the court."[12]

Throughout the autumn of 1571, Jeanne was steadily clamoring for
the restoration of her rights in direct correspondence with the King and
Catherine. In her eyes, the test case of royal sincerity in the execution of
the Peace was the fortified hill-town of Lectoure, capital of the county
of Armagnac, which she held in fief from the crown. Although it was

---

* A reference to one of Catherine's many attempted reconciliations of the factions.
This one was unsuccessful.

only a "small town in Guyenne," to Sir Henry Norris, Lectoure was known as "the key to Gascony," and had been bitterly fought over during the civil wars. Under the terms of the Peace of St. Germain, Jeanne was entitled to resume the government and to place her own officers in command. In spite of her repeated, and specifically documented, demands and the crown's verbal aquiescence, the royal governor, Jean de Nogaret, Marquis de La Valette, would not yield the citadel. Jeanne expended more energy on Lectoure than on all the other disputed places combined, and she managed to snatch back some of the initiative from Catherine by using the King's betrayal of his word on Lectoure to cast doubt on his trustworthiness in the marriage negotiations.[13]

Before Jeanne left Béarn she asked—and was offered—much advice about the desirability of the marriage in relation to the future of the Protestant cause, a matter she took seriously, although she subordinated it to Henri's "destiny." Without mentioning any name except that of Beauvoir (whom he blames for having been "corrupted" at court and then persuading Jeanne to accept the marriage), Bordenave gives a lengthy account of the conflicting opinions in Jeanne's Council in Pau, as well as his own interpretation of the feelings behind Jeanne's decision.

The leaders of her own religion were those who most urged her to do it, assuring themselves that it would bring an end to the calamities of France. . . . The Queen did not wish to cross them since they threatened every hour to abandon her, and said that [if she opposed the marriage] she would be the cause of future misfortunes. . . . Some others, fewer in number and less highly placed . . . warned her not to pay so much attention to the apparent worldly advantages . . . but to the real evil that would ensue. . . . Even the pagans thought that the best marriages were made between persons of the same religion, . . . and God had expressly forbidden the children of Israel to marry their children to idolaters. . . . It was to be feared that the young Prince would be distracted . . . and drawn to the Roman Religion by the King's command . . . the ruses of the Queen Mother, and the blandishments of his wife . . . since [he] was not as wise or steadfast as Solomon, who had been drawn to idolatry by an alliance with Egypt. . . . They also pointed out that the King had . . . broken his word before . . . one of the chief precepts of Machiavellian politics is that men should be deceived with promises as children are with apples . . . and the Roman Religion teaches that one need not keep faith with heretics. . . .

The fact that the evil counselors responsible for the flight [of Condé, Coligny, and Jeanne herself] to La Rochelle were still in power should make her hesitate even more. . . . Those of this opinion took pains to make clear that they were not accusing the King of these deceptions . . . only his mother and his advisers ... who were all in the pay of the King of Spain and the Pope.

This difference of opinion greatly troubled the Queen's mind. She would gladly have followed the second, if she had dared, but she feared to anger the King and those of the Religion who assured her that it was the only way to achieve both the peace of the kingdom and the advancement of the religion. . . . For this reason, after having pointed out the inconveniences and dangers she foresaw from the marriage (fearing more evils than they hoped for benefits), she bowed to their will [*condescendit à leur volonté*] in order that they might not blame her stubbornness for keeping so many good things . . . from coming to pass [*n'etre estimée avoir voulu par son opinastreté reculer tant de biens*]. . . .

She prayed God to bless the decision . . . and to bring about the happy issue so many good men of both religions expected. Nevertheless, she wished also to obtain the opinion of the most learned theologians . . . so that, whatever happened, her conscience and that of her son would be clear.[14]

It is interesting to compare Bordenave's impressions of Jeanne, as she was preparing to meet Catherine, with those expressed by the Florentine agent Fregoso to Petrucci at the same time, the end of November 1571. Fregoso had been deeply involved in the abortive intrigue to marry Henri to Queen Elizabeth, which had permitted repeated contacts with Jeanne at close range over several months. Bordenave had no such advantage. In 1571 he was a mere "minister of the word of God" in the little Béarnais town of Nay, and his history (which Jeanne commissioned at this time), is an official document with a strong Huguenot bias. Since we have Fregoso's opinions in the words of Petrucci, the latter's bias, anti-Huguenot and extremely favorable to Catherine, must also be kept in mind.

In substance, the temper of this Queen is very eccentric [*molto fantastico*], requiring both skill and patience to reach her and to pin her down [*fermarla*]. She changes often and eludes you every minute. In the end she hopes to manage everything her own way. She will arrive in court about the 20th of next month [December], but alone, without the Prince . . . who will come when sent for by her, with a large company. . . . The Huguenot ministers have been preaching that such a marriage cannot take place. . . . M. de Biron . . . has corrupted some of them . . . to change their minds, who now say . . . that each [spouse] can remain in his own religion. . . . The Queen of Navarre wishes to examine and tempt Madame . . . but Her Highness, already warned of the very words that will be used, will answer in a certain way.[15]

Long before the final confrontation, Jeanne's defeat had been assured.

Her correspondence shows that Jeanne left Béarn about the first of December for Nérac, where she had arrived by the eighth. It was the first of a series of farewells. Her departure would have been even harder to bear if she had known that she would never see her son again. She had written ahead to various important vassals in Albret and Armagnac to meet her there and accompany her to court. Her letter to the faithful Caumont de La Force shows her very much on the alert as she gathered her strength, in all senses, for the fray. "In cases of dire necessity, one finds out who is really a friend. . . . If I can count on you in private matters, how much more do I do so when God's service is in question. I need you for a matter closely concerning my son, whom I have brought this far with me . . . I pray you come and meet me as soon as possible . . . *periculum est in mora.*"[16]

On December 10 she was joined by Biron, who had been to court and returned to escort the Queen of Navarre there. He thought that all the obstacles had been overcome and that they would set out immediately upon his arrival, a prevailing illusion in the royal entourage, to judge by November dispatches from Blois announcing Jeanne's arrival "in two or three weeks." Catherine's deputy was soon disabused. On December 12 he reported that a great number of nobles had come to Nérac to support Jeanne and were "casting doubt on [the crown's] good faith." Jeanne had been persuaded to delay her departure and was sending a new letter detailing their complaints. Biron fears that the peace will be broken unless the King acts at once "to snuff out the rumors and suspicions."[17]

Following are parts of the letter Biron was referring to, written on the same day but delivered by Jeanne's own courier.

to my great regret, I am forced to protest, along with others, of those who, by their flagrant disobedience to your express will and command, make it suspect. . . . Up to today I have been deprived of the benefits of the peace . . . unable to enter my towns and chateaux because of the insolence of those who cover their actions with your words. . . . When I tried to use the letters patent [Charles had recently sent] in Lectoure . . . La Vallette flatly refused to honor them. Please listen to [the eyewitness and bearer of the letter] for I beg you to believe, Monseigneur, that all the world is watching to see how you treat me, in view of the honor you do us in proposing so close an alliance with my son. . . . There is a contradiction between . . . what comes directly from you, on the one hand, and the insolence and insults of those who pass for very well-informed . . . about your wishes . . . on the other. . . .

I would much prefer to speak of nothing to Your Majesty but marriages and other happy things . . . but this is too serious a matter . . . and very damaging to your reputation. In order to hasten my arrival, therefore, please send back the present bearer, posthaste.[18]

Four days later Biron brought the King up to date on the latest developments. "Until yesterday there continued to be gatherings of armed men angered over the refusal of La Vallette to surrender Lectoure, but since the arrival of the latest courier, the Queen seems somewhat mollified. . . . She says that when she is satisfied on this point she will no longer doubt either Your Majesty's intentions nor [your] power to be master in your kingdom. . . . She is determined to wait for the return of the messengers she sent to Your Majesties on the 12th, but assures me she will continue on her journey when they have brought your message satisfying her."[19]

The crown's messages, intended to reassure Jeanne, had so far been ineffective. Having also failed to reconcile Coligny and the Guises, Catherine requested the Lorrainers to leave court after Coligny had withdrawn to Châtillon. Jeanne's letter to Charles on December 17 is of particular interest because, in contrast to the many which deal only with her own affairs, it comments on the general policy of the crown:

I would never approve of anyone's bearing arms in your kingdom. Your subjects can yield their natural right to defend themselves and trust you to render justice if they are wronged only if nobody has private recourse to force. . . . I am sure that you are a wise enough king to know that [such uses of force] have as their sole object to trouble the peace of your kingdom and to weaken your authority.[20]

Conflicting reports of Jeanne's plans circulated at court. Petrucci says, "she fears, she hopes, she changes her mind, she does not know how to proceed nor exactly what she wants [ne quel si voglia], not recognizing as an honor what His Majesty proposes for her son, nor the greatness that it could bring him. If [the marriage] does not take place, she will regret it more than they." Catherine then made the necessary gesture of appeasement, which gave Jeanne one real triumph—the yielding of Lectoure. In early January, the Comtesse d'Armagnac visited her "capital" and could express satisfaction with her reception. "I have come to this town of Lectoure, which the Sieur de La Valette has finally returned to me," she wrote Caumont, "I did so partly to erase the evil opinion that he had tried to impress on my subjects, namely that I wished to oppress them, my God! But they are very satisfied with me and I with them."[21]

JEANNE EMBATTLED

Escorted by Biron and her Gascon nobles, Jeanne left Nérac about the middle of January to begin her final journey. From the estate of Biron, on January 21, she wrote eighteen-year-old Henri the first of a series of letters, through which one can follow her changes of mood in the climactic stage of her negotiations with Catherine. Initially, her frame of mind was cheerful and her tone strictly parental.[22]

My son,

I have received your letter and am pleased that you are feeling well and that Pistolle has had her puppies, although I could wish there had been more males than females. Your cousin arrived here the same day I did. He is not nearly as tall as you are, but I think he is more amorously inclined.* You will not doubt that M. de Biron's hospitality is everything one could wish. . . . I remind you of your duty—and the importance of your example—to attend the public sermons regularly and to say your prayers every day, and to believe and obey M. de Beauvoir. . . Also, do not forget your promise to take some lessons from M. de Francourt.†

On January 10, 1572, Killigrew had reported to Burghley, "The Queen of Navarre makes all speed to the court, whereof the King is glad," a prime example of English understatement. But in the meantime another guest, much less welcome, was expected. Cardinal Alexandrini was trying to reach the court before Jeanne and prevent the French crown from proceeding with the marriage without a dispensation. The decision to do so had been taken some time before, and one of Philip's agents had broken the bad news to his master on December 17. "The Nuncio told me in greatest confidence a secret imparted by Cardinal de Bourbon . . . and of his shocked reply." Frangipani also expressed doubts about Charles' orthodoxy and warned the Spaniard that the only effect of the favors heaped on Henri d'Anjou would be to unite the *politiques* and Huguenots more firmly in support of the marriage and against foreign intervention.[23]

Catherine hoped that Jeanne would arrive first, so that the Legate could be kept at a distance geographically and confronted with a *fait accompli* politically. The Cardinal outwitted her, however. Alexandrini

---

* Condé was courting Jeanne's niece Marie de Clèves.

† Barbier de Francourt, Chancellor of Navarre. Jeanne subsequently sent for him to come to Blois and help her with legal details of the marriage contract.

was furious that St. Sulpice, who had been assigned to escort him, kept him waiting six days at Bayonne, and depressed by manifestations of Huguenot strength in the regions he traversed. An English dispatch reports that he made a ceremonial procession through certain towns, "crossing and blessing until he perceived that they did no reverence with knee or cap, but only laughed at him, and after what sort he blessed them afterwards, I leave the reader to think." As soon as he was certain that Jeanne was on her way, Alexandrini left his cumbersome train behind and made as rapid a march as possible, arriving in Blois on February 7. In the final stages of the journey, he and Jeanne crossed on the road, but no greetings were exchanged. The drama of this near-encounter between the Pope's legate and the woman whom he regarded as the embodiment of the devil caught the imagination of contemporary historians.

Correspondence in papal circles shows that Pius was heartened by Jeanne's opposition to the marriage, and Jeanne in turn may have taken some comfort from the Pope's continued pressure, in that she could exploit Catherine's difficulties by raising her own demands in the bargaining over the marriage treaty. The Pontiff's hopes were not shared by Alexandrini, however. From the beginning he was sure that his mission would fail, and after it was over he said, "I leave France having accomplished nothing whatever that I have undertaken. I would have done as well not to come." Catherine's explanations to the King of Spain show that she was determined on the Navarre marriage, even at the price of his displeasure.[24]

Since the Cardinal arrived first at Blois, it was Jeanne who had to be kept at a distance. She stayed at Tours until his departure. It was awkward for Catherine to be obliged to keep Jeanne waiting after so many months of urging her to come without delay. She resolved the problem by inviting Jeanne to meet her for an initial interview at Chenonceaux, taking Marguerite and several ladies with her and risking the possible consequences of leaving the King unsupervised while the Legate was still at court. Petrucci reports on February 14, "today the Queen Mother went to Chenonceaux to meet the Queen of Navarre. The Legate awaits her return in three days to learn the outcome." Of the first meeting, Petrucci says, "the Queen Mother had scarcely crossed the threshold when the Queen of Navarre arrived. Embraces and salutations were exchanged . . . and the Queen of Navarre asked at once for something to eat. Immediately afterward the two queens retired into a room alone. The Queen of Navarre is said to have thanked God for the honor Their Majesties wished to do her son . . . but that she needed to discuss the particulars more fully with the King himself . . . as indeed she will after the Legate departs."[25]

Jeanne's own reactions to the first confrontation are revealed in a letter to Henri on February 21, after she had returned to Tours.

My son,

The long dispatch I am sending contains details of the exchange I have had with the Queen Mother and Madame. . . . I am very much put out not to be able to report a good outcome. . . . Since the matter must be played by ear [*manié au doigt et à l'oeuil*] I urge you not to leave Béarn until you receive word from me. If you are already en route, find some pretext . . . to return. This is my opinion and it is shared by those who best understand matters here. For the talk is of nothing but to hurry you up. . . . It is evident that [Catherine] thinks everything I say is only my own opinion and that you hold another. . . . When you next write, please tell me to remember all that you have told me and especially to sound out Madame on her religious views, emphasizing that this is the only thing holding you back, so that when I show it to her she will tend more to believe that such is your will. This will be very useful. I assure you I am very uncomfortable because they oppose me strongly and I need all the patience in the world.

Madame has paid me great honor . . . assuring me that she favors your suit. . . . Given her influence with the King and her mother . . . if she embraces the Religion, we can count ourselves the luckiest [persons] in the world, and not only our family but the whole kingdom of France. But if, with her caution and judgment, she is determined to stick stubbornly to her religion—as I am told—I fear this marriage will be the ruin, in the first place, of our friends and our domains, and such an aid to the Papists . . . that we and all the churches of France will be destroyed. Therefore, my son, if you are ever to pray to God, let it be now. I assure you I do so constantly, so that this marriage shall not express His wrath, to punish us, but His mercy, to His glory and our tranquillity. . . .

As for other news, my sister the Princess and my niece* are here and like two peas in a pod [*deuz doigts de la main*] in constantly mocking everyone. I find them very much changed in a way as strange as it is unpleasant. If you cannot do your courting better than [Condé] I advise you to give it up. . . .

I will not fail to inform you what happens when I talk to the King. The Queen is unwilling to receive me at Blois until the Legate leaves. I was con-

---

* Condé's widow, Françoise d'Orléans-Longueville, and Marie de Clèves, daughter of Antoine's sister.

stantly pressed to come, but nobody is in any hurry to see me now that I am here. Count Mansfield came to see me, crying for his money. . . . Keep an eye on Lectoure. Your sister is still sick. I am waiting to be summoned to court.

In conclusion, my son, I beg you to pray to God, for if you ever needed His help it is at this hour. Since you are closely spied upon, make a point of attending sermons and prayers. . . . M. de Montgomery who has asked to accompany you, writes me that the King is willing to receive him, but the Queen objects.* . . . I hope in the end she will permit it as a favor to you.

I beg you, my son, not to forget to write what I mentioned above. Take care of our religion and our affairs. . . .

The dispatch referred to has been lost, but there is a postscript to the letter in the hand of Catherine de Bourbon, who had just had her thirteenth birthday: "Monsieur, I have seen Madame and found her very beautiful. I wish you could see her. I spoke of you in such a way that you are in her good graces. . . . She was kind to me and gave me a little dog I like very much."[26]

Developments on the larger scene in the early months of 1572 affected the final struggle between the two queens. The war in the Netherlands was rising to fever pitch; the Sea Beggars were making the Duke of Alva's position untenable in parts of the Low Countries, and France was expected to throw its weight into the scales against Spain—in alliance with England.[27] Smith and Walsingham were in Blois negotiating a treaty. In common with Coligny and Louis of Nassau, the English diplomats thought the success of their enterprise inextricably bound up with the Navarre marriage, indispensable for both a Protestant coalition, which would alter the European balance of power against Spain, and, specifically, the control of the Netherlands. For Louis, of course, the issue was the life or death of his dynasty and of the emerging nation his brother was bringing to birth. For the English, it is always essential to keep the Low Countries out of the grasp of any major continental power; otherwise they become, in Winston Churchill's phrase, "a pistol pointed at the heart of England." For Catherine, the Netherlands war and the Navarre marriage were intended to achieve national unity and strengthen French power against Spain. The motives of the Huguenot leaders are harder to disentangle, with party considerations and Coligny's personal ambition playing a considerable role. For the Admiral, the war in

---

* Catherine never forgave Montgomery because his lance had accidentally killed her husband in 1559.

Flanders was certainly the more important. For Jeanne, while it was desirable to bolster the Protestant cause by any means, the war was peripheral to domestic religious and political considerations and distinctly subordinate to the dynastic question.

Alexandrini left on February 25, "with no great contentment, being much aggrieved to see such small account made of him by those of the court." On March 2, Charles IX went in person to greet the Queen of Navarre outside the town of Blois. "It would be impossible to exaggerate the caresses lavished upon her by the King, the Queens, the brothers and sister of the King, and all the court." The author of this statement was an ardent Huguenot, writing in the aftermath of the Massacre of St. Bartholomew. He continues, "The King was the one who carried this [welcome] to the greatest extremes, but he said in private to his mother, 'Well, Madame, am I not playing my part well? Leave it to me and I will deliver them into your net.' "[28]

Contemporary sources for the final phase of the marriage negotiations have the advantage of not being affected by knowledge of the Massacre; in spite of conflicting interpretations, their accounts of what happened are consistent. Elements which may be distinguished (although they cannot be separated) are the parts played by Louis of Nassau and Walsingham, the differences of opinion—religious and otherwise—among the Huguenots, and Jeanne's relations with her future daughter-in-law. The methods and personalities of Jeanne and Catherine stand out boldly in the running commentary of participants and close observers of developments from day to day, and sometimes from hour to hour. The ultra-Catholic view of Spanish and papal observers is balanced, at the other extreme, by Walsingham's dispatches and the *Avis sur les cérémonies du mariage de M. le Prince de Navarre et de Madame la Soeur du Roy en la convocation des ministres,* wherein we find, respectively, the broader and the narrower Protestant reactions. Catherine's attitude, as well as foreign moderate and French *politique* opinion, is expressed in Petrucci's abundant commentary. Finally, there are Jeanne's letters to Henri and Beauvoir, which show that Catherine was acting on advice given her by the Maréchal de Tavannes:* "as one woman to

---

* Gaspard de Saulx, Maréchal de Tavannes, 1509–1573, was in the intimate counsels of Catherine de Medici. A fanatical Catholic and one of the leaders of the League, he is generally considered to have been among those responsible for the Massacre of St. Bartholomew.

another, make her mad, while staying calm yourself."[29] The result was that for about five weeks, between March 3 and April 4, 1572, the Queen of Navarre was a tigress at bay.

Jeanne may have found comfort in a letter from her son, written on March 1. He acknowledges her letter of February 21, expresses regret about Catherine's illness, and asks for a portrait of Marguerite. Obediently, he says, "I beg you to remember carefully everything I said before you left, and especially to find out the sentiments of Madame about religion. I well understand that they want nothing more than to separate me from the religion and from you, but I assure you they will never succeed . . . for there was never a more obedient son than I am and I am very sensible of the debt I owe you, not only for bringing me into the world but for all the pains you have taken for my welfare and advancement. . . . I pray to God every day for you and ask Him to bless this marriage."[30]

Nevertheless, Jeanne did not trust Henri—or anyone—to withstand the wiles of the court. Among her first acts was a long interview with Fregoso, with only Louis of Nassau as witness. The Florentine informed her of the state of affairs at court and assured her of the Grand Duke's desire to further the marriage as a means to the pacification of the kingdom. Petrucci reported on March 4, "The Queen of Navarre does not wish [Louis of Nassau] to confide in anyone at court, but he is in communication with the Comte de Retz on all matters, intending to get the best of him." Count Louis' stake in the successful outcome of negotiations was such that he exerted every possible effort to bring about concessions that would both appease Jeanne and moderate her resistance. After several unproductive sessions Catherine said to Jeanne on the evening of March 6, according to Petrucci's dispatch of the following day:

"You always talk in generalities and I do not wish to linger over them." The reply was, "If all my demands are not met, I will not go any further." The Queen Mother then said, "There is no need to talk any more. If you stay at court you will be treated with favor, and if you send for the Prince he will be welcomed with open arms." [Jeanne] then jumped to her feet, shouting, "The Prince shall not come until everything is arranged." The Queen Mother wished to avoid a rupture, so she said, "Very well, to wind things up it would be well for these matters to be settled by deputies named by us. You choose two or three and I shall do the same." But the other retorted, "I will not trust any living person, I shall do it all myself."

M. de Biron, seeing the conversation about to break off, intervened, saying that [a break] was not advisable, and giving many reasons. The Queen

Mother then named M. de Morvilliers, M. de Foix,* and one other to represent her. *Navarra* delayed all day today, but it has been decided not to allow
enough time for her to send for those she trusts. (This last is still a secret.)

The Queen Mother has since said that the King must think of his own
interests . . . and that *Navarra* . . . does not wish a resolution. . . .

This is no small break in the negotiations, because *Navarra* is so obsti-
nate . . . and no real results can be obtained without her agreement.[31]

Jeanne's view of the situation is presented in two important letters.
The first, written on March 8, was addressed to Henri.

My son,

I am in agony, in such extreme suffering that if I had not been prepared,
it would overcome me. . . . I am sending this bearer because I am being
obliged to negotiate quite contrary to my hopes—and to their promises. I
am not free to talk with either the King or Madame, only with the Queen
Mother, who goads me [*me traite à la fourche*], as the bearer will tell you.
Monsieur [Anjou] tries to get around me in private with a mixture of mockery and deceit; you know how he is. As for Madame [Marguerite], I only
see her in the Queen's quarters, whence she never stirs except at hours impossible for me to visit her. Moreover, Madame de Curton† is always with
her and overhears everything. I have not yet shown Madame your letter, but
I shall do so. I mentioned it to her but, being very cautious, she answered in
general terms, expressing obedience and reverence for you and for me too,
in case she becomes your wife.

Perceiving that nothing is being accomplished and that they do everything possible to bring about a hasty decision instead of proceeding logically,
I have remonstrated on three separate occasions with the Queen. But all she
does is mock me, and afterward tells others exactly the opposite of what I
have said, with the result that they blame me. I do not know how to give
her the lie, because when I say "Madame, it is reported that I have said such
and such to you"—and she knows perfectly well that she herself said it—she
denies everything, laughing in my face. She treats me so shamefully that you
might say that the patience I manage to maintain surpasses that of Griselda
herself. If I point out how far I find the reality here from the hope she had
given me of negotiating privately and in good faith with her, she denies it
all. You can judge the position I am placed in from the report of the bearer.

When I leave [Catherine's] apartments, I am besieged by a regiment of
Huguenots, who come rather to spy on me than to help me. Some of them
are important to us and I have to be careful not to set them even more

---

* Jean de Morvilliers, 1506–1577, diplomat and *politique;* Paul de Foix, 1528–
1581, diplomat; René de Birague, 1506–1583, Cardinal and Chancellor.

† Marguerite's gouvernante, Charlotte de Vienne, widow of the Sieur de Cha-
bannes, Baron de Curton.

against me. I also have other visitors, who are no less of a hindrance (though I defend myself as best I can), those one might call religious hermaphrodites. I cannot say that I lack advice, but no two opinions agree.

When she realized that I was vacillating, the Queen said that she could not come to an agreement with me and that some of your people should get together and find a solution. She drew up the list [of negotiators on both sides] that I am sending. She decides everything herself, which is the main reason, my son, that I am sending the present bearer—to beg you to send my Chancellor. I have no man here who can equal him in knowledge or ability. If he does not come, I shall give up. I have come this far on the sole understanding that the Queen and I would negotiate and be able to agree. But all she does is mock me. She will not yield at all on the subject of the Mass, which she speaks of in an entirely different tone from formerly.

The King wishes you to write to him. They have permitted me to consult with some of our minsters and I have sent for MMs. de l'Espine, Merlin, and others.

Take note that they are making every effort to get you here, my son, and watch it carefully [advisez-y bien]. For if the King is determined to bring you here—as is rumored—it makes me more troubled than ever.

The bearer has two missions: first, to warn you how their attitude toward me has changed; and, second, to point out how necessary it is for M. de Francourt to come. . . . I beg you, my son, if he raises any objections, persuade and command him.

I am sure that if you knew the pain I feel you would pity me, for they treat me with all the harshness in the world and with empty and facetious remarks instead of behaving with the gravity the issue merits. I am determined not to let anger get the best of me, and my patience is miraculous to behold. I know that I will need it even more than in the past, and I have braced myself. I fear that I may fall sick, for I do not feel at all well.

Your letter is much to my taste and I shall show it to Madame as soon as I can. As for her picture, I'll send you one from Paris. She is beautiful, discreet, and graceful, but she has grown up in the most vicious and corrupt atmosphere imaginable. I cannot see that anyone escapes its poison. Your cousin the Marquise [Marie de Clèves] is so changed that she seems to have no religion at all (unless abstinence from the idolatry of the Mass be a sign of religion, in all other respects she behaves like the Papists), and my sister the Princess [Françoise d'Orléans-Longueville, widow of Condé] is even worse. Keep this to yourself. As for the King, the bearer will tell you how he indulges himself—a pitiful thing.

Not for anything on earth would I have you come to live here. Therefore I wish you to be married and to retire—with your wife—from this corruption. Although I knew it was bad, I find it even worse than I feared. Here women make advances to men rather than the other way around. If you were here you would never escape without a special intervention from God. . . . The men cover themselves with jewels. The King recently spent 100,000 écus on gems, and buys more every day. They say the Queen is about to go to Paris. If I decide to stay on, I shall go to Vendôme.

Send the bearer back right away, I beg you, my son, and when you write, say that you do not dare to write Madame again, not knowing her reaction to your first letter. . . .

You have doubtless realized that their main object, my son, is to separate you from God, and from me . . . you can understand my anxiety for you. . . . I beg you, pray to God. . . .

The letter, signed, *votre bonne mère et meilleure amie,* has a post-script:

My son,

Since writing this letter, I have told Madame the contents of yours to her . . . she replied that when these negotiations began we well knew that she was devout in her religion. I told her that those who made the first overtures to us represented the matter very differently, giving the impression that religion would be no problem as she had already shown some inclination toward ours, and that, had this not been so, I would not have proceeded thus far. . . . When I spoke to her of this matter on earlier occasions she did not answer so peremptorily, even rudely. I think she says what she is told to say. I also believe that what we were told—about her alleged inclination to our religion—was a trap for us. I take every opportunity to draw from her some word of reassurance. Last evening I asked whether she had a message for you. At first she said nothing, then, when I pressed her, admitted, "I can send none without permission," and added that you should come here. But, my son, *I say just the contrary.*[32]

The second letter, to Beauvoir three days later, brings out even more sharply Jeanne's upset state of mind, including bitterness toward some of her fellow-Huguenots. She is obviously exhausted as well as angry. The letter skips from one subject to another and in spots is scarcely coherent, quite different from her usual, rigorously logical, style, which so often resembles a formal debate.

In truth, you are right to pity me. . . . I have never been treated with such disdain. They still do me honor on the surface . . . hoping to get around me with subtleties . . . but I shall win out by being even more subtle. If anything good is to be obtained here, it must be done by surprise, before they realize it. . . . Anything they promise, they renege on.

Jeanne then refers to the support of Elizabeth's ambassadors, who, she claims, will only make a treaty with France if the crown shows good faith in the Navarre marriage. She believes that Catherine intends to deceive them also.

As for myself, I am fortified from hour to hour by the grace of God, and I assure you I often remember your warning not to get angry . . . because I am pushed to the limit. I have the most marvelous patience you have ever heard of. . . .

I am glad to have matters put in writing, on condition that you and my son do not believe what they say. . . . Since the dispute is dragging on and I have no man here who can express himself as well as Francourt, I pray you send him as soon as possible. . . . Plenty of men here offer their services, but I do not trust them . . . such as Cavagnes, Brodeau, . . . and others, who have long talks with the Queen . . . but I clearly see that they have left the straight path.

Jeanne says that it was Catherine's suggestion to send for Francourt, and for Beauvoir himself, "but I told her you could not leave my son . . . who shall not budge from there except to perform the office that cannot be done by proxy."

Your letter said that you expected matters to be well advanced by now, but you see that they are not . . . because everything has been changed from what I was told and all the hopes with which they lured me here have been dashed. . . . The more I see how things are going, the more I fear [Henri's] coming . . . I am glad you are satisfied with his progress . . . above all, see to it that he persists in piety, because here they do not believe it, and say that he will go to Mass and not put up obstacles as I do.

She is indignant that Catherine—and even Brodeau—should claim that Beauvoir, when he was at court the previous autumn, had held out hope that Henri could be married by proxy in a Catholic ceremony. "I said, 'Madame, it is very difficult for me to believe that M. de Beauvoir said that, since he told me himself that he had assured you it was impossible.' . . . Finally, seeing that I did not believe her, she said, 'Well, he said something.' 'I can believe that, Madame,' I replied, 'but nothing like that.' She then burst out laughing, for she never speaks to me except with mockery."

Biron's predicament is revealed by Jeanne's comment that he

is at the end of his subtleties, and no longer knows what to say. On the one hand, he fears the Queen, on the other, I reproach him, laughingly, with having deceived me. He shrugs his shoulders and excuses the Queen's duplicity as best he can. . . . The more I see of the King and his court, the more our opinions of them are confirmed. Madame had been very cool to me in the last two days . . . the King spends much time making love, but he thinks nobody knows it . . . at nine in the evening he goes to his study, pretending to work on a book he is writing. His mistress' room adjoins the study . . . this court inspires pity but I am extremely out of sympathy with it.

As for the beauty of Madame, I admit she has a good figure, but it is too tightly corseted. Her face is spoiled by too much makeup, which displeases me.... You cannot imagine how my daughter shines in this company. Everyone assails her about her religion and she stands up to them all. Everyone loves her. What makes me angriest of all is that they talk of nothing but bringing my son here. Again this evening the Queen said that they wished to deal directly with him because he is so wise.

M. de Beauvoir, the heart of my letter is to pray you to pity me as the most put-upon and harassed person in the world . . . strangely assailed by friends and foes alike, and helped by nobody except [Louis of Nassau] who serves me without stint and backs me up. . . . I say again that if I have to endure another month like the past one I shall fall ill. I do not even know whether I am already sick, because I am not at my ease.[33]

The letter has a long postscript taking up matters of business in Beauvoir's letter to her, which she says she has burned. She is glad to hear that young Condé is going to Béarn, "showing him the country will provide a good excuse for my son to remain there." She repeats, "I do not know how I can stand it, they scratch me, they stick pins into me, they flatter me, they tear out my fingernails, without letup." She ends by asking him to send the bearer of the letter back at once, and reckons the time required (nine days, allowing him two days in Pau). "I have made up my mind to go no further [in the negotiations] until he returns. I am badly lodged, holes have been drilled in the walls of my apartment, and Madame d'Uzès spies on me."

Even more than on earlier occasions, matters had reached a deadlock. It lasted about two weeks. Jeanne threatened to leave court unless she was dealt with more respectfully and more as she had been led to expect. The Spaniard Aguilon, Alava's secretary who had stayed on at the French court so that Philip would have a continuing source of information even if he lacked an ambassador, wrote to the Duke of Alva on March 14, "the Queen of Navarre would rather see her son burn than married according to the rites of the Roman Catholic Church." The form of the ceremonies was indeed the greatest stumbling block, but there were others. Certain articles of the marriage treaty which took a good deal of negotiating were handled by deputies after the most difficult matters had been settled. (This was the principal purpose for which Jeanne needed her chancellor, Francourt.) The third obstacle mentioned in all the sources was the question of where the marriage would take place. "The King wished it to be celebrated in Paris, because it was the custom for daughters of

France to be married in the capital of the kingdom. . . . The Queen of Navarre argued for a long time over this point, knowing what the temper of Paris is, but when the King made so many promises guaranteeing to keep the peace, she let it pass."[34]

The question of the ceremonies symbolized the other issues, since it tested the sincerity of the King's repeated protestations of respect for Huguenot rights as well as the crown's attitude toward Henri. A complicating factor was the declaration of some Huguenots that they would not recognize the legitimacy of any offspring of a marriage performed according to Catholic rites.[35] If Jeanne and Henri could not rally the support of their fellow-Huguenots they would be dangerously isolated.

In this connection, Louis of Nassau and Francis Walsingham became main actors in the drama. On March 16, Petrucci reported, "to the great amazement of everyone, Count Louis has obtained the King's permission to hold a meeting in the Queen of Navarre's apartments with the English ambassador and other leading Huguenots, to work out the form of the marriage . . . I am informed that she told the King she would put this matter in the hands of others she trusted, but that she has not. The King proposed, among others, the Admiral, and she agreed to hear his opinion. He was sent for, and the Prince, her son, was asked to send Francourt, whom she most trusts with her secrets—a man of evil life." Petrucci then casually makes a brief mention of what, about ten days later, turned out to be the most important factor in resolving the crisis. "The King told the Queen of Navarre, with a very angry look, that he did not wish to be troubled further and that on no account did he wish her to talk to the Queen Mother or things would take a bad turn." Charles' intervention and exclusion of his mother, while it cut the Gordian knot, also threw the negotiators into confusion. On March 19, Petrucci writes, "It had been decided that the Duc de Montpensier, as proctor for the Prince de Navarre, would marry Madame in church, according to our religion, but within two days everything was upset . . . nevertheless, the marriage will surely take place, . . . but it is delayed."[36]

These were the days of Jeanne's final resistance. As Petrucci put it on March 24, "The Queen of Navarre remains so hard and unmoving in the negotiations that even Count Louis is in despair and many Huguenots have turned away from her. . . . Two days ago *Navarra* said to [Marguerite] that, since the marriage could from now on be considered a *fait accompli,* she wished to know whether she would be content to follow the religion of the Prince. Madame replied with great wisdom that if it pleased God she would not fail in obedience to her and to the Prince in all reasonable ways, but that even if he were King of the whole world she would never change her religion. Thereupon [Jeanne] said, 'The marriage shall not take place.' Then Madame said she would do as the King wished. . . . So they parted with little satisfaction on either side. Since then, Madame has pretended to be indisposed. *Navarra* avers that things are not as she was led to believe. . . . Even if the marriage is concluded, it will not be until late April."[37]

This was the impression of an observer well-placed to follow the intrigues of the court, one who had the confidence of Catherine de Medici. Other foreign Catholic diplomats concur in their judgment of Jeanne as a *femina terribile, di humore fantastico,* and mention her attempts to cultivate Margot, but their accounts are fragmentary and their understanding limited.[38] Petrucci himself did not know the real details of what was happening behind the scenes, especially on the Protestant side, as we do, thanks in part to Francis Walsingham and to Jeanne herself. In a dispatch to Lord Burghley (March 29) the English ambassador gives the details of the assembly arranged by Count Louis, to which Petrucci had referred.

Immediately upon our coming she showed unto us, that, with the consent of the Queen-Mother, she had sent for us as the ministers and ambassadors of a Christian princess, whom she had sundry causes to honour, to confer with us and certain others in whom she reposed great trust, touching certain difficulties, which were impediments to the marriage, which thing she would communicate to us after dinner. She said unto us, that she had now the wolf by the ear; for that in concluding, or not concluding the marriage, she saw danger every way; and that no matter, though she had dealt in matters of great consequence, did so much trouble her as this; for that she could not tell what to resolve. Among divers causes of fear, she showed us that two things chiefly troubled her. The first, that the King would needs have her son and the lady Marguerite, the marriage proceeding, to be courtiers, and yet would not yield to grant him (the Prince) any exercise of his religion, the next way to make him become an atheist; as also no hope to grow of the conversion of the lady Marguerite, for that it was said she should not resort to any sermon. The second, that they would needs condition that the lady Marguerite, remaining constant in the Catholic religion, should have, wheresoever she went into the country of Béarn, her mass—a thing which, the Queen said, she could in nowise consent unto, having cleansed her said country of all idolatry. Besides, said she, the lady Marguerite remaining a Catholic, whensoever she shall come to inhabit in the country of Béarn, the

Papists there will make a party which will breed divisions in the country, and make them the more unwilling to give ear to the gospel, they having a staff to lean unto.

So dinner ended, the said Queen of Navarre sent for us into an inner chamber, where we found a dozen others of certain chosen gentlemen of the religion, and three ministers. She declared unto us briefly what had passed between the King, the Queen-Mother, and her, touching the marriage; as also, what was the cause of the present stay, of the same wherein she desired us severally to say our opinion, and that as sincerely as we would answer unto God. The stay stood upon three points, and concerned a good conscience. First, whether she might substitute a Papist for her son's procurator in the *fiançailles;* which thing was generally agreed that she might. Secondly, whether the said procurator going to mass, incontinently, after the said *fiançailles,* the same being expressly forbidden in his letters procuratory, it would not breed an offence to the godly. It was agreed that forasmuch as he was expressly forbidden the same by the letters procuratory, the same could justly minister no offence, for he was no longer a procurator than he kept himself within the limits of the letters procuratory. Thirdly, whether she might consent that the words of betrothment should be pronounced by a priest in his priestly attire, with his surplice and stole. This latter point was long debated; and for that, the ministers concluded that the same (though it were a thing indifferent) would breed a general offence unto the godly, the Queen protested that she would never consent to do that thing whereof there might grow a public scandal; for she knew, she said, that she should so incur God's high displeasure; upon which protestation, it was generally concluded, that in no case she might yield thereto, her own conscience gainsaying the same; so that now the marriage is generally holden for broken; notwithstanding, I am of a contrary opinion, and do think assuredly that hardly any cause will make them break—so many necessary causes there are, why the same should proceed.[39]

Walsingham, with his inside knowledge and his Protestant sympathies, proves the astuteness of Petrucci, believing that, despite appearances to the contrary, the marriage would take place. His own concern, as Elizabeth's ambassador, together with the motivation of Count Louis, appears in a sentence at the end of the dispatch, "Upon the success of the Navarre marriage depends the enterprise of Flanders."

While these intrigues and negotiations were developing and interacting, the King himself brought about the denouement. Faced with the refusal of a papal dispensation, Charles decided to go ahead anyway.*

---

* Pius V died on May 1, having resisted to the end. Catherine's correspondence shows that the new pope, Gregory XIII, was on the point of conceding when Jeanne died (June 9), but Charles had already decided to proceed without a dispensation.

Like Henry VIII in an earlier generation, he mobilized the support of "learned doctors" in his kingdom. Petrucci reports on March 24, "The Comte de Retz . . . is consulting many theologians of the Sorbonne to find out if the marriage can be performed in a manner acceptable to Catholics. He finds so many who say no . . . and a few who say that it is possible, so the matter has been dropped . . . it is sufficient that the King has consulted them."[40]

About March 21, Charles let it be known that, providing Henri would come to Paris for the wedding, he would yield to Jeanne on all other issues. This was received by the Huguenots, even the ministers, as a magnificent manifestation of the King's generosity and goodwill—they tended to make much of the alleged differences between Charles and his mother. The result was that all of Jeanne's erstwhile allies deserted her and urged her to give in to what seemed, after all, a reasonable demand, in return for the crown's concessions. Jeanne found herself totally isolated and forced to capitulate. The King's move had trumped all her aces. The one remaining hope was that objections from the Huguenot ministers to details of the ceremony would provide an excuse for further delay. (There was of course no question of their altering the basic decision.) From a document entitled *Avis sur les ceremonies du mariage de M. le Prince de Navarre et de Madame, soeur du Roy, en la convocation des ministres,* we learn that Jeanne took great pains to make clear that she at least was not selling out to the enemy.

When Jeanne asked if the marriage would be deemed legal if it were not celebrated before a Calvinist congregation, the ministers replied, "considering the urgent necessity of the case, if the consent of the sovereign of these realms can be obtained on no other terms, this ceremony may be dispensed with, and the marriage celebrated elsewhere without scandal." Then she inquired whether they would accept a ceremony performed by the Cardinal de Bourbon. They answered, "if it pleases the King to nominate the said Cardinal to perform that office, the troth of the parties may be received by him, provided that at the ceremony he arrays himself only in the vestments which the said Cardinal wears on ordinary occasions, such as when he attends the royal council, or the court of Parlement. Moreover, that during the ceremony he shall content himself with delivering the ring only to the parties without uttering the accustomed nuptial benediction." Jeanne's third question was "whether it would be unlawful for the marriage to be celebrated upon a platform reared at the portal of the great temple [Notre Dame] in Paris, where the daughters of France have been usually espoused?" After some discussion, the decision was that "it might be permitted, provided that the marriage was solemnized according to the above injunctions." Finally, Jeanne wished to know whether they would object, if, after the ceremony, Henri accompanied the King of France when he entered Notre Dame. They conceded the point, "provided that he leave the cathedral before the commencement of the Roman service, and by the same door that he entered; the said Prince taking his departure in as conspicuous a manner as possible in the sight of all, that it may at once be proven that he appeared there with no intention of assisting at Mass, or at any other ceremony whatsoever."[41]

The document concludes with the statement that Jeanne presented these decisions in writing to the King, who accepted them, "though he was not pleased and subsequently changed the formula in agreement with the Prince." But the changes were made after Jeanne's death.

Jeanne's abandonment of the struggle has been variously interpreted. La Ferrière, the editor of Catherine de Medici's letters, thinks that "ambition overrode" all other considerations, while Miss Freer thinks that her strength had given out, she knew she was defeated, "so she struggled no more." It seems possible that she felt there was nothing further to be expected, realistically. In any case, a letter she wrote to Henri on March 25, shows a certain resiliency of spirit, a determination to make the best of the situation, and even a light touch: "Madame does me so much honor . . . that it gives me hope that you will be pleased. I beg you pay attention to three matters: be gracious, but speak boldly, even when you are taken aside by the King, for note that the impression you make on arrival will remain. The final thing is most on my mind. Every enticement will be offered to debauch you, in everything from your appearance to your religion . . . set up an invincible resistance against this. I know it is their object because they do not conceal it. The King will soon write to you personally. Nobody here knows your height; personally, I think you are as tall as M. le Duc [Anjou]. . . . Your sister has a very annoying cough, which keeps her in bed. She drinks donkey's milk and calls the little ass her brother. This is all I have to say, since I am writing the rest to M. de Beauvoir, except this: try to train your hair to stand up and be sure there are no lice in it."[42]

Jeanne had made up her mind to fight no more, either because she thought she had obtained the best possible bargain or because she was overcome by fatigue and discouragement. The official decision was made on April 4, as Jeanne's letter to Queen Elizabeth announcing that the marriage agreement "was concluded yesterday," is dated April 5. It expresses the view she wished to present to the world.

Madame:

Events which order the destinies of great personages are usually so beset with difficulties that it is impossible to divine their conclusion. Such has been the cause, Madame, why I have not sooner informed you of the matters which I came to negotiate at this court. This uncertainty had not its rise, Madame, in the want of goodwill manifested by those chiefly concerned, but through the evil practices and devices of turbulent men, who opposed thus both the public weal and their own private welfare. Despite these impediments, He, who cares especially for those who rest on His wisdom and providence, has looked down upon me with paternal favour, and has at length disposed the hearts of all to take final and determinate resolution to complete the marriage proposed between Madame Marguerite and my son. This, Madame, was concluded yesterday. Although the Evil One, since my arrival here, raised in many the spirit of dissension and opposition, God has manifested His gracious goodness to the overthrow of their malicious intent; and has inspired those animated with benevolence, lovers of concord and repose, to accomplish this union, I would not, therefore, Madame, lose time in informing you of the event, so that I may rejoice with you, who have so wisely foreseen how greatly this alliance may lead, not only to the prosperity and peace of this realm, a thing which interests Your Majesty greatly, but may also extend its real benefits to neighbouring states.

Amongst so many results, which cannot fail to give you content, I will yet add my own peculiar satisfaction, knowing, Madame, the friendship which you bear me, and that you will sympathize with my feelings. I should justly be accused of ingratitude, if I omitted, Madame, to tender you my very humble thanks for the welcome services which MM. your ambassadors have rendered me here; and as they informed me that it was by your special commandment, this knowledge doubles the obligations which I have so long received from Your Majesty. I entreat you, Madame, to pardon the boldness which your goodness inspires, if I venture very earnestly to desire that I may soon have occasion to congratulate you on a similar event personal to yourself: for I will not conceal from you, Madame, that as one wishful for your happiness and prosperity, I fail not daily to pray that God will speedily give you a husband, in whose society and presence yourself, your people, and your realm may enjoy the satisfaction and blessings which God promises to His children.[43]

The marriage contract was signed on April 11. The most important clauses, worked out through tense negotiations by the two sets of deputies, concerned the inheritance of various lands. Religion is never mentioned. As soon as the contract was signed, those to whom it was a means to other ends swiftly turned to their ultimate concerns. The Treaty of Blois between France and England was signed on April 19. Viewed from outside France, this Treaty and the Navarre marriage made it appear that 1572 marked the height of Calvinist power in France. In fact, however, the Huguenot position had been greatly weakened. Both the Treaty and the marriage were adopted by Catherine as means to offset the power of Spain rather than as steps toward Protestantism.[44]

Once it was decided, Catholics who had opposed the marriage with every means at their disposal complacently assumed the eventual conversion of Henri. The Duke of Alva was told that the Cardinal de Bourbon himself had guaranteed that the Prince would convert, in addition to permitting his children to be raised as Catholics. In papal circles it was regarded as a triumph for Catherine over Jeanne. Alamani wrote to Salviati, on April 15, "the Queen Mother has chosen the best possible way . . . she has abased the haughtiness of the Queen of Navarre, overcome her shiftiness [*instabilità*], and made her accept the conditions. . . . This is a beginning from which Your Reverence can be assured that we will soon see the Prince returning to the bosom of Holy Church." Of Marguerite, he says, "one could not ask for anything better than her ardor . . . she and her mother have dealt so cleverly with the Queen of Navarre that one of these days they will lead her to Mass."[45]

This last was totally unrealistic as far as Jeanne was concerned, but she feared it would be Henri's fate. She had finally given the signal for him to come to court and Biron had been sent to escort him, but there was a further delay because Henri had fallen seriously ill. When this news arrived at court in the last days of April, Jeanne decided to leave court alone.[46] She went to Vendôme for a brief rest, to gather strength for the expected ordeal: Henri's exposure to the court and the marriage itself. Afterward, she hoped to take the Prince and his bride home to Béarn.

XIV

THE READINESS IS ALL

IN Vendôme, Jeanne's principal task was a piece of unfinished business: to hold delayed funeral services for Louis de Condé, killed at the Battle of Jarnac three years earlier.[1] Vendôme had not been visited by its Duchess in over five years, when she had visited there with the children during her unannounced·journey home from Paris in January 1567. The rebellions in Navarre, the Third Civil War, and the completion of Jeanne's administrative and religious system in Béarn had since intervened. We can assume that she felt it important to hold fitting ceremonies for Condé as part of her insistence on the position of the Bourbons, so evident during the many months of negotiation of the Peace of St. Germain and the marriage. It was also desirable to renew contact with Henri's principal fief on his father's side at this time when she was putting her house in order for him to inherit as First Prince of the Blood. No mere son-in-law of the King of France, Henri de Navarre must be as secure in his lands and rights as his mother could make him.

Jeanne had first gone to Vendôme on her honeymoon in October 1548. During the early years of her marriage, before she inherited the responsibilities of Béarn, she and Antoine had spent much time there. To Vendôme she had fled after their rupture during the first days of civil war and to Vendôme she had been banished by Catherine in 1564. She had won a series of lawsuits against other members of the Bourbon family for Henri's rights to the duchy, and the last ducal funeral had been that of Antoine himself. If her mind dwelt on these matters there is no evidence of it, and it was not her way to indulge in sentimental reminiscence, at least on paper. Nor do we know how conscious she was of her failing strength. She was undoubtedly exhausted by the activity of the recent months. Since her departure from La Rochelle, she had worked feverishly, traveled constantly about her domains, and labored long hours with vassals, advisers, and Calvinist ministers. Since December she had been on the road, from Pau to Nérac to Lectoure and then to court. Most recently, for two months past, she had been waging the greatest struggle of her life, against Catherine.

Henri was supposed to join her in the seat of his father's family and together they were to proceed to Paris to complete the practical arrangements for the marriage, but his illness forced her to continue on alone. Messages concerning her son's health and plans were undoubtedly delivered to the Queen of Navarre by persons in her own service, but since they have not survived (or been found) we are obliged to depend on Biron's accounts to Charles and Catherine. Biron's tone is apologetic, as if anxious to prove that he was doing his full duty. Possibly his self-esteem was suffering from failure to negotiate the marriage. After many months of patient effort, fatiguing journeys, and frustrating talks on his part, others had done the job. On the present mission, he had gone all the way to Pau to see Henri, whom he described as "crude beyond the pale" [*creu, hors de raison*], adding, *le trouvera-t-on merveilleusement agréable à la cour.* Since both the Prince and Beauvoir seemed anxious to go to court and Henri could obviously not travel—he had five degrees of fever, according to Biron—the latter had decided to proceed to his own estates and attend to other matters until Henri had recovered. This was in late April. His expectation at that time was that Henri would leave Pau for Nérac on May 2 and arrive at court a month later.[2]

On May 20 Henri had not even left Pau, although Beauvoir was by then expecting him in Nérac. Biron told Catherine that in the attempt to speed up Henri's departure he had sent two messengers since the death of the Pope (the crown hoped that the new Pope would prove more obliging about the dispensation), and that he would return in person if necessary. He did not do so, however, and informed the King on May 23 that Henri was supposed to leave Pau that day. He reckoned that sixteen days would be required between Nérac and Tours if Henri stopped only to sleep. He says, "If I had thought that his relapse would cause such a long delay, I would never have left his side." On May 29 Henri had reached Nérac, further delayed because the rivers were in flood. Biron thought he would be in Bergerac on June 6 and in Tours twelve days later, if Biron could prevent him from stopping in Vendôme. He was not confident of his powers of persuasion, and suggested that the King write to the Prince commanding him to travel with all deliberate speed.[3]

Since Henri could not arrive until late June, his mother was obliged to go to Paris without him. She left Vendôme about May 8, arriving in the capital on the 16th.[4] She stayed at the house of Jean de Ferrière, Vidame de Chartres, on the rue St. Honoré-Grenelle (now the rue Jean-Jacques Rousseau) where it crosses the rue du Louvre.[5] Her days in Paris were filled with preparations for the wedding, buying jewels for Marguerite and clothes suitable for Henri to wear at court.[6] She was putting up a brave front, as we see in the postscript of a letter from Anne d'Este to her mother, Renée of Ferrara: "The Queen of Navarre is here, not in very good health but very courageous. She is wearing more pearls than ever."[7] The Duchesse de Nemours had little reason to sympathize with Jeanne and there was bad blood between them on two counts: Anne was prominent in the Guise faction and she had stolen Nemours from Françoise. Yet Jeanne's gallantry wrung this reluctant expression of admiration from the Duchess.

Shortly after her arrival in Paris, Jeanne had to say goodbye to her best ally and greatest comfort, Louis of Nassau, who left on June 19 for the Netherlands. It must have been a poignant moment for Jeanne, but we cannot place much confidence in the veiled references to impending disaster La Huguerye puts in the Count's mouth, "we must flee from the danger . . . if you and your children are exempt by your station, others lack that privilege." In parting, Jeanne is alleged to have said, "I do not wish to detain you, but every time this clock strikes, think of me, and be assured that when you lose me you will have lost the flower of your friends." The clock was Jeanne's gift to Count Louis. Since his business in France was over and Jeanne knew her health to be failing, it is perfectly possible that she never expected to see him again. There is no necessity to read into the words a premonition of foul play.[8]

Catherine de Medici was not in the capital during Jeanne's first days there but she had deputed the Comte de Retz to make Jeanne feel at home. Jeanne referred with appreciation and gaiety to one of their expeditions in the last letter of hers that we possess, written to Catherine on May 23. "I have seen your Tuilleries fountains, when M. de Retz invited me to a private supper. I have found many things for our wedding in this city during my excursions with him. I am in good form awaiting your arrival."[9] The main body of the letter, and of one to Charles on the same day, is taken up with problems still outstanding in the "pacification," such as discharging obligations to the reiters and obtaining fulfillment of royal promises to individuals under Jeanne's protection. Even if she felt trapped in the clutches of the crown, Jeanne was still a power to reckon with. Philip II took pains to warn one of his agents in Paris against "the evils the Queen of Navarre will try to accomplish," instructing him "to penetrate her cadres in order to discover her designs."[10]

Then, suddenly, she was struck down. On the evening of Wednesday, June 4, returning from a shopping trip, she felt very tired and went to bed. She had a slight fever. In the morning it was worse and she had considerable pain in the upper right-hand side of her body.[11]

It took her four and a half days to die. The ministers in her entourage* immediately began to exhort her at length to accept the will of God, who, as a good father, sends only good to His children. Jeanne's response to the first of these harangues was that she believed all things came from God, that she had no complaint despite her suffering, and that she was not afraid to die. When they urged her to look to God for the causes of her illness, she replied that she asked Him to give her what she needed for bodily health as well as for salvation, "adding, nevertheless, that she 'found this life *fort enneuyeuse* on account of the misery I have felt since my youth.' " They took exception to this "pagan" attitude toward death as a release, declaring that Christians had a duty to believe that life was always good, and that she should pray to live if God willed it. "To this she protested that life was a small thing to her personally but that she was concerned to leave her children so young, 'yet I am certain that God will be their father and protector as He has been mine in my

---

* Aside from Pierre Hespérien, it is not easy to determine exactly which ministers were members of Jeanne's own household, because the documents are not precise. Wherever Jeanne was, Calvinist ministers in the vicinity "attended" her in various capacities, including preaching and conducting prayers at her request. In 1572, some of those we know to have been regularly in her service—like Barbaste and Merlin de Vaulx—had been left in Béarn with Henri. When she fell mortally ill, it is probable that most of the Parisian ministers paid their respects and took a turn in the events described. These would include La Roche-Chandieu, Holbrac, and La Fontaine, and probably Jean de l'Espine. The eyewitness account of her death (*Le Bref discours . . .*) was written by one of them for Catherine de Bourbon, with a covering letter dated June 28. The author cannot have been Hespérien, because he says that he has not had the honor of serving her "but visited your most honored mother during her last illness and consequently [was] a spectator and auditor of her virtuous actions and blessed words." J. Bonnet, who edited and published the *Bref discours* (see note 11), finds no clue to the author's identity.

greatest afflictions, therefore I put them entirely in His hands.' " "These are her exact words," says the chronicler. Exhorted to confess her sins, she did so "with hands joined and eyes raised heavenward, and they assured her of God's mercy."

"When the minister stopped talking, fearing to tire her with a longer discourse, the doctors having said that it was bad for her to talk, she begged him to continue and to speak of salvation and eternal life, adding that since arriving in Paris she had neglected to hear the word of God every day." He then read some verses from Isaiah and St. Paul's First Epistle to the Corinthians. Afterward, he asked her whether she believed that Jesus Christ was her Savior and that she would be cleansed by His blood. "She replied that she believed Him to be her only Savior and Mediator and that she was sure of God's mercy, according to His promises." During this long day of spiritual preparation, Jeanne is described as "uttering great sighs to God to testify to the hope and desire she had to go to Him." She spoke also a personal prayer: "O God, my father, deliver me from this body of death and from the miseries of this life, that I may commit no further offenses against Thee and that I may enjoy the felicity Thou hast promised me." During the General Confession which ended the first full day of her illness (Thursday, June 5), "she sighed heavily when God's mercy to sinners was mentioned and it could clearly be seen that she followed in her heart the words pronounced in her presence."

The pain continued to grow worse, "but no word of impatience or complaint ever passed her lips, as many beside the members of her household can testify, even the Queen Mother and Monsieur and Madame, the brother and sister of the King, who came sometimes to visit her." There may have been several visits, but we are sure of only one by the King and Catherine, probably on Friday, June 6. Sir Thomas Smith wrote to Lord Burghley on June 7, "the Queen of Navarre lies without any hope of life . . . whom the Queen-Mother, the King and all his brothers and sisters have visited and departed without any hope of seeing her again."[12] The chronicle continues, "When God granted her some relief from her pain (for no illness is so cruel as to be without intermission) she made it clear that she wished to recover, refusing nothing the doctors gave her to this end. But as soon as the pain increased she did not lose courage, showing an admirable confidence in the last fight and preparing herself gladly for death."

"To her ladies, weeping around her bed, she spoke comforting words, saying that they should not mourn, since God was calling her to a better life . . . that her only regret was that she did not have time to recompense them and others of her household who had served her well. She excused herself for this and said that it was not lack of good will, but that her illness had taken her by surprise, and that she would attend to it as far as possible." She spoke at length to Madame de Tignonville, exhorting Catherine, through her governess, "to stand firm and constant in God's service despite her extreme youth, to heed the good advice of the Prince her brother, and to follow the fine example of the ladies Jeanne had chosen to surround her."

"Finally, feeling her strength ebbing, she drew up her last will and testament,* in which she commanded her children to live in fear of God and in the knowledge of the Gospel, in the light of which they had been brought up, insisting especially that her daughter the Princess be constantly instructed in it and that to this end she remain in Béarn until she was of proper age to marry a Prince of the same religion." The Cardinal de Bourbon, the Duc de Montpensier, and Coligny were named executors. The will was probably drawn up on Saturday, June 7, because the chronicler says "it was read for the second time in Jeanne's presence by the notaries [Gaudicher and Goguyer] on Sunday, June 8. Having a stronger apprehension of death than formerly, she then sent for her ministers and asked them to speak to her of Satan's special temptations for the dying."

Sunday was spent in a series of long religious discourses and another confession on Jeanne's part. When one of the ministers said, " 'see, Madame, with the eye of faith, Jesus Christ the Savior, seated on His Father's right hand, is holding out his arms to receive you. Do you not wish to go to Him?' She replied, 'yes, much more willingly, I assure you, than to remain in this world where I see nothing but vanity.' " Coligny and his chaplain, Pierre Merlin, joined the death-watch on Sunday night, and the ministers took turns in prayers, "admonitions," and readings from the Bible (St. John, Chapters 14–18 and the 31st Psalm) at Jeanne's request. The ministers were impressed that Jeanne expressed no regrets for the worldly life, "all the more remarkable in that in the days before she fell ill she applied herself with great ardor to the preparation of pomps and magnificences for the wedding of her son . . . it is an admir-

* Text in *Mémoires de L'Estat de France sous Charles IX,* I, 314–318.

able thing that from the start of her mortal illness God had so caused her to forget such things that she showed no concern whatever with them."

"After this night, so well spent, the next day, this virtuous princess, persevering in manifestations of piety and ardent faith, passed from this life to the other, gently rendering her soul to God between eight and nine in the morning of Monday, June 9, 1572, in the forty-fourth year of her age. . . . She spoke with perfect lucidity up to the hour of her death and showed herself as sound of mind as ever, not only in regard to her salvation but in other matters as well."

The body lay in state five days, in a room draped entirely in black. The Queen was dressed in a white satin robe and a mantle of purple velvet. Her crown and scepter stood on a table beside her bed. The impression of members of the court who came to pay their respects is described by Marguerite in her *Mémoires*.[13] For Brantôme's benefit, she includes a curious incident, "too amusing not to be shared with you, although unworthy of being recorded in history. Madame de Nevers,* whose temperament you know, had come with the Cardinal de Bourbon, Madame de Guise, the Princesse de Condé and her sisters, and myself . . . to discharge our last duty [at the Queen's lying-in-state, which was signalized] not by the pomp and ceremony of our religion, but with the austerity permitted by *la huguenotterie,* that is, no cross, no priests, no holy water. We were all standing about five or six paces from the bed . . . when Madame de Nevers, who had hated the Queen more than anyone else in the world when she was alive—and which was reciprocated in thought and in words, you know how [the Queen] used to speak to those she hated—approached the bed, making several deep, humble *révérences* . . . took [the Queen's] hand and kissed it. We, who knew their mutual dislike, considered this. . . .†

Marguerite's list of witnesses does not include Charles and Catherine. Henriette de Clèves would probably not have dared to behave so in their presence. One wonders whether the Princesse de Condé found it "amusing." She at least was in constant attendance on her dying sister-in-law, as she wrote to her children's governess a few days after Jeanne's death. "Arriving in this city, I found the Queen of Navarre at death's door. . . .

---

* Henriette de Clèves, eldest daughter of Antoine's sister, Marguerite de Bourbon. See above, Chapter IX.

† Unfortunately, the rest of this provocative sentence is missing in the manuscript.

She has since gone gladly to her God. This is a terrible loss to us . . . and the reason I have not written. . . . I have had so many unhappy duties on this account that I have not been able to buy anything for the children . . . I had to attend the Queen during her illness and left her side only after she died . . . to escort my niece [Catherine de Bourbon] to the King. . . . She made as fine a speech as possible for one of her age. . . . At court, we are all draped in great black veils."[14]

The belief that Jeanne d'Albret was poisoned is an item in Huguenot mythology developed after the Massacre of St. Bartholomew.[15] It first appears in a libelous attack on Catherine de Medici, *Discours merveilleux sur la vie, actions et déportements de Catherine de Médicis,* published in 1574, and was widely repeated in the pamphlets and polemical writings of the later civil wars. The Queen Mother is supposed to have brought about Jeanne's death through the agency of her Florentine perfumer, René Bianco, who sold Jeanne a pair of perfumed gloves (a regular extravagance of hers) during the last shopping trip. The author of the *Mémoires de l'Estat de France sous Charles IX* (1576) repeats the story, claiming that when the autopsy was performed the head was not opened, on Catherine's orders, so that the poison remained undiscovered. The official medical explanation—tuberculosis and an abscess in the right breast—is given but discounted. This is the only substantial respect in which this account differs from a verbatim repetition of the eyewitness account of the *Bref discours sur la mort de la Royne de Navarre,* written immediately afterward and dedicated to Catherine de Bourbon. None of the strictly contemporary accounts of Jeanne's death (including all the diplomatic dispatches) contains the slightest suggestion that it was due to anything but natural causes—in contrast to reports of the deaths of many prominent persons during the civil wars. On the contrary, all state the true explanation in a tone of certainty. As to the head, the family historians of Henri's reign say specifically that it *was* opened, following Jeanne's own orders. Desnoeds, a Parisian surgeon, performed the autopsy in the presence of Caillart, Jeanne's regular physician and a Huguenot, "at the command of the Queen, in order to discover the cause of her frequent violent headaches, hoping that he could thus cure her children of the same."[16]

The perpetuation of the poison rumor down to the middle of the twentieth century, in the absence of all evidence, demonstrates the vitality of the myth of Catherine de Medici as "the wicked Italian Queen," especially in the Huguenot tradition. Even so, few responsible late sixteenth-century writers believed it: Davila, an apologist for Catherine, who accuses Charles of the crime; D'Aubigné, who fell victim to Huguenot legend in this and certain other cases; and Pierre de L'Estoile, who repeats it in a series of random notes on the reigns preceding the start of his *Mémoires-Journaux* in 1574. La Popelinière specifically denies it as a false rumor.

From her childhood Jeanne had poor health and showed signs of the tuberculosis hereditary in her family. During the last years of her life she lived under constant strain. Her strength was utterly spent in the spring of 1572 and her shopping excursions in Paris took place during an intense heat wave. It is possible that only her iron will kept her from succumbing sooner. In the words of Guadet, an editor of Henri's letters, "My God! let us not search so far afield for the causes of this death. Did not the fatigue, the mental anguish, suffice to exhaust the strength and undermine the life-force of a woman, especially a woman who had written a few weeks before, 'I greatly fear that I shall fall ill, because I am not well. I do not know how I am because I am not at ease.'?"

Yet she retained her vitality to the end and her death came as a surprise to anyone not in Paris between June 4 and June 9. To some it was a terrible loss and to others a miraculous deliverance, but all agreed that it was a severe blow to the Huguenot cause. The most objective commentator, the Venetian ambassador Cavalli, says, "She was a very bold woman [*pleine d'audace*] and her death is causing the greatest possible setback to Huguenot affairs."[17] The Princesse de Condé spoke for the party: "it is a terrible loss to us." The international Protestant cause was affected as well. In a letter to Coligny on June 27, the Elector Palatine wrote, "we are very distressed by it, but we accept God's will." He adds, ruefully, "She has trod the road we all must take . . . but if we had been present we might have been able to prevent it."[18]

To judge by the tone of the documents, the Protestants generally took the loss philosophically. The expressions of joy by Jeanne's enemies far surpass expressions of sorrow by her friends. The nuncio Frangipani wrote to the new Pope on the day of Jeanne's death:

> In a great proof of God's almighty power, on this day of Corpus Christi, the Queen of Navarre died in this city, this morning, on the 5th day of her illness . . . at a time when the Huguenots were most happy to have their Queen here and she was most triumphant, preparing for her son's wedding

. . . and other evils for God's dishonor and the disturbance of Christian states. But God—may He be forever praised!—snatched suddenly . . . such an important enemy of His Holy Church. I hope this will liberate Your Holiness from the difficult problems arising from the marriage of her son with the King's sister . . . we must hope now that he will become a Catholic . . . to which there has been no other impediment but his mother, as his uncle, Cardinal de Bourbon, has often told me. . . . This death has struck hard at the Admiral and all the sect, who see themselves lost by it, and has caused universal rejoicing among Catholics.

Ten days later, to the Cardinal of Como, he expanded on the "fortunate consequences": Coligny was ill and "it is possible God will remove him also," and Henri, now recovered, was showing "a good disposition" from the Catholic point of view. Finally, in a letter to the Archbishop of Rossano on June 28, Frangipani is transported into a double metaphor: "The death of the Duchesse de Vendôme is an event happy beyond my highest hopes. It has cut the most vital roots of the evil plant, thanks to which the infamous goods sold in her store have largely ceased to find a market. Her death, a great work of God's own hand, has put an end to this wicked woman, who daily perpetrated the greatest possible evil. Her son and daughter are in the hands of the crown."[19] From the Spaniards also we learn that Catherine de Bourbon was with Catherine de Medici, and that she was still quite sick. The report of Zúñiga to the Duke of Alva is a factual statement about Jeanne's illness, will, and death, including the royal visit to the bedside. In response, he was told, "all Madrid rejoices that the Devil has got her, at last!"[20]

Jeanne left instructions that she was to be buried beside her father in the tomb of her ancestors in the cathedral of Lescar, but they were never carried out. Instead, she was buried beside Antoine in Vendôme. This may have been Henri's decision, as he had intended to preside over the ceremonies on his way to Paris* and wished the separation between his parents to be passed over in silence. The House of Bourbon borrowed 6000 livres tournois to cover Jeanne's funeral expenses.[21] The inscription on the joint tomb in the Collegiale de St. Georges (before it was destroyed in the Revolution) read as follows:

Here lies buried Antoine de Bourbon, King of Navarre, Sovereign of Béarn, Duc de Vendôme, Lieutenant of King Charles, ninth of this name. . . .

---

* Actually, the relapse he suffered in May delayed his arrival in Vendôme until nearly a month after Jeanne's funeral.

In this same sepulcher lies the most high, most wise, and most virtuous lady, Madame Jehanne d'Albret, Queen of Navarre, Sovereign of Béarn, Duchesse de Vendôme, only daughter of Henri d'Albret, King of Navarre, and Marguerite de France, his wife, sister of François, first of this name, King of France, who died in Paris on the 9th day of June 1572.[22]

XV

A RICH LEGACY

DURING the last five years of her life, while she was putting down rebellion, completing religious and administrative reforms, sharing in the leadership of the Huguenot party, and negotiating with the crown, Jeanne was also bringing up her own two children and standing *in loco parentis* to several other members of the next generation. Henri had his thirteenth birthday just before the flight from court in January 1567, and Catherine her eighth within a few days of their arrival in Béarn. For Henri, the following two years—until, as a result of Condé's death at Jarnac, he went off with the army—was the longest period of close association with his mother he had ever had. More is known about Henri's training than about Catherine's, partly because the legend has preserved more detail and partly because Jeanne carried on a maternal tradition, well-established in her mother's family, of concentrating on the sons.

HENRI'S CHILDHOOD, 1553–1567

Jeanne had been allowed little control over her son as an infant. Henri d'Albret took him over from the moment of his birth. There is no record of Jeanne's sentiments—or Antoine's—about the rustic upbringing imposed by the old King of Navarre on his grandson, but Jeanne at least may well have been in sympathy with the plan. She had grown up in the country herself, and she had never liked or approved of the Valois court. Had it been left to her decision, she might not have insisted to the same degree on the toughening process whereby he went

HENRI DE NAVARRE AS A CHILD

barefoot in the mountains and lived his first years virtually as a peasant child, but it was to stand him in good stead in the difficult years (1576–1589) when he lived with his Gascon troops, often in the open and without material resources. Even if the rigor and simplicity of his earliest training has been exaggerated by the legend, his subjects felt that Henri understood the realities of life—unlike most kings, or even nobles. Henri was endowed with a natural genius for dealing with people, both as individuals and in the mass, a gift that would have served him well under any circumstances, but his upbringing developed resourcefulness, adaptability, courage, and self-reliance as a more confined and artificial environment could not have. It also provided him with a variety and depth of experience on which he capitalized fully in later years, as well as with rich material for his famous Gascon wit.

It is a fact, duly registered in the Archives, that Henri had seven wet nurses before Jeanne Fourcade, whose milk agreed with him, was found. Henri maintained an affectionate relationship with a number of them, giving them estates and their children jobs, and he remained on familiar terms with them even as King of France, many years later.[1] Unlike Jeanne, Henri trusted people freely, sometimes to his sorrow, and his capacity to forgive was exceptional. Where Jeanne was suspicious and prone to *brouilles,* Henri repeatedly forgave when he had been betrayed and personally humiliated.

Three different women shared the maternal role in Henri's infancy: his nurse; his gouvernante, Suzanne de Bourbon-Busset, wife of Jean d'Albret-Miossens, both cousins of the D'Albret princes, in whose charge Henri d'Albret placed his heir; and his mother. Of the three, his mother had the least contact with him until he was nearly four years old. Henri was born in December 1553. For the next year and a half Jeanne was away from Béarn a good deal, at court and in the Bourbon estates with Antoine. Henri lived under his grandfather's watchful eye, in the care of the D'Albret-Miossens in their chateau of Coarraze, near the pretty little village of Nay. Until his death in 1555, the paternal role was filled more by Henri d'Albret than by Antoine. While it is doubtful that Henri could remember his grandfather, he resembled him strongly. Even after the old King's death, Henri saw little of his father, who was at court or at war much of the time. Yet Henri did not seem to suffer from this absence and he became a warm loving father himself. (Visitors to the court of France in the opening years of the seventeenth century commented in surprise on the habit of Henri IV, then in his fifties, of surrounding himself with his children, legitimate and illegitimate, playing with them and teasing them as a natural part of the day's routine.)² Possibly Henri's optimistic temperament was inherited from his grandfather and his "good adjustment" derived from his simple upbringing, surrounded by affection, in which his mother had her part.

The first big event in Henri's life provided the boy's first opportunity for regular association with both parents—their official trip to court as King and Queen of Navarre, in the autumn of 1556. The elaborate welcome offered by the city of Limoges, where they spent Christmas, was Henri's initiation into royal ceremonial. The traditional account of the meeting of the future Henri IV with Henri II foreshadows accurately the effect the former's personality would have on the court in later years. His natural fearlessness, unabashed in the King's presence, and his country style expressed in patois, as he politely but firmly declared that he could not be the King's son because he already had a father, were unfamiliar at court. Henri was strikingly different from the Valois princes. He brought with him a breath of mountain air, strongly flavored with the garlic which had been his first food,* and aroused ambivalent feelings at court: envy and reluctant admiration coupled with scorn. He was the butt of many jokes, which he took in stride, but his nimble wit, enabling him to retort in kind, or better, earned him respect.

When his mother turned Calvinist, in December 1560, he was naturally included in the change. Probably he did not know of the growing rift between his parents until faced with it after his mother's sensational arrival at court the following August. He was eight years old when his parents parted in the bitterness, personal and political, that accompanied the outbreak of civil war, and he became the object of a struggle won by Antoine.

His separation from his mother resulted in the replacement of his Protestant attendants by Catholics under Jean de Losses. His first association with boys of his own rank came when he attended the Collège de Navarre in Paris with three other Henris whose lives were dramatically intertwined with his: Henri de Valois, Duc d'Anjou, later Henri III, to whom Henri de Navarre was alternately an enemy and an ally, whom he succeeded as King of France in 1589; Henri de Guise, standard-

* Both his wives complained that Henri smelled of garlic.

bearer in his generation of the ultra-Catholic party, whose greatest ambition was to prevent Jeanne's son from becoming King so that he could do so himself; and Henri de Condé, his first cousin, who shared the Huguenot leadership until his death in 1588.

The sources do not reveal Henri's reaction to the dismissal of his mother from court (March 1562) and to the emotional warning she is alleged to have addressed to him in farewell. It must have had some effect, because the eight-year-old Prince resisted for three months more the combined pressure of his father, his Catholic tutors, and the royal family, before he capitulated. Philip's ambassador Chantonay reported frequently on the situation to his master, and on May 19 a reluctant admiration creeps into his account. Despite a series of severe punishments, including beatings, "everything remains as before . . . the young man is still very much a child, although he is lively, intelligent, and very handsome. He shows himself very firm in the opinions of his mother." Henri did not consent to attend Mass with his father until the first day of June.[3]

Within a few weeks Henri came down with the measles, and was taken to Renée of Ferrara at Montargis when his father went to the front —never to return. The brief letter he wrote in September, after his return to court, asking for news of his mother, proves that he was conscious of her plight and, probably, of his own, now alone at court. After Antoine's death in November, Henri was a hostage in the hands of the crown for four years. He continued to be the object of a power struggle, but the contestants had changed; instead of Antoine, Catherine de Medici was now his mother's opponent.

Catherine permitted the Protestants Jeanne had originally chosen to resume their functions in 1563. Palma Cayet, also a member of the household, says that La Gaucherie, Henri's *précepteur* until he died in 1566, was "very learned in the Greek language, which he taught in the way one teaches the mother tongue, in daily life. . . . He made the Prince learn by heart selected Greek phrases, without either reading or writing. . . . I had the honor of serving the Prince and of drilling him in these."[4] Among the maxims which appealed to the Prince, says the ex-tutor (but many years later, when Henri was king) were "sedition must be banished from the city," and "victory or death." Occasional glimpses of Henri during this first of his periods of captivity at court are provided by remarks of foreign ambassadors when Henri made himself conspicuous either by taking the lead in the games of the royal children or by falling and injuring himself.[5] One letter to his mother which has survived from these years shows that in some ways Henri at court resembled every child away from home. He encloses a list of books (unfortunately lost) needed for his studies, and says, "I beg you to be so kind as to add some money, as much as you wish, as I have very little left. Please thank good Madame de Tignonville for her gift, although I cannot use it now, such artillery would frighten the Romans here."[6] The present was probably a Huguenot tract, since Madame de Tignonville, Catherine de Bourbon's governess, was exceedingly devout and no doubt apprehensive of the Catholic influence on the boy.

It has not been possible to determine whether Henri spent any time in his own domains with his mother between her flight from court in March 1562 and their reunion at Mâcon (on the tour of France) in June 1564. We know for certain that they did not meet until after the end of the First Civil War in the spring of 1563. Henri was still —or again—at court the following August when Charles IX was declared of age in Rouen.[7] Some writers assert, without evidence, that Catherine permitted Henri to visit Jeanne as part of the goodwill campaign toward the Protestants following the Pacification of Amboise. It is possible that there was such a visit, in the autumn of 1563;[8] but if so, it was brief, and Catherine insisted upon his early return to court. Henri was not with Jeanne in March 1564 when she left Béarn; her chief objective in going to court was to get him back.

Writers hostile to Henri IV, especially Huguenots, are prone to assert that it was during the years 1562–1567, that he was fatally infected with the "poisons" Jeanne so feared: worldliness, vanity, deceit, and corrupt morals. They are scornful of Henri's intellectual attainments, claiming that he did not take his studies seriously.[9] This is in direct contradiction to the accounts of his love for ancient history and his translations of Caesar and Plutarch, emphasized by the family "historians." While it is evident that book learning was not Henri's strong point and that he drew from his studies what he needed as a man of action, he was not without cultivation. A letter he wrote to Marie de Medici, not long after their marriage in 1601, throws an interesting light on the question and on Jeanne's role in Henri's education.

God be praised! Nothing you could tell me would give me more pleasure than the news that you are enjoying Plutarch . . . I never tire of him and always find something new. To love him is to love me, for he was my first teacher. My good mother, to whom I owe everything, and who supervised my upbringing with such care and affection—she used to say that she did not want a son who was an illustrious ignoramus—put this book into my hands when I was scarcely weaned. [Plutarch] has been like a conscience to me ever since, and has whispered in my ear much good advice, both for myself and for the conduct of the government.[10]

Moreover, to read Henri's important speeches, such as the discourse to the Parlement of Paris on the necessity of registering the Edict of Nantes, is to realize that he was a very effective orator.[11] If his speeches are not studded with classical quotations, like those of "the wisest fool in Christendom" (Henri's characterization of James I of England), they show a natural verbal facility and a sophisticated, forceful style. An editor of Henri's letters considers him also a master of epistolary style, combining elegance with spontaneity. He contrasts the King's use of the spoken language with the artificial style of most writers of the period, and regrets that certain of Henri's locutions have not become part of the language—such as *démariage* for *divorce, partement* for *départ* and *de bien en mieux* instead of *de mieux en mieux*. Most of all, Guadet wishes that Henri's use of *du tout,* meaning "entirely," had become standard French. (This usage, among others, is also found in Jeanne's letters; her son unquestionably picked them up from her).[12] It may be that Henri was never properly aroused to intellectual pursuits. We remember that his mother told Beza that he had learned more in a few months from that man of dangerous thoughts, Morély, "than from dear old La Gaucherie in seven years."

There are several anecdotes about Henri on the tour of France. One concerns an episode at Bayonne, when he supposedly overheard the Spaniards plotting to massacre the Huguenot leaders. Their distrust of Catherine's promises is sometimes dated from the Prince's report to his mother, at Nérac a few weeks later. The story is almost certainly apocryphal, yet there is no doubt of Philip's desire to eliminate Calvinism, in France and elsewhere. Such tales indicate that Jeanne's son was an unusual child with a well-developed personality, more than a little conspicuous among the children of the court—and not only because he was a country cousin.

TRAINING FOR KINGSHIP, 1567–1572

After the return to Béarn, Henri's academic education continued (he was just thirteen years old), under the humanist Florent Chrétien,* but his childhood was over. For the next two years, until the Battle of Jarnac, his mother was training him for his future responsibilities, moral and political. "She wished him to grow up, as she put it, 'in the respect and loyalty he owed to the King and his own position.' " Even after his elevation to the supreme command, "what pains she took to overcome the budding passions of her son! She supervised him so closely that one day when she noticed that he had more money than usual, she asked him how he had come by it. The Prince admitted, blushing, that he had won it in a game of dice—something she had absolutely forbidden. The Queen ordered him to be severely punished, although he had been declared chief of the Huguenot party, but he won her forgiveness by objecting, in a tone half-serious and half-joking, that 'it would not be to her credit to treat a general like a child.' "[13] We know from her son himself that Jeanne was a strict disciplinarian and—at least in later years—he approved of this. In a letter to the governess of six-year-old Louis XIII in 1607, he says, "you have not reported beating my son . . . please understand that I wish you to do so every time he stubbornly persists in wrongdoing, for I know well, from my own experience, that there is nothing that can do him more good. When I was his age I was severely punished, by the command of the world's best mother. For this reason I wish you [to punish him] and to let him know that such is my will."[14]

The practical side of Henri's training took the form of accompanying his mother as she moved about her domains in 1567 and 1568, picking up the threads of her administration after her long absence. "She allowed him freedom . . . so that he could enjoy pleasures natural to his age . . . and everyone became attached to him . . . he had the graces of a courtier, and also the tastes of one . . . gambling, dancing, eating, and drinking . . . were his delight . . . women lost their heads over him . . . such a life involved great expense." In order to finance his pleasures, Henri began early to borrow freely; "one can well imagine that nobody refused him." At the same time, Jeanne insisted that he continue his studies. She took

* Florent Chrétien, "long-time retainer of the Vendôme family, and cultivated in literary matters," according to Palma Cayet, *Chron. Nov.* I, 179.

the trouble to explain her policies to him, pointing out that "he could learn from history how little respect was accorded to kings whose lack of learning and knowledge of their people kept them from being able to do their duty . . . she said that he should not be a donkey with a crown on his head, like them . . . and she taught him to distinguish in every party and in both religions those who were really in earnest about the service of God and the King."[15]

The impression made by the Prince on at least some observers is revealed by letters of a member of the Parlement of Bordeaux, which show that the child resembled the future King, both in his virtues and in his vices. "We have here the prince of Béarn; it must be confessed that he is a charming youth. At thirteen years of age, he has all the riper qualities of eighteen or nineteen: he is agreeable, polite, obliging, and behaves to every one with an air so easy and engaging, that wherever he is, there is always a crowd. He mixes in conversation like a wise and prudent man, speaks always to the purpose, and when it happens that the court is the subject of discourse, it is easy to see that he is perfectly well acquainted with it, and he never says more nor less than he ought, in whatever place he is. I shall all my life hate the new religion for having robbed us of so worthy a subject." [And in another letter], "His hair is a little red, yet the ladies think him not less agreeable on that account: his face is finely shaped, his nose neither too large nor too small, his eyes full of sweetness, his skin brown but clear, and his whole countenance animated with an uncommon vivacity: with all these graces, if he is not well with the ladies, he is extremely unfortunate." [Again], "He loves diversions and the pleasures of the table. When he wants money, he has the address to procure it in a manner quite new, and very agreeable to others as well as himself; to those, whether men or women, whom he thinks his friends, he sends a promissory-note, written and signed by himself, and entreats them to send him back the note, or the sum mentioned in it. Judge, if there is a family that can refuse him: everyone looks upon it as an honour to have a note from this Prince."[16]

The first independent assignment with which Jeanne entrusted Henri combined military with political experience, when she sent him to Basse-Navarre in February 1568, as commander of a small but effective armed force. The rebellion had already been put down; Henri's task was to "pacify" the region.

The Prince pursued [the rebels] to the far side of St. Jean-Pied-de-Port, and then, since he could not capture them, he assembled the people . . . and demonstrated how wrong they had been to follow the leaders of this sedition . . . in a speech translated into their language [Basque]. He said that his mother, like all good mothers, wished her children to be strong rather than weak, alive rather than dead, rich rather than poor . . . and free rather than enslaved . . . and that they had no reason to resort to arms . . . since they never appealed to her without receiving a fair hearing and redress for their grievances to the extent that the law and reason permitted. . . . He hoped that his coming would make them wiser . . . so that in future . . . [they would] consider the horrible consequences of sedition before undertaking it. [He pointed out] the ruin of their property and the misery of their families . . . and he assured them that as their fathers had benefited from the benevolence of their predecessors, the Queen his mother and he himself . . . would never be surpassed in justice and good will toward their subjects. . . . If they proved themselves worthy and obedient [his mother] would never infringe upon their liberties . . . and privileges . . . nor force them in their religion. . . . He also offered to act as their advocate to her and told them to address themselves to him without fear.

"The People listened very attentively," continues Bordenave, "and with great acclaim promised in future to be more faithful to the Queen and not to allow themselves to be deceived by those who used their pretended religious zeal . . . to advance their own foul designs."[17]

This account is from the pen of an admirer, but any student of the techniques of the first Bourbon king in the greater "pacifications" of later years will be struck by the fact that his style was already apparent at the age of fourteen. Charm, flattery, appeals to personal loyalty, magnanimity, and wit sweetened the dose to be swallowed, especially when the real message was, "I will be obeyed." The basic formula is familiar, but Henri was to develop it into a superb instrument, on which he alone —among the Bourbon kings—could play.

It was Jeanne's deliberate intention to include Henri in her important acts and to create the impression that he was fully capable and aware of what he was doing. In the *Mémoires,* a political manifesto drawn up to justify her participation in the Third Civil War, she inserts a conversation between Henri and Fénelon which makes the point neatly. When Fénelon asked Henri why he had left his own lands, "to meddle in the troubles . . . my son replied, with the fearlessness of his age and of a true Béarnais, that it was in order that all the Princes of the Blood could die at once and thus save the expenses of mourning.* I believe that [Fénelon] thought my son so young and ill-informed that he was there without knowing why, but [Henri] showed him the next day that he well knew what torch had set fire to France, when the said Seigneur was complaining [about the civil war] . . . my son said that he could put it out with one bucket of water. Asked how . . . he explained, 'by making the Cardinal de Lorraine drink it until he chokes to death.' I have not written down these two anecdotes about my son," adds Jeanne, "in order to boast about him . . . but so that everyone will know that he has not come to the Cause as a child led by his mother, but that his own personal will is joined to mine in recognition of the worth of our Cause, that is, the service of God, the service of the King, and affection for those closely related to us."[18]

Within a few days of this exchange, Jeanne and Henri, having joined Condé, made their entrance into La Rochelle. The official who welcomed them made an elaborate allusion to Henri in the peroration of his speech, comparing the Prince to the sun which would dissipate the clouds. To this Henri replied simply and briefly: "I have not studied enough to speak as well as you do, but I assure you that if I cannot speak very well I can act better, for I am much more accomplished at doing than at speaking." "Remarkable words," adds the chronicler, "revealing a great soul and a lively awareness of his own greatness." With all his precocious skill in politics and diplomacy, Henri was still an active fourteen-year-old boy, full of energy and curiosity and prone to take foolish risks. Shortly after their arrival at La Rochelle, he ventured too far out on one of the dikes, lost his balance, fell into the sea, and started to drown. Fortunately a Rochelais captain saw him struggling and rescued him.[19]

From 1569 on Henri was closely studied by foreign observers at court. The Venetian ambassador Correro includes remarks on the Prince of Navarre in the *Relazione* of his embassy, which presents the First Prince of the Blood at the time of the Third Civil War: "a young man full of wit, very carefully brought up in the new religion by his mother. The general opinion is that he will become the scourge of our times

---

* It was the custom for the ranking member of a branch of the royal family to pay the expenses of mourning apparel for all the surviving members, as well as that of their officers and servants.

HENRI DE NAVARRE AT EIGHTEEN

unless God applies some remedy." Guadet, piecing together many separate remarks, describes him thus: "on the tall side of normal height, with a straight figure and robust limbs; his step was light, his movements fast, but he knew how to be serious and dignified when necessary. His features combined to make his face very attractive: high forehead, eyes full of warmth under their heavy brows, aquiline nose, firm cheeks of good color like his lips, luxurious beard. He felt the need for violent exercise, in arms, horseback riding, and dancing, which he enjoyed more if pretty women were watching. . . . Henri needed much affection, openly expressed. His own emotions were strong and impulsive, his heart overflowed, while his wit . . . scintillated in many jokes . . . which did not prevent his reason from having absolute control [*empire absolu*] over his acts, or from seeing that he carried out his decisions."[20]

Such was the new titular leader of the Huguenot army, proudly presented to the troops by his mother after the disaster at Jarnac. The fifteen-year-old acquitted himself creditably during the war, but we should not take the family historians seriously when they say, for instance, that the Huguenots would have won the battle of Moncontour if Coligny had followed his advice.[21] While Henri took no direct part in the peace negotiations, he and Condé acted in concert with Jeanne during the long preliminaries, writing to Charles IX that they could not consider coming to the peace table until certain conditions were met, especially in regard to the right of public worship for Calvinists. Similarly, in the months that followed the signing of the Treaty of St. Germain, both boys wrote letters to foreign princes in the name of the Huguenot party and the Bourbon family.[22]

Henri's own letters in the two years between the end of the war and his mother's death are echoes of Jeanne's and may be taken as evidence of his continuing apprenticeship—or, that she found it effective to push him in front of her. As early as the summer of 1568, Jeanne had included him in all her dealings with the crown. The restoration of Lectoure, the invitation to Beza to preside at the Synod of La Rochelle, and the demand for the Bishopric of Comminges for his bastard brother were among the important matters on which Henri wrote letters similar in argument and phrasing to hers in 1571.[23] Jeanne also sent him on several missions to Béarn, before her return in 1571. Jeanne's insistence that Antoine's son by Mademoiselle de Rouet be given special consideration reveals the extent to which dynastic concerns outweighed her personal feelings. Henri was probably glad to make a gesture indicating solidarity between his parents; historians in his reign never mention the ill-feeling and separation between them. Palma Cayet and Olhagaray say that Jeanne returned to Béarn in March 1562 because she anticipated the renewal of civil war and for reasons of health. They pass directly to the death of Antoine and the problems faced by Jeanne "unprotected" in Béarn, a flagrant suppression of one of the most important events in Jeanne's life, and Henri's.[24]

It seems that Henri was not as uncritically admiring of Coligny as the young Condé, who called him *mon oncle* and held him in filial affection. Nor was Henri de Navarre ever as much dominated by the Admiral as was Charles IX in the months between Coligny's return to court and St. Bartholomew. Since his father's death, in Henri's ninth year, the boy had not been closely associated with a man who could provide a satisfactory father-substitute (except for Condé in the few months between the flight to La Rochelle and the Battle of Jarnac). Coligny was a strong man and an able commander. When Henri was first exposed to his influence, the Spanish ambassador remarked sourly "he constantly sucks the Admiral's milk," yet by the spring of 1570 observers were saying that Henri was being "dragged" by the Admiral and that he wished to desert the Cause and go to court.[25] Certainly the crown was making every effort to separate the Huguenot leaders, and the Huguenot historians interpret Henri's "restlessness" as proof of the success of Catherine's strategy. On the other hand, Henri's growing independence may have derived from his political sagacity—opportunism, if one prefers—in view of the fact that he had already developed his own style, had been entrusted with important responsibilities by his mother, and was highly conscious of his position and destiny. One cannot help wondering whether he would not have developed considerable restlessness under his mother's tutelage also, if she had lived longer.

Henri received word of Jeanne's illness on June 12, 1572 at Verteuil-sur-Charente; the next day, at Chaunay, he learned of her death. Letters to Charles IX from both Beauvoir and Biron, traveling with Henri to Paris, show his reaction. Beauvoir asks the King to excuse Henri for not writing to him personally by the same courier, "because he is so hard hit by this devastating news which he has just heard." Biron says, "we had decided not to tell the Prince . . . until some hours later . . . but he realized it . . . during the prayers, as the minister was overcome by emotion when he named the Queen, his mistress, so recently dead. . . . It was a bloody blow [*coup sanglant*] to M. le Prince, who . . . rose after prayers with a frozen expression and retired into another room . . . we could hear his anguished sorrow at losing his mother. About an hour later, I went to see him . . . and found him greatly affected, but in a way that showed . . . both piety and courage."[26]

The new King of Navarre immediately asserted his authority over his kingdom. He appointed the faithful D'Arros Lieutenant-General; with the letters patent went a personal letter:

M. d'Arros:

I have received the saddest news in the world, which is the loss of my mother, whom God has called to Himself in these recent days. She died of pleurisy after only five days and four hours. I cannot describe . . . my mourning and anguish . . . so extreme that I find it hard to bear. Nevertheless, I praise God in this, as in all things. Since . . . I succeed to her position . . . it is necessary that I take care of everything for her . . . which is why I beg you, M. d'Arros, to continue as in her lifetime and with the same faithfulness and affection you always showed her. Especially, see to it that the edicts and ordinances of Her Majesty are obsérved without violation, so that nothing contrary to them can be done in the future. Such is my will. I am confident that you will do everything in your power to this end and you, in turn, can be sure that I shall never forget all your good offices, which I will reward whenever and in any way I can, as gladly as I pray to God, M. d'Arros, to hold you in His holy keeping.

Your good master and friend,
Henri

A postscript adds, "Above all, I beg you, keep your eye on the observation of the Ecclesiastical Ordinances, for so the late Queen, my mother, specifically charged me, in her will."[27]

After the Massacre of St. Bartholomew, which followed his marriage (August 18, 1572) by only four days, Henri had to endure another captivity at the Valois court—three and one-half years. He was forced to convert to Catholicism and to revoke Jeanne's religious legislation in Béarn. The Huguenot cause staggered and nearly fell. But in February 1576, he succeeded in escaping, under cover of a hunting expedition, displaying guile like his mother's.[28] His first act, once clear of the pursuing royal forces, was to return to his mother's faith; the second, to rally the weakened followers of her Cause; and the third, to restore her legislation in the kingdom he had inherited from her. In the words of one

Spanish dispatch, "he wishes the heretical ordinances of his mother to be observed, which puts heart in all the heretics and Guyenne is once more bursting into flame."[29]

Henri fought for the Bourbon and Protestant causes, joined and embodied in his person, through the long drama-laden civil wars under the last Valois kings. For nearly four years after he became King of France he remained a Calvinist. Only when he had to choose between the survival of France and his own religious preference did he elect the former. In so doing he displayed the same values as his mother: France came first. Despite the bitterness of Huguenot historians about Henri's desertion, Jeanne probably would have understood, while deeply regretting the necessity. Furthermore, his argument with the Catholic theologians sent to "instruct" him at the time of his conversion to Catholicism in 1593[30] shows that he knew what he believed and why, and that it was not the lighthearted change suggested by the phrase, *Paris vaut bien une messe.** When the enemy, domestic and foreign, was finally defeated, after thirty-six years of civil war, Henri granted his former coreligionists the Edict of Nantes (1598), which fulfilled the demands of the Huguenots of his mother's generation and since. It gave French Calvinists legal standing and rights greater than any religious minority had ever before enjoyed in a large European kingdom.†

CATHERINE DE BOURBON AND ADOPTED DAUGHTERS

In contrast to Henri, Catherine de Bourbon spent most of her first thirteen years at her mother's side but received much less of her attention.[31] She was given a good humanist education, with Florent Chrétien, Palma Cayet, and Charles Macrin‡ as her tutors. Her gouvernante, Marguerite de Selve, Baronne de Tignonville, was assisted by Mademoiselle du Perray and Mesdames de Fontrailles and de Vaux, "all

---

* I cannot find that Henri ever made this point in these exact words, so often quoted. They nevertheless express his dilemma accurately. Until the capital accepted him, the civil war would continue. There are many other documented sayings to the same effect. One involves an old Huguenot friend whom Henri met coming out of Mass a few months after his own conversion. When the King asked what he was doing there, the man replied, "I am here because you are, Sire." "Oh," said Henri, "I understand: you have some crown to gain." (L'Estoile, *Mémoires-Journaux,* Brunet edition, VI, 155; Roelker edition 252.)

† Similar policies had been adopted earlier in some autonomous cities in the Netherlands and Germany.

‡ "Son of the learned Salomon Macrin, colleague of Budé," according to Palma Cayet, *Chron. Nov.,* 179.

women whose entire lives provide a good example," to quote Jeanne's will. Among Catherine's playmates were the Tignonville daughter and Gramont's daughter, Diane d'Andoins, the famous Corisande, later Comtesse de Guiche. Jeanne had built a playhouse for Catherine in the park of the chateau at Pau, *Château-Chéri* (or *Castel-Beziat*, in Béarnais). There mother and daughter spent some of Jeanne's rare leisure hours; she read aloud to the child or worked on her needlepoint while Catherine played the lute and sang.

Catherine, small and slight, suffered from a deformity recurrent in the Bourbon family—although both Antoine and Henri escaped it: one leg was shorter than the other and she limped all her life. Her health, like her mother's, was frail, and she lived only a little longer, dying a few days after her forty-fifth birthday. She was reputed to have a lively intelligence and considerable intellectual cultivation. Unlike her brother, she wrote poetry and cared for the arts and music, but like him she had the gift of inspiring loyalty. Names of Jeanne's old servants (and their children) fill the rolls of her retainers; she maintained warm friendships in a flood of correspondence with such leading Huguenots as DuPlessis-Mornay.

When the Queen Mother took over the orphaned princess in her fourteenth year, Catherine de Bourbon was obliged to submit to instruction at the hands of an apostate from Calvinism, Sureau du Rosier, as preparation for an enforced conversion to Catholicism.[32] After the Peace of Monsieur had ended the Fifth Civil War in the spring of 1576, she was allowed to return to Béarn, a concession to Henri's repeated demands. She dismissed her Catholic chaplain at the gates of Paris and is described as "running" to attend the Protestant services at Châteaudun. Later she and Henri made public profession of their mother's faith in La Rochelle. Then, at the age of seventeen, Catherine became her brother's deputy in Béarn. With assistance from Armand de Gontaut, Seigneur d'Audaux, whom Henri had reinstated as Sénéchal de Béarn, she proved to be an efficient administrator and was very popular with her subjects.

In the two dramas of Catherine's mature life, both of which brought her into conflict with her brother, she displayed temperament and attitudes similar to those of her mother. The first crisis arose from her desire to marry Charles de Bourbon, Comte de Soissons, son of her uncle Condé by his second wife, Françoise d'Orléans-Longueville. She fell in love with him at the age of twenty-eight in 1587. In the words of the editor of her letters, it was *l'amour brusque, absolu, sans réserve et pour toujours.* Although initially he had appeared to favor the match, Henri soon became suspicious of Soissons' ambition and impulsive nature. The situation was not clarified for five years. Henri did not permit them to see each other, but took no coercive measures against either until the Count went to Pau (taking advantage of the King's preoccupation with the siege of far-off Rouen in 1592) and persuaded Catherine to sign a secret marriage contract. Henri's officers arrested him, for his mere presence in Béarn, and Catherine wrote an anguished appeal to her brother: "I have no intention of running away . . . please let me come and talk to you." She speaks of the "insolence of *ceux de Pau*" as if informing him of it. "You are my only support. For God's sake, my King, make clear that you are a good King and a good brother. If I were the meanest woman in the kingdom, you would not deny me justice. If I were to be abandoned by you, I would no longer wish to live . . . I beg you, very humbly, with hands joined, and not without many tears, to receive me."[33]

Henri was not only adamant but furious. When he and Catherine met in Tours the following February, he wrung from her a confession of the secret betrothal and threatened to imprison her in Sedan, at the other end of France. This was the beginning of a desperate struggle between them, which was to last six years. He offered her a choice of husbands: another cousin, Henri de Bourbon, Prince de Dombes, Duc de Montpensier; or Henri de Lorraine, Marquis du Pont, Duc de Bar, son and heir of the Duc de Lorraine. But he absolutely refused to consider Soissons. In an exchange of letters on this matter, Catherine's method of argument is reminiscent of Jeanne's. She boldly refutes his charges of disloyalty, then takes the offensive, accusing him of encouraging his officers to insult her while lacking the courage to admit it, and of keeping her in awkward financial straits by delaying the distribution of properties left to her by their mother.[34] Henri insisted on Catherine's marriage to the ultra-Catholic Duc de Bar. By so doing the King not only allowed considerations of policy to override his affection for his sister, but he violated their mother's deathbed injunction: to keep Catherine in Béarn and to marry her to a prince of her own religion. Catherine would not agree to marry the Lorrainer until 1597, and the struggle was prolonged for two years more because the religious question held up the signing of the marriage treaty.

Catherine de Bourbon
sœur unique du Roi

CATHERINE DE BOURBON, DUCHESSE DE BAR, ABOUT 1600

Catherine's resistance to Henri's pressures for her conversion to Catholicism constituted the second crisis. Ever since his own conversion in 1593 he had been trying to bring this about, in line with his general policy and because Catherine's persistent Calvinism was constantly thrown in his face as a sign of insincerity in his new profession. Many of his former coreligionists had capitulated, but, along with Mornay and Sully, Catherine was prominent in the stubborn minority. When it was rumored (1594) that she had given in, she wrote to Mornay in her mother's tone, combining categorical statements with irony: "I have this one word for you. Whatever is said about my having been to Mass, I have done so in neither deed nor thought . . . I am waiting to go until they make you Pope. . . . Rest assured then, and tell all good men, that I remain steadfast in my religion and that I always will." Enclosing some of her poems in a letter to Beza, in June 1596, she emphasizes "the desire, not only to continue in the holy fellowship of God's church, in which I was brought up from infancy, but also to make sure that all good men and especially faithful members of the church know and rest assured that by the grace of God I will never change." She was true to her word. Not content to remain steadfast herself, Catherine, like her mother, went out of her way to intercede for others and her apartments at court furnished a rallying place for the Cause. She also actively encouraged her brother to force through the Edict of Nantes in the face of violent opposition.[35]

The marriage took place at St. Germain-en-Laye on January 31, 1599. Catherine was then sent to Lorraine. The state of her health obliged her to stop en route and she did not arrive in Bar until March 1599. During the trip she wrote the King. "I have been so sick that I have had to stop for two or three days . . . I shall let you know how I am as I go along, hoping that it does not displease you to be reminded of your little sister and of her undying devotion . . . oh, my dear King, how I miss you. I am sure that the cruel necessity of saying goodbye to you is the cause of my present illness."[36]

Unknown to her, Henri had dealt Catherine the worst blow of all, and perpetrated his greatest betrayal of his mother's wishes: he had instructed Catherine's new father-in-law, the Duc de Lorraine, to dismiss her Protestant ladies-in-waiting. When she learned this, during the journey, Catherine was distraught and she asked him to write her about it directly, "a blow so cruel and hard to believe . . . indeed, I cannot believe it until I hear it from you. . . . I cannot imagine that after obeying you . . . in taking a husband of the other religion . . . you would do such a cruel thing. . . . I beg you, deliver me from this suffering . . . by honoring the promises . . . you gave me when we parted . . . which have been my only consolation for leaving you, without which it would have been unbearable." Referring to continual pressure brought to bear to make her change her religion, she cries, "Have pity on your little sister! . . . I can bear everything else, but this reduces me to despair."[37]

Once in Lorraine, Catherine showed a determination to put the best possible face on the marriage. Her letters in the summer of 1599 make exaggerated assertions of marital happiness in the hope of regaining Henri's favor. In one she says, her husband "loves me passionately and I love him no less. I know this will please you, which is why I am sending you a special messenger." She claims to have been so affected by a portrait of Henri, seen unexpectedly in the ducal palace at Nancy, that she burst into tears. She begs forgiveness for writing so often, "but it relieves the pain of the separation, which otherwise would be more than I could bear."[38]

The main themes of Catherine's letters near the end of her life were her passion for her brother and her longing for a son to serve him. She drank special waters, reputed to be efficacious in combating sterility, brought from Béarn. On August 18, 1599 she wrote, "I love you more than myself . . . Command me, my King, to make you a little page, for I fear that unless you command it yourself, he will not consent to lodge in my body." She tells him that she has had a miscarriage [*j'en ay bien pleuré*] but that she did not dare to tell her husband.[39] The resemblance to Marguerite d'Angoulême's letters to François I is striking, but in Catherine the attachment to her brother was combined with her mother's resolute Calvinism and tenacity in claiming her rights—even against Henri. This same summer of 1599 she reminded him with some asperity of his promise to release her share of their inheritance once the kingdom was at peace and she was married.[40]

One letter of this period reflects Catherine's memory of her mother. She says that if her husband brings down a stag worthy of the King he intends to send him the head as a gift. "How I would love to be the bearer. This is the only way I would ever wish to bear horns, because in this regard I am my mother's own daughter, that is, of a jealous disposition." Like her mother too, Catherine suffered from long, severe migraine headaches, often a sign of repressed anger. In May 1595, she told Caumont-La Force that she was suffering from a headache so bad that she could hardly write: "I fear it may be like the one I had in Pau that lasted for fourteen months."[41]

Although she made two brief visits to the French court toward the end of her life, Catherine never returned to Béarn. She had the comfort of attending her own church only when she was at Nancy and could find a pretext to go to the outskirts of the town where there was a Calvinist temple. Henri, despite a number of half-promises, never visited Lorraine. When his sister died (February 1604) he seemed depressed for a few days but he did not go to Vendôme for the services when she was buried beside their parents in the royal chapel.[42]

Catherine's exploitation by and sacrifice to Henri continues the pattern of the Angoulême family established by Louise de Savoie nearly a century earlier. Marguerite had imposed it on Jeanne, who, despite her own sufferings as a daughter downgraded in favor of (in Jeanne's case nonexistent) brothers, had transmitted it to her own daughter. Hence the echo of the relationship between Marguerite and François in that of Catherine with Henri, with the sister so identified with her brother that her exaggerated devotion seemed undiminished by his egotistical—not to say brutal—violation of her human dignity for his own ends. Transmission of this emotional dependence may well have been a logical extension of the extraordinary external power of kings over others. If she thought about it at all, Jeanne may have considered it necessary for dynastic reasons, or, she may have resented it as a particularly burdensome disadvantage of being female, but accepted it as an example of *la force des choses*. As a child Jeanne had learned to face unpleasant facts. She knew, in another expression of French realism, that *la vie n'est pas pour s'amuser*. If she had cooperated with the inevitable in this respect, Jeanne had nevertheless passed on to Catherine a belief in personal rights, even for women, and the courage to fight for them. Circumstances made religion the most obvious vehicle—and the most acceptable socially—for the assertion of a woman's independence in the sixteenth century. Catherine's long struggle is a striking instance but it is not unique, nor is it the only one in which Jeanne's teaching and example played an important part.

Jeanne stood in a quasi-parental relationship to a number of young people. Some came under her wing because they were orphaned or because their surviving parent was in trouble and had a claim to Jeanne's protection. Among these were Françoise de Rohan's son, young Condé, and Marie de Clèves. Others, such as Catherine du Bellay, sought her protection from positions more remote in terms of family obligation but appealing to Jeanne on religious grounds. In 1561 Jeanne supported the girl against her mother, Madame de Langey, made sure that she became a good Huguenot, and took parental charge of her in every respect. They disagreed again in 1564, over the choice of a husband for Catherine. In an unpublished letter, showing a good deal of realism and common sense, Jeanne says of Madame de Langey's candidate, "it seems to me that if you consider their ages . . . your daughter will be old when the Seigneur is at the age when trouble often starts. . . . [Jeanne's choice] has less fortune, but he also has no sisters to provide for. . . . His affection for your daughter, and hers for him, is beyond question. You will wrong her if you withhold your consent. . . . I am showing you how strongly I feel in this matter because . . . it is much better not to let things drag along . . . but to settle them."[43] In the end they compromised on a third man, Charles de Beaumanoir, Marquis de Lavardin, but it was really a victory for Jeanne, since he was a zealous Huguenot and her devoted vassal.

With her niece Marie de Clèves, on the other hand, Jeanne's training was a failure. She had given her a Calvinist upbringing and arranged for her marriage to young Condé, but by 1572 Marie's behavior at court disgusted her. The marriage was unhappy; Marie, soon mistress of Henri d'Anjou, became involved in unsavory scandals. When she died in childbirth two years later, it was widely believed that Catherine de Medici had had her poisoned.[44]

Historically, the most important young woman Jeanne ever helped to defy her parents and assert her independence via la Cause, was her distant cousin, Charlotte de Bourbon, daughter of Louis, Duc de Montpensier,* and Jacqueline de Longwy.[45] Jacqueline had been much beloved and influential with all court factions before her death in 1561. As lady-in-waiting and close friend of Catherine de Medici, she had often interceded for Huguenots, and Jeanne credits her with saving Antoine's life in 1560. Although Jacqueline had been known for her liberal religious ideas, she had placed Charlotte—the second of five daughters in a family of high station but little money—in a convent. The court was

* Father of the man mentioned as a suitor of Catherine de Bourbon.

shocked in 1571 when the Abbesse de Jouarre fled in disguise, renounced her vows, and became a Calvinist. On Jeanne's advice she went first to Sedan, to the protecting roof of her older sister, Françoise, whose husband, the Duc de Bouillon, was influential—and a Calvinist. Her father's rage and that of the King made it unsafe for Charlotte to stay in France and in February 1572, she went to the court of the Count Palatine, where she spent two years.* Charlotte appealed again to Jeanne, the highest ranking Protestant in France, to intercede for her. The request came at the most awkward time possible—late March 1572—as Jeanne was waging her final battle with Catherine de Medici. On April 5, the same day that she announced the conclusion of the marriage negotiations to Queen Elizabeth, Jeanne replied that she had written to thank the German prince for his hospitality to Charlotte and that she hoped the marriage between Henri and Marguerite would serve Charlotte's cause. "I shall have more credit and you can make use of it, as is always the case with children of good parents." She reports that she has appealed to Charlotte's father in vain, "but I shall never weary of doing what a mother should for you."[46] Utterly spent, with only a few weeks to live, it was in character for the woman who had defied François I at the age of twelve to risk further trouble in order to help another young woman to fight against injustice imposed by superior force and to assert her own identity.

If self-reliance in the child is a sound criterion of a parent's success, Jeanne's achievement was considerable. Both her children demonstrated in their mature lives the ability to know what they wanted and to pursue it courageously in the face of difficulty. Both showed, in their separate ways, respect for her values. Each built on some aspect of her achievement and reflected the devotion Jeanne had given them.

---

* Charlotte de Bourbon became the third wife of William of Orange in 1574. In an ironic twist, one of their six daughters turned Catholic, went to France, and became Abbess of a convent near Poitiers.

EPILOGUE

DESPITE Henri's devotion to his mother and her Cause, he disposed of her earthly remains to suit his own purposes, in disregard of her wishes. There is a certain classic symmetry in the fact. Her father and uncle had used her for their own ends in her childhood and her husband had exploited her in her prime. The strength of her will as she resisted her fate, even when she could not change it, is striking. Calvinist eulogies emphasize her constancy and courage; the very intensity of her enemies' hatred and fear testifies to the force of her character. Neither the highhandedness of François I nor the egotism of Henri d'Albret nor the treachery of Antoine nor the guile of Catherine de Medici could break her spirit. On the contrary, in each struggle she was able to perfect her weapons for use in the succeeding one. The qualities of constancy, single-mindedness, and perseverence can also be described as rigidity, self-will, and stubbornness. Jeanne developed all these qualities at a very young age, and they matured with the years.

The factors contributing to her strength included a keen intelligence, freely conceded by her worst enemies; extraordinary willpower, enabling her to achieve self-reliance at an early age; boldness or audacity; and an exceptional nervous vitality and stamina, despite poor physical health. The fruits of this combination were realism and toughness, seen in her ability to stand pain and discouragement; a sense of timing suited to the fulfillment of her wishes; and a capacity for sublimation. On the other hand, severe inner pressures partially blocked the free operation of these assets. At the root of these lay anger. Jeanne's childhood belief that she had scores to settle is amply documented in the letters of her mature life and in the *Mémoires*—catalogues of "wrongs," injustices, and demands. At least in her later years, Jeanne was conscious of her anger; she describes efforts to control it. She had a suspicious nature, at times verging on a persecution complex—especially in relation to the Guises—and

4 1 9

habitually became *brouillée* with anybody who would not knuckle under to her imperious will.

Jeanne's inner pressures were reinforced by external circumstances—opposition by others, often more powerful than she was—so that her strength often took the form of inflexibility, authoritarianism, or aggressiveness. She seems to have believed that offense was the best defense. Her dealings with opponents exhibit a consistent pattern: a brief but effective refutation of their charges, followed by counteraccusations. In the latter phase she showed great resourcefulness. The confrontations with Monluc, Descurra, Armagnac, and Spifâme illustrate the pattern. The struggle with Catherine constitutes a series of self-justifications and counteroffensives. The power of the crown was so much greater than Jeanne's that she could not win, but she extracted every possible advantage from her few assets and made Henri's position much stronger than it would otherwise have been.

Conflict between the effort to control anger and her clearly articulated wishes produced much tension, resulting in violent headaches, pessimism, a tendency to obsession—especially with injustice—and what others described as Jeanne's *humore fantastico*. When the pressures were particularly severe or when she was unsure how to proceed, she would shift from one idea, policy, or means to another, with a suddenness startling to observers and disconcerting to those dealing with her. Sometimes she resorted to apparent helplessness: for example, her disarming request to Descurra for advice about her religious policy in 1563. This may have been an unconscious way of testing out different tools or weapons. The effect of these moods on others was their conclusion that it was necessary to "handle" (*ménager*) her.

Jeanne tended to fasten on small, sometimes ridiculous, incidents, and blow them up out of all proportion, so that they became, for her, important symbols. For example, just before Jeanne left the royal tour in 1564, frustrated by Catherine's refusal to let her go home or to take Henri with her into "exile," a scrap of paper was retrieved from the mouth of a small dog by one of Jeanne's servants. Although it lacked salutation and signature, it appeared to be a letter from Catherine de Medici about her troubles with the Huguenots. Because Anne d'Este, Duchesse de Guise, had a room opening off the same balcony as her own, Jeanne concluded that the dog had found the paper in the Duchess' wastebasket, and she insisted on confronting Catherine with it, as evidence of complicity with Spain, in the presence of a secretary of state. Four years later, she was still angry enough to tell the story at length in the *Mémoires,* concluding, "this shows how God finds out the most closely guarded secrets . . . it revealed the evil designs of *ceux de Guise* against us."[1]

Jeanne was not only touchy about her rights, but about her intelligence and about the competence of women in general. She took pains to refute charges of "imbecility" (when, where, or by whom, is not on record) in her move to La Rochelle, and she added, "I will not stoop to refute [the argument that women are imbeciles] but if I wished to undertake the defense of my sex, I could find plenty of examples . . . these people [who say so] deserve only pity . . . for their ignorance."[2] These sudden bursts of anger were more frequent toward the end, when she was physically worn out and involved in the most important fight of her life. More characteristic were confident aggressiveness or dissimulation. When circumstances made aggressiveness impracticable, Jeanne deliberately laid a false scent to mislead the enemy. Outstanding instances of this are her concealment of her religious views until 1560; her apparent docility in Paris in 1566, and her dealings with Monluc, with the Navarre rebels, and with the crown in 1568. In each case dissimulation was the only means by which she could reduce the odds against her, and it was usually successful. When conditions changed, favoring her designs, Jeanne would revert to aggression and intransigence, as we see in the substitution of a rigid, authoritarian religious policy after Montgomery's victory for the greater toleration of the earlier years, when her rule was less secure. If others reacted to her temperamental outbursts by trying to manage her, experience with her dissimulation made them distrust her. Hence the repeated attempts of royal, Spanish, and papal agents to "discover her designs" or to corner her so that she would have to "declare her real intentions." Although Jeanne frequently fooled others, she rarely fooled herself. She was aware that she was *ung petite glorieuse* and several times boasted of her ability to outwit her opponents.

Rumors of a mysterious episode toward the end of her life must be mentioned while considering Jeanne's dissimulation. Some writers have believed that Jeanne contracted a secret marriage in La Rochelle, sometime between the Peace of St. Germain and the synod held there in April 1571. But the alleged sources do not stand up under scholarly scrutiny and failing reliable proof the story must be rejected as apocryphal (see

Appendix D). Given the watch her enemies kept on Jeanne and the efforts they made to discredit her, such a secret would have been very hard to keep. An item in one Spanish dispatch virtually proves the point. On December 11, 1569, Alava wrote to Philip II, from Tours, "they say the Queen of Navarre is so sick in La Rochelle that she cannot come to see the Queen. Some even say it is because she cannot conceal the fact that she is pregnant."[3] Philip's agents surely made an effort to follow up this item, and if they had discovered anything of this nature at any time, they would have made use of it.

Jeanne's suspiciousness and aggressiveness isolated her from others. There is abundant evidence that she inspired respect, sometimes awe, in those who hated her, but little spontaneous affection, even in those who agreed with and obeyed her. Her relations with her parents, Aymée, and Antoine were strained—in the last two cases to the breaking point. Renée of Ferrara tried to love her like a daughter but found her hard to live with. Françoise de Rohan, nearest in age and blood and almost like a sister, has left no first-hand record of her feelings, but Marguerite's poem shows that Jeanne tyrannized over her. With two exceptions— Viret and Louis of Nassau—her colleagues and allies do not seem to have been her friends. A lonely child, Jeanne was even more solitary as a woman. Her religion was undoubtedly important in relieving this situation; only God was reliable, and only He did not talk back.

Resentful of those above her in station and cut off from friendship, Jeanne's most successful human relationships were with those who were dependent upon her: children, her own and others, servants, officers in her employ, and faithful vassals. A considerable range in her epistolary style reflects this. Formal or "polite" letters, such as those to Montmorency or Queen Elizabeth, are written in long, involved sentences, almost impossible to translate literally, although their style is less artificial and self-conscious than the youthful letters-in-verse to Marguerite. Her official or "royal" style, in letters to her vassals or to the Council of Geneva, is much more straightforward, with a self-confident dignity. In correspondence with the crown, the elements of self-pity and self-justification are sometimes uppermost; the best example of this mood, and its incoherence, is the letter to Beauvoir in March 1572. At other times, as in the letter to Armagnac, "debater's" style predominates. Even in her angriest letters to Catherine or Charles Jeanne could not give rein to her anger as she could to the Cardinal, who owed his original rise in the world to her mother's patronage. Her vocabulary with those she could not control is thick with words that express anger, *faschée, marrie, navrée, contrariée, tracassée, outrée. . . .*

Jeanne's letters to her dependents, on the other hand, are more directly expressed and seem to flow naturally from her pen. They are more eloquent, sometimes lightened with warmth and wit. Her feelings toward a particular correspondent or her mood when writing are often discernible. Her correspondence with the faithful Caumont-La Force shows affectionate concern for his welfare and that of his family. The sharpness for which she was known among her enemies is totally lacking in letters to the few persons she trusted—except when referring to her opponents. Conversely, when she was angry or on the defensive, pretentious stylistic devices creep in. Letters to Beza are of special interest because he was one of a small number of persons whom Jeanne really respected and because they cover a wide variety of subjects, from personal matters like her health or her opinions of Henri's tutors to her political philosophy and the state of the Cause. Most interesting of all are the letters to Catherine, which bring out every facet of Jeanne's mind except the affection and trust she held in reserve for the privileged few.

Letters thanking those who had been faithful to her service and missives embodying pardons, gifts, or favors to those dependent upon her bounty show the most agreeable, and most womanly, side of Jeanne's character. Much has been made of Jeanne's masculine characteristics. To cite only two opinions—from spokesmen of the two camps in the generation following Jeanne's—De Thou said that she had the mind of a man and D'Aubigné that she had only the body (*le sexe*) of a woman. It is true that her aggressiveness and audacity in the face of danger were of a kind more usually found in men. On the other hand, Jeanne's power of endurance, her periodic spells of self-pity, her tendencies to lose her temper and to hold grudges, as well as her maternal sense of responsibility are "feminine" characteristics, as is the projection of her ambition onto her son.

It remains to consider whether Jeanne's public career affected the history of France in any way whatever. Three distinct but interrelated influences are discernible. There is no doubt that "the little corner of Béarn" bore the imprint of her legislation and administration as long as it remained a separate political unit. Since its absorption into France, Béarn, like other former feudal sovereignties, has retained local particularities beneath the high degree of national centralization; but these are the heritage of many generations, of which Jeanne represents only one. On the national scale, the Huguenot party and the Calvinist movement—overlapping but not quite identical—reached their apex between 1561 and 1572, precisely when Jeanne shared in the leadership of both. Given her single-mindedness and effectiveness, it seems logical to conclude that she contributed to their temporary success. The Edict of Nantes fulfilled Jeanne's demands for her coreligionists and Henri's settlement of the war with Spain pacified the kingdom as she had wished. Even since the fall of the House of Bourbon, for which she sacrificed so much, Henri's special place in French hearts continues some aspects of the "destiny" she wished for him. On balance, Jeanne d'Albret probably left as much of a mark as most women who seek fulfillment in causes doomed to be lost.

Jeanne's life illustrates the interaction between a human being and her environment, or, between "life history" and history. Because she was a woman, only a princess could have had Jeanne's career. The lives of at least two other French princesses (her own mother and Renée) exhibited some of the same elements. Yet neither of them had the special quality that made it necessary for Jeanne to choose the hard way, to "take arms against a sea of troubles," from the time of the Cleves marriage to the day she rendered her spirit to her God and her kingdom and Cause to her son.

APPENDIX A

A Note on Estates

Under the *ancien régime,* French society was divided into three Estates of the realm: clergy; nobility; and the third estate, which included the peasants as well as the middle class. The Estates-General were sessions called by the King when he needed financial, military, and moral support from all classes. Since they were also dismissed at the royal will and had never acquired the power of the purse, they had not become a check on the crown. Yet because the meetings were largely bargaining sessions in which the representatives agreed to vote subsidy or raise armies in return for the redress of grievances, the Estates-General were regarded as a recourse against misgovernment, especially by the third estate.

The Estates-General of 1484 (under Charles VIII) had been the most effective in French history. Neither François I nor Henri II, both strong kings, had recourse to them. Demands for a meeting of the Estates-General were a natural reaction to the situation in 1560: a seventeen-year-old-king (François II), dominated by powerful, nonroyal uncles. The Guises were generally unpopular, but the Princes of the Blood and the Huguenots were most threatened by them. The Bourbons had been supplanted at court and the Calvinists faced extermination if the ultra-Catholic policy of the Guises was not checked. (The 1560 session of the Estates-General has been ably studied by J. R. Major, *The Estates-General of 1560* [Princeton, 1951].)

In the Estates-General, the representatives of each order met separately, except in the ceremonial opening and closing sessions. Members of the clergy and nobility were called by royal writ, by name, for example, Bishop of Chartres, Duc de Guise. The third estate elected its members. (For details see R. Doucet, *Les Institutions de la France au seizième siècle* [Paris, 1948], I, 312–337). Although the third estate constituted the vast majority of the population, its influence in the Estates was often slight, since the two others were really representative of the same class, the landed aristocracy, and the vote was registered "by order" and not "by head."

Béarn like many other provinces had its own Estates. Unlike the Estates-General, however, they played an important part in the regular process of government, with annual meetings. Between sessions their interests were represented by officers elected for the purpose, *jurats* and syndics. The Estates had many specific rights and privileges and were generally regarded as guardians of the *fors,* Béarn's charter of liberties. The vicomtes were obliged to respect the wishes of the Estates if they were to receive necessary subsidies and to rule successfully. A special feature of the Béarnais Estates was the custom of meeting in two Houses instead of three; the five ranking members of the clergy (two bishops and three abbots) sat with the nobility. (Dartigue, whose studies are frequently cited throughout the text, is the foremost authority on the subject: *La Vicomté de Béarn sous Henri d'Albret* [Paris, 1934] and *Jeanne d'Albret et le Béarn* [Mont-de-Marsan, 1934].)

APPENDIX B

The Wars of Religion
and Huguenot Resistance Theory

Historians have distinguished eight separate Wars of Religion in France. The fighting which began in April 1562 and ended in the Pacification of Amboise, March 19, 1563, counts as the First. The Second and Third Civil Wars also took place in Jeanne's lifetime, and during the latter she reached the height of her career. For the nonspecialist, it is sufficient to realize that there were thirty-six years of civil war, punctuated by periods of truce, involving two generations of Frenchmen. Political factors were at least as important as religious factors. The basic configuration was constant: the crown and the majority of Frenchmen were Gallican in sentiment, while the French arm of the Counter Reformation, led by the House of Guise-Lorraine, brought pressure on the crown to prevent concessions, political or religious, to the Calvinists. The weakness of the last Valois Kings (François II, 1559–1560; Charles IX, 1560–1574; Henri III, 1574–1589) obliged their mother, Catherine de Medici, *de facto* ruler until the 1580's, to make concessions, sometimes to the Huguenots and sometimes to the Guises. From the earliest days of the struggle she learned to play them off against each other, favoring the weaker when she could.

Although the religious affiliation of the Guise party was heavily emphasized by their publicists, scholars agree that political factors were more important. (See L. Romier, *Les Origines politiques des guerres de religion* [Paris, 1913–1914]; N. M. Sutherland, "The Foreign Policy of Philip II and the French Catholic League," in *History* [October 1966], 322–331: "primarily a conflict of power, patronage and security"; and De Lamar Jensen, *Diplomacy and Dogmatism* [Cambridge, Mass., 1964].) Astute *politique* contemporaries, like Pierre de L'Estoile, had already realized this. L'Estoile often refers to the use of the "mantle of religion" by the Guises.

To some extent, but much less, the same can be said of the Huguenots. The strength of the Huguenot party lay not in its religious adherents, a small minority despite their aggressiveness and fortitude, but in the fact that an important section of the nobility, led by some members of the Bourbon branch of the royal family, had turned Calvinist. Some at least had political motives: to keep the Valois weak, to oppose the Guises, and to retain or revive their own traditional privileges.

In the first decade, or first three "wars," 1562–1572, the Guise faction was led by the Cardinal de Lorraine and his brother Duc François de Guise; the Huguenot faction by the Prince de Condé (until his death in 1569), Admiral Gaspard de Coligny, and Jeanne d'Albret. In the second generation, the Holy League, as the ultra-Catholic party called itself after about 1575, was led by Duc Henri de Guise, son of François, and after his assassination (at the hands of Henri III) in 1588, by his brother Claude, Duc de Mayenne. The Huguenot party in the second generation was led by Henri de Navarre (Henri IV after 1589), until his conversion to Catholicism in 1593.

In the course of the wars there gradually emerged a third party, the *politiques,* Catholic (in the Gallican sense) and royalist, who preferred to make some concessions to the Huguenots rather than see France fall under Spanish domination, as seemed inevitable in case of a victory for the League. Some *politiques* rallied to Henri IV immediately upon his accession, and by his conversion he became their leader; the moderate majority could then prevail. Nevertheless, it took him nine years (to 1598) to end the civil wars, partly by defeating the Spaniards and the League forces in battle, partly by political ingenuity and charismatic leadership, and partly by granting limited freedom of worship and political equality (the Edict of Nantes) to his former coreligionists.

Details of the earlier wars and treaties are given in the text or in footnotes only insofar as they are needed to follow Jeanne's career. A reader wishing fuller information should consult J. W. Thompson, *The Wars of Religion in France* (New York, 1909); E. Armstrong, *The French Wars of Religion* (London, 1904); or the relevant sections of volumes V and VI of Lavisse, *Histoire de France.*

HUGUENOT THEORY ON THE RIGHT OF RESISTANCE

Huguenot thinkers differed among themselves about the right to resist established authority. Calvin and Beza maintained that only spiritual and "constitutional" means were legitimate, but a certain evolution is discernible in their definition of the latter term. Calvin, while condemning the Conspiracy of Amboise, said that he would regard differently a movement led by a Prince of the Blood (Antoine or Condé), whom he recognized as "natural and legal defenders" of the peoples' rights. Both he and Beza encouraged the notion that an Estates-General ("lesser magistrates") might legally oppose the crown. The secular Huguenot leaders, therefore, felt it necessary constantly to justify their resort to arms in their many manifestoes, including Jeanne's *Ample Déclaration* or *Mémoires.* Toward the end of the wars a theory of legitimate resistance to tyranny, including tyrannicide, was

428

developed on the Catholic side, especially by Jesuit writers. Because the Huguenots were pioneers in the development of "constitutional" theories of monarchy, and because the Puritans in seventeenth-century England were influenced by their arguments, modern scholars have paid considerable attention to Huguenot political thought. The principal works on this subject are listed in Chapter XI, note 33.

Church-State Relations in Béarn, as decreed in the Ecclesiastical Ordinances of Jeanne d'Albret, November 1571

Excerpts from C. Dartigue, *Jeanne d'Albret et le Béarn*, pp. 145–164

PREAMBLE

Jehanne, by grace of God Queen of Navarre, Sovereign Lady of Béarn and Domezan, Duchesse de Vendômois, Beaumont, Albret . . . Comtesse de Foix, Armagnac, Périgord . . . Vicomtesse de Limoges. . . .

To all present and to come: health and joy.

There is no monarch alive who is not obligated to use his full powers to place his subjects under the rule of Jesus Christ, since the Eternal Father has given Him all power in Heaven and earth and commanded all His creatures to seek Him above all things. How much greater is the obligation of princes whom He has saved from sin and death by his grace and goodness alone to procure the complete establishment and advancement of [Christ's] kingdom. If it be their duty to conserve the public peace, which affects only their own estates, how much greater [is their duty] to establish piety so that the administration will not fail to destroy anything by which God is not purely served according to His word. Who then can doubt that princes who do not follow the examples of Josiah, Ezechial, and Theodosius will fall under the wrath of God in the end? These [princes] . . . were moved by the spirit of God to eject all idolatry and superstition from their domains and to enthrone instead the true religion. . . .

The punishment [of princes who do not follow such examples] would be all the more justified if, their subjects being ready to embrace the Gospel (as in the case of our own) they failed in any degree to assure the eternal salvation of those for whom they shall have to answer if they neglect to do so.

In order, therefore, to obey the Lord's commandment, to fulfill the obligations of a Christian, to respond to the vocation given us by God, to procure the salvation of our subjects, to assure the unity of our administration and of the public peace, to follow the example of good princes and kings, to avoid the terrible wrath of God's judgment, and to comply with the request of the latest Estates of Béarn, the sovereign country bound to obey us, legitimately assembled, in which they begged us, of their own free will, to banish all false services, idolatries, and superstitions and to declare the pure word of God and to administer the baptism and Holy Communion according [to His word], we have said and declared, and now do ordain, say, and declare by this present edict, perpetual and irrevocable, that it is our will that all subjects of the said country, of whatever quality, condition, sex, or estate, shall profess publicly the Confession of Faith that we here publish by our authority as surely founded on the doctrine and writings of the Prophets and of the Apostles.

And so that none shall be in ignorance, we have ordained that it be here inserted, word for word (Dartigue, 147–148). [Here is inserted the Confession of La Rochelle, as formulated by the synod held in that city in April 1571.]

[Even in matters under the jurisdiction of the clergy, the final authority rests with the secular magistrates, by decree of their sovereign. The following excerpts are particularly relevant.]

Article 1 (*ibid.*, 148)

The clergy . . . shall be subject not only to the magistrates and to our laws, but to all points established by our authority in consultation with the national synod of the said country . . . and if anyone attempts to exercise a ministry without an authorized vocation . . . he shall bow to the discipline of the church and be punished and chastised by our magistrates by banishment from our said country for two years . . . and may only return when the national synod is satisfied that he has repented and abandoned his rebellion, scandalous behavior, and obstinacy.

Article 11 (*ibid.*, 152)

Those who are legitimately called to the consistory . . . before exercising their charge in any manner whatever, . . . shall take an oath before the magistrates of their place of residence . . . to eliminate all idolatry, superstitions, and everything contrary to God's commandments . . . and if anyone is summoned before the consistory and fails to obey . . . it is our will that he be constrained by our judges and magistrates.

Article 15 (*ibid.*, 153)

. . . We ordain that every year the national synod of our country of Béarn, meeting at such times and in such places as we ordain, shall proceed under our authority to establish a council, which shall consist of nine persons, zealous in piety and filled with the word of God . . . to seek out, conserve, and distribute ecclesiastical wealth . . . after they have been commissioned by us and have sworn an oath of loyalty to us, or, if we are absent, to our legitimate deputy. . . .

Article 25 (*ibid.,* 158)

Since all civil jurisdiction belongs originally to princes and their magistrates . . . all degrees of judicial authority [*haute, moyenne, basse,* and so on] are hereby removed from ecclesiastics [who formerly exercised them] and reunited in our hands and those of our magistrates. . . .

In many other articles religious practices and ceremonies are described and decreed by authority of the sovereign and the secular authorities empowered to assure their execution. In Article 3 (*ibid.,* 149), for instance, specific punishments are established for the offense of failing to attend public prayers and religious instruction, ranging from small fines for the first offense to imprisonment for the third. The list is followed by this sentence: "It is our express command that the members of our Council, our magistrates, officers, consuls, *jurats,* and deputies shall execute this article, under pain of deprivation of their offices and estates if they are negligent." Variations in the wording are many, but every power granted to the Béarnais church is ultimately checked or controlled by the sovereign's authority, and every religious duty of Jeanne's subjects is decreed by her and is to be enforced by the secular arm.

APPENDIX D

Jeanne's Alleged Secret Marriage

The prime evidence cited by those who believe in the marriage consists of two documents.* First, an *Avis* of three of Jeanne's ministers in Pau (Viret, Barbaste, and Hespérien), signed on February 23, 1571, which states that Jeanne and an unnamed man "had married by mutual consent before two or three witnesses," and asks whether it could be considered a legal union "even without a Calvinist blessing, in public." The Béarnais ministers said that they would consider the marriage "real and indissoluble," but that "for the sake of the example, the couple should repeat their vows in the presence of a goodly number of witnesses." Subsequently, on April 2, 1571, this document is alleged to have been submitted to Beza, Gallars, and Chandieu in La Rochelle. Hespérien and Barbaste were included in the second *Avis* also, as they were attending the Synod; Viret had died en route to it. The second opinion was that "the said marriage should be announced as soon as possible . . . with recognition by the parties that they had failed in their duty . . . by not having the accustomed blessing, and that they repent thereof."

Both documents are to be found in the *Mémoires et correspondence de DuPlessis-Mornay,* but no responsible modern scholar considers them authentic. Neither names the man or gives reasons for keeping the marriage secret. The first *Avis* contains one obvious error, it is dated "Paris," while the three ministers are known to have been in Pau. The second is not mentioned in the *Procès-Verbaux* of the Synod, in Beza's correspondence, or any other source.

Only two authors since the seventeenth century have believed in Jeanne's secret marriage. Bascle de Lagrèze tells the story in a chapter entitled, "Les Amours de Jeanne d'Albret" of his book *Henri IV*. Among other statements for which there is no evidence, he claims that Jeanne tortured Roman Catholics in *oubliettes* beneath the chateau of Pau. An editor of Catherine de Medici's letters, Bagenault de Puchesse, a responsible scholar, also believes

---

* The various opinions and sources are summarized by N. Weiss, "La Vertu de Jeanne d'Albret," in BHPF (1915), 64:708–712. *Mémoires et correspondance de DuPlessis-Morney,* C. A. de Mornay ed., (2 vols., Paris, 1824), II, 18–19; L'Estoile, Brunet edition, II, 131; Roelker edition, 95; D'Aubigné, VIII, 333; P. Bayle, *Dictionnaire historique et critique* (Paris, 1820), XI, 77; Archives des Basses-Pyrénées, B 148, fol. 114v.

in the marriage, and speculates that Jeanne's husband was Jean de Salettes, who had an illegitimate son, "nourished by the charity of the Queen of Navarre," according to D'Aubigné. As evidence, he cites an exchange between Henri III and Henri IV in 1583, when the Valois King was trying to persuade the Béarnais to take back Marguerite as his wife despite her loose behavior. Henri III said, "Kings are often deceived and the most virtuous princesses do not escape calumny. You know what has been said of your late mother." (Henri's comment was, "The King does me too much honor; first, he calls me a cuckold and then the son of a whore.")

Pierre Bayle thought that Jeanne's last husband was a certain Comte de Goyon and that a refugee Calvinist minister in Amsterdam was the child of the marriage. A genuine document in the Archives des Basses-Pyrénées, dated May 23, 1572, about two weeks before Jeanne's death in Paris, reads: "Paid to Raymond Chamgrant, *régent* of Lescar, the sum of 75 livres tournois for a year's room and board for a small child that the Queen placed in *pension.*" Above the words, "small child," in another (later) hand, is written, "named François Goyon." Jeanne's correspondence and the archives in her various domains contain numerous examples of such charity on her part. There is no evidence to connect Jeanne personally with this child, still less with the child of De Salettes. (D'Aubigné does not suggest that it was Jeanne's child.) Both children were probably illegitimate offspring of members of her household.

Not one of the scholars concerned with Jeanne in the nineteenth or twentieth centuries—the Haags, Rochambeau, De Ruble, Weiss, Dartigue, or even Dubarat—finds any evidence for either of these hypotheses despite painstaking (and independent) research in all relevant records.

BIBLIOGRAPHICAL COMMENT
NOTES
INDEX

BIBLIOGRAPHICAL COMMENT

Since every source directly used is cited in the notes and a full formal bibliography would be very long, it seems necessary here only to indicate the range and kind of sources for this study. Three main areas are involved: Jeanne's role in the Wars of Religion; her administration and policy in her several domains; personal materials on Jeanne.

I. For her public career on the national level, 1562–1572, all the important primary sources for the early Wars of Religion are relevant. The principal subdivisions, with examples which are particularly full on Jeanne d'Albret, are: (1) Archival materials and public documents (Edicts of Toleration, Treaties between the Crown and the Huguenots, Registers of the Parlements); (2) Correspondence of the political leaders (Catherine de Medici, Charles IX, Antoine de Bourbon, members of the royal council like Montmorency, Coligny, L'Hôpital, and the Cardinal de Lorraine) and religious leaders (Calvin and Beza); (3) Diplomatic correspondence and dispatches (Simancas Archives, English Calendars of State Papers, reports of Florentine, Venetian, and papal diplomats in France and French ambassadors or agents in Madrid, London, and Rome); (4) *Receuils,* the big collections of manifestoes and documents produced during the first three Wars of Religion (*Mémoires de Condé, Mémoires de l'estat de France sous Charles IX, Histoire de nostre temps . . .*); (5) Memoirs of important individuals (Castelnau, Monluc, Tavannes); (6) Pamphlets and polemical writings which were the weapons of the ideological struggle, abundant in the Houghton Library at Harvard and the Newbury Library in Chicago; (7) Histories written shortly after the events (De Thou, D'Aubigné, Palma Cayet); (8) Literary sources (Brantôme). Although they are few in number, the scholarly studies dealing with France during the first ten years of the Wars of Religion (1562–1572) are also essential. I have drawn most heavily on the work of De Ruble, Delaborde, La Ferrière, Romier, Kingdon, and Sutherland.

II. Knowledge of Jeanne as an administrator is drawn chiefly from her legislation and public documents in departmental and communal archives in her former domains. The legislation and debates of the Estates of Béarn in the Archives des Basses-Pyrénées have been translated and calendared by C. Dartigue, *Jeanne d'Albret et le Béarn* (Mont-de-Marsan, 1934). Other Béarnais archival materials are less complete, owing to the fire of 1716, but those remaining have been inventoried by M. Raymond, *Inventaire-sommaire des archives départementales anterieures à 1790;* Basses-Pyrénées (6 volumes, Paris, 1863–1874) and capital documents on religious policy have been preserved in Pierre de Salefranque's *Histoire de l'hérésie en Béarn (Bulletin*

437

de la société des sciences, lettres et arts de Pau, 1921–22). Registers of the Parlements of Bordeaux and Toulouse are essential. Departmental and communal archives in Jeanne's other domains are also valuable but in many cases they are incomplete; for example, the Nérac Archives for the key years were entirely destroyed and those of Vendôme are fragmentary. Jeanne's miscellaneous *mandements* (commands, pardons, judgments, rulings that interpret her decrees, and so on) constitute a very valuable source for the practical implementation of policy. Only a few of these have been published, chiefly in the *Bulletin de la société de l'histoire du protestantisme français*, or in regional and local periodicals such as the *Bulletin de Pau* and the *Bulletin de la société archéologique, scientifique et littéraire du Vendômois*. The Simancas Archives (K, nos. 55–57) contain several hundred of these documents.

III. Jeanne's own letters are the most important single source for her public career as well as for her character and ideas. I have found about 300, more than one-third of which have never been published. The rest are to be found in a variety of publications, chiefly De Ruble's studies, the correspondence of Catherine de Medici and the reformers, and Pierre de Salefranque and Felix Frank, *Le Dernier voyage de la Royne de Navarre, Marguerite d'Angoulême, avec sa fille, Jeanne d'Albret, aux bains de Cauterets, 1549* (Paris, 1897). The largest collection (60 letters, some of which have been published elsewhere) is that of the Marquis de Rochambeau, *Lettres de Antoine de Bourbon et de Jehanne d'Albret* (Société de l'Histoire de France, Paris, 1877). There are very few from the early years—only 15 before Jeanne became Queen in 1555. By far the largest number (130) were written in 1571, including 80 unpublished. Two important groups in the Bibliothèque Nationale have been cited or excerpted in previous publications, but never critically edited or published in full: the 9 letters to the Vicomte de Gourdon (F fr, 17,044); and the 54 to members of the royal family or their officers, formerly in the Imperial Library in St. Petersburg (LIII), copied by Doat and catalogued as Nouv. aquis. françaises, 21, 603, of which 9 have been published. I plan in the near future to publish a complete calendar of Jeanne's known letters, with the full text of those previously unpublished, identification of her correspondents, and their letters when available. The *Ample Déclaration* . . . edited by De Ruble under the title, *Mémoires et poésies de Jeanne d'Albret* (Paris, 1893) and N. de Bordenave's *Histoire de Béarn et Navarre* (ed. P. Raymond, Société de l'Histoire de France, Paris, 1873) are also capital sources since they were written at Jeanne's command by people in her employ. The *Mémoires*, in the first person, bear the marks of her personal style.

Direct sources for the twelve years before the Cleves marriage and for the years 1545–1548 are very scarce. The biographer is therefore dependent on materials dealing with Jeanne's parents for the former and on indirect sources concerning the court for the latter. Thanks to the fine work of P.

Jourda, *Marguerite d'Angoulême* (2 volumes, Paris, 1930) and *Correspond-ance de Marguerite d'Angoulême* (published in the same year), and to De Ruble's extensive research into the policy of Henri d'Albret in *Le Mariage de Jeanne d'Albret* (Paris, 1877), I have been able to locate what sources there are, but they leave many gaps, particularly of the personal kind so precious for a biography that seeks to go behind the public facade of the subject.

Three biographies of Jeanne d'Albret were written in the nineteenth century. Mademoiselle de Vauvilliers, *Histoire de Jeanne d'Albret* (3 volumes, Paris 1818?) is the earliest, the fullest, and in my opinion the best. Although she often fails to identify her sources or to discriminate between reliable, first-hand documents and hearsay, propaganda, or legend, she was familiar with a great quantity of the important sources in the Bibliothèque Royale, as the B.N. was then called. M. W. Freer, *The Life of Jeanne d'Albret, Queen of Navarre* (London, 1862), the only previous work in English, leans heavily on Mademoiselle de Vauvilliers, but the author was a less sophis-ticated scholar and more of an apologist. Chiefly concerned to prove Jeanne a heroine and a martyr, Miss Freer makes a number of serious errors in chronology. T. Muret, *Histoire de Jeanne d'Albret* (Paris, 1862), is the least reliable factually and presents the most biased interpretation. Muret's object is to defend the Huguenot leaders from the charge of having betrayed France and to prove that Jeanne's prime concern was the promotion of the "true faith"—Calvinism.

De Ruble's six volumes (*Le Mariage de Jeanne d'Albret* [Paris, 1877] *Antoine de Bourbon et Jeanne d'Albret* [4 volumes, Paris, 1881–1886], and *Jeanne d'Albret et la guerre civile* [Paris, 1897]), are excellent on the aspects which interested him, that is, the diplomatic intrigues arising from the Navarre question. His interest in Jeanne as a person was slight and his interpretation limited by his view of her as a "pure" woman sacrificed to the ambitions of her father and husband and "wronged" by the politico-religious instability and marital infidelity of the latter. De Ruble died just as he reached the beginning of Jeanne's independent career, after the death of Antoine de Bourbon in November 1562, so that he could not use much of the vast quantity of material he had collected with the intention of con-tinuing the series. I seem to have been the first person to use the sixty large cartons he left to the Bibliothèque de la Faculté de Lettres of the University of Bordeaux. Without his careful and extensive work, both in the published volumes and in his papers, nobody could have written a new biography of Jeanne d'Albret without years of full-time research. He is, therefore, the most important of the predecessors to whom I am indebted. Another aspect of the present study, Jeanne as Queen and administrator, has been made possible by the work of Dartigue, whose studies of the institutions of Béarn under Henri d'Albret and Jeanne are indispensable (*La Vicomté de Béarn sous Henri d'Albret* [Paris, 1934], and *Jeanne d'Albret et le Béarn* [Mont-de-Marsan, 1934]). Lacking the work of Dartigue, a biographer would have had to learn Béarnais and then spend many months in the Archives des Basses-Pyrénées—or omit this facet of Jeanne's life, as indeed all previous biographers have done. Finally, I should acknowledge my debt to Jules Delaborde and Hyppolite Aubert de la Rue, both of whom began collecting Jeanne's letters and other source materials before they died. They left their papers to the Société de l'Histoire du Protestantisme français (ms. 755'; 880; 881 B; 882) where I made extensive use of them.

Except where otherwise noted, all translations are my own.

NOTES

PROLOGUE

1. P. Jourda, *Marguerite d'Angoulême* (2 vols., Paris, 1930). In addition to extensive biographical detail on Marguerite, this admirable study contains much material on the court, the French Renaissance, and the reign of François I.

2. *Ibid.*, 150.

3. *Ibid.*, 136.

4. E. Lavisse, ed., *Histoire de France* (10 vols., Paris, 1911), V, pt. 1 (H. Le Monnier), 187–204. Hereafter cited as Lavisse.

5. See J. R. Major, "Crown and Aristocracy in Renaissance France," *American Historical Review* (April 1964), 631–635, for an analysis of the role of the "new" feudal aristocracy in limiting the crown.

6. C. Dartigue, *La Vicomté de Béarn sous Henri d'Albret* (Paris, 1934), 147–154. Hereafter cited as Dartigue, *Vicomté*.

7. *Ibid.*, 153–154; N. de Bordenave, *Histoire de Béarn et Navarre*, ed. P. Raymond, Société de l'Histoire de France (Pau, 1873), 30. Commissioned by Jeanne in 1571 and finished in the 1590's, during her son's reign, this is the most reliable contemporary history of Navarre.

8. Jourda, *Marguerite d'Angoulême*, I, 146.

9. *Ibid.*, 150.

10. *Ibid.*, 151–152.

11. P. Jourda, ed., *Correspondance de Marguerite d'Angoulême* (Paris, 1930), no. 424, Marguerite to François I, October 1528; no. 427, Marguerite to François I, November 1528. Hereafter cited as Jourda, ed., *Correspondance*.

12. Jourda, *Marguerite d'Angoulême*, I, 152–153, footnote. Bibliothèque Nationale (hereafter cited as B.N.), F Clairambault 312, fol. 254. Louise de Savoie to Montmorency, November 16, 1528.

CHAPTER I

THE TWIG IS BENT

1. *Catalogue des Actes de François I,* ed. G. Picot (2 vols., Paris, 1887), I, 628. The number of masters was limited partly because a sizable fee was a prerequisite. French kings sometimes waived the requirement to celebrate fortunate events, losing revenue but gaining popularity.

2. In matters of chronology, the dating of letters, and the movements of Marguerite and Henri d'Albret, I have followed Jourda, *Marguerite d'Angoulême,* I, 154–208, and Jourda, ed., *Correspondance.* Also important for Marguerite's public career, DeCrue de Stoutz, *Anne de Montmorency* (Paris, 1885).

3. B.N., F Clairambault 331, fol. 233, Bishop of Rodez to Montmorency, March 1530.

4. "Journal de Versoris," *Mémoires de la société de l'histoire de Paris* (1886), 12:210, and "Journal de Driart," *ibid.* (1895), 22:136, mention Jeanne's birth without additional comment.

5. Archives du Palais de Monaco, J 18, fol. 50, cited in *Correspondance de Joachim de Mattignon,* ed. I.-H. Labande (Monaco, 1914), xxi. The Mattignons descended from Aymée de Lafayette.

6. Jourda, ed., *Correspondance;* nos. 428–464 constitute Marguerite's letters between December 1528 and April 1530.

7. *Ibid.,* no. 474, Marguerite to François I, July 1530.

8. *Ibid.,* no. 476, Marguerite to Montmorency, July 1530.

9. *Ibid.,* no. 478, Marguerite to Montmorency, July 1530.

10. Full discussion in Jourda, *Marguerite d'Angoulême,* II, 1138–1162.

11. Documents relating to the Alençon crisis of 1533 are published in the *Bulletin de la société de l'histoire du protestantisme français* (1884), 33:113. Hereafter cited as BHPF.

12. Jourda, ed., *Correspondance,* nos. 572, 573, Marguerite to François, June–July 1533.

13. *Ibid.,* no. 566, Marguerite to Montmorency, summer, 1533.

14. *Ibid.,* nos. 581, 583, Clement VII to Marguerite, October 21 and November 8, 1533.

15. B.N. F fr 17,044, fol. 446 (Collection Vallant), Jeanne to Gourdon, August 1555. See Chapter V, note 15.

16. Jourda, *Marguerite d'Angoulême,* I, 196–197.

17. B. Fontana, *Renata di Francia, Duchessa di Ferrara* (Rome, 1889–1899), I, 321 ff. This three-volume study of Renée contains many documents on the French Reformation up to 1575. The text must be used with caution, since Fontana's object is to clear Renée of all suspicion of heresy. A new study of Renée is needed.

18. The dispatches of Descurra in the Simancas Archives are of major importance, not only for the life of Jeanne d'Albret but for the entire relationship of the Navarre question to French and Spanish diplomacy. This is the first of several dispatches which are the only source for a particular question. Documents for Descurra's first mission are in Simancas K, 1484, nos. 45, 69.

19. Jourda, ed., *Correspondance,* no. 644, Marguerite to Renée, October 1536; also BHPF (1866) 15:129.

20. *Ibid.,* no. 555, Marguerite to Montmorency, 1532.

21. *Ibid.,* no. 580, Marguerite to Montmorency, Summer 1533.

A NORMAN CHILDHOOD

22. For the history of the fief of Lonray and information about the Renaissance chateau, I am much indebted to M. Thillier, Directeur des Services d'Archives at the Archives Départementales de l'Orne in Alençon, who led me to the sources and helped me to straighten out some of the inconsistencies and fill in some of the gaps. The principal sources are: *Inventaire-sommaire des archives départementales de l'Orne,* ed. L. Duval (8 vols., Alençon, 1899), III, xv–xvii; L. Duval, *La Normandie monumentale et pittoresque, Orne,* (2 vols., Le Havre, 1896), I, 57–59; L. Dubois, "Lonray," *Archives annuelles de la Normandie* (Caen, 1826), 1–6; L. de la Sicotière and A. Poulet-Malassis, *Le Département*

de l'Orne archéologique et pittoresque (Laigle, 1845), 59–67; P. J. Odolant-Desnos, *Mémoires historiques sur la ville d'Alençon* (2 vols., Alençon, 1757), II, 562–567.

The origins of the fief are lost in obscurity owing to the disappearance of early charters, but a papal bull of 1148 confirms to the Abbey of Séez certain of its revenues. In the thirteenth and fourteenth centuries it belonged to a succession of Seigneurs de Neuilly, descended from an illegitimate son of the third Comte d'Alençon. The estate was later owned by the family of Aymée's grandson, Maréchal Jacques de Mattignon. In the seventeenth century it passed, through marriage, into a branch of Colbert's family, and in the eighteenth, in the same way, to Charles-François de Montmorency-Luxembourg, Governor of Normandy and Maréchal de France. Just before the Revolution, it was bought by a prosperous merchant of Alençon, M. Mercier, who was given the title of Baron by Napoleon. A decree of June 11, 1810, gave Mercier the right to tear down the village church and add the land upon which it stood to his own, on condition that he build another church for the village at his own expense. Disappearance of the Registre des Délibérations du Conseil Municipal for the years 1806 to 1824 has made it impossible to determine exactly when, why, or how the chateau was destroyed. There was nothing left of it when the estate was purchased by the father of the present owner, Comte Le Marois, about 1870.

Genealogical information about Aymée's family is found in M. Beziers, *Chronologie historique des baillis et des gouverneurs de Caen* (Caen, 1769), 97, and *Correspondance de Joachim de Mattignon.*

23. Dubois, in the article cited (1826), describes this tomb but does not say where he saw it. He also mentions that the church had been torn down. There is no record of what happened to the tomb after the destruction of the church. This is one of several confusing matters arising from Dubois' article. He describes the chateau and refers to "le Baron Mercier" as if he knew them at first hand, yet M. Thillier is reasonably sure that the chateau was destroyed between 1806 and 1824, since these are the only years for which there are no records.

24. H. de La Ferrière-Percy, *Marguerite d'Angoulême, son livre de dépenses, 1540–1549* (Paris, 1862). Hereafter cited as *Livre de dépenses.* This is the *Registre* of Jehan de Frotté, Marguerite's Controleur-Général des Finances, with some comment by La Ferrière-Percy.

25. Pierre de Bourdeille, Seigneur de Brantôme, *Oeuvres completes,* ed. L. Lalanne (11 vols., Paris, 1864–1881), IX, 475–477. Hereafter cited as Brantôme.

26. Jourda, *Marguerite d'Angoulême,* II, 765, 876–877. Since the Tales in the *Heptameron* have the same numbers in all editions, no page references to a particular edition are cited.

27. Marquis de Rochambeau, *Lettres de Antoine de Bourbon et de Jehanne d'Albret,* Société de l'Histoire de France (Paris, 1877), no. XLVIII, 64–65. Hereafter cited as Rochambeau. Roman numerals indicate Rochambeau's chronological ordering. See Chapter III.

28. *Livre de dépenses,* 191–192. The *Registre* contains many references to members of the staff and to Jeanne herself. We cannot assume that all those mentioned in the 1540's, when Jeanne had a larger household, at Plessis, had necessarily also been at Lonray. On the other hand, the fact that many of the

same names appear in the Archives des Basses-Pyrénées (Series B) in later years, when Jeanne had become Queen, suggests that they may have been in her service for most of her life.

29. *Ibid.,* 165–190. Foreign observers remarked on the contrast between the formality of life at the French court and the informality of nobles on their estates; see, for example, the impressions of Suriano, Venetian ambassador in 1561, cited by A. Lefranc, *La Vie quotidienne de la Renaissance* (Paris, 1938), 108.

30. "Le Journal du Sieur de Gouberville," published in full in *Mémoires de la société de Normandie,* 1892–1895. Excerpts of the Journal in English in K. Fedden, *Manor Life in Old France* (New York, 1933).

31. In addition to Gouberville, see Rabelais, Montaigne, Brantôme, Pasquier (*Recherches de la France* [Amsterdam, 1725]), Castiglione (first French edition, Paris and Lyons, 1537). Among secondary works which interpret these and other sources well are A. Lefranc, *La Vie quotiedienne;* L. Batiffol, *Le Siècle de la Renaissance* (Paris, 1909); P. de Vaissière, *Gentilhommes de l'ancienne France* (Paris, 1903); W. L. Wiley, *The Gentlemen of Renaissance France* (Cambridge, Mass., 1954); E. S. Teall, "The Seigneur of Renaissance France: Advocate or Oppressor?," *Journal of Modern History* (1965), 37:131–150.

32. *Livre de dépenses,* 19.

33. P. Ariès, *Centuries of Childhood* (New York, 1962); see 37–39; 58; 62–66; 359–361, for references in these paragraphs.

EDUCATION OF A PRINCESS

34. Jourda, *Marguerite d'Angoulême,* I, 151; *Livre de dépenses,* 191.

35. On Nicolas Bourbon, see L. Febvre, *Le Problème de l'incroyance, la religion de Rabelais* (Paris, 1942), for biographical data and an excellent analysis of Bourbon's thought. For the French translation of the *Nugae,* see E. Saulnier, *Nicolas Bourbon, Bagatelles* (Paris, 1945).

On Humanist education in general see: E. Garin, *L'educazione in Europa,* 1400–1600 (Bari, 1958); J. H. Hexter, "The Education of the Aristocracy in the Renaissance," *Reappraisals in History* (N.Y., 1961), 45–70; A. Renaudet, *Préréforme et humanisme* (Paris, 1916); E. F. Rice, *The Renaissance Idea of Wisdom* (Cambridge, Mass., 1958); R. Weiss, "Learning and Humanism in Western Europe, 1470–1520," *New Cambridge Modern History* (1957), I, chapter V; W. H. Woodward, *Studies in Education during the Age of the Renaissance* (Cambridge, 1906).

36. Febvre, *Incroyance,* 41–43.

37. Joachim du Bellay, cited in Saulnier, 45. *Nugae* becomes *Bagatelles* in French; in English, "trifles" comes closest.

LA MIGNONNE DE DEUX ROIS?

38. For the movements of Marguerite and Henri d'Albret, and for details of the Spanish intrigues in 1537, see Jourda, *Marguerite d'Angoulême,* I, 213–227; also A. de Ruble, *Le Mariage de Jeanne d'Albret* (Paris, 1877), 19–25; hereafter cited as De Ruble, *Mariage.*

39. Jourda, *Marguerite d'Angoulême,* I, 224.

40. C. Marot, *Oeuvres,* ed. P. Jannet (4 vols., Paris, 1868–1872), II, 201.

41. Jourda, ed., *Correspondance,* no. 661, Marguerite to Montmorency, March 1537.

42. F. Génin, ed., *Nouvelles lettres de Marguerite d'Angoulême* (2 vols., Paris, 1842), II, no. XC, 148–150; Marguerite to François I, 1537. Hereafter cited as Génin.

43. Marot (ed. Jannet), III, 49.

44. Jourda, ed., *Correspondance,* no. 699, Marguerite to Montmorency, September 15, 1537; Jourda, *Marguerite d'Angoulême,* I, 221.

45. Jourda, ed., *Correspondance,* no. 700, Marguerite to François I, late in 1537.

46. Marot (ed. Jannet), I, 205–207.

47. Jourda, ed., *Correspondance,* no. 709, Marguerite to François I, December 1537.

48. *Ibid.,* no. 711, Marguerite to Montmorency, December 1537.

49. Jourda, *Marguerite d'Angoulême,* I, 227.

50. Odolant-Desnos, *Mémoires historiques sur la ville d'Alençon,* II, 562–567.

CHAPTER II
ADOLESCENT PAWN

1. P. de Comines, *Mémoires,* ed. L. Dupont, Société de l'Histoire de France (3 vols., Paris, 1840–1847), II, 267.

2. Cited in P. Vitry, *Tours et les chateaux de Touraine* (Paris, 1905), 74–76. See also R. Vivier, *La Touraine artistique* (Tours, 1926).

3. P. Olhagaray, *Histoire des comtes de Foix et de Navarre* (Paris, 1609), 503.

4. C. Dartigue, *Jeanne d'Albret et le Béarn* (Mont-de-Marsan, 1934), xv. Hereafter cited as Dartigue, *Jeanne d'Albret.*

PARENTAL AMBITIONS AND FRUSTRATIONS

5. For the movements of the D'Albrets in 1538, see Jourda, *Marguerite d'Angoulême,* I, 228–235, and De Ruble, *Mariage,* 25–29.

6. Jourda, *Marguerite d'Angoulême,* I, 229–234.

7. Jourda, ed., *Correspondance,* no. 793, Marguerite to Charles V, October 1539.

8. *Chronique du Roy François I,* ed. G. Guiffrey (Paris, 1860), 291. Hereafter cited as *Chronique.*

9. C. de Sainte-Marthe, *Oraison funèbre de la Reine de Navarre* (1550). For Jourda's dating of the episode see *Marguerite d'Angoulême,* I, 239–240 (footnote 203).

10. Génin, I, no. 146, p. 363, Marguerite to Montmorency, December 1537.

THE CLEVES MARRIAGE

11. For the movements of the D'Albrets in 1540–1541 see Jourda, *Marguerite d'Angoulême,* I, 251–274, and De Ruble, *Mariage,* 58–88 (details of the kipnaping plot 69–74).

12. Archives des Basses-Pyrénées, E 572.

13. Simancas K, 1492, no. 14. This key document has been translated into French by De Ruble, who makes extensive use of it, with his own interpretation, in *Mariage*, 80–110. I copied it from his papers in the Bibliothèque de la Faculté de Lettres in Bordeaux.

14. Jourda, *Marguerite d'Angoulême*, I, 254–256.

15. Archives of Düsseldorf, Jülich-Berg, no. 17, fol. 432 (De Ruble, *Mariage*, 289–290), Marguerite to the Duke of Cleves, April 1541.

16. Bordenave, 32; Archives des Basses-Pyrénées C 683.

17. De Ruble, *Mariage*, 93.

18. Jourda, ed., *Correspondance*, no. 839, Marguerite to François I, May 1541; italics mine.

19. Unless otherwise indicated, descriptions of ceremonies come from *Chronique*, 365–383.

20. "Chronique du Docteur Olisleger," cited by De Ruble, *Mariage*, 115.

21. Bordenave, 39.

22. Archives des Basses-Pyrénées, E 572 and 573, published in Génin, II, 291–292.

23. *Ibid.*, II, 292–293, and *Papiers d'état du Cardinal Granvelle*, ed. C. Weiss (3 vols., Paris, 1842), III, 112–113. Hereafter cited as Granvelle.

24. Brantôme, VIII, 117–118; *Chronique*, 369.

25. Bordenave, 39.

26. Olisleger, cited in De Ruble, *Mariage*, 120.

27. *Livre de dépenses*, 37.

28. Jourda, *Marguerite d'Angoulême*, I, 262–264; italics mine.

29. De Ruble, *Mariage*, 113.

30. Bordenave, 38; italics mine.

31. J. Sleidan, *De l'estat de la religion chrestienne et des quatres monarchies* (Strasbourg, 1564), 203, cited in Jourda, *Marguerite d'Angoulême*, I, 261.

DENOUEMENT OF THE CLEVES MARRIAGE

32. Jourda, ed., *Correspondance*, no. 581, Marguerite to Calvin, July 25, 1541.

33. Archives of Düsseldorf, Jülich-Berg, no. 17, fol. 466 (De Ruble, *Mariage*, 300–301), Marguerite to Cleves, November 1541.

34. *Ibid.*, no. 17, fol. 330 (De Ruble, *Mariage*, 302–303), Marguerite to Chancellor, November 1541.

35. *Ibid.*, no. 17, fol. 449 (De Ruble, *Mariage*, 310), Jeanne to William of Cleves, June 1541.

36. *Ibid.*, no. 17, fol. 465 (De Ruble, *Mariage*, 311), Jeanne to William of Cleves, November 1541.

37. *Ibid.*, no. 17, fol. 463 (De Ruble, *Mariage*, 312), Jeanne to William of Cleves, November 1541.

38. *Ibid.*, no. 17, fol. 427 (De Ruble, *Mariage*, 303–304), Marguerite to Cleves, November 1541.

39. *Ibid.*, no. 17, fol. 425 (De Ruble, *Mariage*, 305–307), Marguerite to Cleves, January 1542.

40. Jourda, ed., *Correspondance*, no. 916, Marguerite to François I, December 1542; Jourda, *Marguerite d'Angoulême*, I, 275–278.

41. *Correspondance de François, Cardinal de Tournon,* ed. M. François (Paris, 1946), no. 356, Tournon to Du Bellay, July 14, 1543.

42. De Ruble, *Mariage,* 182–188, summarizes the events and the sources.

43. Jourda, ed., *Correspondance,* no. 947, Marguerite to François I, October 1543, italics mine; Jourda, *Marguerite d'Angoulême,* I, 281.

44. Génin, II, no. CXXXIII, 235–238, Marguerite to François I, October 1543; *ibid.,* 240–241 (footnote 2).

45. Archives of Düsseldorf, Jülich-Berg, no. 17, fol. 504 (De Ruble, *Mariage,* 312–313), Jeanne to Drimborn, October 1543.

46. Archives de Bruxelles, Collection de documents historiques, VII, 123; De Ruble, *Mariage,* 196–203.

47. Génin, II, 289–294; Granvelle, III, 212–216.

48. Granvelle, III, 237.

49. De Ruble, *Mariage,* 199.

50. Génin, II, 289–294; Granvelle, III, 112–113; De Ruble, *Mariage,* 197–201; Jourda, *Marguerite d'Angoulême,* I, 305–306.

51. *Négociations diplomatiques de la France avec la Toscane,* ed. C. Desjardins (5 vols., Paris, 1861–1865), III, 152–153, Bernardo de Medici to Cosimo I, April 8, 1545. Hereafter cited as Desjardins, ed.

52. De Ruble, *Mariage,* 201.

53. Jourda, ed., *Correspondance,* no. 1000, Marguerite to Paul III, November 1545.

54. Fontana, II, 215–216, Jeanne to Paul III, November 1545.

55. De Ruble, *Mariage,* 200–203.

56. B.N., F fr 662, fol. 199, Jeanne to François I, undated, probably 1545 or 1546.

57. De Ruble, *Mariage,* 208–210.

ADOLESCENT REBELLION

58. Dartigue, *Vicomté,* 168.

59. *Livre de dépenses,* 19 (footnote 1).

60. *Ibid.,* 24 (footnote 2).

61. *Ibid.,* 19.

62. Jourda, *Marguerite d'Angoulême,* I, 329; *Livre de dépenses,* 19.

63. Génin, I, no. 158, 390–392, Marguerite to Izernay, January 20, 1548.

64. Jourda, *Marguerite d'Angoulême,* I, 324.

65. *Livre de dépenses,* 54–57, 79–80.

66. Jourda, *Marguerite d'Angoulême,* I, 322; De Ruble, *Mariage,* 267.

67. Jourda and La Ferrière-Percy, for instance. These authors are influenced by letters from Henri II to Montmorency, cited below.

68. Lyons, 1547, published by De Ruble, *Mariage,* 11.

69. De Ruble, *Mariage,* 10.

CONTENTED PAWN

70. Dispatches of Charles V's ambassador, Jean de St. Mauris, 1547–1548, C. Paillard, ed., *Revue historique* (1877), 5:100–120.

71. B.N., F fr 326, fol. 24, Cardinal de Guise to Henri II, July 1547.

72. Granvelle, III, 312, Charles V to Philip, January 18, 1548. "In my opinion, we should turn our sights to the Princesse de Béarn, on condition that

she renounce all pretensions to the Kingdom of Navarre and that the Princess herself leave France."

73. *Livre de dépenses*, 112–113, Henri d'Albret to Henri II, 1548.

74. *Ibid.*, 113, Marguerite to Henri II, 1548.

75. *Ibid.*, 114, Henri II to Montmorency, 1548.

76. Jourda, *Marguerite d'Angoulême*, I, 327.

77. *Livre de dépenses*, 126, Henri II to Montmorency, September 1548.

78. *Ibid.*, 127, Henri II to Montmorency, October 10, 1548.

79. Simancas K, 1498, no. 78, St. Mauris to Maximilian, November 9, 1548, cited in De Ruble, *Mariage*, 26. On the wedding see Jourda, *Marguerite d'Angoulême*, I, 328, and De Ruble, *Mariage*, 263–265.

80. *Livre de dépenses*, 128, Henri II to Montmorency, October 21, 1548.

81. B.N., F fr 20,449, fol. 119, Brissac to Aumale, October 23, 1548.

82. Cited in De Ruble, *Mariage*, 266, Henri II to Montmorency, October 22, 1548.

83. *Livre de dépenses*, 128–129, Henri II to Montmorency, October 24, 1548.

84. Brantôme, VIII, 58.

CHAPTER III

BRIDE AND DAUGHTER

1. The Salic law prevented the French crown from passing to a woman or through the female line. When the sons of Henri II had all died, leaving no heirs, Antoine's son (Henri IV) came to the throne, in 1589.

As explained in the text, Protestant historians are very severe in their judgments of Antoine, royalist historians are lenient. The very full study of Antoine's political career, A. de Ruble, *Antoine de Bourbon et Jeanne d'Albret* (4 vols., Paris, 1881–1886), is not a biography but contains much material on which a biographer might draw. Hereafter cited as De Ruble, *Antoine de Bourbon*. The best analysis of Antoine's career, excluding the Navarre question as such, is L. Romier, *Catholiques et Huguenots à la cour de Charles IX* (Paris, 1924). Hereafter cited as Romier, *Catholiques et Huguenots*. The best short biographical summaries are E. and E. Haag, *La France protestante* (9 vols., Paris, 1846), II, 429–437 (hereafter cited as Haag); and *Biographie universelle* (Paris, 1847–1865), II, 77–78.

2. Brantôme, IV, 361–373; *Relations des ambassadeurs vénétiens*, ed. N. Tommaseo (2 vols., Paris, 1838), I, 429, *Relazione* of Mihieli; 494–499, *Relazione* of Suriano (hereafter cited as Tommaseo, ed.); De Ruble, *Antoine de Bourbon*, IV, 374.

3. Brantôme, IV, 370; De Ruble, *Antoine de Bourbon*, IV, 372; the four volumes of *Antoine de Bourbon et Jeanne d'Albret* devote much more space to Antoine than to Jeanne.

4. Brantôme, IV, 363; Tommaseo, ed., I, 429–431, *Relazione* of Mihieli; A. d'Aubigné, *Histoire universelle*, ed. A. de Ruble, Société de l'Histoire de France (10 vols., Paris, 1886–1909), I, 290. All D'Aubigné references are to this edition.

5. Simancas K, 1485, no. 111, St. Mauris to Philip, November 20, 1547, cited in De Ruble, *Mariage*, 245.

THE BRIDE AND HER MOTHER

6. Rochambeau, no. X, 15–16, Antoine to Jeanne, August 8, 1549.

7. *Livre de dépenses,* 132–133; Jourda, *Marguerite d'Angoulême,* I, 326–343. Both authors describe and document the movements of Marguerite and Jeanne in the last months of 1548 and the first months of 1549.

8. Olhagaray, 505.

9. Relations with the Spaniards in 1549 in De Ruble, *Antoine de Bourbon,* I, 10–18. His major sources are the correspondence of the Duke of Maqueda and the dispatches of Descurra, Archives de la Secretariat d'Etat d'Espagne, leg. 353, fols. 70, 72, 76, 78, 81, 89; leg. 354, fols. 80, 226.

10. Included in F. Frank, *Le Dernier voyage de la Royne de Navarre, Marguerite d'Angoulême, avec sa fille, Jeanne d'Albret, aux bains de Cauterets,* 1549 (Paris, 1897). This correspondence is summarized by Jourda, *Marguerite d'Angoulême,* I, 332–336.

11. This was an unusual attitude in the sixteenth century. Although it deals only incidentally with France, Marjorie Nicolson's study, *Mountain Gloom and Mountain Glory* (Ithaca, N.Y., 1959), shows that until the eighteenth century mountains did not usually inspire romantic admiration.

12. Jourda, *Marguerite d'Angoulême,* I, 335–336.

13. *Ibid.*

14. Rochambeau, no. XII, 17–18, Antoine to Jeanne, 1549, probably June.

15. *Ibid.,* no. X, cited in note 6 above; De Ruble, *Antoine de Bourbon,* I, 29–30.

16. Archives de la Secretariat d'Etat d'Espagne, leg. 353, fols. 94, 96, 100, interpreted by De Ruble, *Antoine de Bourbon,* I, 31; Jourda, *Marguerite d'Angoulême,* I, 340.

17. Rochambeau, no. LXXI, 92–93, Jeanne to La Connêtable de Montmorency, 1555.

A SOLDIER'S WIFE

18. Archives de la Secretariat d'Etat d'Espagne, leg. 354, fols. 10, 57, interpreted by De Ruble, *Antoine de Bourbon,* I, 40–42; *Calendar of State Papers, Foreign Series, Edward VI,* 1547–1553, ed. W. B. Turnbull (London, 1861), no. 237, John Mason to the Council, September 10, 1550. Hereafter cited as *CSP For.* with particular volume.

19. Archives de la Secretariat d'Etat d'Espagne, leg. 354, fol. 108, Maqueda to Princess Juana, June 16, 1551; De Ruble, *Antoine de Bourbon,* I, 47–48; Archives de la Secretariat d'Etat d'Espagne, leg. 354, fols. 12, 17, Maqueda to Prince Philip, November 1 and 8, 1551.

20. *CSP For. Ed. VI* no. 332, John Mason to the Council, April 29, 1551; Rochambeau, nos. XVI, XVII, XVIII, 22–25, on May 20, July 21, August 9, written from La Fère, are Antoine's only letters before September in the year 1551.

21. *Mémoire* of Claude Régin, Bishop of Oloron, on the vital statistics of Jeanne's children, B.N., Dupuy, no. 88, fol. 3, published by Rochambeau, 395–399.

22. De Ruble, *Antoine de Bourbon,* I, 54, summarizes Antoine's movements at this time, from the provenance of his letters.

23. Archives des Basses-Pyrénées, E 887.

24. De Ruble, *Antoine de Bourbon,* I, 56–63. Among the sources for the Artois campaign is a long letter from the Duke of Albuquerque to Philip, January 30, 1553, in Archives de la Secretariat d'Etat d'Espagne, leg. 355, fol. 60.

25. Rochambeau, no. XXIV, 31–33, Antoine to Jeanne, probably December 1551.

26. *Ibid.,* no. XXVI, 35–37, Antoine to Jeanne, 1552.

27. *Ibid.,* no. XXXI, 41–42, Antoine to Jeanne, 1552.

28. *Ibid.,* no. XXXIII, 45–46, Antoine to Jeanne, 1552.

29. *Ibid.,* no. XXXII, 42–45, Antoine to Jeanne, 1552.

30. *Ibid.,* no. XXXIV, 46–47, Antoine to Jeanne, 1552.

31. De Ruble, *Antoine de Bourbon,* I, 66–82 covers the fighting of the summer of 1553; Archives des Basses-Pyrénées, E 262.

32. Rochambeau, no. XLIII, 57–59, Antoine to Jeanne, 1553.

33. *Ibid.,* no. XLIV, 59–60, Antoine to Jeanne, July 1553.

34. *Ibid.,* 397, *Mémoire* of Régin.

35. Archives de la Secretariat d'Etat d'Espagne, leg. 355, fol. 87, Albuquerque to Charles V, August 1553.

36. Palma Cayet, *Chronologie Novenaire,* 1608, ed. J. A. C. Buchon (3 vols., Paris, 1836), I, 172. All references to Palma Cayet in this edition.

37. Rochambeau, no. XLV, 61–62, Antoine to Jeanne, August 1553.

38. *Ibid.,* no. XLVIII, 64–65, Antoine to Jeanne, August 1553; italics mine.

39. Archives des Basses-Pyrénées, B, 1556.

40. Rochambeau, no. XLIX, 66, Antoine to Jeanne, August 1553.

41. *Ibid.,* no. L, 67, Antoine to Jeanne, late summer 1553.

42. *Ibid.,* no. LI, 67–68, Antoine to Jeanne, late summer 1553.

43. *Ibid.,* no. XLVI, 63, Jeanne to Antoine, late summer 1553.

44. *Ibid.,* no. LIII, 70–71, Antoine to Jeanne, late summer 1553.

45. *Ibid.,* no. LV, 72–73, Henri d'Albret to Jeanne, probably September 1553.

46. *Ibid.,* no. LVII, 74–75, Antoine to Jeanne, probably early autumn, 1553.

47. *Ibid.,* no. LVIII, 75–76, Antoine to Jeanne, probably early autumn 1553.

48. *Ibid.,* no. LIX, 76–77, Antoine to Jeanne, probably early autumn 1553.

49. De Ruble, *Antoine de Bourbon,* I, 77–78.

BITTERSWEET MOTHERHOOD

50. Palma Cayet, I, 173–174. This story is repeated by every historian of Henri IV, and by the twentieth-century expert on the royal family of Béarn, Dartigue, *Vicomté,* 182.

51. Archives des Basses-Pyrénées, C 683, fol. 220; Etablissements de Béarn, vol. V.

52. For the legends of Henri IV's infancy and childhood, see Chapter XV, and De Ruble, *Antoine de Bourbon,* I, 83–86.

53. Dartigue, *Vicomté,* 179.

54. Archives de la Secretariat d'Etat d'Espagne, leg. 356, fol. 81, and leg. 355, fol. 101, Albuquerque to Philip, December 1553; leg. 356, fol. 83, Memorandum of the Spanish Chancery, based on Descurra's reports.

55. Rochambeau, no. LXIV, 82–83, Antoine to Jeanne, 1554.

56. *Ibid.,* no. LXX, 91–92, Antoine to Jeanne, December 30, 1554.

57. *Ibid.,* no. LXVIII, 89–90, Jeanne to Anne d'Este, Duchesse de Guise, 1554.

58. *Ibid.,* no. LXXIV, 95–96, Antoine to Jeanne, 1554 or 1555.

59. *Ibid.,* 397, *Mémoire* of Régin.

60. Palma Cayet, I, 175.

61. Rochambeau, no. CIX, 144–145, Antoine to the Duchesse de Nevers, March 21, 1557.

62. Archives de la Secretariat d'Etat d'Espagne, leg. 357, fol. 42, Dispatch of Don Sancho, November 23, 1557; fol. 174, Dispatch of Descurra, November 30, 1557; De Ruble, *Antoine de Bourbon,* I, 103 (footnote).

FATHER AND DAUGHTER

63. Dartigue, *Vicomté,* 187.

64. Rochambeau, no. LXXXII, 103–104, Antoine to Jeanne, 1554.

65. For a twentieth-century example of the continuation of this view of Jeanne's attitude toward Marguerite, see N. Williams, *The Pearl of Princesses* (New York, 1916), 333, where he writes that, although Jeanne possessed a "remarkable faculty for absorbing knowledge," like her mother, in other respects, "she was the exact opposite, a person of convictions rather than sympathies, seeing one thing at a time and not wanting to see more." He further says, "Marguerite worshipped her, but the little girl, far from returning her affection, appears to have disliked her mother and to have regarded her confiding and generous nature with something very like contempt, although she was only too willing to take advantage of her liberality in money matters."

CHAPTER IV

KING AND QUEEN

1. De Ruble, *Antoine de Bourbon,* I, 113; Dartigue, *Vicomté,* 187. The movements of Antoine and Jeanne in these years are thoroughly covered and the sources indicated in the first volume of De Ruble's study.

2. Archives de la Secretariat d'Etat d'Espagne, leg. 356, fol. 10, Albuquerque to Philip, June 19, 1555.

3. Archives des Basses-Pyrénées, C 683.

4. De Ruble, *Antoine de Bourbon,* I, 110–114; Olhagaray, 508; Archives de la Secretariat d'Etat d'Espagne, leg. 356, fols. 80, 172, 173.

5. Bordenave, 52–53; Coronation Oath in Archives des Basses-Pyrénées, E 1229, published in De Ruble, *Antoine de Bourbon,* I, 119–121.

6. *Etats de Béarn,* 1555. Calendared in Dartigue, *Jeanne d'Albret,* 1–12; summarized in De Ruble, *Antoine de Bourbon,* I, 121–124.

7. Archives des Basses-Pyrénées, B 6 (Comptes de la Maison de la Reine de Navarre, 1555).

8. Archives des Basses-Pyrénées, B 7.

9. Rochambeau, no. XCIX, 131–133, Antoine to Jeanne, 1555.

10. *Ibid.,* no. LXXXVII, 111–112, Antoine to Montmorency, April 26, 1556. In January, Jeanne had asked the advice of the Vicomtesse de Turenne about a governess "for her daughters." It is evident that she did not wish to employ any of the ladies currently in her service, who had served with Aymée. *Ibid.,* no. LXXXIV, 105, Jeanne to Vicomtesse de Turenne, January 15, 1556.

11. *Ibid.,* nos. LXXXV-XC, 106–119, are the relevant letters. The King's informant was Jacques Benoît de Lagebaston, Premier Président of the Parlement of Bordeaux; see p. 115 of text.

12. *Ibid.,* no. XCII, 121–122, Antoine to Jeanne, July 7, 1556.

13. *Ibid.,* no. XCV, 126–127, Antoine to Jeanne, summer 1556.

14. *Ibid.,* no. CII, 136–137, Antoine to Jeanne, summer 1556.

15. *Ibid.,* no. CIII, 138, Jeanne to Montmorency, summer 1556.

16. Archives de la Secretariat d'Etat d'Espagne, leg. 356, fol. 96, Albuquerque to Princess Juana, August 1556.

17. Rochambeau, nos. CV, CVI, 140–141, Antoine to Jeanne, 1556.

18. *CSP, For.* 1553–1558, ed. W. P. Turnbull (London, 1861), no. 554, Wotton to Petre and Bourne, November 8, 1556; Archives de la Secretariat d'Etat d'Espagne, leg. 356, fol. 127, Albuquerque to Princess Juana, November 23, 1556.

19. Details of the Limoges visit in *Registres consulaires de la ville de Limoges,* ed. Ruben (Limoges, 1869), II, 103ff.

20. Palma Cayet, I, 176.

21. Brantôme, VIII, 44, Jeanne to the Sénéchale de Poitou, 1557; Rochambeau, no. CIX, 144–145, Antoine to the Duchesse de Nevers, March 21, 1557.

22. Archives des Basses-Pyrénées, C 684, fol. 70 (ordinance signed by Jeanne in Pau, March 25, 1557).

23. Registres Secrets du Parlement de Bordeaux, copy in Bibliothèque de Toulouse, B 94; summarized in De Ruble, *Antoine de Bourbon,* I, 143–144.

24. Archives des Basses-Pyrénées, AA 1; Tamizey de Larroque, *Antoine de Noailles à Bordeaux* (Bordeaux, 1878), 34.

25. *CSP, For. Elizabeth,* 1558–1559, ed. J. Stevenson (London, 1863), no. 833(5), Throckmorton to the Queen, June 13, 1559.

26. Rochambeau, no. CXIX, 157–158, Antoine to Jeanne, August 20, 1558.

ANTOINE AND THE HAPSBURGS

27. For this story of intrigue in detail, see De Ruble, *Antoine de Bourbon,* I, 147–210.

28. Archives de la Secretariat d'Etat d'Espagne, leg. 356, fol. 27, Albuquerque to Princess Juana, July 27, 1555.

29. *Ibid.,* leg. 355, fol. 172, Albuquerque to Philip, July 7, 1555.

30. *Ibid.,* leg. 356, fol. 87, Albuquerque to Philip, September 1, 1555.

31. *Ibid.,* 356, fol. 85, Albuquerque to Princess Juana, November 1555.

32. *Ibid.,* leg. 356, fol. 22, *Avis de France,* November 1555.

33. L. P. Gachard, *Retraite et mort de Charles-Quint* (2 vols., Brussels, 1854–1855), II, 105, Charles V to Philip, November 1556.

34. Simancas K, 1489, 108, Secretary of the Duc de Vendôme to Descurra, November 8, 1556.

35. De Ruble, *Antoine de Bourbon,* I, 168–173, summarizes the Lagebaston affair.

36. Archives de la Secretariat d'Etat d'Espagne, leg. 356, fol. 93, Philip to Albuquerque, December 2, 1556.

37. *Ibid.,* leg. 356, fol. 54. The account of Descurra's interview with Antoine in Vendôme is *ibid.,* leg. 357, fol. 31, Albuquerque to Philip, February 21, 1557.

38. De Ruble, *Antoine de Bourbon,* I, 181–184.

39. Archives de la Secretariat d'Etat d'Espagne, leg. 357, fols. 5, 6, Philip to Albuquerque, April 13, 1557.

40. There are several copies of this document. It is summarized in De Ruble, *Antoine de Bourbon,* I, 189–191.

41. Gachard, I, 162.

42. Archives de la Secretariat d'Etat d'Espagne, leg. 357, fol. 13, Albuquerque to Princess Juana, August 29, 1557.

43. Gachard, I, 259, Charles V to Albuquerque, October 24, 1557.

44. Archives de la Secretariat d'Etat d'Espagne, leg. 357, fols. 42, 173, Don Sancho to Descurra, November 24, 1557.

45. Gachard, I, 247, Charles V to Albuquerque, January 25, 1558.

46. Archives de la Secretariat d'Etat d'Espagne, leg. 357, fol. 143, unsigned dispatch, January 30, 1558.

47. L. E. Arcère, *Histoire de la ville de La Rochelle* (3 vols., La Rochelle, 1756–1757), I, 333–334.

CHAPTER V

THE PATH TO CONVERSION

1. Lavisse, *Histoire de France,* V, part 2 (H. Le Monnier), 187–196. The reader will find the relevant sections of Lavisse helpful for all aspects of the Huguenot story at the national level. A. Renaudet, *Pré-réforme et humanisme* (Paris, 1916), gives full detail on the earlier stages, and L. Romier, *Les Origines politiques des guerres de religion* (Paris, 1913–1914), documents the political and diplomatic aspects. Relations with Geneva in R. M. Kingdon, *Geneva and the Coming of the Wars of Religion in France* (Geneva, 1956). All have good bibliographies.

2. Kingdon, *Geneva ... Wars of Religion,* 54–55.

3. See, for instance, *Mémoires-Journaux de Pierre de L'Estoile,* ed. G. Brunet *et al.* (12 vols., Paris, 1888–1896), vols. VII-XI *passim,* and N. L. Roelker, "A Sympathetic View of the Huguenots in the Paris of Henry of Navarre," *Transactions* of the Huguenot Society of South Carolina, Charleston, 1958.

4. Kingdon, *Geneva ... Wars of Religion,* 59–61.

5. Cited in Lavisse, V, 2, 193.

6. Archives des Basses-Pyrénées, C 84.

7. Dartigue, *Vicomté,* 464–468, 471–472.

8. Pierre de Salefranque, *Histoire de l'hérésie en Béarn,* ed. V. Dubarat, in *Bulletin de la société des sciences, lettres et arts de Pau,* 1921, 39–40, 68–69, 74–80. Hereafter cited as Salefranque, *Bulletin de Pau,* with year and page numbers. Document numbers will be given for the *Preuves.* Simple page numbers refer to Salefranque's text.

9. Dartigue, *Vicomté,* 478–480.

ANTOINE, JEANNE, AND THE REFORM, 1555–JULY 1559

10. Brantôme, IV, 362; De Ruble, *Antoine de Bourbon,* I, 221.

11. Dartigue, *Jeanne d'Albret,* xliv.

12. Bordenave, 53–58.

13. *Mémoires et poésies de Jeanne d'Albret*, ed. A. de Ruble (Paris, 1893), 2–3. Hereafter cited as *Mémoires*. The word *Mémoires* is De Ruble's. The document is a political pamphlet with some autobiographical detail. The original, called *Ample Déclaration*, is found in a larger polemical collection, *L'Histoire de nostre temps contenant un receuil des choses memorables passées et publiées pour le faict de la religion et estat de la France despuis l'édict de paciffication du 23 jour de mars, jusqu'au présent* (probably La Rochelle, 1570). The *Ample Déclaration* itself was written and published in the autumn of 1568 and the edict referred to is the Peace of Longjumeau, March 23, 1568. See E. Droz, *L'Imprimerie à La Rochelle* (3 vols., Geneva, 1960), I, 80–83, 98–99.

14. De Ruble, *Antoine de Bourbon*, I, 221.

15. B.N., F fr 17,044, fol. 446, Jeanne to the Vicomte de Gourdon, August 22, 1555; italics mine.

16. Salefranque, *Bulletin de Pau*, 1921, nos. 13, 14, 15.

17. *Ibid.*, 1921, 123; G. Bourgeon, *La Réforme à Nérac* (Toulouse, 1880), 49–50.

18. Salefranque, *Bulletin de Pau*, 1921, 124.

19. *Ibid.*, no. 10, Jeanne to the Bishop of Lescar, March 2, 1556.

20. *Ibid.*, nos. 17, 18, 19, Armagnac to the Bishop of Lescar, August 28, September 12, December 17, 1556.

21. *Ibid.*, p. 129 and no. 20, Chapter of Lescar to the Bishop, March 29, 1557.

22. *Ibid.*, 130.

23. Archives des Basses-Pyrénées, B 7.

24. De Ruble, *Antoine de Bourbon*, I, 221–222; Lavisse, V, 2, *Affaire de la rue St. Jacques*, 220–221; D'Andelot, 240–242.

25. *Ioannis Calvini Opera*, ed. G. Baum, E. Cunitz, E. Reuss (50 vols., Brunswick, Germany, 1863–1900), XVI, no. 2274, cols. 730–734, Calvin to the King of Navarre, December 14, 1557. Hereafter cited as CO. See Haag, I, 153 for listing of the pamphlet: *Supplex exhortatio ad invictissim. Caesarem Carolum V et illustriss. principes aloisque ordines Spirae nunc Imperii conventum agentes: ut restituendae ecclesiae curam serio velint suscipere*, 1534.

26. Salefranque, *Bulletin de Pau*, 1921, 129, 147.

27. *Ibid.*, 31 (from Salefranque's preface).

28. De Ruble, *Antoine de Bourbon*, I, 227; Brantôme, IV, 361.

29. Lavisse, V, 2, 222, 240–242; Kingdon, *Geneva . . . Wars of Religion*, 62.

30. CO, XVII, no. 2819, cols. 69–71; no. 2885, cols. 196–198, Calvin to King of Navarre, February and June 1558.

31. Bourgeon, 96–102, Boisnormand to Calvin, September 10, 1558; also CO XVII, no. 2956, cols. 329–333.

32. Bordenave, 56–61; M. Forissier, *La Réforme en Béarn* (2 vols., Tarbes, France, 1950), 107–108.

33. De Ruble, *Antoine de Bourbon*, I, 419–421, Jeanne to Montmorency, 1558.

34. B.N., F fr 17,044, fol. 447, Jeanne to the Vicomte de Gourdon. This is dated by the copyist of the Collection Vallant as February 1558, but I am sure this is an error; from internal evidence it was probably written in the late summer or autumn.

35. Salefranque, *Bulletin de Pau*, 1921, 152-156; italics mine. It is noteworthy that, although Salefranque pushes Jeanne's conversion further back chronologically than is usual, he does not consider it complete until after the death of Antoine, almost two years after the official announcement. It is true that she did not begin to "establish" Calvinism until the early months of 1563. See Chapter VIII.

36. "La Seigneurie de Longjumeau," BHPF (1898), 48:393-410.

37. De Ruble, *Antoine de Bourbon*, I, 281-314.

38. *Ibid.*, I, 317 (footnote 1).

39. *Ibid.*, II, 29; Olhagaray, 520.

40. Rochambeau, no. CXXXV, 183-184, Antoine to Henri II, July 8, 1559.

ANTOINE, JEANNE, AND THE REFORM,
JULY 1559-DECEMBER 1560

41. *CSP, For. Eliz.*, 1558-1559, no. 1008, Cecil's Memorandum, July 18, 1559; no. 1018, Elizabeth to the King of Navarre, July 19, 1559; no. 1020, Elizabeth to the Queen of Navarre, July 19, 1559. See also N. M. Sutherland, "The Origins of Queen Elizabeth's Relations with the Huguenots, 1559-1562," *Proceedings of the Huguenot Society of London* (1962), XX, 626-648.

42. De Ruble, *Antoine de Bourbon*, II, 31-49, covers the movements of Antoine, July-October 1559, and cites the sources.

43. *Ibid.*, II, 44; Simancas K, 1492, fol. 67, Chantonay to Philip, August 22, 1559.

44. De Ruble, *Antoine de Bourbon*, II, 52-58.

45. N. M. Sutherland, "Antoine de Bourbon King of Navarre and the French Crisis of Authority, 1559-1562," unpublished paper delivered at the Anglo-French Conference (September 1967), under the auspices of the International Historical Congress. Cited with the author's permission.

46. De Ruble, *Antoine de Bourbon*, II, 75-120, covers the trip of Antoine and Jeanne with Elizabeth de Valois in November-December 1559.

47. Registres Secrets du Parlement de Bordeaux, Bibliothèque de Toulouse, B 94.

48. De Ruble, *Antoine de Bourbon*, II, 82.

49. *Ibid.*, 83; *CSP, For. Eliz.* 1559-1560, ed. J. Stevenson (London, 1865), no. 449(1), anonymous dispatch, December 29, 1559.

50. See De Ruble, *Antoine de Bourbon*, II, 86-120, for Antoine's dealings with the Spaniards.

51. *Mémoires*, 5-7.

52. See Lavisse, V, 2, 245, on Henri II and Du Bourg; *ibid.*, VI, 1 (J.-H. Mariéjol), 10-12, on events at the turn of the year 1559-60.

53. P. Geisendorf, *Théodore de Bèze* (Geneva, 1949), 116; *Correspondance de Théodore de Bèze*, ed. H. Meylan, A. Dufour, *et al.* (4 vols., Geneva, 1960-1965), III, no. 50, Beza to Bullinger, September 12, 1559. Hereafter cited as *Correspondance de Bèze*. See also Appendix B.

54. Kingdon, *Geneva . . . Wars of Religion*, 69-74.

55. Desjardins, ed., III, 408-418, Dispatches of Tornabuoni, March-April 1560.

56. Lavisse, VI, 1, 12-19, provides a good summary of the Conspiracy of

Amboise. It is treated with emphasis on Antoine by De Ruble, *Antoine de Bourbon*, II, 121–229. The most detailed studies are L. Romier, *La Conjuration d'Amboise* (Paris, 1923), and H. Naef, *La Conjuration d'Amboise* (Paris and Geneva, 1922). The most recent treatment is N. M. Sutherland, "Calvinism and the Conspiracy of Amboise," *History* (1962) 47:111–138.

57. De Ruble, *Antoine de Bourbon*, II, 217–228.

58. *Mémoires de Condé* (6 vols., London ed., 1740), I, 529; De Ruble, *Antoine de Bourbon*, II, 221.

59. Kingdon, *Geneva . . . Wars of Religion*, 75, and 78 (footnote 46) (which covers Calvin's opinion also).

60. Bourgeon, 105, La Motte to Calvin, July 1560; also CO, XVIII, no. 3231, cols. 152–154.

61. N. Weiss, "La Conversion de Jeanne d'Albret," BHPF (1923), 72: 127; Geisendorf, 120–121.

62. *Histoire Ecclésiastique*, ed. G. Baum and E. Cunitz (3 vols., Paris, 1883–1889), I, 325–326; Bordenave, 115.

63. Bourgeon, 108–109, Beza to Calvin, August 25, 1560; also *Correspondance de Bèze*, III, 161. The main subject of the letter was another conspiracy, centering in Lyons. See A. Dufour, "L'Affaire de Maligny," *Cahiers d'histoire publiés par les universités Clermont–Lyon–Grenoble* (1963), 8, 269–280.

64. Bordenave, 86.

65. De Ruble, *Antoine de Bourbon*, II, 467 (analysis of documents).

66. Forissier, I, 113–116.

67. Events of the last three months of 1560 in Bordenave, 103–108, and De Ruble, *Antoine de Bourbon*, II, 360–443. See also Lavisse, VI, 1, 24–28.

68. J. Héritier, *Catherine de Médicis* (Paris, 1940), 202–204.

69. Geisendorf, 122–123.

70. *CSP, For. Eliz.* 1560, ed. J. Stevenson (London, 1865), no. 716(18), Throckmorton to the Queen, November 17, 1560.

71. Simancas K, 1493, fol. 106, Chantonay to Philip, November 13, 1560.

72. Cited by De Ruble, *Antoine de Bourbon*, II, 411.

73. *Mémoires*, 7–12 (excerpts).

74. Bordenave, 107.

75. Sources on the condemnation of Condé are summarized by De Ruble, *Antoine de Bourbon*, II, 429–430.

76. Registres du Parlement de Paris, B.N., F fr 18,534, fol. 387; De Ruble, *Antoine de Bourbon*, II, 432.

77. Simancas K, 1493, fols. 113, 115, Chantonay to Philip, December 3 and 8, 1560. These dispatches are our most important source for the confrontation between Catherine and Antoine.

78. De Ruble, *Antoine de Bourbon*, II, 436.

79. *Ibid.*, II, 439–443, covers the death and funeral of François II.

80. Bordenave, 108.

81. "That was the Reformation that was," *The New York Review of Books*, December 29, 1966.

82. *Lettres de Calvin*, ed. J. Bonnet (2 vols., Paris, 1854), II, 265–268, Calvin to Jeanne, January 1561; also CO XVIII, no. 3315, cols. 313–314.

83. *CSP, For. Eliz.* 1560–1561, ed. J. Stevenson (London, 1865), no. 900,

Throckmorton to the Queen of Navarre, January 20, 1561. No source known to me indicates a meeting, or even correspondence, between Jeanne and Elizabeth's ambassador before Jeanne's conversion. It is certain that she was not with Antoine when he met Throckmorton in mid-September 1560, in St. Denis.

CHAPTER VI

A HUSBAND LOST, A PARTY GAINED

(The year of letters cited is 1561 unless otherwise indicated.)

1. L. Romier's *Catholiques et Huguenots à la cour de Charles IX* is a masterful analysis of the factions at court in the year covered by this chapter, which depends heavily on Romier for Catherine's policy and for the sources. Little reference is made, however, to his important original interpretations, unless they relate directly to Jeanne.

2. *CSP, For. Eliz.* 1560–1561, no. 77(9), Throckmorton to the Queen, March 31; Suriano to the Signoria, April 4, calendared in De Ruble, *Antoine de Bourbon,* III, 341; Simancas K, 1494, no. 75, Chantonay to Philip, April 9.

3. De Ruble, *Antoine de Bourbon,* III, 77–78, summarizes the Châtillon episode, with sources; see *ibid.,* 59, for the actions of the royal council.

4. Romier, *Catholiques et Huguenots,* 54.

5. *Lettres de Catherine de Médicis,* ed. H. de La Ferrière and B. de Puchesse (5 vols., Paris, 1880–1909), I, 181, Catherine to the Bishop of Rennes, March 29; 599–600, Catherine to Sébastien l'Aubespine, Bishop of Limoges, June 20.

6. *CSP, For. Eliz.* 1560–1561, no. 984 (1)(3), Bedford to Cecil, February 11; Simancas K, 1494, nos. 55, 56, Chantonay to Philip, January 28.

7. *Lettres de Calvin,* II, 363–365, Calvin to Antoine, January; also, CO, XVIII, no. 3314, cols. 311–312; BHPF (1860), 9:32, Hotman to Antoine, December 31, 1560.

8. *CSP. For. Eliz.* 1560–1561, no. 1012, Antoine to Elizabeth, February 20; Romier, *Catholiques et Huguenots,* 62; De Ruble, *Antoine de Bourbon,* III, 44–48.

9. Romier, *Catholiques et Huguenots,* 15; Simancas K, 1494, no. 68, Chantonay to Philip, March 26; Desjardins, ed., III, 449, Tornabuoni to Cosimo I, March 27; Romier, *Catholiques et Huguenots,* 98; De Ruble, *Antoine de Bourbon,* III, 66.

10. A. H. Layard, *Dispatches of the Venetian Ambassadors* (Lymington, England, 1891), 21, Dispatch of Suriano, March 29.

11. On the Triumvirate, see Romier, *Catholiques et Huguenots,* 99–128; De Ruble, *Antoine de Bourbon,* III, 70, 76; J. W. Thompson, *Wars of Religion in France* (New York, 1909), 97–100.

12. Rochambeau, no. CLVIII, 225–227, Antoine to Jeanne, January 21.

13. Dartigue. *Jeanne d'Albret,* 37–43 (Calendar of the Estates of 1561); Archives des Basses-Pyrénées, C 884, fol. 52.

14. Dartigue, *Jeanne d'Albret,* li.

15. *Ibid.,* 43.

16. Romier, *Catholiques et Huguenots,* 124.

17. B.N., F fr 17,044, fol. 447v, Jeanne to Gourdon, probably July 1561.

18. Romier, *Catholiques et Huguenots,* 160–162.

19. Simancas K, 1495, no. 62, Chantonay to Philip, August 15; K, 1494, no. 94, Chantonay to Philip, August 31. Calendared in De Ruble, *Antoine de Bourbon*, II, 365–366, 367.

20. *CSP, For. Eliz.* 1560–1561, no. 735(4), Throckmorton to Challoner, December 20.

21. Simancas K, 1494, no. 97, Chantonay to Philip, September 4; Dispatch of Suriano, August 24, calendared in De Ruble, *Antoine de Bourbon*, III, 366; Desjardins, ed., III, 461, Dispatch of Tornabuoni, September 4. See Chapter VIII for the question of Jeanne's residence in Paris.

22. Dispatches of Suriano, May 14 and July 27, calendared in De Ruble, *Antoine de Bourbon*, III, 354, 362; Simancas K, 1494, no. 77; K, 1495, no. 50, Chantonay to Philip, April 4 and July 7.

23. Layard, 39, Dispatch of Suriano, August 24; De Ruble, *Antoine de Bourbon*, III, 121.

24. Simancas K, 1495, no. 47, Chantonay to Philip, June 19.

25. *Lettres de Calvin*, II, 399–402, Calvin to the King of Navarre, May; also CO, XVIII, no. 3393, cols. 457–459.

26. Romier, *Catholiques et Huguenots*, 205; *Lettres de Calvin*, II, 420, Calvin to the King of Navarre, August; also CO, XVIII, no. 3502, cols. 659–661.

27. Archives des Basses-Pyrénées, E 584.

28. Simancas K, 1494, no. 94; K, 1495, no. 64, Chantonay to Philip, October 14.

29. Simancas K, 1495, no. 62, Chantonay to Philip, August 15.

30. *Ibid.;* K, 1494, no. 97, Chantonay to Philip, September 4.

THE FLOOD TIDE OF CALVINISM

31. On the *Colloque de Poissy,* see Thompson, 106–130; Romier, *Catholiques et Huguenots*, 139–237; H. O. Evennett, *The Cardinal of Lorraine and the Council of Trent* (Cambridge, 1930).

32. Romier, *Catholiques et Huguenots*, 250–251.

33. *Ibid.,* 252–258 surveys this phenomenon.

34. P. Courteault, *Monluc, historien* (Paris, 1908), 397–398.

35. C. Hatton, *Mémoires,* ed. F. Bourquelot (2 vols., Paris, 1857), I, 155.

36. Romier, *Catholiques et Huguenots*, 204–205.

37. Hatton, I, 156, cited in J. Delaborde, *Les Protestants à la cour de St. Germain* (Paris, 1874), 15 (note 1). Delaborde includes many sources important for this section.

38. Romier, *Catholiques et Huguenots*, 205, and Delaborde, *Protestants,* 13–15, where Beza's letter is published; also *Correspondance de Bèze,* III, no. 186, Beza to Calvin, August 25, 1561.

39. Delaborde, *Protestants,* 53–57, gives the service verbatim; *CSP, For. Eliz.* 1561–1562, ed. J. Stevenson (London, 1867), no. 619 (3), Throckmorton to the Queen, October 10; other sources summarized in De Ruble, *Antoine de Bourbon*, III, 194.

40. Romier, *Catholiques et Huguenots*, 204.

41. *Mémoires de Marguerite de Valois,* ed. L. Lalanne (Paris, 1842), 6, and Delaborde, *Protestants,* 41.

42. Romier, *Catholiques et Huguenots*, 204; Simancas K, 1495, no. 86;

K, 1494, nos. 105, 108, Chantonay to Philip, October 24, October 28, November 13.

43. Romier, *Catholiques et Huguenots*, 268–269.

44. *Correspondance de Bèze*, III, nos. 209, 211, 212, 220. See especially, pp. 214–215 (note 7), p. 217 (note 4), p. 210 (note 4); Romier, *Catholiques et Huguenots*, 270.

45. Geisendorf, 175.

46. *Correspondance de Bèze*, III, no. 216; De Ruble, *Antoine de Bourbon*, III, 207–208; Jeanne's letter, written on November 25, is in Archives de Genève, 1713. Romier (262, note 1) scorns De Ruble's interpretation of this episode as the first step in the founding of a national Calvinist church, calling it "a great blunder." While the sources do not justify the assumption that it was a definite plan, no evidence rules the notion out—as a hope. Although the forces that would reverse the Protestant tide were already in motion, this was not evident until early in 1562.

47. Tommaseo, ed., II, 69, *Relazione* of M. A. Barbaro, 1563; Hubert Languet's *Epistles*, II, 56, cited in Delaborde, *Protestants*, 37. Further evidence of Jeanne's proseletyzing activity comes in a letter from the Poitiers church to Calvin, December 30, 1561, reporting that she has written in their behalf to the city of Berne, BHPF (1865), 14:327.

48. *Correspondance de Bèze*, III, nos. 220, 222; Simancas K, 1495, no. 103, Chantonay to Philip, December 21; De Ruble, *Antoine de Bourbon*, III, 224. Estimates of crowds must be viewed with caution when no reliable method of counting exists.

49. Romier, *Catholiques et Huguenots*, 270; De Ruble, *Antoine de Bourbon*, III, 213–215; Delaborde, *Protestants*, 70, all give the sources. This episode was very fully reported by the ambassadors each with his own bias. For the attempt to poison Jeanne and Antoine see *CSP, For. Eliz.* 1561–1562, no. 659(1), Throckmorton to the Queen, November 14.

50. *CSP, For. Eliz.* 1561–1562, no. 682(3), Throckmorton to the Queen, November 26.

51. *Ibid.*, no. 682(4), Throckmorton to the Queen, November 26.

52. Rochambeau, no. CLXIV, 240–242, Jeanne to Madame de Langey, October 3.

53. *Ibid.*, no. CLXVII, 245–246, Jeanne to Madame de Langey, November.

54. *Ibid.*, no. CLXXI, 251, Jeanne to Madame de Langey, May 3, 1562.

55. On the Edict of January see Romier, *Catholiques et Huguenots*, 285–317; Thompson, 128–130.

56. Hubert Languet, Epistle LXIII in Delaborde, *Protestants*, 84–85.

57. *Archives Curieuses*, ed. M. Cimber (pseud.) (27 vols., Paris, 1834–1840), VI, 16–20, Santa Croce to Borromeo, January 7, 1562.

COUNTEROFFENSIVE

58. Summarized by Romier, *Catholiques et Huguenots*, 306–310.

59. *Ibid.*, 278–279.

60. De Ruble, *Antoine de Bourbon*, III, 251–314 contains thorough coverage of Antoine's Spanish intrigues; Simancas K, 1494, no. 98, Memorandum of Philip to D'Auzance, December 15.

61. Simancas K, 1497, no. 3, Chantonay to Philip, January 5, 1562.

62. *Ibid.*, K, 1494, no. 115, Chantonay to Philip, December 3, 1561.

63. *Histoire ecclésiastique*, I, 769. *Lettres de Calvin*, II, 441–447; also CO, XIX, no. 3664, cols. 198–202.

64. *CSP, For. Eliz.* 1561–1562, no. 934(1), Throckmorton to Cecil, March 14, 1562.

65. Romier, *Catholiques et Huguenots*, 309.

66. *Archives Curieuses*, VI, 37–43, Santa Croce to Borromeo, February 22, 1562; Desjardins, ed., III, 471, 474, Dispatches of Tornabuoni, January 3 and March 25, 1562; *CSP. For. Eliz.* 1561–1562, nos. 924, 934, Throckmorton to the Queen, March 6 and 14, 1562.

THE PARTING OF THE WAYS

67. *CSP, For. Eliz.* 1561–1562, no. 534, Narrative of the Vicomte de Gruz, September 24, 1561.

68. Simancas K, 1494, nos. 109, 110, 115; K, 1495, no. 103, Chantonay to Philip, November 18 and 21, December 3 and 21.

69. Tommaseo, ed., II, 81, *Relazione* of Barbaro.

70. *CSP, For. Eliz.* 1561–1562, no. 924(8), Throckmorton to the Queen, March 6, 1562.

71. *Histoire ecclésiastique*, I, 771; De Ruble, *Antoine de Bourbon*, IV, 78.

72. Simancas K, 1497, nos. 3, 7, Chantonay to Philip, January 3 and 30, 1562.

73. Simancas K, 1497, no. 120; K, 1495, no. 100; K, 1497, no. 10, Chantonay to Philip, November 26, December 15, 1561, and February 14, 1562.

74. Simancas K, 1494, no. 110, Chantonay to Philip, November 21, 1561; *Négociations du Cardinal de Ferrare* (Paris, 1650), 11; De Ruble, *Antoine de Bourbon*, IV, 80–83; *CSP, For. Eliz.* 1561–1562, no. 792(10), Intelligences from France, January 10, 1562.

75. Bordenave, 110; E. Davila, *The Civil Wars in France* (2 vols., London, 1758), I, 89; Brantôme, VII, 420; De Ruble, *Antoine de Bourbon*, IV, 52.

76. Simancas K, 1496, no. 31, Alva to Chantonay, January 23, 1562.

77. Simancas K, 1497, no. 9, Chantonay to Philip, February 11, 1562.

78. *CSP, For. Eliz.* 1561–1562, no. 924(4), Throckmorton to the Queen, March 6, 1562; Simancas K, 1497, no. 9 (see note 91).

79. "Journal de 1562," *Revue Retrospective*, ser. 1 (1836), 5:81.

80. Simancas K, 1497, no. 3, Chantonay to Philip, January 5, 1562. Unfortunately there is no record of what the Duchess said.

81. *CSP, For. Eliz.* 1561–1562, no. 965(1), Queen to Throckmorton, March 31, 1562.

82. *Lettres de Calvin*, II, 458–461, Calvin to the Queen of Navarre, March 22, 1562; also CO, XIX, no. 3748, cols. 347–349.

83. Delaborde, *Protestants*, 38–39.

84. *CSP, For. Eliz.* 1561–1562, no. 934(2), Throckmorton to Cecil, March 14, 1562; no. 924(8), Throckmorton to the Queen, March 6, 1562.

85. See De Ruble, *Antoine de Bourbon*, IV, 86–89, for summary, with sources (quotation is from letter cited in note 86).

86. Simancas K, 1497, no. 17, Chantonay to Philip, March 25, 1562.

87. Simancas K, 1497, no. 11, Chantonay to Philip, February 23, 1562;

K, 1496, no. 48, undated report of the Spanish Chancery; *Négociations du Cardinal de Ferrare,* 136.

88. *Mémoires,* 4.

89. Rochambeau, no. CLXX, 250, Antoine to Artus de Cossé, March 8, 1562.

90. J. W. Baum, *Theodor Beza* (2 vols., Leipzig, 1843–1851), *Preuves* (vol. II), 176–177.

91. *Mémoires de Castelnau de la Mauvissière,* ed. J. Le Laboureur (2 vols., Paris, 1731), I, 857; De Ruble, *Antoine de Bourbon,* IV, 77.

CHAPTER VII
STRATEGIC NEUTRALITY: THE FIRST CIVIL WAR

1. *Mémoires,* 18–25. The Queen Mother's position was ambiguous in the early stages of the civil wars but circumstances later forced her into alignment with the ultra-Catholic party. See, N. M. Sutherland, *Catherine de Medici and the Ancien Régime* (London, 1966), Historical Association Pamphlet, no. 62.

2. Rochambeau, no. CLXXII, 251–253, Jeanne to Catherine de Medici, 1562 (probably May).

3. A. de Ruble, *Jeanne d'Albret et la guerre civile* (Paris, 1897), 188. Hereafter cited as De Ruble, *Guerre civile.* One of Catherine's biographers, J.-H. Mariéjol, *Catherine de Médicis* (Paris, 1940), 257–258, states categorically that Jeanne "insisted" on the taking of Orléans.

4. B.N., F fr 17,044, fol. 448, Jeanne to Gourdon, March 1562; fol. 450, Jeanne to Gourdon, May 1562.

5. Rochambeau, no. CXCI, 282–283, Jeanne to the Duc de Nemours, 1565.

6. *Mémoires,* 25; Bordenave, 110; Simancas K, 1498, no. 6, Chantonay to Philip, June 6, 1562.

7. B.N., F fr 17,044, fol. 448, Jeanne to Gourdon, March 1562.

8. *Ibid.,* fol. 449, Gourdon to Jeanne, March 1562.

9. Kingdon, *Geneva . . . and Wars of Religion,* 60, 66 (notes 42–45).

10. *Mémoires,* 23. We know that Beza had returned to Orléans by April 5, when he wrote Calvin from there. See *Correspondance de Bèze,* IV, no. 248.

11. Simancas K, 1497, no. 36, Chantonay to Philip, May 28, 1562; De Ruble, *Antoine de Bourbon,* IV, 94–98, and *Guerre civile,* 191–192. Abbé Métais, "Jeanne d'Albret et la Spoliation de l'Eglise de St. Georges de Vendôme," *Bulletin de la société archéologique, scientifique et littéraire du Vendômois* (1882), published an inventory of treasures confiscated from the chapter, which was drawn up on May 19, and Jeanne's receipt for coin received after they were melted down, May 27 (about 30,000 livres tournois). The Abbé believed that the sack occurred first, in an "excess of fury," and that a remorseful Jeanne had an inventory of the remainder made and the receipt given to regularize the situation and make it appear like a loan to her from the chapter. Indeed, the chapter tried to collect from the crown (Louis XVI, in 1780) on the grounds that the money had been loaned to Henri IV. Even the most hostile sources do not suggest that Jeanne kept any of the treasure, or the money, although she was in dire financial straits. (See Chapter X.) Rochambeau, *Galerie des hommes illustrés du Vendômois* (Vendôme, 1878), gives slightly different dates and emphasizes Jeanne's demand that the inhabitants of the town deposit their arms in the chateau. He places the sack at the *end* of the sequence: "having nothing more to

fear, she gave rein to her religious fanaticism." He also repeats, without documentation, the local legend that Jeanne gave orders for the relics themselves—inside the gold or silver vessels—to be thrown in the river, whence they were rescued by a devout Catholic who bribed the man entrusted with the task.

12. De Ruble, *Guerre civile*, 191.

13. *Correspondance de Bèze*, IV, no. 252, Beza to Jeanne, May 23, 1562.

14. *Ibid.*, 94 (note 4).

15. Simancas K, 1497, no. 36, Chantonay to Philip, May 28, 1562.

16. *Correspondance de Bèze*, IV, 95, note 10.

JEANNE AND MONLUC: THE INITIAL CONFLICT

17. Simancas K, 1495, nos. 93, 95, Chantonay to Philip, December 7 and 10, 1561.

18. *Commentaires et lettres de Blaise de Monluc*, ed. A. de Ruble, Société de l'Histoire de France (5 vols., Paris, 1864–1867), IV, 138. Hereafter cited as *Commentaires de Monluc*.

19. *Mémoires*, 25. Chantonay's dispatches show that Antoine was proclaiming his intention to have Jeanne arrested. Simancas K, 1498, no. 6, June 30, 1562.

20. *Commentaires de Monluc*, II, 424.

21. Registre du Parlement de Bordeaux, B.N., F fr 22,372, fol. 1044.

22. *Mémoires*, 28.

23. B.N., F fr 15,876, fol. 440, cited in De Ruble, *Guerre civile*, 197.

24. Archives des Basses-Pyrénées, C 682 (Etablissements de Béarn, IV, 188).

25. *Mémoires*, 25, 28.

26. *Ibid.*, 26. Jeanne had many dealings with her vassals in this family, especially with François (III) de Caumont, Sieur de Castelnau de La Force, killed at St. Bartholomew, to whom she wrote a series of letters that have survived.

27. *CSP, For. Eliz.* 1562, ed. J. Stevenson (London, 1867), no. 497(4), Occurrences in France, August 17, 1562.

28. Archives des Basses-Pyrénées, C 682 and C 684 (documents signed by Jeanne on August 19).

29. *Commentaires de Monluc*, II, 441.

30. De Ruble, *Guerre civile*, 201–263, gives details of the war in Guyenne. For a summary see Thompson, 155–161.

31. *Commentaires de Monluc*, II, 443.

32. *Ibid.*, IV, 180.

33. *Lettres de Catherine de Médicis*, I, 402 (footnote). Letters exchanged by Catherine and Throckmorton reveal that an Englishman defending Jeanne's honor had a fight with Monluc, which created a public disturbance and became a matter for diplomatic negotiation.

34. *Commentaires de Monluc*, III, 58.

35. De Ruble, *Guerre civile*, 311–312. De Ruble's opinion carries weight since he spent years studying Monluc. See also La Ferrière, *Deux années de mission à St. Petersbourg* (Paris, 1867), 220. Hereafter cited as La Ferrière, *Deux années*.

36. De Ruble, *Guerre civile*, 344–346; Thompson, 214.

37. *Commentaires de Monluc*, III, 68; B.N., F fr 20,624, fol. 69v; De Ruble, *Guerre civile*, 347.

JEANNE AND ANTOINE: THE FINAL PHASE

38. Archives des Basses-Pyrénées, C 684, and Archives du Syndicat d'Ossau, EE1.

39. *Mémoires,* 29–30.

40. Bordenave, 113.

41. Archives des Basses-Pyrénées, E 585.

42. Bordenave, 113.

43. *Mémoires de Condé* (8 vols., London, ed., 1743), II, 92, Chantonay to Philip, October 2, 1562. Details in De Ruble, *Antoine de Bourbon,* IV, 337–352; summary in Thompson, 165–170.

44. Simancas K, 1496, no. 119, Chantonay to Philip, October 19, 1562. It is beyond the scope of this book to attempt either to substantiate or to refute the persistent rumors that Antoine was shot by somebody on his own side. There was plenty of motive for wanting him out of the way. Jeanne's letter to Catherine, cited below, shows that she blamed Antoine's death, like all the other evils of the time, on the Guises.

45. *Archives curieuses,* VI, 114, Santa Croce to Borromeo, October 22, 1562.

46. *CSP, For. Eliz.* 1562, no. 950(8)(10), News from France, October 31, 1562.

47. De Ruble, *Antoine de Bourbon,* IV, 363, Dispatch of Barbaro, November 8, 1562.

48. *Ibid.,* IV, 365–369, summarizes the situation, with sources.

49. *Ibid.,* 369–379.

50. Bordenave, 114.

51. *Histoire ecclésiastique,* II, 173; De Ruble, *Antoine de Bourbon,* IV, 369–370.

52. De Ruble, *Antoine de Bourbon,* IV, 370–371, paraphrases the document, published in full in *Mémoires de Condé* (1743 ed.), II, 116–118. Up to the last hours of his life Antoine's shifts had been between Calvinism and Roman Catholicism. He had nevertheless shown some interest in the Augsburg Confession at the time of the Colloquy, and had cooperated with the Cardinal de Lorraine in his attempt at a compromise solution to the religious conflict. H. O. Evenett, in *The Cardinal of Lorraine and the Council of Trent,* 333, says, "Catherine and Antoine were trying to use Lutheranism as a kind of theological sticking-plaster."

53. Tommaseo, ed., II, 95, *Relazione* of Barbaro.

54. *Archives curieuses,* VI, 115, Santa Croce to Borromeo, November 23, 1562.

55. De Ruble, *Guerre civile,* 302.

56. *Mémoires,* 30.

57. *CSP, For. Eliz.* 1562, no. 950(8), News from France, October 31, 1562.

58. M. Moliner and F. Mazcrolle, eds., *Inventaire du trésor du chateau de Pau,* Société des Bibliophiles français (Paris, 1891). See Chapter X.

59. Archives de la Secretariat d'Etat d'Espagne (Navarre), no. 358, Albuquerque to Philip, December 1, 1562.

60. *Ibid.,* no. 52, cited in De Ruble, *Antoine de Bourbon,* IV, 378.

61. Bordenave, 115.

62. De Ruble, *Antoine de Bourbon,* IV, 314–315.

63. B.N., F fr 15,877, fol. 98.
64. Bordenave, 115.
65. *Lettres missives de Henri IV*, ed. B. de Xivrey (9 vols., Paris, 1843–1876), I, 3. Hereafter cited as *Lettres missives*.
66. De Ruble, *Guerre civile*, 348.
67. B.N., Nouvelles acquisitions françaises, 21,603, fols. 91–97 (St. Petersburg, LIII, fols. 60–63, no. 50) published in full by De Ruble, *Guerre civile*, 348–353, Jeanne to Catherine de Medici, March 1563.
68. B.N., F fr 17,044, fol. 451, Jeanne to Gourdon, March 28, 1563.

CHAPTER VIII

PRECARIOUS INDEPENDENCE

(The year of letters cited is 1563 unless otherwise indicated.)

REFORM AND SELF-DEFENSE

1. *Lettres de Calvin*, II, 488–493, Calvin to Jeanne, January 20; see also CO, XIX, no. 3904, cols. 643–647.
2. L. Cadier, "Documents sur Jean-Raymond Merlin," in *Bulletin de Pau* (1941), 149–158.
3. *CSP, For. Eliz.* 1563, ed. J. Stevenson (London, 1869), no. 228, Montgomery to Cecil, February 3; *Documents inédits sur l'histoire de France* (3 vols., Paris, 1847), III, 577; De Ruble, *Guerre civile*, 307–308, Jeanne to the Seigneur de Bories, March 3.
4. Dartigue, *Jeanne d'Albret*, 1–132, calendars all sessions of the Estates in Jeanne's reign, with names, votes, and many verbatim citations. Details on the religious program of 1563 are also to be found in Merlin's letters (note 10) and Descurra's dispatch (note 11). See also Chapter X.
5. *Lettres de Calvin*, II, 519–522, Calvin to Jeanne, June 1; see also CO, XX, no. 3961, cols. 34–36.
6. Bordenave, 116.
7. Bibliothèque de la Société de l'Histoire du Protestantisme français, ms. 433/4, *Receuil des procès-verbaux des synodes de Béarn,* a remarkable document discovered in 1921 in Bordeaux by Jules Farans. There are two sets of page numbers. The first synod (1563) is 29–40 or 59–81. Hereafter cited as *Receuil*.
8. *Revue historique* (1876), 2:45, François Hotman to the Duke of Wurtemburg, October 3.
9. Fontana, III, 94, Santa Croce to Borromeo, June 11; see also Merlin to Calvin, July 23 (note 10); Archives des Basses-Pyrénées, C 684, fol. 128v; see also Dartigue, *Jeanne d'Albret*, 50–54.
10. BHPF (1865), 14:230–248, Merlin to Calvin, July 23 and December 25; see also CO, XX, no. 3988, cols. 85–101, no. 4061, cols. 216–222.
11. R. Ritter, "Jeanne d'Albret et les Troubles de Béarn," *Revue de Béarn* (1929). Simancas numbers given by Ritter are omitted here except for documents quoted at length.
12. Simancas K, 1499, no. 85 (Ritter, "Jeanne d'Albret," 68–73), Descurra to Erasso, August 14.
13. Ritter, "Jeanne d'Albret," 85.

14. De Ruble, *Guerre civile,* 305–306; Courteault, 479 (note 3, where sources are cited).

15. *Mémoires de Condé* (6 vols., London, 1740 ed.), VI, 155–163; Armagnac also wrote a long disciplinary letter to Louis d'Albret, Bishop of Lescar, *ibid.,* 207–212.

16. Olhagaray, 540.

17. *Mémoires de Condé* (1740 ed.), VI, 163–171.

18. *CSP, For. Eliz.* 1563, no. 1546(7), Occurrences in France, December 27.

19. *Ibid.,* no. 1445(7), Occurrences in France, December 1; no. 1508(13), Challoner to the Queen, December 19; Bordenave, 121.

20. *Ambassade en Espagne de Jean d'Ebrard, Seigneur de St. Sulpice, 1562–1565,* ed. E. Cabié (Albi, France, 1903), 167, Catherine to St. Sulpice, October 18. Hereafter cited as St. Sulpice.

21. St. Sulpice, 186–187, Charles IX to St. Sulpice, November 30.

22. *CSP, For. Eliz.* 1563, no. 1463, G. Bertano to A. Bruschetto, November 27.

23. *Lettres de Catherine de Médicis,* II, 119–120 (note), Catherine to Gramont, undated; St. Sulpice, 224, Instructions of the Queen Mother to Lansac, January 1564.

24. *CSP, For. Eliz.* 1563, no. 1233(6), Throckmorton to Cecil, September 20; Courteault, 484; St. Sulpice, 183, St. Sulpice to the Queen of Spain, about November 25; H. Forneron, *Histoire de Philippe II* (2 vols., Paris, 1881), I, 303–306.

25. Olhagaray, 551.

26. B.N., Nouv. acquis. frçses. 21,603, fols. 87–88 (St. Petersburg, LIII, fol. 58, no. 48) published in La Ferrière, *Deux années,* 35–36, Jeanne to Catherine, probably December 1563.

27. Bordenave, 123.

28. A. Communay, ed., *Les Huguenots dans le Béarn et la Navarre* (Paris, 1885), 9, Queen of Navarre to Montmorency, November or December 1563. There are several letters from Jeanne to the Constable within a short period. See Communay, 13, and *Archives historiques de la Gironde* (58 vols., Bordeaux, 1859–1932), X, 375.

29. *CSP, For. Eliz.* 1563, no. 1508(10), Challoner to Queen, December 19, Merlin to Calvin, December 25; see note 10.

30. *Lettres de Catherine de Médicis,* II, 119–120 (note), Catherine to Gramont, probably December 1563.

31. Dartigue, *Jeanne d'Albret,* lxii, lxiii-lxviv; 61–70 calendars the legislation of January 12–February 11, 1564.

32. Archives de Genève, 1713, Queen of Navarre to the Seigneurie de Genève, January 1564.

33. *Receuil,* 40–45 or 81–92.

34. *Lettres de Catherine de Médicis,* II, 145–146 (note), Gramont to Catherine, March 21, 1564.

35. Communay, 17–18, Queen of Navarre to the King of Spain, April 1564; St. Sulpice, 256, St. Sulpice to Catherine, April 28, 1564.

36. St. Sulpice, 246, Queen of Navarre to St. Sulpice, March 26, 1564; 247–248, Instructions of the Queen of Navarre to the Baron de Larboust, about March 26, 1564.

JEANNE AND THE CROWN

37. B.N., Nouv. acquis. frçses. 21,603, fols. 85–86 (St. Petersburg, LIII, fol. 56, no. 47), Jeanne to Catherine, spring 1564 (undated).

38. La Ferrière's Introduction to volume II, *Lettres de Catherine de Médicis,* and P. Champion, *Catherine de Médicis presente à Charles IX son royaume,* 1564–1566 (Paris, 1937). Both of these draw on the account of a member of Catherine's entourage during the tour, Abel Jouan, *Receuil et discours du voyage du Roy, Charles IX. . . .* (Paris, 1566) (*Archives curieuses,* V and VI).

39. Fontana, III, 103–111, Renée to Calvin, March 1564 (excerpts from 108–109); see also CO, XX, No. 4085, cols. 266–273.

40. BHPF (1865), 14:125–127.

41. Archives de Genève, 1713, Jeanne to the Seigneurie, May 16, 1564 (published in BHPF [1865], 14:63–64). See H. Schlaeffer, "Laurent de Normandie," *Aspects de la propagande religieuse* (Humanisme et Renaissance, XXVIII, Geneva, 1958), 177–183. De Normandie had been a fellow-citizen of Calvin's, in Noyon. He is described as "a personage of great stature, known throughout Europe. . . . This Picard . . . was a sort of Calvinist minister of propaganda. . . . Although he had lost everything when he left Noyon . . . he died possessed of . . . 35,000 volumes . . . the greatest reformed publicity enterprise in the French language." Unpublished letters from Jeanne to De Normandie and his widow will appear in the forthcoming Calendar of Jeanne's letters, thanks to the generosity of M. Alain Dufour, in whose family collection of valuable papers they belong.

42. Abel Jouan, cited in Champion, 93–94.

43. Fontana, III, 124–125, Santa Croce to Borromeo, June 18, 1564.

44. *Lettres de Catherine de Médicis,* II, 193 (note), Oysel to Catherine, May 31, 1564.

45. Abel Jouan, cited in Champion, 103–104.

46. Fontana, III, 128–129, Santa Croce to Borromeo, June 17 and 21, 1564; on the encounters between Viret and various Catholic doctors in Lyons see R. L. Linder, *The Political Ideas of Pierre Viret* (Geneva, 1964), 54–60.

47. *Lettres de Catherine de Médicis,* II, 190–191, Catherine to the Parlement of Paris, June 15, 1564; 196, Charles IX to the Parlement, June 21, 1564. Du Moulin continued to be controversial. His *Conseil sur le fait du Conseil de Trente* (Lyons, 1564) and other books were condemned in Geneva as well as in Rome. He fell out with the Calvinist leaders and turned Lutheran in 1565, but returned to the Roman Church before his death in 1566. See M. Reulos, "Le Jurisconsulte Charles du Moulin en conflit avec les Eglises Réformées de France," BHPF (1954), 100:12; R. M. Kingdon, *Geneva and the Consolidation of the French Protestant Movement* (Geneva, 1967), 138–149.

48. *Lettres de Catherine de Médicis,* II, l.

49. Rochambeau, no. CLXXXIX, 280, Jeanne to the Comtesse de la Rochefoucauld, undated, probably early August 1564; Fontana, III, 128, Santa Croce to Borromeo, August 1564; Simancas K, 1502, no. 16, Alava to Philip, August 13, 1564, cited in *Mémoires,* 36 (note 2).

50. *CSP, For. Eliz.* 1564–1565, ed. J. Stevenson (London, 1870), no. 1091 (17), Occurrences in France, April 11, 1565.

51. B.N., Nouv. acquis. frçses. 21,603, fols. 100–101 (St. Petersburg, LIII, fols. 66–67, no. 52), Jeanne to Catherine, undated, probably 1565.

52. *CSP, For. Eliz.* 1564–1565, no. 775(2), Advices from Italy, November 30, 1564; no. 1092(5), Occurrences in France, April 11, 1565.

53. St. Sulpice, 321, Charles IX to St. Sulpice, November 28, 1564; 353, St. Sulpice to the Queen of Spain, March 8, 1565; 357, St. Sulpice to Catherine, March 16, 1565; 366, St. Sulpice to Philip II, April 3, 1565; 369, St. Sulpice to Catherine, April 13, 1565; 371–372, Catherine to St. Sulpice, about April 15, 1565; 375–376, *Mémoire* from St. Sulpice to Catherine, May 1565.

54. *Ibid.*, 376; for a general summary of the Massacre of St. Bartholomew, see Thompson, 449–453.

55. Simancas K, 1503, no. 11, published in *Lettres de Catherine de Médicis,* II, lxxiii; K, 1504, cited in *ibid.,* II, lxxxii.

56. *Ibid.,* xl; Champion, *passim.*

57. C. de Batz-Trenquelléon, *Henri IV en Gascogne* (Paris, 1885), 43–44; Davila, I, 165; *CSP, For. Eliz.* 1564–1565, no. 1369(3)(6), Smith to Leicester and Cecil, August 8, 1565.

58. *Lettres de Catherine de Médicis,* II, 332 (note 1), Charles IX to Fourquevaux, December 6, 1565.

59. Thompson, 299–300, summarizes the situation and gives the sources.

60. *CSP, For. Eliz.* 1564–1565, no. 1728(2), Smith to Cecil, December 10, 1565; no. 1729(1), Smith to Leicester and Cecil, December 11, 1565.

61. Abel Jouan, cited in Champion, 395, 431.

JEANNE IN PARIS

62. H. Sauval, *Histoire et recherches des antiquités de la ville de Paris* (3 vols., Paris, 1724), II, 249; M. Félibien and G.-A. Lobineau, *Histoire de Paris* (5 vols., Paris, 1725), I, 662; *Dictionnaire historique des rues de Paris,* ed. J. Hillairet (2 vols., Paris, 1962).

63. B.N., F fr 22,562, fol. 130, published in M. W. Freer, *The Life of Jeanne d'Albret* (London, 1862), 254.

64. The Italian translations are, Jean de Vauzelles, *La Passion de Iesu Christ, vifvement descripte, par le divin engin de Pierre Aretin, Italien* (Lyons, 1540), and Claude de Taillemont, *Orlando furioso* (Lyons, 1556) (parts only). Works dedicated to Jeanne are to be found in the following bibliographical sources: *Catalogue des livres composant la bibliothèque du Baron J. de Rothschild* (Paris, 1920), V, 442; P. Renouard, *Imprimeurs et libraires parisiens du seizième siècle* (Paris, 1964), I, no. 686; *French Sixteenth Century Books* (2 vols., Harvard College Library, Department of Printing and Graphic Arts, Catalogue, ed. R. Mortimer, Cambridge, Mass., 1964), I, no. 117. Because of the number of printers and the small quantity and obscurity of many editions, only extensive bibliographical research (which I have not undertaken) would permit a relatively complete list to be drawn up. When the Renouard Catalogue is finished, information on Parisian printers will be complete. Lyons and La Rochelle are also important. For Lyonnais works, see A. Claudin, *L'Imprimerie en France, au quinzième et seizième siècles* (Paris, 1915), and H. L. Baudrier, *Bibliographie lyonnaise* (13 vols., Lyons, 1895–1921); on La Rochelle see E. Droz, *L'Imprimerie à la Rochelle* (Travaux d'Humanisme et Renaissance, no. XXXIV, Geneva, 1960). Some verses of Jeanne's in acknowledgment of Du Bellay's, probably written in 1559, are included in the 1573 edition of his works. The themes

are conventional, not to say banal, and the style stilted. Some have been published by De Ruble in *Mémoires et poésies de Jeanne d'Albret*, 129–132.

65. Anne de Marquets, Rothschild Catalogue, IV, no. 2918; for Georgette de Montenay, see Chapter VI, note 98.

66. C. Jouhanneaud, *Jeanne d'Albret et les Limousins* (Limoges, 1897); F. Marvaud, *Histoire des vicomtes de Limoges* (2 vols., Paris, 1873), II, 221, 226.

67. N. Valois, *Le Conseil de roi au XIV, XV et XVI siècles* (Paris, 1880), 202–208.

68. *Mémoires*, 44.

69. Dartigue, *Jeanne d'Albret*, 72, Estates of September 25, 1565; 75, Estates of May 1566.

70. *Receuil*, 68–83 or 138–167; on Viret see J. Barnaud, *Pierre Viret, sa vie et son oeuvre* (St. Amans, Tarn, France, 1911), 635–648; Linder, 50–51; Dartigue, *Jeanne d'Albret*, 78–79 (Ordinances of July 1566); Bordenave, 125. See also Chapter X.

71. CSP, For. Eliz. 1566–1568, ed. J. Crosby (London, 1871), no. 907, Sir Henry Norris to the Queen, January 26, 1567. See also Chapter IX.

72. Palma Cayet, I, 178; *Mémoires*, 45–46.

73. BHPF (1867), 16:66, Jeanne to Beza, December 6, 1566. See also Chapter IX.

74. Simancas K, 1507, no. 57, Alava to Philip, February 19, 1567. It is not certain that Catherine de Bourbon was with her mother during Jeanne's earlier participation in the tour of France (1564), but she was included in the final months, after the court's visit to Nérac.

CHAPTER IX

JEANNE BROUILLÉE

1. L. Wylie, *Village in the Vaucluse* (Cambridge, Mass., 1958), 196–197, 200.

2. A. de Ruble, *Le Duc de Nemours et Mademoiselle de Rohan, 1551–1592* (Paris, 1881), contains full documentation and a comprehensive interpretation of the case in the legal and political context. Hereafter cited as De Ruble, *Duc de Nemours*.

3. *Ibid.*, 121–123 (B.N., F fr 6606, fol. 30).

4. Abel Jouan, cited in Champion, 431–432.

5. De Ruble, *Duc de Nemours*, 124–125.

6. *Chronique inédit*, B.N., F fr 12,795, fol. 484.

7. BHPF (1867), 16:66, Jeanne to Beza, December 1566; *Mémoires*, 39–42.

8. De Ruble, *Duc de Nemours*, 147–160; see also *Mémoires-Journaux de Pierre de L'Estoile*, ed. Brunet, II, 30–31, 179–180.

9. Fontana, III, 145–146, Gianelli to the Duke of Ferrara, June 2, 1566; CSP, For. Eliz. 1566–1568, no. 406(4), Sir Thomas Hoby to Cecil, May 21, 1566.

10. E. Saulnier, *Le Rôle politique du Cardinal de Bourbon* (Paris, 1912), 54.

11. E. Courbet, "Jeanne d'Albret et le Heptameron," *Bulletin du bibliophile*

et du bibliothecaire, 1904, 277–290; Jourda, *Marguerite d'Angoulême,* II, 655–657.

12. On Pedro d'Albret, see *Revue de Gascogne,* 1871, 320ff.; *Commentaires de Monluc,* IV, 328–333, 338 (footnote); St. Sulpice, 263–264, 280–281, 284, 293, 299–300, 324.

13. Bibliothèque de Rouen, Fonds Leber, ms. 5721.

14. J.-A. Gautier, *Histoire de Genève* (8 vols., Geneva, 1896–1911), IV, 541–590; A. Roget, *Histoire du peuple de Genève* (7 vols., Geneva, 1870–1883), VII, 173–187; A. Delmas, "Le Procès de Spifâme," *Humanisme et renaissance* (1944), 105–137; Geisendorf, 293ff. Sources summarized in Delmas. Where there is a conflict between him and Geisendorf, I have followed the latter. Roget's comment on Jeanne, VII, 184.

15. La Fontaine to Beza, August 8; Gallars to Beza, August 12; La Mare to Beza, September 25. All documents cited on *l'Affaire Morély* are in the Baum copies of Beza's correspondence, Bibliothèque de la Société de l'Histoire du Protestantisme français, *ms.* no. 880B. The most important ones are: Hespérien to Beza, November 26; an unsigned account of the hearing, dated only "November, 1566"; Morély's letters to Beza of December 7, 1566, and January 10, 1567, and to De Normandie, December 4, 1566; Jeanne's letter to Beza, December 6, 1566 (published in BHPF [1867], 16:64–67); La Mare to Beza, January 5, 1567; Merlin to Beza, January 10, 1567; Beza to Hespérien, January 1567. This episode is treated in a broader context by Kingdon, *Geneva and the Consolidation . . . ,* 82–96. See 48–62 on Morély's ideas, 65–82 on his relations with the pastors.

16. For this information I am indebted to Professor Kingdon, who brought it to my attention while he was reading the manuscript of this book and before the publication of his own, *Geneva and the Consolidation. . . .* On Chrétien, see Chapter XV; on Martinius, see Chapter XI.

17. *Mémoires,* 42–49.

18. Wylie, 204.

CHAPTER X
QUEEN AND ADMINISTRATOR

1. There is considerable literature on Béarn's geography, history, and economy, including two relatively recent works, C. Dartigue, *Vicomté,* and J.-B. Laborde, *Précis de l'histoire de Béarn* (Pau, 1941). I have drawn on them for general information in this section, supplemented by E. Soulice, "Notice historique sur les Eaux-Chaudes et les Eaux-Bonnes," *Bulletin de Pau,* ser. II (1876–1877), 6:231.

2. E. Molinier et F. Mazerolle, eds., *Inventaire du chateau de Pau,* 1562, published by the Société des Bibliophiles français, 1891 (original in B.N., F fr 16,812). Responsibility for the Inventory was given to the Bishops of Lescar (Louis d'Albret) and Oloron (Régin). Presumably, the actual listing was done by secretaries under their supervision. There are 1361 articles in the document, many of which list several objects; provenance and workmanship are specified, but dimensions are rarely given. All other material in this section drawn from Archives des Basses-Pyrénées (*Inventaire* ed. by P. Raymond, Paris, 1863), chiefly series B.

HENRI D'ALBRET'S SUCCESSOR

3. For material in this and the following sections I am greatly indebted to the works of Dartigue, *Vicomté* (cited above) and *Jeanne d'Albret*. The operations of the Estates of Béarn and other aspects of the government are fully explained in the latter work, and all the sessions in Jeanne's reign are calendared, with notes that explain the votes and identify important persons. Arabic numerals refer to documents, small Roman numerals to Dartigue's text. His knowledge of the materials in the Archives des Basses-Pyrénées was very thorough.

4. Dartigue, *Vicomté,* 261.

5. *Ibid.,* 263–283, 302–306; Dartigue, *Jeanne d'Albret,* xxxviii; see also L. Lacaze, *Les Imprimeurs et les libraires de Béarn,* 1552–1883 (Pau, 1884), chapter I. The expenses were borne by the Estates (Archives des Basses-Pyrénées, B 5958). While they were in the Vicomté, the two printers also produced *The Constitution of the Church and Diocese of Lescar,* for Jacques de Foix. *Los Fors et costumes de Béarn* was bound by Mathurien Chèze, a bookseller in Pau.

6. Dartigue, *Jeanne d'Albret,* xxxii–xxxiv.

7. *Ibid.,* xxxi–xlii.

8. *Ibid.,* xxxvii, xxxviii, 63. This latter provision was only partially carried out. Letters patent, for instance, continued to be issued in French.

9. *Ibid.,* xxxix–xlii.

10. *Ibid.,* xli–xlii; Dartigue, *Vicomté,* chapter X.

THE RELIGIOUS ESTABLISHMENT

11. P. Tucoo-Chala, *La Vicomté de Béarn et le problème de sa souveraineté des origines jusqu'à* 1620 (Bordeaux, 1961), 123–126, gives a clear analysis of a thorny legal problem, containing criticism of the sources and of all former treatments.

12. Dartigue, *Vicomté,* 470–480.

13. Dartigue, *Jeanne d'Albret,* 33–34.

14. *Ibid.,* 41–43.

15. Forissier, I, 132.

16. Dartigue, *Jeanne d'Albret,* 69, 79, 114, xcii–xcvii.

17. *Ibid.,* lxiii–lxiv; Forissier, 163.

18. Dartigue, *Jeanne d'Albret,* lxvii–lxviii, 72, 75, 77; *Receuil,* 68–88 or 138–177.

19. Dartigue, *Jeanne d'Albret,* 79.

20. *Ibid.,* 78–80, lxviii; Salefranque, *Bulletin de Pau,* 1921, 195–198, nos. 56–63; Dubarat, *Le Protestantisme en Béarn et au Pays Basque* (Pau, 1898), 112–119. No ecclesiastic might in future appoint holders of benefices, and laymen, although they retained the right, were obliged to appoint Calvinists. As benefices were suppressed, their resources were taken over by the treasurer of the Vicomté for the support of poor adherents of the reform. Dartigue, *Jeanne d'Albret,* 79–80.

21. Dartigue, *Jeanne d'Albret,* 80.

22. *Ibid.,* lxxi.

23. *Ibid.,* 85.

24. Bordenave, 137–138.

25. Dartigue, *Jeanne d'Albret,* lxiv–lxv, lxxi.

26. *Ibid.,* lxxiii, 99–101.

27. For the Béarnais phase of the Third Civil War see *ibid.,* lxxvi–lxxxvii; Forissier, I, 208–267; Communay, *passim* (a precious collection of documents); Salefranque, *Bulletin de Pau,* 1922, 70–80, 105–120, 141–160; Bordenave, 168–310.

28. Dartigue, *Jeanne d'Albret,* lxxix–lxxx, 109–111.

29. *Ibid.,* 111–113.

30. *Ibid.,* lxxxviii.

31. *Ibid.,* xc, 117–118, 122–123.

32. *Ibid.,* text (French), 145–164, xci–xcviii; Forissier, I, 296–304 (Ecclesiastical Ordinances ms B.N., Brienne, vol. 217, fol. 145ff.).

33. *Receuil,* 139v–149; Dartigue, *Jeanne d'Albret,* xcii–xcvi, and articles 15–26 of the Ecclesiastical Ordinances.

34. On the Academy of Orthez see Lourde-Rocheblave, "L'Académie d'Orthez," BHPF (1885), 34:280; P. de Félice, *Les Lois collegiales de l'académie de Béarn, 1568–1580* (Paris, 1889); A. Planté, *L'Université protestante de Béarn, documents inédits du seizième siècle* (Pau, 1886); J. Conderille, *Etude sur l'académie d'Orthez à la fin du seizième siècle* (Orthez, 1885). On the educational system as a whole, see also Dartigue, *Vicomté,* 383–398, and *Jeanne d'Albret,* xcviii–ic, and articles 31–32 of the Ecclesiastical Ordinances; Forissier, I, 177–185, 282–284. The *collège* was what we would call a secondary school. When it became an academy, more advanced instruction was offered. Henri IV raised it to the status of a university in 1583 and its greatest period was in the following generation. Jeanne had ordered the Academy to return to Orthez in 1571 but the obstructionist tactics of the officials at Lescar prevented execution of her will.

35. On Viret see Barnaud, 638–648; Linder, 50–51; Dartigue, *Jeanne d'Albret,* lxxxix (footnote 153), 116 (footnote 27); Forissier, I, 186–190.

36. Archives de Genève, 1713, Jeanne to the Council, April 22, 1571. The Academy inherited Viret's collection of books, which gave it the finest library in southern France in the succeeding half-century. Unfortunately the collection cannot be described, since the library of the University at Orthez was absorbed by the Capuchins in the seventeenth century. See BHPF (1897), 46:18, 483.

37. The two important treatments are Dubarat, *Le Protestantisme en Béarn et au Pays Basque* (Pau, 1895), and the articles of N. Weiss and L. Cadier, BHPF (1885), 34:89, 258, 266; (1891), 40:261–295, 443; (1893), 42: 107–111, 667; (1895), 44:638–663. Each author sums up the arguments of his own side and attempts to refute those of the opposition. Dubarat, a Catholic priest, chaplain of the *lycée* in Pau, and editor of the Salefranque *Histoire de l'hérésie,* is much less objective than his seventeenth-century predecessor. Weiss, for many years president of the Société de l'Histoire du Protestantisme français, respects the sources and is trustworthy in that he is not merely trying to defend Jeanne, but he fails to distinguish between sixteenth- and nineteenth-century meanings of toleration or between religious dissent and lese majesty.

38. The edict of D'Arros is in Dartigue, *Jeanne d'Albret,* 117–118. Jeanne's open letter, unpublished, is Simancas K, 100 B no. 57, fol. 1.

39. See, for example, W. K. Jordan, *The Development of Religious Toleration in England to the Death of Queen Elizabeth* (Cambridge, Mass., 1932);

T. H. Clancey, *Papist Pamphleteers: the Allen-Parsons Party and the Political Thought of the Counter-Reformation in England,* 1572–1616 (Chicago, 1964).

VENGEANCE OR JUSTICE?

40. Documents for this section are in Simancas K, 100 B, nos. 54–57. Dartigue, *Jeanne d'Albret;* Communay; and Salefranque. The subject is also extensively treated by two relatively objective Calvinist historians, Bordenave in the late sixteenth century and Forissier in the twentieth.

41. Olhagaray, 373.

42. Dartigue, *Jeanne d'Albret,* lxxvii (footnote 121); Communay, 129–130 (foonote 1).

43. Salefranque, *Bulletin de Pau,* 1922, no. 116.

44. Bordenave, 134, 222, 253, 301; Dartigue, *Jeanne d'Albret,* lxxx–lxxxi; Forissier, I, 216.

45. Bordenave, 179, 212–213, 253; Dartigue, *Jeanne d'Albret,* lxxviii; Forissier, I, 233; Communay, 99–100 (footnote 2).

46. Bordenave, 199–200; Dartigue, *Jeanne d'Albret,* lxxviii; Forissier, I, 214, 234; Communay, 109.

47. Communay, 29–32; De Salles to the Queen of Navarre, April 4, 1569.

48. Bordenave, 126, 224, 262–264, 277, 280; Forissier, I, 225–226, 259–260; Communay, 59 (footnote 1).

49. Accounts of the fall of Orthez in Bordenave, 267–276; Dartigue, *Jeanne d'Albret,* lxxxiv–lxxxv; Forissier, I, 252–257; Salefranque (text), *Bulletin de Pau,* 1922, 76–78. Documents containing the terms of the capitulation, Communay, 49–53.

50. Forissier, I, 262; Communay, 59 (footnote 1).

51. Bordenave, 282–283; Dartigue, *Jeanne d'Albret,* lxxxv (footnote 145 sums up all the theories on this subject); Forissier, I, 254–256, 263–267; Communay, 50–53, lists the prisoners, 69 (footnote 1), those who were executed, 69–71, Jeanne's official explanation as reported in an anonymous *Mémoire,* B.N., F fr 15,550. fol. 53. Dubarat believes that Jeanne "had plenty of time to receive messages sent and to give orders," and therefore that she was personally responsible for the "massacre." He bases his case on a message sent to her at La Rochelle on August 11, however, whereas the prisoners in question were not captured until August 15. Moreover, we do not know whether the August 11 message ever reached La Rochelle. *Bulletin de Pau,* 1925, 112–113, "Journal du Siège de Navarrenx."

52. Salefranque, *Bulletin de Pau,* 1922, no. 117.

53. Communay, 72–73, 72 (footnote 3); Bordenave, 284.

54. Communay, 57–58, Montamat to Jeanne, August 23, 1569.

55. *Ibid.,* 61, 64–65, Montgomery to Jeanne, September 5 and September 11, 1569.

56. *Ibid.,* 68, Montgomery to Jeanne, September 28, 1569.

57. Montgomery's edicts after his victory are in Dartigue, *Jeanne d'Albret,* 112–113; Salefranque, *Bulletin de Pau,* 1922, nos. 128, 119.

58. Dartigue, *Jeanne d'Albret,* 114; Salefranque, *Bulletin de Pau,* 1922, no. 122.

59. Dartigue, *Jeanne d'Albret,* lxxxvi–lxxxvii; Forissier, I, 277–281; see

also the report of Jeanne's secretary Enecot de Sponde on September 29; Communay, 71–80.

60. Communay, 81–92 (Archives des Basses-Pyrénées E 340); Salefranque, *Bulletin de Pau,* 1922, nos. 136, 143; Communay, 122–125.

61. Dartigue, *Jeanne d'Albret,* 121.

62. Communay, 107, Montamat to Jeanne, February 25, 1570; Salefranque, *Bulletin de Pau,* nos. 136, 143; Communay, 122–125.

63. J. Aymon, *Tous les synodes nationaux des églises réformées de France* (2 vols., The Hague, 1710), I, 108. See also J. Quick, *Synodicon in Gallia Reformata* (2 vols., London, 1692), I, 99.

64. Aymon, I, 110; Quick, I, 99.

65. *Receuil,* 146r.

66. Forissier, I, 279–280; the entire correspondence is in Communay, 129–139.

67. Simancas K, 100 B, nos. 54 (1570), 55–57 (1571) (55 and 56 are bound together). Registres du Secretariat de la Reine de Navarre.

68. Archives des Basses-Pyrénées, E 586.

69. P. Erlanger, *L'Etrange mort d'Henri IV* (Paris, 1957).

CHAPTER XI
PARTY LEADER AND DIPLOMAT

THE GREAT DECISION

1. Thompson, 357–358, considers the Montmorency actions at this time "the germ of the *politique* party."

2. *Lettres de Catherine de Médicis,* III, xxiv–xxv.

3. Thompson, 350, cites the sources.

4. See C. Hirschauer, *La Politique de St. Pie V en France* (Paris, 1922), 29–37 for relations between France and Rome between the Second and Third Civil Wars.

5. Thompson, 305–361 *passim,* deals with relations between the Dutch rebels and the Huguenots in 1568.

6. *Lettres de Catherine de Médicis,* III, xxii–xxiii; Thompson, 346–348.

7. Desjardins, ed., III, 573, Petrucci to François de Médicis, April 9, 1568.

8. Thompson, 351–358.

9. *Ibid.,* 351.

10. B.N., F fr 22,373, fol. 308, Registres du Parlement de Bordeaux, January 19, 1568.

11. *Mémoires,* 54–55; Communay, 19–21, contains letters authorizing Fénelon's mission, Charles IX to the Queen of Navarre and to Antoine de Noailles, February 13, 1568.

12. B.N., F fr 22,373, fol. 373, Registres du Parlement de Bordeaux, February 25, 1568.

13. *Commentaires de Monluc,* V, 115–122, Monluc to Charles IX, April 2, 1568.

14. B.N., Nouv. acquis. frçses. 21,603, fols. 28–29 (St. Petersburg, LIII, fol. 19, no. 18), Jeanne to Catherine, undated, probably spring 1568.

15. *Lettres de Catherine de Médicis,* III, 136, Catherine to Monluc, April 14, 1568. The Queen Mother's reply to Jeanne has not survived.

16. B.N., F fr 22,373, fol. 410, Registres du Parlement de Bordeaux, May 12, 1568.

17. *Mémoires*, 55.

18. *Ibid.*, 56-58 (excerpts).

19. *Ibid.*, 60-66 (excerpts); for these articles and the King's response see *Mémoires*, 165-193.

20. *Ibid.*, 70-77, for excerpts cited in this paragraph.

21. *Ibid.*, 81-82.

22. *Ibid.*, 86-87, 90-91 (excerpts).

23. *Ibid.*, 107-120, gives Jeanne's itinerary and detailed account of her escape.

24. See *Commentaires de Monluc,* III, 173-175; Courtenault, 514-515, for Monluc's version.

25. Archives d'Agen BB 1, cited in *Mémoires,* 108 (note 3).

26. Olhagaray, 575.

27. Registres du Parlement de Bordeaux, ms. 369, 3, fol. 123.

28. A. Barbot, *Histoire de la Rochelle. Archives historiques de la Saintonge et de l'Aunis,* 1889, 316. See Note 75.

MINISTER OF PROPAGANDA AND FOREIGN AFFAIRS

29. The sources for Jeanne's propaganda are the following five letters and the *Mémoires.* Other places where the letters may be found in print are Jean de Serres, *Histoire de la troisième guerre civile,* 1571 and J. Delaborde, *Gaspard de Coligny* (3 vols., Paris, 1872), III. (1) Jeanne to Charles IX, Bergerac, September 16, 1568: *Mémoires,* 205-208; De Serres, 174-177; Delaborde, *Coligny,* III, 516-517; Bordenave, 157-158. (2) Jeanne to Catherine de Medici, Bergerac, September 16, 1568: *Mémoires,* 209-214; De Serres, 177-184; Delaborde, *Coligny,* III, 518-520; Bordenave, 159-163. (3) Jeanne to the Duc d'Anjou, Bergerac, September 16, 1568: *Mémoires,* 215-216; De Serres, 185-186; Delaborde, *Coligny,* III, 520-521. (4) Jeanne to the Cardinal de Bourbon, Bergerac, September 16, 1568: *Mémoires,* 217-218; De Serres, 187-188; Delaborde, *Coligny,* III, 521-522. (5) Jeanne to Queen Elizabeth of England, La Rochelle, October 16, 1568: *Mémoires,* 219-222; Bordenave, 164-167. See also E. Droz, *L'Imprimerie à La Rochelle,* I, *Barthélemy Breton,* 1563-1573 (Geneva, 1960), 73-74. Condé's manifestoes are in Delaborde, *Coligny,* III, 479-536. For his arguments, succinctly stated in his *Déclaration relative à la nouvelle prise d'armes,* 1568, see Delaborde, Coligny, III, 527.

30. Valois, *Conseil du roi, passim.*

31. In justice to Jeanne's apprehension, the Cardinal de Lorraine, by aligning himself with Anjou at this time, pushed Catherine further into the Catholic camp, thus helping to force the Huguenots into opposition. See N. M. Sutherland, *Catherine de Medici and the Ancien Régime* (Historical Association Pamphlet, London, 1966), 17-19.

32. *Correspondance diplomatique de Bertrand de Salignac, Seigneur de La Mothe-Fénelon* (7 vols., Paris and London, 1838-1840), I, 28 Dispatch of December 5, 1568. Hereafter cited as Fénelon.

33. See J. W. Allen, *A History of Political Thought in the Sixteenth Century* (London, 1941); W. F. Church, *Constitutional Thought in Sixteenth-Century*

France (Cambridge, Mass., 1941); J. N. Figgis, *Political Thought from Gerson to Grotius* (Cambridge, 1931); R. M. Kingdon, "Calvinism and Democracy: Some Political Implications of Debates on French Reformed Church Government, 1562–1572," *American Historical Review* (January 1964), 68:393–401; R. M. Kingdon, "William Allen's use of Protestant political arguments," *From the Renaissance to the Counter-Reformation; Essays in Honor of Garrett Mattingly* (New York, 1965), 164–178; H. G. Koenigsberger, "The Organization of Revolutionary Parties in France and the Netherlands during the Sixteenth Century," *The Journal of Modern History* (December 1955), 27:335–351; R. D. Linder, *The Political Ideas of Pierre Viret*; W. J. Stankewicz, *Politics and Religion in Seventeenth-Century France* (Berkeley, 1960), chapter I; G. Weill, *Les Théories sur le pouvoir royal en France pendant les guerres de religion* (Paris, 1892). The most recent over-all treatment of the problem is V. de Caprariis, *Propaganda e pensiero politico in Francia durante le guerre di religione* (Naples, 1959).

34. Fénelon, I, 62–63, Dispatch of December 28, 1568. For many interesting details on Odet and for an excellent account of English opinion about the Huguenots in general, see E. G. Atkinson, 'The Cardinal of Châtillon in England, 1568–1571," *Proceedings of the Huguenot Society of London* (1888–1891), 3: 172–285.

35. *Lettres de Catherine de Médicis,* III, 222–225, Catherine to Fénelon, February 10, 1569 and Henri de Navarre to Cecil, January 10, 1569; La Ferrière, *Le Seizième siècle et les Valois* (Paris, 1879), 230, Condé to Cecil, December 31, 1568; 231, Jeanne to Cecil, January 16, 1569; 236–237, Condé to Elizabeth and Coligny to Elizabeth, January 11, 1569. Hereafter cited as La Ferrière, *Seizième siècle. Lettres de Catherine de Médicis,* III, 225 (footnote), Jeanne to Elizabeth, February 1, 1569.

36. Arcère, I, 372.

37. Delaborde, *Coligny,* III, 535–538, D'Andelot, Jeanne and Henri de Navarre to Louis, Duke of Wurtemburg, all on January 31, 1569, and Condé to the Duke, February 1, 1569; La Ferrière, *Seizième Siècle,* 236–237, D'Andelot to the Elector of Brandenburg, January 30, 1569 and Jeanne to the Elector, January 31, 1569. La Ferrière, *Seizième siècle,* 238, Condé, Coligny and Henri de Navarre to the Duc de Deux-Ponts, February 11, 1569.

38. See A. N. Whitehead, *Gaspard de Coligny, Admiral of France* (London, 1904), 204–209, for the sources and summary of Condé's death.

39. Rochambeau, no. CCIII, 296, Jeanne to the Prince de Condé, March, 1569.

40. *CSP, For. Eliz.* 1569–1571, ed. A. J. Crosby (London, 1874), no. 182, Jeanne to Cecil, March 21, 1569; (also La Ferrière, *Seizième siècle,* 240).

41. Delaborde, *Coligny,* III, 543–545, *Mémoire* of Cardinal de Châtillon to Jeanne, March, 1569; La Ferrière, *Seizième siècle,* 241, Queen Elizabeth to the Duc d'Anjou, April 17, 1569; Delaborde, *Coligny,* III, 109 (footnote).

42. BHPF (1928), 77:23–25, Jeanne to Beza, April 19, 1569.

43. Fénelon, I, 385–387, Dispatch of May 19, 1569.

44. *CSP, For. Eliz.* 1569–1571, no. 286, Norris to the Queen, June 3, 1569; Simancas K, 1514, no. 118, Alava to Philip, June 11, 1569.

45. Delaborde, *Coligny,* III, 135–138.

46. Fénelon, II, 98, Dispatch of July 27, 1569; 140–141, Dispatch of

August 5, 1569. See also La Ferrière, *Seizième siècle,* 244–245, Henri de Navarre to Cecil, June 6, 1569, offering Jeanne's jewels as collateral.

47. British Museum, Cotton, Caligula, E VI, fol. 106, Jeanne to Elizabeth, July 19, 1569 (excerpt in *Lettres de Catherine de Médicis,* III, 260–261 [note].

48. Thompson, 381; Desjardins, ed., III, 601–604, Petrucci's dispatches of October 1569 (excerpts).

49. *CSP, For. Eliz.* 1569–1571, no. 376, Norris to Cecil, August 11, 1569.

ACTIVE LEADERSHIP

50. Simancas K, 1510, no. 27, Alava to Philip, December 10, 1568.

51. "Le Conseil de la Reine de Navarre à La Rochelle," J. de Gaulle, ed., BHPF (1865), 14:123–137.

52. *Ibid.,* 127–128.

53. J.-B. E. Jourdan, *Ephémerides historiques de la Rochelle* (see Note 75), 21; Barbot, *Archs. hists. Saintonge* (1889), 330; Arcère, I, 373–374.

54. J.-A. De Thou, *Histoire universelle* (6 vols., Basle, ed., 1742), IV, 178; Simancas K, 1514, no. 80, Alava to Philip, April 7, 1569.

55. De Thou, IV, 187.

56. Thompson, 383, summarizes the situation; Fénelon, II, 69, Dispatch of June 28, 1569.

57. Delaborde, *Coligny,* III, 134; De Thou, IV, 188–189.

58. *Lettres de Catherine de Médicis,* III, 243, Catherine to Charles IX, June 9, 1569.

59. Bordenave, 255.

60. Dubarat, ed., "Couriers de Jeanne d'Albret entre Béarn et La Rochelle, 1569," *Bulletin de Pau* (1930), 283–296. The key document is Archives des Basses-Pyrénées, B 954.

61. D'Aubigné, III, 75–79.

62. *Histoire de notre temps* . . . , 617–619, Jeanne to M. de Puyviaut and Jeanne to MMs. de Puyviaut et de La Brosse, undated, probably July 1569. We do not possess the originals of these letters, only the report of them, in indirect discourse, included in the Receuil, *L'Histoire de notre temps* . . . ; see E. Droz, *Imprimerie,* 98–99.

63. *CSP, For. Eliz.* 1569–1571, no. 434, Norris to Cecil, September 11, 1569.

64. Simancas K, 1512, no. 69, Alava to Gabriel de Cayas, September 5, 1569.

65. D'Aubigné, III, 130–131.

66. Barbot, *Archs. hists. Saintonge* (1889), 358.

67. Simancas K, 1512, no. 98, Alava to Philip, October 4, 1569.

68. *CSP, For. Eliz.* 1569–1571, no. 514, Jeanne to the Princes, November 24, 1569.

69. Desjardins, ed., III, 605, Petrucci to François de Mèdicis, November 24, 1569; Barbot, *Archs. hists. Saintonge* (1889), 361.

70. Jourdan, II, 449; Barbot, *Archs. hists. Saintonge* (1889), 368–372.

71. *CSP, For. Eliz.* 1569–1571, nos. 625, 772, Elizabeth to Jeanne, January 15 and March 23, 1570.

72. See Delaborde, *Coligny,* III, 165–213, and Whitehead, 224–226, on

Coligny between Moncontour and the Peace of St. Germain (October 1569–August 1570).

73. H. Hauser, *François de La Noue* (Paris, 1892), 22; Delaborde, *Coligny*, III, 289 (footnote).

74. De Thou, IV, 324.

QUEEN OF HUGUENOT FRANCE: JEANNE AT LA ROCHELLE.

75. There are several historians of La Rochelle used as sources for this section. The earliest and most reliable is Amos Barbot, 1566–1625. Member of an important family in the municipal government, Barbot is more than a chronicler, and considerably more objective than the later historians, who, however, draw heavily on him. (See L. Delayant, *Historiens de La Rochelle* [La Rochelle, 1863], for evaluation of the various manuscript histories.) Barbot's *Histoire de La Rochelle* was published in *Archives historiques de la Saintonge et de l'Aunis* (1889), 17:1–381, and (1890), 18:1–241. J.-B. E. Jourdan, *Ephémerides historiques de La Rochelle* (2 vols., La Rochelle, 1861), had access to documentary sources to supplement Barbot. The greatest amount of detail—and of local bias—is to be found in the three volumes of the eighteenth-century historian, L. E. Arcère, *Histoire de la ville de La Rochelle* (La Rochelle, 1756). The only twentieth-century study is primarily topographical, by an archivist of the Departement of Charente Inferieure (now Maritime): François de Vaux de Foletier, *La Rochelle d'autrefois et d'à present* (La Rochelle, 1923). I have also used the notes on Rabelaisian topography by H. Patry, *Revue des études rabelaisiennes* (1906), 4:373–376.

76. Discussion of l'Hôtel d'Huré in Jourdan, II, 316–318; Arcère, I, 290; Foletier, 163. It does not seem to be certain how the house was destroyed, possibly by fire, in the eighteenth century. Henri's lease is in Archives des Basses-Pyrénées, B 3068.

77. Arcère, I, 197.

78. Jeanne's correspondence for the years 1570 and 1571, in large part unpublished, is the authority for this statement. The present writer is preparing a calendar of her letters for publication.

79. Barbot, *Archs. hists. Saintonge* (1889), 381; Jourdan, I, 84; Arcère, I, 388, 392–393.

80. Arcère, I, 193–198, describes the operation of the municipal government. The article in Larousse, *Dictionnaire du dix-neuvième siècle* (1876), 207, summarizes the history of the city in relation to the French crown.

81. Arcère, I, 377–378.

82. Barbot, *Archs. hists. Saintonge* (1889), 374.

83. *CSP, For. Eliz.* 1569–1571, no. 516, Norris to the Queen, November 25, 1569.

84. Barbot, *Archs. hists. Saintonge* (1889), 373.

85. *Ibid.*, 377.

86. *Ibid.* (1890), 5.

87. *Ibid.*, 1; Jourdan, II, 156; Arcère, I, 308; Foletier, 168.

88. Aymon, I, 98–111. See also Geisendorf, 301–303; Quick, I, 89–101.

89. Aymon, I, 109; Quick, I, 100.

90. Barbot, *Archs. hists. Saintonge* (1890), 4; Jourdan, I, 192; Arcère, I, 399. Following Barbot, all the Rochelais historians place this speech in March

1572, but this is probably an error. The documentary sources on Jeanne's movements are quite explicit—since royal agents were reporting regularly on them—from the time she left Pau, the end of November 1571, until her arrival in Blois, March 4, 1572. (See Chapter XIII.) She spent several weeks in Nérac and a few days in Lectoure before proceeding to Biron, where she had arrived by January 21. From there she went directly to Tours and then to Blois. If she made a detour to La Rochelle on this last trip it must have been in January and not in March, and it would almost surely have been mentioned by Biron. It is true that Jeanne, in a letter to Gourdon of November 29, 1571, just as she was departing from Pau, mentions her intention to return to La Rochelle "very shortly" (B.N., F fr 17,044, fol. 454v) but there is no evidence that she did so. I believe the speech was made in August 1571, when Jeanne left La Rochelle, after nearly three years' residence there, to return to Béarn. The error probably crept in from the context of Barbot's statement that "she was leaving to arrange the marriage of her son." We know that all preliminary negotiations took place between Jeanne and Biron in Béarn, in the autumn of 1571, and that only the confrontation with Catherine took place in Blois in March 1572. Further support for this hypothesis lies in the fact that the matter is mentioned as a subordinate clause in a sentence whose main point is the relief of the Rochelais at Jeanne's departure.

CHAPTER XII
JEANNE AND CATHERINE DE MEDICI

EARLIER CONTACTS

1. Simancas K, 1494, no. 94, Chantonay to Philip, August 31, 1561.
2. Simancas K, 1495, no. 70, Chantonay to Philip, September 21, 1561; Desjardins, ed., III, 461, Tornabuoni, Dispatch of September 4, 1561.
3. *Mémoires,* 112–113 (note); Thompson, 390.

NEGOTIATING THE PEACE

4. Desjardins, ed., III, 609, Petrucci, Dispatch of January 24, 1570.
5. *CSP, For. Eliz.* 1569–1571, no. 620, M. de Mongueville to M. Nicolas Carrée, January 11, 1570.
6. On Monluc and Damville, see Thompson, 347–348, 400; on Charles and Anjou, see Desjardins, ed., III, 639, Petrucci, Dispatch of August 10, 1570.
7. *Mémoires de Michel de Castelnau,* I, bk. VII, X, 256.
8. M. W. Freer, *The Life of Jeanne d'Albret, Queen of Navarre* (London, 1862), 301–303 [Collection of Louis Paris] Jeanne to Catherine, undated, probably December 1569. This is Miss Freer's translation; the original is no longer available.
9. *CSP, For. Eliz.* 1569–1571, no. 644, January 1570.
10. There is no general treatment of these negotiations in English and no single adequate treatment in French. A part of La Ferrière's introduction to volume III of *Lettres de Catherine de Médicis,* lii–lxvii, is good as far as it goes, as is De Thou, IV, 301–329. The Protestant side of the story is very fully documented—although inadequately interpreted, I believe—in Delaborde, *Coligny,* III, 177–237; the actions and opinions of the various papal representatives are thoroughly covered in Hirschauer, *La Politique de St. Pie V en France,* 44–62.

11. Hirschauer, 47.

12. *Lettres de Catherine de Médicis,* III, 294–295, Catherine and Charles to Fourquevaux, February 7, 1570; Spanish and Vatican observers give an even more lurid picture of the state of the kingdom in 1570. Simancas K, 1516, no. 15, Martin to Gabriel, July 14.

13. *Lettres de Catherine de Médicis,* III, 346–352, Jeanne to Catherine, February 10, 1570.

14. *CSP, For. Eliz.,* 1569–1571, no. 689, Norris to Cecil, February 17, 1570.

15. On the Montréal conference, see D'Aubigné, III, 161–162; Proclamation of the Princes, *CSP, For. Eliz.,* 1569–1571, no. 820, the Princes to Charles IX, April 17, 1570; no. 742, Odet de Châtillon to Cecil, March 9, 1570.

16. B.N., F fr 6621, fol. 161, Biron to Charles, March 12, 1570.

17. Fénelon, III, 115, Dispatch of April 13, 1570; Simancas K, 1515, no. 78, Anonymous report, April 11, 1570; Rochambeau, no. CCV, 298–301 [Collection Laverdet], Jeanne to Charles IX, April 27, 1570.

18. De Thou, IV, 315; *Lettres de Catherine de Médicis,* III, lix, lxiii.

19. Desjardins, ed., III, 630, Petrucci, Dispatch of June 25, 1570.

20. *Ibid.,* III, 633, Petrucci, Dispatch of July 4, 1570.

21. Simancas K, 1517, no. 62, Alava to Alva, April 2, 1570.

22. Desjardins, ed., III, 626, Petrucci, Dispatch of May 5, 1570.

23. Delaborde, *Coligny,* III, 212, Artus de Cossé-Brissac to the King and Catherine, July 4, 1570 (B.N., F fr 15,552, fol. 104).

24. Desjardins, ed., III, 634, Petrucci, Dispatch of July 4, 1570; Fénelon, III, 257, secret *Mémoire* added to Dispatch of July 25, 1570.

25. *Lettres de Catherine de Médicis,* III, lxvi; Thompson, 416–417.

26. Desjardins, ed., III, 640, Anonymous dispatch, August 20, 1570.

27. *Lettres de Catherine de Médicis,* III, lxvii; *CSP, For. Eliz.* 1569–1571, no. 1109, Norris to the Queen, July 23, 1570.

28. B.N., Nouv. acquis. frçses. 21,603, fols. 30–31 (St. Petersburg, LIII, fol. 21, no. 19), Jeanne to Catherine, August 15, 1570; fol. 32 (St. Petersburg, LIII, fol. 22, no. 20), Jeanne to Catherine, also August 15, 1570; fol. 58 (St. Petersburg, LIII, fol. 38, no. 31), Jeanne to Charles IX, August 15, 1571.

IMPLEMENTING THE PEACE

29. *CSP, For. Eliz.* 1569–1571, no. 1198, Norris to Cecil, August 23, 1570; no. 1377, Occurrences in France, October 1570.

30. Simancas K, 1518, no. 10, Alava to Philip, October 14, 1570; no. 18, Alava to Philip, October 31, 1570; no. 64, Alava to Philip, December 22, 1570; *CSP, For. Eliz.* 1569–1571, no. 1216, Norris to Queen, August 31, 1570; no. 1422, Advices from Venice, December 1570.

31. B.N., Nouv. acquis. frçses., 21,603, fol. 9 (St. Petersburg, LIII, fol. 13, no. 13), Jeanne to Catherine, August 22, 1570.

32. B.N., F fr 15,552, fol. 237, Jeanne to Charles IX, August 25, 1570.

33. *Commentaires de Monluc,* III, 354–355.

34. B.N., Nouv. acquis. frçses., 21,603, fols. 27–29 (St. Petersburg, LIII, fol. 25, no. 23), Jeanne to Charles IX, September 5, 1570.

35. *Ibid.,* fol. 6 (St. Petersburg, LIII, fol. 4, no. 4), Jeanne to Charles, October 4, 1570.

36. *Ibid.*, fol. 18 (St. Petersburg, LIII, fol. 12, no. 12), Jeanne to Charles, October 17, 1570; Bibliothèque de la Société de l'Histoire du Protestantisme français, Collection Labouchère, II, fol. 56, Jeanne to Charles IX, 1570.

37. Delaborde, *Coligny,* III, 266–285; D'Aubigné, III, 274.

38. D. Digges, *The Compleat Ambassador* (London, 1655), 18.

39. *Lettres de Catherine de Médicis,* III, xvi–xix.

40. Hirschauer, 107–130, Dispatches of Frangipani, August 19–November 12, 1570.

41. *Ibid.*, 127, Dispatch of November 6, 1570.

42. *Ibid.*, 120, Dispatch of September 30, 1570.

43. *Ibid.*, 123, 134, Frangipani and Bramante to Rusticucci, October 14 and November 28, 1570. The notion that the Massacre of St. Bartholomew was premeditated is partially based on statements of this kind by agents of the Papacy and the King of Spain. For a recent discussion of this matter see H. Butterfield, *Man on his Past* (Boston, 1960), chapter VI.

44. Simancas K, 1516, no. 50, Alava to Philip, August 2, 1570; K, 1517, no. 114, Alava to Philip, September 20, 1570.

45. *Mémoires de l'estat de France sous Charles IX* (3 vols., Meidleburg? 1576), I, 46; Delaborde, *Coligny,* III, 266; *Lettres de Catherine de Médicis,* IV, 22–24, Catherine to Jeanne and Jeanne to Catherine, both January 3, 1571 (Jeanne's in footnote).

46. B.N., Nouv. acquis. frçses. 21,603, fols. 71–77 (St. Petersburg, LIII, fol. 51, no. 42), Jeanne to Quincé, January 8, 1571; B.N., F fr 15,553, fol. 12, Jeanne to Artus Cossé-Brissac, January 19, 1571; fol. 34, Jeanne to the Marquis de Villars, January 27, 1571.

47. Desjardins, ed., III, 648, Dispatch of Petrucci, February 23, 1571.

48. B.N., Nouv. acquis. frçses. 21,603, fols. 40–43 (St. Petersburg, LIII, fol. 27, no. 24), Jeanne to Charles IX, February 4, 1571.

49. *Ibid.*, fols. 69–70 (St. Petersburg, LIII, fol. 45, no. 39), Jeanne to Charles and Catherine, February 22, 1571.

50. *Archives historiques de la Gironde,* XIV, 43–44, Biron to Cossé, March 1571.

51. *Ibid.*, XIV, 44–45, Biron to Charles IX, March 7, 1571.

52. Rochambeau, no. CCXV, 317–318, Jeanne to Charles IX, May 6, 1571; B.N., Nouv. acquis. frçses., 21,603, fols. 16–17 (St. Petersburg, LIII, fol. 11, no. 11), Jeanne to Charles IX, May 21, 1571; fol. 68 (St. Petersburg, LIII, fol. 45, no. 38), Jeanne to the Duc d'Anjou, May 25, 1571.

53. B.N., F fr 15,553, fol. 105, Castelnau to Catherine, June 12, 1571.

54. B.N., Nouv. acquis. frçses., 21,603, fols. 35–36 (St. Petersburg, LIII, fol. 24, no. 22), Jeanne to Catherine, June 21, 1571.

55. *Ibid.*, fols. 63–64 (St. Petersburg, LIII, fol. 42, no. 35), Jeanne to Charles IX, August 17, 1571.

56. Hirschhauer, 131, Frangipani to Rusticucci, November 12, 1570; 133, Bramante to Rusticucci, November 14, 1570.

57. Simancas K, 1520, no. 59, Alava to Philip, April 15, 1571.

58. Desjardins, ed., III, 686, 695, Dispatches of Petrucci, July 26 and August 10, 1571; *CSP, For. Eliz.* 1569–1571, no. 1849, Walsingham to Burghley, July 8, 1571.

59. B.N., F fr 15,553, fol. 212, Coligny to Catherine, August 2, 1571; fol.

233, Cossé to Catherine, August 18, 1571; Delaborde, *Coligny,* III, 325, where other sources are summarized.

60. Hirschauer, 78 (footnote), Frangipani to Rusticucci, August 31, 1570. The Spaniards say the same thing; Simancas K, 1530, no. 77, Alava to Alva, September 12, 1570.

61. *Mémoires inédits de La Huguerye,* ed. A. de Ruble, Société de l'Histoire de France (3 vols., Paris, 1877), I, 20–91 *passim.*

62. La Huguerye, I, 20–21 (note giving opinion of De Ruble); H. Hauser, *Les Sources de l'histoire de France au seizième siècle* (4 vols., Paris, 1906–1915), III (1915), no. 1461, p. 60; Delaborde, *Coligny,* III, 318–319; C. Read, *Mr. Secretary Walsingham* (3 vols., Cambridge, Mass., 1925), I, 156–158. La Huguerye clearly was acting as a double spy in this episode (see his *Mémoires,* 33–40). There are many inaccuracies and anachronisms in his account. Jeanne is the villain of the story, partly because she would not cooperate in the scheme but chiefly because La Huguerye is prejudiced against the House of Navarre. He says that two of its kings "had already inflicted a thousand ills upon France," and that Jeanne was jealous of Condé before Jarnac because she feared he would usurp Henri's position as First Prince of the Blood. H. Hauser, an authority on the sources of the period, considers the *Mémoires* a polemical document, *condéen,* because La Huguerye opposes the Condés, as heroes, to the villains, Jeanne, Antoine, and Henri de Navarre. La Huguerye's *Mémoires* were written in the service of the Condés about 1604.

63. La Huguerye, I, 66–69, 72–77, 85–87.

64. *Ibid.,* I, 22.

65. *Ibid.,* I, 47.

66. *Ibid.,* I, 83.

67. *Ibid.,* I, 41. A marriage between Henri and Elizabeth would have served Coligny's ambition very well, by reinforcing Elizabeth's connection with the Huguenots and removing the First Prince of the Blood from France; but he probably never expected it to come about because of the intensity of Jeanne's opposition. (With hindsight, one can also state that Elizabeth would almost certainly not have carried the plan out.) The Navarre-Valois marriage was the second-best chance for the success of the Admiral's policy. Since, unlike the English marriage, it also advanced Jeanne's ambition for her son, her opposition was even more frustrating to Coligny.

68. *Mémoires de l'estat de France sous Charles IX,* I, 82–83.

69. B.N., Nouv. acquis. frçses., 21,603, fols. 63–64 (St. Petersburg, LIII, fol. 42, no. 35), Jeanne to Charles IX, August 17, 1571.

70. *Ibid.,* fols. 1–2 (St. Petersburg, LIII, fol. 1, no. 1), Jeanne to Charles IX, August 24, 1571, published in La Ferrière, *Deux années,* 31–32.

71. *Ibid.,* fol. 60 (St. Petersburg, LIII, fol. 40, no. 33), Jeanne to Charles IX, September 9, 1571.

CHAPTER XIII

CONFRONTATION: THE MARRIAGE TREATY

CATHERINE'S OFFENSIVE

1. *Mémoires de Marguerite de Valois,* 24. Marguerite says that the Montmorencys first proposed the alliance to Catherine.

2. *Lettres de Catherine de Médicis,* IV, 59, Catherine to Charles, August 1571; B.N., Nouv. acquis. frçses. 21,603, fols. 61–62 (St. Petersburg, LIII, fol. 41, no. 34), Jeanne to Catherine de Medici, August 7, 1571.

3. Simancas K, 1520, no. 77, Alava to Alva, September 12, 1571; Desjardins, ed., III, 706–707, Dispatch of Petrucci, September 20, 1571; *CSP, For. Eliz.* 1569–1571, no. 2049, Walsingham to Burghley, September 26, 1571; Simancas K, 1522, no. 40, Alava to Alva, September 1571; Fénelon, IV, 246, Dispatch of September 30, 1571.

4. Desjardins, ed., III, 711, Dispatch of Petrucci, September 29, 1571; 721–722, Dispatch of October 16, 1571.

5. Delaborde, *Coligny,* III, 345, 346–348; De Thou, IV, 494.

6. Simancas K, 1522, no. 68, Alava to Philip, November 6, 1571; Read, I, 167–171; Fénelon, VII, 277, Dispatch of November 30, 1571.

7. *Lettres de Catherine de Médicis,* IV, 76, Catherine to the Grand Duke of Tuscany, October 8, 1571.

8. Hirschauer, 80–86, 79 (note 1), 172 (note 1), Dispatch of Frangipani, October 10, 1571; B.N., F fr 3951, fol. 135, Charles to M. de Ferrals, October 1571.

9. A letter from Charles to Ferrals suggesting that he try to obtain a "private dispensation" was never sent, according to a marginal notation in a contemporary hand B.N., F fr 2899, fol. 295 (published in *Lettres de Catherine de Médicis,* IV, 75 [note 1]). The substitution of the menace of disinheriting Henri was the reason. Later, after Jeanne's death, Catherine again asked for a secret dispensation.

10. La Huguerye, I, 79, 82–83; Bordenave, 318–319; Simancas K, 1522, no. 68, Alava to Philip, November 6, 1571.

11. *Archs. hists. Gir.,* XIV, 46–49, Biron to Catherine, November 12, 1571.

12. *Ibid.,* 49–50, Biron to the King, November 20, 1571; *CSP, For. Eliz.* 1569–1571, no. 2157, News from France, December 3, 1571; no. 2196, Killigrew to Burghley, December 29, 1571.

13. *Commentaires de Monluc,* III, 104, 178; Courteault, 500ff.; B.N., Nouv. acquis. frçses., 21,603, fols. 44–46 (St. Petersburg, LIII, fol. 29, no. 25), Jeanne to Charles IX, undated, probably autumn, 1571.

14. Bordenave, 313–319 (excerpts).

15. Archives de Nay, CCII, and Archives des Basses-Pyrénées, B 148, fol. 21; Desjardins, ed., III, 733–734, Dispatch of Petrucci, November 30, 1571.

16. Rochambeau, no. CCXXII, 326–327, Jeanne to Caumont-La Force, December 1571.

17. Desjardins, ed., III, 725, 727, Dispatches of Petrucci, November 4 and 20, 1571; *Archs. hists. gir.,* XIV, 53–54, Biron to Charles, December 12, 1571.

18. B.N., Nouv. acquis. frçses., 21,603, fols. 71–74 (St. Petersburg, III, fols. 48–49, no. 40), Jeanne to Charles, December 12, 1571.

19. *Archs. hists. Gir.,* XIV, 54–55, Biron to Charles, December 16, 1571.

20. Desjardins, ed., III, 743, Dispatch of Petrucci, December 24, 1571; B.N., Nouv. acquis. frçses., 21,603, fols. 52–53 (St. Petersburg, LIII, fol. 34, no. 28), Jeanne to Charles, December 17, 1571.

21. Desjardins, ed., III, 743, Petrucci to François de Médicis, December 24, 1571; Rochambeau, no. CCXXX, 335, Jeanne to Caumont, probably January 1572.

JEANNE EMBATTLED

22. B.N., Dupuy, 211, fol. 42 (published in Freer, 370–371), Jeanne to Henri, January 21, 1572.

23. Simancas K, 1524, no. 55, Aguilon to Philip, December 17, 1571; *CSP, For. Eliz.* 1572–1574, ed. A. J. Crosby (London, 1876), no. 27, Killigrew to Burghley, January 10, 1572.

24. *Ibid.*, no. 109 (2), News from France, February 3, 1572; Hirschauer, 85–89, 181 (note 2); De Thou, IV, 535; La Huguerye, I, 96 (note 1); *Lettres de Catherine de Médicis,* IV, xli, 315–316, Catherine to Philip, February 1572.

25. Desjardins, ed., III, 748–749, Dispatches of Petrucci, February 14 and 18, 1572; *CSP, Venetian,* ed. R. Brown (London, 1890), VII, no. 539, Anonymous Dispatch, February 24, 1572.

26. B.N., Dupuy, 211, fol. 39 (Freer, 374–376), Jeanne to Henri, February 21, 1572.

27. Thompson, 444–446; Archives de la Secretariat d'Etat d'Espagne, leg. 359, fol. 14, January 30, 1572.

28. *CSP, For. Eliz.* 1572–1574, no. 148, Occurrences in France, March 1572; *Mémoires de l'estat de France sous Charles IX,* I, 283.

29. *Mémoires du Maréchal de Tavannes,* ed. J. J. F. Poujoulat and J. Micaud, Nouvelle Collection des Mémoires pour servir à l'Histoire de France (32 vols., Paris, 1836–39), VIII, 354.

30. *CSP, For. Eliz.* 1572–1574, no. 149 (Public Records Office, vol. 70, no. 123), Henri to Jeanne, March 1, 1572.

31. Desjardins, ed., III, 751, Petrucci to François de Médicis, March 4, 1572; 752–753, Petrucci to François de Médicis, March 7, 1572.

32. *Mémoires de Michel de Castelnau,* I, 858 (also Freer, 380–383), Jeanne to Henri, March 8, 1572.

33. Rochambeau, no. CCXXXVI, 345–353 (also *Bulletin de la société de l'histoire de France* [1835], 2:169–172), Jeanne to Beauvoir, March 11, 1572.

34. Simancas K, 1526, no. 11, Aguilon to Alva, March 14, 1572; *Mémoires de l'estat de France,* I, 284.

35. Simancas K, 1525, no. 29, Aguilon to Philip, February 1, 1572.

36. Desjardins, ed., III, 754–755, Dispatch of Petrucci, March 16, 1572, 756, Dispatch of Petrucci, March 19, 1572.

37. *Ibid.,* 757–758, Dispatch of Petrucci, March 24, 1572.

38. For example, Simancas K, 1526, Dispatches of Aguilon, March 21 and 28; see Hirschauer, 88 (note 5) for list of sources.

39. British Museum Cott. Vesp. France/VI, fol. 1 (Freer, 385–386), Walsingham to Burghley, March 29, 1572.

40. Desjardins, ed., III, 758, Dispatch of Petrucci, March 24; *Lettres de Catherine de Médicis,* IV, liv–lviii, 106–107, Catherine to Pope, July 3, 1572.

41. B.N., Dupuy, 591, fol. 41, *Avis sur les cérémonies du mariage de M. le Prince de Navarre et de Madame la soeur du roy en la convocation des ministres.*

42. Freer, 388; *Lettres de Catherine de Médicis,* IV, xviv; Rochambeau, no. CCXXXIV, 343–344, Jeanne to Henri, March 25, 1572.

43. British Museum Cott. Vesp. F VI, fol. 9 (Freer, 391–392), Jeanne to Elizabeth, April 5, 1572.

44. *Mémoires de l'estat de France,* I, 285–290; Read, I, 176–197.

45. Desjardins, ed., III, 765, Alamani to Salviati, April 15, 1572; Siman-

cas K, 1526, no. 34, Aguilon to Alva, April 9, 1572; Hirschauer, 87–92.

46. Desjardins, ed., III, 771, Dispatch of Petrucci, April 28; also see Biron letters in Chapter XIV.

CHAPTER XIV
THE READINESS IS ALL

1. Simancas K, 1529, B 32, Aguilon to Alva, May 5, 1572.

2. *Archs. hists. Gir.*, XIV, 52–53, Biron to Villeroy, April 27, 1572.

3. *Ibid.*, 58–59, Biron to Catherine, May 20; Biron to Charles IX, May 23 and 29, 1572.

4. Archives des Basses-Pyrénées, B 35.

5. *Dictionnaire historique des rues de Paris,* I, 675.

6. *Mémoires de l'estat de France sous Charles IX,* I, 298.

7. B.N., F fr 3120, fol. 21, Duchesse de Nemours to Duchess of Ferrara, May 1572.

8. *La Huguerye,* I, 102–104.

9. B.N., Nouv. acquis. frçses., 21,603, fols. 33–34 (St. Petersburg, LIII, fol. 23, no. 21), Jeanne to Catherine de Medici, May 23, 1572.

10. Simancas K, 1529, no. 33, Philip to Cuniga [Zúñiga?], May 28, 1572.

11. Except where other sources are cited, all details of Jeanne's last illness and death are from the eyewitness account *Bref discours sur la mort de la Royne de Navarre,* BHPF (1882), 31:12–30 (ed. J. Bonnet).

12. *CSP, For. Eliz.* 1572–1574, no. 401, Smith to Burghley, June 7, 1572.

13. *Mémoires de Marguerite de Valois,* ed. L. Lalanne (Paris, 1858), 24–25.

14. *Cabinet historique* (1856), II, part 1, 229, Françoise d'Orléans Princesse de Condé, to Mademoiselle de Guillerville, June 12, 1572.

15. On the poison rumor see: De Ruble's opinion in *Mémoires de la Huguerye,* I, 114, and his edition of D'Aubigné, III, 290–291; Davila, I, 303; J. R. L. Desormeaux, *Histoire de la Maison de Bourbon* (5 vols., Paris, 1772–1788), IV, 476; Freer, 402–403; Muret, *Histoire de Jeanne d'Albret* (Paris, 1862), 409–413; Mlle. de Vauvilliers, *Histoire de Jeanne d'Albret* (3 vols., Paris, 1818?), III, 193–194; La Popelinière, *Histoire des histoires . . .* (1581), II, XXVII. Bordenave, 333–334, and the Haags, I, 57–58 (ed. 1846), give all the opinions and take no definite position. The Haags consider that the "moral presumption" (that Catherine had Jeanne poisoned) is affirmative, but the "political presumption" negative. Believing in Catherine's responsibility for the massacre in August, the Haags argue that foul play against Jeanne in June would have put the Huguenots on guard and thus would not have served Catherine's interests. See also Guadet, *Henri IV, sa vie, son oeuvre, ses écrits* (Paris, 1879), 47.

16. Favyn, *Histoire de Navarre* (Paris, 1612), 862, cited in Desormeaux, IV, 476.

17. Kervyn de Lettenhove, *Les Huguenots et les Gueux* (6 vols., Bruges, 1883–1888), II, 449.

18. B.N., Moreau, 719, fol. 40, Elector Palatine to Coligny, June 1572.

19. Fontana, III, 254–256; Hirschauer, 185–186 (Archivo Vaticano, Nunziature di Francia, V, 10–13, Frangipani to Gregory XIII, June 9, 19–22, Frangi-

pani to Cardinal of Como, June 20); Simancas K, 1529, no. 101, Frangipani to Archbishop of Rossano, June 28, 1572.

20. Simancas K, 1529, no. 81, Cuniga [Zúñiga?] to Alva, June 10, 1572; K, 1529, no. 92, Gabriel de Cayas to Zúñiga, June 20, 1572.

21. Archives des Basses-Pyrénées, B 35.

22. Rochambeau, *Galerie des hommes illustrés du Vendômois* (Vendôme, 1878), 113.

CHAPTER XV
A RICH LEGACY

HENRI'S CHILDHOOD

1. Archives des Basses-Pyrénées, B 8, 9, 11, analyzed by De Ruble, *Antoine de Bourbon,* I, 84–85.

2. Examples given by Guadet, 95–97; see also L'Estoile, *Mémoires-Journaux* (Brunet edition), VIII, *passim.*

3. De Ruble, *Antoine de Bourbon,* IV, 91–93; Bordenave, 115; Simancas K, 1497, no. 33; K, 1498, Chantonay to Philip, May 19 and June 3, 1562.

4. Palma Cayet, I, 178–179.

5. *CSP, For. Eliz.* 1563, no. 736(4), Smith to the Queen, May 11, 1563, no. 748(5), Occurrences in France, May 15, 1563.

6. BHPF (1855), 3:524, Henri to Jeanne, 1563 or 1564.

7. *Lettres missives,* I, xxxi.

8. *CSP, For. Eliz.* 1563, no. 1508(10), Challoner to the Queen, December 19, 1563.

9. For example, Haag, III, 458, V, 447.

10. *Lettres missives,* V, 462–463, Henri to Marie de Medici, September 3, 1601.

11. L'Estoile (Brunet edition), VII, 164–168; excerpts in English in *The Paris of Henry of Navarre,* ed. N. L. Roelker (Cambridge, Mass., 1958), 295–296. Hereafter cited as L'Estoile (Roelker edition).

12. Guadet, 262–272.

TRAINING FOR KINGSHIP

13. Desormeaux, IV, 367, 474.

14. *Lettres missives,* VII, 385, Henri to Madame de Montglat, November 14, 1607.

15. Desormeaux, IV, 368.

16. *Memoirs of the Duke of Sully* (5 vols., Edinburgh, 1819), I, 12. I have retained here the English translation (anonymous) in an eighteenth-century edition of Sully's *Memoirs.* The originals are in the *Mémoires de Nevers,* a *Receuil* of the second half of the sixteenth century.

17. Bordenave, 146–149 (excerpts).

18. *Mémoires,* 114–115.

19. Arcère, I, 370 (quoting Amos Barbot).

20. Tommaseo, ed., II, 153–155, *Relazione* of Correro, 1569; Guadet, 38.

21. Palma Cayet, I, 180.

22. *Lettres missives,* I, 8–10, Henri de Navarre and Henri de Condé to the Dukes of Brunswick and Savoy, August 1570.

23. *Ibid.,* I, 10–11, Henri de Navarre to Cardinal de Bourbon, September 13, 1570; 12–13, Henri de Navarre to François de Montmorency, September 13, 1570; 14–15, Henri de Navarre to the Marquis de Villars, January 24 and February 6, 1571.

24. Palma Cayet, I, 178; Olhagaray, 530–531; Desormeaux, IV, 361–362.

25. Simancas K, 1512, no. 68, Alava to Gabriel de Cayas, September 5, 1569; K, 1517, no. 62, Alava to Alva, April 2, 1570; Desjardins, ed., III, 622–623, Dispatch of Petrucci, April 15, 1570.

26. BHPF (1912), 61:140–143, Beauvoir to Charles IX, June 13, 1572 and Biron to Charles IX, the same day.

27. Salefranque, *Bulletin de Pau,* 1922, 200, Henri to D'Arros, June 15, 1572.

28. L'Estoile (Roelker edition), 47–48 (February 1576).

29. Simancas K, 1500, no. 61, Avis de France, March 1576.

30. L'Estoile (Roelker edition), 237–238 (July 1593).

CATHERINE DE BOURBON AND ADOPTED DAUGHTERS

31. The principal source on Catherine is the collection of her letters, edited and fully annotated by R. Ritter, *Lettres et poésies de Catherine de Bourbon* (Paris, 1927), hereafter cited as Ritter. It is the authority for all statements about Catherine unless otherwise indicated. Ritter also published some of the letters in BHPF, vols. 73–75 (1924, 1925, 1926).

32. See R. M. Kingdon, "Problems of Religious Choice for Sixteenth Century Frenchmen," *Journal of Religious History* (December 1966), 105–112; Kingdon, *Geneva and Consolidation,* 83–86.

33. BHPF (1926), 75:259–262, Catherine to Henri, May 1592.

34. Ritter, 118–123, no. CXI, Catherine to Henri, September 22, 1595.

35. Ritter, 114, no. CV, Catherine to DuPlessis-Mornay, 1594; *ibid.,* 125–126, no. CXVI, Catherine to Beza, June 26, 1596; L'Estoile (Brunet edition), VII, *passim,* especially, 100–101, 117–118, 126, 131, 137, 157.

36. Ritter, 147–148, no. CXLVII, Catherine to Henri, March 1599.

37. *Ibid.,* 148–149, no. CXLVIII, Catherine to Henri, March 1599.

38. *Ibid.,* 158–161, nos. CLXIII, CLXV, CLXII, Catherine to Henri, July 1599.

39. *Ibid.,* 166–167, no. CLXXIII, Catherine to Henri, August 18, 1599.

40. *Ibid.,* 161–162, no. CLXXVII, Catherine to Henri, July 1599.

41. *Ibid.,* 157–158, no. CLXII, Catherine to Henri, June 1599; 116–117, no. CIX, Catherine to Caumont-La Force, May 1595.

42. L'Estoile (Brunet edition), VII, 121–122 (February 1604).

43. Archives Nationales, M 273, XVI, fols. 24v–25r, Jeanne to Madame de Langey, 1564.

44. *Bulletin de la société de l'histoire de France* (1835), 2:166–171, Jeanne to Henri, March 8, 1572; Jeanne's correspondence with the royal family about the marriage of Marie and Condé is B.N., Nouv. acquis. frçses. 21,603, fols. 10, 4–5, 24–25 (St. Petersburg, LIII, fol. 7, no. 7 is the letter to the King, the others are variations and shorter). On the Clèves family see Haag, III, 503.

45. Haag, II, 479; J. Delaborde, *Charlotte de Bourbon, Princesse d'Orange* (Paris, 1888).

46. Rochambeau, no. CCXVI, 319–320, Jeanne to Charlotte, July 28, 1571, no. CCXXXIX, 356–357, Jeanne to Charlotte, April 5, 1572. The third surviving letter is no. CCXL, 357–358, Jeanne to Charlotte de Bourbon, May 5, 1572.

EPILOGUE

1. *Mémoires,* 32–36.
2. *Ibid.,* 49, 91–93.
3. Simancas K, 1513, no. 140, Alava to Philip, December 11, 1569.

INDEX

Due 28 Days From Latest Date